SQL Server 2012

Administration

Kalman Toth

SQL Server 2012 Administration

Copyright © 2013 by Kalman Toth

Contents at a Glance

About the Author

Kalman Toth has been working with relational database technology since 1990 when one day his boss, at a commodity brokerage firm in Greenwich, Connecticut, had to leave early and gave his SQL Server login & password to Kalman along with a small SQL task. Kalman was a C/C++ developer fascinated by SQL, therefore, he studied a Transact-SQL manual 3 times from start to end "dry", without any server access. His boss was satisfied with the execution of SQL task and a few days later Kalman's dream came true: he got his very own SQL Server login. His relational database career since then includes database design, database development, database administration, OLAP architecture and Business Intelligence development. Applications included enterprise-level general ledger & financial accounting, bond funds auditing, international stock market feeds processing, broker-dealer firm risk management, derivative instruments analytics, consumer ecommerce database management for online dating, personal finance, physical fitness, diet and health. Currently he is Principal Trainer at www.sqlusa.com. His MSDN forum participation in the Transact-SQL and SQL Server Tools was rewarded with the Microsoft Community Contributor award. Kalman has a Master of Arts degree in Physics from Columbia University and a Master of Philosophy degree in Computing Science also from Columbia. Microsoft certifications in database administration, development and Business Intelligence. The dream SQL career took him across United States & Canada as well as South America & Europe. SQL also involved him in World History. At one time he worked for Deloitte & Touche on the 96th floor of World Trade Center North. On September 11, 2001, he was an RDBMS consultant at Citibank on 111 Wall Street. After escaping at 10:30 on that fateful Tuesday morning in the heavy dirt smoke, it took 10 days before he could return to his relational database development job just 1/2 mile from the nearly three thousand victims buried under steel. What Kalman loves about SQL is that the same friendly, yet powerful, commands can process 2 records or 2 million records or 200 million records the same easy way. His current interest is Artificial Intelligence. He is convinced that machine intelligence will not only replace human intelligence but surpass it million times in the near future. His hobby is flying gliders & vintage fighter planes. Accessibility: http://twitter.com/sqlusa, http://www.sqlusa.com/contact2005/.

V

CONTENTS

This page is intentionally left blank.

INTRODUCTION

SQL Server and Database Administration is a challenging job. A DBA has to learn how to install SQL Server 2012 instances and manage them. Also the database administrator has to master creating a database, backing it up and restoring it when it becomes necessary. Preparing for a disaster and recovering from it is a must skill for a database administrator. A DBA has to master RDBMS security and learn how to automate with SQL Server Agent and other tools. In addition to server and database management, a database administrator has to know SQL programming and database design as well.

Developers across the world are facing database issues daily. While they are immersed in procedural languages with loops , RDBMS forces them to think in terms of sets without loops. It takes transition. It takes training. It takes experience. Developers are exposed also to Excel worksheets or spreadsheets as they were called in the not so distant past. So if you know worksheets how hard databases can be? After all worksheets look pretty much like database tables? The big difference is connections among well-designed tables. A database is a set of connected tables which represent entities in the real world. A database can be 100 connected tables or 3000. The connection is very simple: row A in table Alpha has affiliated data with row B in table Beta. But even with 200 tables and 300 connections (FOREIGN KEY references), it takes a good amount of time to familiarize to the point of acceptable working knowledge.

In SQL you are thinking at a high level. In C# or Java, you are dealing with details, lots of them. That is the big difference. Why is so much of the book dedicated to database design? Why not plunge into SQL coding and sooner or later the developer will get a hang of the design? Because high level thinking requires thinking at the database design level. A farmer has 6 mules, how do we model it in the database? We design the Farmer and FarmAnimal tables, then connect them with FarmerID FOREIGN KEY in FarmAnimal referencing the FarmerID PRIMARY KEY in the Farmer table. What is the big deal about it, looks so simple? In fact, how about just calling the tables Table1 & Table2 to be more generic? Ouch... meaningful naming is the very basis of good database design. Relational database design is truly simple for simple well-understood models. The challenge starts in modeling complex objects such as financial derivative instruments, airplane passenger scheduling or social network website. When you need to add 5 new tables to a 1000 tables database and hook them in (define FOREIGN KEY references) correctly, it is a huge challenge. To begin with, some of the 5 new tables may already be redundant, but you don't know that until you understand what the 1000 tables are really storing. Frequently, learning the application area is the biggest challenge for a developer when starting a new job.

The SQL language is simple to program and read even if when touching 10 tables. Complexities are abound though. The very first one: does the SQL statement touch the right data set? 999 records and 1000 or 998? T-SQL statements are turned into Transact-SQL scripts, stored procedures, user-defined functions and triggers, server-side database objects. They can be 5 statements or 1000 statements long programs. The style of Transact-SQL programming is different from the style in procedural programming languages. There are no arrays, only tables or table variables. Typically there is no looping, only set-based operations. Error control is different. Testing & debugging is relatively simple in Transact-SQL due to the interactive environment and the magic of selecting & executing a part without recompiling the whole.

WHO THIS BOOK IS FOR

Database administrators, developers, programmers and systems analysts who are new to relational database technology. Also developers, designers and BI consumers, who know some SQL programming and database design, wish to expand their RDBMS design & development technology horizons. Familiarity with other computer language is assumed. The book has lots of queries, lots of T-SQL scripts, plenty to learn. The best way to learn it is to type in the query in your own SQL Server copy and test it, examine it, change it. Wouldn't it be easier just to copy & paste it? It would but the learning value would diminish. You need to feel the SQL language in your fingers. SQL queries must "pour" out from your fingers into the keyboard. Why is that so important? After everything can be found on the web and just copy & paste? Well not exactly. If you want to be an expert, it has to be in your head not on the web. Second, when your supervisor is looking over your shoulder, "Charlie, can you tell me what is the total revenue for March?", you have to be able to type in the query without SQL forum search and provide the results to your superior promptly.

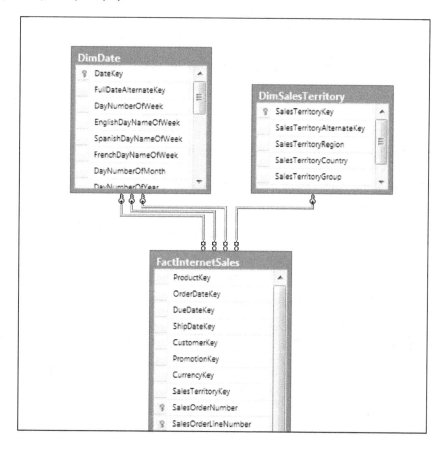

ABOUT THIS BOOK

Beginning SQL Server Administration, beginning relational database design and beginning Transact-SQL programming. It is not a reference manual, rather learn by examples: there are hundreds of administration screen images and over 700 SELECT queries in the book. Instead of imaginary tables, the book uses the SQL Server sample databases for explanations and examples: pubs (PRIMARY KEYs 9, FOREIGN KEYs 10), Northwind (PRIMARY KEYs 13, FOREIGN KEYs 13) and the AdventureWorks family. Among them: AdventureWorks, AdventureWorks2008, AdventureWorks2012 (PRIMARY KEYs 71, FOREIGN KEYs 90), & AdventureWorksDW2012 (PRIMARY KEYs 27, FOREIGN KEYs 44). The book introduces relational database design concepts, then reinforces them again and again, not to bore the reader, rather indoctrinate with relational database design principles. Light weight SQL starts at the beginning of the book, because working with database metadata (not the content of the database, rather data which describes the database) is essential for understanding database design. By the time the reader gets to T-SQL programming, already knows basic SQL programming from the database design section of the book. The book was designed to be readable in any environment, even on the beach laptop around or no laptop in sight at all. All queries are followed by results row count and /or full/partial results listing in tabular (grid) format. For full benefits though, the reader should try out the T-SQL queries and scripts as he progresses from page to page, topic to topic. Example for SQL Server 2012 T-SQL query and results presentation.

```
SELECT          V.Name                          AS Vendor,
                FORMAT(SUM(POH.TotalDue), 'c', 'en-US')   AS [Total Purchase],
                FORMAT(AVG(POH.TotalDue), 'c', 'en-US')   AS [Average Purchase]
FROM AdventureWorks.Purchasing.Vendor AS V
    INNER JOIN AdventureWorks.Purchasing.PurchaseOrderHeader AS POH
        ON V.VendorID = POH.VendorID
GROUP BY V.Name  ORDER BY Vendor;
-- (79 row(s) affected) - Partial results.
```

Vendor	Total Purchase	Average Purchase
Advanced Bicycles	$28,502.09	$558.86
Allenson Cycles	$498,589.59	$9,776.27
American Bicycles and Wheels	$9,641.01	$189.04
American Bikes	$1,149,489.84	$22,539.02

CONVENTIONS USED IN THIS BOOK

The Transact-SQL queries and scripts (sequence of statements) are shaded.

The number of resulting rows is displayed as a comment line: -- (79 row(s) affected) .

The results of the queries is usually displayed in grid format.

Less frequently the results are enclosed in comment markers: /*...... */ .

When a query is a trivial variation of a previous query, no result is displayed.

While the intention of the book is database design & database development, SQL Server installation and some database administration tasks are included.

"Apparatus Intelligentia

vincet

Humanum Intelligentia"

Dedicated to

Ron Soukup

One of the Founding Fathers of

Microsoft SQL Server

This page is intentionally left blank.

CHAPTER 1: Editions & Installing SQL Server 2012

SQL Server 2012 Express Edition Installation

The **Express Edition** is free. It can be installed from the following webpage.

http://www.microsoft.com/sqlserver/en/us/editions/2012-editions/express.aspx

Installation instructions provided.

SQL Server 2012 Evaluation Edition Installation

The **Evaluation Edition** is free for a certain time period like 6 months. It can be installed from the following webpage.

http://www.microsoft.com/en-us/download/details.aspx?id=29066

Installation instructions provided.

SQL Server 2012 Pay Edition Installation

The installation process from the distribution DVD is fairly automatic. Product key (4 x 5 alphanumeric) entry is required near the beginning of the installation.

Planning tab has the preparation steps.

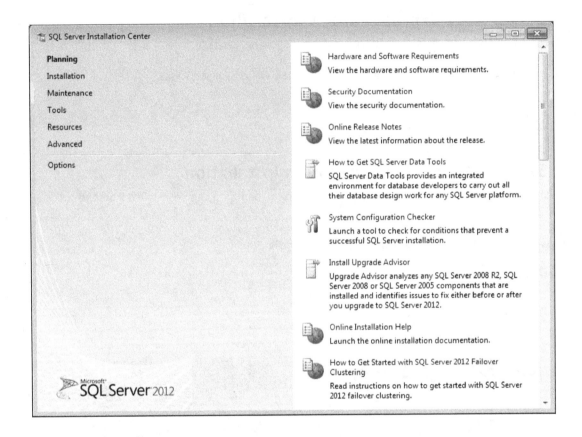

The Installation tab has the SQL Server and Client Tools (SS Management Studio is a client tool) install options.

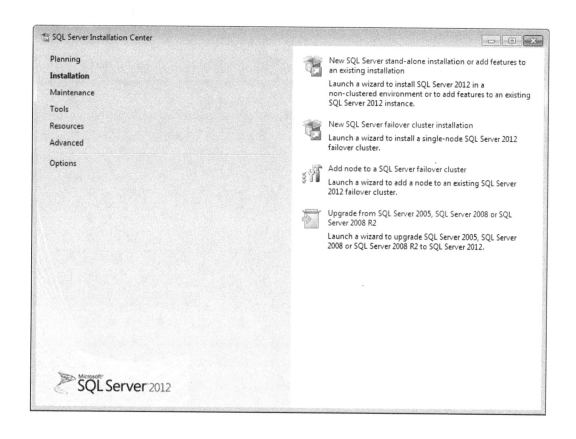

Setup Support Rules page shows the results of preliminary checks for installation readiness. Failed issues require fix.

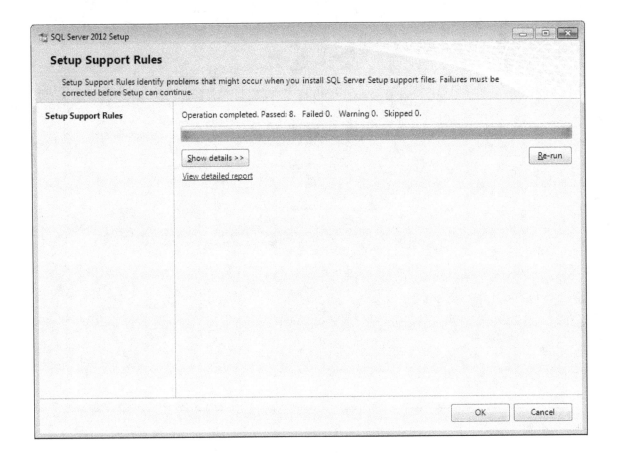

Product Updates page checks the web for latest updates.

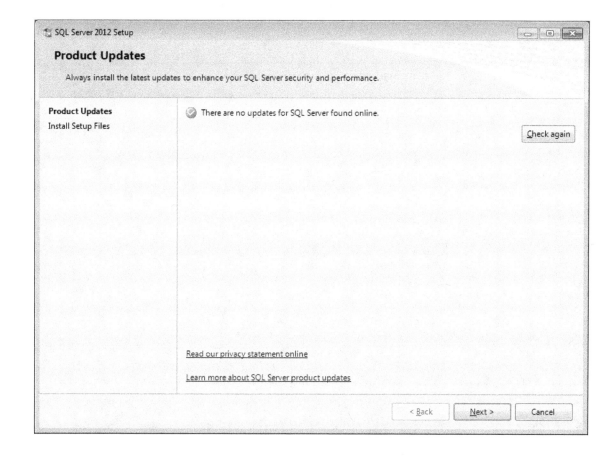

Setup Support Rules page performs a number of internal system checks.

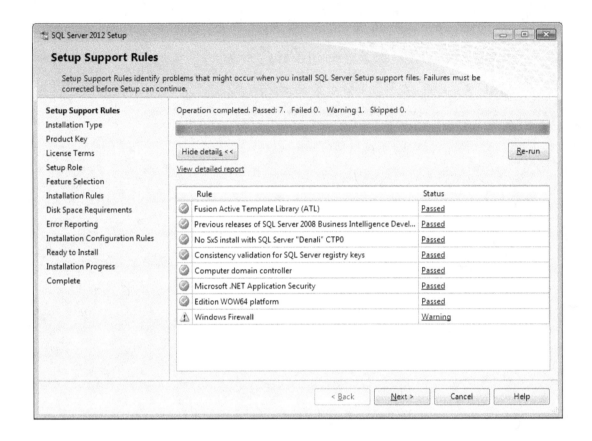

Installation Type page displays currently installed SQL Server products.

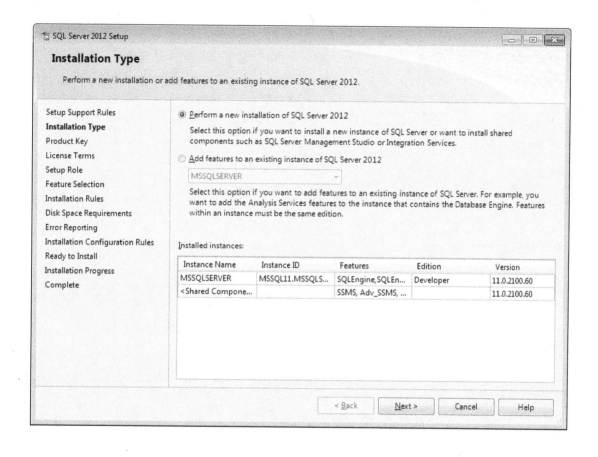

Product Key page requests key entry from packaging box inside cover.

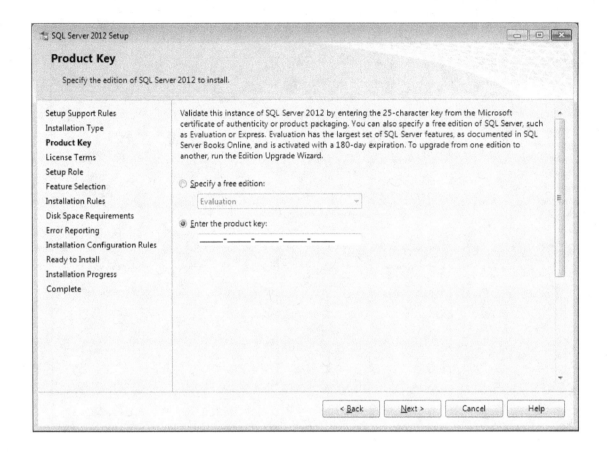

License terms page requires acceptance checkmark.

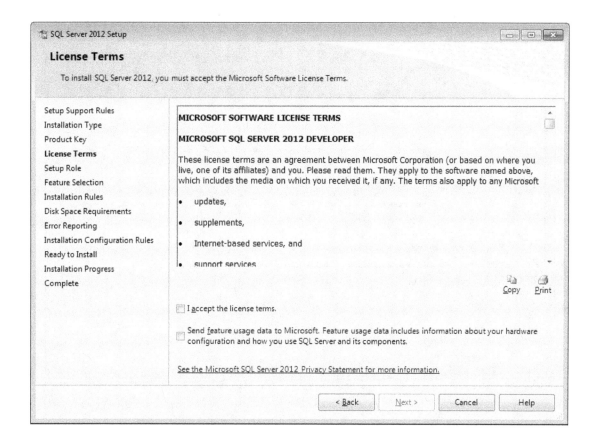

Setup Role page lists installation options. "All Features with Defaults" is the easiest to install.

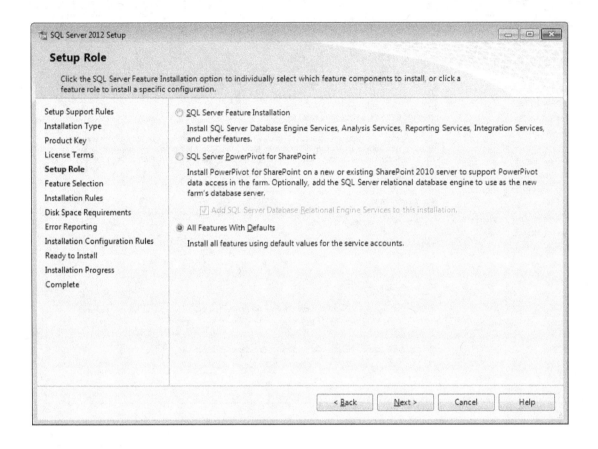

Feature Selection page can be used to pick & choose features.

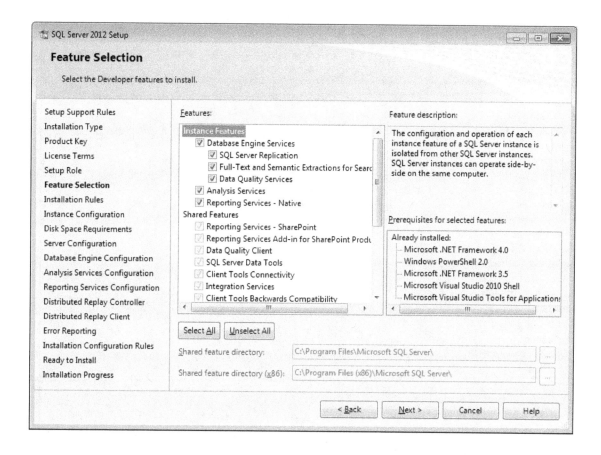

Installation Rules page performs further internal system checks.

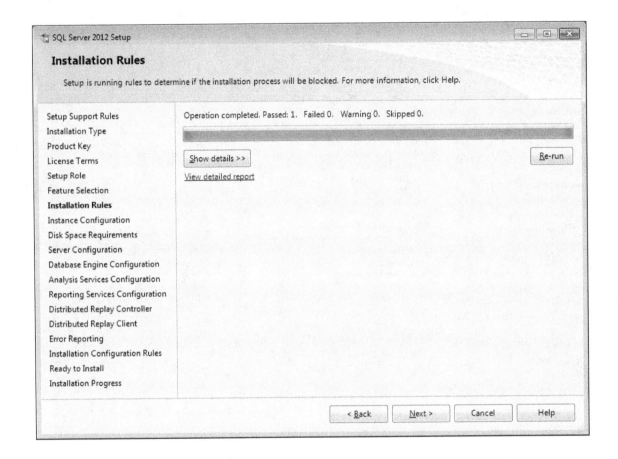

Instance Configuration page requires name entrance for the named instance since the default instance is already installed.

The SQL Server reference is [YOURSERVER] for the default instance and [YOURSERVER\INSTANCENAME] for the named instance.

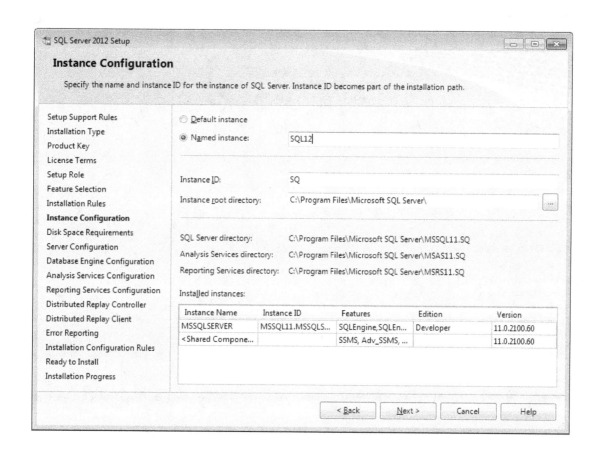

Disk Space Requirements page checks for available disk space.

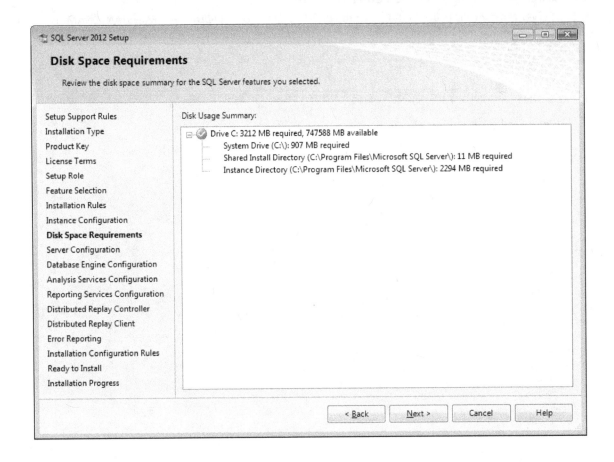

The Server Configuration page covers accounts, startup type and collation.

For example, SQL Server Agent (job management) can be set to automatic instead of manual startup.

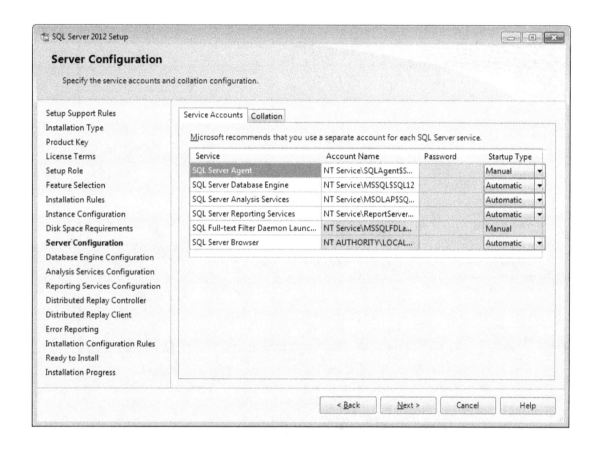

The collation page offers choosing a different collation from the default. Note: selecting collation requires quite an expertise, safest choice is the default.

The "_CI_AS" suffix in the collation name means Case Insensitive, Accent Sensitive (foreign word with accent marks on E & O: PÉNZSZERZŐ).

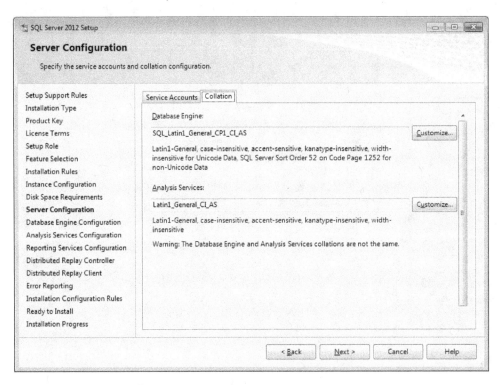

-- Case Insensitive, Accent Sensitive sort
DECLARE @Words TABLE ([Foreign] nvarchar(32)); INSERT @Words VALUES
(N'PÉNZSZERZŐ'),(N'Pénzszerző'), (N'PENZSZERZŐ'), (N'pÉNZSZERZŐ'), (N'PÉNZSZERZŐ'), (N'pENZSZERZŐ'),
(N'pénzszerző'), (N'péNZSZERZŐ') ;
SELECT * FROM @Words ORDER BY [Foreign];

Foreign
PENZSZERZŐ
pENZSZERZŐ
pénzszerző
péNZSZERZŐ
pÉNZSZERZŐ
PÉNZSZERZŐ
PÉNZSZERZŐ
Pénzszerző

The Database Engine Configuration page offers administrator accounts, data directories and FILESTREAM setup options.

FILESTREAM is required for FileTable, a new feature of SQL Server 2012.

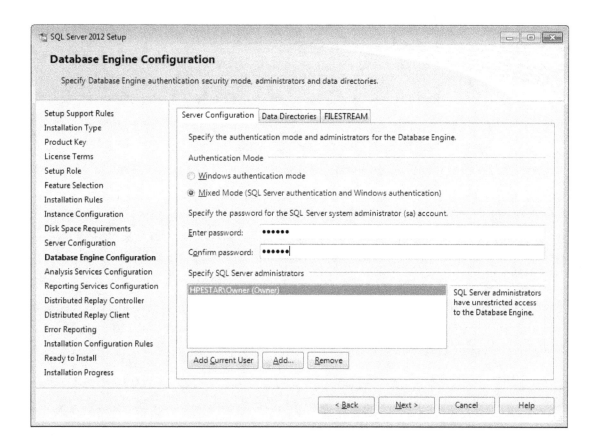

Error Reporting page has checkmark option to report errors automatically.

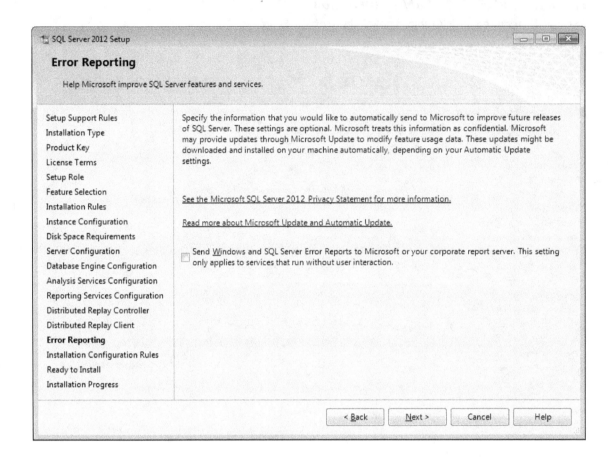

Installation Configuration Rules page performs a final check.

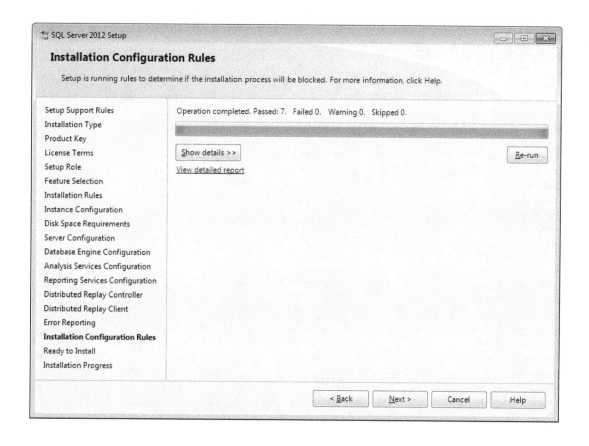

Ready to Install page shows the action plan.

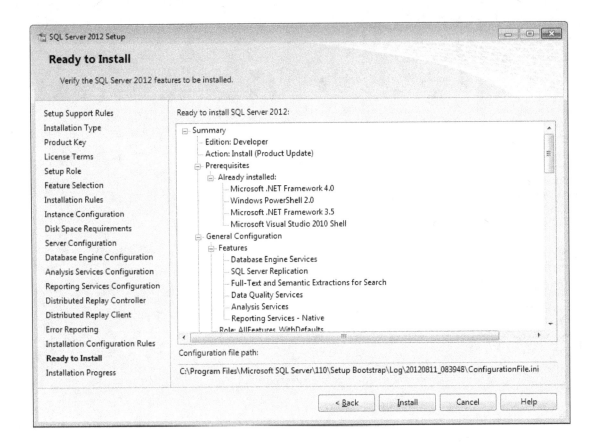

Installation Progress page displays progress messages (this part will take a few minutes).

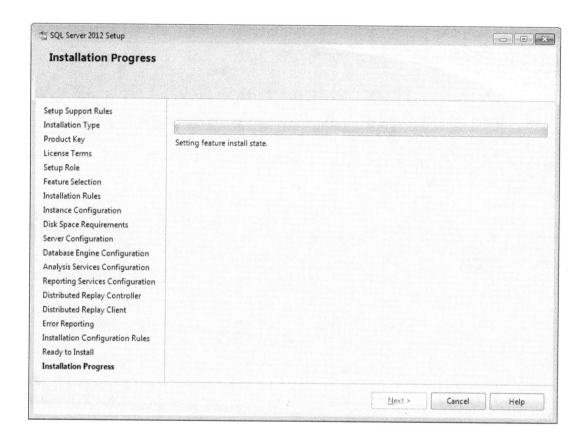

The Complete page displays successful installation information or failure.

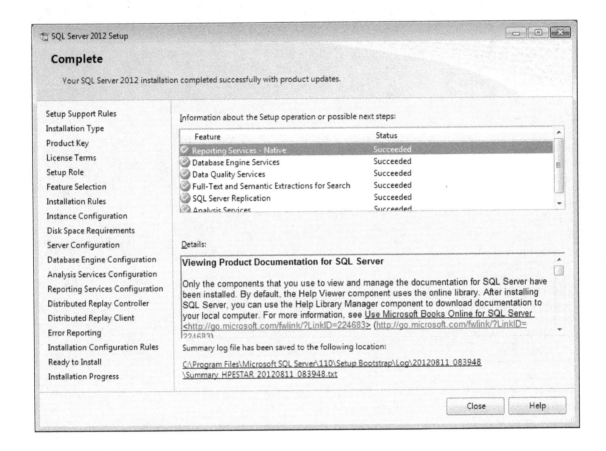

Start Menu for SQL Server 2012

The Start Menu has all the components related to SQL Server including Management Studio and SQL Server Data Tools for Business Intelligence (SSAS, SSIS & SSRS) application design.

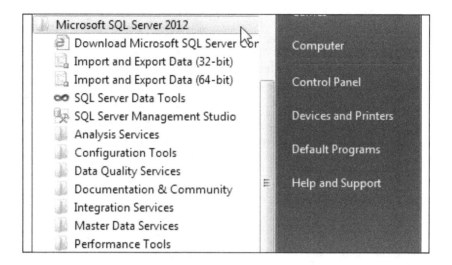

Creating Shortcut for Management Studio on Desktop

Management Studio can also be pinned to the Start Menu or Taskbar from the right-click drop-down menu.

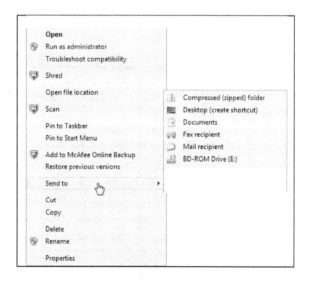

Launching SQL Server Configuration Manager

Expand (left click) the Configuration Tools tab on the Start Menu and click on SQL Server Configuration Manager.

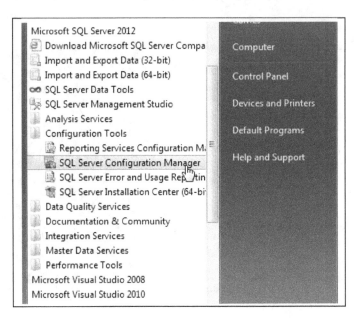

SQL Server should be running by itself after installation, if not, it can be started and/or reconfigured.

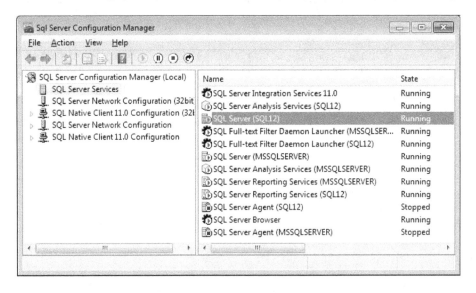

Starting, Restarting & Stopping SQL Server

Right click on the server name in Configuration Manager launches the control menu. To start the server, click on Start.

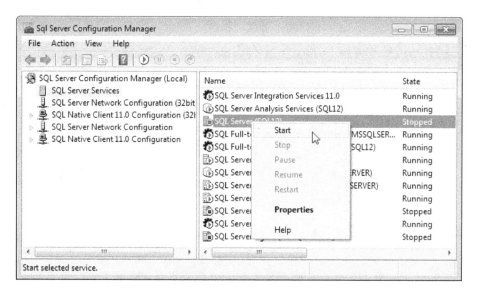

Message window pops up.

To stop a running server or restart it, click on the menu item respectively.

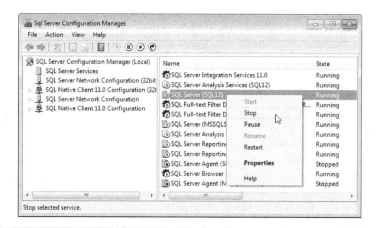

Connecting to the New Named SQL Server Instance

The newly installed SS instance is ready for use. Here is how we can connect to it from SSMS Object Explorer. NOTE: on your computer you will see YOURCOMPUTERNAME instead of "HPESTAR".

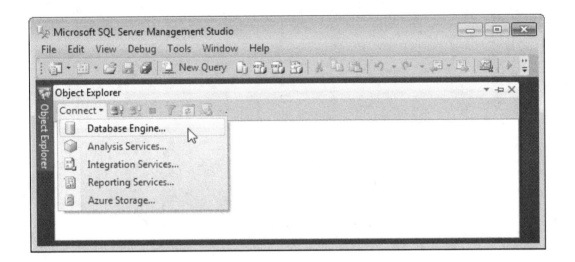

Investigating the New SQL Server Instance

We can start discovering the new SQL Server instance in Query Editor & Object Explorer.

SELECT @@version;
-- Microsoft SQL Server 2012 - 11.0.2100.60 (X64)

SELECT @@SERVERNAME;
-- YOURSERVERNAME\SQL12;

-- SS Version, Level (service pack), Edition
SELECT   CONCAT ('Microsoft SQL Server ',convert(varchar, SERVERPROPERTY('ProductVersion')), ' -- ',
         convert(varchar, SERVERPROPERTY('ProductLevel')), ' -- ',convert(varchar,
SERVERPROPERTY('Edition')));
-- Microsoft SQL Server 11.0.2100.60 -- RTM -- Developer Edition (64-bit)

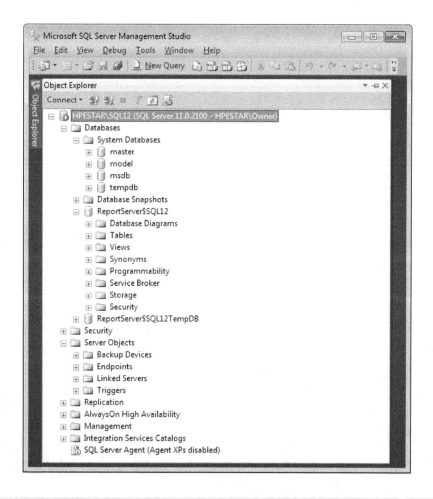

Connecting to 2 SQL Server Instances Simultaneously

SSMS Object Explorer support multiple SS instances connections. Warning: **Production, QA and Development SS instances may look similar, an opportunity to get confused and carry out actions on the wrong server**. Best prevention: **take regular database backups and connect only to one SQL Server instance at one time**.

The first connection is the named instance, the second is the default instance.

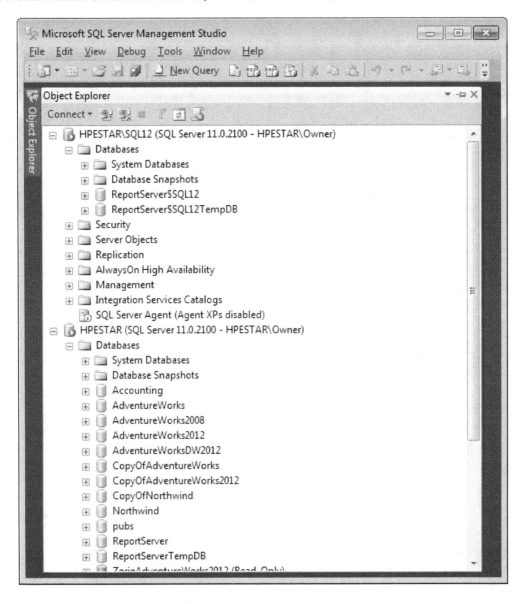

BACKUP DATABASE Command

Database backup command; the backup filename can be changed at will to reflect the backup date.

```
BACKUP DATABASE [AdventureWorks2012] TO  DISK = N'F:\data\backup\AW20161023.bak';


-- Dynamic backup filename with datestamp
DECLARE @Filename nvarchar(64) = CONCAT(N'F:\data\backup\AW', CONVERT(varchar, CONVERT(DATE, getdate())),'.bak');
BACKUP DATABASE [AdventureWorks2012] TO  DISK = @Filename;
-- AW2018-08-23.bak
```

Installing Books Online - BOL

Books Online can be installed from the web or from the distribution DVD. Select Manage Help Settings from the Help menu in Management Studio.

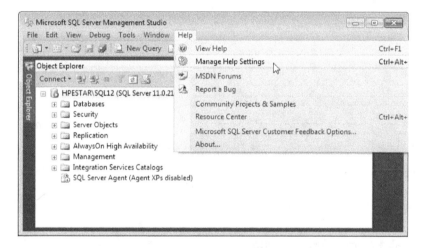

Select **Install content from online** from the pop-up panel.

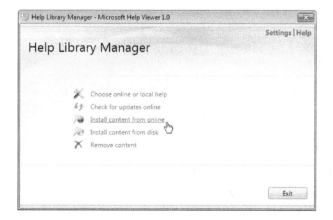

Add Books Online to the to do list on the dialog box.

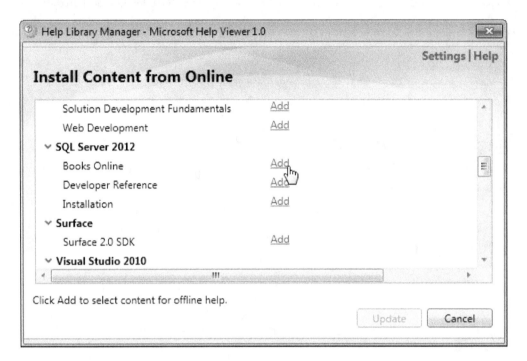

Click on UPDATE button.

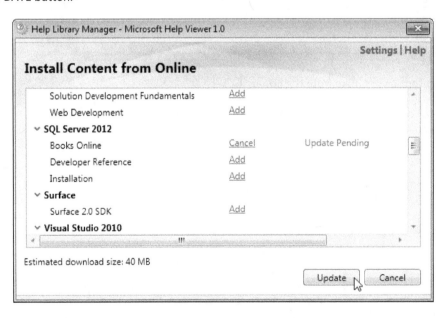

Updating will take a few minutes.

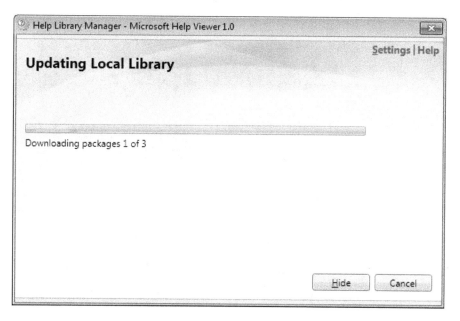

Finish panel. Click in Finish button.

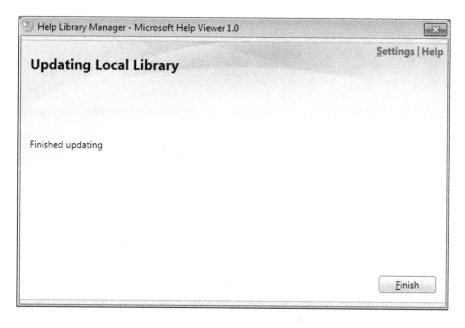

Creating Shortcut for Books Online on Desktop.

Follow the usual process for shortcut creation, start with right click on SQL Server Documentation.

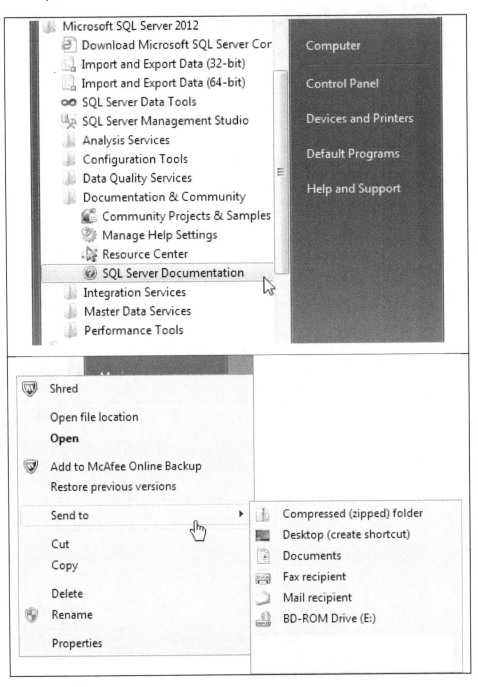

Installing Developer Reference

To install Developer Reference follow the same process as for Book Online.

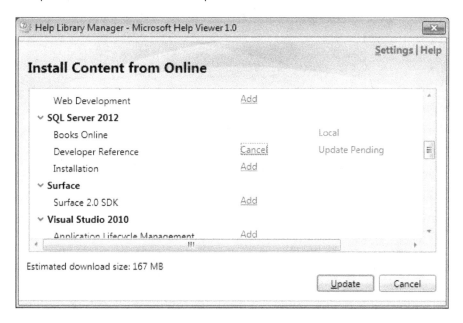

Click on Update button. Update will take a few minutes.

Developer Reference will install into Books Online.

Desktop segment with SSMS, SSDT and Books Online (includes Developer Reference).

Searching Books Online Contents Mode

Books Online is the complete reference tool for SQL Server. The implementation in Microsoft Help Viewer is new to SQL Server 2012. In the Contents mode, you drill-down in the left pane and read the article in the right pane.

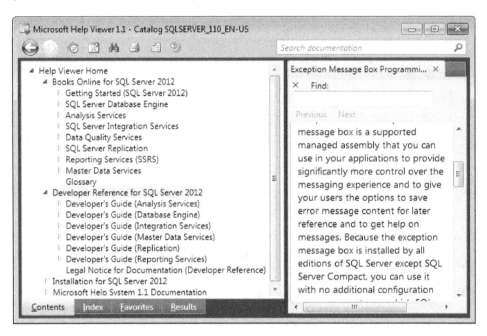

When you click on a Contents item, the corresponding article pops up in the right pane.

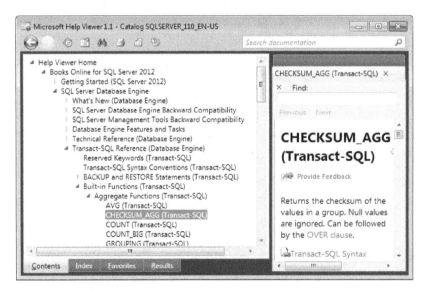

Searching Books Online Index Mode

In the Index Mode, items are listed alphabetically. When you click on an item, the corresponding article pops up in the right pane.

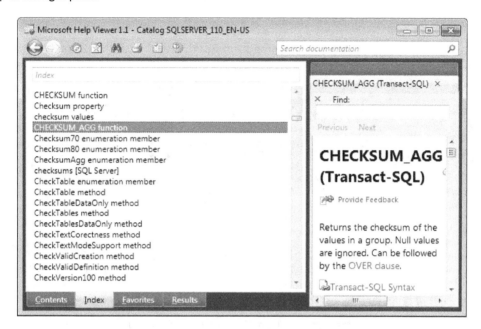

Searching the Web for SQL Server MSDN Articles

When searching the web for SS documentation use the prefix "SQL SERVER" or "T-SQL" before the keyword.

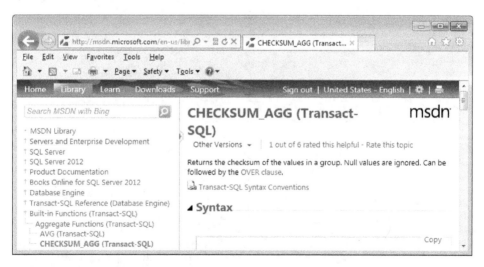

Installing AdventureWorks2012 Sample Database

AdventureWorks2012 and other related databases can be installed from the following webpage:
http://msftdbprodsamples.codeplex.com/releases/view/55330

Community Projects & Samples from the Start Menu will bring up the following site:
http://sqlserversamples.codeplex.com/

Installing Northwind & pubs Sample Databases

Here is the download website with instructions. http://www.microsoft.com/en-us/download/details.aspx?displaylang=en&id=23654

Server Properties

All information on server instance definition is presented on the properties pages.

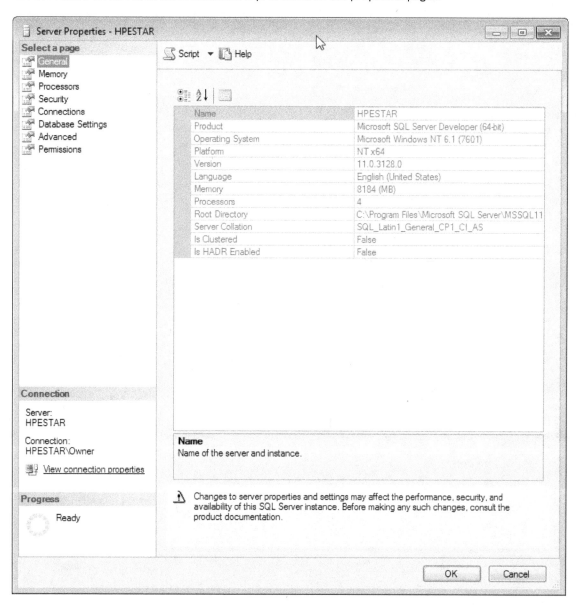

Server Properties Security Page

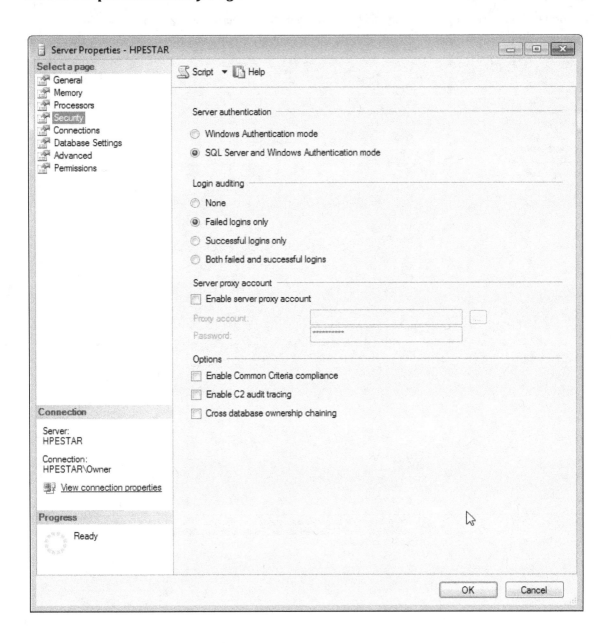

Server Properties Connections Page

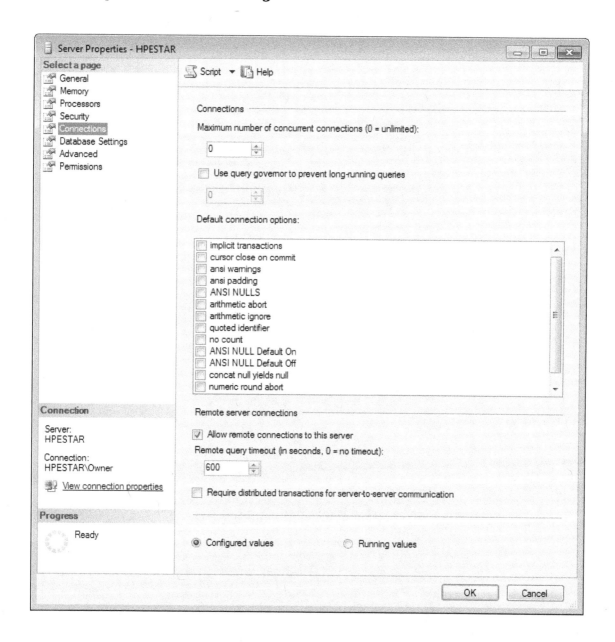

Server Properties Advanced Page

Server Properties Memory Page

Memory max should be set. For example, it can be set 54GB for a server with 64GB of memory.

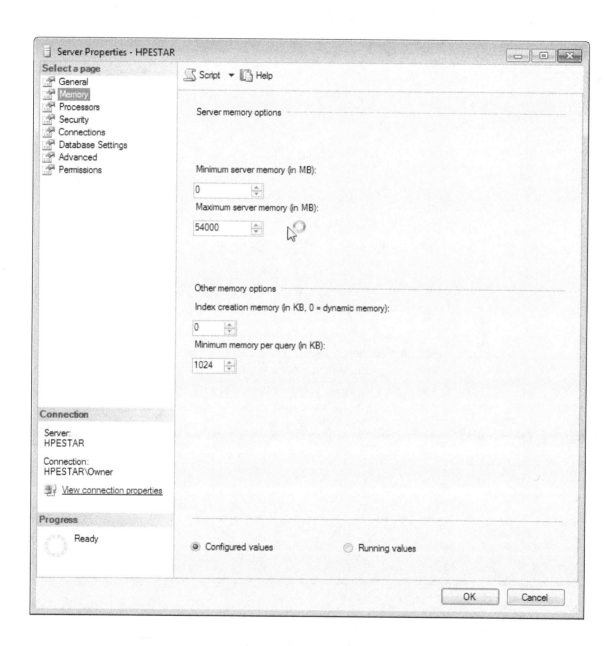

Server Properties Database Settings Page

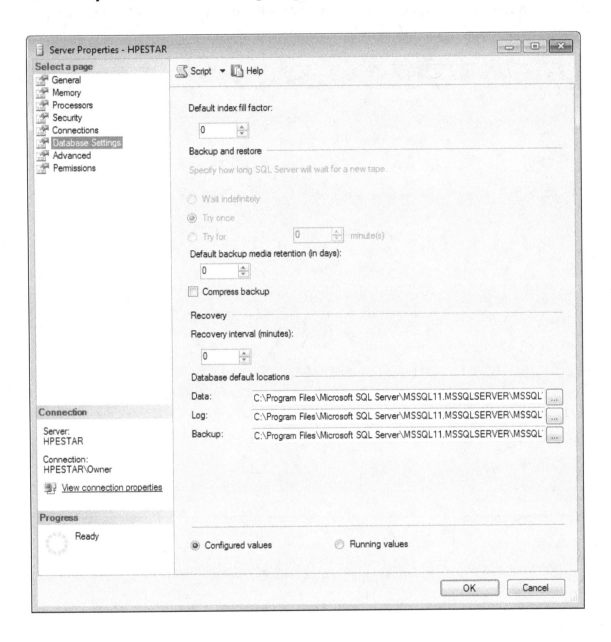

Server Properties Processors Page

Server Properties Permissions Page

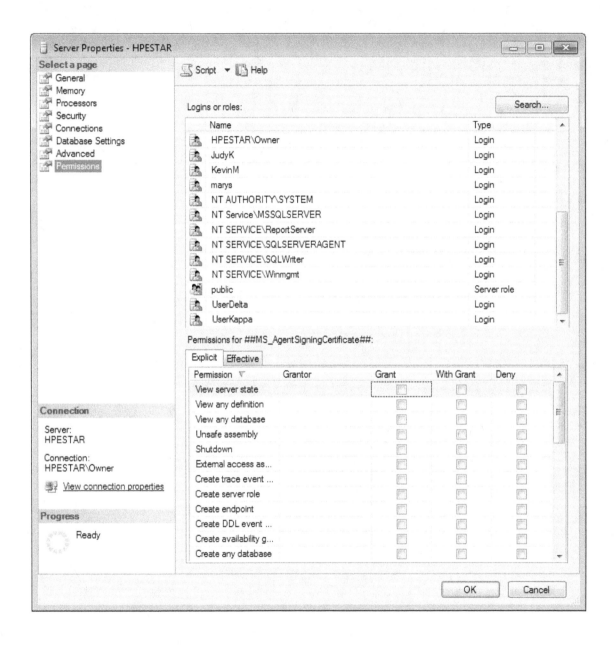

CHAPTER 2: Sample Application & System Databases

AdventureWorks Series of OLTP Databases

AdventureWorks sample On Line Transaction Processing (OLTP) database has been introduced with SQL Server 2005 to replace the previous sample database Northwind, a fictional gourmet food items distributor. The intent of the AdventureWorks sample database is to support the business operations of AdventureWorks Cycles, a fictitious mountain, touring and road bike manufacturer. The company sells through dealer network and online on the web. In addition to bikes, it sells frames and parts as well as accessories such as helmets, biking clothes and water bottles. The AdventureWorks2012 database image of Touring-1000 Blue, 50 bike in Production.ProductPhoto table.

T-SQL query to generate list of tables of AdventureWorks2012 in 5 columns. The core query (bolded) is simple. Presenting results in 5 columns instead of 1 column adds a bit of complexity.

```
;WITH cteTableList AS (      SELECT CONCAT(SCHEMA_NAME(schema_id), '.', name)          AS TableName,
  (( ROW_NUMBER() OVER( ORDER BY CONCAT(SCHEMA_NAME(schema_id),'.', name)) ) % 5)   AS Remainder,
  (( ROW_NUMBER() OVER( ORDER BY CONCAT(SCHEMA_NAME(schema_id),'.', name)) - 1 )/ 5)  AS Quotient
                    FROM AdventureWorks2012.sys.tables),
CTE AS (SELECT TableName, CASE WHEN Remainder=0 THEN 5 ELSE Remainder END AS Remainder, Quotient
        FROM cteTableList)
SELECT    MAX(CASE WHEN Remainder = 1 THEN TableName END),
          MAX(CASE WHEN Remainder = 2 THEN TableName END),
          MAX(CASE WHEN Remainder = 3 THEN TableName END),
          MAX(CASE WHEN Remainder = 4 THEN TableName END),
          MAX(CASE WHEN Remainder = 5 THEN TableName END)
FROM  CTE GROUP BY Quotient ORDER BY Quotient;
GO
```

The query result set in grid format: tables in AdventureWorks2012

dbo.AWBuildVersion	dbo.DatabaseLog	dbo.ErrorLog	HumanResources.Department	HumanResources.Employee
HumanResources.EmployeeDepartmentHistory	HumanResources.EmployeePayHistory	HumanResources.JobCandidate	HumanResources.Shift	Person.Address
Person.AddressType	Person.BusinessEntity	Person.BusinessEntityAddress	Person.BusinessEntityContact	Person.ContactType
Person.CountryRegion	Person.EmailAddress	Person.Password	Person.Person	Person.PersonPhone
Person.PhoneNumberType	Person.StateProvince	Production.BillOfMaterials	Production.Culture	Production.Document
Production.Illustration	Production.Location	Production.Product	Production.ProductCategory	Production.ProductCostHistory
Production.ProductDescription	Production.ProductDocument	Production.ProductInventory	Production.ProductListPriceHistory	Production.ProductModel
Production.ProductModelIllustration	Production.ProductModelProductDescriptionCulture	Production.ProductPhoto	Production.ProductProductPhoto	Production.ProductReview
Production.ProductSubcategory	Production.ScrapReason	Production.TransactionHistory	Production.TransactionHistoryArchive	Production.UnitMeasure
Production.WorkOrder	Production.WorkOrderRouting	Purchasing.ProductVendor	Purchasing.PurchaseOrderDetail	Purchasing.PurchaseOrderHeader
Purchasing.ShipMethod	Purchasing.Vendor	Sales.CountryRegionCurrency	Sales.CreditCard	Sales.Currency
Sales.CurrencyRate	Sales.Customer	Sales.PersonCreditCard	Sales.SalesOrderDetail	Sales.SalesOrderHeader
Sales.SalesOrderHeaderSalesReason	Sales.SalesPerson	Sales.SalesPersonQuotaHistory	Sales.SalesReason	Sales.SalesTaxRate
Sales.SalesTerritory	Sales.SalesTerritoryHistory	Sales.ShoppingCartItem	Sales.SpecialOffer	Sales.SpecialOfferProduct
Sales.Store	NULL	NULL	NULL	NULL

CHAPTER 2: Sample Application & System Databases

Diagram of Person.Person & Related Tables

Database diagram displays the Person.Person and related tables. PRIMARY KEYs are marked with a gold (in color display) key. The "oo-------->" line is interpreted as many-to-one relationship. For example a person (one) can have one or more (many) credit cards. The "oo" side is the table with **FOREIGN KEY** referencing the gold key side table with the **PRIMARY KEY**.

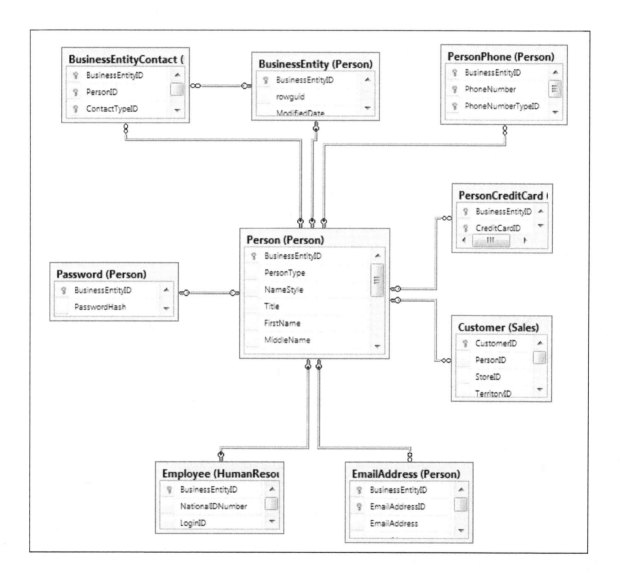

Diagram of Sales.SalesOrderHeader and Related Tables

Database diagram displays Sales.SalesOrderHeader and all tables related with **FOREIGN KEY** constraints. The SalesOrderHeader table stores the general information about each order. Line items, e.g. 5 Helmets at $30 each, are stored in the SalesOrderDetail table.

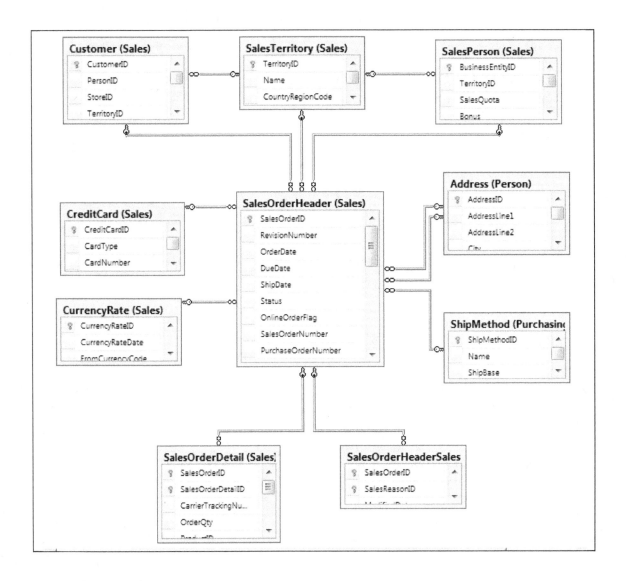

SELECT Query Basics

We have to use "light-weight" SQL (Structured Query Language) in the database design lessons. The reason is that rather difficult to discuss any database related topic without demonstration T-SQL scripts, in fact it would not make sense. **Relational database** and the **SQL language** are "married" to each other forever and ever.

The Simplest SELECT Statement

The simplest SELECT statement is "SELECT * FROM TableNameX" as demonstrated following. The "*" means wildcard inclusion of all columns in the table. Since there is no any other clause in the SELECT statement, it means also to retrieve all rows in the **table in no particular order**. Small tables which were populated in order are usually retrieved in order even though there is no ORDER BY clause. But this behaviour is purely coincidental. **Only ORDER BY clause can guarantee a sorted output.**

```
SELECT * FROM AdventureWorks2012.HumanResources.Department;
-- (16 row(s) affected)
```

DepartmentID	Name	GroupName	ModifiedDate
1	Engineering	Research and Development	2002-06-01 00:00:00.000
2	Tool Design	Research and Development	2002-06-01 00:00:00.000
3	Sales	Sales and Marketing	2002-06-01 00:00:00.000
4	Marketing	Sales and Marketing	2002-06-01 00:00:00.000
5	Purchasing	Inventory Management	2002-06-01 00:00:00.000
6	Research and Development	Research and Development	2002-06-01 00:00:00.000
7	Production	Manufacturing	2002-06-01 00:00:00.000
8	Production Control	Manufacturing	2002-06-01 00:00:00.000
9	Human Resources	Executive General and Administration	2002-06-01 00:00:00.000
10	Finance	Executive General and Administration	2002-06-01 00:00:00.000
11	Information Services	Executive General and Administration	2002-06-01 00:00:00.000
12	Document Control	Quality Assurance	2002-06-01 00:00:00.000
13	Quality Assurance	Quality Assurance	2002-06-01 00:00:00.000
14	Facilities and Maintenance	Executive General and Administration	2002-06-01 00:00:00.000
15	Shipping and Receiving	Inventory Management	2002-06-01 00:00:00.000
16	Executive	Executive General and Administration	2002-06-01 00:00:00.000

When tables are JOINed, SELECT * returns all the columns with all the data in the participant tables.

```
SELECT TOP 3 * FROM Sales.SalesOrderHeader H
            INNER JOIN Sales.SalesOrderDetail D
                ON H.SalesOrderID = D.SalesOrderID;
-- 121,317 rows in the JOIN
```

CHAPTER 2: Sample Application & System Databases

Query Result Set In Text Format

If no grid format available, text format can be used. While it works, it is a challenge to read it, but computer geeks are used to this kind of data dump.

```
/* SalesOrderID RevisionNumber OrderDate        DueDate        ShipDate        Status OnlineOrderFlag SalesOrderNumber
PurchaseOrderNumber    AccountNumber   CustomerID SalesPersonID TerritoryID BillToAddressID ShipToAddressID ShipMethodID CreditCardID
CreditCardApprovalCode CurrencyRateID SubTotal        TaxAmt        Freight        TotalDue        Comment
rowguid              ModifiedDate        SalesOrderID SalesOrderDetailID CarrierTrackingNumber    OrderQty ProductID SpecialOfferID UnitPrice
UnitPriceDiscount    LineTotal        rowguid        ModifiedDate
----------- -------------- ----------------------- ----------------------- ----------------------- ------ -------------- ------------------------ -------------------------------- ---------------------------------- -------------------- ----------- -
----------- -------------- ----------------------- ----------------------- ----------------------- ------ -------------- ------------------------ -------------------------------- ---------------------------------- -------------------- -------
---- ----------------------- -------- -------- ----------------------- -------------------------------- ---------------------------------- ------
---- -----------------------
43735   3       2005-07-10 00:00:00.000 2005-07-22 00:00:00.000 2005-07-17 00:00:00.000 5   1       SO43735         NULL            10-
4030-016522 16522   NULL    9   25384   25384   1   6526    1034619Vi33896      119    3578.27     286.2616
89.4568     3953.9884   NULL                    98F80245-C398-4562-BDAF-
EA3E9A0DDFAC 2005-07-17 00:00:00.000 43735    391     NULL    1   749   1   3578.27   0.00      3578.270000
74838EF7-FDEB-4EB3-8978-BA310FBA82E6 2005-07-10 00:00:00.000
43736   3       2005-07-10 00:00:00.000 2005-07-22 00:00:00.000 2005-07-17 00:00:00.000 5   1       SO43736         NULL            10-
4030-011002 11002   NULL    9   20336   20336   1   1416    1135092Vi7270       119    3399.99     271.9992
84.9998     3756.989    NULL                    C14E29E7-DB11-44EF-943E-
143925A5A9AE 2005-07-17 00:00:00.000 43736    392     NULL    1   773   1   3399.99   0.00      3399.990000
3A0229FA-0A03-4126-97CE-C34259688670 2005-07-10 00:00:00.000
43737   3       2005-07-11 00:00:00.000 2005-07-23 00:00:00.000 2005-07-18 00:00:00.000 5   1       SO43737         NULL            10-
4030-013261 13261   NULL    8   29772   29772   1   NULL    NULL                136    3578.27     286.2616
89.4568     3953.9884   NULL                    0B3E274D-E5A8-4E8C-A417-
0EAFABCFF162 2005-07-18 00:00:00.000 43737    393     NULL    1   750   1   3578.27   0.00      3578.270000
65AFCCE8-CA28-41C4-9A07-0265FB2DA5C8 2005-07-11 00:00:00.000       (3 row(s) affected)  */
```

```sql
SELECT MatchingRows = COUNT(*) FROM AdventureWorks2012.Sales.SalesOrderHeader H
    INNER JOIN AdventureWorks2012.Sales.SalesOrderDetail D
        ON H.SalesOrderID = D.SalesOrderID;    -- INNER JOIN MatchingRows 121317
```

```sql
SELECT AllRowsInDetail = COUNT(*) FROM AdventureWorks2012.Sales.SalesOrderDetail
-- AllRowsInDetail 121317
```

The SOUNDEX() Function to Check Sound Alikes

The soundex() function is very interesting for testing different spelling of words such as names.

```sql
USE AdventureWorks2012;
SELECT DISTINCT LastName   FROM Person.Person
WHERE soundex(LastName)  = soundex('Steel');
```

LastName
Seidel
Sotelo
Stahl
Steel
Steele

SELECT Query with WHERE Clause Predicate

Query to demonstrate how can we be selective with columns, furthermore, filter returned rows (WHERE clause) and sort them (ORDER BY clause).

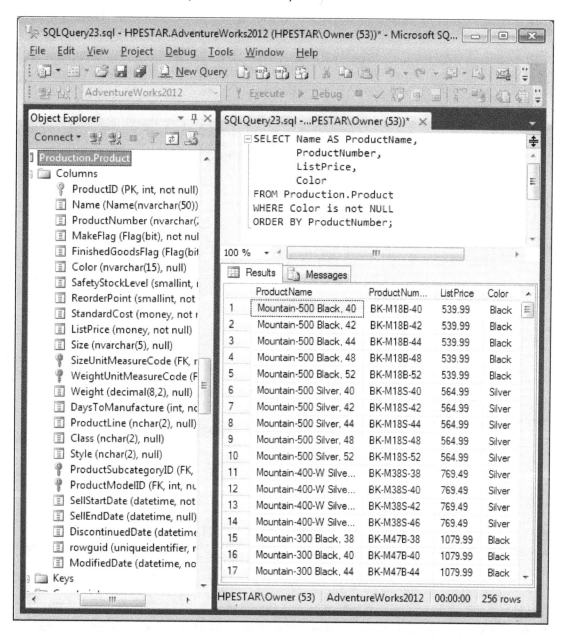

Aggregating Data with GROUP BY Query

The second basic query is GROUP BY aggregation which creates a **summary** of detail data. GROUP BY query can be used to preview, review, survey , assess, and analyze data at a high level.

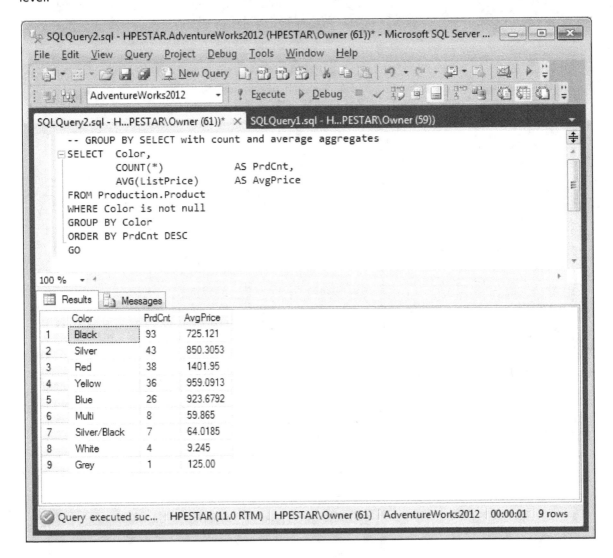

NOTE
GROUP BY aggregate queries can efficiently "fingerprint" (profile) data in tables, even millions of rows.
GROUP BY aggregates form the computational base of Business Intelligence.

GROUP BY Query with 2 Tables & ORDER BY for Sorting

JOINing two tables on matching KEYs, FOREIGN KEY to PRIMARY KEY, to combine the data contents in a consistent fashion.

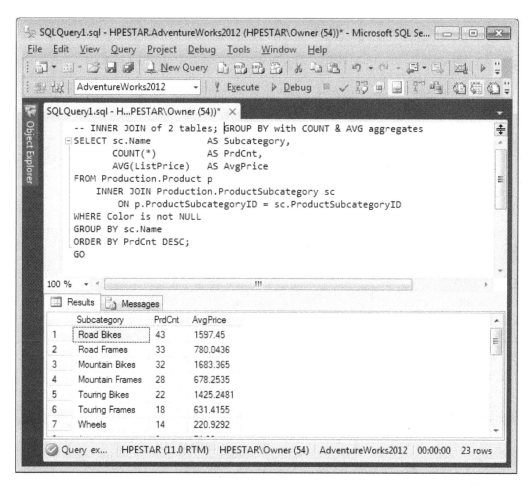

LEN(), DATALENGTH(), LTRIM() & RTRIM() Functions

The LEN() function counts characters without the trailing spaces. DATALENGTH() counts storage bytes including trailing spaces. LTRIM() trims leading spaces, RTRIM() trims trailing spaces.

```
DECLARE @W varchar(32)= CHAR(32)+'Denver'+CHAR(32);
DECLARE @UW nvarchar(32) = CHAR(32)+N'MEGŐRZÉSE'+CHAR(32); -- UNICODE 2 bytes per character
SELECT Length=LEN(@W), DLength=DATALENGTH (@W);                              -- 7  8
SELECT Length=LEN(@UW), DLength=DATALENGTH (@UW);                           -- 10 22
SELECT Length=LEN(LTRIM(RTRIM(@W))), DLength=DATALENGTH (LTRIM(RTRIM(@W)));  -- 6  6
SELECT Length=LEN(LTRIM(RTRIM(@UW))), DLength=DATALENGTH (LTRIM(RTRIM(@UW))); -- 9 18
```

CHAPTER 2: Sample Application & System Databases

Finding All Accessories in Production.Product Table

Query to list all accessories (a category) for sale.

```
USE AdventureWorks2012;

SELECT      UPPER(PC.Name) AS Category, PSC.Name          AS Subcategory,
            P.Name AS Product, FORMAT(ListPrice, 'c', 'en-US')   AS ListPrice,
            FORMAT(StandardCost, 'c', 'en-US')            AS StandardCost
FROM Production.Product AS P
   INNER JOIN Production.ProductSubcategory AS PSC
            ON PSC.ProductSubcategoryID = P.ProductSubcategoryID
   INNER JOIN Production.ProductCategory AS PC
            ON PC.ProductCategoryID = PSC.ProductCategoryID
WHERE PC.Name = 'Accessories'
ORDER BY Category, Subcategory, Product;      -- (29 row(s) affected) - Partial results.
```

Category	Subcategory	Product	ListPrice	StandardCost
ACCESSORIES	Bike Racks	Hitch Rack - 4-Bike	$120.00	$44.88
ACCESSORIES	Bike Stands	All-Purpose Bike Stand	$159.00	$59.47
ACCESSORIES	Bottles and Cages	Mountain Bottle Cage	$9.99	$3.74
ACCESSORIES	Bottles and Cages	Road Bottle Cage	$8.99	$3.36
ACCESSORIES	Bottles and Cages	Water Bottle - 30 oz.	$4.99	$1.87
ACCESSORIES	Cleaners	Bike Wash - Dissolver	$7.95	$2.97

Using Implicit or Explicit Conversion

Implicit conversion results in simpler code and may even be faster. However, if we really need a specific conversion, explicit conversion should be used. In the ShipDate datetime column example, the implicit & explicit conversions yield the same results.

```
SELECT SalesOrderID, OrderDate, ShipDate, CustomerID, SubTotal
FROM Sales.SalesOrderHeader
WHERE ShipDate = '2008-03-08';                    -- Implicit conversion to datetime

/*     WHERE Shipdate = CONVERT(DATETIME, '2008-03-08');    -- Explicit conversion
       WHERE Shipdate = CONVERT(DATE, '2008-03-08');        -- Explicit conversion */
-- (247 row(s) affected) - Partial results.
```

SalesOrderID	OrderDate	ShipDate	CustomerID	SubTotal
65089	2008-02-29 00:00:00.000	2008-03-08 00:00:00.000	30079	1466.01
65090	2008-02-29 00:00:00.000	2008-03-08 00:00:00.000	29812	98.774
65151	2008-03-01 00:00:00.000	2008-03-08 00:00:00.000	30072	76.20

How Can SQL Work without Looping?

Looping is implicit in the SQL language. The commands are set oriented and carried out for each member of the set be it 5 or 500 millions in an unordered manner.

SELECT * FROM AdventureWorks2012.Sales.SalesOrderDetail;   (121317 row(s) affected)

SQL Server database engine looped through internally on all rows in SalesOrderDetail table in an unordered way. In fact the database engine may have used some ordering for efficiency, but that behaviour is a blackbox as far as programming concerned. Implicit looping makes SQL statements so simple, yet immensely powerful for information access from low level to high level.

Single-Valued SQL Queries

Single-valued SQL queries are very important because **we can use them where ever the T-SQL syntax requires a single value just by enclosing the query in parenthesis**. The next T-SQL query returns a single value, a cell from the table which is the intersection of a row and a column.

SELECT ListPrice FROM AdventureWorks2012.Production.Product WHERE ProductID = 800;
-- (1 row(s) affected)

ListPrice
1120.49

The ">" comparison operator requires a single value on the right hand side so we plug in the single-valued query. The WHERE condition is evaluated for each row (implicit looping).

```
SELECT ProductID, Name AS ProductName, ListPrice
FROM AdventureWorks2012.Production.Product                         -- 504 rows
WHERE ListPrice > 2 *  (
                SELECT ListPrice FROM AdventureWorks2012.Production.Product
                WHERE ProductID = 800
                )
ORDER BY ListPrice DESC, ProductName;    -- (35 row(s) affected) - Partial results.
```

ProductID	ProductName	ListPrice
750	Road-150 Red, 44	3578.27
751	Road-150 Red, 48	3578.27
752	Road-150 Red, 52	3578.27
753	Road-150 Red, 56	3578.27
749	Road-150 Red, 62	3578.27
771	Mountain-100 Silver, 38	3399.99

CHAPTER 2: Sample Application & System Databases

Data Dictionary Description of Tables in the Sales Schema

It is not easy to understand a database with 70 tables, even harder with 2,000 tables. Documentation is very helpful, if not essential, for any database. SQL Server provides Data Dictionary facility for documenting tables and other objects in the database. Data which describes the design & structure of a database is called **metadata**. Here is the high level documentation of tables in the Sales schema using the fn_listextendedproperty system function.

```
SELECT
        CONCAT('Sales.', objname COLLATE DATABASE_DEFAULT)      AS TableName,
        value                                                   AS [Description]
FROM fn_listextendedproperty (NULL, 'schema', 'Sales', 'table', default, NULL, NULL)
ORDER BY TableName;
```

TableName	Description
Sales.ContactCreditCard	Cross-reference table mapping customers in the Contact table to their credit card information in the CreditCard table.
Sales.CountryRegionCurrency	Cross-reference table mapping ISO currency codes to a country or region.
Sales.CreditCard	Customer credit card information.
Sales.Currency	Lookup table containing standard ISO currencies.
Sales.CurrencyRate	Currency exchange rates.
Sales.Customer	Current customer information. Also see the Individual and Store tables.
Sales.CustomerAddress	Cross-reference table mapping customers to their address(es).
Sales.Individual	Demographic data about customers that purchase Adventure Works products online.
Sales.SalesOrderDetail	Individual products associated with a specific sales order. See SalesOrderHeader.
Sales.SalesOrderHeader	General sales order information.
Sales.SalesOrderHeaderSalesReason	Cross-reference table mapping sales orders to sales reason codes.
Sales.SalesPerson	Sales representative current information.
Sales.SalesPersonQuotaHistory	Sales performance tracking.
Sales.SalesReason	Lookup table of customer purchase reasons.
Sales.SalesTaxRate	Tax rate lookup table.
Sales.SalesTerritory	Sales territory lookup table.
Sales.SalesTerritoryHistory	Sales representative transfers to other sales territories.
Sales.ShoppingCartItem	Contains online customer orders until the order is submitted or cancelled.
Sales.SpecialOffer	Sale discounts lookup table.
Sales.SpecialOfferProduct	Cross-reference table mapping products to special offer discounts.
Sales.Store	Customers (resellers) of Adventure Works products.
Sales.StoreContact	Cross-reference table mapping stores and their employees.

NULL Values in Tables & Query Results

NULL means no value. If so why do we capitalize it? We don't have to. Somehow, it became a custom in the RDBMS industry, nobody knows anymore how it started. Since the U.S. default collation for server and databases are case insensitive, we can just use "null" as well. **NULL value is different from empty string ('') or 0 (zero) which can be tested by the "=" or "!=" operators.** If a database table does not have a value in a cell for whatever reason, it is marked (flagged) as NULL by the database engine. When a value is entered, the NULL marking goes away. **NULL values can be tested by "IS NULL" or "IS NOT NULL" operators, but not the "=" or "!=" operators.**

The likelihood is high that the color attribute is not applicable to items like tire tube, that is the reason that some cell values were left unassigned (null).

```
SELECT TOP 5    Name                                AS ProductName,
                ProductNumber,
                ListPrice,
                Color
FROM AdventureWorks2012.Production.Product
WHERE Color IS NULL  ORDER BY ProductName DESC;
```

ProductName	ProductNumber	ListPrice	Color
Water Bottle - 30 oz.	WB-H098	4.99	NULL
Touring Tire Tube	TT-T092	4.99	NULL
Touring Tire	TI-T723	28.99	NULL
Touring Rim	RM-T801	0.00	NULL
Touring End Caps	EC-T209	0.00	NULL

We can do random selection as well and get a mix of products with color and null value.

```
SELECT TOP 5    Name AS ProductName,
                ProductNumber,
                ListPrice,
                Color
FROM AdventureWorks2012.Production.Product  ORDER BY NEWID();    -- Random sort
```

ProductName	ProductNumber	ListPrice	Color
Touring-1000 Yellow, 46	BK-T79Y-46	2384.07	Yellow
HL Spindle/Axle	SD-9872	0.00	NULL
ML Mountain Tire	TI-M602	29.99	NULL
Road-650 Red, 60	BK-R50R-60	782.99	Red
Pinch Bolt	PB-6109	0.00	NULL

NULL Values Generated by Queries

NULL values can be generated by queries as well. Typically, LEFT JOIN, RIGHT JOIN and some functions generate NULLs. The meaning of OUTER JOINs: include no-match rows from the left or right table in addition to the matching rows.

```
SELECT TOP 5
          PS.Name                AS Category,
          P.Name                 AS ProductName,
          ProductNumber,
          ListPrice,
          Color
FROM AdventureWorks2012.Production.Product P
   RIGHT JOIN AdventureWorks2012.Production.ProductSubcategory PS
        ON    PS.ProductSubcategoryID = P.ProductSubcategoryID
              AND ListPrice >= 3500.0
ORDER BY newid();
GO
```

Category	ProductName	ProductNumber	ListPrice	Color
Road Bikes	Road-150 Red, 62	BK-R93R-62	3578.27	Red
Road Bikes	Road-150 Red, 52	BK-R93R-52	3578.27	Red
Bib-Shorts	NULL	NULL	NULL	NULL
Socks	NULL	NULL	NULL	NULL
Cranksets	NULL	NULL	NULL	NULL

Some system functions, like the brand new TRY_CONVERT(), can generate NULL values as well. If the PostalCode cannot be converted into an integer, TRY_CONVERT() returns NULL.

```
SELECT TOP 5   ConvertedZip = TRY_CONVERT(INT, PostalCode),
          AddressLine1,
          City,
          PostalCode
FROM Person.Address  ORDER by newid();
```

ConvertedZip	AddressLine1	City	PostalCode
91945	5979 El Pueblo	Lemon Grove	91945
NULL	7859 Green Valley Road	London	W1V 5RN
3220	6004 Peabody Road	Geelong	3220
NULL	6713 Eaker Way	Burnaby	V3J 6Z3
NULL	5153 Hackamore Lane	Shawnee	V8Z 4N5

DATETIME Conversion to Text with the CONVERT Function

DATETIME data type stored internally in a special 8-bytes binary format. Externally it is represented in various string formats which changes from country to country. The CONVERT function with style number parameter is used to translate from datetime to text and vice versa.

```
DECLARE @DT datetime = '2016-10-23T11:20:30.456';
SELECT CONVERT(VARCHAR, @DT, 100);                          -- 100 is the style number
-- Oct 23 2016 11:20AM    -- one string representation of @DT datetime value

SELECT @DT = CONVERT(datetime, 'Oct 23 2016 11:20AM');
SELECT @DT;  -- 2016-10-23 11:20:00.000 -- different string representation of datetime value
SELECT @DT = '2016-10-23T11:20:30.456'; -- restore initial value
```

Standard	SQL Statement	Input/Output Format	Sample Date/Time
USA default	SELECT CONVERT(VARCHAR, @DT);	Mon DD YYYY HH:MIAM/PM	Oct 23 2016 11:20AM
USA	SELECT CONVERT(VARCHAR, @DT, 100);	Mon DD YYYY HH:MIAM/PM	Oct 23 2016 11:20AM
USA without century	SELECT CONVERT(VARCHAR, @DT, 1);	MM/DD/YY	10/23/16
USA with century	SELECT CONVERT(VARCHAR, @DT, 101);	MM/DD/YYYY	10/23/2016
ANSI	SELECT CONVERT(VARCHAR, @DT, 2);	YY.MM.DD	16.10.23
with century	SELECT CONVERT(VARCHAR, @DT, 102);	YYYY.MM.DD	2016.10.23
British/French	SELECT CONVERT(VARCHAR, @DT, 3);	DD/MM/YY	23/10/16
with century	SELECT CONVERT(VARCHAR, @DT, 103);	DD/MM/YYYY	23/10/2016
German	SELECT CONVERT(VARCHAR, @DT, 4);	DD.MM.YY	23.10.16
with century	SELECT CONVERT(VARCHAR, @DT, 104);	DD.MM.YYYY	23.10.2016
Italian	SELECT CONVERT(VARCHAR, @DT, 5);	DD-MM-YY	23-10-16
with century	SELECT CONVERT(VARCHAR, @DT, 105);	DD-MM-YYYY	23-10-2016
UK	SELECT CONVERT(VARCHAR, @DT, 106);	DD Mon YYYY	23 Oct 2016
USA	SELECT CONVERT(VARCHAR, @DT, 107);	Mon DD, YYYY	Oct 23, 2016
time only	SELECT CONVERT(VARCHAR, @DT, 108);	HH:MM:SS	11:20:30
Default + milliseconds	SELECT CONVERT(VARCHAR, @DT, 109);	Mon DD YYYY HH:MI:SS:MMMAM/PM	Oct 23 2016 11:20:30:457AM
USA	SELECT CONVERT(VARCHAR, @DT, 110);	MM-DD-YYYY	10-23-2016
Japan	SELECT CONVERT(VARCHAR, @DT, 111);	YYYY/MM/DD	2016/10/23
ISO	SELECT CONVERT(VARCHAR, @DT, 112);	YYYYMMDD	20161023
Europe default + milliseconds	SELECT CONVERT(VARCHAR, @DT, 113);	DD Mon YYYY HH:MM:SS:MMM(24h)	23 Oct 2016 11:20:30:457
time only	SELECT CONVERT(VARCHAR, @DT, 114);	HH:MI:SS:MMM(24H)	11:20:30:457
ODBC Canonical	SELECT CONVERT(VARCHAR, @DT, 120);	YYYY-MM-DD HH:MI:SS(24h)	2016-10-23 11:20:30
ODBC (with milliseconds)	SELECT CONVERT(VARCHAR, @DT, 121);	YYYY-MM-DD HH:MI:SS.MMM(24h)	2016-10-23 11:20:30.457
ISO8601	SELECT CONVERT(VARCHAR, @DT, 126);	YYYY-MM-DDTHH:MM:SS:MMM	2016-10-23T11:20:30.457
Hijri	SELECT CONVERT(NVARCHAR(40), @DT, 130);	DD Mon YYYY HH:MI:SS:MMMAM	محرم 1438 11:20:30:457AM 22
Hijri	SELECT CONVERT(NVARCHAR(40), @DT, 131);	DD/MM/YYYY HH:MI:SS:MMMAM	22/01/1438 11:20:30:457AM

DATETIME Conversion with the FORMAT Function

Starting with SQL Server 2012 the FORMAT function can be used for DATETIME to text conversion.

```
DECLARE @DT datetime = '2016-10-23T11:20:30.456';
SELECT FORMAT(@DT, 'MMM dd, yyyy hh:mm:ss', 'en-US');          -- Oct 23, 2016 11:20:30
SELECT FORMAT(@DT, 'dd MMMMMMMMMMMMM, yyyy hh:mm:ss', 'en-GB');  -- 23 October, 2016 11:20:30
SELECT FORMAT(@DT, 'MMM dd, yyyy hh:mm:ss', 'de-DE');          -- Okt 23, 2016 11:20:30
SELECT FORMAT(@DT, 'MMM dd, yyyy hh:mm:ss', 'hu-HU');          -- okt. 23, 2016 11:20:30
SELECT FORMAT(@DT, 'MMM dd, yyyy hh:mm:ss', 'es-ES');          -- oct 23, 2016 11:20:30
SELECT FORMAT(@DT, 'MMM dd, yyyy hh:mm:ss', 'ru-RU');          -- окт 23, 2016 11:20:30
```

CHAPTER 2: Sample Application & System Databases

Building an FK-PK Diagram in AdventureWorks2012

The **FOREIGN KEY - PRIMARY KEY** diagram of AdventureWorks2012 database with over 70 tables can be built just by adding the tables to the diagram. The FK-PK lines are automatically drawn. An FK-PK line represents a predefined referential constraint.

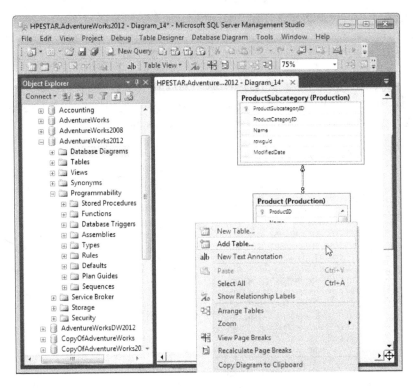

While all tables are important in a database, tables with the most connections play central roles, in a way analogous to the Sun with planets around it.

```
-- PRIMARY KEY tables with the most FOREIGN KEY references
SELECT          schema_name(schema_id)          AS SchemaName,
                o.name                           AS PKTable,
                count(*)                         AS FKCount
FROM sys.sysforeignkeys s    INNER JOIN sys.objects o      ON s.rkeyid = o.object_id
GROUP BY schema_id, o.name    HAVING count(*) >= 5   ORDER BY FKCount DESC;
```

SchemaName	PKTable	FKCount
Production	Product	14
Person	Person	7
HumanResources	Employee	6
Person	BusinessEntity	5
Sales	SalesTerritory	5

CHAPTER 2: Sample Application & System Databases

AdventureWorksDW2012 Data Warehouse Database

AdventureWorksDW series contain second hand data only since they are Data Warehouse databases. All data originates from other sources such as the AdventureWorks OLTP database & Excel worksheets. Tables in the data warehousing database are divided into two groups: dimension tables & fact tables.

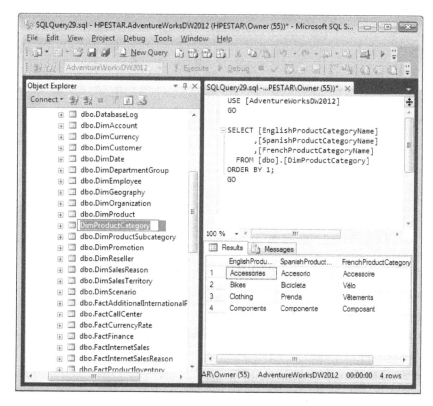

Simple data warehouse query.

```
SELECT          D.CalendarYear AS [Year], C.SalesTerritoryCountry AS [Country],
                FORMAT(SUM(S.SalesAmount),'c0','en-US') AS TotalSales
FROM FactInternetSales AS S  INNER JOIN DimDate AS D ON S.OrderDateKey = D.DateKey
        INNER JOIN DimSalesTerritory AS C ON S.SalesTerritoryKey = C.SalesTerritoryKey
GROUP BY D.CalendarYear, C.SalesTerritoryCountry  ORDER BY Year DESC, SUM(S.SalesAmount) DESC;
```

Year	Country	TotalSales
2008	United States	$3,324,031
2008	Australia	$2,563,884
2008	United Kingdom	$1,210,286
2008	Germany	$1,076,891
2008	France	$922,179

CHAPTER 2: Sample Application & System Databases

Diagram of a Star Schema in AdventureWorksDW2012

The high level star schema diagram in AdventureWorksDW2012 Data Warehouse database with FactResellerSales fact table and related dimension tables. The temporal dimension table DimDate plays a central role in Business Intelligence data analytics.

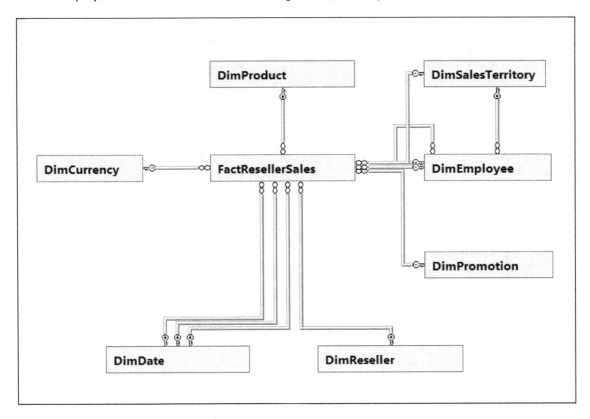

Distribution of **PRIMARY KEY - FOREIGN KEY** relationships can be generated from metadata (system views) for the entire Data Warehouse.

```
SELECT  schema_name(schema_id) AS SchemaName, o.name AS PKTable,  count(*) AS FKCount
FROM sys.sysforeignkeys s  INNER JOIN sys.objects o    ON s.rkeyid = o.object_id
GROUP BY schema_id, o.name  HAVING COUNT(*) > 2 ORDER BY FKCount DESC;
```

SchemaName	PKTable	FKCount
dbo	DimDate	12
dbo	DimCurrency	4
dbo	DimSalesTerritory	4
dbo	DimEmployee	3
dbo	DimProduct	3

CHAPTER 2: Sample Application & System Databases

AdventureWorks2008 Sample Database

There were substantial changes made from the prior version of the sample database. Among them demonstration use of the **hierarchyid** data type which has been introduced with SS 2008 to support sophisticated tree hierarchy processing. In addition employee, customer and dealer PRIMARY KEYs are pooled together and called BusinessEntityID.

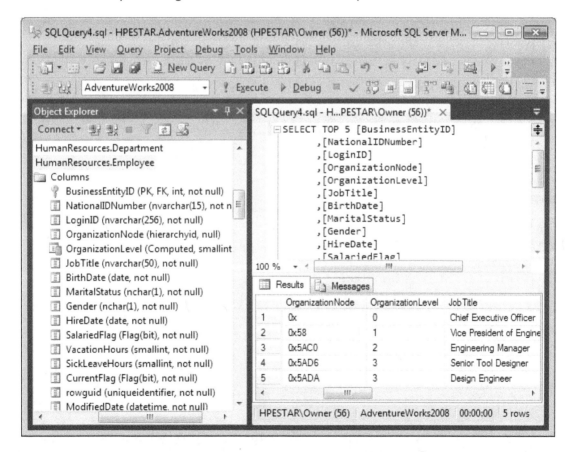

AdventureWorks2012 Sample Database

There were no apparent design changes made from the prior version of the sample database. A significant content change: dates were advanced 4 years. An OrderDate (Sales.SalesOrderHeader table) of 2004-02-01 in previous versions is now 2008-02-01.

The OrderDate statistics in the two sample databases.

```
SELECT [Year]          = YEAR(OrderDate),     OrderCount    = COUNT(*)
FROM AdventureWorks2008.Sales.SalesOrderHeader GROUP BY YEAR(OrderDate)
ORDER BY [Year];
```

Year	OrderCount
2001	1379
2002	3692
2003	12443
2004	13951

```
SELECT [Year]          = YEAR(OrderDate),     OrderCount    = COUNT(*)
FROM AdventureWorks2012.Sales.SalesOrderHeader GROUP BY YEAR(OrderDate)
ORDER BY [Year];
```

Year	OrderCount
2005	1379
2006	3692
2007	12443
2008	13951

Starting with SQL Server 2012, numeric figures, among others, can be formatted with the FORMAT function.

```
SELECT [Year]          = YEAR(OrderDate),
       OrderCount      = FORMAT(COUNT(*), '###,###')
FROM AdventureWorks2012.Sales.SalesOrderHeader
GROUP BY YEAR(OrderDate)  ORDER BY [Year];
```

Year	OrderCount
2005	1,379
2006	3,692
2007	12,443
2008	13,951

Production.Product and Related Tables

The Product table is the "center" of the database. The reason is that AdventureWorks Cycles is a product base company selling through dealers and directly to consumers through the internet. You may wonder why are we pushing **FOREIGN KEY - PRIMARY KEY** relationship so vehemently? Because there is nothing else to a database just **well-designed tables and their connections which are FK-PK constraints**.

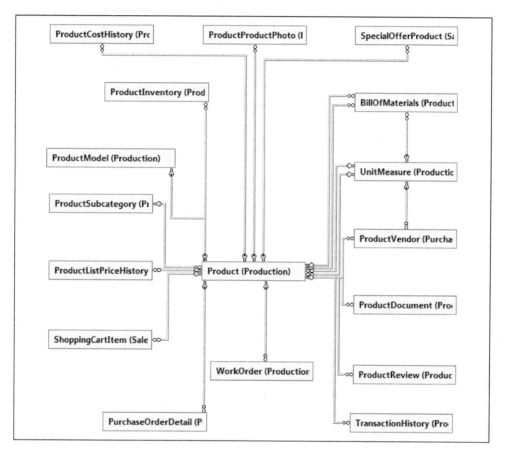

Simple OLTP query.

```
SELECT Color, WOCount=COUNT(*)  FROM Production.WorkOrder W
       INNER JOIN Production.Product P   ON W.ProductID = P.ProductID  WHERE Color != ''
GROUP BY Color ORDER BY WOCount DESC;
```

Color	WOCount
Black	18952
Silver	6620
Yellow	5231
Red	4764
Blue	2319

CHAPTER 2: Sample Application & System Databases

Descriptions of Columns in Production.Product Table

Queries to list the description of table and columns from Extended Property (data dictionary).

```
USE AdventureWorks2012;
SELECT          objname AS TableName, value   AS [Description]
FROM fn_listextendedproperty( NULL, 'schema', 'Production', 'table', 'Product', NULL, NULL);
```

TableName	Description
Product	Products sold or used in the manfacturing of sold products.

```
SELECT          'Production.Product'          AS TableName,          -- String literal
                objname                        AS ColumnName,
                value                          AS [Description]
FROM fn_listextendedproperty( NULL, 'schema', 'Production', 'table',
                            'Product', 'column', default);
```

TableName	ColumnName	Description
Production.Product	ProductID	Primary key for Product records.
Production.Product	Name	Name of the product.
Production.Product	ProductNumber	Unique product identification number.
Production.Product	MakeFlag	0 = Product is purchased, 1 = Product is manufactured in-house.
Production.Product	FinishedGoodsFlag	0 = Product is not a salable item. 1 = Product is salable.
Production.Product	Color	Product color.
Production.Product	SafetyStockLevel	Minimum inventory quantity.
Production.Product	ReorderPoint	Inventory level that triggers a purchase order or work order.
Production.Product	StandardCost	Standard cost of the product.
Production.Product	ListPrice	Selling price.
Production.Product	Size	Product size.
Production.Product	SizeUnitMeasureCode	Unit of measure for Size column.
Production.Product	WeightUnitMeasureCode	Unit of measure for Weight column.
Production.Product	Weight	Product weight.
Production.Product	DaysToManufacture	Number of days required to manufacture the product.
Production.Product	ProductLine	R = Road, M = Mountain, T = Touring, S = Standard
Production.Product	Class	H = High, M = Medium, L = Low
Production.Product	Style	W = Womens, M = Mens, U = Universal
Production.Product	ProductSubcategoryID	Product is a member of this product subcategory. Foreign key to ProductSubCategory.ProductSubCategoryID.
Production.Product	ProductModelID	Product is a member of this product model. Foreign key to ProductModel.ProductModelID.
Production.Product	SellStartDate	Date the product was available for sale.
Production.Product	SellEndDate	Date the product was no longer available for sale.
Production.Product	DiscontinuedDate	Date the product was discontinued.
Production.Product	rowguid	ROWGUIDCOL number uniquely identifying the record. Used to support a merge replication sample.
Production.Product	ModifiedDate	Date and time the record was last updated.

Mountain Bikes in Production.Product Table

Query to list all mountain bikes offered for sale by AdventureWorks Cycles with category, subcategory, list price and standard cost information.

```
USE AdventureWorks2012;
SELECT  UPPER(PC.Name) AS Category, PSC.Name AS Subcategory,
        P.Name AS Product, FORMAT(ListPrice, 'c', 'en-US') AS ListPrice,
        FORMAT(StandardCost, 'c', 'en-US') AS StandardCost
FROM Production.Product AS P
   INNER JOIN Production.ProductSubcategory AS PSC
            ON PSC.ProductSubcategoryID = P.ProductSubcategoryID
   INNER JOIN Production.ProductCategory AS PC
            ON PC.ProductCategoryID = PSC.ProductCategoryID
WHERE PSC.Name = 'Mountain Bikes'
ORDER BY Category, Subcategory, Product;                -- Partial results.
```

Category	Subcategory	Product	ListPrice	StandardCost
BIKES	Mountain Bikes	Mountain-100 Black, 38	$3,374.99	$1,898.09
BIKES	Mountain Bikes	Mountain-100 Black, 42	$3,374.99	$1,898.09
BIKES	Mountain Bikes	Mountain-100 Black, 44	$3,374.99	$1,898.09
BIKES	Mountain Bikes	Mountain-100 Black, 48	$3,374.99	$1,898.09
BIKES	Mountain Bikes	Mountain-100 Silver, 38	$3,399.99	$1,912.15
BIKES	Mountain Bikes	Mountain-100 Silver, 42	$3,399.99	$1,912.15
BIKES	Mountain Bikes	Mountain-100 Silver, 44	$3,399.99	$1,912.15
BIKES	Mountain Bikes	Mountain-100 Silver, 48	$3,399.99	$1,912.15
BIKES	Mountain Bikes	Mountain-200 Black, 38	$2,294.99	$1,251.98
BIKES	Mountain Bikes	Mountain-200 Black, 42	$2,294.99	$1,251.98
BIKES	Mountain Bikes	Mountain-200 Black, 46	$2,294.99	$1,251.98
BIKES	Mountain Bikes	Mountain-200 Silver, 38	$2,319.99	$1,265.62
BIKES	Mountain Bikes	Mountain-200 Silver, 42	$2,319.99	$1,265.62
BIKES	Mountain Bikes	Mountain-200 Silver, 46	$2,319.99	$1,265.62
BIKES	Mountain Bikes	Mountain-300 Black, 38	$1,079.99	$598.44
BIKES	Mountain Bikes	Mountain-300 Black, 40	$1,079.99	$598.44
BIKES	Mountain Bikes	Mountain-300 Black, 44	$1,079.99	$598.44
BIKES	Mountain Bikes	Mountain-300 Black, 48	$1,079.99	$598.44
BIKES	Mountain Bikes	Mountain-400-W Silver, 38	$769.49	$419.78
BIKES	Mountain Bikes	Mountain-400-W Silver, 40	$769.49	$419.78
BIKES	Mountain Bikes	Mountain-400-W Silver, 42	$769.49	$419.78
BIKES	Mountain Bikes	Mountain-400-W Silver, 46	$769.49	$419.78
BIKES	Mountain Bikes	Mountain-500 Black, 40	$539.99	$294.58
BIKES	Mountain Bikes	Mountain-500 Black, 42	$539.99	$294.58
BIKES	Mountain Bikes	Mountain-500 Black, 44	$539.99	$294.58
BIKES	Mountain Bikes	Mountain-500 Black, 48	$539.99	$294.58

Nested CONVERTs for hex to String Conversion

```
SELECT  CONVERT(VARCHAR(MAX),
       CONVERT(VARBINARY(MAX), '0xFFF4662D8A4422CDED95CB505C269CC897BAFF'));
-- 0xFFF4662D8A4422CDED95CB505C269CC897BAFF
```

CHAPTER 2: Sample Application & System Databases

Prior SQL Server Sample Databases

There are two other sample databases used in the releases of SQL Server: **Northwind** and **pubs**. Northwind has been introduced with SQL Server 7.0 in 1998. That SQL Server version had very short lifetime, replaced with SQL Server 2000 in year 2000. The pubs sample database originates from the time Microsoft & Sybase worked jointly on the database server project around 1990. Despite the relative simplicity of pre-2005 sample databases, they were good enough to demonstrate basic RDBMS SQL queries.

Book sales summary GROUP BY aggregation query.

```
USE pubs;
SELECT pub_name          AS Publisher,
    au_lname             AS Author,
    title                AS Title,
    SUM(qty)             AS SoldQty
FROM   authors
    INNER JOIN titleauthor
        ON authors.au_id = titleauthor.au_id
    INNER JOIN titles
        ON titles.title_id = titleauthor.title_id
    INNER JOIN publishers
        ON publishers.pub_id = titles.pub_id
    INNER JOIN sales
        ON sales.title_id = titles.title_id
GROUP  BY     pub_name,
              au_lname,
              title
ORDER BY Publisher, Author, Title;
-- (23 row(s) affected) - Partial results.
```

Publisher	Author	Title
Algodata Infosystems	Bennet	The Busy Executive's Database Guide
Algodata Infosystems	Carson	But Is It User Friendly?
Algodata Infosystems	Dull	Secrets of Silicon Valley
Algodata Infosystems	Green	The Busy Executive's Database Guide
Algodata Infosystems	Hunter	Secrets of Silicon Valley
Algodata Infosystems	MacFeather	Cooking with Computers: Surreptitious Balance Sheets
Algodata Infosystems	O'Leary	Cooking with Computers: Surreptitious Balance Sheets
Algodata Infosystems	Straight	Straight Talk About Computers
Binnet & Hardley	Blotchet-Halls	Fifty Years in Buckingham Palace Kitchens
Binnet & Hardley	DeFrance	The Gourmet Microwave

Northwind Sample Database

The Northwind database contains well-prepared sales data for a fictitious company called Northwind Traders, which imports & exports specialty gourmet foods & drinks from wholesale suppliers around the world. The company's sales offices are located in Seattle & London. Among gourmet food item products: Carnarvon Tigers, Teatime Chocolate Biscuits, Sir Rodney's Marmalade, Sir Rodney's Scones, Gustaf's Knäckebröd, Tunnbröd & Guaraná Fantástica.

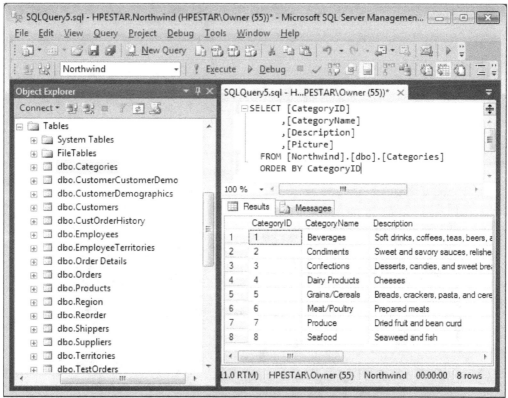

Diagram of Northwind Database

The basic diagram of Northwind database excluding a few ancillary tables. The Orders table is central since the business is wholesale distribution (reselling) of high-end food products.

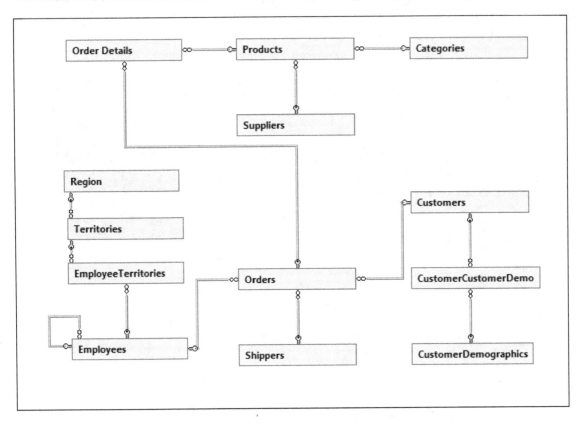

CHAPTER 2: Sample Application & System Databases

pubs Sample Database

The pubs database is a very small and simple publishing database, yet it demonstrates the main features of database design such as PRIMARY KEYs, FOREIGN KEYs, and junction table reflecting many-to-many relationship. The main entities (tables) are: (book) titles, authors, titleauthor (junction table), publishers, sales & royalties.

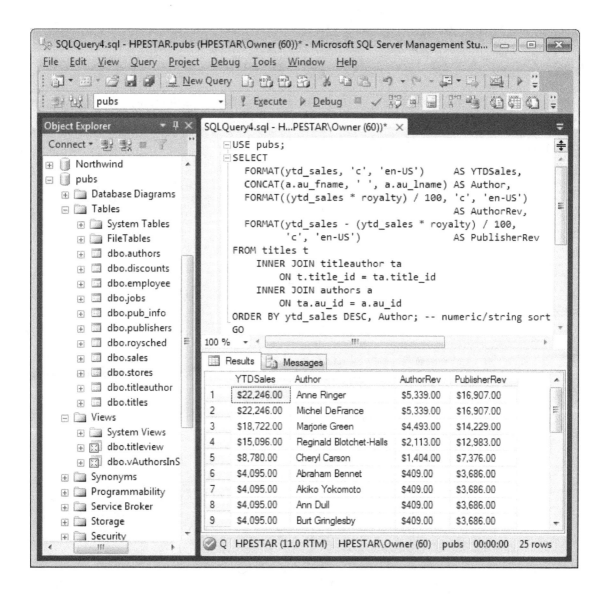

Book Titles in pubs Database

The titles table has the most interesting content in the pubs database as demonstrated by the following T-SQL query.

```
SELECT  TOP 4 title_id AS TitleID, title AS Title, type               AS Type,
        pub_id AS PubID, FORMAT(price, 'c','en-US')                   AS Price,
        FORMAT(advance, 'c','en-US')                                  AS  Advance,
        FORMAT(royalty/100.0, 'p') AS Royalty, FORMAT(ytd_sales, 'c', 'en-US')  AS YTDSales,
        Notes
FROM pubs.dbo.titles
ORDER BY title;
```

TitleID	Title	Type	PubID	Price	Advance	Royalty	YTDSales	Notes
PC1035	But Is It User Friendly?	popular_comp	1389	$22.95	$7,000.00	16.00 %	$8,780.00	A survey of software for the naive user, focusing on the 'friendliness' of each.
PS1372	Computer Phobic AND Non-Phobic Individuals: Behavior Variations	psychology	0877	$21.59	$7,000.00	10.00 %	$375.00	A must for the specialist, this book examines the difference between those who hate and fear computers and those who don't.
BU1111	Cooking with Computers: Surreptitious Balance Sheets	business	1389	$11.95	$5,000.00	10.00 %	$3,876.00	Helpful hints on how to use your electronic resources to the best advantage.
PS7777	Emotional Security: A New Algorithm	psychology	0736	$7.99	$4,000.00	10.00 %	$3,336.00	Protecting yourself and your loved ones from undue emotional stress in the modern world. Use of computer and nutritional aids emphasized.

Diagram of pubs Database

Since pubs is a small database, the diagram conveniently fits on a page.

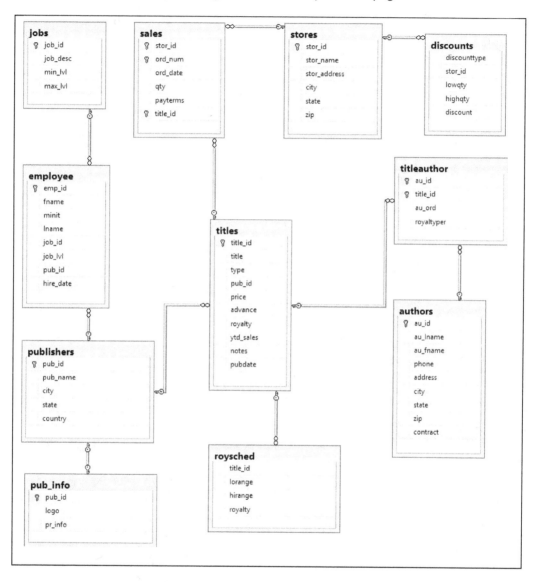

Simple JOIN on non-key columns.

```
USE pubs; SELECT p.*, a.* FROM authors AS a
INNER JOIN publishers AS p ON a.city = p.city ORDER BY p.city, a.au_lname;
```

pub_id	pub_name	city	state	country	au_id	au_lname	au_fname	phone	address	city	state	zip	contract
1389	Algodata Infosystems	Berkeley	CA	USA	409-56-7008	Bennet	Abraham	415 658-9932	6223 Bateman St.	Berkeley	CA	94705	1
1389	Algodata Infosystems	Berkeley	CA	USA	238-95-7766	Carson	Cheryl	415 548-7723	589 Darwin Ln.	Berkeley	CA	94705	1

CHAPTER 2: Sample Application & System Databases

SQL Server System Databases

The master, model, tempdb and msdb are system databases for special database server operations purposes. SSMS Object Explorer drill-down listing of system databases.

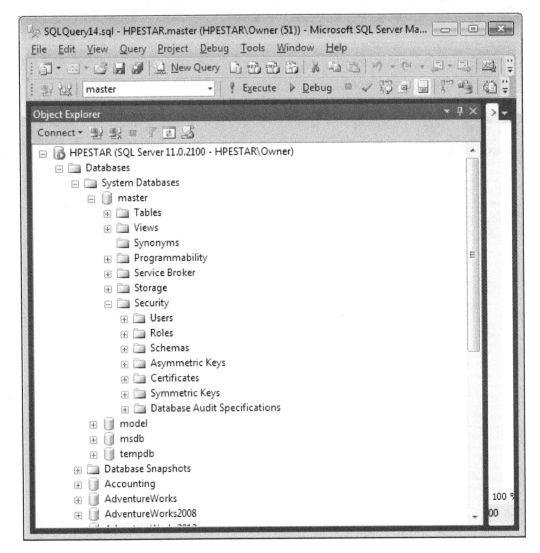

Query to create a new table in tempdb for development purposes.

```
SELECT * INTO tempdb.dbo.Product
FROM AdventureWorks2012.Production.Product
WHERE ListPrice > 0.0;
-- (304 row(s) affected)
```

CHAPTER 2: Sample Application & System Databases

The master Database

The master system database is the nerve center of SQL Server. It contains tables and db objects essential for server operations. System tables are accessible only through read-only views. System tables cannot be changed by users. A subset of the system views are called Dynamic Management Views (DMV) which return server state information for monitoring the operational aspects of a SQL Server instance, diagnosing problems, and performance tuning. Dynamic Management Functions (DMF) are applied in conjunction with DMVs.

```
SELECT TOP 5    ST.text,
                EQS.*
FROM master.sys.dm_exec_query_stats AS EQS                     -- DMV
CROSS APPLY master.sys.dm_exec_sql_text(EQS.sql_handle) as ST  -- DMF
ORDER BY last_worker_time DESC;
```

SQL Server Management Studio Object Explorer display of some objects in the master database and a query listing all databases.

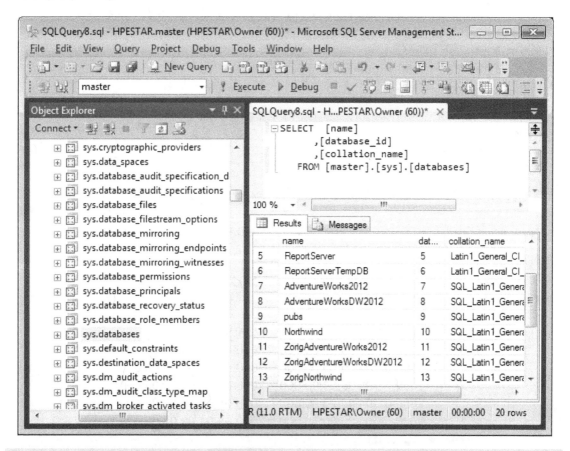

An Important System View In master Database: sys.databases

```
SELECT TOP (10) name, database_id
FROM master.sys.databases
ORDER BY database_id;
```

name	database_id
master	1
tempdb	2
model	3
msdb	4
ReportServer	5
ReportServerTempDB	6
AdventureWorks2012	7
AdventureWorksDW2012	8
pubs	9
Northwind	10

spt_values table in master database can be used for integer sequence with a range of 0 - 2047.

```
-- End of the range - BOTTOM
SELECT TOP 5 number FROM master.dbo.spt_values WHERE TYPE='P'
ORDER BY number DESC;
```

number
2047
2046
2045
2044
2043

Example for using the sequence in spt_values to generate DATE and MONTH sequences.

```
SELECT TOP 5 number,  dateadd(day, number, '20000101')       AS "Date",
                  dateadd(mm, number, '20000101')       AS "Month"
FROM master.dbo.spt_values  WHERE type = 'P'  ORDER BY number;
```

number	Date	Month
0	2000-01-01 00:00:00.000	2000-01-01 00:00:00.000
1	2000-01-02 00:00:00.000	2000-02-01 00:00:00.000
2	2000-01-03 00:00:00.000	2000-03-01 00:00:00.000
3	2000-01-04 00:00:00.000	2000-04-01 00:00:00.000
4	2000-01-05 00:00:00.000	2000-05-01 00:00:00.000

CHAPTER 2: Sample Application & System Databases

The model Database

The model database serves as prototype for a new database. The model database is also the prototype for tempdb when the SQL Server instance started. Upon server shutdown or restart everything is wiped out of tempdb, it starts with a clean slate as a copy of the model database. Therefore we should only place objects into the tempdb can be purged any time.

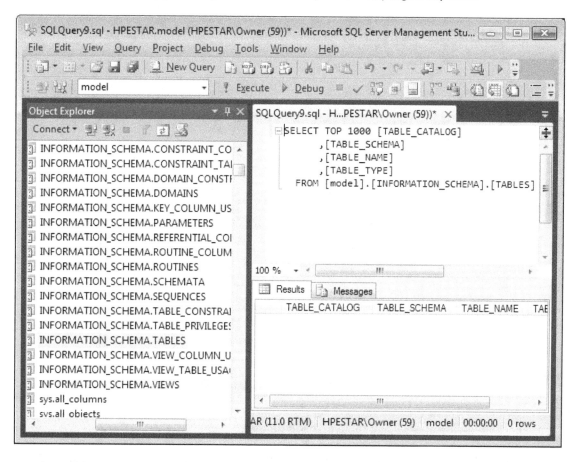

CHAPTER 2: Sample Application & System Databases

The msdb Database

The msdb database is used for server internal operations such as support for SQL Server Agent job scheduling facility or keeping track of database the all important backups and restores.

Database backup history query using table in msdb database.

```
SELECT  s.name AS Name, CONVERT(DATE,MAX(b.backup_finish_date)) AS LastGoodBackup,
        b.type AS Type
FROM master.dbo.sysdatabases AS s
LEFT OUTER JOIN msdb.dbo.backupset AS b ON s.name = b.database_name
GROUP BY s.name, b.type ORDER BY Name, Type;
```

Name	LastGoodBackup	Type
Accounting	2016-11-29	D
AdventureWorks	2016-11-29	D
AdventureWorks2008	2016-11-29	D
AdventureWorks2012	2016-11-29	D

The tempdb Database

The tempdb serves as temporary database for system operations such as sorting. Temporary tables (#temp1) and global temporary tables (##globaltemp1) are stored in the tempdb as well. "Permanent" tables can be created in tempdb with a short lifetime which lasts till shutdown or restart.

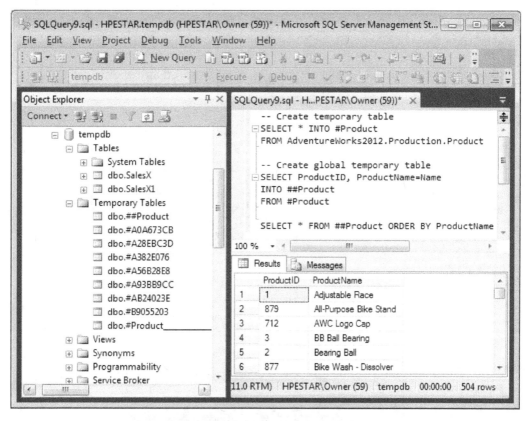

CHAPTER 2: Sample Application & System Databases

Sudden Death in tempdb When Server Restarts

Even though a temporary table and a global temporary table are created and queried in the context setting for AdventureWorks2012 database, they are placed into tempdb automatically. Same consideration when a temporary table is created from a stored procedure which is compiled in an application database. Upon server restart everything is wiped out of tempdb, rebirth follows as a copy of model db. We should not place anything into tempdb we cannot afford to lose. tempdb is also used by SQL Server engine for operations such as version control, sorting and more.

> Instead of GUI & mouse use T-SQL scripts which can be saved as .sql disk files.

CHAPTER 3: Easy SELECT Queries

The SELECT Clause

The SELECT clause is the only required clause in a SELECT statement, all the other clauses are optional. The SELECT columns can be literals (constants), expressions, table columns and even subqueries. Lines can be commented with "--".

```
SELECT 15 * 15;                                        -- 225
```

```
SELECT Today = convert(DATE, getdate());              -- 2016-07-27    -- getdate() T-SQL only
SELECT Today = convert(DATE, CURRENT_TIMESTAMP);       -- 2016-07-27    -- ANSI SQL
```

```
SELECT          Color,
                ProdCnt                = COUNT(*),
                AvgPrice               = FORMAT(AVG(ListPrice),'c','en-US')
FROM AdventureWorks2012.Production.Product p
WHERE Color is not null
GROUP BY Color
        HAVING count(*) > 10
ORDER BY AvgPrice DESC;
```

Color	ProdCnt	AvgPrice
Yellow	36	$959.09
Blue	26	$923.68
Silver	43	$850.31
Black	93	$725.12
Red	38	$1,401.95

```
-- Equivalent with column aliases on the right
SELECT          Color,
                COUNT(*)                               AS ProdCnt,
                FORMAT(AVG(ListPrice),'c','en-US')       AS AvgPrice
FROM AdventureWorks2012.Production.Product p  WHERE Color is not null
GROUP BY Color HAVING count(*) > 10  ORDER BY AvgPrice DESC;
GO
```

SELECT with Search Expression

SELECT statement can have complex expressions for text or numbers as demonstrated in the next T-SQL query for finding the street name in AddressLine1 column.

```
SELECT  AddressID,
        SUBSTRING(AddressLine1, CHARINDEX(' ', AddressLine1+' ', 1) +1,
        CHARINDEX(' ', AddressLine1+' ', CHARINDEX(' ', AddressLine1+' ', 1) +1) -
        CHARINDEX(' ', AddressLine1+' ', 1) -1)                               AS StreetName,
        AddressLine1,
        City
FROM AdventureWorks2012.Person.Address
WHERE ISNUMERIC (LEFT(AddressLine1,1))=1
  AND City = 'Seattle'
ORDER BY AddressLine1;
-- -- (141 row(s) affected)- Partial results.
```

AddressID	StreetName	AddressLine1	City
13079	boulevard	081, boulevard du Montparnasse	Seattle
859	Oak	1050 Oak Street	Seattle
110	Slow	1064 Slow Creek Road	Seattle
113	Ravenwood	1102 Ravenwood	Seattle
95	Bradford	1220 Bradford Way	Seattle
32510	Steven	1349 Steven Way	Seattle
118	Balboa	136 Balboa Court	Seattle
32519	Mazatlan	137 Mazatlan	Seattle
25869	Calle	1386 Calle Verde	Seattle
114	Yorba	1398 Yorba Linda	Seattle
15657	Book	151 Book Ct	Seattle
105	Stillman	1619 Stillman Court	Seattle
18002	Carmel	1635 Carmel Dr	Seattle
19813	Acardia	1787 Acardia Pl.	Seattle
16392	Orchid	1874 Orchid Ct	Seattle
18053	Green	1883 Green View Court	Seattle
13035	Mt.	1887 Mt. Diablo St	Seattle
29864	Valley	1946 Valley Crest Drive	Seattle
13580	Hill	2030 Hill Drive	Seattle
106	San	2144 San Rafael	Seattle

```
-- Search for Crest in the middle of AddessLine1
SELECT * FROM AdventureWorks2012.Person.Address
WHERE AddressLine1 LIKE '% Crest %';
-- (21 row(s) affected)
```

CHAPTER 3: Easy SELECT Queries

SELECT Statement with Subquery

Two Northwind category images, Beverages & Dairy Products, from the dbo.Categories table.

The following SELECT statement involves a subquery which is called a derived table. It also demonstrates that INNER JOIN can be performed with a GROUP BY subquery as well not only with another table or view.

```
USE Northwind;
SELECT          c.CategoryName                      AS Category,
                cnum.NoOfProducts                   AS CatProdCnt,
                p.ProductName                       AS Product,
                FORMAT(p.UnitPrice,'c', 'en-US')    AS UnitPrice
 FROM    Categories c
                INNER JOIN Products p       ON c.CategoryID = p.CategoryID
                INNER JOIN (    SELECT           c.CategoryID,
                                                 NoOfProducts = count(* )
                                FROM     Categories c
                                INNER JOIN Products p
                                ON c.CategoryID = p.CategoryID
                                GROUP BY c.CategoryID
                        ) cnum                              -- derived table
                ON c.CategoryID = cnum.CategoryID
ORDER BY Category, Product;      -- (77 row(s) affected) - Partial results.
```

Category	CatProdCnt	Product	UnitPrice
Dairy Products	10	Mozzarella di Giovanni	$34.80
Dairy Products	10	Queso Cabrales	$21.00
Dairy Products	10	Queso Manchego La Pastora	$38.00
Dairy Products	10	Raclette Courdavault	$55.00
Grains/Cereals	7	Filo Mix	$7.00
Grains/Cereals	7	Gnocchi di nonna Alice	$38.00
Grains/Cereals	7	Gustaf's Knäckebröd	$21.00
Grains/Cereals	7	Ravioli Angelo	$19.50
Grains/Cereals	7	Singaporean Hokkien Fried Mee	$14.00
Grains/Cereals	7	Tunnbröd	$9.00

CHAPTER 3: Easy SELECT Queries

Creating Delimited String List (CSV) with XML PATH

The XML PATH clause , the text() function and correlated subquery is used to create a comma delimited string within the SELECT columns. Note: it cannot be done using traditional (without XML) SQL single statement, it can be done with multiple SQL statements only. STUFF() string function is applied to replace the leading comma with an empty string.

```
USE AdventureWorks;

SELECT  Territory        = st.[Name],
        SalesYTD =   FORMAT(floor(SalesYTD), 'c', 'en-US'), -- currency format
        SalesStaffAssignmentHistory =

          STUFF((SELECT CONCAT(', ', c.FirstName, SPACE(1), c.LastName)      AS [text()]
                  FROM   Person.Contact c
                  INNER JOIN Sales.SalesTerritoryHistory sth
                  ON c.ContactID = sth.SalesPersonID
                  WHERE  sth.TerritoryID =  st.TerritoryID
                  ORDER  BY StartDate
                  FOR XML Path ('')), 1, 1, SPACE(0))

FROM   Sales.SalesTerritory st
ORDER  BY SalesYTD DESC;
GO
```

Territory	SalesYTD	SalesStaffAssignmentHistory
Southwest	$8,351,296.00	Shelley Dyck, Jauna Elson
Canada	$6,917,270.00	Carla Eldridge, Michael Emanuel, Gail Erickson
Northwest	$5,767,341.00	Shannon Elliott, Terry Eminhizer, Martha Espinoza
Central	$4,677,108.00	Linda Ecoffey, Maciej Dusza
France	$3,899,045.00	Mark Erickson
Northeast	$3,857,163.00	Maciej Dusza, Linda Ecoffey
United Kingdom	$3,514,865.00	Michael Emanuel
Southeast	$2,851,419.00	Carol Elliott
Germany	$2,481,039.00	Janeth Esteves
Australia	$1,977,474.00	Twanna Evans

```
-- Comma delimited list of column names
SELECT CONCAT(',', c.name)  AS [text()]
FROM  sys.columns c   WHERE c.[object_id] = OBJECT_ID('Purchasing.PurchaseOrderDetail')
ORDER BY column_id FOR XML PATH('');
```

CHAPTER 3: Easy SELECT Queries

Logical Processing Order of the SELECT Statement

The results from the previous step will be available to the next step. The logical processing order for a SELECT statement is the following. Actual processing by the database engine may be different due to performance and other considerations.

1.	FROM
2.	ON
3.	JOIN
4.	WHERE
5.	GROUP BY
6.	WITH CUBE or WITH ROLLUP
7.	HAVING
8.	SELECT
9.	DISTINCT
10.	ORDER BY
11.	TOP

As an example, it is logical to filter with the WHERE clause prior to applying GROUP BY. It is also logical to sort when the final result set is available.

```
SELECT Color, COUNT(*) AS ColorCount  FROM AdventureWorks2012.Production.Product
WHERE Color is not NULL  GROUP BY Color ORDER BY ColorCount DESC;
```

Color	ColorCount
Black	93
Silver	43
Red	38
Yellow	36
Blue	26
Multi	8
Silver/Black	7
White	4
Grey	1

The TOP Clause

The TOP clause filters results according the sorting specified in an ORDER BY clause, otherwise random filtering takes place.

Simple TOP usage to return 10 rows only.

SELECT TOP 10 SalesOrderID, OrderDate, TotalDue
FROM AdventureWorks2012.Sales.SalesOrderHeader ORDER BY TotalDue DESC;

SalesOrderID	OrderDate	TotalDue
51131	2007-07-01 00:00:00.000	187487.825
55282	2007-10-01 00:00:00.000	182018.6272
46616	2006-07-01 00:00:00.000	170512.6689
46981	2006-08-01 00:00:00.000	166537.0808
47395	2006-09-01 00:00:00.000	165028.7482
47369	2006-09-01 00:00:00.000	158056.5449
47355	2006-09-01 00:00:00.000	145741.8553
51822	2007-08-01 00:00:00.000	145454.366
44518	2005-11-01 00:00:00.000	142312.2199
51858	2007-08-01 00:00:00.000	140042.1209

TOP function usage: not known in advance how many rows will be returned due to "TIES".

SELECT   TOP 1 WITH TIES coalesce(Color, 'N/A')   AS Color,
         FORMAT(ListPrice, 'c', 'en-US')   AS ListPrice,
         Name   AS ProductName,
         ProductID
FROM   AdventureWorks2012.Production.Product
ORDER BY ROW_NUMBER() OVER(PARTITION BY Color ORDER BY ListPrice DESC);

Color	ListPrice	ProductName	ProductID
N/A	$229.49	HL Fork	804
Black	$3,374.99	Mountain-100 Black, 38	775
Red	$3,578.27	Road-150 Red, 62	749
Silver	$3,399.99	Mountain-100 Silver, 38	771
Blue	$2,384.07	Touring-1000 Blue, 46	966
Grey	$125.00	Touring-Panniers, Large	842
Multi	$89.99	Men's Bib-Shorts, S	855
Silver/Black	$80.99	HL Mountain Pedal	937
White	$9.50	Mountain Bike Socks, M	709
Yellow	$2,384.07	Touring-1000 Yellow, 46	954

The DISTINCT Clause to Omit Duplicates

The DISTINCT clause returns only unique results, omitting duplicates in the result set.

```
USE AdventureWorks2012;
SELECT DISTINCT Color FROM Production.Product
WHERE Color is not NULL
ORDER BY Color;
GO
```

Color
Black
Blue
Grey
Multi
Red
Silver
Silver/Black
White
Yellow

```
SELECT DISTINCT ListPrice
FROM Production.Product
 WHERE ListPrice > 0.0
ORDER BY ListPrice DESC;
GO
-- (102 row(s) affected) - Partial results.
```

ListPrice
3578.27
3399.99
3374.99
2443.35

```
-- Using DISTINCT in COUNT - NULL is counted
SELECT          COUNT(*)                    AS TotalRows,
                COUNT(DISTINCT Color)       AS ProductColors,
                COUNT(DISTINCT Size)        AS ProductSizes
FROM AdventureWorks2012.Production.Product;
```

TotalRows	ProductColors	ProductSizes
504	9	18

CHAPTER 3: Easy SELECT Queries

The CASE Conditional Expression

The CASE conditional expression evaluates to a **single value of the same data type**, therefore **it can be used anywhere in a query where a single value is required.**

```
SELECT          CASE ProductLine
                      WHEN 'R' THEN 'Road'
                      WHEN 'M' THEN 'Mountain'
                      WHEN 'T' THEN 'Touring'
                      WHEN 'S' THEN 'Other'
                      ELSE 'Parts'
                END                     AS Category,
                Name                    AS ProductName,
                ProductNumber
FROM AdventureWorks2012.Production.Product
ORDER BY ProductName;
GO
-- (504 row(s) affected) - Partial results.
```

Category	ProductName	ProductNumber
Touring	Touring-3000 Blue, 62	BK-T18U-62
Touring	Touring-3000 Yellow, 44	BK-T18Y-44
Touring	Touring-3000 Yellow, 50	BK-T18Y-50
Touring	Touring-3000 Yellow, 54	BK-T18Y-54
Touring	Touring-3000 Yellow, 58	BK-T18Y-58
Touring	Touring-3000 Yellow, 62	BK-T18Y-62
Touring	Touring-Panniers, Large	PA-T100
Other	Water Bottle - 30 oz.	WB-H098
Mountain	Women's Mountain Shorts, L	SH-W890-L

Query to return different result sets for repeated execution due to newid().

```
SELECT  TOP 3 CompanyName,   City=CONCAT(City, ', ', Country),        PostalCode,
        [IsNumeric] =  CASE     WHEN PostalCode like '[0-9][0-9][0-9][0-9][0-9]'
                            THEN '5-Digit Numeric'   ELSE 'Other' END
FROM    Northwind.dbo.Suppliers
ORDER BY NEWID();                       -- random sort
GO
```

CompanyName	City	PostalCode	IsNumeric
PB Knäckebröd AB	Göteborg, Sweden	S-345 67	Other
Gai pâturage	Annecy, France	74000	5-Digit Numeric
Heli Süßwaren GmbH & Co. KG	Berlin, Germany	10785	5-Digit Numeric

Same query as above expanded with ROW_NUMBER() and another CASE expression column.

```
SELECT          ROW_NUMBER() OVER (ORDER BY Name)            AS RowNo,
                CASE ProductLine
                  WHEN 'R' THEN 'Road'
                  WHEN 'M' THEN 'Mountain'
                  WHEN 'T' THEN 'Touring'
                  WHEN 'S' THEN 'Other'
                  ELSE 'Parts'
                END                           AS Category,
                Name                          AS ProductName,
                CASE WHEN Color is null THEN 'N/A'
                        ELSE Color END        AS Color,
                ProductNumber
FROM Production.Product   ORDER BY ProductName;
-- (504 row(s) affected) - Partial results.
```

RowNo	Category	ProductName	Color	ProductNumber
1	Parts	Adjustable Race	N/A	AR-5381
2	Mountain	All-Purpose Bike Stand	N/A	ST-1401
3	Other	AWC Logo Cap	Multi	CA-1098
4	Parts	BB Ball Bearing	N/A	BE-2349
5	Parts	Bearing Ball	N/A	BA-8327
6	Other	Bike Wash - Dissolver	N/A	CL-9009
7	Parts	Blade	N/A	BL-2036
8	Other	Cable Lock	N/A	LO-C100
9	Parts	Chain	Silver	CH-0234
10	Parts	Chain Stays	N/A	CS-2812

Testing PostalCode with ISNUMERIC and generating a flag with CASE expression.

```
SELECT  TOP (4) AddressID,  City,   PostalCode                        AS Zip,
        CASE WHEN ISNUMERIC(PostalCode) = 1 THEN 'Y'  ELSE 'N'  END    AS IsZipNumeric
FROM    AdventureWorks2008.Person.Address  ORDER BY NEWID();
```

AddressID	City	Zip	IsZipNumeric
16704	Paris	75008	Y
26320	Grossmont	91941	Y
27705	Matraville	2036	Y
18901	Kirkby	KB9	N

CHAPTER 3: Easy SELECT Queries

The OVER Clause

The OVER clause defines the partitioning and sorting of a rowset (intermediate result set) preceding the application of an associated window function, such as ranking. Window functions are also dubbed as ranking functions.

```
USE AdventureWorks2012;
-- Query with three different OVER clauses
SELECT  ROW_NUMBER() OVER ( ORDER BY SalesOrderID, ProductID)          AS RowNum
        ,SalesOrderID, ProductID, OrderQty
        ,RANK() OVER(PARTITION BY SalesOrderID ORDER BY OrderQty DESC)  AS Ranking
        ,SUM(OrderQty) OVER(PARTITION BY SalesOrderID)                  AS TotalQty
        ,AVG(OrderQty) OVER(PARTITION BY SalesOrderID)                  AS AvgQty
        ,COUNT(OrderQty) OVER(PARTITION BY SalesOrderID)  AS "Count"  -- T-SQL keyword, use "" or []
        ,MIN(OrderQty) OVER(PARTITION BY SalesOrderID)                  AS "Min"
        ,MAX(OrderQty) OVER(PARTITION BY SalesOrderID)                  AS "Max"
FROM Sales.SalesOrderDetail
WHERE SalesOrderID BETWEEN 61190 AND 61199
ORDER BY RowNum;
-- (143 row(s) affected) - Partial results.
```

RowNum	SalesOrderID	ProductID	OrderQty	Ranking	TotalQty	AvgQty	Count	Min	Max
1	61190	707	4	13	159	3	40	1	17
2	61190	708	3	18	159	3	40	1	17
3	61190	711	5	8	159	3	40	1	17
4	61190	712	12	2	159	3	40	1	17
5	61190	714	3	18	159	3	40	1	17
6	61190	715	5	8	159	3	40	1	17
7	61190	716	5	8	159	3	40	1	17
8	61190	858	4	13	159	3	40	1	17
9	61190	859	7	6	159	3	40	1	17
10	61190	864	8	4	159	3	40	1	17
11	61190	865	3	18	159	3	40	1	17
12	61190	870	9	3	159	3	40	1	17
13	61190	876	4	13	159	3	40	1	17
14	61190	877	5	8	159	3	40	1	17
15	61190	880	1	34	159	3	40	1	17
16	61190	881	5	8	159	3	40	1	17
17	61190	883	2	26	159	3	40	1	17
18	61190	884	17	1	159	3	40	1	17
19	61190	885	3	18	159	3	40	1	17
20	61190	886	1	34	159	3	40	1	17
21	61190	889	2	26	159	3	40	1	17
22	61190	892	4	13	159	3	40	1	17
23	61190	893	3	18	159	3	40	1	17
24	61190	895	1	34	159	3	40	1	17

FROM Clause: Specifies the Data Source

The FROM clause specifies the source data sets for the query such as tables, views, derived tables and table-valued functions. Typically the tables are JOINed together. The most common JOIN is INNER JOIN which is based on equality between FOREIGN KEY and PRIMARY KEY values in the two tables.

PERFORMANCE NOTE
All FOREIGN KEYs should be indexed. PRIMARY KEYs are indexed automatically with unique index.

```
USE AdventureWorks2012;
GO
SELECT
  ROW_NUMBER() OVER(ORDER BY SalesYTD DESC)                         AS RowNo,
  ROW_NUMBER() OVER(PARTITION BY PostalCode ORDER BY SalesYTD DESC)   AS SeqNo,
              CONCAT(p.FirstName, SPACE(1), p.LastName)          AS SalesStaff,
              FORMAT(s.SalesYTD,'c','en-US')                     AS YTDSales,
              City,
              a.PostalCode                                       AS ZipCode
FROM Sales.SalesPerson AS s
   INNER JOIN Person.Person AS p
     ON s.BusinessEntityID = p.BusinessEntityID
   INNER JOIN Person.Address AS a
     ON a.AddressID = p.BusinessEntityID
WHERE TerritoryID IS NOT NULL   AND SalesYTD <> 0 ORDER BY ZipCode, SeqNo;
```

RowNo	SeqNo	SalesStaff	YTDSales	City	ZipCode
1	1	Linda Mitchell	$4,251,368.55	Issaquah	98027
3	2	Michael Blythe	$3,763,178.18	Issaquah	98027
4	3	Jillian Carson	$3,189,418.37	Issaquah	98027
8	4	Tsvi Reiter	$2,315,185.61	Issaquah	98027
12	5	Garrett Vargas	$1,453,719.47	Issaquah	98027
14	6	Pamela Ansman-Wolfe	$1,352,577.13	Issaquah	98027
2	1	Jae Pak	$4,116,871.23	Renton	98055
5	2	Ranjit Varkey Chudukatil	$3,121,616.32	Renton	98055
6	3	José Saraiva	$2,604,540.72	Renton	98055
7	4	Shu Ito	$2,458,535.62	Renton	98055
9	5	Rachel Valdez	$1,827,066.71	Renton	98055
10	6	Tete Mensa-Annan	$1,576,562.20	Renton	98055
11	7	David Campbell	$1,573,012.94	Renton	98055
13	8	Lynn Tsoflias	$1,421,810.92	Renton	98055

The WHERE Clause to Filter Records (Rows)

The WHERE clause filters the rows generated by the query. Only rows satisfying (TRUE) the
WHERE clause predicates are returned.

```
PERFORMANCE NOTE
All columns in WHERE clause should be indexed.
```

USE AdventureWorks2012;

String equal match predicate - equal is TRUE, not equal is FALSE.

SELECT ProductID, Name, ListPrice, Color
FROM Production.Product WHERE Name = 'Mountain-100 Silver, 38' ;

ProductID	Name	ListPrice	Color
771	Mountain-100 Silver, 38	3399.99	Silver

-- Function equality predicate
SELECT * FROM Sales.SalesOrderHeader WHERE YEAR(OrderDate) = 2008;
-- (13951 row(s) affected)

```
PERFORMANCE NOTE
When a column is used as a parameter in a function ( e.g. YEAR(OrderDate) ), index (if any) usage is voided.
Instead of random SEEK, all rows are SCANned in the table.  The predicate is not SARGable.
```

-- String wildcard match predicate
SELECT ProductID, Name, ListPrice, Color
FROM Production.Product WHERE Name LIKE ('%touring%');

-- Integer range predicate
SELECT ProductID, Name, ListPrice, Color
FROM Production.Product WHERE ProductID >= 997 ;

-- Double string wildcard match predicate
SELECT ProductID, Name, ListPrice, Color
FROM Production.Product WHERE Name LIKE ('%bike%') AND Name LIKE ('%44%');

-- String list match predicate
SELECT ProductID, Name, ListPrice, Color FROM Production.Product
WHERE Name IN ('Mountain-100 Silver, 44', 'Mountain-100 Black, 44');

CHAPTER 3: Easy SELECT Queries

The GROUP BY Clause to Aggregate Results

The GROUP BY clause is applied to partition the rows and calculate aggregate values. An extremely powerful way of looking at the data from a summary point of view.

```
SELECT
            V.Name                              AS Vendor,
            FORMAT(SUM(TotalDue), 'c', 'en-US') AS TotalPurchase,
            A.City,
            SP.Name                             AS State,
            CR.Name                             AS Country
FROM Purchasing.Vendor AS V
   INNER JOIN Purchasing.VendorAddress AS VA
            ON VA.VendorID = V.VendorID
   INNER JOIN Person.Address AS A
            ON A.AddressID = VA.AddressID
   INNER JOIN Person.StateProvince AS SP
            ON SP.StateProvinceID = A.StateProvinceID
   INNER JOIN Person.CountryRegion AS CR
            ON CR.CountryRegionCode = SP.CountryRegionCode
   INNER JOIN Purchasing.PurchaseOrderHeader POH
            ON POH.VendorID = V.VendorID
GROUP BY V.Name, A.City, SP.Name, CR.Name
ORDER BY SUM(TotalDue) DESC, Vendor;  -- TotalPurchase does a string sort instead of numeric
GO
-- (79 row(s) affected) - Partial results.
```

Vendor	TotalPurchase	City	State	Country
Superior Bicycles	$5,034,266.74	Lynnwood	Washington	United States
Professional Athletic Consultants	$3,379,946.32	Burbank	California	United States
Chicago City Saddles	$3,347,165.20	Daly City	California	United States
Jackson Authority	$2,821,333.52	Long Beach	California	United States
Vision Cycles, Inc.	$2,777,684.91	Glendale	California	United States
Sport Fan Co.	$2,675,889.22	Burien	Washington	United States
Proseware, Inc.	$2,593,901.31	Lebanon	Oregon	United States
Crowley Sport	$2,472,770.05	Chicago	Illinois	United States
Greenwood Athletic Company	$2,472,770.05	Lemon Grove	Arizona	United States
Mitchell Sports	$2,424,284.37	Everett	Washington	United States
First Rate Bicycles	$2,304,231.55	La Mesa	New Mexico	United States
Signature Cycles	$2,236,033.80	Coronado	California	United States
Electronic Bike Repair & Supplies	$2,154,773.37	Tacoma	Washington	United States
Vista Road Bikes	$2,090,857.52	Salem	Oregon	United States
Victory Bikes	$2,052,173.62	Issaquah	Washington	United States
Bicycle Specialists	$1,952,375.30	Lake Oswego	Oregon	United States

The HAVING Clause to Filter Aggregates

The HAVING clause is similar to the WHERE clause filtering but applies to GROUP BY aggregates.

```
USE AdventureWorks;
SELECT
            V.Name                              AS Vendor,
            FORMAT(SUM(TotalDue), 'c', 'en-US') AS TotalPurchase,
            A.City,
            SP.Name                             AS State,
            CR.Name                             AS Country
FROM Purchasing.Vendor AS V
   INNER JOIN Purchasing.VendorAddress AS VA
            ON VA.VendorID = V.VendorID
   INNER JOIN Person.Address AS A
            ON A.AddressID = VA.AddressID
   INNER JOIN Person.StateProvince AS SP
            ON SP.StateProvinceID =  A.StateProvinceID
   INNER JOIN Person.CountryRegion AS CR
            ON CR.CountryRegionCode = SP.CountryRegionCode
   INNER JOIN Purchasing.PurchaseOrderHeader POH
            ON POH.VendorID = V.VendorID
GROUP BY  V.Name, A.City, SP.Name, CR.Name
HAVING SUM(TotalDue) < $26000   -- HAVING clause predicate
ORDER BY SUM(TotalDue) DESC,  Vendor;
```

Vendor	TotalPurchase	City	State	Country
Speed Corporation	$25,732.84	Anacortes	Washington	United States
Gardner Touring Cycles	$25,633.64	Altadena	California	United States
National Bike Association	$25,513.90	Sedro Woolley	Washington	United States
Australia Bike Retailer	$25,060.04	Bellingham	Washington	United States
WestAmerica Bicycle Co.	$25,060.04	Houston	Texas	United States
Ready Rentals	$23,635.06	Kirkland	Washington	United States
Morgan Bike Accessories	$23,146.99	Albany	New York	United States
Continental Pro Cycles	$22,960.07	Long Beach	California	United States
American Bicycles and Wheels	$9,641.01	West Covina	California	United States
Litware, Inc.	$8,553.32	Santa Cruz	California	United States
Business Equipment Center	$8,497.80	Everett	Montana	United States
Bloomington Multisport	$8,243.95	West Covina	California	United States
International	$8,061.10	Salt Lake City	Utah	United States
Wide World Importers	$8,025.60	Concord	California	United States
Midwest Sport, Inc.	$7,328.72	Detroit	Michigan	United States
Wood Fitness	$6,947.58	Philadelphia	Pennsylvania	United States
Metro Sport Equipment	$6,324.53	Lebanon	Oregon	United States
Burnett Road Warriors	$5,779.99	Corvallis	Oregon	United States
Lindell	$5,412.57	Lebanon	Oregon	United States
Consumer Cycles	$3,378.17	Torrance	California	United States
Northern Bike Travel	$2,048.42	Anacortes	Washington	United States

The ORDER BY Clause to Sort Results

The ORDER BY clause sorts the result set. It guarantees ordering according to the columns or expressions listed from major to minor keys. Unique ordering requires a set of keys which generate unique data rows. The major key, YEAR(HireDate), in the first example is not sufficient for uniqueness.

```
USE AdventureWorks2012;          -- Sort on 2 keys
SELECT BusinessEntityID AS EmployeeID, JobTitle, HireDate
FROM HumanResources.Employee  ORDER BY YEAR(HireDate) DESC, EmployeeID;
-- (290 row(s) affected) - Partial results.
```

EmployeeID	JobTitle	HireDate
285	Pacific Sales Manager	2007-04-15
286	Sales Representative	2007-07-01
288	Sales Representative	2007-07-01

```
-- Sort on CASE conditional expression
SELECT   BusinessEntityID AS SalesStaffID, CONCAT(LastName, ', ', FirstName) AS FullName,
        CASE CountryRegionName WHEN 'United States' THEN TerritoryName
            ELSE '' END AS TerritoryName, CountryRegionName
FROM Sales.vSalesPerson   WHERE TerritoryName IS NOT NULL        -- view
ORDER BY CASE WHEN CountryRegionName != 'United States' THEN  CountryRegionName
            ELSE TerritoryName  END;
```

SalesStaffID	FullName	TerritoryName	CountryRegionName
286	Tsoflias, Lynn		Australia
278	Vargas, Garrett		Canada
282	Saraiva, José		Canada

The EXCEPT & INTERSECT Set Operators

The EXCEPT operator & the INTERSECT operator require the column lists are compatible for the comparison.

```
USE tempdb;  -- Prepare two tables with 400 random(newid()) picks from the Product table
SELECT TOP (400) * INTO Prod1 FROM AdventureWorks2012.Production.Product ORDER BY NEWID();
SELECT TOP (400) * INTO Prod2 FROM AdventureWorks2012.Production.Product ORDER BY NEWID();

-- EXCEPT SET OPERATOR - no match rows
SELECT * FROM PROD1 EXCEPT SELECT * FROM PROD2;  -- (81 row(s) affected)

-- INTERSECT SET OPERATOR - matching rows
SELECT * FROM PROD1 INTERSECT SELECT * FROM PROD2;  -- (319 row(s) affected)
```

CHAPTER 3: Easy SELECT Queries

CTE - Common Table Expression

CTE helps with structured programming by the definition of named subqueries at the beginning of the query. It supports nesting and recursion.

```
USE AdventureWorks;
-- Testing CTE
WITH CTE (SalesPersonID, NumberOfOrders, MostRecentOrderDate)
   AS  (      SELECT SalesPersonID, COUNT(*), CONVERT(date, MAX(OrderDate))
              FROM Sales.SalesOrderHeader
              GROUP BY SalesPersonID  )
SELECT * FROM CTE;
-- (18 row(s) affected) - Partial results.
```

SalesPersonID	NumberOfOrders	MostRecentOrderDate
284	39	2004-05-01
278	234	2004-06-01
281	242	2004-06-01

```
-- Using CTE in a query
;WITH CTE (SalesPersonID, NumberOfOrders, MostRecentOrderDate)
   AS ( SELECT SalesPersonID, COUNT(*), CONVERT(date, MAX(OrderDate))
        FROM Sales.SalesOrderHeader   GROUP BY SalesPersonID        )
-- Start of outer (main) query
 SELECT        E.EmployeeID,
               OE.NumberOfOrders              AS EmpOrders,
               OE.MostRecentOrderDate         AS EmpLastOrder,
               E.ManagerID,
               OM.NumberOfOrders              AS MgrOrders,
               OM.MostRecentOrderDate         AS MgrLastOrder
 FROM   HumanResources.Employee AS E
        INNER JOIN CTE AS OE            ON E.EmployeeID = OE.SalesPersonID
        LEFT OUTER JOIN CTE AS OM       ON E.ManagerID = OM.SalesPersonID
ORDER BY EmployeeID;
-- (17 row(s) affected) - Partial results.
```

EmployeeID	EmpOrders	EmpLastOrder	ManagerID	MgrOrders	MgrLastOrder
268	48	2004-06-01	273	NULL	NULL
275	450	2004-06-01	268	48	2004-06-01
276	418	2004-06-01	268	48	2004-06-01
277	473	2004-06-01	268	48	2004-06-01
278	234	2004-06-01	268	48	2004-06-01

Combining Results of Multiple Queries with UNION

UNION and UNION ALL (no duplicates elimination) operators can be used to **stack result sets from two or more queries into a single result set**.

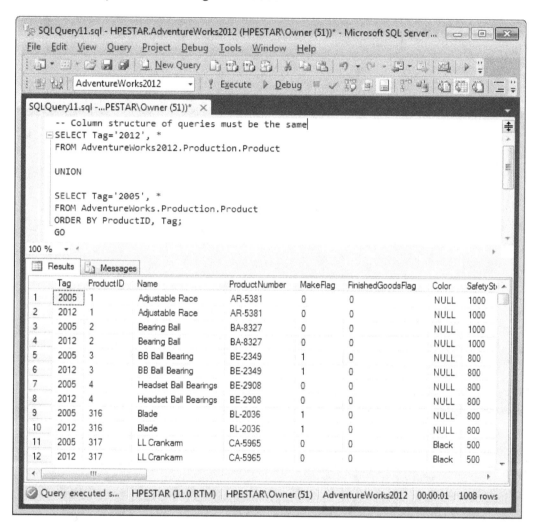

```
-- Combining data from OLTP & data warehouse databases
SELECT FirstName,LastName, 0 AS TotalChildren
FROM AdventureWorks2012.Person.Person
UNION ALL
SELECT FirstName,LastName, TotalChildren
FROM AdventureWorksDW2012..DimCustomer;
```

CHAPTER 3: Easy SELECT Queries

TOP n by Group Query with OVER PARTITION BY

OVER PARTITION BY method is very convenient for TOP n by group selection. List of top 3 orders placed by resellers (customers of AdventureWorks Cycles).

-- Row numbering by partitioning view results
SELECT ROW_NUMBER() OVER(PARTITION BY PhoneNumberType ORDER BY SalesYTD DESC) RN,
      CONCAT(FirstName, ' ', LastName) as Name, ROUND(SalesYTD,2,1) AS YTDSales,
      PhoneNumberType
FROM AdventureWorks2012.Sales.vSalesPerson
ORDER BY PhoneNumberType, RN;

CHAPTER 4: Management Studio as Comprehensive DBA Tool

SQL Server Programming, Administration & Management Tool

SQL Server Management Studio (SSMS) is a GUI (Graphical User Interface) tool for accessing, configuring, managing, administering, and developing all major components of SQL Server with the exception of Business Intelligence components: SSAS (Analysis Services), SSRS (Reporting Services) & SSIS (Integration Services). The two main environments in SSMS: Object Explorer and Query Editor. Object Explorer is used to access servers, databases and db objects. Query Editor is to develop and execute queries. SSMS is used by a DBA (Data Base Administrator) for administrative and programming functions. SSMS can also be used by a database developer to develop application related db objects such as stored procedures, functions and triggers. Some developers prefer to stay in Visual Studio environment which has features to support database development albeit not as extensive as Management Studio. A typical screen display of Management Studio.

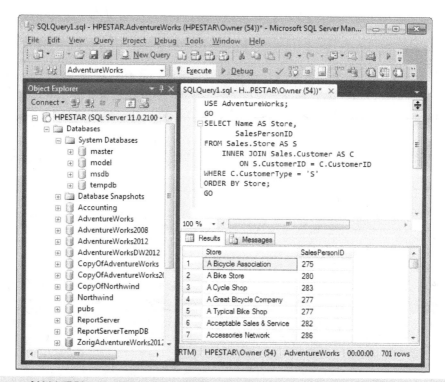

CHAPTER 4: Management Studio as Comprehensive DBA Tool

Query Editor

The Query Editor is used to type in queries, edit them and submit them for execution by the
server. Queries can also be loaded from a disk file, typically with .sql extension. In addition to
textual query development, a number of special tools available such as graphical query
designer, debugger, execution plan display and query analysis by the Database Engine Tuning
Advisor. IntelliSense provides contextual assistance with SQL syntax checking and guessing
object names in a drop-down menu based on the typed prefix.

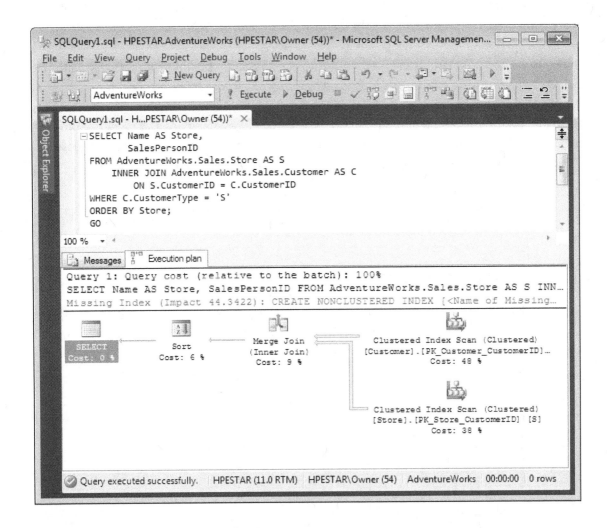

Execute All Batches in Query Editor

The entire content of the Query Editor is executed when we click on the Execute button. Batches typically separated by "GO" on a separate line.

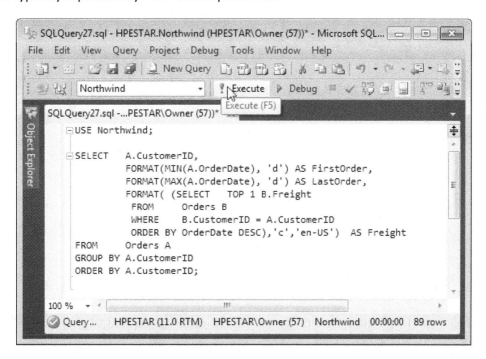

The Significance of GO in T-SQL Scripts

"GO" is not transmitted to SQL Server. "GO" indicates the end of batch to the client software such as SSMS. "GO" also indicates the end of a logical unit to the human reader. Certain statements must be the first line, or have "GO" preceding them.

```
USE AdventureWorks2012;
CREATE FUNCTION Z () RETURNS TABLE AS
RETURN  SELECT * FROM Production.ProductSubcategory;
GO    /* Msg 111, Level 15, State 1, Line 2   'CREATE FUNCTION' must be the first statement in a
query batch. */
```

```
USE AdventureWorks2012;
GO
CREATE FUNCTION Z () RETURNS TABLE AS RETURN SELECT * FROM
Production.ProductSubcategory;
GO
-- Command(s) completed successfully.
```

The Results Pane contains the result rows of the query. It is currently set to Grid format.

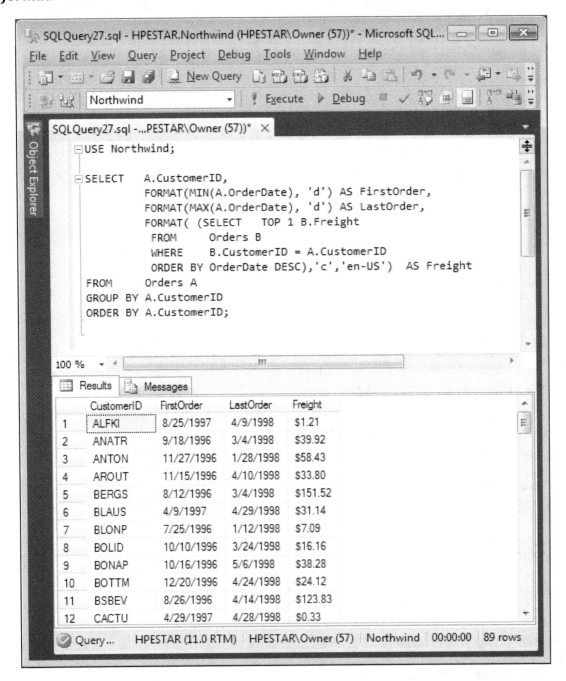

The Messages Pane gets the row count values, warning & error messages as well as the output of the PRINT & RAISERROR statements if any.

The client software also gets the same messages following query execution.

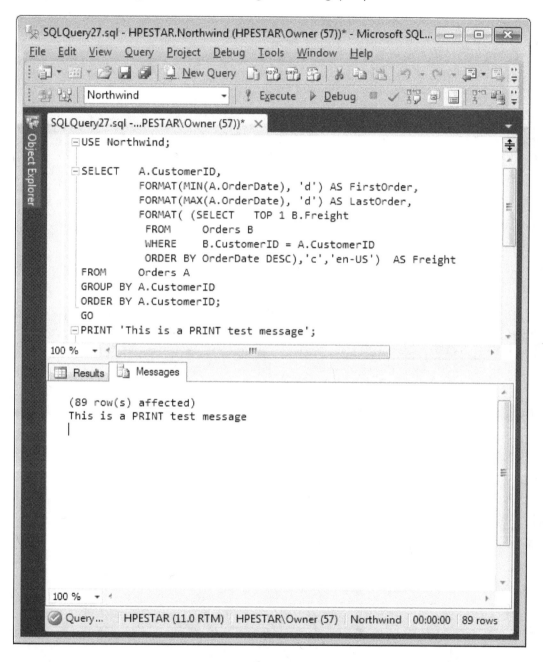

Routing Results to Grid, Text or File

Results can be routed to Grid, Text or File from the right-click menu or the Query drop-down menu.

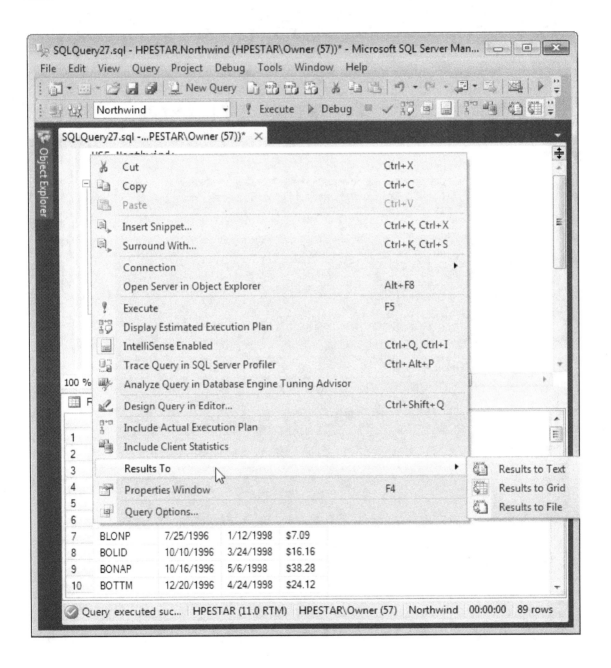

Routing Results to Text

The following screen window image displays results in text format. Messages also come to the Results window, following the results rows.

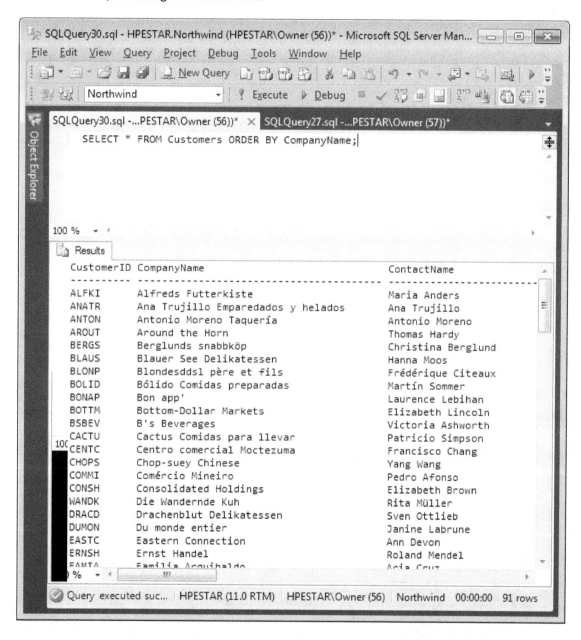

Routing Results to File

When the routing option is file, the file save window pops up upon query execution.

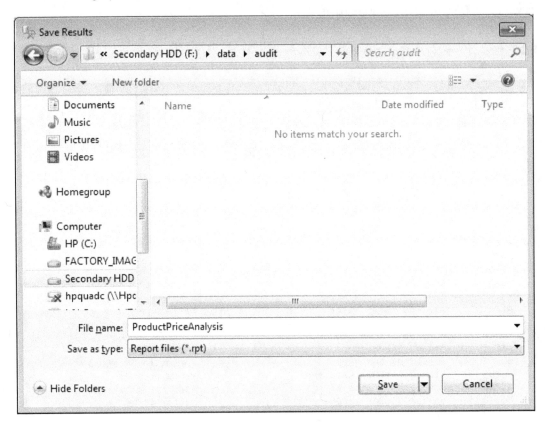

Part of the file in Notepad.

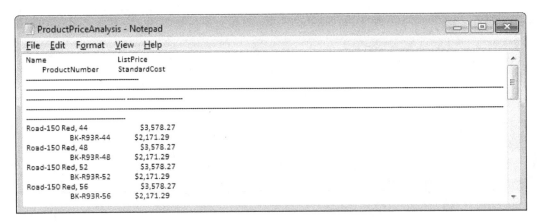

Saving Results in CSV Flat File Format

Results can also be saved in CSV (comma separated values) format which can be read by Excel and other software.

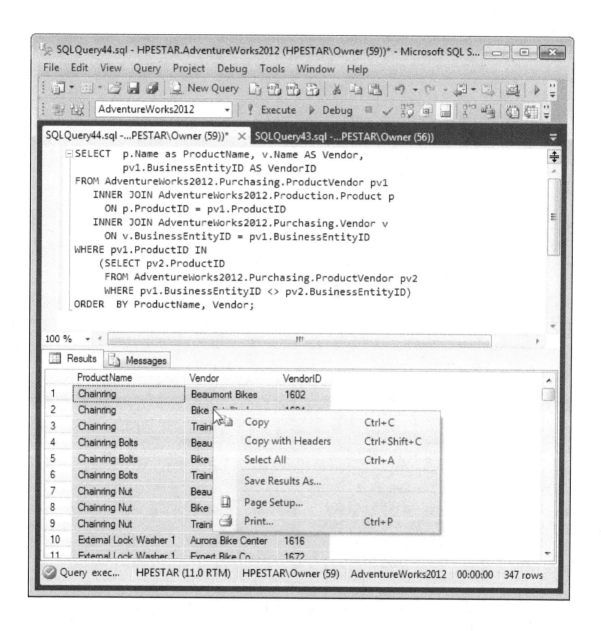

The saving file dialog box is configured automatically to csv saving.

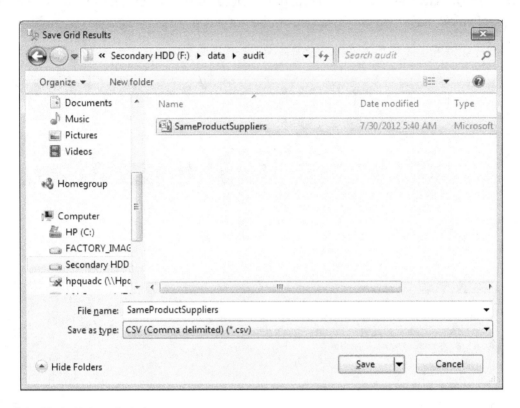

Part of the file in Notepad window.

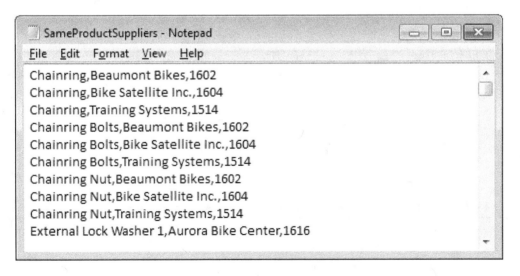

CHAPTER 4: Management Studio as Comprehensive DBA Tool

Copy & Paste Results to Excel

Using the copy / copy with headers option in SSMS result window, the query results can simply be pasted into an Excel worksheet. Excel may do implicit conversions on some columns.

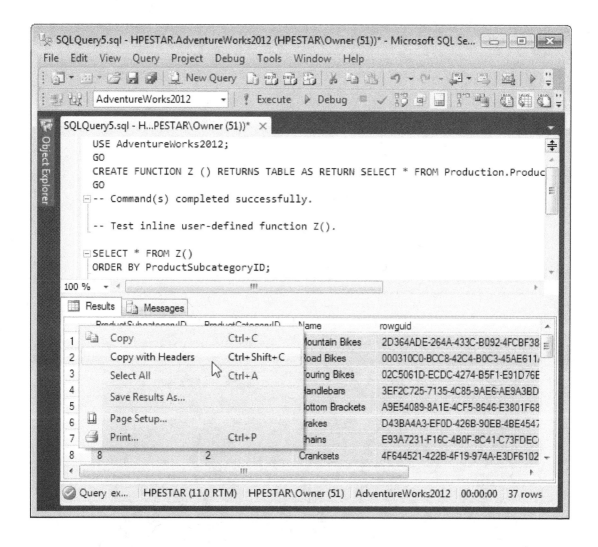

After pasting into an Excel worksheet some formatting may be necessary such as for datetime columns.

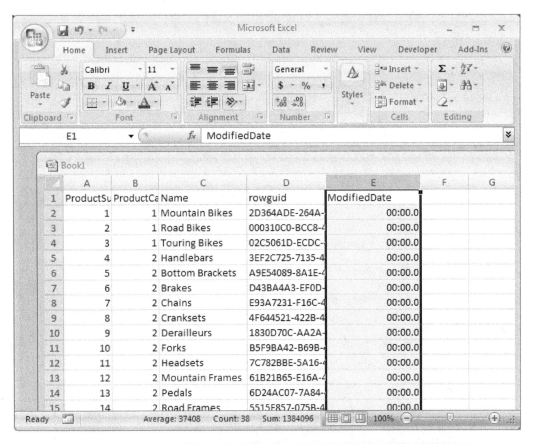

Error Handling & Debugging

Error handling and debugging is a major part of database development work. When there is an error, it is displayed in the Messages area (or returned to the application client software) which automatically becomes active. In the following example, we introduced an invalid column name which resulted in error. The error message line reference starts with the top line of the batch which is the first line after the first "GO" which indicates a new batch. The red wave-underlining comes from optional IntelliSense and not related to the execution attempt error message. IntelliSense gives warning ahead of time if it detects a potential error. Simple errors can be corrected with help from the error message. Complex errors may required web search and/or examining the query in parts.

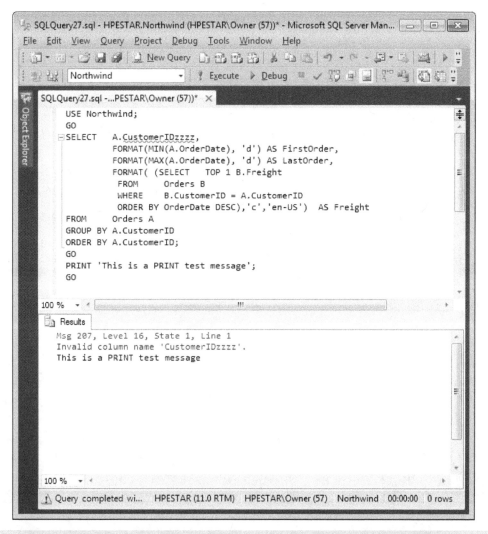

Locating the Error Line in a Query

Position the cursor on the error and double click. The error line will be highlighted. This method does not work for all errors.

Error Message Pointing to the Wrong Line

For some errors, the first line of the query (3) is returned by the database engine not the actual error line (13). The error message is still very helpful though in this instance.

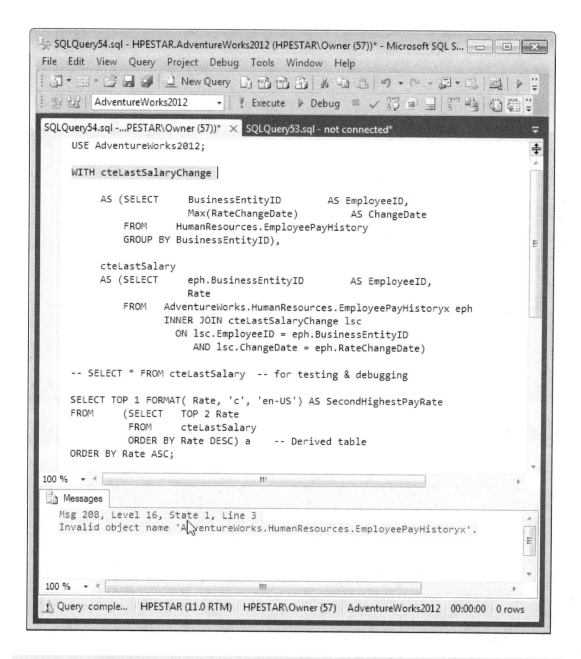

Parsing a Query for Syntax Errors

A query (or one or more batches) can be parsed for syntax errors. Parsing catches syntax errors such as using "ORDER" instead of "ORDER BY" for sorting.

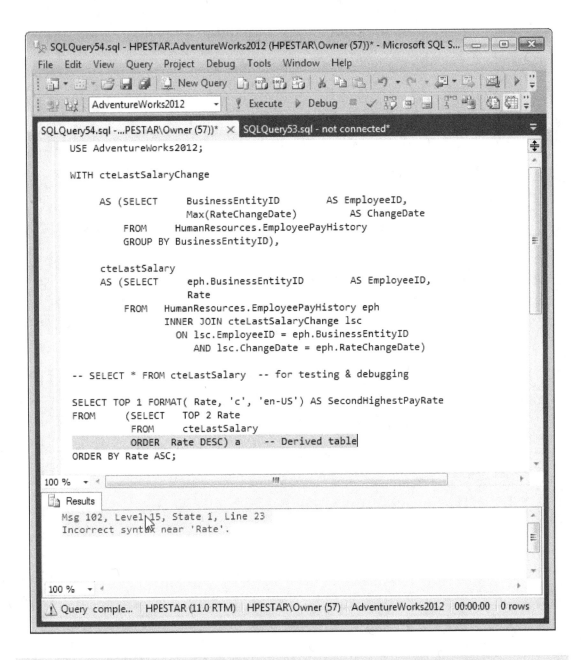

Deferred Name Resolution Process

Deferred Name Resolution Process: Only syntax errors are caught when parsed, not execution
(runtime) errors as shown in the following demo which has an invalid table reference
(EmployeePayHistoryx). Similarly, **stored procedures can be compiled without errors with
invalid table references**. A table need not exist for stored procedure compilation, only for
execution.

Executing Single Batch Only

A single batch can be executed by selecting (highlighting) it and clicking on Execute.

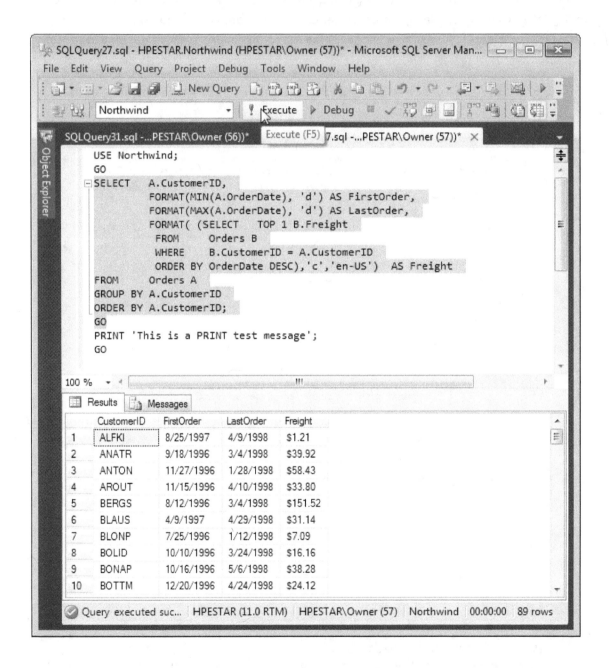

Executing Part of a Query

A part of a query can be executed as long as it is a valid query, otherwise error results. The query part has to be selected (highlighted) and the Execute button has to be pushed. The selected part of the query is considered a batch which is sent to the server. In this example, we executed the subquery (inner query) in the WHERE clause predicate.

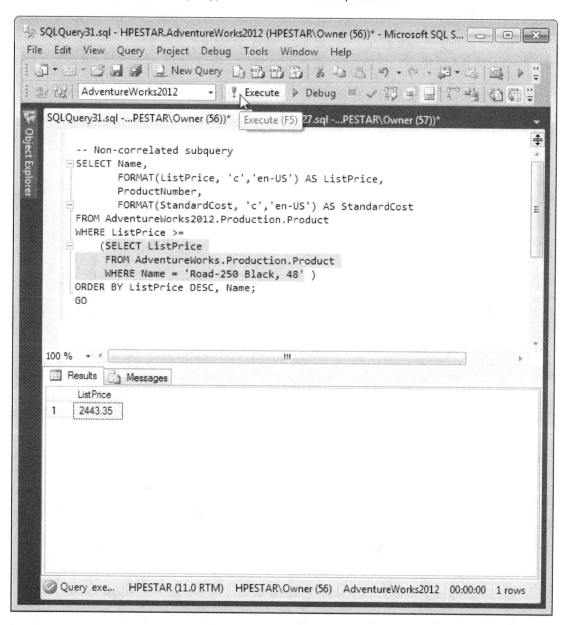

Object Explorer

SSMS Object Explorer functions as:

➢ A tree-based directory of all database objects
➢ A launching base for graphical user-interface tools
➢ An access way to object properties

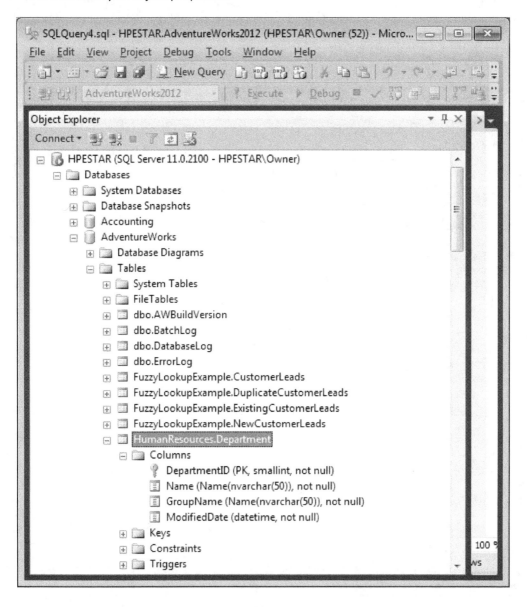

Context-Sensitive Right-Click Menu

Based on what object the cursor is on, right-click menu changes accordingly, it is context-sensitive. In the following demo the cursor is on table object when we right click on the mouse.

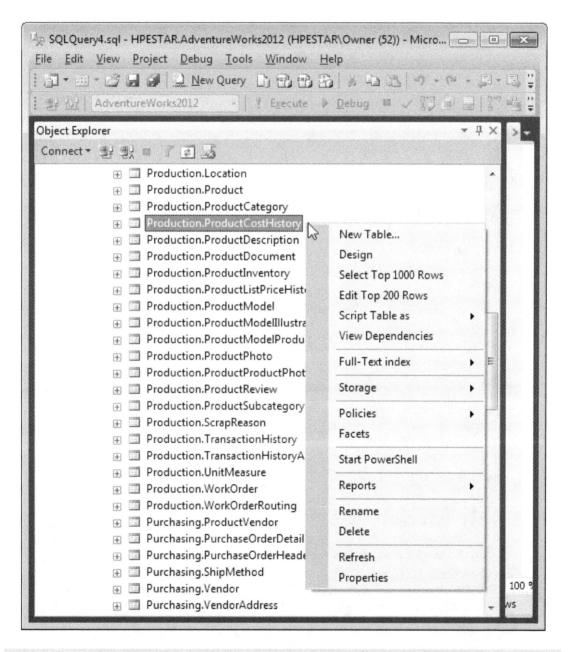

Server Administration & Management Tools

All the available SQL Server administration and management tools can be accessed from the
Object Explorer. Usually the Database Administrator (DBA) uses these tools.

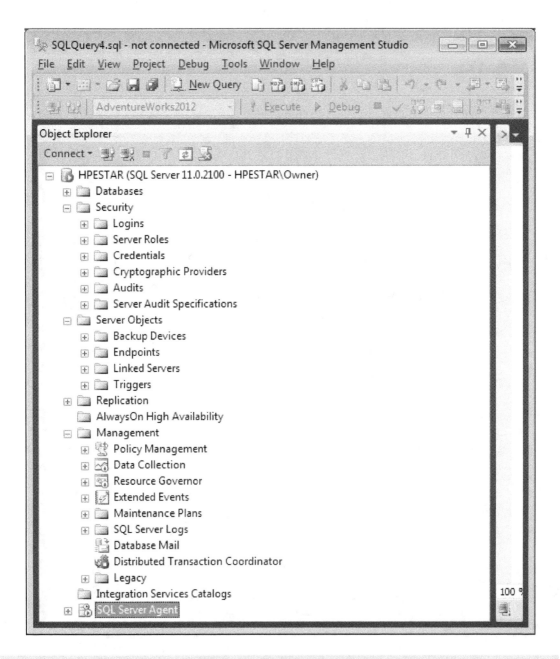

SQL Server Agent Jobs to Automate Administration Tasks

SQL Server Agent is a job creation and scheduling facility with notification features. For example, database backup job can be scheduled to execute 2:15AM every night as shown on the following dialog box. Stored procedure execution can also be setup as a job and scheduled for periodic execution.

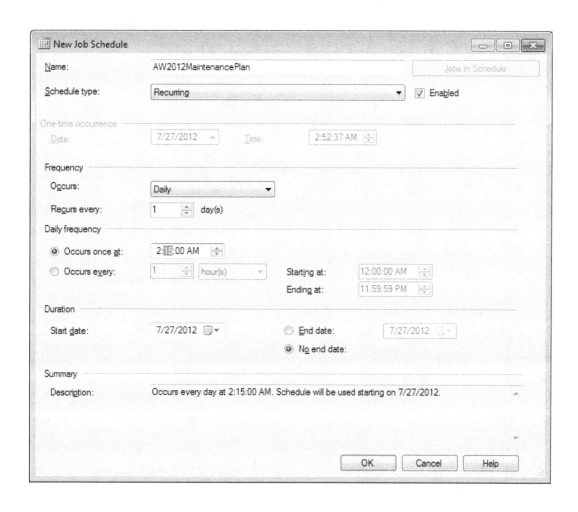

Job properties panel can be used to create and manage jobs with multiple job steps and multiple schedules.

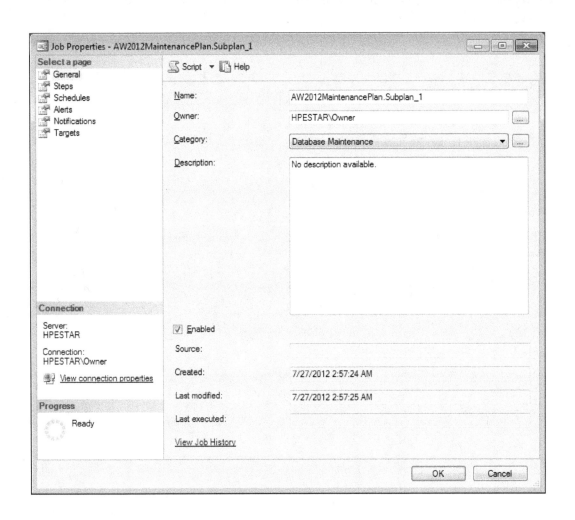

Graphical Query Designer

The Design Query in Editor entry on the Query drop-down menu launches the graphical Query Designer which can be used to design the query with GUI method and the T-SQL SELECT code will be generated automatically upon completion.

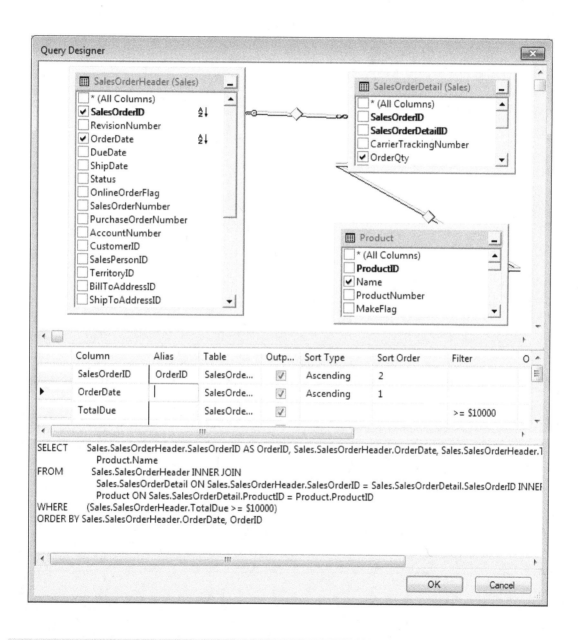

Designing a GROUP BY Query in Query Designer

Query Designer can be used to design from simple to complex queries. It can also serve as a starter query for a more complex query. It is really easy to get the tables JOINs graphically.

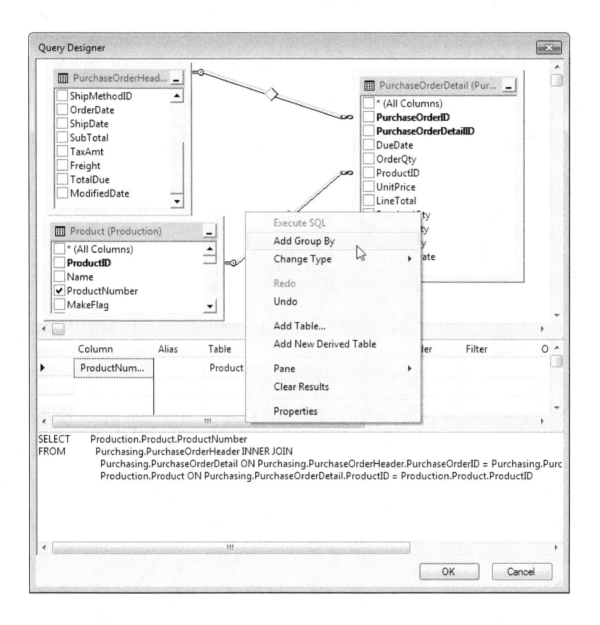

The Production.Product.Name column will also be configured as GROUP BY (drop-down default).

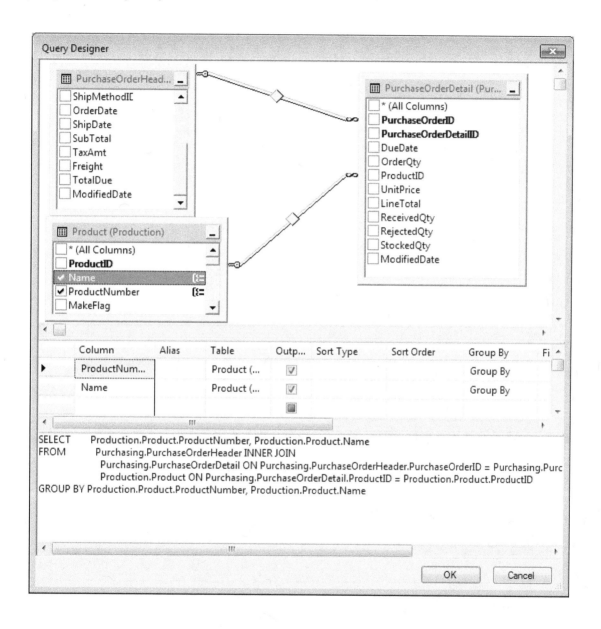

We add the TotalDue column and change the summary function to "SUM" from "Group by" and configure sorting on the first column.

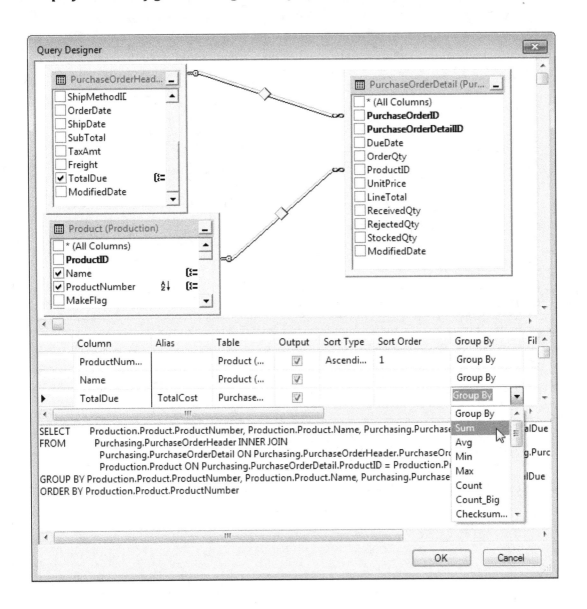

After pressing OK, the query is moved into the Query Editor window. Frequently it requires reformatting.

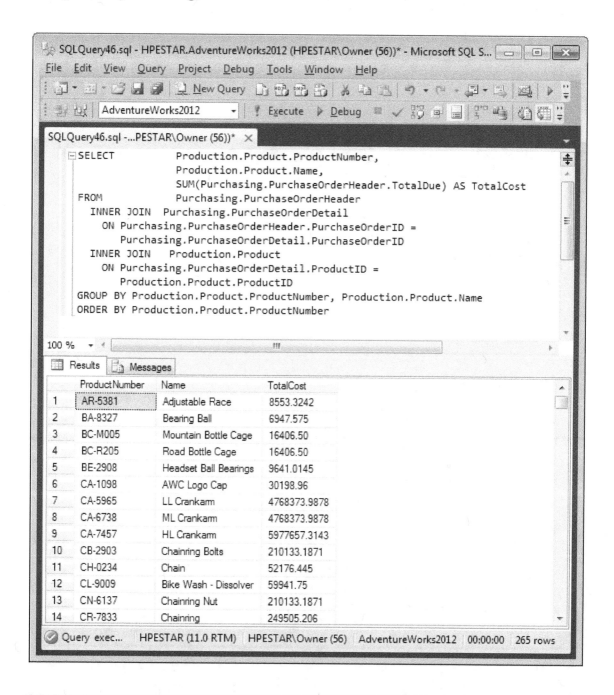

The only remaining issue with the query is the 3-part column references which is hard to read. We can change the query for readability improvement by using table aliases.

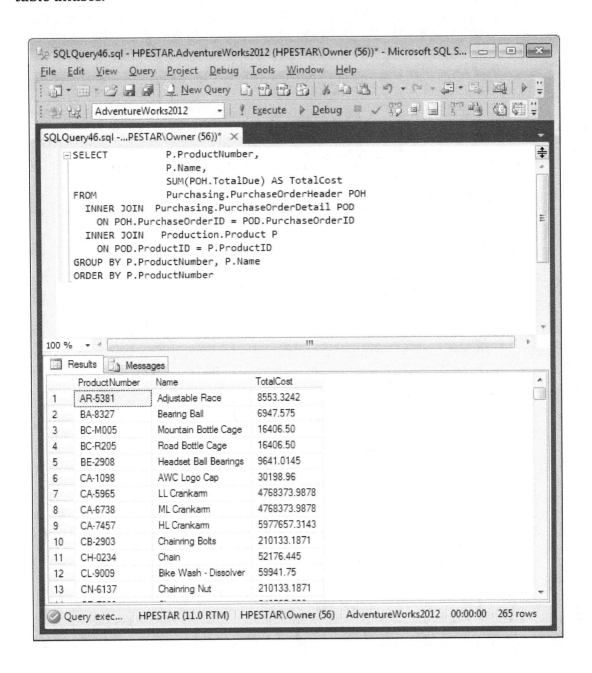

Graphically Editing of an Existing Query

An existing query, exception certain complex queries, can be uploaded into the Graphical Query Designer the following way: select (highlight) the query and right-click for the drop-down menu; click on Design Query in Editor.

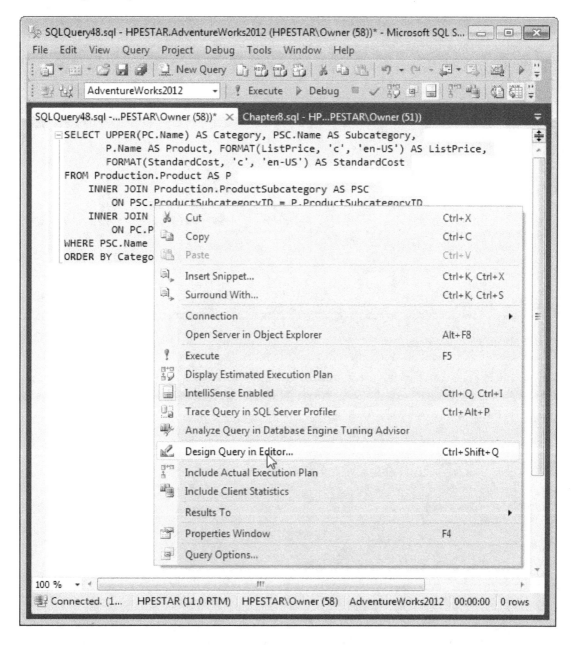

Following screen image shows the query in the Graphical Query Designer after some manual beautifying such as moving the tables for better display.

The query can be edited graphically and upon clicking on "OK", the query text is updated in the Query Editor window.

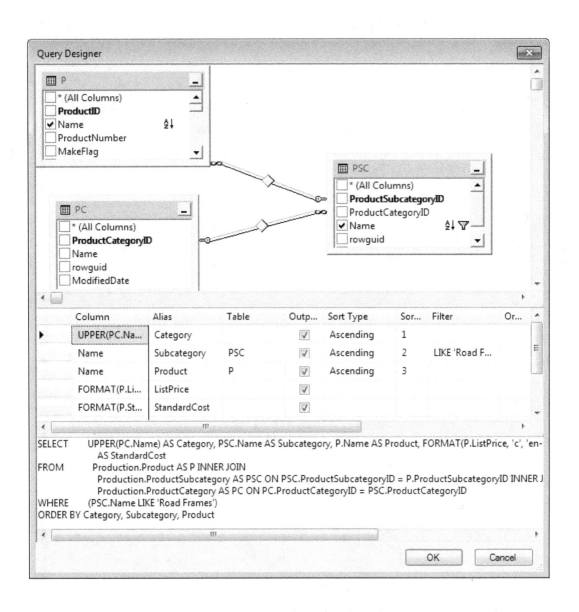

Configuring Line Numbers in Query Editor

Line numbering is an option which is off by default. Line numbers are helpful to find errors in large queries or T-SQL scripts (a sequence of T-SQL statements) when the error references a line number. Following is an example an error which includes the line number.

The Display Line Numbers option in the query editor can be activated from Options.

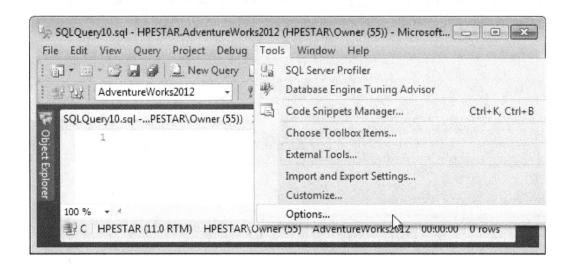

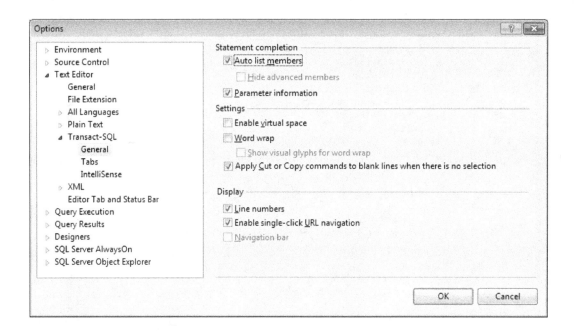

IntelliSense - Your Smart Assistant

IntelliSense is a smart agent in Query Editor. It helps completing long object names and pointing out potential errors by red wave-lining (squiggly) them.

The Options configuration screen for IntelliSense.

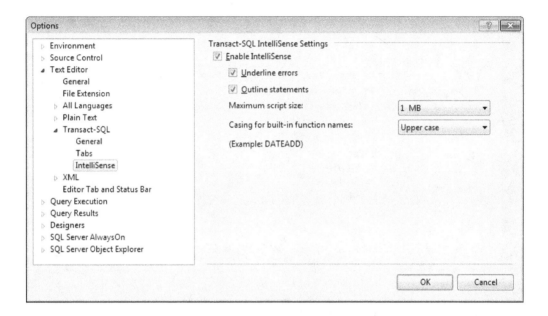

Underlining with red wave-line potential errors such as misspelling of a column name.

```
⊟SELECT TOP 1000 [BillOfMaterialsID]
       ,[ProductAssemblyID]
       ,[ComponentID]
       ,[StartDate]
       ,[EndDate]
       ,[UnitMeasureCodex]
       ,[BOMLevel]
       ,[PerAssemblyQty]
       ,[ModifiedDate]
   FROM [AdventureWorks2012].[Production].[BillOfMaterials]
```

100 %

IntelliSense Guessing and Completing Object Names

Screenshots show IntelliSense in action when typing queries.

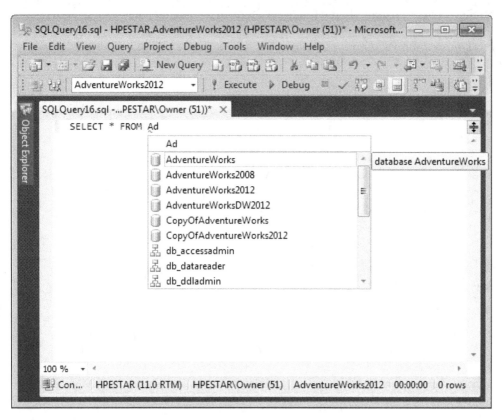

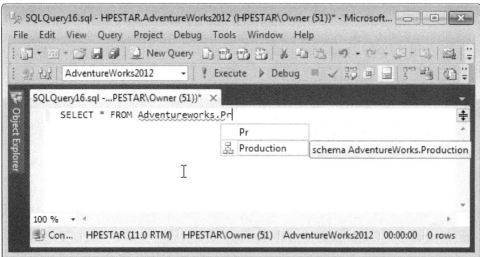

CHAPTER 4: Management Studio as Comprehensive DBA Tool

IntelliSense drop-down menu for "Prod".

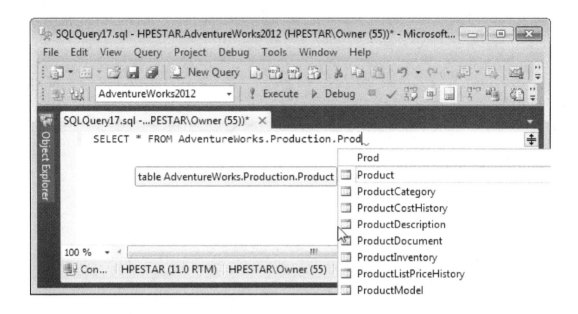

IntelliSense drop-down menu for "ProductS".

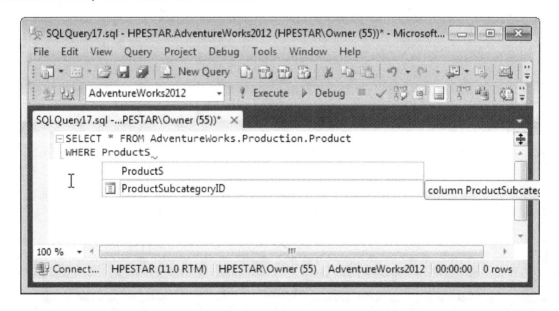

IntelliSense completion assistance for "ProductN"

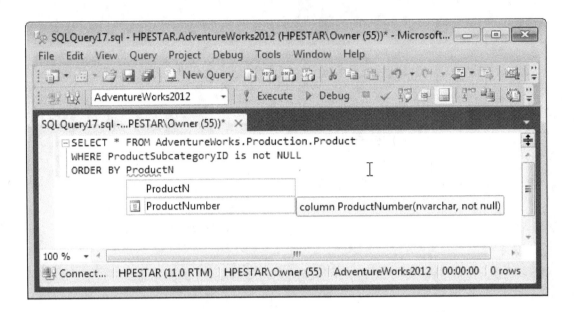

IntelliSense completion assistance for "Produ"

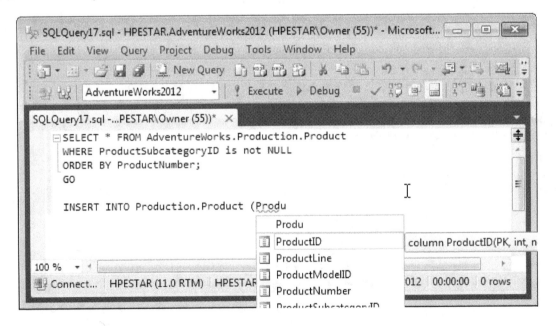

CHAPTER 4: Management Studio as Comprehensive DBA Tool

IntelliSense Assisting with User-Defined Objects

IntelliSense helps out with a user-defined stored procedure execution.

IntelliSense Smart Guessing Partial Word in Middle of Object Names

You don't have to remember how an object name starts. You just have to remember some part of the name. Looking for the system view associated with "waits".

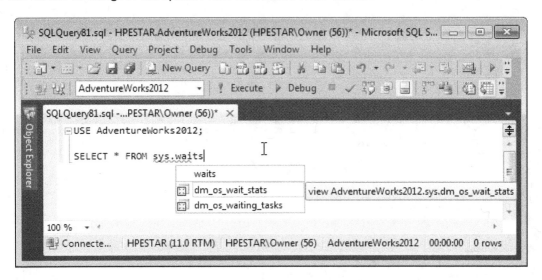

Looking for the SalesOrderHeader table but only remembering "head".

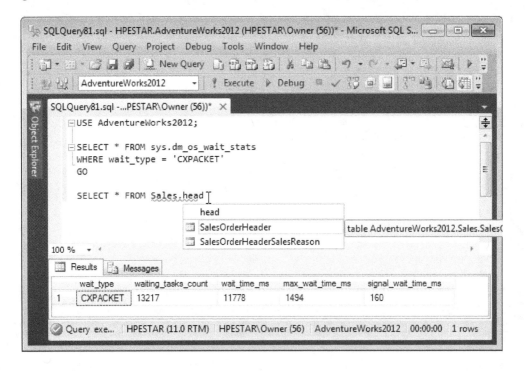

Hovering over Red Squiggly Underline Errors for Explanation

IntelliSense red wave (squiggly) underlining of errors which is caused, actually, by a single invalid table reference.

Common Error: The multi-part identifier "abc" could not be bound.

Hovering over the first error results in an explanation pop-up. This is a distant error, the kind usually the hardest to solve, because, actually, it is a secondary error caused by the primary error which is located on a different line. In this instance, there are few lines difference only, but in a large stored procedure the difference can be 200 lines as an example.

```
PSC.Name AS Subcategory,
```
The multi-part identifier "PSC.Name" could not be bound.

Hovering over the second error yields the cause of all errors: "ProductSubZcategory".

```
Production.ProductSubZcategory AS PSC
```
Invalid object name 'Production.ProductSubZcategory'.

The remaining error messages are all "multi-part..." caused by the solitary invalid table reference.

```
PSC.ProductSubcategoryID = P.ProductSubcategoryID
```
The multi-part identifier "PSC.ProductSubcategoryID" could not be bound.

After fixing the table name, all errors are gone.

```
SELECT          UPPER(PC.Name)                          AS Category,
                PSC.Name                                AS Subcategory,
                P.Name                                  AS Product,
                FORMAT(P.ListPrice, 'c', 'en-US')       AS ListPrice,
                FORMAT(P.StandardCost, 'c', 'en-US')    AS StandardCost,
                P.ProductNumber
FROM     Production.Product AS P
            INNER JOIN  Production.ProductSubcategory AS PSC
                        ON PSC.ProductSubcategoryID = P.ProductSubcategoryID
            INNER JOIN  Production.ProductCategory AS PC
                        ON PC.ProductCategoryID = PSC.ProductCategoryID
WHERE       (PSC.Name LIKE 'Touring Frames')
ORDER BY Category, Subcategory, Product;
```

Refreshing IntelliSense Cache for New DB Objects

IntelliSense cache is not updated real-time. If new objects are created in another connection (session), they will not be seen until exit SSMS/reenter or IntelliSense cache is updated. No red-wave underline for the **newly created object SOD** in the same connection.

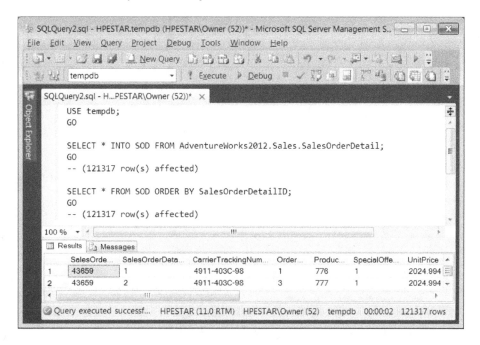

In another connection, the query works, but there are red squiggly underlining for the new table & column.

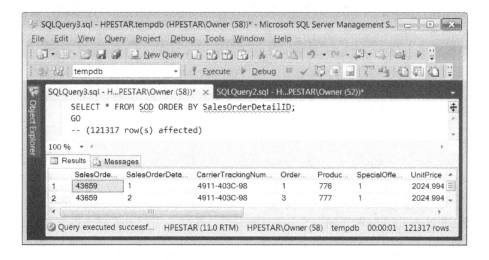

Refreshing IntelliSense Local Cache

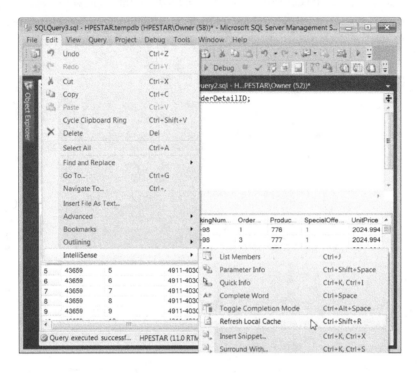

Squiggly red line goes away in all connections for the new database objects.

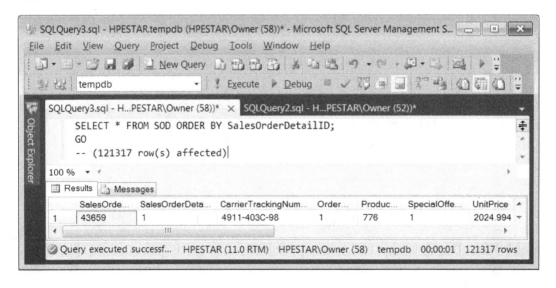

CHAPTER 4: Management Studio as Comprehensive DBA Tool

Scripting DB Objects With Script Wizard

The Script Wizard is a sophisticated tool for scripting out multiple objects, in fact all objects can be scripted in a single setup and execution. The generated script can be saved to single/multiple files, new query window or the Clipboard. **Data can be scripted as well (INSERT statements).** The launching sequence of menus starts with Right Click on the database.

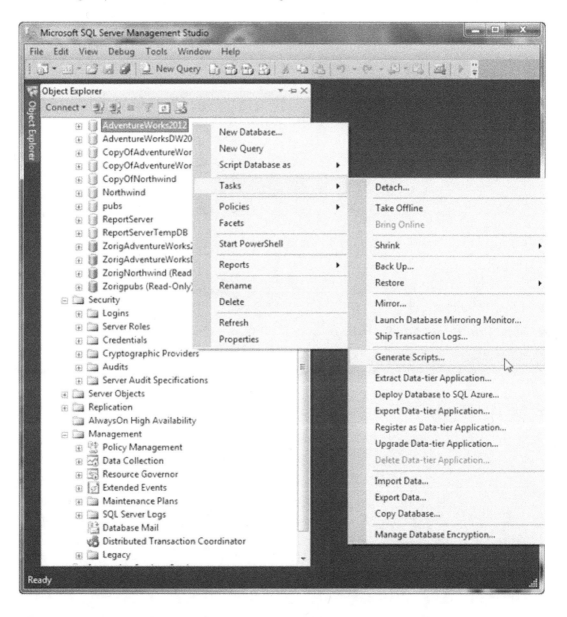

Script Wizard Optional Description Page

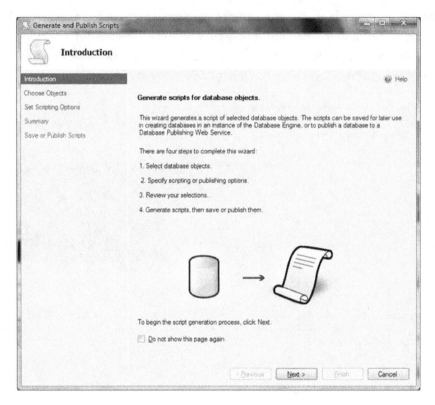

Object Selection Panel For Scripting

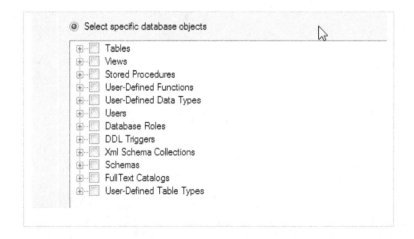

A number of options can be set for generation, including scripting of related objects.

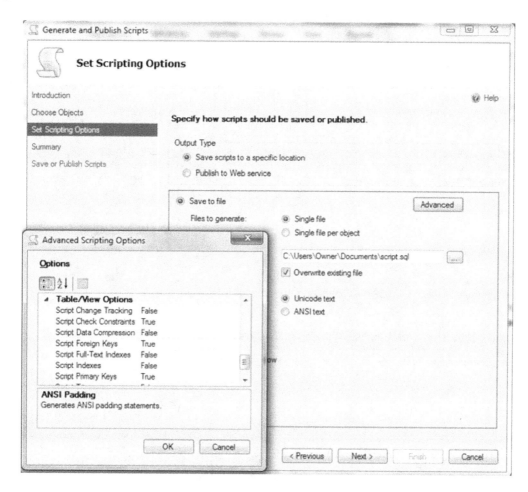

The script generated by the Script Wizard for the Banking.Loan table and related objects

```
USE [AdventureWorks2012]
GO
SET ANSI_NULLS ON
GO
SET QUOTED_IDENTIFIER ON
GO
SET ANSI_PADDING ON
GO
```

CHAPTER 4: Management Studio as Comprehensive DBA Tool

The script generated by the Script Wizard for the Banking.Loan table and related objects (continued)

```
CREATE TABLE [Banking].[Loan](
        [LoanID] [int] IDENTITY(1,1) NOT NULL,
        [BranchID] [int] NOT NULL,
        [LoanNumber] [char](20) NOT NULL,
        [LoanType] [varchar](30) NOT NULL,
        [Amount] [money] NOT NULL,
        [ModifiedDate] [datetime] NULL,
PRIMARY KEY CLUSTERED  (  [LoanID] ASC) WITH (PAD_INDEX = OFF, STATISTICS_NORECOMPUTE = OFF,
IGNORE_DUP_KEY = OFF,  ALLOW_ROW_LOCKS = ON, ALLOW_PAGE_LOCKS = ON) ON [PRIMARY],
UNIQUE NONCLUSTERED (     [LoanID] ASC ) WITH (PAD_INDEX = OFF, STATISTICS_NORECOMPUTE = OFF,
IGNORE_DUP_KEY = OFF, ALLOW_ROW_LOCKS = ON, ALLOW_PAGE_LOCKS = ON) ON [PRIMARY],
UNIQUE NONCLUSTERED (     [LoanNumber] ASC ) WITH (PAD_INDEX = OFF, STATISTICS_NORECOMPUTE = OFF,
IGNORE_DUP_KEY = OFF, ALLOW_ROW_LOCKS = ON, ALLOW_PAGE_LOCKS = ON) ON [PRIMARY]
) ON [PRIMARY]

GO
SET ANSI_PADDING ON
GO

ALTER TABLE [Banking].[Loan] ADD  DEFAULT (getdate()) FOR [ModifiedDate]
GO

ALTER TABLE [Banking].[Loan]  WITH CHECK ADD FOREIGN KEY([BranchID])
REFERENCES [Banking].[Branch] ([BranchID])
ON DELETE CASCADE
GO
```

CHAPTER 5: Server Architecture & Configuration Best Practices

Client - Server Relational Database Management System

The "server" is SQL Server, operating on a powerful hardware platform, managing databases and related items. The client is application software. The real client is naturally a human user who runs the application software. Automated software which uses the database for one thing or another is also considered a "client". The client computer, in the next room or thousands of miles away, is connected to the server through communications link. The client software sends a request, a query, to SQL Server, after execution the server returns the results to the client. An example for a query sent by the client to the server:

SELECT ListPrice FROM AdventureWorks2012.Production.Product WHERE ProductID = 800;

SQL Server executes the query and returns "1120.49" to the client with a flag indicating successful query execution. A tempting analogy is a restaurant: kitchen is the server, patrons are the clients and the communications / delivery done by waiters & waitresses.

Screenshot displays SQL Server (highlighted) along with other related software such as SQL Server Agent (job scheduling facility) , SSIS (data transformation & transfer), SSRS (Reporting), SSAS (OLAP Cube) and other auxiliary software.

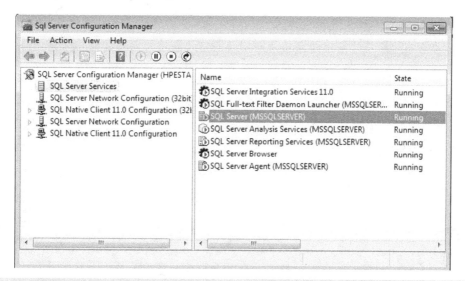

CHAPTER 5: Server Architecture & Configuration Best Practices

Database Objects on Server-Side

Screenshot of Object Explorer displays almost all important database objects with the exception of constraints, triggers and indexes.

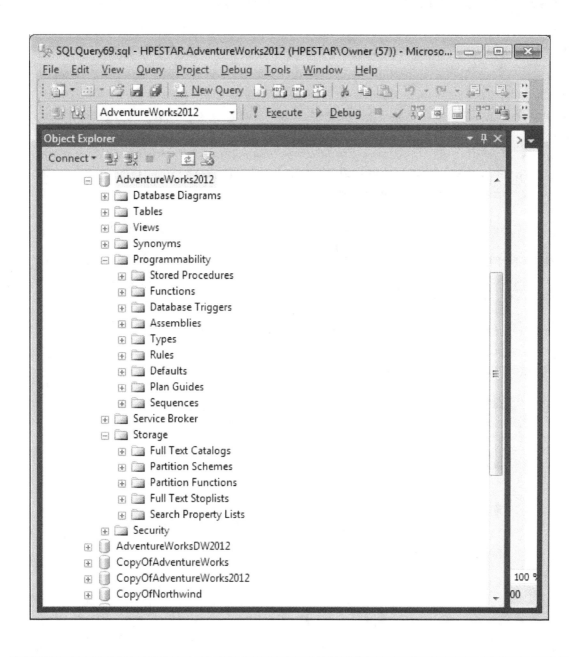

Database Related Items on Client-Side

On the client side the following items:

- ➢ SQL Server client libraries to access the server and database
- ➢ SQL queries imbedded in application programs
- ➢ Stored procedure calls imbedded in application software

Queries by themselves are not database object. To make them database objects we have to build stored procedures, functions or views around them.

The following code segment illustrates database connection and query from ASP to Inventory database. In ANSI SQL terminology catalog means database.

```
' Connect
<%
Dim StrConnInventory
Dim ConnInventory

StrConnInventory = "Provider=SQLOLEDB.1;Data Source=LONDONHEADOFFICE;Initial
Catalog=Inventory;User ID=finance;Password=fa$nAnCe#9*"

Set ConnInventory = Server.CreateObject("ADODB.Connection")

ConnInventory.ConnectionTimeout = 4000
ConnInventory.CommandTimeout = 4000
ConnInventory.Open StrConnInventory

' Query
Dim YourQuery As String = "SELECT Name, Price FROM Product"
 Dim YourCommand As New SqlCommand(YourQuery)
 YourCommand.Connection = ConnInventory
 YourConnection.Open()
 YourCommand.ExecuteNonQuery()
 Response.Write(YourCommand)
 YourCommand.Connection.Close()
%>
' Disconnect
<%
ConnInventory.Close
Set ConnInventory = Nothing
%>
```

SQL Server Profiler to Monitor Client-Server Communications

SQL Server Profiler, a tool in SSMS, has two modes of operations: interactive GUI and silent T-SQL script based operation. The simplest use of the Profiler is to check what queries are sent to the server (SQL Server) from the client and how long does processing take (duration). The client software sending the queries is SSMS. Even though SSMS appears as the "face of SQL Server", it is only a client software.

```
USE pubs;
GO
SELECT * FROM titles;
GO
```

```
USE Northwind;
GO
SELECT * FROM Products ORDER BY ProductName;
GO
```

```
USE AdventureWorks2012;
GO
SELECT * FROM Sales.SalesOrderHeader WHERE OrderDate='20080201';
GO
```

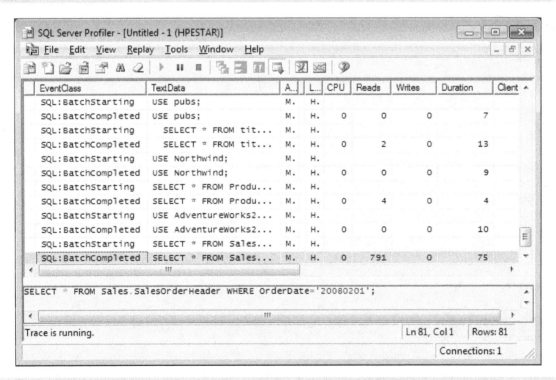

Table - Database Object

A database table holds data in tabular format by rows and columns. The main method of connecting tables is FOREIGN KEY referencing PRIMARY KEY. A set of connected tables makes up the database. Screenshot displays the structure and partial content of Northwind database Products table.

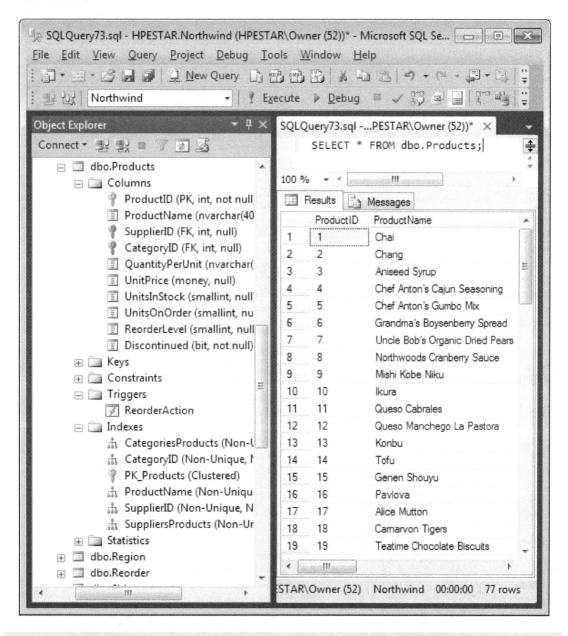

Tables in Production Schema

The listing and data dictionary description of tables in AdventureWorks2012 Production schema.

```
USE AdventureWorks2012;

SELECT  CONCAT('Production.', objname COLLATE DATABASE_DEFAULT) AS TableName,
        value                                               AS [Description]
FROM fn_listextendedproperty (          NULL,
                    'schema', 'Production',
                    'table', default,
                    NULL, NULL)
ORDER BY TableName;
```

TableName	Description
Production.BillOfMaterials	Items required to make bicycles and bicycle subassemblies. It identifies the hierarchical relationship between a parent product and its components.
Production.Culture	Lookup table containing the languages in which some AdventureWorks data is stored.
Production.Document	Product maintenance documents.
Production.Illustration	Bicycle assembly diagrams.
Production.Location	Product inventory and manufacturing locations.
Production.Product	Products sold or used in the manfacturing of sold products.
Production.ProductCategory	High-level product categorization.
Production.ProductCostHistory	Changes in the cost of a product over time.
Production.ProductDescription	Product descriptions in several languages.
Production.ProductDocument	Cross-reference table mapping products to related product documents.
Production.ProductInventory	Product inventory information.
Production.ProductListPriceHistory	Changes in the list price of a product over time.
Production.ProductModel	Product model classification.
Production.ProductModelIllustration	Cross-reference table mapping product models and illustrations.
Production.ProductModelProductDescriptionCulture	Cross-reference table mapping product descriptions and the language the description is written in.
Production.ProductPhoto	Product images.
Production.ProductProductPhoto	Cross-reference table mapping products and product photos.
Production.ProductReview	Customer reviews of products they have purchased.
Production.ProductSubcategory	Product subcategories. See ProductCategory table.
Production.ScrapReason	Manufacturing failure reasons lookup table.
Production.TransactionHistory	Record of each purchase order, sales order, or work order transaction year to date.
Production.TransactionHistoryArchive	Transactions for previous years.
Production.UnitMeasure	Unit of measure lookup table.
Production.WorkOrder	Manufacturing work orders.
Production.WorkOrderRouting	Work order details.

Index - Database Object

An index on a table is a B-tree based structure which speeds up random searches. **Typically PRIMARY KEY (automatic), FOREIGN KEY and WHERE clause columns have indexes.** If the index is constructed on more than one column, it is called **composite index**. If all the columns in a query are in the index, it is called **covering index**. Properties dialog box displays the PRIMARY KEY composite index of the EmployeeDepartmentHistory table.

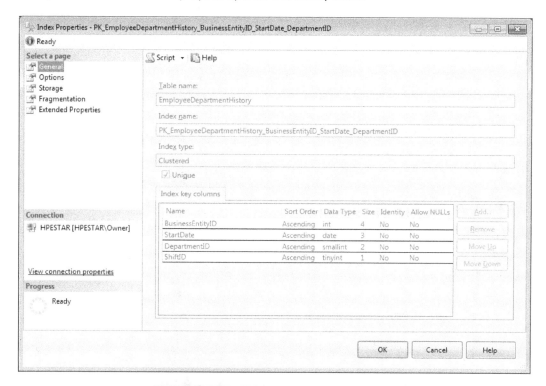

Diagram of EmployeeDepartmentHistory and Related Tables

EmployeeDepartmentHistory is a simple junction table with three FOREIGN KEYS to the
Employee, Shift and Department tables respectively.

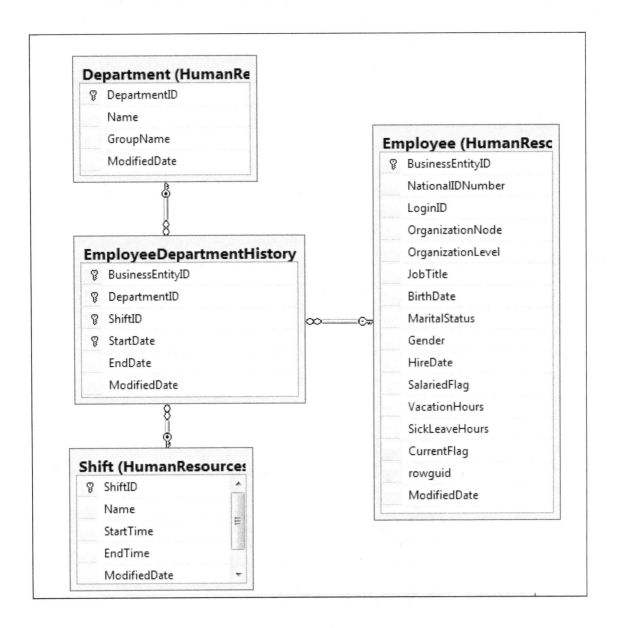

Index Description in Data Dictionary

The indexes listing for Product, SalesOrderHeader & SalesOrderDetail tables.

USE AdventureWorks2012;

```
SELECT   objtype                        AS ObjectType,
         'Sales.SalesOrderHeader'       AS TableName,
         objname                        AS ObjectName,
         value                          AS [Description]
FROM fn_listextendedproperty (NULL, 'schema', 'Sales', 'table', 'SalesOrderHeader', 'index', default)


UNION


SELECT objtype, 'Sales.SalesOrderDetail', objname, value
FROM fn_listextendedproperty (NULL, 'schema', 'Sales', 'table', 'SalesOrderDetail', 'index', default)


UNION


SELECT objtype, 'Production.Product', objname,  value
FROM fn_listextendedproperty (NULL, 'schema', 'Production', 'table', 'Product', 'index', default)
ORDER BY TableName;
GO
```

ObjectType	TableName	ObjectName	Description
INDEX	Production.Product	AK_Product_Name	Unique nonclustered index.
INDEX	Production.Product	AK_Product_ProductNumber	Unique nonclustered index.
INDEX	Production.Product	AK_Product_rowguid	Unique nonclustered index. Used to support replication samples.
INDEX	Production.Product	PK_Product_ProductID	Clustered index created by a primary key constraint.
INDEX	Sales.SalesOrderDetail	AK_SalesOrderDetail_rowguid	Unique nonclustered index. Used to support replication samples.
INDEX	Sales.SalesOrderDetail	IX_SalesOrderDetail_ProductID	Nonclustered index.
INDEX	Sales.SalesOrderDetail	PK_SalesOrderDetail_SalesOrderID_SalesOrderDetailID	Clustered index created by a primary key constraint.
INDEX	Sales.SalesOrderHeader	AK_SalesOrderHeader_rowguid	Unique nonclustered index. Used to support replication samples.
INDEX	Sales.SalesOrderHeader	AK_SalesOrderHeader_SalesOrderNumber	Unique nonclustered index.
INDEX	Sales.SalesOrderHeader	IX_SalesOrderHeader_CustomerID	Nonclustered index.
INDEX	Sales.SalesOrderHeader	IX_SalesOrderHeader_SalesPersonID	Nonclustered index.
INDEX	Sales.SalesOrderHeader	PK_SalesOrderHeader_SalesOrderID	Clustered index created by a primary key constraint.

Constraint - Database Object

The PRIMARY KEY constraint ensures that each row has a unique ID. The FOREIGN KEY constraint ensures that the FK points to (references) a valid PK. CHECK constraint enforces formulas (check clauses) defined for a column such as OrderQty > 0. If the formula evaluates to TRUE, the CHECK constraint satisfied, otherwise ERROR condition is generated by the database engine. SSMS screenshot shows a CHECK constraints listing query and results in the Northwind database.

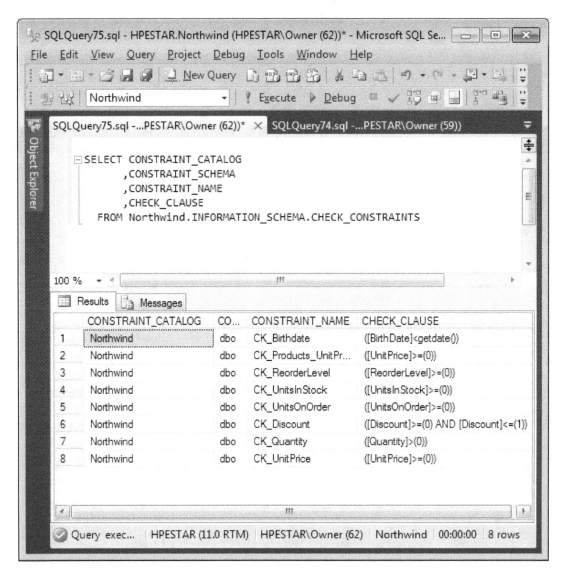

PRIMARY KEY & FOREIGN KEY Constraint Descriptions in Data Dictionary
Query to retrieve constraint descriptions (extended properties) for Product, SalesOrderHeader & SalesOrderDetail tables. Note: *description* not definition.

```
USE AdventureWorks2012;

-- UNION of 3 result sets
SELECT objtype AS ObjectType, 'Sales.SalesOrderHeader' AS TableName,
        objname as ObjectName, value AS [Description]
FROM fn_listextendedproperty (NULL, 'schema', 'Sales', 'table', 'SalesOrderHeader', 'constraint', default)
WHERE left(convert(varchar,value),7)='Foreign' or left(convert(varchar,value),7)='Primary'
UNION
SELECT objtype, 'Sales.SalesOrderDetail', objname,  value
FROM fn_listextendedproperty (NULL, 'schema', 'Sales', 'table', 'SalesOrderDetail', 'constraint', default)
WHERE left(convert(varchar,value),7)='Foreign' or left(convert(varchar,value),7)='Primary'
UNION
SELECT objtype, 'Production.Product', objname,  value
FROM fn_listextendedproperty (NULL, 'schema', 'Production', 'table', 'Product', 'constraint', default)
WHERE left(convert(varchar,value),7)='Foreign' or left(convert(varchar,value),7)='Primary'
ORDER BY TableName, ObjectName DESC;
GO
```

ObjectType	TableName	ObjectName	Description
CONSTRAINT	Production.Product	PK_Product_ProductID	Primary key (clustered) constraint
CONSTRAINT	Production.Product	FK_Product_UnitMeasure_WeightUnitMeasureCode	Foreign key constraint referencing UnitMeasure.UnitMeasureCode.
CONSTRAINT	Production.Product	FK_Product_UnitMeasure_SizeUnitMeasureCode	Foreign key constraint referencing UnitMeasure.UnitMeasureCode.
CONSTRAINT	Production.Product	FK_Product_ProductSubcategory_ProductSubcategoryID	Foreign key constraint referencing ProductSubcategory.ProductSubcategoryID.
CONSTRAINT	Production.Product	FK_Product_ProductModel_ProductModelID	Foreign key constraint referencing ProductModel.ProductModelID.
CONSTRAINT	Sales.SalesOrderDetail	PK_SalesOrderDetail_SalesOrderID_SalesOrderDetailID	Primary key (clustered) constraint
CONSTRAINT	Sales.SalesOrderDetail	FK_SalesOrderDetail_SpecialOfferProduct_SpecialOfferIDProductID	Foreign key constraint referencing SpecialOfferProduct.SpecialOfferIDProductID.
CONSTRAINT	Sales.SalesOrderDetail	FK_SalesOrderDetail_SalesOrderHeader_SalesOrderID	Foreign key constraint referencing SalesOrderHeader.PurchaseOrderID.
CONSTRAINT	Sales.SalesOrderHeader	PK_SalesOrderHeader_SalesOrderID	Primary key (clustered) constraint
CONSTRAINT	Sales.SalesOrderHeader	FK_SalesOrderHeader_ShipMethod_ShipMethodID	Foreign key constraint referencing ShipMethod.ShipMethodID.
CONSTRAINT	Sales.SalesOrderHeader	FK_SalesOrderHeader_SalesTerritory_TerritoryID	Foreign key constraint referencing SalesTerritory.TerritoryID.
CONSTRAINT	Sales.SalesOrderHeader	FK_SalesOrderHeader_SalesPerson_SalesPersonID	Foreign key constraint referencing SalesPerson.SalesPersonID.
CONSTRAINT	Sales.SalesOrderHeader	FK_SalesOrderHeader_Customer_CustomerID	Foreign key constraint referencing Customer.CustomerID.
CONSTRAINT	Sales.SalesOrderHeader	FK_SalesOrderHeader_CurrencyRate_CurrencyRateID	Foreign key constraint referencing CurrencyRate.CurrencyRateID.
CONSTRAINT	Sales.SalesOrderHeader	FK_SalesOrderHeader_CreditCard_CreditCardID	Foreign key constraint referencing CreditCard.CreditCardID.
CONSTRAINT	Sales.SalesOrderHeader	FK_SalesOrderHeader_Address_ShipToAddressID	Foreign key constraint referencing Address.AddressID.
CONSTRAINT	Sales.SalesOrderHeader	FK_SalesOrderHeader_Address_BillToAddressID	Foreign key constraint referencing Address.AddressID.

CHAPTER 5: *Server Architecture & Configuration Best Practices*

View - Database Object

A SELECT query, with some restrictions, can be repackaged as view and thus become a server-side object, a coveted status, from "homeless" to "mansion". The creation of view is very simple, basically a name assignment is required as shown in the following demonstration. As soon as the CREATE VIEW statement is executed successfully the query, unknown to the SQL Server so far, becomes an "official" SQL Server database object, stored in the database. A view, a virtual table, can be used just like a table in SELECT queries. A note about the query: **the column aliases FirstAuthor and SecondAuthor cannot be used in the WHERE clause, only in the ORDER BY clause if present.**

SELECT results from views require ORDER BY if sorting is desired. There is no way around it.

```
USE pubs;
GO
```

```
CREATE VIEW vAuthorsInSameCity
AS
SELECT          FirstAuthor        = CONCAT(au1.au_fname,' ', au1.au_lname),
                SecondAuthor       = CONCAT(au2.au_fname,' ', au2.au_lname),
                FirstCity          = au1.city,
                SecondCity         = au2.city
FROM    authors au1
     INNER JOIN authors au2
      ON au1.city = au2.city
WHERE   CONCAT(au1.au_fname,' ', au1.au_lname) < CONCAT(au2.au_fname,' ', au2.au_lname)
GO
```

```
SELECT * FROM vAuthorsInSameCity
ORDER BY FirstAuthor, SecondAuthor
GO
-- (13 row(s) affected) - Partial results.
```

FirstAuthor	SecondAuthor	FirstCity	SecondCity
Abraham Bennet	Cheryl Carson	Berkeley	Berkeley
Albert Ringer	Anne Ringer	Salt Lake City	Salt Lake City
Ann Dull	Sheryl Hunter	Palo Alto	Palo Alto
Dean Straight	Dirk Stringer	Oakland	Oakland
Dean Straight	Livia Karsen	Oakland	Oakland
Dean Straight	Marjorie Green	Oakland	Oakland
Dean Straight	Stearns MacFeather	Oakland	Oakland
Dirk Stringer	Livia Karsen	Oakland	Oakland

View Descriptions in Data Dictionary

Query to list view descriptions in selected schemas.

```
USE AdventureWorks2012;
SELECT   CONCAT('Sales.', objname COLLATE DATABASE_DEFAULT)              AS ViewName,
         value                                                          AS [Description]
FROM fn_listextendedproperty (NULL, 'schema', 'Sales', 'view', default, NULL, NULL)
UNION
SELECT   CONCAT('Production.', objname COLLATE DATABASE_DEFAULT),  value
FROM fn_listextendedproperty (NULL, 'schema', 'Production', 'view', default, NULL, NULL)
UNION
SELECT   CONCAT('HumanResources.', objname COLLATE DATABASE_DEFAULT),  value
FROM fn_listextendedproperty (NULL, 'schema', 'HumanResources', 'view', default, NULL, NULL)
UNION
SELECT   CONCAT('Person.', objname COLLATE DATABASE_DEFAULT),   value
FROM fn_listextendedproperty (NULL, 'schema', 'Person', 'view', default, NULL, NULL)
ORDER BY ViewName;  -- (18 row(s) affected) - Partial results.
```

ViewName	Description
HumanResources.vEmployee	Employee names and addresses.
HumanResources.vEmployeeDepartment	Returns employee name, title, and current department.
HumanResources.vEmployeeDepartmentHistory	Returns employee name and current and previous departments.
HumanResources.vJobCandidate	Job candidate names and resumes.

CREATE Indexed View for Business Critical Queries

An indexed view is stored like a table unlike a standard view which is a virtual table with a query that is evaluated upon view invocation. Performance is the main benefit of an indexed view, but it comes at a cost: it slows down INSERTs and other operations in the underlying tables.

```
IF OBJECT_ID ('Sales.vSalesByDateByProduct', 'V') IS NOT NULL DROP VIEW Sales.vSalesByDateByProduct ;
GO
CREATE VIEW Sales.vSalesByDateByProduct WITH SCHEMABINDING  AS
   SELECT OrderDate, ProductNumber, SUM(LineTotal) AS TotalSales, COUNT_BIG(*) AS Items
   FROM Sales.SalesOrderDetail AS sod INNER JOIN Sales.SalesOrderHeader AS soh
     ON soh.SalesOrderID = sod.SalesOrderID   INNER JOIN Production.Product p ON sod.ProductID=p.ProductID
     GROUP BY OrderDate, ProductNumber;
GO
CREATE UNIQUE CLUSTERED INDEX idxVSalesCI ON Sales.vSalesByDateByProduct (OrderDate, ProductNumber);
GO
SELECT * FROM Sales.vSalesByDateByProduct ORDER BY OrderDate, ProductNumber;
GO  -- (26878 row(s) affected) - Partial results.
```

OrderDate	ProductNumber	TotalSales	Items
2005-07-01 00:00:00.000	BK-M82B-38	44549.868000	7
2005-07-01 00:00:00.000	BK-M82B-42	32399.904000	8
2005-07-01 00:00:00.000	BK-M82B-44	46574.862000	7

Graphical View Designer

A view can be designed graphically or an existing view altered by using the Design option on the View drop-down menu in SSMS Object Explorer. First we create a view, then enter the graphical view designer to take a look.

```
USE [Northwind];
GO
CREATE VIEW [dbo].[ListOfProducts] AS
SELECT Categories.CategoryName as Category, ProductName, CompanyName AS Supplier
FROM Categories         INNER JOIN Products  ON Categories.CategoryID = Products.CategoryID
                        INNER JOIN Suppliers  ON Suppliers.SupplierID = Products.SupplierID
WHERE (((Products.Discontinued)=0));
GO
```

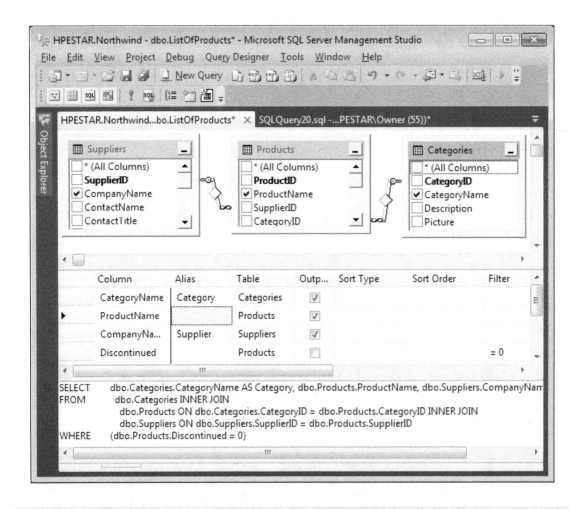

Stored Procedure: Server-Side Program

Stored procedures are T-SQL programs with optional input/output parameters. They vary from very simply to extremely complex. Following is the query which we will transform into a stored procedure, a server-side database object. Typical stored procedure returns table-like results to the client application software just like a SELECT query. That is though not a requirement.

```
USE AdventureWorks2012;
GO
SELECT          P.Name                          AS Product,
                L.Name                          AS [Inventory Location],
                SUM(PI.Quantity)                AS [Qty Available]
FROM Production.Product AS P
   INNER JOIN Production.ProductInventory AS PI
            ON P.ProductID = PI.ProductID
   INNER JOIN Production.Location AS L
            ON PI.LocationID = L.LocationID
   INNER JOIN Production.ProductSubcategory SC
            ON P.ProductSubcategoryID = SC.ProductSubcategoryID
WHERE SC.Name = 'Touring Bikes'
GROUP BY P.Name, L.Name
ORDER BY P.Name;
GO
-- (44 row(s) affected) - Partial results.
```

Product	Inventory Location	Qty Available
Touring-1000 Blue, 46	Final Assembly	86
Touring-1000 Blue, 46	Finished Goods Storage	99
Touring-1000 Blue, 50	Final Assembly	81
Touring-1000 Blue, 50	Finished Goods Storage	67
Touring-1000 Blue, 54	Final Assembly	60
Touring-1000 Blue, 54	Finished Goods Storage	73
Touring-1000 Blue, 60	Final Assembly	99
Touring-1000 Blue, 60	Finished Goods Storage	30
Touring-1000 Yellow, 46	Final Assembly	83
Touring-1000 Yellow, 46	Finished Goods Storage	65
Touring-1000 Yellow, 50	Final Assembly	62
Touring-1000 Yellow, 50	Finished Goods Storage	75
Touring-1000 Yellow, 54	Final Assembly	40
Touring-1000 Yellow, 54	Finished Goods Storage	35
Touring-1000 Yellow, 60	Final Assembly	100

Stored Procedure with Input Parameters

To make the stored procedure even more useful, we replace the literal 'Touring Bikes' with an input parameter. BEGIN & END are of control-of-flow language keywords.

```
CREATE PROC uspProductInventoryLocation @Subcategory nvarchar(50)
AS
BEGIN
SELECT          P.Name                          AS Product,
                L.Name                          AS [Inventory Location],
                SUM(PI.Quantity)                AS [Qty Available]
FROM Production.Product AS P
    INNER JOIN Production.ProductInventory AS PI
            ON P.ProductID = PI.ProductID
    INNER JOIN Production.Location AS L
            ON PI.LocationID = L.LocationID
    INNER JOIN Production.ProductSubcategory SC
            ON P.ProductSubcategoryID = SC.ProductSubcategoryID
WHERE SC.Name = @Subcategory
GROUP BY P.Name, L.Name
ORDER BY P.Name;
END
GO
```

```
-- Execute stored procedure with parameter
EXEC uspProductInventoryLocation 'Touring Bikes';
-- (44 row(s) affected)

EXEC uspProductInventoryLocation 'Mountain Bikes';        -- (64 row(s) affected) - Partial results.
```

Product	Inventory Location	Qty Available
Mountain-100 Black, 38	Final Assembly	56
Mountain-100 Black, 38	Finished Goods Storage	99
Mountain-100 Black, 42	Final Assembly	116
Mountain-100 Black, 42	Finished Goods Storage	78
Mountain-100 Black, 44	Final Assembly	100
Mountain-100 Black, 44	Finished Goods Storage	49
Mountain-100 Black, 48	Final Assembly	65
Mountain-100 Black, 48	Finished Goods Storage	88
Mountain-100 Silver, 38	Final Assembly	100
Mountain-100 Silver, 38	Finished Goods Storage	49
Mountain-100 Silver, 42	Final Assembly	65
Mountain-100 Silver, 42	Finished Goods Storage	88
Mountain-100 Silver, 44	Final Assembly	75
Mountain-100 Silver, 44	Finished Goods Storage	83
Mountain-100 Silver, 48	Final Assembly	102

CHAPTER 5: Server Architecture & Configuration Best Practices

Stored Procedure Descriptions in Data Dictionary

Query to list stored procedure descriptions in selected schemas.

```
USE AdventureWorks2012;

SELECT
        CONCAT('dbo.', objname COLLATE DATABASE_DEFAULT)              AS SprocName,
        value                                                        AS [Description]
FROM fn_listextendedproperty (NULL, 'schema', 'dbo', 'procedure', default, NULL, NULL)
WHERE LEN(convert(nvarchar(max),value)) > 4
UNION
SELECT
        CONCAT('dbo.', objname COLLATE DATABASE_DEFAULT),
        value
FROM fn_listextendedproperty (NULL, 'schema', 'HumanResources', 'procedure', default, NULL, NULL)
ORDER BY SprocName;
```

SprocName	Description
dbo.uspGetBillOfMaterials	Stored procedure using a recursive query to return a multi-level bill of material for the specified ProductID.
dbo.uspGetEmployeeManagers	Stored procedure using a recursive query to return the direct and indirect managers of the specified employee.
dbo.uspGetManagerEmployees	Stored procedure using a recursive query to return the direct and indirect employees of the specified manager.
dbo.uspGetWhereUsedProductID	Stored procedure using a recursive query to return all components or assemblies that directly or indirectly use the specified ProductID.
dbo.uspLogError	Logs error information in the ErrorLog table about the error that caused execution to jump to the CATCH block of a TRY...CATCH construct. Should be executed from within the scope of a CATCH block otherwise it will return without inserting error information.
dbo.uspPrintError	Prints error information about the error that caused execution to jump to the CATCH block of a TRY...CATCH construct. Should be executed from within the scope of a CATCH block otherwise it will return without printing any error information.
dbo.uspUpdateEmployeeHireInfo	Updates the Employee table and inserts a new row in the EmployeePayHistory table with the values specified in the input parameters.
dbo.uspUpdateEmployeeLogin	Updates the Employee table with the values specified in the input parameters for the given BusinessEntityID.
dbo.uspUpdateEmployeePersonalInfo	Updates the Employee table with the values specified in the input parameters for the given EmployeeID.

Trigger: Event Fired Server-Side Program

Trigger is like a stored procedure with four differences:

- ➢ Trigger is fired by an event such as table insert not by a call like a stored procedure.
- ➢ Trigger has the deleted (old row copy) and inserted (new row copy) tables available.
- ➢ Trigger does not have input/output parameter option.
- ➢ Trigger never returns table-like results.

Trigger to synchronize data in StateTaxFreeBondArchive table if data is inserted or updated in the StateTaxFreeBond table.

```
CREATE TRIGGER trgFillInMissingCouponRate

ON [dbo].StateTaxFreeBond

FOR INSERT,UPDATE

AS

BEGIN

    UPDATE StateTaxFreeBondArchive

        SET CouponRate = isnull(i.CouponRate,m.CouponRate)

    FROM StateTaxFreeBondArchive m

        INNER JOIN inserted i

            ON m.MBCID = i.MBCID

END
GO
```

Once a trigger is compiled, it is active and working silently in the background whenever insert, update or delete event fires it up.

It is important to note that there is a downside to the trigger "stealth" operation: if a trigger is dropped , it may not be noticed as part of the day-to-day operation. This behaviour is unlike stored procedure whereby if dropped, it causes error in the calling application software which can be noticed by users.

Function: Read-Only Server-Side Program

A user-defined function is also a program like a stored procedure, however, **no database change can be performed within a function, read only**. The database can be changed both in a trigger and a stored procedure. The following T-SQL script demonstrates the creation and use of a table-valued user-defined function. The other function type is scalar-valued, returns only a single value. WHILE is control-of-flow construct for looping. BREAK & CONTINUE keywords can be used within the WHILE loop to control the loop.

```
CREATE FUNCTION dbo.ufnSplitCommaDelimitedIntegerString (@NumberList nvarchar(max))
RETURNS @SplitList TABLE ( Element INT )
AS
 BEGIN
   DECLARE @Pointer   int,
       @Element nvarchar(32)
   SET @NumberList = LTRIM(RTRIM(@NumberList))
   IF ( RIGHT(@NumberList, 1) != ',' )
    SET @NumberList=@NumberList + ','
   SET @Pointer = CHARINDEX(',', @NumberList, 1)
   IF REPLACE(@NumberList, ',', '') <> ''
    BEGIN
      WHILE ( @Pointer > 0 )
       BEGIN
         SET @Element = LTRIM(RTRIM(LEFT(@NumberList, @Pointer - 1)))
         IF ( @Element <> '' )
          INSERT INTO @SplitList
          VALUES    (CONVERT(int, @Element))
         SET @NumberList = RIGHT(@NumberList, LEN(@NumberList) - @Pointer  )
         SET @Pointer = CHARINDEX(',', @NumberList, 1)
       END
    END
   RETURN
 END;
GO
SELECT * FROM  dbo.ufnSplitCommaDelimitedIntegerString ('1, 2, 4, 8, 16, 32, 64, 128, 256');
```

Element
1
2
4
8
16
32
64
128
256

CHAPTER 5: Server Architecture & Configuration Best Practices

User-Defined Function Descriptions in Data Dictionary

Query to list user-defined function descriptions in the default "dbo" schema. "dbo" stands for database owner, a database role.

```
USE AdventureWorks2012;
GO

SELECT
        CONCAT('dbo.', objname COLLATE DATABASE_DEFAULT)          AS UDFName,
        value                                                     AS [Description]
FROM fn_listextendedproperty (    NULL,
                                  'schema',
                                  'dbo',
                                  'function',
                                  default, NULL, NULL)
WHERE LEN(convert(nvarchar(max),value)) > 4
ORDER BY UDFName;
GO
```

UDFName	Description
dbo.ufnGetAccountingEndDate	Scalar function used in the uSalesOrderHeader trigger to set the starting account date.
dbo.ufnGetAccountingStartDate	Scalar function used in the uSalesOrderHeader trigger to set the ending account date.
dbo.ufnGetContactInformation	Table value function returning the first name, last name, job title and contact type for a given contact.
dbo.ufnGetDocumentStatusText	Scalar function returning the text representation of the Status column in the Document table.
dbo.ufnGetProductDealerPrice	Scalar function returning the dealer price for a given product on a particular order date.
dbo.ufnGetProductListPrice	Scalar function returning the list price for a given product on a particular order date.
dbo.ufnGetProductStandardCost	Scalar function returning the standard cost for a given product on a particular order date.
dbo.ufnGetPurchaseOrderStatusText	Scalar function returning the text representation of the Status column in the PurchaseOrderHeader table.
dbo.ufnGetSalesOrderStatusText	Scalar function returning the text representation of the Status column in the SalesOrderHeader table.
dbo.ufnGetStock	Scalar function returning the quantity of inventory in LocationID 6 (Miscellaneous Storage)for a specified ProductID.
dbo.ufnLeadingZeros	Scalar function used by the Sales.Customer table to help set the account number

Sequence - Database Object

The INT IDENTITY(1,1) function commonly used as **SURROGATE PRIMARY KEY** is limited to the host table. Sequence object, new in SQL Server 2012, can be shared by tables and programs. T-SQL script to demonstrate how two tables can share an integer sequence.

```
USE AdventureWorks2012;
GO
CREATE SEQUENCE CustomerSequence as INT
START WITH 1  INCREMENT BY 1;
GO
CREATE TABLE LONDONCustomer
(
        CustomerID      INT PRIMARY KEY,
        Name            NVARCHAR(64) UNIQUE,
        ModifiedDate    DATE default (CURRENT_TIMESTAMP)    );
GO
CREATE TABLE NYCCustomer
(
        CustomerID      INT PRIMARY KEY,
        Name            NVARCHAR(64) UNIQUE,
        ModifiedDate    DATE default (CURRENT_TIMESTAMP)    );
GO
INSERT NYCCustomer (CustomerID, Name)
VALUES
        (NEXT VALUE FOR CustomerSequence, 'Richard Blackstone'),
        (NEXT VALUE FOR CustomerSequence, 'Anna Smithfield');
GO
SELECT * FROM NYCCustomer;
```

CustomerID	Name	ModifiedDate
1	Richard Blackstone	2016-07-18
2	Anna Smithfield	2016-07-18

```
INSERT LONDONCustomer (CustomerID, Name)
VALUES
        (NEXT VALUE FOR CustomerSequence, 'Kevin Lionheart'),
        (NEXT VALUE FOR CustomerSequence, 'Linda Wakefield');
GO

SELECT * FROM LONDONCustomer;
```

CustomerID	Name	ModifiedDate
3	Kevin Lionheart	2016-07-18
4	Linda Wakefield	2016-07-18

ROW_NUMBER() and Ranking Functions

Ranking functions (window functions), introduced with SQL Server 2005, provide sequencing and ranking items in a partition or all. ROW_NUMBER() (sequence) function is the most used.

```
SELECT  CustomerID,
        CONVERT(date, OrderDate)                          AS OrderDate,
        RANK() OVER (    PARTITION BY CustomerID
                         ORDER BY OrderDate DESC)          AS RankNo
FROM   AdventureWorks2012.Sales.SalesOrderHeader
ORDER  BY CustomerID,  RankNo;
GO
-- (31465 row(s) affected) - Partial results.
```

CustomerID	OrderDate	RankNo
11014	2007-11-01	1
11014	2007-09-24	2
11015	2007-07-22	1
11016	2007-08-13	1
11017	2008-04-16	1
11017	2007-07-05	2
11017	2005-07-15	3
11018	2008-04-26	1
11018	2007-07-20	2
11018	2005-07-20	3
11019	2008-07-15	1
11019	2008-07-14	2
11019	2008-06-12	3
11019	2008-06-02	4
11019	2008-06-01	5
11019	2008-04-28	6
11019	2008-04-19	7
11019	2008-03-22	8
11019	2008-03-11	9
11019	2008-02-23	10
11019	2008-01-24	11
11019	2007-11-26	12
11019	2007-11-09	13
11019	2007-10-30	14
11019	2007-09-14	15
11019	2007-09-05	16
11019	2007-08-16	17
11020	2007-07-02	1

Partition data by CustomerID and rank it OrderDate DESC (most recent orders first).

```
SELECT *
FROM   (SELECT CustomerID,
           CONVERT(date, OrderDate)        AS OrderDate,
           RANK()  OVER (
               PARTITION BY CustomerID
               ORDER BY OrderDate DESC)       AS RankNo
        FROM   AdventureWorks2012.Sales.SalesOrderHeader)  x -- derived table
WHERE  RankNo  BETWEEN 1 AND 4
ORDER  BY CustomerID;
GO
-- (29383 row(s) affected)  - Partial results.
```

CustomerID	OrderDate	RankNo
11675	2007-08-13	1
11675	2006-04-27	2
11676	2008-06-11	1
11676	2008-02-21	2
11677	2008-06-02	1
11677	2008-03-24	2
11677	2008-03-17	3
11677	2008-03-07	4
11678	2007-08-09	1
11678	2006-04-12	2
11679	2008-06-01	1
11679	2008-04-15	2
11680	2008-07-22	1
11680	2008-03-04	2
11681	2008-05-28	1
11681	2007-09-08	2
11682	2008-06-11	1
11682	2008-03-08	2
11683	2007-08-11	1
11683	2006-04-07	2
11684	2008-06-14	1
11684	2008-01-02	2
11685	2008-06-15	1
11685	2007-09-12	2
11686	2007-10-26	1
11686	2007-09-09	2
11687	2007-12-23	1
11687	2007-10-14	2
11688	2007-08-18	1
11688	2006-04-04	2
11689	2008-03-05	1
11689	2008-02-27	2

CHAPTER 5: Server Architecture & Configuration Best Practices

Query to compare RANK, DENSE_RANK and NTILE.

```
USE AdventureWorks;

SELECT c.AccountNumber                          AS CustAccount,
    FLOOR(h.SubTotal / 1000)                    AS [SubTotal (Thousands $)],
    ROW_NUMBER() OVER(
        ORDER BY FLOOR(h.SubTotal /1000) DESC)   AS RowNumber,
    RANK()  OVER(
        ORDER BY FLOOR(h.SubTotal /1000) DESC)  AS Rank,
    DENSE_RANK()  OVER(
        ORDER BY FLOOR(h.SubTotal /1000) DESC)  AS DenseRank,
    NTILE(5)  OVER(
        ORDER BY FLOOR(h.SubTotal /1000) DESC)  AS NTile
FROM   Sales.Customer c
    INNER JOIN Sales.SalesOrderHeader h
        ON c.CustomerID = h.CustomerID
    INNER JOIN Sales.SalesTerritory t
        ON h.TerritoryID = t.TerritoryID
WHERE  t.Name = 'Germany'
        AND OrderDate >= '20040101' AND OrderDate  <  DATEADD(yy, 1, '20040101' )
        AND SubTotal >= 4000.0
ORDER  BY RowNumber;
```

CustAccount	SubTotal (Thousands $)	RowNumber	Rank	DenseRank	NTile
AW00000230	100.00	1	1	1	1
AW00000230	88.00	2	2	2	1
AW00000302	77.00	3	3	3	1
AW00000320	68.00	4	4	4	1
AW00000536	68.00	5	4	4	1
AW00000536	64.00	6	6	5	1
AW00000266	58.00	7	7	6	1
AW00000302	44.00	8	8	7	2
AW00000687	43.00	9	9	8	2
AW00000482	36.00	10	10	9	2
AW00000176	36.00	11	10	9	2
AW00000464	35.00	12	12	10	2
AW00000320	35.00	13	12	10	2
AW00000176	34.00	14	14	11	2
AW00000464	34.00	15	14	11	3

Dynamic SQL To Soar Beyond the Limits of Static SQL

Static (regular) T-SQL syntax does not accept variables at all places in a query. With dynamic SQL we can overcome the limitation. Dynamic SQL script uses table list metadata from the INFORMATION_SCHEMA.TABLES system view to build a COUNT() query for all tables. COUNT(*) returns 4 bytes integer. For large values COUNT_BIG() returns an 8 bytes integer.

```
DECLARE @SQL nvarchar(max) = '', @Schema sysname, @Table sysname;
SELECT TOP 20 @SQL = CONCAT(@SQL , 'SELECT "',QUOTENAME(TABLE_SCHEMA),'.',
        QUOTENAME(TABLE_NAME),'"',
        '= COUNT(*) FROM ', QUOTENAME(TABLE_SCHEMA),'.',QUOTENAME(TABLE_NAME) , ';',
        CHAR(10))
FROM INFORMATION_SCHEMA.TABLES
WHERE TABLE_TYPE='BASE TABLE';
PRINT @SQL;            -- Test & debug - Partial results.
```

```
SELECT "[Production].[BillOfMaterials]"= COUNT(*) FROM [Production].[BillOfMaterials];
SELECT "[Production].[Culture]"= COUNT(*) FROM [Production].[Culture];
```

```
EXEC sp_executesql @SQL   -- Dynamic SQL query execution
-- Partial results.
```

```
[Production].[ScrapReason]
16
```

```
[HumanResources].[Shift]
3
```

Parameterized Dynamic SQL Query Execution

The dynamic SQL string has a parameterized query. It can only be executed if the parameter(s) is supplied when dynamic execution is called thus provides protection against SQL injection attack.

```
DECLARE @LastName varchar(30) = 'O''Brien';
DECLARE @DynamicSQL nvarchar(max)= 'SELECT BusinessEntityID, FirstName, LastName
            FROM AdventureWorks2012.Person.Person ';
SET @DynamicSQL = CONCAT(@DynamicSQL, 'WHERE LastName = @pLastName');
PRINT @DynamicSQL;   -- testing & debugging
```

```
EXEC sp_executesql  @DynamicSQL, N'@pLastName varchar(40)', @pLastName = @LastName;
```

BusinessEntityID	FirstName	LastName
1553	Tim	O'Brien

CHAPTER 5: Server Architecture & Configuration Best Practices

Built-in System Functions

SQL Server T-SQL language has a large collection of system functions such as date & time, string and math function. The nested REPLACE string function can be used to remove unwanted characters from a string.

```
DECLARE @text nvarchar(128) = '#1245! $99^@';
SELECT REPLACE(REPLACE(REPLACE(REPLACE(REPLACE(REPLACE(REPLACE(REPLACE(REPLACE(@text,
    '!',''),'@',''),'#',''),'$',''),'%',''),'^',''),'&',''),'*',''),' ','');     -- 124599
```

All the system functions are listed in SSMS Object Explorer under the Programmability tab.

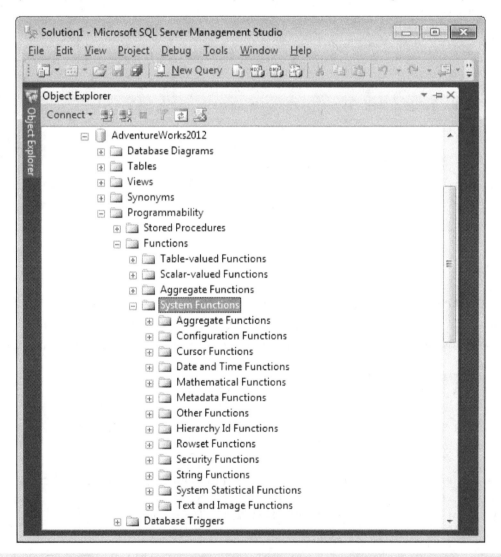

Local Variables & Table Variables in T-SQL

Local variables with different data types have scope of a batch or a stored procedure/trigger/function. Note that a "GO" in T-SQL script indicates end of batch, therefore the end of scope for local variables. Table variable is a virtual table with similar scope to local variable. Script to demonstrate local and table variables.

```
DECLARE @i INT;  SET @i = 999;

SELECT @i + @i;
-- 1998

SELECT @i = 555;  -- assignment
SELECT @i + @i;
GO
-- 1110

DECLARE @i INT = 999;          -- new in SQL Server 2008
SET @i += 1;                   -- new in SQL Server 2008

SELECT @i;
GO
-- 1000

DECLARE @OrderShipperJunction TABLE              -- Table variable
  (
   ShipperID            SMALLINT IDENTITY ( 1, 1 ) PRIMARY KEY,
   ShipperName          NVARCHAR(64),
   PurchaseOrderID      INT,
   ShipDate             DATE DEFAULT (CURRENT_TIMESTAMP),
   FreightCost          SMALLMONEY
  ) ;
INSERT @OrderShipperJunction
    (ShipperName,
     PurchaseOrderID,
     FreightCost)
VALUES('Custom Motor Bike Distributor',     11111,     177.34)

SELECT * FROM   @OrderShipperJunction
GO
```

ShipperID	ShipperName	PurchaseOrderID	ShipDate	FreightCost
1	Custom Motor Bike Distributor	11111	2016-07-18	177.34

Metadata Visibility Through System Views

The system views provide SQL Server and database metadata which can be used just for viewing in SSMS Object Explorer or programmatically in T-SQL scripts. The system views are based on system tables which are no longer accessible since SQL Server 2005. The system view sys.objects contains all the basic info on each and every user objects in the database with the exception of indexes. Query to retrieve partial data form sys.objects system view.

```
select
    s.name                  as [Schema],
    o.name                  as [Name],
    o.type_desc             as [Type],
    o.create_date           as CreateDate
from    sys.objects o
        inner join sys.schemas s
            on s.schema_id = o.schema_id
where is_ms_shipped = 0
order by [Type], [Schema], [Name]
-- (722 row(s) affected)  -  Partial results.
```

Schema	Name	Type	CreateDate
HumanResources	Department	USER_TABLE	2012-03-14 13:14:19.267
HumanResources	Employee	USER_TABLE	2012-03-14 13:14:19.303
HumanResources	EmployeeDepartmentHistory	USER_TABLE	2012-03-14 13:14:19.313
HumanResources	EmployeePayHistory	USER_TABLE	2012-03-14 13:14:19.320
HumanResources	JobCandidate	USER_TABLE	2012-03-14 13:14:19.337
HumanResources	Shift	USER_TABLE	2012-03-14 13:14:19.593
Person	Address	USER_TABLE	2012-03-14 13:14:19.140
Person	AddressType	USER_TABLE	2012-03-14 13:14:19.150
Person	BusinessEntity	USER_TABLE	2012-03-14 13:14:19.183
Person	BusinessEntityAddress	USER_TABLE	2012-03-14 13:14:19.190
Person	BusinessEntityContact	USER_TABLE	2012-03-14 13:14:19.197
Person	ContactType	USER_TABLE	2012-03-14 13:14:19.207
Person	CountryRegion	USER_TABLE	2012-03-14 13:14:19.220
Person	EmailAddress	USER_TABLE	2012-03-14 13:14:19.290
Person	Password	USER_TABLE	2012-03-14 13:14:19.350
Person	Person	USER_TABLE	2012-03-14 13:14:19.357
Person	PersonPhone	USER_TABLE	2012-03-14 13:14:19.370
Person	PhoneNumberType	USER_TABLE	2012-03-14 13:14:19.377
Person	StateProvince	USER_TABLE	2012-03-14 13:14:19.623
Production	BillOfMaterials	USER_TABLE	2012-03-14 13:14:19.170
Production	Culture	USER_TABLE	2012-03-14 13:14:19.237

Constructing T-SQL Identifiers

Identifiers are the names given to SQL Server & database objects such as linked servers, tables, views or stored procedures.

Very simple rule: **do not include any special character in an identifier other than single underscore (_). Double underscore in an identifier inevitably leads to confusion, loss of database developer productivity.**

Creating good identifiers helps with productivity in database development, administration and maintenance. Using names AccountsPayable1 and AccountsPayable2 as variations for AccountsPayable is not good because the 1,2 suffixes are meaningless. On the other hand AccountsPayableLondon & AccountsPayableNYC are good, meaningful names. The list of identifiers can be enumerated from AdventureWorks2012.sys.objects.

SELECT name FROM AdventureWorks2012.sys.objects   ORDER BY name; -- (820 row(s) affected)

Selected results with comments.

Identifier(name)	Style Comment
Account	single word
AddressType	double words CamelCase style
BillOfMaterials	CamelCase (also known as Pascal case)
BusinessEntityContact	CamelCase
CK__ImageStore__67152DD3	double underscore separator, CK prefix for CHECK CONSTRAINT
CK_Document_Status	single underscore separator
CK_EmployeeDepartmentHistory_EndDate	mixed - CamelCase and underscore
DF__ImageStor__is_sy__75634D2A	database engine (system) generated name
sp_creatediagram	old-fashioned, sp prefix for system procedure
syscscolsegments	old-fashioned with abbreviations
ufnGetProductDealerPrice	Hungarian naming, ufn stands for user(-defined) function
vSalesPersonSalesByFiscalYears	Hungarian naming, v prefix is for view

The Use of [] - Square Brackets in Identifiers

Each identifier can be enclosed in square brackets, but not required. If the identifier is the same as a T-SQL reserved keyword, then it is required. Square brackets are also required when the identifier includes a special character such as space. Double quotes can be used also but that becomes very confusing when single quotes are present. The use of brackets is demonstrated in the following T-SQL script.

```
USE Northwind;
```

```
-- Syntax error without brackets since table name has space
SELECT * FROM Order Details;
/* ERROR
Msg 156, Level 15, State 1, Line 3
Incorrect syntax near the keyword 'Order'.
*/
```

```
-- Valid statement with brackets around table name
SELECT * FROM [Order Details];
-- (2155 row(s) affected)
```

```
-- Create and populate table with SELECT INTO
-- Error since ORDER is a reserved keyword
SELECT * INTO Order FROM Orders;
/* ERROR
Msg 156, Level 15, State 1, Line 1
Incorrect syntax near the keyword 'Order'.
*/
```

```
-- With brackets, query is valid
SELECT * INTO [Order] FROM Orders;
-- (830 row(s) affected)
```

When a database object is scripted out in SSMS Object Explore, the identifiers are surrounded with square brackets even when not needed as shown in the following demonstration.

```
CREATE TABLE [dbo].[Order Details](
        [OrderID] [int] NOT NULL,
        [ProductID] [int] NOT NULL,
        [UnitPrice] [money] NOT NULL,
        [Quantity] [smallint] NOT NULL,
        [Discount] [real] NOT NULL,
 CONSTRAINT [PK_Order_Details] PRIMARY KEY CLUSTERED
(       [OrderID] ASC,
        [ProductID] ASC));
```

CHAPTER 5: Server Architecture & Configuration Best Practices

CHAPTER 6: Business Intelligence via SSAS, SSIS & SSRS

Business Intelligence in the Enterprise

SQL Server Analysis Services (SSAS), SQL Server Integration Services (SSIS) & SQL Server Reporting Services (SSRS) are the server side Business Intelligence software components. Easy to remember associations: SSAS: OLAP cubes and more, SSIS: ETL (extract, transform, load) data transfer system & SSRS: traditional reports, interactive & OLAP reports. SQL Server Data Tools (SSDT) provides 3 customized templates as design environments.

SSRS: Designing Complex Interactive Reports

SSDT report design environment: product catalog in the report design editor.

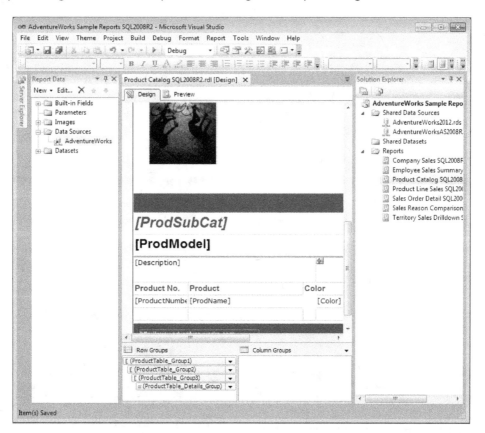

Previewing the Report Design

The product catalog is interactive with a drill down directory on the left which is based on the Production.ProductCategory and Production.ProductSubcategory tables. The Product, ProductSubcategory & ProductCategory tables form a hierarchy which is neatly exploited in the product catalog report. What makes the report design environment extremely powerful that you can try the look & feel of a report just by clicking a tab and staying in the studio environment. The product images are from the ProductPhoto table(in Management Studio we cannot see the images, only the binary code).

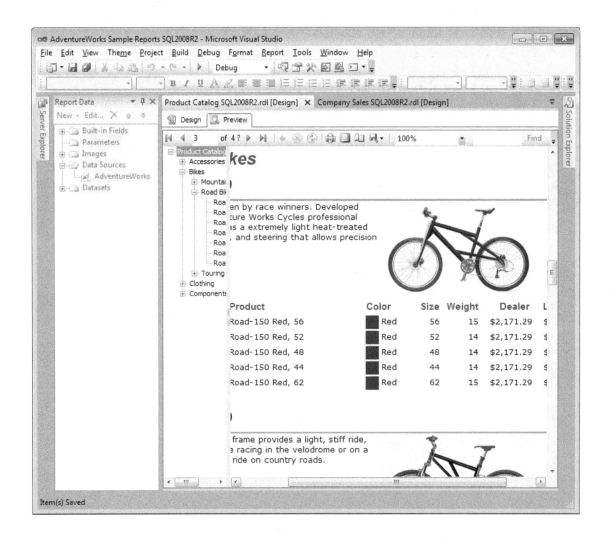

Detailed Preview of AWC Product Catalog

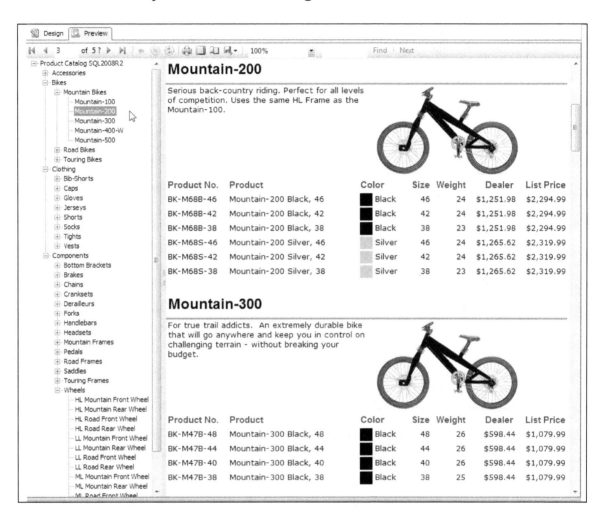

SSAS: Designing Multi-Dimensional Cubes

SSAS cubes contain millions of pre-calculated answers just waiting for the question like: what was the net revenue in Florida for the 3rd Quarter of 2016? Since the answer is ready, the response time is sub-second. AS cubes are derived from dimension tables and fact tables in a data warehouse database.

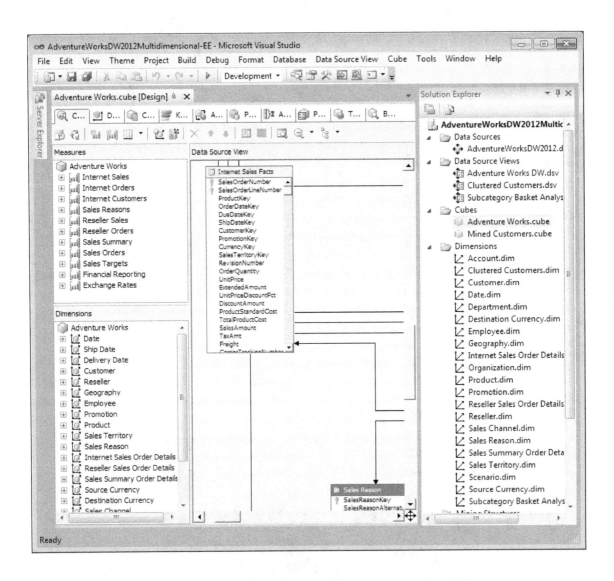

Test OLAP Analysis Services Cube Design with Browser

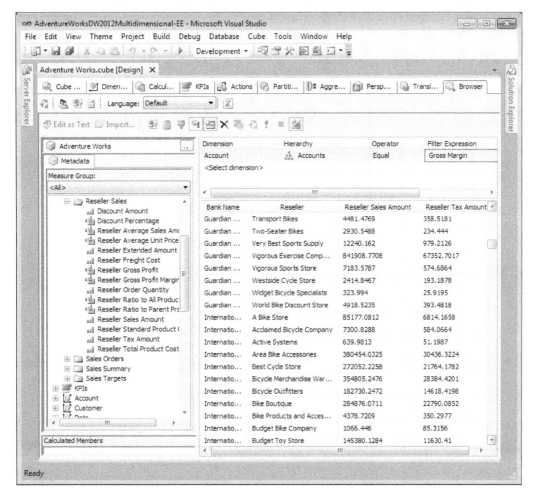

Dimension Usage Display

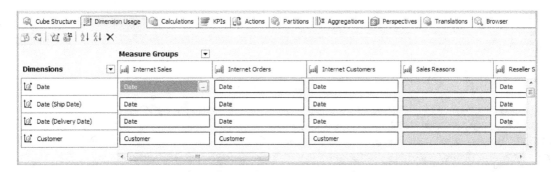

CHAPTER 6: Business Intelligence via SSAS, SSIS & SSRS

Browsing Multidimensional Cube in Management Explorer

In Object Explorer we can connect to Analysis Server and browse the available multidimensional cubes.

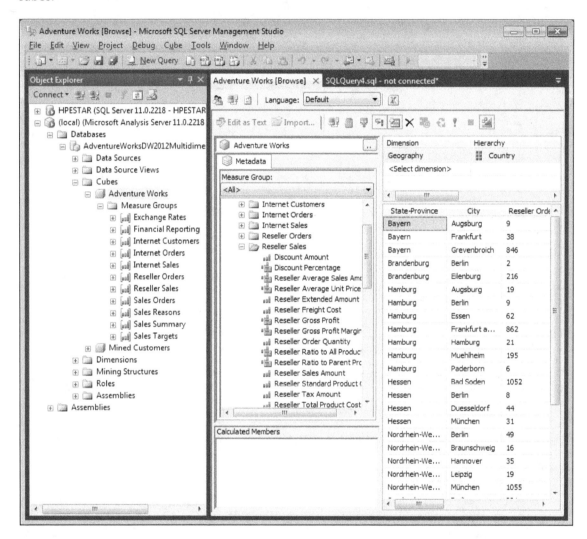

```
USE AdventureWorksDW2012;
-- Searching data warehouse database metadata for table objects
SELECT  CONCAT(schema_name(O.schema_id),'.', O.NAME) AS ObjectName,
        O.TYPE AS ObjectType,      C.NAME AS ColumnName
FROM sys.objects O INNER JOIN sys.columns C ON O.OBJECT_ID = C.OBJECT_ID
WHERE  O.type='U' AND O.NAME LIKE '%sales%' AND C.NAME LIKE '%price%'
ORDER BY ObjectName, ColumnName;   -- Partial results.
-- dbo.FactInternetSales    U           UnitPrice
```

Excel PivotTable Report Using AS Cube Datasource

Excel can use as datasource SQL Server database and Analysis Services database(bottom image). Actually PivotTable is a very good match for browsing multidimensional cubes since the underlying concepts are very similar: summary data tabulations by dimensions.

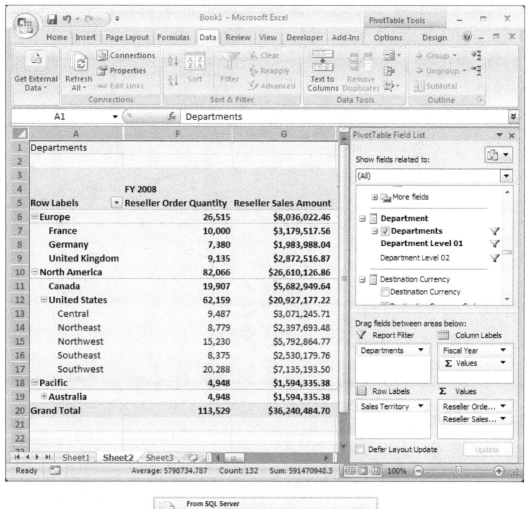

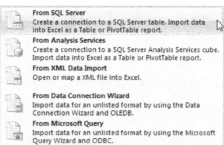

Sales Reason Comparison Report Based on AS Cube

The Sales Reason Comparison report (converted to 2012) is based on the multidimensional
AdventureWorksAS AS cube. Design mode and report segment in preview mode.

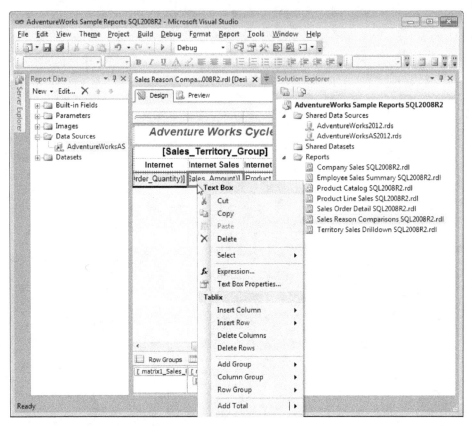

Sales Reason	Europe			North America		
	Internet Orders	Internet Sales Amount	Internet Total Product Cost	Internet Orders	Internet Sales Amount	Interr Prod
Manufacturer	$352	$1,206,594	$733,050	$803	$2,765,552	$
On Promotion	$1,118	$2,009,804	$1,182,740	$1,298	$2,217,191	$
Other	$111	$65,666	$39,932	$109	$62,743	
Price	$2,275	$3,586,028	$2,120,140	$2,630	$4,158,322	$
Quality	$316	$1,130,733	$686,129	$718	$2,569,198	$
Review	$226	$436,477	$250,168	$319	$578,245	

SSIS: Enterprise Level Data Integration

SSIS is an enterprise level data integration and data transformation software tool. Transmit (clean, transformed) data from different data sources to the database and vice versa. The Data Flow editor in SSDT for an SSIS sample project.

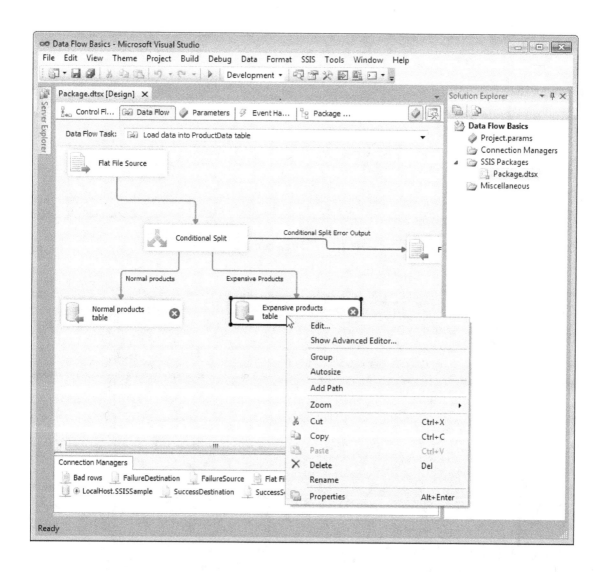

SSAS, SSIS, SSRS in Configuration Manager

SSIS is shared for all instances. SSAS & SSRS are per instance. MSSQLSERVER means the default instance, HPESTAR. SQL12 means the names instance HPESTAR\SQL12.

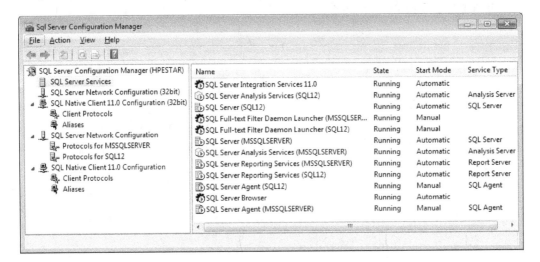

ReportServer & ReportServerTempDB Databases

Each Reporting Services instance is supported by two databases.

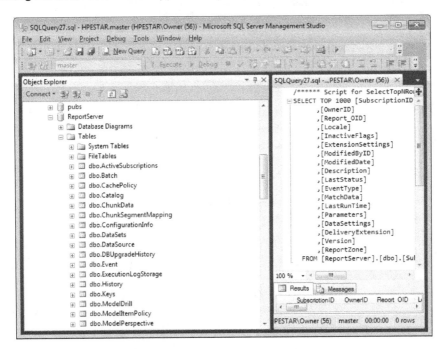

CHAPTER 7: Database Infrastructure Design

Create a New Database

Easiest to create a new database by Object Explorer GUI. The action can be scripted, saved, modified and reused.

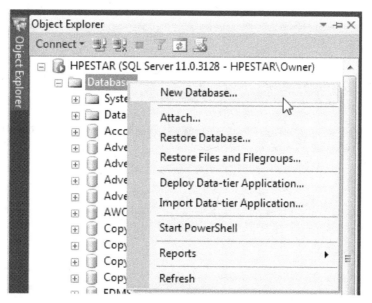

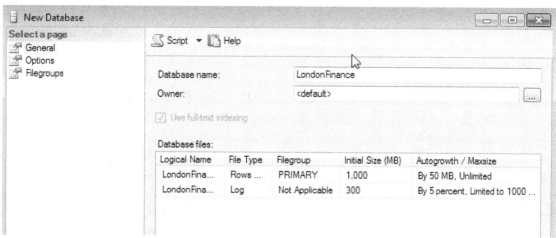

CHAPTER 7: Database Infrastructure Design

Specifying Database Files

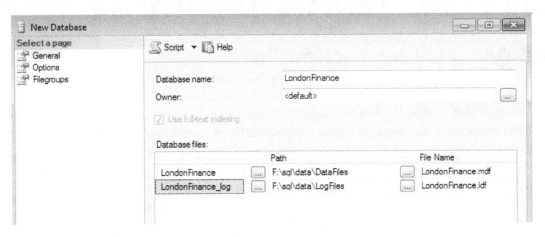

New Database Filegroups Page

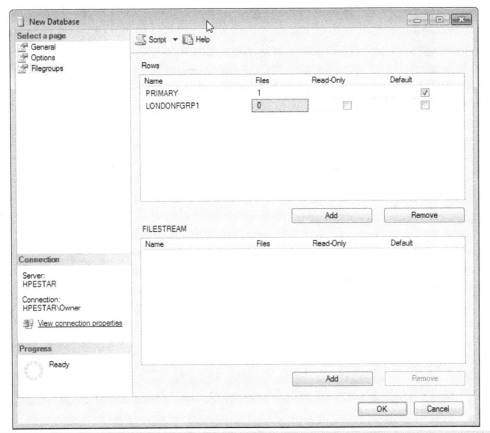

CHAPTER 7: Database Infrastructure Design

New Database Options Page

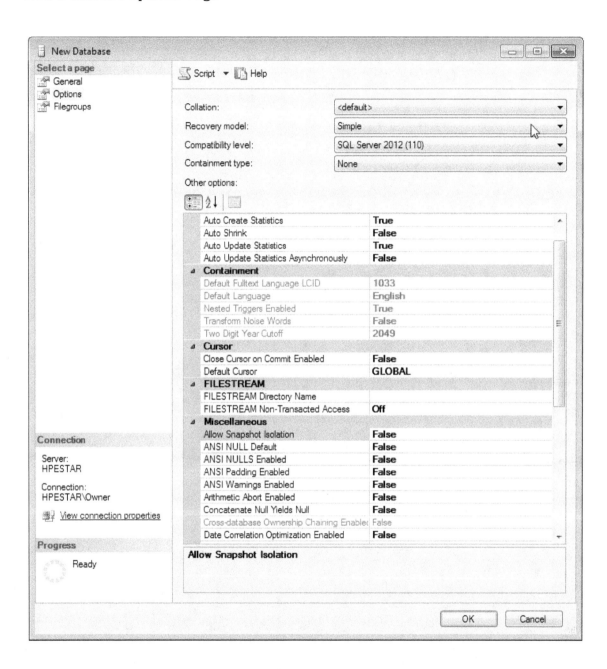

Adding Data File in a New Filegroup and Scripting Action

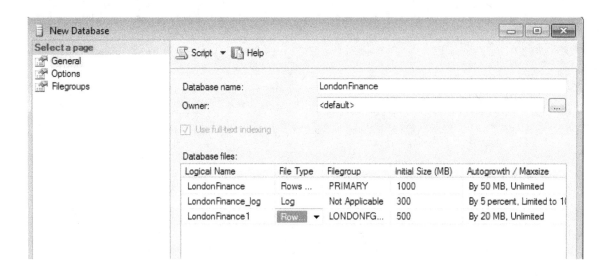

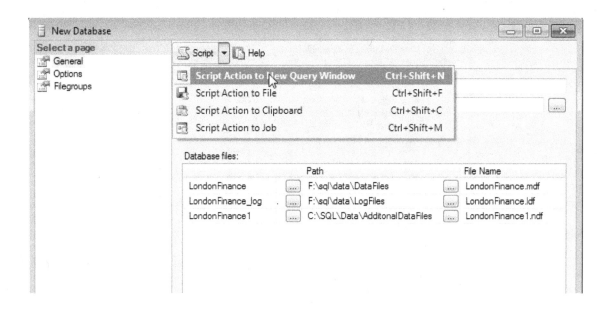

CREATE DATABASE Script

Here is the generated CREATE DATABASE T-SQL script.

```
CREATE DATABASE [LondonFinance]
 CONTAINMENT = NONE
 ON  PRIMARY
( NAME = N'LondonFinance', FILENAME = N'F:\sql\data\DataFiles\LondonFinance.mdf' ,
SIZE = 1024000KB , FILEGROWTH = 51200KB ),
 FILEGROUP [LONDONFGRP1]
( NAME = N'LondonFinance1', FILENAME =
N'C:\SQL\Data\AdditonalDataFiles\LondonFinance1.ndf'
, SIZE = 512000KB , FILEGROWTH = 20480KB )
 LOG ON
( NAME = N'LondonFinance_log', FILENAME = N'F:\sql\data\LogFiles\LondonFinance.ldf' ,
SIZE = 307200KB , MAXSIZE = 1024000KB , FILEGROWTH = 5%)
GO
ALTER DATABASE [LondonFinance] SET COMPATIBILITY_LEVEL = 110
GO
ALTER DATABASE [LondonFinance] SET ANSI_NULL_DEFAULT OFF
GO
ALTER DATABASE [LondonFinance] SET ANSI_NULLS OFF
GO
ALTER DATABASE [LondonFinance] SET ANSI_PADDING OFF
GO
ALTER DATABASE [LondonFinance] SET ANSI_WARNINGS OFF
GO
ALTER DATABASE [LondonFinance] SET ARITHABORT OFF
GO
ALTER DATABASE [LondonFinance] SET AUTO_CLOSE OFF
GO
ALTER DATABASE [LondonFinance] SET AUTO_CREATE_STATISTICS ON
GO
ALTER DATABASE [LondonFinance] SET AUTO_SHRINK OFF
GO
ALTER DATABASE [LondonFinance] SET AUTO_UPDATE_STATISTICS ON
GO
ALTER DATABASE [LondonFinance] SET CURSOR_CLOSE_ON_COMMIT OFF
GO
ALTER DATABASE [LondonFinance] SET CURSOR_DEFAULT  GLOBAL
GO
ALTER DATABASE [LondonFinance] SET CONCAT_NULL_YIELDS_NULL OFF
GO
```

```
ALTER DATABASE [LondonFinance] SET NUMERIC_ROUNDABORT OFF
GO
ALTER DATABASE [LondonFinance] SET QUOTED_IDENTIFIER OFF
GO
ALTER DATABASE [LondonFinance] SET RECURSIVE_TRIGGERS OFF
GO
ALTER DATABASE [LondonFinance] SET  DISABLE_BROKER
GO
ALTER DATABASE [LondonFinance] SET AUTO_UPDATE_STATISTICS_ASYNC OFF
GO
ALTER DATABASE [LondonFinance] SET DATE_CORRELATION_OPTIMIZATION OFF
GO
ALTER DATABASE [LondonFinance] SET PARAMETERIZATION SIMPLE
GO
ALTER DATABASE [LondonFinance] SET READ_COMMITTED_SNAPSHOT OFF
GO
ALTER DATABASE [LondonFinance] SET  READ_WRITE
GO
ALTER DATABASE [LondonFinance] SET RECOVERY SIMPLE
GO
ALTER DATABASE [LondonFinance] SET  MULTI_USER
GO
ALTER DATABASE [LondonFinance] SET PAGE_VERIFY CHECKSUM
GO
ALTER DATABASE [LondonFinance] SET TARGET_RECOVERY_TIME = 0 SECONDS
GO
USE [LondonFinance]
GO
IF NOT EXISTS (SELECT name FROM sys.filegroups WHERE is_default=1 AND name =
N'PRIMARY')
ALTER DATABASE [LondonFinance] MODIFY FILEGROUP [PRIMARY] DEFAULT
GO
```

CHAPTER 7: Database Infrastructure Design

Database Properties

Database Properties provides all the metadata on the database and options for changing some of the properties.

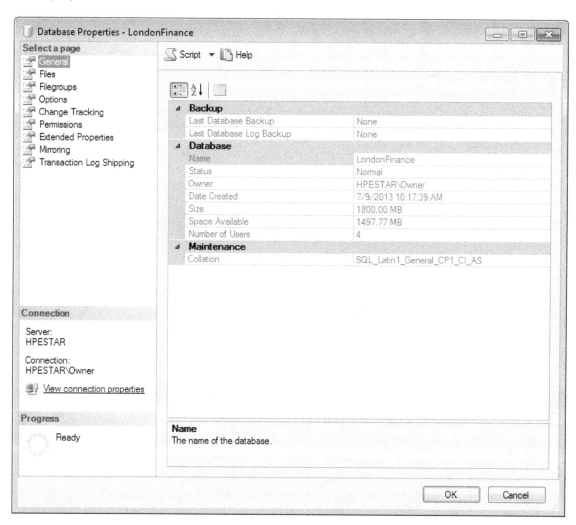

Database Properties Options Page

As usual script can be generated, tentative changes made, action scripted and Cancel clicked
(abandon action).

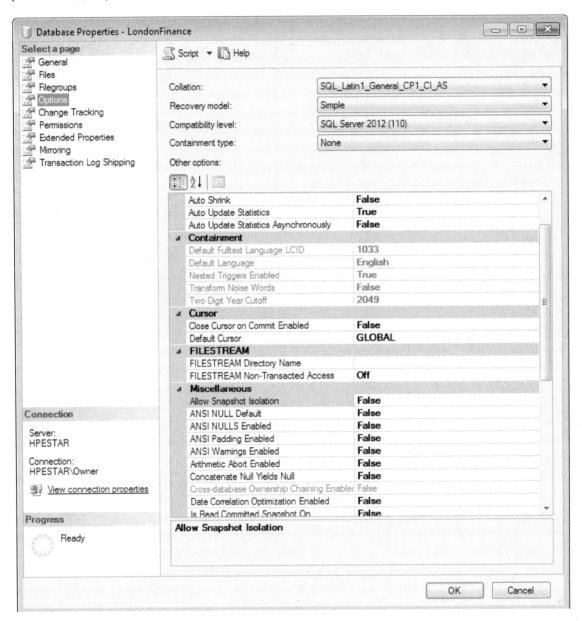

Database Properties Files Page

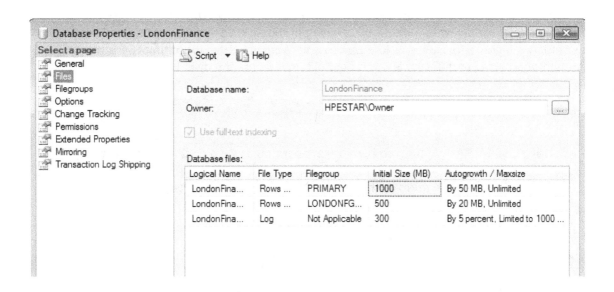

Database Properties Filegroups Page

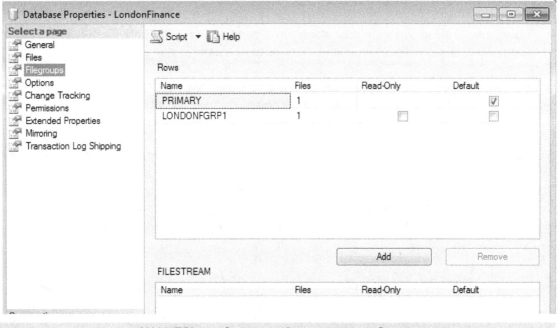

Disk Configuration for Best Performance

Disk is the slowest part of the computer. Physical movements involved two ways: disk read/write head positioning to a track and spinning of the disk. Therefore it is imperative to have sufficient high-performance disk resources and configure them for optimal performance. RAM memory caching at different levels is helpful to overcome the disk sluggishness.

The following SQL Server disk drive configuration is reliable, high performance and relatively low cost:

- ➢ Drive C 60 GB RAID 1 mirrored hard drive: operating system / SQL Server software

- ➢ Drive D 60 GB RAID 1 mirrored hard drive: temporary database (tempdb) data file

- ➢ Drive E 300 GB RAID 5 hard drive array: application database data files

- ➢ Drive F 60 GB RAID 1 mirrored hard drive: transaction logs

- ➢ Drive G 60 GB RAID 1 mirrored hard drive: temporary database (tempdb) log file

- ➢ Drive F 120 GB RAID 0 hard drive: staging files - feeds, disk-to-disk-to-tape backups, etc.

While mirrored RAID 1 drive appears to be perfect for redundancy, errors on source drive are automatically duplicated to the mirror drive.

Ideally busy tables and indexes should be placed on separate independent drives. However, server computer disk arrays have some limitations as to how can they be configured.

Articles: **Hard Drive Configurations for SQL Server**   http://bit.ly/W5gLLc
http://www.mssqltips.com/sqlservertip/1328/hard-drive-configurations-for-sql-server/

Deciding the best disk configuration for your SQL Server   http://bit.ly/13zHiVb
http://www.tek-tips.com/faqs.cfm?fid=5747

SAN Storage Best Practices for SQL Server   http://bit.ly/9Crc4N
http://www.brentozar.com/sql/sql-server-san-best-practices/

CHAPTER 8: Advanced Database Architecture

How to Read varbinary(max) Columns

Usually the binary objects such as images or Word documents in varbinary(max) columns have to be exported to the file system and the appropriate software is used to "read" them. Clean plain text is readable after conversion to varchar(max) or nvarchar(max).

```
SELECT  Title AS DocTitle, LEN(Document) AS Length,
     CONVERT(varchar(max), substring(Document,1806, 60)) AS DocumentSegment
FROM Production.Document WHERE DocumentNode = 0x6B40;
```

DocTitle	Length	DocumentSegment
Lubrication Maintenance	22528	NG: Do not over lubricate parts. If oil gets on the wheel ri

FileTable - Integrating Folders with Database

Storing large number of binary files such as images was a challenge until SQL Server 2012: FileTable integrates files in a folder into the database, yet keep them accessible at Windows file system level. In the past, there were two solutions:

- ➢ Keep only the filenames in the database table.
- ➢ Keep both the filenames and binary file objects (varbinary(max)) in the table.

Using the first method, the files were not backed up with the database since they were not part of the database. Applying the second method, the binary objects were in the database, but as a deadweight, since not much can be done with them. FileTable is the best of both worlds: files are backed up / restored with the database, yet they remain visible at the file system level. So if a new file is dropped (copied) into the folder, it becomes visible to SQL Server instantaneously. FileTable requires the FILESTREAM feature as shown on the Server Properties dialog box.

The CREATE TABLE statement for a FileTable

```
-- Create FileTable  -- new to SQL Server 2012
CREATE TABLE ImageStore
AS FileTable
  WITH (
     FileTable_Directory = 'ImageStore',
     FileTable_Collate_Filename = database_default
     );
GO  -- (1 row(s) affected)
```

We can determine the FileTable folder name which is visible at the file system level the following way.

```
SELECT DBName=DB_NAME ( database_id ), directory_name
   FROM sys.database_filestream_options
       WHERE directory_name is not null;
```

DBName	directory_name
AdventureWorks2012	FSDIR

FileTable directory(path): \\YOURSERVER\MSSQLSERVER\FSDIR\ImageStore

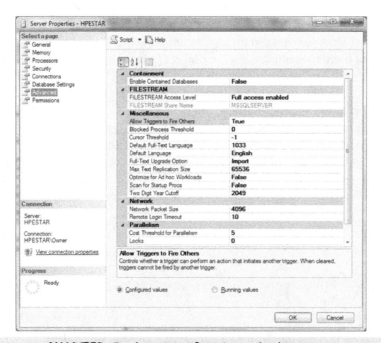

The dialog box for database options setup as related to FILESTREAM

"hpestar" is the name of the SQL Server instance (default instance, same name as the computer).

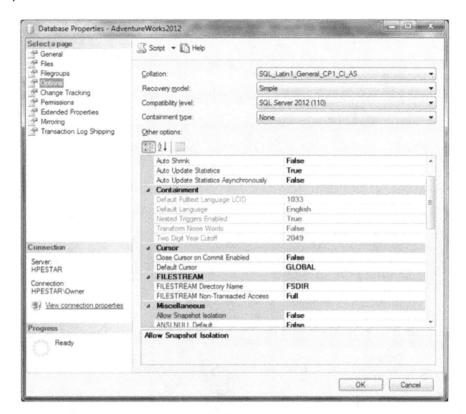

CHAPTER 8: Advanced Database Architecture

The FileTable folder is currently empty.

We shall now copy 3 photos in the ImageStore folder using Windows Copy & Paste operation.

The photos are "visible" from the database side as well.

The INSERT, UPDATE and DELETE commands are operational on FileTable, however, a new column cannot be added as demonstrated in the following script:

```
SELECT * FROM ImageStore;
GO
UPDATE ImageStore SET name='RollerCoaster.jpg'
WHERE stream_id='E73EA731-AAAA-E111-9078-D8D3857FC43E';
GO
SELECT * FROM ImageStore;
```

CHAPTER 8: Advanced Database Architecture

Adding Files to FileTable Using T-SQL

There are two T-SQL methods available. **Note: xp_cmdshell should be disabled on prodution server due to security reasons.**

```
-- Adding files from T-SQL - method 1 xp_cmdshell copy
EXEC xp_cmdshell 'copy "C:\photo\000Test\xBermuda.jpg"
"\\HPESTAR\mssqlserver\FSDIR\ImageStore\xBermuda.jpg"'
GO
```

```
-- Adding files from T-SQL - method 2 OPENROWSET
INSERT INTO [dbo].[ImageStore] ([name],[file_stream])
SELECT 'Bermuda9.jpg', * FROM
    OPENROWSET(BULK N'C:\photo\2012\BERMUDA\BERMUDA\IMG_1154.jpg', SINGLE_BLOB)
            AS FileUpload
```

Deleting Files from FileTable Using T-SQL

```
SELECT * FROM ImageStore
GO
```

```
DELETE ImageStore
WHERE stream_id = '62F55342-ABAA-E111-9078-D8D3857FC43E'
GO
```

```
SELECT * FROM ImageStore
GO
```

```
-- Column(s) cannot be added to a FileTable
ALTER TABLE ImageStore
ADD AddDate smalldatetime NULL
CONSTRAINT AddDateDflt
DEFAULT CURRENT_TIMESTAMP WITH VALUES ;
GO
/* Msg 33422, Level 16, State 1, Line 2
The column 'AddDate' cannot be added to table 'ImageStore' as it is a FileTable.
Adding columns to the fixed schema of a FileTable object is not permitted.
*/
```

```
DROP TABLE ImageStore
GO
```

Data Compression: Compressed Table

The table compression option has been introduced with SQL Server 2008. Data is compressed inside a database table, and it reduces the size of the table. Performance benefit in addition to space saving: "reads" reduction; queries need to read fewer pages from the disk. Sufficient CPU resources are required for the SQL Server instance to compress and decompress table data, when data is read (SELECT) or written (INSERT, UPDATE, MERGE). Analysis is required to ensure that table compression has no adverse effect on business critical query performance. Data compression may not be available in all editions of SQL Server. In the demonstration, first we create a new table for testing.

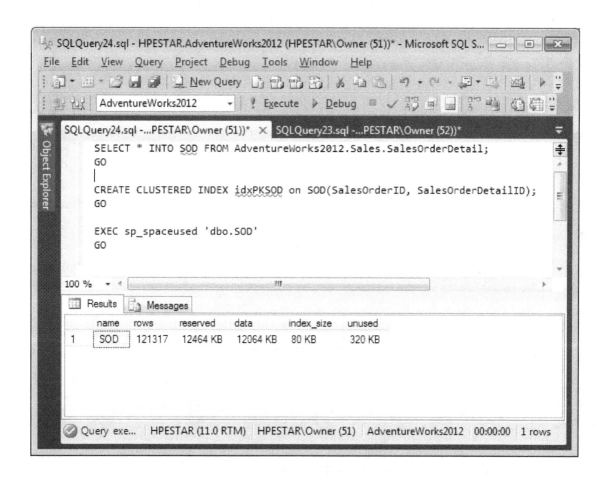

Switching to PAGE-LEVEL Compression

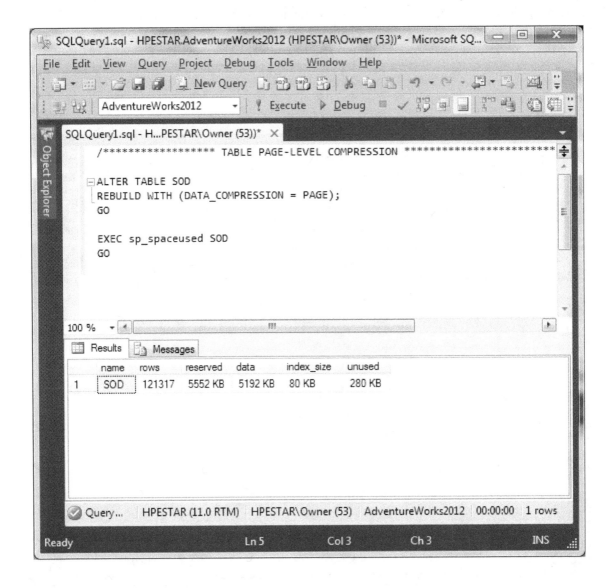

Data storage size decreased from around 12 MB to around 5 MB.

Testing ROW-LEVEL Compression

We can see the space reduction from 12MB to around 7.5MB.

Space reduction can be estimated with a system stored procedure.

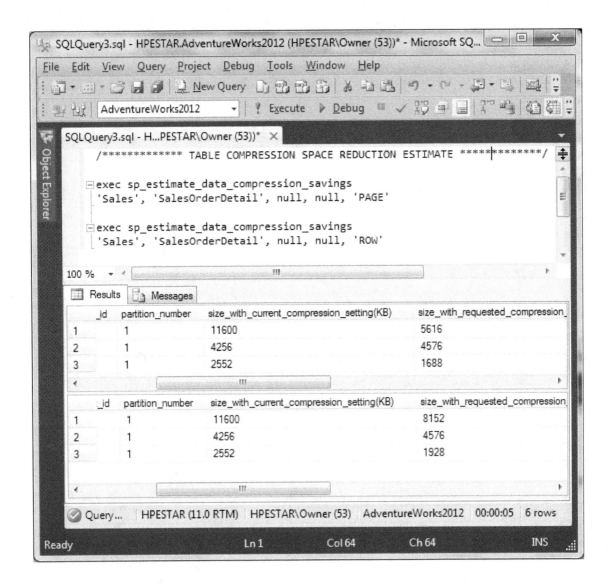

Careful and extensive considerations are required to decide to apply row, page or no compression to a table.

Query To Check How Many Rows Are Stored In An 8K Page In The Original Non-Compressed Table

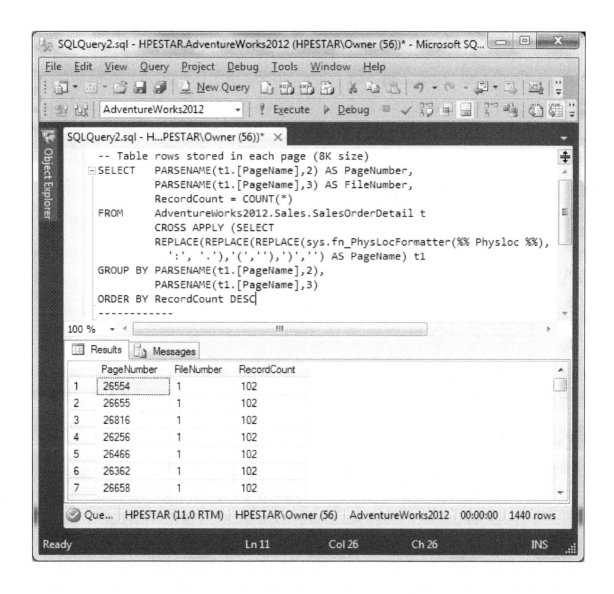

Query to check the same for the compressed table SOD

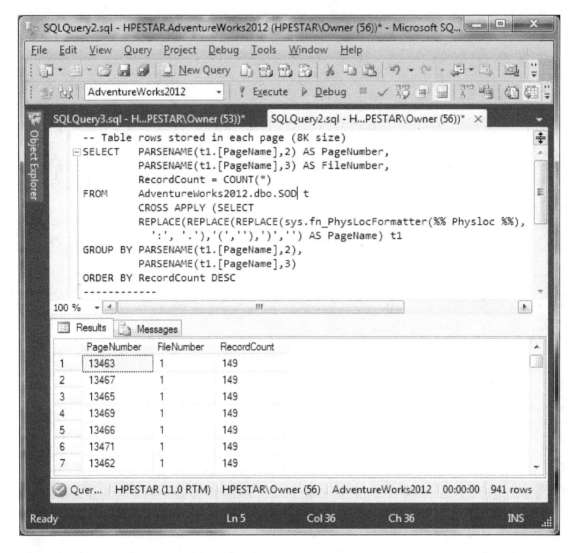

We can see that the best record (rows) count is 149 per page as opposed to 102 when the rows are not compressed. Since compression and decompression are processing intensive, we are trading CPU load vs. disk load. Which one to choose? PAGE compression is the true compression with maximum space saving. Choose PAGE compression for best disk IO reduction. As mentioned earlier careful preparation is required to make sure there are no undesirable side effects.

CHAPTER 8: Advanced Database Architecture

Data Compression: Compressed Index

Index can also be compressed. The following script creates and compresses an index with included columns.

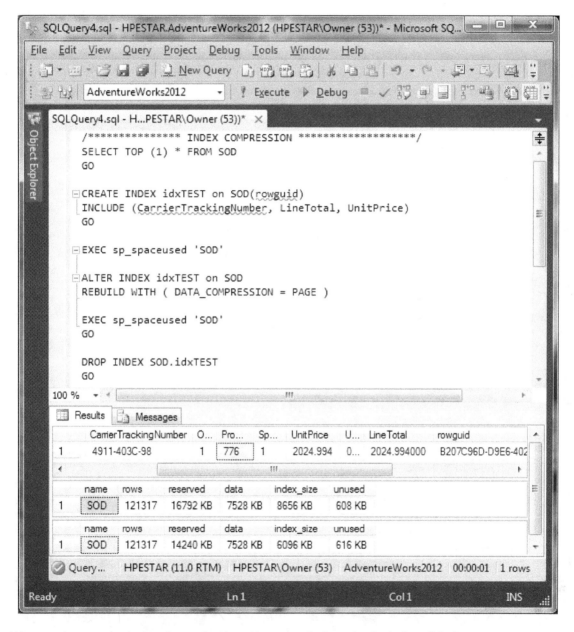

We can observe the index size reduction. Note that index_size includes all indexes.

The GUI Data Compression Wizard

The wizard can be started with Right Click on the table in SSMS Object Explorer.

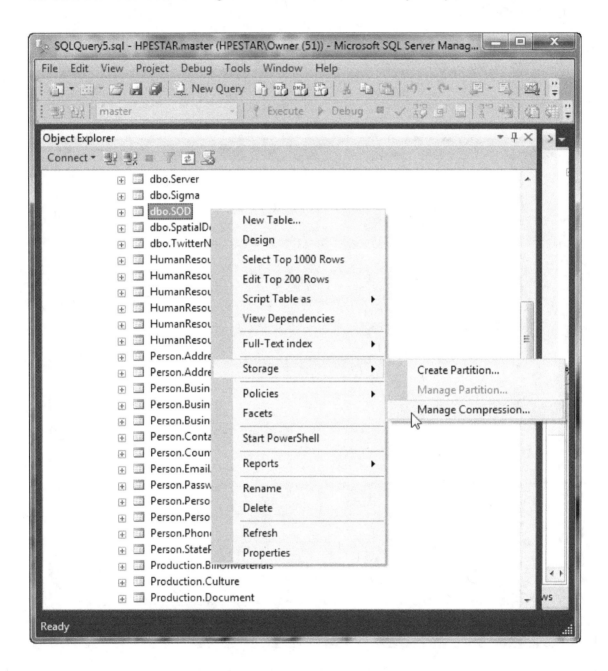

Space Saving Calculation Wizard Page
The figures include table & indexes total size.

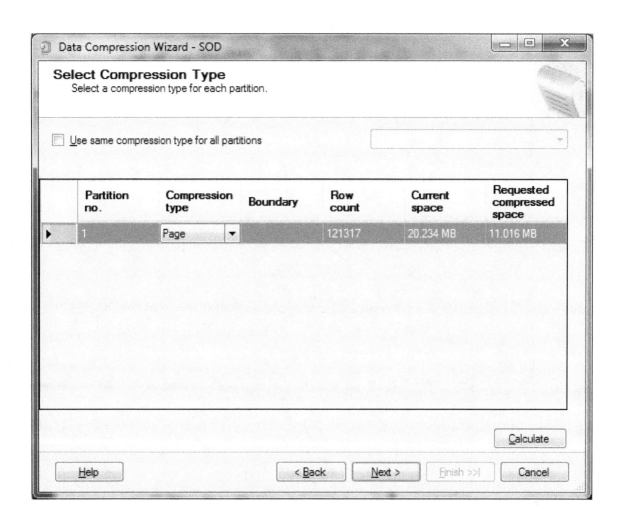

Output Panel Offers Scripting And Execution Options

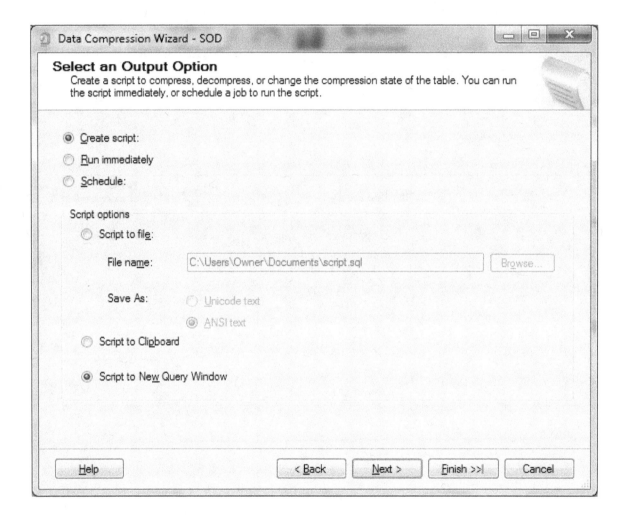

Testing the generated script with the sp_spaceused system stored procedure

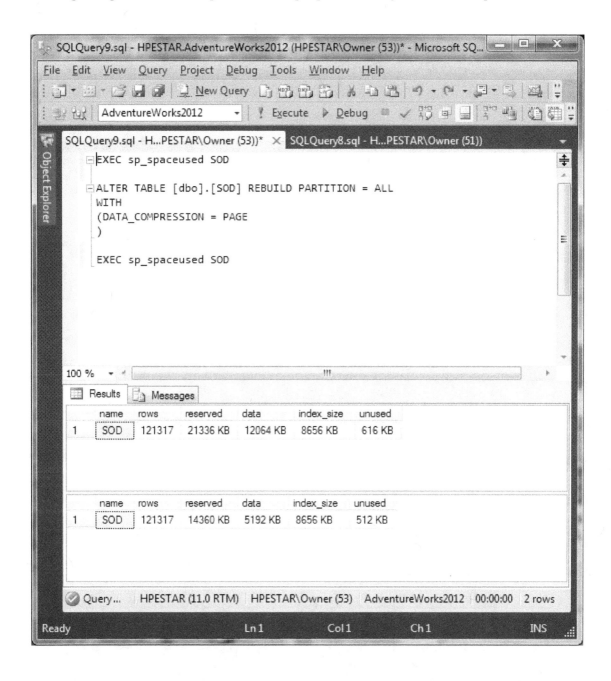

Indexes Can Be Compressed With The Wizard As Well

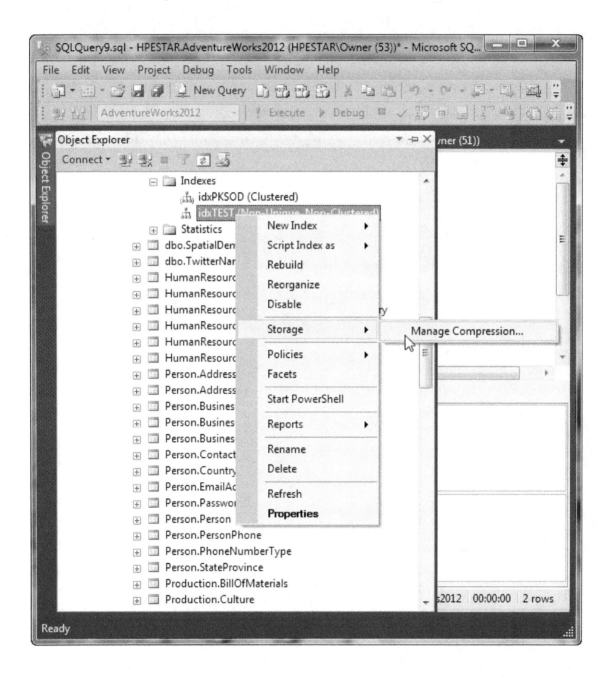

The generated script follows with measurement before and after index compression.

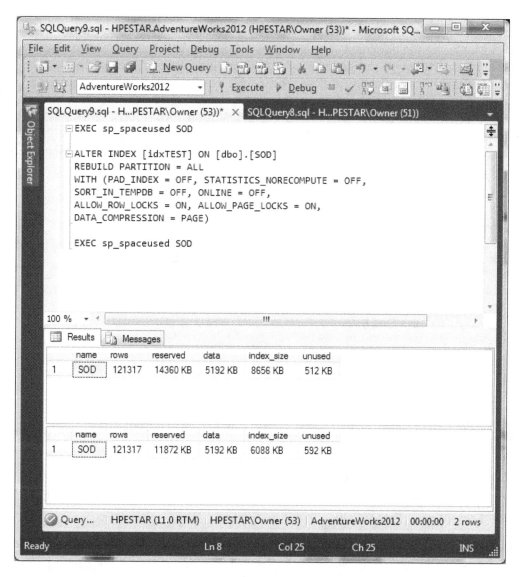

We can observe that the index size has been reduced from 8656KB to 6088 KB.

Articles
Data Compression: Strategy, Capacity Planning and Best Practices
http://msdn.microsoft.com/en-us/library/dd894051(v=sql.100).aspx
Data Compression http://msdn.microsoft.com/en-us/library/cc280449.aspx

---

Partitioned Table, Partition Function & Partition Scheme

When data is stored from New York, Chicago, Houston, London and Hong Kong operations in a table, it makes you wonder if the server trips over NYC data when looking for London information. Analogous, 95% of the time in a typical business the last 30 days data may be accessed in a table, yet the dominant storage is for the 5% access of the 5 years prior data. The solution is logical: partition the data according to a usage-based scheme. Partitioning can improve performance, the scalability and manageability of large tables and tables that have varying query access patterns. **Gains with partitioning is not automatic.** Careful design studies are necessary for a successful table partitioning implementation.

In order to carry out a demonstration, first we create a copy of AdventureWorks2012 database from a backup file.

```
/* RESTORE script to create a new copy of AdventureWorks2012
 * Folder  FS1 should exist; FSBeta should not exist; AW12 should exist
 * Folder Backup should exist */
USE [master]
GO
```

```
BACKUP DATABASE [AdventureWorks2012] TO
DISK = N'C:\Data\Backup\AW12.bak'
GO
```

```
RESTORE DATABASE [CopyOfAdventureWorks2012]
FROM  DISK = N'C:\Data\Backup\AW12.bak'
WITH  FILE = 1,  MOVE N'FSAlpha' TO N'F:\data\FS1\FSBeta',
MOVE N'AdventureWorks2012_Data' TO N'F:\AW12\xAdventureWorks2012_Data.mdf',
MOVE N'AdventureWorks2012_Log' TO N'F:\AW12\xAdventureWorks2012_log.ldf',
NOUNLOAD,  STATS = 5
GO
```

Remap database user's id after copying (restoring under new name) database.

```
EXEC sp_change_users_login 'Auto_Fix', 'Mary', NULL, 'srvLoginMary'
```

Partition a table with SalesOrderDetail subset information. First a partition function is created.

```
USE CopyOfAdventureWorks2012;
CREATE PARTITION FUNCTION pfSOD (int)
AS RANGE LEFT FOR VALUES (1, 20000, 40000, 60000, 80000, 150000) ;
GO
```

CHAPTER 8: Advanced Database Architecture

The next step is to test the partition function to make sure it works as intended.

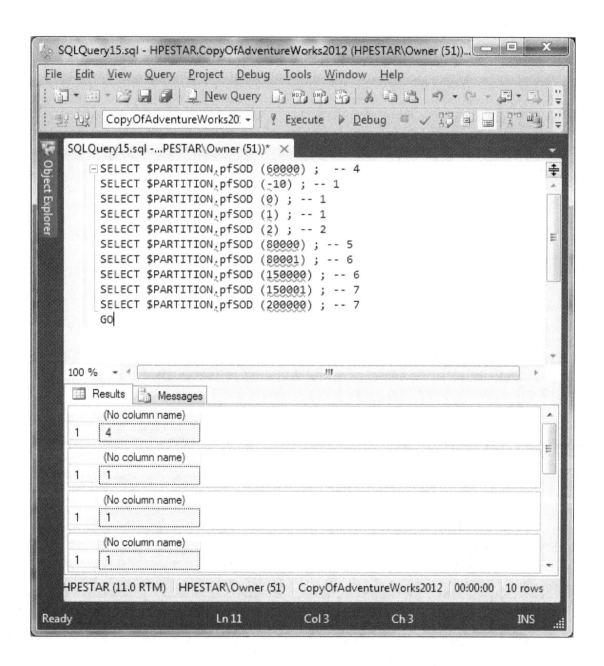

T-SQL scripts to create FILEGROUPs for the partitions

```
USE [master]
GO
```

```
ALTER DATABASE [CopyOfAdventureWorks2012] ADD FILEGROUP [Test1FileGroup]
ALTER DATABASE [CopyOfAdventureWorks2012] ADD FILEGROUP [Test2FileGroup]
ALTER DATABASE [CopyOfAdventureWorks2012] ADD FILEGROUP [Test3FileGroup]
ALTER DATABASE [CopyOfAdventureWorks2012] ADD FILEGROUP [Test4FileGroup]
ALTER DATABASE [CopyOfAdventureWorks2012] ADD FILEGROUP [Test5FileGroup]
ALTER DATABASE [CopyOfAdventureWorks2012] ADD FILEGROUP [Test6FileGroup]
ALTER DATABASE [CopyOfAdventureWorks2012] ADD FILEGROUP [Test7FileGroup]
GO
```

```
ALTER DATABASE [CopyOfAdventureWorks2012]
ADD FILE ( NAME = N'Test1', FILENAME = N'F:\UTIL\Microsoft\sampledatabases\Test1.ndf' ,
SIZE = 3072KB , FILEGROWTH = 1024KB ) TO FILEGROUP [Test1FileGroup]
ALTER DATABASE [CopyOfAdventureWorks2012]
ADD FILE ( NAME = N'Test2', FILENAME = N'F:\UTIL\Microsoft\sampledatabases\Test2.ndf' ,
SIZE = 3072KB , FILEGROWTH = 1024KB ) TO FILEGROUP [Test2FileGroup]
ALTER DATABASE [CopyOfAdventureWorks2012]
ADD FILE ( NAME = N'Test3', FILENAME = N'F:\UTIL\Microsoft\sampledatabases\Test3.ndf' ,
SIZE = 3072KB , FILEGROWTH = 1024KB ) TO FILEGROUP [Test3FileGroup]
ALTER DATABASE [CopyOfAdventureWorks2012]
ADD FILE ( NAME = N'Test4', FILENAME = N'F:\UTIL\Microsoft\sampledatabases\Test4.ndf' ,
SIZE = 3072KB , FILEGROWTH = 1024KB ) TO FILEGROUP [Test4FileGroup]
ALTER DATABASE [CopyOfAdventureWorks2012]
ADD FILE ( NAME = N'Test5', FILENAME = N'F:\UTIL\Microsoft\sampledatabases\Test5.ndf' ,
SIZE = 3072KB , FILEGROWTH = 1024KB ) TO FILEGROUP [Test5FileGroup]
ALTER DATABASE [CopyOfAdventureWorks2012]
ADD FILE ( NAME = N'Test6', FILENAME = N'F:\UTIL\Microsoft\sampledatabases\Test6.ndf' ,
SIZE = 3072KB , FILEGROWTH = 1024KB ) TO FILEGROUP [Test6FileGroup]
ALTER DATABASE [CopyOfAdventureWorks2012]
ADD FILE ( NAME = N'Test7', FILENAME = N'F:\UTIL\Microsoft\sampledatabases\Test7.ndf' ,
SIZE = 3072KB , FILEGROWTH = 1024KB ) TO FILEGROUP [Test7FileGroup]
GO
```

T-SQL scripts to create a partition scheme, a partitioned table and populate the new table with INSERT SELECT

```
USE CopyOfAdventureWorks2012;
GO
```

```
CREATE PARTITION SCHEME psSOD
AS PARTITION pfSOD
TO (Test1FileGroup, Test2FileGroup, Test3FileGroup, Test4FileGroup,
Test5FileGroup, Test6FileGroup, Test7FileGroup) ;
GO
```

```
CREATE TABLE SODPartitioned   (col1 int, col2 char(30))  ON psSOD (col1) ;
GO
```

```
insert SODPartitioned
select    SalesOrderDetailID, 'Unit Price: '+convert(varchar,UnitPrice)
from AdventureWorks2012.Sales.SalesOrderDetail;
GO
```

```
insert SODPartitioned
select SalesOrderDetailID+1,  'Unit Price: '+convert(varchar,UnitPrice+1)
from AdventureWorks2012.Sales.SalesOrderDetail;
GO
```

```
insert SODPartitioned select SalesOrderDetailID+2,  'Unit Price: '+convert(varchar,UnitPrice+2)
from AdventureWorks2012.Sales.SalesOrderDetail;
```

Query To Check The Data Distribution Within The Partitions

A few more counting queries to check entire table and a single partition population

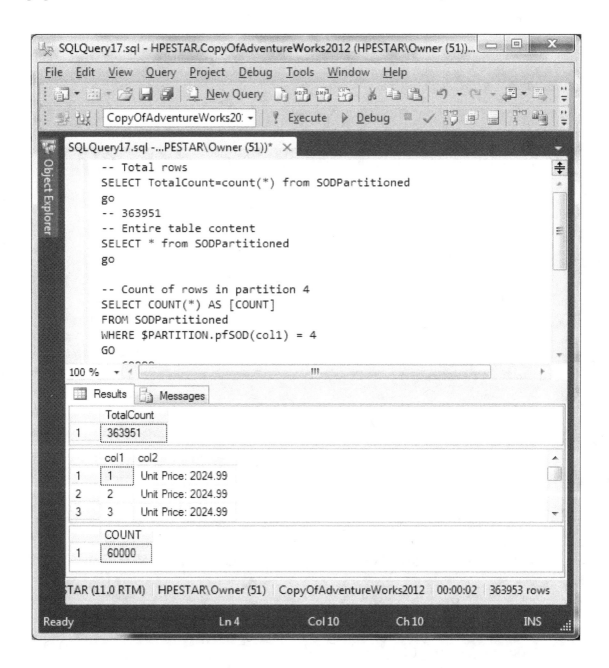

System views with "partition" prefix contain metadata on partitions.

In the following example, we partition for "UK", "US" and other countries.

The GUI Create Partition Wizard

SSMS Object Explorer Create Partition Wizard provides GUI environment for partition design and setup.

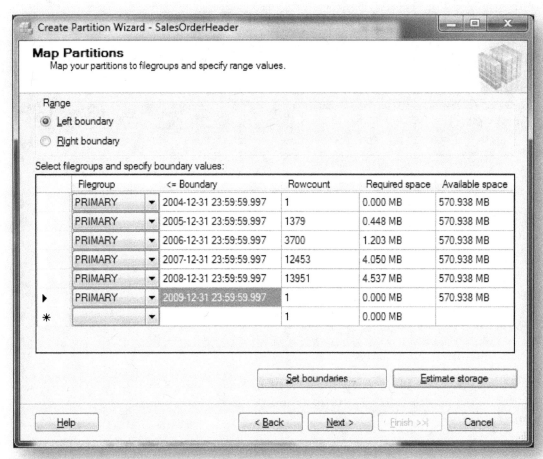

CHECKSUM_AGG Function to Compare Tables

CHECKSUM_AGG group checksum function can be applied to test if tables with content are potentially the same. The following two tables may be the same with high likelihood.

```
SELECT CHECKSUM_AGG(Binary_CheckSum(*)) From Sales.SalesOrderHeader With (NOLOCK);
-- -1271394099

SELECT * INTO #SOH From Sales.SalesOrderHeader;
SELECT CHECKSUM_AGG(Binary_CheckSum(*)) From #SOH With (NOLOCK);    -- -1271394099
```

Columnstore Index for Data Warehouse Performance

Columnstore index for static tables, new to SQL Server 2012, is designed for Data Warehouse performance enhancement. The first script is a timing script for a GROUP BY summary query, and the second script is the creation of the columnstore index.

```
-- Timing before creating Columnstore index (5th timing)
USE AdventureWorksDW2012;
dbcc dropcleanbuffers;
declare @start datetime = getdate()
SELECT SalesTerritoryKey, SUM(ExtendedAmount) AS SalesByTerritory
FROM FactResellerSales   GROUP BY SalesTerritoryKey;
select [Timing]=datediff(millisecond, @Start, getdate());
GO 5
-- 190 msec
```

```
CREATE NONCLUSTERED COLUMNSTORE INDEX [idxColStoreResellerSales]
ON [FactResellerSales]
(
    [ProductKey],
    [OrderDateKey],
    [ShipDateKey],
    [EmployeeKey],
    [PromotionKey],
    [CurrencyKey],
    [SalesTerritoryKey],
    [SalesOrderNumber],
    [SalesOrderLineNumber],
    [OrderQuantity],
    [UnitPrice],
    [ExtendedAmount],
    [UnitPriceDiscountPct],
    [DiscountAmount],
    [ProductStandardCost],
    [TotalProductCost],
    [SalesAmount],
    [TaxAmt],
    [Freight],
    [CarrierTrackingNumber],
    [CustomerPONumber],
    [OrderDate],
    [DueDate],
    [ShipDate]
);
```

Checking the same query after creating the index.

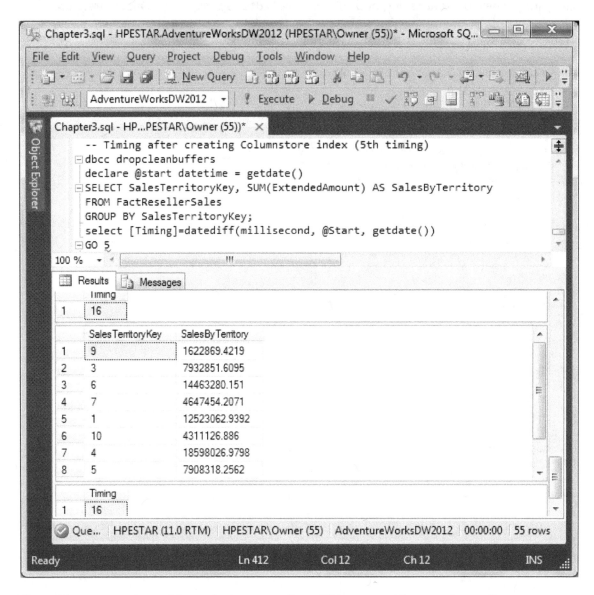

The performance gain on this particular query: from 190 msec to 16 msec. Generally columnstore index leads to significant query performance improvement in Data Warehouse environment.

CHAPTER 8: Advanced Database Architecture

DATE Data Type Solves Many Problems with DATETIME

DATE columns should be DATE type (3 bytes) not DATETIME type (8 bytes) with exception when time is needed for the record such as credit card or online banking transaction.

Example: Sales.Customer table create with one computed column which has unique index defined on AccountNumber(computed).

```
CREATE TABLE Sales.Customer(
        CustomerID int IDENTITY(1,1) PRIMARY KEY,
        PersonID int              REFERENCES Person.Person,
        StoreID int               REFERENCES Sales.Store,
        TerritoryID int           REFERENCES Sales.SalesTerritory,
        AccountNumber  AS (isnull('AW'+dbo.ufnLeadingZeros(CustomerID),'')) ,
        RowGuid uniqueidentifier ROWGUIDCOL  NOT NULL default (newid()),
        ModifiedDate DATE  NOT NULL default (CURRENT_TIMESTAMP));

SELECT TOP 2 * FROM Sales.Customer  ORDER BY AccountNumber;
```

CustomerID	PersonID	StoreID	TerritoryID	AccountNumber	rowguid	ModifiedDate
1	NULL	934	1	AW00000001	3F5AE95E-B87D-4AED-95B4-C3797AFCB74F	2008-10-13
2	NULL	1028	1	AW00000002	E552F657-A9AF-4A7D-A645-C429D6E02491	2008-10-13

Pad with Leading Zeros

Padding with leading zeros is a frequent business requirement. The ufnLeadingZeros() scalar-valued user-defined function converts the number into a string and pads it with leading zeros. The new **FORMAT command** can be utilized as well for leading zeros.

```
SELECT [dbo].[ufnLeadingZeros] (999);    -- 00000999
```

```
-- T-SQL script to pad with leading zeros
USE AdventureWorks2012;  DECLARE @Len tinyint=8;
SELECT   BusinessEntityID AS EmployeeID,    Rate,
        RIGHT(REPLICATE('0',@Len) + CAST(Rate AS VARCHAR(20)),@Len) AS PaddedRate
FROM   HumanResources.EmployeePayHistory;
```

EmployeeID	Rate	PaddedRate
1	125.50	00125.50
2	63.4615	00063.46
3	43.2692	00043.27

```
SELECT TOP(1) FORMAT(ProductID, '00000') FROM Production.Product;  -- 00980
SELECT FORMAT(999, '00000'); -- 00999
```

CHAPTER 8: Advanced Database Architecture

Database Design & Programming Standards

Standards have multiple purposes:

> ➢ Increase the productivity of the database developer.
> ➢ Increase the productivity of the project team.
> ➢ Decrease future maintenance cost of the RDBMS system.

Standards are about communications among project team members and among future software engineers who will come in contact with the work done presently by the software project team. Software standards are simple ordinary rules which should be followed. It is like when you turn on the left-turn signal in your car, the driver behind you anticipates you slowing down and making the next left turn. The situation is a little bit different though with software standards: there is no enforcing authority like the state authority in case of traffic rules. Many times argument can break out within the project team: "I like it this way", "it is really stupid to do it that way", "database expert Q says to do it this way in a blog" and so on. The following standards are pretty reasonable, and are based on industry acceptance, albeit not universal acceptance. The project manager has to enlist the support of all of the project team members for successful standards implementation. Database Design & Programming Standards to aid in optimal usability of SQL Server schema, scripts and stored procedures, user defined functions developed for applications by defining a reasonable, consistent and effective coding style. The identifier segment of the standard will formalize naming conventions. Without standards, database design, function, stored procedure and script development may become sloppy and unreadable, resulting in diminished productivity, usability, reusability, maintainability and extendibility.

Database Design Standards

Base design is normalized to 3NF or higher. History, log, Data Warehouse and reporting tables, containing second-hand data, need not be normalized. Similar considerations for staging and lookup tables. Each OLTP table has the following layout:

```
TableNameID (PRIMARY KEY) - commonly int identity(1,1) SURROGATE PRIMARY KEY
TableNameAlphaID (FOREIGN KEY if any)
TableNameBetaID (FOREIGN KEY if any)
natural-key column(s)
non-key columns
row maintenance columns
  RowGuid           uniqueidentifier
  IsActive          maintenance flag (bit 0 = not active, 1 = active)
  CreateDate        maintenance date (datetime if necessary)
  ModifiedDate      maintenance date (datetime if necessary)
  ModifiedByUser    last user who modified the record
```

Identifiers

CamelCase (Pascal case) naming convention: OrderDetail, ShippingCompany

With prefix example: vInvoiceHistory (view - Hungarian naming after Charles Simonyi)

Old-style naming example: sales_order_detail

Space usage is not a good idea in identifier: confusing & forces square brackets or double quotation marks use (delimited identifier).

Using spaces example: [sales order detail]

PREFIX ASSIGNMENT

Primary Key Clustered	pk
Primary Key Nonclustered	pknc
Index Clustered	idxc
Index Nonclustered	idxnc
Foreign Key	fk
Unique Constraint	uq
Check Constraint	chk
Column Default	dflt
Synonym	syn

Passed Parameter @p (input/output parameter) or @ - Example: @pStartDate, @StartDate

Local Variable @ - Example: @WeekOfTransaction

Table   usually no prefix; exception large number of tables

Reporting table	rpt
Log table	log
History table	hist or arch
Date Warehouse table	dw, dim, fact
Common Table Expression	cte
View	v or view
User Defined Scalar Function	udf or fns or ufn or fn
User Defined Table Function	udf or fnt or ufn or fn
Stored Procedure	usp, sproc, or none

CHAPTER 8: Advanced Database Architecture

Principles of T-SQL Identifier Architecture

Each word in the naming must be functional. The first word must be the highest level category or action indicator. Examples for stored procedure names:

> uspAccountPayableSummary
> uspInsertAccountPayableTransaction
> uspUpdateStockPrice
> sprocInsertInventoryItem
> sprocAccountReceivableSummary
> AccountReceivableMonthly

Commonly accepted or easily understood abbreviations are allowed. Examples for business abbreviations usage in view naming:

> vAPSummary
> vAPDetail
> vARSummary
> vARMonthly
> vGLTrialBalance

AdventureWorks2012 long stored procedure and view names.

SELECT name, type FROM sys.objects WHERE LEN(name) > 20 AND type in ('V', 'P') ORDER BY name;

name	type
uspGetBillOfMaterials	P
uspGetEmployeeManagers	P
uspGetManagerEmployees	P
uspGetWhereUsedProductID	P
uspSearchCandidateResumes	P
uspUpdateEmployeeHireInfo	P
uspUpdateEmployeeLogin	P
uspUpdateEmployeePersonalInfo	P
vAdditionalContactInfo	V
vEmployeeDepartmentHistory	V
vJobCandidateEducation	V
vJobCandidateEmployment	V
vProductAndDescription	V
vProductModelCatalogDescription	V
vProductModelInstructions	V
vSalesPersonSalesByFiscalYears	V
vStateProvinceCountryRegion	V
vStoreWithDemographics	V

CHAPTER 8: Advanced Database Architecture

Stored Procedure Outline

```
use {DatabaseName};
if (objectProperty(object_id('{schema}.{ProcedureName}'),
'IsProcedure') is not null)
    drop procedure {schema}.{ProcedureName}
go

create procedure {schema}.{ProcedureName}
  [{parameter} {data type}]....
as
/*****************************************************************
* PROCEDURE: {ProcedureName}
* PURPOSE: {brief procedure description}
* NOTES: {special set up or requirements, etc.}
* CREATED:  {developer name} {date}
* LAST MODIFIED: {developer name} {date}

* DATE          AUTHOR              DESCRIPTION
-----------------------------------------------------------------
* {date}       {developer} {brief modification description}
*****************************************************************/
BEGIN
[declare {variable name} {data type}....
[{set session}] e.g. SET NOCOUNT ON
[{initialize variables}]

{body of procedure - comment only what is not obvious}

return (Value if any)

{error handler}
return (Value if any)
END
 go
```

User-Defined Function Outline
Similar to stored procedure outline

How to Create a Database with T-SQL Script

Database can be created by a script (CREATE DATABASE) or in SSMS Object Explorer using GUI. Here is a T-SQL script version.

```
-- SQL CREATE DATABASE
USE master;
GO


-- F:\DB\DATA\ folder should exist

CREATE DATABASE [Finance]
ON  PRIMARY
( NAME = N'Finance_Data',
FILENAME = N'F:\DB\DATA\Finance.mdf' , SIZE = 217152KB ,
MAXSIZE = UNLIMITED, FILEGROWTH = 16384KB )
LOG ON
( NAME = N'Finance_Log',
FILENAME = N'F:\DB\DATA\Finance_1.ldf' ,
SIZE = 67584KB , MAXSIZE = 2048GB , FILEGROWTH = 16384KB )
GO


-- SQL compatibility level 110 is SQL Server 2012
ALTER DATABASE [Finance] SET COMPATIBILITY_LEVEL = 110
GO


USE Finance;
-- SQL select into table create
SELECT * INTO POH
FROM AdventureWorks2012.Purchasing.PurchaseOrderHeader;
GO


-- SQL select query for 3 random records
SELECT TOP (3) * FROM POH ORDER BY NEWID()
GO
```

PurchaseOrderID	RevisionNumber	Status	EmployeeID	VendorID
3506	1	4	261	1666
233	1	4	257	1578
84	1	3	261	1654

CHAPTER 8: Advanced Database Architecture

Adding New Column to a Table with ALTER TABLE

It happens quite often that a table in production for years needs a new column. While adding a new column to a populated table is relatively simple, there is a downside: application software needs to be retested to make sure it still works with the new table. One offending statement is "SELECT * FROM". The application software was programmed, let's say for example, 6 columns, after the addition SELECT * is sending 7 columns which causes error in the application. T-SQL scripts to demonstrate the addition of a new column to a table for sequencing or other purposes.

```
USE AdventureWorks2012;

SELECT NewProductID = ROW_NUMBER()    OVER (   ORDER BY ProductID),
    *
INTO   #Product
FROM   AdventureWorks.Production.Product
GO
-- (504 row(s) affected)
```

```
ALTER TABLE #Product ADD CountryOfOrigin nvarchar(32) not null DEFAULT ('USA');
GO
-- Command(s) completed successfully.
```

```
SELECT          ProductID,
                Name                        AS ProductName,
                ProductNumber,
                ListPrice,
                COALESCE(Color,'')          AS Color,
                CountryOfOrigin
FROM   #Product
ORDER BY ProductName;
GO
```

ProductID	ProductName	ProductNumber	ListPrice	Color	CountryOfOrigin
1	Adjustable Race	AR-5381	0.00		USA
879	All-Purpose Bike Stand	ST-1401	159.00		USA
712	AWC Logo Cap	CA-1098	8.99	Multi	USA
3	BB Ball Bearing	BE-2349	0.00		USA
2	Bearing Ball	BA-8327	0.00		USA
877	Bike Wash - Dissolver	CL-9009	7.95		USA
316	Blade	BL-2036	0.00		USA
843	Cable Lock	LO-C100	25.00		USA
952	Chain	CH-0234	20.24	Silver	USA
324	Chain Stays	CS-2812	0.00		USA
322	Chainring	CR-7833	0.00	Black	USA
320	Chainring Bolts	CB-2903	0.00	Silver	USA

```
-- Cleanup
DROP TABLE #Product
```

CHAPTER 8: Advanced Database Architecture

IDENTITY Column in a Table Variable

Using IDENTITY function for row numbering in new column with table variable. Statements must be in one batch, that is the scope of table variable.

```
DECLARE @Product TABLE
 (
   ID        INT IDENTITY(1, 1),   -- new column
   ProductID  int,
   ProductName varchar(64),
   ListPrice   money,
   Color     varchar(32)
 ) ;

INSERT @Product
    (ProductID,
     ProductName,
     ListPrice,
     Color)
SELECT ProductID,
     Name,
     ListPrice,
     Color
FROM  AdventureWorks2012.Production.Product
WHERE  ListPrice > 0
     AND Color IS NOT NULL
ORDER  BY Name;

SELECT TOP(7) *
FROM   @Product
ORDER  BY ID;
GO
```

ID	ProductID	ProductName	ListPrice	Color
1	712	AWC Logo Cap	8.99	Multi
2	952	Chain	20.24	Silver
3	866	Classic Vest, L	63.50	Blue
4	865	Classic Vest, M	63.50	Blue
5	864	Classic Vest, S	63.50	Blue
6	948	Front Brakes	106.50	Silver
7	945	Front Derailleur	91.49	Silver

Note: the above "GO" (ending the batch) terminated the scope of @Product table variable.

```
SELECT TOP(7) * FROM  @Product ;
/* Msg 1087, Level 15, State 2, Line 1     Must declare the table variable "@Product" */
```

CHAPTER 8: Advanced Database Architecture

Partition Data By Country Query

Partition sales data by country and sequence sales staff from best to worst.

NOTE: **ROW_NUMBER()** only sequencing; to rank data with ties use the **RANK()** function.

```
SELECT CONCAT(LastName,', ', FirstName)                    AS SalesPerson,
       CountryRegionName                                   AS Country,
       ROW_NUMBER()  OVER(
                    PARTITION BY CountryRegionName
                    ORDER BY SalesYTD DESC)                AS 'Row Number',
       FORMAT( SalesYTD, 'c', 'en-US')                     AS SalesYTD
INTO  #SalesPersonRank  FROM  AdventureWorks2012.Sales.vSalesPerson
WHERE  TerritoryName IS NOT NULL    AND SalesYTD <> 0;
```

```
-- Add new column StarRank, which is 1 "*" for each $1,000,000 of sales
ALTER TABLE #SalesPersonRank ADD StarRank varchar(32) NOT NULL DEFAULT ('');
--Command(s) completed successfully.
```

```
-- New column empty so far, population follows with UPDATE
UPDATE #SalesPersonRank SET StarRank =
REPLICATE ('*', FLOOR(CONVERT(Money, REPLACE(SalesYTD,',','')) / 1000000.0));  -- (14 row(s) affected)
```

```
SELECT * FROM  #SalesPersonRank  ORDER BY Country,   [Row Number];     -- Partial results.
```

SalesPerson	Country	Row Number	SalesYTD	StarRank
Tsoflias, Lynn	Australia	1	$1,421,810.92	*
Saraiva, José	Canada	1	$2,604,540.72	**
Vargas, Garrett	Canada	2	$1,453,719.47	*
Varkey Chudukatil, Ranjit	France	1	$3,121,616.32	***
Valdez, Rachel	Germany	1	$1,827,066.71	*
Pak, Jae	United Kingdom	1	$4,116,871.23	****

Free Disk Space Available Query

The legacy method is the undocumented system command xp_fixeddrives. Currently, DMV/DMF query can be applied.

```
SELECT   DISTINCT vs.volume_mount_point as Volume,
              FLOOR(cast(vs.available_bytes as decimal)/1073741824) as [FreeSpaceGB]
 FROM sys.master_files AS mf
         CROSS APPLY sys.dm_os_volume_stats(mf.database_id, mf.file_id) vs ORDER BY Volume;
```

Volume	FreeSpaceGB
C:\	669
F:\	1460

CHAPTER 8: Advanced Database Architecture

Diagram of Sales.SalesPerson & Related Tables

The sales staff is crucial in any business organization. It is reflected on the following diagram.

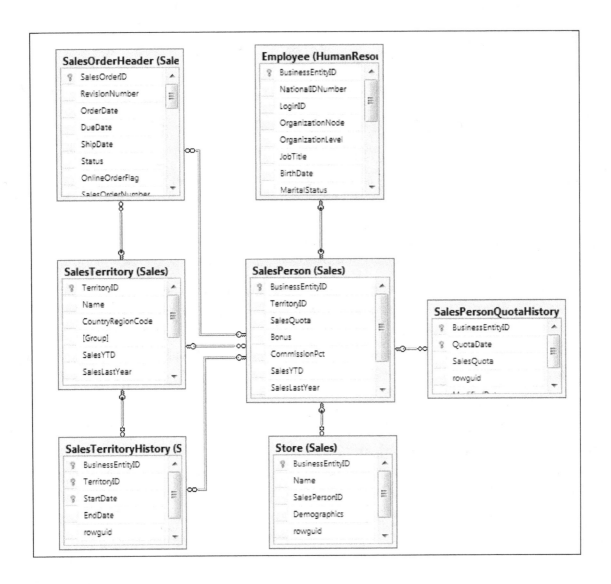

Adding IDENTITY Column To Empty Table
Add IDENTITY column to a table for sequential unique numbering (autonumber).

```
USE tempdb;
CREATE TABLE Department
 (
   Name      varchar(32)  UNIQUE,
   GroupName   varchar(256),
   ModifiedDate date default (CURRENT_TIMESTAMP)
 );
GO -- Command(s) completed successfully.
```

```
-- Add new IDENTITY column
ALTER TABLE Department    ADD DepartmentID smallint IDENTITY(1, 1) PRIMARY KEY;
GO
-- Command(s) completed successfully.
```

```
-- Only one identity column per table
ALTER TABLE Department
 ADD SecondIdentity smallint IDENTITY(1, 1);
GO
/* Msg 2744, Level 16, State 2, Line 1
Multiple identity columns specified for table 'Department'. Only one identity  column per table is allowed.
*/
```

```
INSERT INTO Department ( DepartmentID, Name, Groupname) VALUES (17, 'Student Affairs', 'Executive');
/* Msg 544, Level 16, State 1, Line 1
Cannot insert explicit value for identity column in table 'Department'  when IDENTITY_INSERT is set to
OFF. */
```

SET IDENTITY INSERT tablename ON

```
-- SQL identity insert enabled
SET IDENTITY_INSERT Department ON;
```

```
INSERT INTO Department ( DepartmentID, Name, Groupname) VALUES (17, 'Student Affairs', 'Executive');
-- (1 row(s) affected)
```

```
-- SQL identity insert disabled (default)
SET IDENTITY_INSERT Department OFF;
GO
```

CHAPTER 8: Advanced Database Architecture

DBCC CHECKIDENT Command

DBCC CHECKIDENT can be used to check and reseed IDENTITY parameters.

```
DBCC CHECKIDENT('Production.Product');
/*Checking identity information: current identity value '999', current column value '999'.
DBCC execution completed. If DBCC printed error messages, contact your system administrator. */
```

```
-- SQL reseeding identity column;  reset identity column
DBCC CHECKIDENT ("dbo.Department", RESEED, 999);
/*Checking identity information: current identity value '17'.
DBCC execution completed. If DBCC printed error messages, contact your system administrator. */
```

```
INSERT INTO Department (Name, Groupname) VALUES ( 'Alumni Affairs', 'Executive');
```

```
SELECT * FROM Department;
```

Name	GroupName	ModifiedDate	DepartmentID
Student Affairs	Executive	2016-07-19	17
Alumni Affairs	Executive	2016-07-19	1000

```
-- Add more records to table with INSERT SELECT
INSERT INTO Department (Name, Groupname)
SELECT Name, GroupName  FROM AdventureWorks2012.HumanResources.Department;
```

```
SELECT * FROM Department ORDER BY DepartmentID;
```

Name	GroupName	ModifiedDate	DepartmentID
Student Affairs	Executive	2012-07-19	17
Alumni Affairs	Executive	2012-07-19	1000
Engineering	Research and Development	2012-07-19	1001
Tool Design	Research and Development	2012-07-19	1002
Sales	Sales and Marketing	2012-07-19	1003
Marketing	Sales and Marketing	2012-07-19	1004
Purchasing	Inventory Management	2012-07-19	1005
Research and Development	Research and Development	2012-07-19	1006
Production	Manufacturing	2012-07-19	1007
Production Control	Manufacturing	2012-07-19	1008
Human Resources	Executive General and Administration	2012-07-19	1009
Finance	Executive General and Administration	2012-07-19	1010
Information Services	Executive General and Administration	2012-07-19	1011
Document Control	Quality Assurance	2012-07-19	1012
Quality Assurance	Quality Assurance	2012-07-19	1013
Facilities and Maintenance	Executive General and Administration	2012-07-19	1014
Shipping and Receiving	Inventory Management	2012-07-19	1015
Executive	Executive General and Administration	2012-07-19	1016

```
DROP TABLE tempdb.dbo.Department;
```

ADD Partitioned Sequence Number to Table

Partition table by subcategory (ProductSubcategoryID) by applying ROW_NUMBER for sequencing within each partition.

```
SELECT ROW_NUMBER()    OVER (  PARTITION BY p.ProductSubcategoryID
                               ORDER BY ProductID)              AS RowID,
    ps.Name                                                     AS SubCategory,
    p.Name                                                      AS ProductName,
    ProductNumber,
    Color,
    ListPrice
INTO   #ProductsByCategory
FROM   AdventureWorks.Production.Product p
    INNER JOIN AdventureWorks.Production.ProductSubcategory ps
        ON p.ProductSubcategoryID = ps.ProductSubcategoryID ;
GO
```

```
-- Add new column for display in currency format
ALTER TABLE #ProductsByCategory ADD Dollar varchar(32) not null DEFAULT ('');
GO
-- Command(s) completed successfully.
```

```
-- Populate new column with UPDATE
UPDATE #ProductsByCategory  SET Dollar = FORMAT(ListPrice, 'c', 'en-US');
GO
-- (295 row(s) affected)
```

```
SELECT * FROM  #ProductsByCategory  ORDER BY Subcategory,  RowID;
```

RowID	SubCategory	ProductName	ProductNumber	Color	ListPrice	Dollar
1	Bib-Shorts	Men's Bib-Shorts, S	SB-M891-S	Multi	89.99	$89.99
2	Bib-Shorts	Men's Bib-Shorts, M	SB-M891-M	Multi	89.99	$89.99
3	Bib-Shorts	Men's Bib-Shorts, L	SB-M891-L	Multi	89.99	$89.99
1	Bike Racks	Hitch Rack - 4-Bike	RA-H123	NULL	120.00	$120.00
1	Bike Stands	All-Purpose Bike Stand	ST-1401	NULL	159.00	$159.00
1	Bottles and Cages	Water Bottle - 30 oz.	WB-H098	NULL	4.99	$4.99
2	Bottles and Cages	Mountain Bottle Cage	BC-M005	NULL	9.99	$9.99
3	Bottles and Cages	Road Bottle Cage	BC-R205	NULL	8.99	$8.99
1	Bottom Brackets	LL Bottom Bracket	BB-7421	NULL	53.99	$53.99
2	Bottom Brackets	ML Bottom Bracket	BB-8107	NULL	101.24	$101.24
3	Bottom Brackets	HL Bottom Bracket	BB-9108	NULL	121.49	$121.49
1	Brakes	Rear Brakes	RB-9231	Silver	106.50	$106.50
2	Brakes	Front Brakes	FB-9873	Silver	106.50	$106.50
1	Caps	AWC Logo Cap	CA-1098	Multi	8.99	$8.99
1	Chains	Chain	CH-0234	Silver	20.24	$20.24

```
-- Cleanup
DROP TABLE #ProductsByCategory
```

CHAPTER 8: Advanced Database Architecture

Add ROW_NUMBER & RANK Columns to Table

Add row number and rank number to SELECT INTO table create without partitioning and rank (dense ranking) high price items to low price items.

```
SELECT ROW_NUMBER()
    OVER(
    ORDER BY Name ASC)                          AS ROWID,
  DENSE_RANK()
    OVER(
    ORDER BY ListPrice DESC)                     AS RANKID,
  ListPrice                                      AS Price,
    *
INTO   tempdb.dbo.RankedProduct
FROM   AdventureWorks2012.Production.Product
ORDER  BY        RANKID,
                 ROWID;
GO
-- (504 row(s) affected)
```

```
SELECT * FROM   tempdb.dbo.RankedProduct;
GO
-- (504 row(s) affected) - Partial results.
```

ROWID	RANKID	Price	ProductID	Name	ProductNumber	MakeFlag	FinishedGoodsFlag	Color
376	1	3578.27	750	Road-150 Red, 44	BK-R93R-44	1	1	Red
377	1	3578.27	751	Road-150 Red, 48	BK-R93R-48	1	1	Red
378	1	3578.27	752	Road-150 Red, 52	BK-R93R-52	1	1	Red
379	1	3578.27	753	Road-150 Red, 56	BK-R93R-56	1	1	Red
380	1	3578.27	749	Road-150 Red, 62	BK-R93R-62	1	1	Red
332	2	3399.99	771	Mountain-100 Silver, 38	BK-M82S-38	1	1	Silver
333	2	3399.99	772	Mountain-100 Silver, 42	BK-M82S-42	1	1	Silver
334	2	3399.99	773	Mountain-100 Silver, 44	BK-M82S-44	1	1	Silver

```
DROP TABLE tempdb.dbo.RankedProduct;
GO
```

3-Part Name Table Reference

The above script can be executed from any database on this server instance since we are using three-part name as table reference. Referencing a table on a linked server requires 4-part name. Double dot in table reference means default value between dots. Example:

[LONDONPROD1].TranMaster..OnlineOrderDetail is equivalent to
[LONDONPROD1].TranMaster.dbo.OnlineOrderDetail .

CHAPTER 8: Advanced Database Architecture

The Nature of Connection Between Tables

There is only **one kind of connection between tables** which is defined as FOREIGN KEY **references** the PRIMARY KEY or UNIQUE KEY. Nonetheless, the application functional meaning of the connections can be many, for example, star schema in a data warehouse.

Categorical Relationship

```
USE AdventureWorks2012;

CREATE TABLE Production.ProductSubcategoryTest(
       ProductSubcategoryID int IDENTITY(1,1) PRIMARY KEY,
       ProductCategoryID int NOT NULL
               REFERENCES Production.ProductCategory(ProductCategoryID),
       Name dbo.Name NOT NULL,
       rowguid uniqueidentifier ROWGUIDCOL  NOT NULL DEFAULT( NEWID() ),
       ModifiedDate datetime NOT NULL DEFAULT( CURRENT_TIMESTAMP ));
-- (1 row(s) affected)
```

Based on the naming, with the help of our Human Intelligence, we conclude the connection is **categorization**, from subcategory to (super)category. The example clearly illustrates the importance of good naming in database design. SQL Server would work equally well with Table1 and Table2, but that would make the design practically unreadable.

The connection between Production.Product and Production.ProductSubcategory is also categorization at the bottom level of the Product --> Subcategory --> Category hierarchy.

```
ALTER TABLE Production.Product
       WITH CHECK
       ADD  CONSTRAINT FK_Product_ProductSubcategory_ProductSubcategoryID
       FOREIGN KEY(ProductSubcategoryID)
       REFERENCES Production.ProductSubcategory (ProductSubcategoryID)
GO
```

Information Object Belongs To Relationship

Since we are working with information in the data processing industry, it may not come as a big surprise that frequently we are dealing with information object rather than real world objects. The products in the AdventureWorks2012 database have information objects associated with them: photos, documents and reviews for example. The relationship is many information objects to one product.

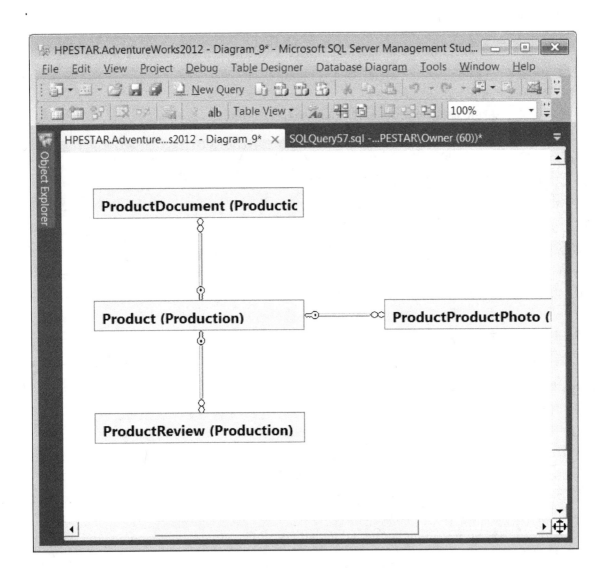

Checking Out Information Objects

Let's take a look at the ProductReview table. The information object is customer review about a product.

```
SELECT  P.Name                      AS ProductName,
        R.ReviewerName,
        LEFT(R.Comments,256)        AS Comments
FROM Production.ProductReview R
        INNER JOIN Production.Product P
            ON P.ProductID = R.ProductID
ORDER BY     ProductName,
             ReviewerName;

GO
```

ProductName	ReviewerName	Comments
HL Mountain Pedal	David	A little on the heavy side, but overall the entry/exit is easy in all conditions. I've used these pedals for more than 3 years and I've never had a problem. Cleanup is easy. Mud and sand don't get trapped. I would like them even better if there was a w
HL Mountain Pedal	Jill	Maybe it's just because I'm new to mountain biking, but I had a terrible time getting use to these pedals. In my first outing, I wiped out trying to release my foot. Any suggestions on ways I can adjust the pedals, or is it just a learning curve thing?
Mountain Bike Socks, M	John Smith	I can't believe I'm singing the praises of a pair of socks, but I just came back from a grueling 3-day ride and these socks really helped make the trip a blast. They're lightweight yet really cushioned my feet all day. The reinforced toe is nearly bulle
Road-550-W Yellow, 40	Laura Norman	The Road-550-W from Adventure Works Cycles is everything it's advertised to be. Finally, a quality bike that is actually built for a woman and provides control and comfort in one neat package. The top tube is shorter, the suspension is weight-tuned and th

The Bike Photo Information Object

The digital bike photo is stored in binary format in the Production.ProductPhoto table. Visualization requires Reporting Services report or external graphics software. SSMS cannot display the image, only the binary content.

```
SELECT          P.Name                              AS ProductName,
                PP.ThumbnailPhotoFilename,
                PP.LargePhotoFilename
FROM Production.ProductProductPhoto PPP
        INNER JOIN Production.Product P
                ON P.ProductID = PPP.ProductID
        INNER JOIN Production.ProductPhoto PP
                ON PPP.ProductPhotoID = PP.ProductPhotoID
WHERE P.Name = 'Road-550-W Yellow, 40'
ORDER BY        ProductName;
GO
```

ProductName	ThumbnailPhotoFilename	LargePhotoFilename
Road-550-W Yellow, 40	racer02_yellow_f_small.gif	racer02_yellow_f_large.gif

The photo of the yellow road bike.

XML Diagram Object

The AdventureWorks2012 sample database includes a number of XML data type columns. These columns cannot be displayed in a formatted fashion using Management Studio, rather they require special software for formatting or visualization.

```
SELECT Diagram FROM AdventureWorks2012.Production.Illustration WHERE IllustrationID = 4;
-- Partial results
```

```xml
<Canvas>
    <!-- Layer 1/<Path> -->
    <Path StrokeThickness="0.500000" Stroke="#ff656565" StrokeMiterLimit="1.000000" Fill="#ff656565" Data="F1 M
111.049805,46.655762 L 114.526367,48.509766 L 112.671875,52.911621 L 109.694336,51.374512 L 111.049805,46.655762 Z" />
    <!-- Layer 1/<Path> -->
    <Path StrokeThickness="1.202600" Stroke="#ff989898" StrokeMiterLimit="1.000000" Data="F1 M 155.380859,314.981934" />
    <!-- Layer 1/<Path> -->
    <Path StrokeThickness="1.000000" Stroke="#ff000000" StrokeMiterLimit="1.000000" Data="F1 M 88.621094,132.691406 C
88.621094,132.691406 89.542969,135.905762 88.029785,130.630371 C 86.841797,126.486328 88.501953,126.418457
91.141113,125.661621 C 93.777832,124.904785 116.826172,118.705566 120.486328,117.249512 C 124.144531,115.791504
125.061523,117.566406 125.819336,120.205566 C 126.576172,122.842285 126.205078,121.554688 126.205078,121.554688 L
122.169922,123.121582 L 164.131836,264.715332 L 161.495117,268.324707 L 163.008789,273.599121 L 141.530273,279.757324 L
139.910156,274.105957 L 134.900391,272.280762 L 93.264160,131.816406 L 88.621094,132.691406 Z">
      <Path.Fill>
       <LinearGradientBrush MappingMode="Absolute" StartPoint="87.639160,198.240234" EndPoint="164.131836,198.240234">
        <LinearGradientBrush.GradientStops>
         <GradientStop Offset="0.000000" Color="#ffffffff" />
         <GradientStop Offset="0.258800" Color="#fffcfcfc" />
         <GradientStop Offset="0.396200" Color="#fff4f4f4" />
```

The diagram can be visualized by special XAML software.

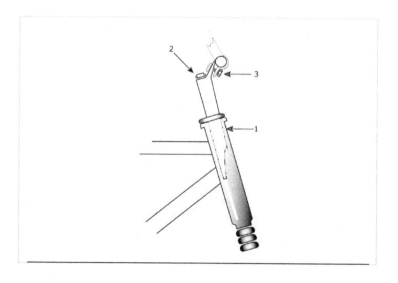

Exporting & Presenting XML Data from Production.ProductModel

XML columns contain semi-structured data. There is no general software which can make the XML data presentable. Each XML data requires specialized software for presentation. The Production.ProductModel table contains 2 XML columns. We export one cell from the first XML column, CatalogDescription, using bcp into an xhtml fil.

bcp "SELECT CatalogDescription FROM AdventureWorks2012.Production.ProductModel WHERE ProductModelID=19" queryout f:\data\xml\Product19.xhtml -c -t -S yourserver -T

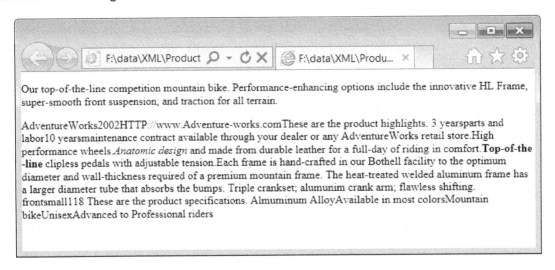

When we double click on the new .xhtml file, the information appears in a presentable format without the XML tags.

Product, ProductPhoto & ProductProductPhoto Tables Diagram

The ProductProductPhoto is a junction table representing many to many relationship between the Product and ProductPhoto. A product may have many photos and a photo may belong to many products.

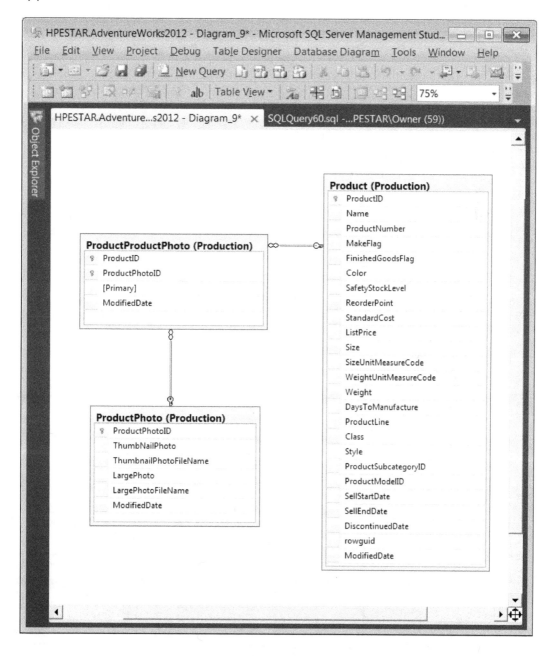

Graphical Query Design Using the Product & Photo Tables

The good database design lends itself to easy query building with Query Designer. To alias a table requires right click on the table and setting the Alias property.

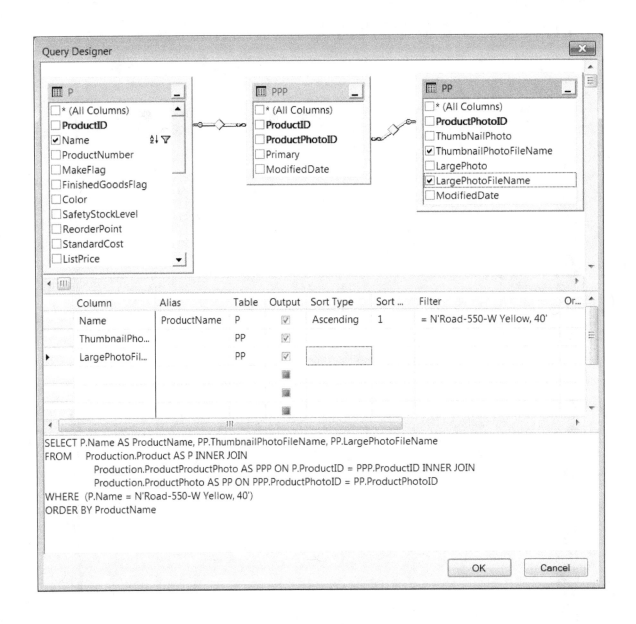

Company Received an Order Relationship

Vendor is a company supplying parts or finished product to AdventureWorks Cycles. Here is the relationship diagram. The purchase order to vendor FOREIGN KEY means a sale for the vendor. The detail to header FOREIGN KEY means the detail belongs to the header.

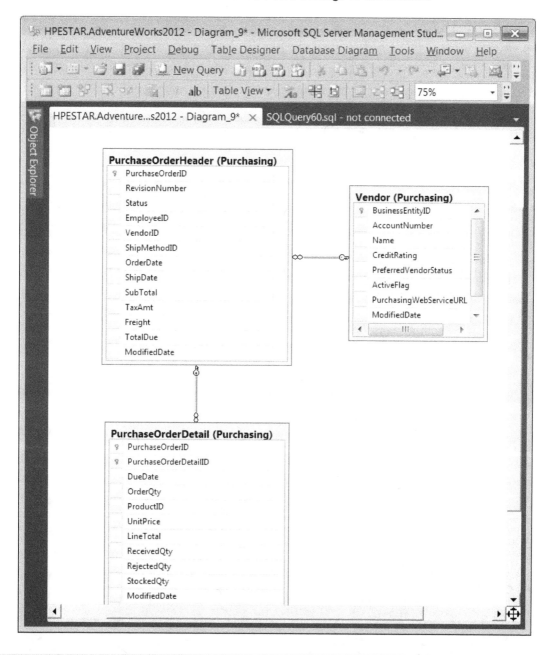

Querying the Vendor & Purchase Order Tables

The query list all purchase orders issued by AdventureWorks Cycles on a particular day.

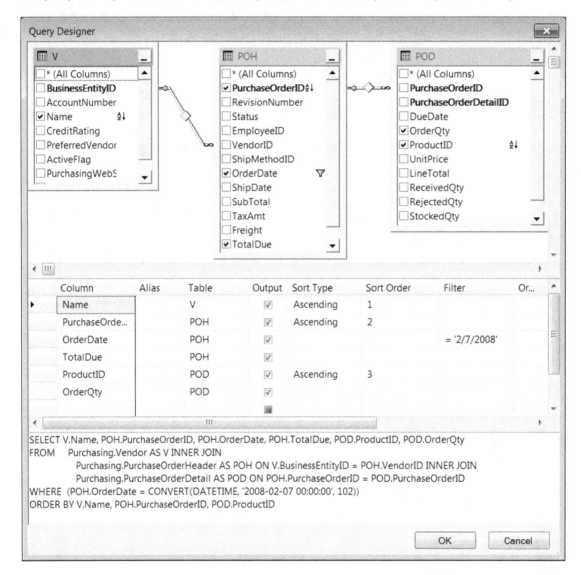

Upon execution the query returns 34 rows. Partial results.

Name	PurchaseOrderID	OrderDate	TotalDue	ProductID	OrderQty
Advanced Bicycles	1641	2008-02-07 00:00:00.000	555.9106	369	3
Allenson Cycles	1642	2008-02-07 00:00:00.000	9776.2665	530	550
American Bicycles and Wheels	1643	2008-02-07 00:00:00.000	189.0395	4	3

Type Relationship

A very frequent FOREIGN KEY representing an attribute of an object. For example a celebrity is a singer, actor, fashion model, writer, talk show host, sports figure and so on.

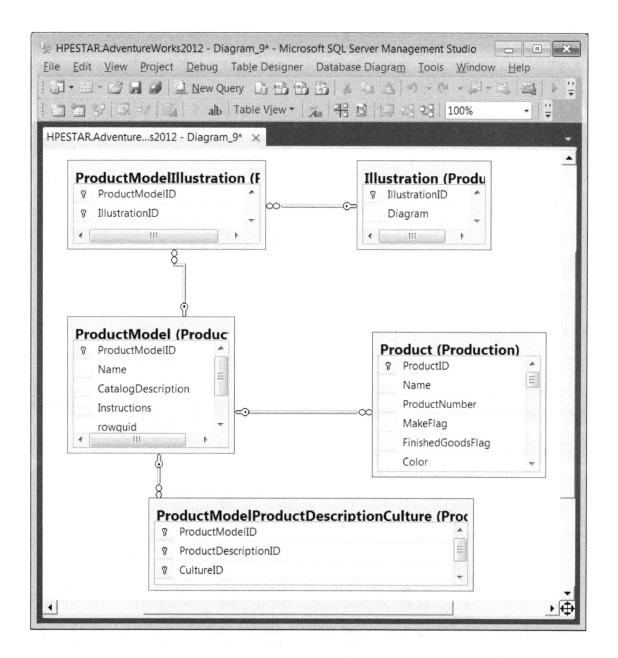

Obtaining Model Information for a Bike

We use the graphical query designer to see Model information for high-priced bikes.

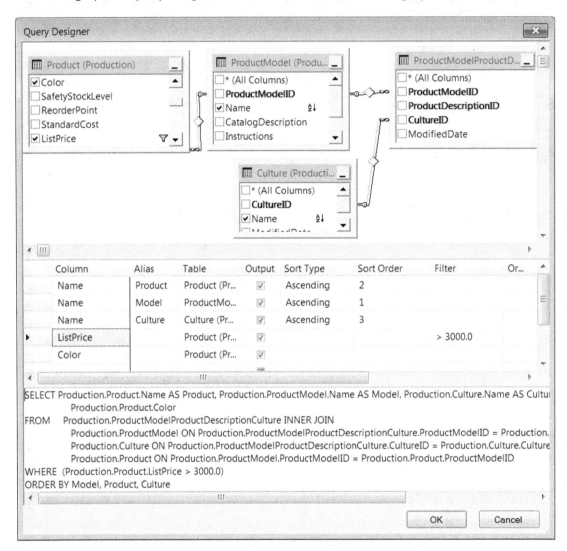

Partial results from the generated query.

Product	Model	Culture	ListPrice	Color
Mountain-100 Silver, 48	Mountain-100	English	3399.99	Silver
Mountain-100 Silver, 48	Mountain-100	French	3399.99	Silver
Mountain-100 Silver, 48	Mountain-100	Hebrew	3399.99	Silver
Mountain-100 Silver, 48	Mountain-100	Thai	3399.99	Silver
Road-150 Red, 44	Road-150	Arabic	3578.27	Red
Road-150 Red, 44	Road-150	Chinese	3578.27	Red

When to Use & Not to Use Composite PRIMARY KEYs

A composite PRIMARY KEY can be used in a junction table if it is unlikely that FOREIGN KEY reference needed from other tables. AdventureWorks2012 example of composite PRIMARY KEY with 4 columns in a junction table.

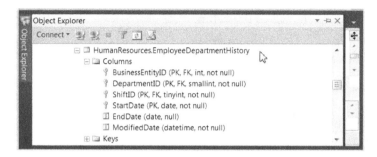

Composite PRIMARY KEY should not be used if FOREIGN KEY reference is necessary today or in the future: ineffective to have FOREIGN KEYs consisting of multiple columns & subtle violation of 3NF rules by duplication of PK table content in other tables as FKs. **The bottom line: COMPOSITE PRIMARY KEYs should not be used in regular tables.** Instead of the composite PRIMARY KEY design:

```
CREATE TABLE AlbumSong(
  AlbumTitle NVARCHAR(64) not null,
  DiskNo INTEGER not null,
  TrackNo INTEGER not null,
  PRIMARY KEY (AlbumTitle, DiskNo, TrackNo),
  Song NVARCHAR(128) not null,
  ModifiedDate DATE default(CURRENT_TIMESTAMP));
```

Design with **SURROGATE PRIMARY KEY** and apply composite **UNIQUE KEY** constraint:

```
CREATE TABLE AlbumSong(
  AlbumSongID INT IDENTITY(1,1) PRIMARY KEY NONCLUSTERED,
  AlbumTitle NVARCHAR(64) not null,
  DiskNo INTEGER not null,
  TrackNo INTEGER not null,
  UNIQUE CLUSTERED (AlbumTitle, DiskNo, TrackNo),
  Song NVARCHAR(128) not null,
  ModifiedDate DATE default(CURRENT_TIMESTAMP));
```

Where to place the clustered index should be based on performance considerations.

CHAPTER 8: Advanced Database Architecture

How To Design a Table

It is very important that we follow in order. Rules are with reference to the Celebrity table.

➢ Identify the NATURAL KEY column(s) (LastName, FirstName) & set it as UNIQUE (KEY)
➢ Design the non-key columns (BirthDate, BirthPlace, NameAtBirth)
➢ Design the row maintenance columns (CreatedDate)
➢ Configure the FOREIGN KEY(s) (CountryID)
➢ Configure the IDENTITY SURROGATE PRIMARY KEY (CelebrityID)

```
CREATE TABLE Profession (
        ProfessionID TINYINT IDENTITY(1,1) PRIMARY KEY,
        Name varchar(50) NOT NULL UNIQUE,
        CreatedDate DATETIME DEFAULT(CURRENT_TIMESTAMP) );
```

```
CREATE TABLE Country (
        ID TINYINT IDENTITY(1,1) PRIMARY KEY,
        Name varchar(128) NOT NULL UNIQUE,
        CreatedDate DATETIME DEFAULT(CURRENT_TIMESTAMP) );
```

```
CREATE TABLE Celebrity(
        CelebrityID SMALLINT IDENTITY(1,1) PRIMARY KEY nonclustered,
        CountryID TINYINT REFERENCES Country(ID),
        LastName nvarchar(40) NOT NULL CHECK( LEN(LastName) > 4),
        FirstName nvarchar(40),
        UNIQUE clustered (LastName, FirstName),
        BirthDate DATE NOT NULL,
        BirthPlace nvarchar(50),
        NameAtBirth nvarchar(60),
        CreatedDate DATETIME DEFAULT(CURRENT_TIMESTAMP) );
```

```
CREATE TABLE CelebrityProfessionXref(
        CelebrityID SMALLINT NOT NULL REFERENCES Celebrity(CelebrityID),
        ProfessionID TINYINT NOT NULL REFERENCES Profession(ProfessionID),
        PRIMARY KEY (CelebrityID, ProfessionID),
        CreatedDate DATETIME DEFAULT(CURRENT_TIMESTAMP) );
```

Without NATURAL KEY we don't have a table. The NATURAL KEY can be set as UNIQUE KEY or PRIMARY KEY. We can tentatively move the clustered index away from the PRIMARY KEY (default), however, final decision point is when we identify the business critical queries. Clustered index is helpful with range query performance.

CHAPTER 8: Advanced Database Architecture

Table-Related Database Objects

Table is the content object in a database. It has a number of supporting objects to keep the content accurate and accessible. The list of database object types in sys.objects system view.

```
SELECT SeqNo=ROW_NUMBER() OVER (ORDER BY type_desc),
    *
FROM ( SELECT DISTINCT type, type_desc
            FROM sys.objects ) x
ORDER BY SeqNo;
```

SeqNo	type	type_desc
1	C	CHECK_CONSTRAINT
2	D	DEFAULT_CONSTRAINT
3	F	FOREIGN_KEY_CONSTRAINT
4	IT	INTERNAL_TABLE
5	PK	PRIMARY_KEY_CONSTRAINT
6	SO	SEQUENCE_OBJECT
7	SQ	SERVICE_QUEUE
8	IF	SQL_INLINE_TABLE_VALUED_FUNCTION
9	FN	SQL_SCALAR_FUNCTION
10	P	SQL_STORED_PROCEDURE
11	TF	SQL_TABLE_VALUED_FUNCTION
12	TR	SQL_TRIGGER
13	S	SYSTEM_TABLE
14	TT	TYPE_TABLE
15	UQ	UNIQUE_CONSTRAINT
16	U	USER_TABLE
17	V	VIEW

Indexes have their own system view.

```
SELECT          OBJECT_NAME(object_ID)      AS TableName,
                name                        AS IndexName,
                 index_id,
                 type_desc
FROM AdventureWorks2012.sys.indexes  ORDER BY TableName, index_id;
-- (333 row(s) affected) - Partial Results
```

TableName	IndexName	index_id	type_desc
Address	PK_Address_AddressID	1	CLUSTERED
Address	AK_Address_rowguid	2	NONCLUSTERED
Address	IX_Address_AddressLine1_AddressLine2_City_StateProvinceID_PostalCode	3	NONCLUSTERED
Address	IX_Address_StateProvinceID	4	NONCLUSTERED

Listing All PRIMARY KEYs

Getting database object information can start in sys.objects system view.

```
SELECT SCHEMA_NAME(schema_id)           AS SchemaName,
         OBJECT_NAME(parent_object_id)    AS TableName,
         name                             AS PKName
FROM AdventureWorks2012.sys.objects WHERE type = 'PK'
ORDER BY SchemaName, TableName;
GO
```

SchemaName	TableName	PKName
dbo	AWBuildVersion	PK_AWBuildVersion_SystemInformationID
dbo	DatabaseLog	PK_DatabaseLog_DatabaseLogID
dbo	ErrorLog	PK_ErrorLog_ErrorLogID
HumanResources	Department	PK_Department_DepartmentID
HumanResources	Employee	PK_Employee_BusinessEntityID
HumanResources	EmployeeDepartmentHistory	PK_EmployeeDepartmentHistory_BusinessEntityID_StartDate_DepartmentID
HumanResources	EmployeePayHistory	PK_EmployeePayHistory_BusinessEntityID_RateChangeDate
HumanResources	JobCandidate	PK_JobCandidate_JobCandidateID
HumanResources	Shift	PK_Shift_ShiftID
Person	Address	PK_Address_AddressID
Person	AddressType	PK_AddressType_AddressTypeID
Person	BusinessEntity	PK_BusinessEntity_BusinessEntityID
Person	BusinessEntityAddress	PK_BusinessEntityAddress_BusinessEntityID_AddressID_AddressTypeID
Person	BusinessEntityContact	PK_BusinessEntityContact_BusinessEntityID_PersonID_ContactTypeID
Person	ContactType	PK_ContactType_ContactTypeID
Person	CountryRegion	PK_CountryRegion_CountryRegionCode
Person	EmailAddress	PK_EmailAddress_BusinessEntityID_EmailAddressID
Person	Password	PK_Password_BusinessEntityID
Person	Person	PK_Person_BusinessEntityID
Person	PersonPhone	PK_PersonPhone_BusinessEntityID_PhoneNumber_PhoneNumberTypeID
Person	PhoneNumberType	PK_PhoneNumberType_PhoneNumberTypeID
Person	StateProvince	PK_StateProvince_StateProvinceID
Production	BillOfMaterials	PK_BillOfMaterials_BillOfMaterialsID
Production	Culture	PK_Culture_CultureID
Production	Document	PK_Document_DocumentNode
Production	Illustration	PK_Illustration_IllustrationID
Production	Location	PK_Location_LocationID
Production	Product	PK_Product_ProductID
Production	ProductCategory	PK_ProductCategory_ProductCategoryID
Production	ProductCostHistory	PK_ProductCostHistory_ProductID_StartDate
Production	ProductDescription	PK_ProductDescription_ProductDescriptionID
Production	ProductDocument	PK_ProductDocument_ProductID_DocumentNode
Production	ProductInventory	PK_ProductInventory_ProductID_LocationID
Production	ProductListPriceHistory	PK_ProductListPriceHistory_ProductID_StartDate
Production	ProductModel	PK_ProductModel_ProductModelID
Production	ProductModelIllustration	PK_ProductModelIllustration_ProductModelID_IllustrationID
Production	ProductModelProductDescriptionCulture	PK_ProductModelProductDescriptionCulture_ProductModelID_ProductDescriptionID_CultureID
Production	ProductPhoto	PK_ProductPhoto_ProductPhotoID
Production	ProductProductPhoto	PK_ProductProductPhoto_ProductID_ProductPhotoID
Production	ProductReview	PK_ProductReview_ProductReviewID
Production	ProductSubcategory	PK_ProductSubcategory_ProductSubcategoryID
Production	ScrapReason	PK_ScrapReason_ScrapReasonID
Production	TransactionHistory	PK_TransactionHistory_TransactionID
Production	TransactionHistoryArchive	PK_TransactionHistoryArchive_TransactionID
Production	UnitMeasure	PK_UnitMeasure_UnitMeasureCode
Production	WorkOrder	PK_WorkOrder_WorkOrderID
Production	WorkOrderRouting	PK_WorkOrderRouting_WorkOrderID_ProductID_OperationSequence
Purchasing	ProductVendor	PK_ProductVendor_ProductID_BusinessEntityID
Purchasing	PurchaseOrderDetail	PK_PurchaseOrderDetail_PurchaseOrderID_PurchaseOrderDetailID
Purchasing	PurchaseOrderHeader	PK_PurchaseOrderHeader_PurchaseOrderID
Purchasing	ShipMethod	PK_ShipMethod_ShipMethodID
Purchasing	Vendor	PK_Vendor_BusinessEntityID
Sales	CountryRegionCurrency	PK_CountryRegionCurrency_CountryRegionCode_CurrencyCode
Sales	CreditCard	PK_CreditCard_CreditCardID

Sales	Currency	PK_Currency_CurrencyCode
Sales	CurrencyRate	PK_CurrencyRate_CurrencyRateID
Sales	Customer	PK_Customer_CustomerID
Sales	PersonCreditCard	PK_PersonCreditCard_BusinessEntityID_CreditCardID
Sales	SalesOrderDetail	PK_SalesOrderDetail_SalesOrderID_SalesOrderDetailID
Sales	SalesOrderHeader	PK_SalesOrderHeader_SalesOrderID
Sales	SalesOrderHeaderSalesReason	PK_SalesOrderHeaderSalesReason_SalesOrderID_SalesReasonID
Sales	SalesPerson	PK_SalesPerson_BusinessEntityID
Sales	SalesPersonQuotaHistory	PK_SalesPersonQuotaHistory_BusinessEntityID_QuotaDate
Sales	SalesReason	PK_SalesReason_SalesReasonID
Sales	SalesTaxRate	PK_SalesTaxRate_SalesTaxRateID
Sales	SalesTerritory	PK_SalesTerritory_TerritoryID
Sales	SalesTerritoryHistory	PK_SalesTerritoryHistory_BusinessEntityID_StartDate_TerritoryID
Sales	ShoppingCartItem	PK_ShoppingCartItem_ShoppingCartItemID
Sales	SpecialOffer	PK_SpecialOffer_SpecialOfferID
Sales	SpecialOfferProduct	PK_SpecialOfferProduct_SpecialOfferID_ProductID
Sales	Store	PK_Store_BusinessEntityID

UNIQUEIDENTIFIER As PRIMARY KEY

For most applications INT IDENTITY(1,1) (SURROGATE) PRIMARY KEY is the perfect choice.
However, some enterprise applications require the generation of a random rowid without any
reference to a database. For those, UNIQUEIDENTIFIER can be used with NEWID() or
NEWSEQUENTIALID() fill. **The latter is faster but not completely random therefore should not
be used for secure applications.** INT IDENTITY() is fastest of the three (not in following test).

```
USE tempdb; SET NOCOUNT ON;
DECLARE @MaxCount Int = 100000,@START DATETIME,@END DATETIME, @i INT
CREATE TABLE TESTID ( ID UNIQUEIDENTIFIER DEFAULT NEWID() PRIMARY KEY,
-- CREATE TABLE TESTID ( ID UNIQUEIDENTIFIER DEFAULT NEWSEQUENTIALID() PRIMARY KEY,
COL1 CHAR(256) DEFAULT 'Everglades', COL2 CHAR(256) DEFAULT 'Everglades',
COL3 CHAR(256) DEFAULT 'Everglades', COL4 CHAR(256) DEFAULT 'Everglades',
COL5 CHAR(256) DEFAULT 'Everglades', COL6 CHAR(256) DEFAULT 'Everglades',
COL7 CHAR(256) DEFAULT 'Everglades', COL8 CHAR(256) DEFAULT 'Everglades',
COL9 CHAR(256) DEFAULT 'Everglades', COL10 CHAR(256) DEFAULT 'Everglades');
SELECT TOP(0) * INTO #Result FROM TESTID;
DBCC DROPCLEANBUFFERS;  SET @START = GETDATE(); SET @i = 1;
WHILE (@i < @MaxCount)
BEGIN INSERT TESTID DEFAULT VALUES; SET @i += 1; END
INSERT #Result SELECT t1.* FROM TESTID t1 INNER JOIN TESTID t2 ON t1.ID=t2.ID
SELECT  DATEDIFF(ms,@START,GETDATE());  DROP TABLE #Result; DROP TABLE TESTID;


-- Test with newid(): 22,436 msec
-- Test with newid(): 14,866 msec
-- Test with newid(): 14,576 msec


-- Test with newsequentialid(): 12,126 msec
-- Test with newsequentialid(): 11,290 msec
-- Test with newsequentialid(): 10,713 msec
```

List All PK & FK Columns in the Database

We can use INFORMATION_SCHEMA metadata system views for the task. The position indicates the placement of the column within a composite key.

```
USE AdventureWorks2012;
SELECT  k.table_schema            AS SchemaName,
        k.table_name              AS  TableName,
        k.column_name             AS ColumnName,
        k.ordinal_position        AS Position,
        c.constraint_type         AS KeyConstraint
FROM   information_schema.table_constraints c
    INNER JOIN information_schema.key_column_usage k
     ON c.table_name = k.table_name
        AND c.constraint_name = k.constraint_name
ORDER BY SchemaName, TableName, KeyConstraint DESC, Position, ColumnName;
GO
-- (194 row(s) affected) - Partial results
```

SchemaName	TableName	ColumnName	Position	KeyConstraint
HumanResources	Department	DepartmentID	1	PRIMARY KEY
HumanResources	Employee	BusinessEntityID	1	PRIMARY KEY
HumanResources	Employee	BusinessEntityID	1	FOREIGN KEY
HumanResources	EmployeeDepartmentHistory	BusinessEntityID	1	PRIMARY KEY
HumanResources	EmployeeDepartmentHistory	StartDate	2	PRIMARY KEY
HumanResources	EmployeeDepartmentHistory	DepartmentID	3	PRIMARY KEY
HumanResources	EmployeeDepartmentHistory	ShiftID	4	PRIMARY KEY
HumanResources	EmployeeDepartmentHistory	BusinessEntityID	1	FOREIGN KEY
HumanResources	EmployeeDepartmentHistory	DepartmentID	1	FOREIGN KEY
HumanResources	EmployeeDepartmentHistory	ShiftID	1	FOREIGN KEY
HumanResources	EmployeePayHistory	BusinessEntityID	1	PRIMARY KEY
HumanResources	EmployeePayHistory	RateChangeDate	2	PRIMARY KEY
HumanResources	EmployeePayHistory	BusinessEntityID	1	FOREIGN KEY
HumanResources	JobCandidate	JobCandidateID	1	PRIMARY KEY
HumanResources	JobCandidate	BusinessEntityID	1	FOREIGN KEY
HumanResources	Shift	ShiftID	1	PRIMARY KEY
Person	Address	AddressID	1	PRIMARY KEY
Person	Address	StateProvinceID	1	FOREIGN KEY
Person	AddressType	AddressTypeID	1	PRIMARY KEY
Person	BusinessEntity	BusinessEntityID	1	PRIMARY KEY
Person	BusinessEntityAddress	BusinessEntityID	1	PRIMARY KEY
Person	BusinessEntityAddress	AddressID	2	PRIMARY KEY
Person	BusinessEntityAddress	AddressTypeID	3	PRIMARY KEY
Person	BusinessEntityAddress	AddressID	1	FOREIGN KEY
Person	BusinessEntityAddress	AddressTypeID	1	FOREIGN KEY
Person	BusinessEntityAddress	BusinessEntityID	1	FOREIGN KEY
Person	BusinessEntityContact	BusinessEntityID	1	PRIMARY KEY
Person	BusinessEntityContact	PersonID	2	PRIMARY KEY
Person	BusinessEntityContact	ContactTypeID	3	PRIMARY KEY
Person	BusinessEntityContact	BusinessEntityID	1	FOREIGN KEY
Person	BusinessEntityContact	ContactTypeID	1	FOREIGN KEY
Person	BusinessEntityContact	PersonID	1	FOREIGN KEY
Person	ContactType	ContactTypeID	1	PRIMARY KEY

How to Get Database Object Definition Information

There are alternate ways of getting object definition metadata.

Scripting Object CREATE Definitions

This is the easiest and most reliable way. Start with a right click on the object in Object Explorer.

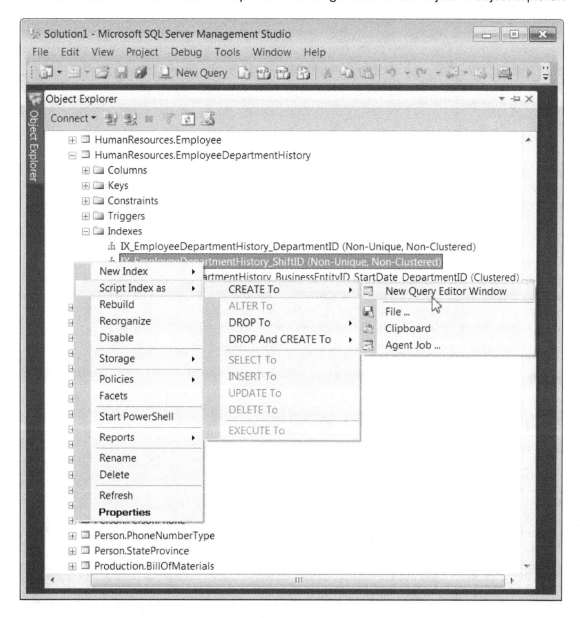

Single Object CREATE & Other Scripts from SSMS Object Explorer

Some of the scripts are generated complete. Others are just templates which require completion and testing.

Index CREATE Script

```
USE [AdventureWorks2012]
GO


/****** Object:  Index [IX_EmployeeDepartmentHistory_ShiftID]   Script Date: .... ******/
CREATE NONCLUSTERED INDEX [IX_EmployeeDepartmentHistory_ShiftID]
ON [HumanResources].[EmployeeDepartmentHistory]
(
        [ShiftID] ASC
)
WITH (PAD_INDEX = OFF, STATISTICS_NORECOMPUTE = OFF, SORT_IN_TEMPDB = OFF,
DROP_EXISTING = OFF, ONLINE = OFF, ALLOW_ROW_LOCKS = ON, ALLOW_PAGE_LOCKS = ON,
FILLFACTOR = 85) ON [PRIMARY]
GO

EXEC sys.sp_addextendedproperty @name=N'MS_Description',
@value=N'Nonclustered index.' ,
@level0type=N'SCHEMA',@level0name=N'HumanResources',
@level1type=N'TABLE',@level1name=N'EmployeeDepartmentHistory',
@level2type=N'INDEX',@level2name=N'IX_EmployeeDepartmentHistory_ShiftID'
GO
```

Index DROP Script

```
/****** Object:  Index [IX_EmployeeDepartmentHistory_ShiftID]   Script Date: ..... ******/
DROP INDEX [IX_EmployeeDepartmentHistory_ShiftID] ON
[HumanResources].[EmployeeDepartmentHistory]
GO
```

View DELETE Script

```
USE [AdventureWorks2012]
GO

DELETE FROM [Person].[vStateProvinceCountryRegion]
      WHERE <Search Conditions,,>
GO
```

CHAPTER 8: Advanced Database Architecture

View UPDATE Script

```
USE [AdventureWorks2012]
GO
UPDATE [Production].[vProductAndDescription]
  SET [ProductID] = <ProductID, int,>
    ,[Name] = <Name, Name,>
    ,[ProductModel] = <ProductModel, Name,>
    ,[CultureID] = <CultureID, nchar(6),>
    ,[Description] = <Description, nvarchar(400),>
 WHERE <Search Conditions,,>
GO
```

Inline Table-Valued User-Defined Function ALTER Script

```
USE [AdventureWorks2012]
GO
/****** Object:  UserDefinedFunction [Sales].[ufnStaffSalesByFiscalYear]    Script Date: ...... ******/
SET ANSI_NULLS ON
GO
SET QUOTED_IDENTIFIER ON
GO
ALTER FUNCTION [Sales].[ufnStaffSalesByFiscalYear] (@OrderYear INT)
RETURNS TABLE  AS
RETURN
SELECT
    CONVERT(date, soh.OrderDate)                                      AS OrderDate
    ,CONCAT(p.FirstName, ' ', COALESCE(p.MiddleName, ''), ' ', p.LastName)   AS FullName
    ,e.JobTitle
    ,st.Name                                                          AS SalesTerritory
    ,FORMAT(soh.SubTotal, 'c', 'en-US')                               AS SalesAmount
    ,YEAR(DATEADD(mm, 6, soh.OrderDate))                              AS FiscalYear
FROM Sales.SalesPerson sp
    INNER JOIN Sales.SalesOrderHeader soh
        ON sp.BusinessEntityID = soh.SalesPersonID
    INNER JOIN Sales.SalesTerritory st
        ON sp.TerritoryID = st.TerritoryID
    INNER JOIN HumanResources.Employee e
        ON soh.SalesPersonID = e.BusinessEntityID
    INNER JOIN Person.Person p
        ON p.BusinessEntityID = sp.BusinessEntityID
WHERE           soh.OrderDate >= datefromparts(@OrderYear, 1, 1)
        AND soh.OrderDate < dateadd(yy,1, datefromparts(@OrderYear, 1, 1));
GO
```

Searching for Database Objects in Object Explorer Details

We start by positioning on AdventureWorks2012 in Object Explorer. We activate the Object Explorer Details window from the Views tab. Enter the keyword or wildcard in the search box and press the Enter key.

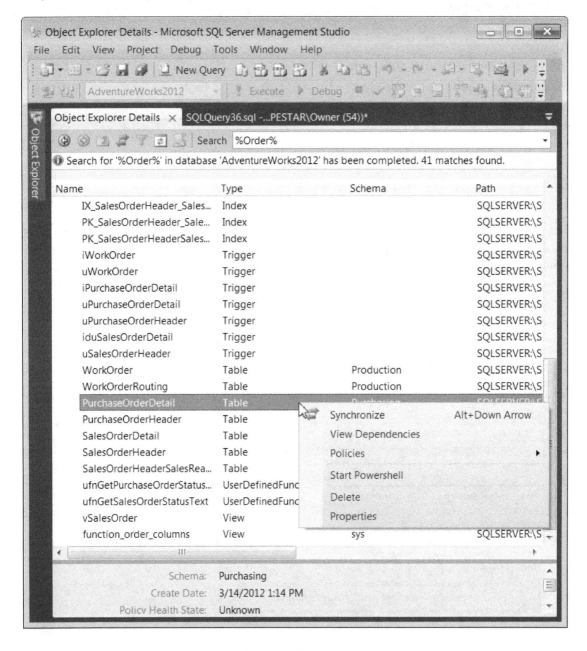

OBJECT_DEFINITION() Function for Getting Source Code

The OBJECT_DEFINITIION() function can be used to retrieve the database object definition source text for some objects such as view, stored procedure, trigger & function.

```
SELECT OBJECT_DEFINITION(object_id('INFORMATION_SCHEMA.TABLES'));
```

```
CREATE VIEW INFORMATION_SCHEMA.TABLES
AS
SELECT
            DB_NAME()                         AS TABLE_CATALOG,
            s.name                            AS TABLE_SCHEMA,
            o.name                            AS TABLE_NAME,
            CASE o.type
                    WHEN 'U' THEN 'BASE TABLE'
                    WHEN 'V' THEN 'VIEW'
            END                               AS TABLE_TYPE
FROM
            sys.objects o LEFT JOIN sys.schemas s
            ON s.schema_id = o.schema_id
WHERE
                        o.type IN ('U', 'V')
```

```
SELECT OBJECT_DEFINITION(object_id('Sales.vSalesPersonSalesByFiscalYears'));
```

```
CREATE VIEW [Sales].[vSalesPersonSalesByFiscalYears] AS
SELECT    pvt.[SalesPersonID]
  ,pvt.[FullName]
  ,pvt.[JobTitle]
  ,pvt.[SalesTerritory]
  ,pvt.[2006]
  ,pvt.[2007]
  ,pvt.[2008]
FROM (SELECT       soh.[SalesPersonID]
    ,p.[FirstName] + ' ' + COALESCE(p.[MiddleName], '') + ' ' + p.[LastName] AS [FullName]
    ,e.[JobTitle]
    ,st.[Name] AS [SalesTerritory]
    ,soh.[SubTotal]
    ,YEAR(DATEADD(m, 6, soh.[OrderDate])) AS [FiscalYear]
  FROM [Sales].[SalesPerson] sp
    INNER JOIN [Sales].[SalesOrderHeader] soh
    ON sp.[BusinessEntityID] = soh.[SalesPersonID]
    INNER JOIN [Sales].[SalesTerritory] st
    ON sp.[TerritoryID] = st.[TerritoryID]
    INNER JOIN [HumanResources].[Employee] e
    ON soh.[SalesPersonID] = e.[BusinessEntityID]
                    INNER JOIN [Person].[Person] p
                    ON p.[BusinessEntityID] = sp.[BusinessEntityID]  ) AS soh
PIVOT (
  SUM([SubTotal])
  FOR [FiscalYear]
  IN ([2006], [2007], [2008])
) AS pvt;
```

Scripting Database Objects with PowerShell

PowerShell script can be used to script database object including tables. Scripting tables in the Purchasing schema of AdventureWorks2012 sample database. In all Command Prompt scripts the lines must be without carriage return or new line breaks (CR/NL).

```
sqlps
Set-Location SQLSERVER:\SQL\HPESTAR\DEFAULT\Databases\AdventureWorks2012\Tables;
ForEach ($item in Get-ChildItem | Where-Object { $_.Schema -eq "Purchasing" })
{$item.Script()}
```

```
Command Prompt - sqlps
C:\Users\Owner>sqlps
Microsoft SQL Server PowerShell
Version 11.0.2100.60
Microsoft Corp. All rights reserved.

PS SQLSERVER:\> Set-Location SQLSERVER:\SQL\HPESTAR\DEFAULT\Databases\AdventureW
orks2012\Tables;
PS SQLSERVER:\SQL\HPESTAR\DEFAULT\Databases\AdventureWorks2012\Tables> ForEach (
$item in Get-ChildItem | Where-Object { $_.Schema -eq "Purchasing" }) {$item.Sc
ript()}
SET ANSI_NULLS ON
SET QUOTED_IDENTIFIER ON
CREATE TABLE [Purchasing].[ProductVendor](
        [ProductID] [int] NOT NULL,
        [BusinessEntityID] [int] NOT NULL,
        [AverageLeadTime] [int] NOT NULL,
        [StandardPrice] [money] NOT NULL,
        [LastReceiptCost] [money] NULL,
        [LastReceiptDate] [datetime] NULL,
        [MinOrderQty] [int] NOT NULL,
        [MaxOrderQty] [int] NOT NULL,
        [OnOrderQty] [int] NULL,
        [UnitMeasureCode] [nchar](3) COLLATE SQL_Latin1_General_CP1_CI_AS NOT NU
LL,
        [ModifiedDate] [datetime] NOT NULL
```

Instead of the console the scripting output can be piped to a .sql file.

```
ForEach ($item in Get-ChildItem | Where-Object { $_.Schema -eq "Purchasing" }) {$item.Script()
| Out-File "f:data\sql\PurchasingTables.sql" -Append }
```

CHAPTER 8: Advanced Database Architecture

System Views since SQL Server 2005

SQL Server 2005 has introduced a large collection, 400 in SS 2012, of system views providing detail metadata and operational data which was not available before. As an example, the full-text index & full-text search functionalities have a number of supporting system views. The system tables are no longer accessible. System views cannot be altered or updated. **System views are read only**. The head of systems views list.

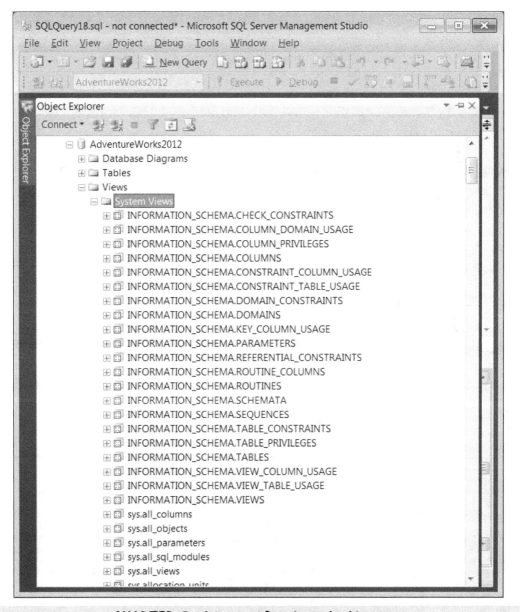

CHAPTER 8: Advanced Database Architecture

Querying Systems Views

Querying system views is not a trivial task. Frequently a group of tables involved and a Dynamic Management Function (DMF) CROSS APPLY may be necessary for useful results.

Download site for SQL Server 2008 R2 System Views Map:
http://www.microsoft.com/en-us/download/details.aspx?id=722 .

```
USE AdventureWorks2012;
SELECT ReferencedObject = CONCAT(SCHEMA_NAME(o2.schema_id), '.',
                          ed.referenced_entity_name),
      ReferencedObjectType = o2.type,
      ReferencingObjectType = o1.type,
      ReferencingObject = CONCAT(SCHEMA_NAME(o1.schema_id), '.', o1.name)
FROM   sys.sql_expression_dependencies ed
    INNER JOIN sys.objects o1
        ON ed.referencing_id = o1.object_id
    INNER JOIN sys.objects o2
        ON ed.referenced_id = o2.object_id
WHERE  o1.type IN ( 'P', 'TR', 'V', 'TF' )
ORDER  BY       ReferencedObjectType, ReferencedObject, ReferencingObject;
-- (163 row(s) affected) - Partial results
```

ReferencedObject	ReferencedObjectType	ReferencingObjectType	ReferencingObject
HumanResources.Department	U	V	HumanResources.vEmployeeDepartment
HumanResources.Department	U	V	HumanResources.vEmployeeDepartmentHistory
HumanResources.Employee	U	TF	dbo.ufnGetContactInformation
HumanResources.Employee	U	P	dbo.uspGetEmployeeManagers
HumanResources.Employee	U	P	dbo.uspGetManagerEmployees
HumanResources.Employee	U	P	HumanResources.uspUpdateEmployeeHireInfo
HumanResources.Employee	U	P	HumanResources.uspUpdateEmployeeLogin
HumanResources.Employee	U	P	HumanResources.uspUpdateEmployeePersonalInfo
HumanResources.Employee	U	V	HumanResources.vEmployee
HumanResources.Employee	U	V	HumanResources.vEmployeeDepartment
HumanResources.Employee	U	V	HumanResources.vEmployeeDepartmentHistory
HumanResources.Employee	U	V	Sales.vSalesPerson
HumanResources.Employee	U	V	Sales.vSalesPersonSalesByFiscalYears
HumanResources.EmployeeDepartmentHistory	U	V	HumanResources.vEmployeeDepartment
HumanResources.EmployeeDepartmentHistory	U	V	HumanResources.vEmployeeDepartmentHistory
HumanResources.EmployeePayHistory	U	P	HumanResources.uspUpdateEmployeeHireInfo
HumanResources.JobCandidate	U	P	dbo.uspSearchCandidateResumes
HumanResources.JobCandidate	U	V	HumanResources.vJobCandidate
HumanResources.JobCandidate	U	V	HumanResources.vJobCandidateEducation
HumanResources.JobCandidate	U	V	HumanResources.vJobCandidateEmployment

Listing All System Views

Since SQL Server 2005 system tables are off limits, replaced by system views, 400 in SS 2012.

The dm_ prefix indicates **Dynamic Management View** (DMV) such as dm_exec_requests.

```
;WITH cteTableList AS (       SELECT CONCAT(SCHEMA_NAME(schema_id), '.', name)          AS TableName,
  (( ROW_NUMBER() OVER( ORDER BY CONCAT(SCHEMA_NAME(schema_id),'.', name)) ) % 3)        AS Remainder,
  (( ROW_NUMBER() OVER( ORDER BY CONCAT(SCHEMA_NAME(schema_id),'.', name)) - 1 )/ 3)     AS Quotient
                    FROM AdventureWorks2012.sys.system_views),
CTE AS (SELECT TableName, CASE WHEN Remainder=0 THEN 3 ELSE Remainder END AS Remainder, Quotient
       FROM cteTableList)
SELECT    MAX(CASE WHEN Remainder = 1 THEN TableName END),
          MAX(CASE WHEN Remainder = 2 THEN TableName END),
          MAX(CASE WHEN Remainder = 3 THEN TableName END)
FROM  CTE GROUP  BY Quotient ORDER  BY Quotient;
```

INFORMATION_SCHEMA.CHECK_CONSTRAINTS	INFORMATION_SCHEMA.COLUMN_DOMAIN_USAGE	INFORMATION_SCHEMA.COLUMN_PRIVILEGES
INFORMATION_SCHEMA.COLUMNS	INFORMATION_SCHEMA.CONSTRAINT_COLUMN_USAGE	INFORMATION_SCHEMA.CONSTRAINT_TABLE_USAGE
INFORMATION_SCHEMA.DOMAIN_CONSTRAINTS	INFORMATION_SCHEMA.DOMAINS	INFORMATION_SCHEMA.KEY_COLUMN_USAGE
INFORMATION_SCHEMA.PARAMETERS	INFORMATION_SCHEMA.REFERENTIAL_CONSTRAINTS	INFORMATION_SCHEMA.ROUTINE_COLUMNS
INFORMATION_SCHEMA.ROUTINES	INFORMATION_SCHEMA.SCHEMATA	INFORMATION_SCHEMA.SEQUENCES
INFORMATION_SCHEMA.TABLE_CONSTRAINTS	INFORMATION_SCHEMA.TABLE_PRIVILEGES	INFORMATION_SCHEMA.TABLES
INFORMATION_SCHEMA.VIEW_COLUMN_USAGE	INFORMATION_SCHEMA.VIEW_TABLE_USAGE	INFORMATION_SCHEMA.VIEWS
sys.all_columns	sys.all_objects	sys.all_parameters
sys.all_sql_modules	sys.all_views	sys.allocation_units
sys.assemblies	sys.assembly_files	sys.assembly_modules
sys.assembly_references	sys.assembly_types	sys.asymmetric_keys
sys.availability_databases_cluster	sys.availability_group_listener_ip_addresses	sys.availability_group_listeners
sys.availability_groups	sys.availability_groups_cluster	sys.availability_read_only_routing_lists
sys.availability_replicas	sys.backup_devices	sys.certificates
sys.change_tracking_databases	sys.change_tracking_tables	sys.check_constraints
sys.column_store_dictionaries	sys.column_store_segments	sys.column_type_usages
sys.column_xml_schema_collection_usages	sys.columns	sys.computed_columns
sys.configurations	sys.conversation_endpoints	sys.conversation_groups
sys.conversation_priorities	sys.credentials	sys.crypt_properties
sys.cryptographic_providers	sys.data_spaces	sys.database_audit_specification_details
sys.database_audit_specifications	sys.database_files	sys.database_filestream_options
sys.database_mirroring	sys.database_mirroring_endpoints	sys.database_mirroring_witnesses
sys.database_permissions	sys.database_principals	sys.database_recovery_status

sys.database_role_members	sys.databases	sys.default_constraints
sys.destination_data_spaces	sys.dm_audit_actions	sys.dm_audit_class_type_map
sys.dm_broker_activated_tasks	sys.dm_broker_connections	sys.dm_broker_forwarded_message s
sys.dm_broker_queue_monitors	sys.dm_cdc_errors	sys.dm_cdc_log_scan_sessions
sys.dm_clr_appdomains	sys.dm_clr_loaded_assemblies	sys.dm_clr_properties
sys.dm_clr_tasks	sys.dm_cryptographic_provider_prop erties	sys.dm_database_encryption_keys
sys.dm_db_file_space_usage	sys.dm_db_fts_index_physical_stats	sys.dm_db_index_usage_stats
sys.dm_db_log_space_usage	sys.dm_db_mirroring_auto_page_rep air	sys.dm_db_mirroring_connections
sys.dm_db_mirroring_past_actions	sys.dm_db_missing_index_details	sys.dm_db_missing_index_group_st ats
sys.dm_db_missing_index_groups	sys.dm_db_partition_stats	sys.dm_db_persisted_sku_features
sys.dm_db_script_level	sys.dm_db_session_space_usage	sys.dm_db_task_space_usage
sys.dm_db_uncontained_entities	sys.dm_exec_background_job_queue	sys.dm_exec_background_job_queu e_stats
sys.dm_exec_cached_plans	sys.dm_exec_connections	sys.dm_exec_procedure_stats
sys.dm_exec_query_memory_grant s	sys.dm_exec_query_optimizer_info	sys.dm_exec_query_resource_sema phores
sys.dm_exec_query_stats	sys.dm_exec_query_transformation_s tats	sys.dm_exec_requests
sys.dm_exec_sessions	sys.dm_exec_trigger_stats	sys.dm_filestream_file_io_handles
sys.dm_filestream_file_io_requests	sys.dm_filestream_non_transacted_h andles	sys.dm_fts_active_catalogs
sys.dm_fts_fdhosts	sys.dm_fts_index_population	sys.dm_fts_memory_buffers
sys.dm_fts_memory_pools	sys.dm_fts_outstanding_batches	sys.dm_fts_population_ranges
sys.dm_fts_semantic_similarity_pop ulation	sys.dm_hadr_auto_page_repair	sys.dm_hadr_availability_group_sta tes
sys.dm_hadr_availability_replica_cl uster_nodes	sys.dm_hadr_availability_replica_clust er_states	sys.dm_hadr_availability_replica_st ates
sys.dm_hadr_cluster	sys.dm_hadr_cluster_members	sys.dm_hadr_cluster_networks
sys.dm_hadr_database_replica_clus ter_states	sys.dm_hadr_database_replica_states	sys.dm_hadr_instance_node_map
sys.dm_hadr_name_id_map	sys.dm_io_backup_tapes	sys.dm_io_cluster_shared_drives
sys.dm_io_pending_io_requests	sys.dm_logpool_hashentries	sys.dm_logpool_stats
sys.dm_os_buffer_descriptors	sys.dm_os_child_instances	sys.dm_os_cluster_nodes
sys.dm_os_cluster_properties	sys.dm_os_dispatcher_pools	sys.dm_os_dispatchers
sys.dm_os_hosts	sys.dm_os_latch_stats	sys.dm_os_loaded_modules
sys.dm_os_memory_allocations	sys.dm_os_memory_broker_clerks	sys.dm_os_memory_brokers
sys.dm_os_memory_cache_clock_h ands	sys.dm_os_memory_cache_counters	sys.dm_os_memory_cache_entries
sys.dm_os_memory_cache_hash_ta bles	sys.dm_os_memory_clerks	sys.dm_os_memory_node_access_s tats
sys.dm_os_memory_nodes	sys.dm_os_memory_objects	sys.dm_os_memory_pools
sys.dm_os_nodes	sys.dm_os_performance_counters	sys.dm_os_process_memory
sys.dm_os_ring_buffers	sys.dm_os_schedulers	sys.dm_os_server_diagnostics_log_ configurations
sys.dm_os_spinlock_stats	sys.dm_os_stacks	sys.dm_os_sublatches
sys.dm_os_sys_info	sys.dm_os_sys_memory	sys.dm_os_tasks

sys.dm_os_threads	sys.dm_os_virtual_address_dump	sys.dm_os_wait_stats
sys.dm_os_waiting_tasks	sys.dm_os_windows_info	sys.dm_os_worker_local_storage
sys.dm_os_workers	sys.dm_qn_subscriptions	sys.dm_repl_articles
sys.dm_repl_schemas	sys.dm_repl_tranhash	sys.dm_repl_traninfo
sys.dm_resource_governor_configuration	sys.dm_resource_governor_resource_pool_affinity	sys.dm_resource_governor_resource_pools
sys.dm_resource_governor_workload_groups	sys.dm_server_audit_status	sys.dm_server_memory_dumps
sys.dm_server_registry	sys.dm_server_services	sys.dm_tcp_listener_states
sys.dm_tran_active_snapshot_database_transactions	sys.dm_tran_active_transactions	sys.dm_tran_commit_table
sys.dm_tran_current_snapshot	sys.dm_tran_current_transaction	sys.dm_tran_database_transactions
sys.dm_tran_locks	sys.dm_tran_session_transactions	sys.dm_tran_top_version_generators
sys.dm_tran_transactions_snapshot	sys.dm_tran_version_store	sys.dm_xe_map_values
sys.dm_xe_object_columns	sys.dm_xe_objects	sys.dm_xe_packages
sys.dm_xe_session_event_actions	sys.dm_xe_session_events	sys.dm_xe_session_object_columns
sys.dm_xe_session_targets	sys.dm_xe_sessions	sys.endpoint_webmethods
sys.endpoints	sys.event_notification_event_types	sys.event_notifications
sys.events	sys.extended_procedures	sys.extended_properties
sys.filegroups	sys.filetable_system_defined_objects	sys.filetables
sys.foreign_key_columns	sys.foreign_keys	sys.fulltext_catalogs
sys.fulltext_document_types	sys.fulltext_index_catalog_usages	sys.fulltext_index_columns
sys.fulltext_index_fragments	sys.fulltext_indexes	sys.fulltext_languages
sys.fulltext_semantic_language_statistics_database	sys.fulltext_semantic_languages	sys.fulltext_stoplists
sys.fulltext_stopwords	sys.fulltext_system_stopwords	sys.function_order_columns
sys.http_endpoints	sys.identity_columns	sys.index_columns
sys.indexes	sys.internal_tables	sys.key_constraints
sys.key_encryptions	sys.linked_logins	sys.login_token
sys.master_files	sys.master_key_passwords	sys.message_type_xml_schema_collection_usages
sys.messages	sys.module_assembly_usages	sys.numbered_procedure_parameters
sys.numbered_procedures	sys.objects	sys.openkeys
sys.parameter_type_usages	sys.parameter_xml_schema_collection_usages	sys.parameters
sys.partition_functions	sys.partition_parameters	sys.partition_range_values
sys.partition_schemes	sys.partitions	sys.plan_guides
sys.procedures	sys.registered_search_properties	sys.registered_search_property_lists
sys.remote_logins	sys.remote_service_bindings	sys.resource_governor_configuration
sys.resource_governor_resource_pool_affinity	sys.resource_governor_resource_pools	sys.resource_governor_workload_groups
sys.routes	sys.schemas	sys.securable_classes
sys.sequences	sys.server_assembly_modules	sys.server_audit_specification_details
sys.server_audit_specifications	sys.server_audits	sys.server_event_notifications
sys.server_event_session_actions	sys.server_event_session_events	sys.server_event_session_fields

CHAPTER 8: Advanced Database Architecture

sys.server_event_session_targets	sys.server_event_sessions	sys.server_events
sys.server_file_audits	sys.server_permissions	sys.server_principal_credentials
sys.server_principals	sys.server_role_members	sys.server_sql_modules
sys.server_trigger_events	sys.server_triggers	sys.servers
sys.service_broker_endpoints	sys.service_contract_message_usages	sys.service_contract_usages
sys.service_contracts	sys.service_message_types	sys.service_queue_usages
sys.service_queues	sys.services	sys.soap_endpoints
sys.spatial_index_tessellations	sys.spatial_indexes	sys.spatial_reference_systems
sys.sql_dependencies	sys.sql_expression_dependencies	sys.sql_logins
sys.sql_modules	sys.stats	sys.stats_columns
sys.symmetric_keys	sys.synonyms	sys.sysaltfiles
sys.syscacheobjects	sys.syscharsets	sys.syscolumns
sys.syscomments	sys.sysconfigures	sys.sysconstraints
sys.syscurconfigs	sys.syscursorcolumns	sys.syscursorrefs
sys.syscursors	sys.syscursortables	sys.sysdatabases
sys.sysdepends	sys.sysdevices	sys.sysfilegroups
sys.sysfiles	sys.sysforeignkeys	sys.sysfulltextcatalogs
sys.sysindexes	sys.sysindexkeys	sys.syslanguages
sys.syslockinfo	sys.syslogins	sys.sysmembers
sys.sysmessages	sys.sysobjects	sys.sysoledbusers
sys.sysopentapes	sys.sysperfinfo	sys.syspermissions
sys.sysprocesses	sys.sysprotects	sys.sysreferences
sys.sysremotelogins	sys.sysservers	sys.system_columns
sys.system_components_surface_area_configuration	sys.system_internals_allocation_units	sys.system_internals_partition_columns
sys.system_internals_partitions	sys.system_objects	sys.system_parameters
sys.system_sql_modules	sys.system_views	sys.systypes
sys.sysusers	sys.table_types	sys.tables
sys.tcp_endpoints	sys.trace_categories	sys.trace_columns
sys.trace_event_bindings	sys.trace_events	sys.trace_subclass_values
sys.traces	sys.transmission_queue	sys.trigger_event_types
sys.trigger_events	sys.triggers	sys.type_assembly_usages
sys.types	sys.user_token	sys.via_endpoints
sys.views	sys.xml_indexes	sys.xml_schema_attributes
sys.xml_schema_collections	sys.xml_schema_component_placements	sys.xml_schema_components
sys.xml_schema_elements	sys.xml_schema_facets	sys.xml_schema_model_groups
sys.xml_schema_namespaces	sys.xml_schema_types	sys.xml_schema_wildcard_namespaces
sys.xml_schema_wildcards	NULL	NULL

CHAPTER 8: Advanced Database Architecture

List of master database System Functions

Some are internal and undocumented functions. Some are used for special tasks: fn_listextendedproperty, fn_trace_getinfo, fn_my_permissions & fn_varbintohexstr. The dm_prefix indicates Dynamic Management Function (DMF) such as dm_exec_sql_text.

```
SELECT * FROM sys.all_objects where is_ms_shipped=1
          AND     ( TYPE_DESC = 'SQL_TABLE_VALUED_FUNCTION'         OR
                   TYPE_DESC = 'SQL_SCALAR_FUNCTION'                OR
                   TYPE_DESC = 'SQL_INLINE_TABLE_VALUED_FUNCTION')
ORDER BY name;  -- (96 row(s) affected)
```

List of System Tables Prior to SQL Server 2005

Some of the system tables were updatable in SQL Server 2000 and previous versions. SS 2005 introduced system views which are not updatable and barred access to system tables.

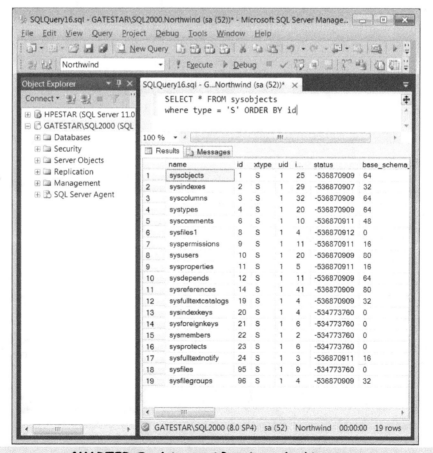

Other Methods of Metadata Access

Graphical Dependency Information

Object dependencies can be launched by a right click on the object.

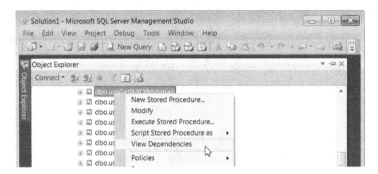

The dependency chart for the uspGetBillOfMaterials stored procedure.

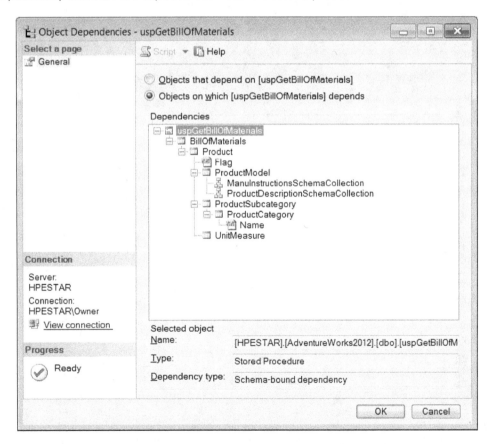

Scripting GUI Object Change

Most of the dialog panels have scripting options. In fact we don't even have to perform the action, we can just script it and execute the script in a (new) connection. The advantage of this approach that the generated script can be modified and saved for future use or reference. We start an index change with right click and properties.

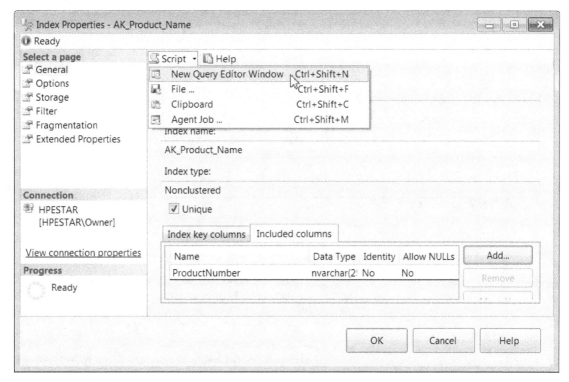

The generated script.

```
USE [AdventureWorks2012]
GO
SET ANSI_PADDING ON
GO
CREATE UNIQUE NONCLUSTERED INDEX [AK_Product_Name] ON [Production].[Product] (
[Name] ASC )
INCLUDE (        [ProductNumber]) WITH (PAD_INDEX = OFF, STATISTICS_NORECOMPUTE = OFF,
SORT_IN_TEMPDB = OFF,
IGNORE_DUP_KEY = OFF, DROP_EXISTING = ON, ONLINE = OFF, ALLOW_ROW_LOCKS = ON,
ALLOW_PAGE_LOCKS = ON, FILLFACTOR = 85) ON [PRIMARY]
GO
```

The sp_helpdb System Procedure

The sp_helpdb system procedure returns information on all or a specified database.

EXEC sp_helpdb;   -- Partial results

Accounting	3.88 MB	HPESTAR\Owner	17	May 24 2012	Status=ONLINE, Updateability=READ_WRITE, UserAccess=MULTI_USER, Recovery=FULL, Version=706, Collation=SQL_Latin1_General_CP1_CI_AS, SQLSortOrder=52, IsAutoCreateStatistics, IsAutoUpdateStatistics, IsFullTextEnabled	110
AdventureWorks	213.94 MB	HPESTAR\Owner	16	May 24 2012	Status=ONLINE, Updateability=READ_WRITE, UserAccess=MULTI_USER, Recovery=SIMPLE, Version=706, Collation=SQL_Latin1_General_CP1_CI_AS, SQLSortOrder=52, IsAnsiNullsEnabled, IsAnsiPaddingEnabled, IsAnsiWarningsEnabled, IsArithmeticAbortEnabled, IsAutoCreateStatistics, IsAutoUpdateStatistics, IsFullTextEnabled, IsNullConcat, IsQuotedIdentifiersEnabled, IsRecursiveTriggersEnabled	90

EXEC sp_helpdb AdventureWorks2012;

name	db_size	owner	dbid	created	status	compatibility_level
AdventureWorks 2012	3118.38 MB	sa	7	May 19 2012	Status=ONLINE, Updateability=READ_WRITE, UserAccess=MULTI_USER, Recovery=SIMPLE, Version=706, Collation=SQL_Latin1_General_CP1_CI_AS, SQLSortOrder=52, IsAnsiNullsEnabled, IsAnsiPaddingEnabled, IsAnsiWarningsEnabled, IsArithmeticAbortEnabled, IsAutoCreateStatistics, IsAutoUpdateStatistics, IsFullTextEnabled, IsNullConcat, IsQuotedIdentifiersEnabled	110

Data only Database Size

Query to calculate the data size within a database.

```
SELECT SUM(size * 8192.0) / (1024.0 * 1024.0 * 1024.0) AS TotalDataSizeGB
FROM AdventureWorks2012.sys.database_files;
-- 0.185050
```

CHAPTER 8: Advanced Database Architecture

The sp_help and sp_helptext System Procedures

The sp_help and sp_helptext provides database metadata in various formats including multiple result sets.

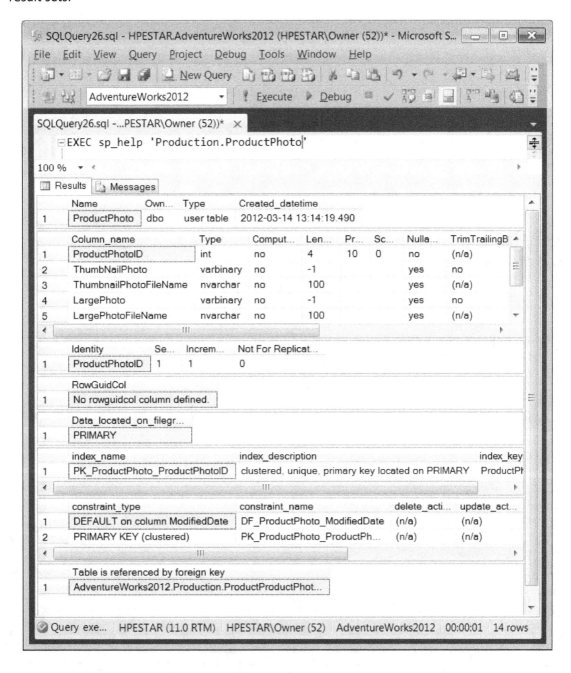

Using sp_helptext for Obtaining Definition

sp_helptext works only for some database objects. Table definition cannot be obtained by command, any command.

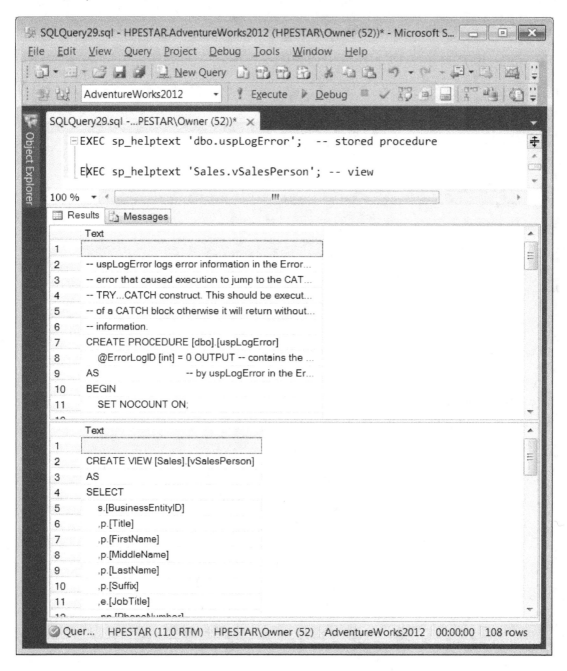

Partial List of sp_helpx System Procedures

The following list is from the master database System Stored Procedures.

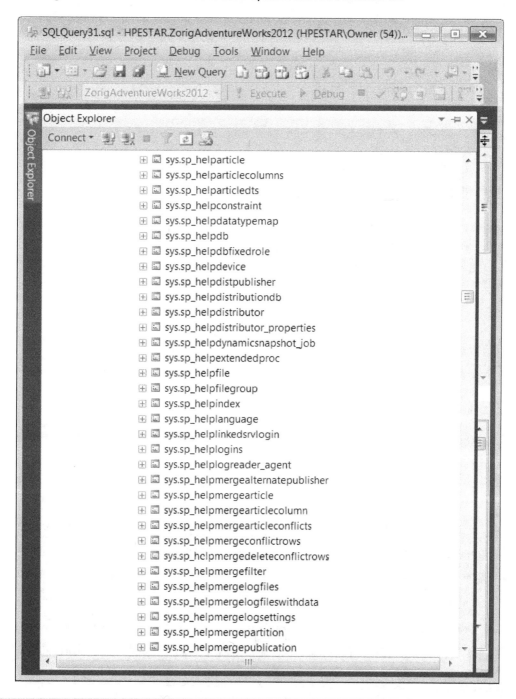

Listing All CHECK Constraints in a Database

We can use INFORMATION_SCHEMA views to perform this task.

```
USE AdventureWorks2012;
GO
```

```
SELECT        cc.CONSTRAINT_SCHEMA                    AS SCHEMA_NAME,
              TABLE_NAME,
              COLUMN_NAME,
              CHECK_CLAUSE,
              cc.CONSTRAINT_NAME
FROM     INFORMATION_SCHEMA.CHECK_CONSTRAINTS cc
              INNER JOIN INFORMATION_SCHEMA.CONSTRAINT_COLUMN_USAGE c
                    ON cc.CONSTRAINT_NAME = c.CONSTRAINT_NAME
ORDER BY      SCHEMA_NAME,
              TABLE_NAME,
              COLUMN_NAME;
-- (105 row(s) affected) - Partial results.
```

SCHEMA_NA ME	TABLE_NAME	COLUMN_NA ME	CHECK_CLAUSE	CONSTRAINT_NAME
HumanResour ces	Employee	BirthDate	([BirthDate]>='1930-01-01' AND [BirthDate]<=dateadd(year,(-18),getdate()))	CK_Employee_BirthDate
HumanResour ces	Employee	Gender	(upper([Gender])='F' OR upper([Gender])='M')	CK_Employee_Gender
HumanResour ces	Employee	HireDate	([HireDate]>='1996-07-01' AND [HireDate]<=dateadd(day,(1),get date()))	CK_Employee_HireDate
HumanResour ces	Employee	MaritalStatus	(upper([MaritalStatus])='S' OR upper([MaritalStatus])='M')	CK_Employee_MaritalStatus
HumanResour ces	Employee	SickLeaveHour s	([SickLeaveHours]>=(0) AND [SickLeaveHours]<=(120))	CK_Employee_SickLeaveHours
HumanResour ces	Employee	VacationHours	([VacationHours]>=(-40) AND [VacationHours]<=(240))	CK_Employee_VacationHours
HumanResour ces	EmployeeDepartment History	EndDate	([EndDate]>=[StartDate] OR [EndDate] IS NULL)	CK_EmployeeDepartmentHistory_ EndDate
HumanResour ces	EmployeeDepartment History	StartDate	([EndDate]>=[StartDate] OR [EndDate] IS NULL)	CK_EmployeeDepartmentHistory_ EndDate
HumanResour ces	EmployeePayHistory	PayFrequency	([PayFrequency]=(2) OR [PayFrequency]=(1))	CK_EmployeePayHistory_PayFreq uency
HumanResour ces	EmployeePayHistory	Rate	([Rate]>=(6.50) AND [Rate]<=(200.00))	CK_EmployeePayHistory_Rate
Person	Person	EmailPromotio n	([EmailPromotion]>=(0) AND [EmailPromotion]<=(2))	CK_Person_EmailPromotion

Creating a UDF CHECK Constraint

UDF CHECK constraint relies on a user-defined function for logic rather than the simple constraint expression. Demonstration script creates a test table with UDF check constraint.

```
USE tempdb;
SELECT TOP 10  P.BusinessEntityID, FirstName, LastName,          -- Create test table
              Email=convert(varchar(64),EmailAddress)
INTO Person FROM AdventureWorks2012.Person.Person P
              INNER JOIN AdventureWorks2012.Person.EmailAddress E
                ON E.BusinessEntityID = P.BusinessEntityID;
GO
-- Create user-defined function (UDF) for checking
CREATE FUNCTION ufnEmailValidityCheck (@Email varchar(64))
RETURNS BIT  AS
BEGIN
IF EXISTS(SELECT 1 WHERE
    CHARINDEX('.',@Email,CHARINDEX('@',@Email))-CHARINDEX('@',@Email)>1
    AND CHARINDEX('.',REVERSE(LTRIM(RTRIM(@Email)))) > 2
    AND CHARINDEX('@',LTRIM(@Email)) > 2) RETURN(1)
RETURN (0)
END;
GO
 -- Create UDF check constraint
ALTER TABLE [dbo].[Person]  WITH CHECK
ADD CONSTRAINT [EmailCheck] CHECK (   dbo.ufnEmailValidityCheck (Email) = 1);
GO
 -- SQL check constraint violated missing . (period)
INSERT Person (BusinessEntityID, FirstName, LastName, Email)
VALUES (100000, 'Elvis', 'Presley', 'elvispresley@thekingcom');
/*  Msg 547, Level 16, State 0, Line 5
The INSERT statement conflicted with the CHECK constraint "EmailCheck". The conflict occurred
in database "tempdb", table "dbo.Person", column 'Email'.*/
 -- SQL check constraint met
INSERT Person (BusinessEntityID, FirstName, LastName, Email)
VALUES (100000, 'Elvis', 'Presley', 'elvispresley@theking.com');
GO   -- (1 row(s) affected)
 SELECT * FROM Person ORDER BY Email;  -- Partial results.
```

BusinessEntityID	FirstName	LastName	Email
8	Diane	Margheim	diane1@adventure-works.com
7	Dylan	Miller	dylan0@adventure-works.com
100000	Elvis	Presley	elvispresley@theking.com

List All DEFAULT Constraint Definitions

We can use system views to carry out the task.

USE AdventureWorks2012;

```
SELECT
    SCHEMA_NAME(o.schema_id)        AS SchemaName,
    o.name                          AS TableName,
    c.name                          AS ColumnName,
    d.definition                    AS DefaultDefinition,
    d.name                          AS ConstraintName
FROM sys.default_constraints d
        INNER JOIN sys.columns c
            ON d.parent_object_id = c.object_id
            AND d.parent_column_id = c.column_id
        INNER JOIN sys.objects o
            ON o.object_id = c.object_id
ORDER BY SchemaName, TableName, ColumnName;
-- (152 row(s) affected) - Partial results.
```

SchemaName	TableName	ColumnName	DefaultDefinition	ConstraintName
dbo	AWBuildVersion	ModifiedDate	(getdate())	DF_AWBuildVersion_ModifiedDate
dbo	ErrorLog	ErrorTime	(getdate())	DF_ErrorLog_ErrorTime
HumanResources	Department	ModifiedDate	(getdate())	DF_Department_ModifiedDate
HumanResources	Employee	CurrentFlag	((1))	DF_Employee_CurrentFlag
HumanResources	Employee	ModifiedDate	(getdate())	DF_Employee_ModifiedDate
HumanResources	Employee	rowguid	(newid())	DF_Employee_rowguid
HumanResources	Employee	SalariedFlag	((1))	DF_Employee_SalariedFlag
HumanResources	Employee	SickLeaveHours	((0))	DF_Employee_SickLeaveHours
HumanResources	Employee	VacationHours	((0))	DF_Employee_VacationHours
HumanResources	EmployeeDepartmentHistory	ModifiedDate	(getdate())	DF_EmployeeDepartmentHistory_ModifiedDate
HumanResources	EmployeePayHistory	ModifiedDate	(getdate())	DF_EmployeePayHistory_ModifiedDate
HumanResources	JobCandidate	ModifiedDate	(getdate())	DF_JobCandidate_ModifiedDate
HumanResources	Shift	ModifiedDate	(getdate())	DF_Shift_ModifiedDate
Person	Address	ModifiedDate	(getdate())	DF_Address_ModifiedDate
Person	Address	rowguid	(newid())	DF_Address_rowguid
Person	AddressType	ModifiedDate	(getdate())	DF_AddressType_ModifiedDate
Person	AddressType	rowguid	(newid())	DF_AddressType_rowguid
Person	BusinessEntity	ModifiedDate	(getdate())	DF_BusinessEntity_ModifiedDate
Person	BusinessEntity	rowguid	(newid())	DF_BusinessEntity_rowguid
Person	BusinessEntityAddress	ModifiedDate	(getdate())	DF_BusinessEntityAddress_ModifiedDate
Person	BusinessEntityAddress	rowguid	(newid())	DF_BusinessEntityAddress_rowguid
Person	BusinessEntityContact	ModifiedDate	(getdate())	DF_BusinessEntityContact_ModifiedDate
Person	BusinessEntityContact	rowguid	(newid())	DF_BusinessEntityContact_rowguid
Person	ContactType	ModifiedDate	(getdate())	DF_ContactType_ModifiedDate
Person	CountryRegion	ModifiedDate	(getdate())	DF_CountryRegion_ModifiedDate

Database Object-Definition from sys.sql_modules System View

The sys.sql_modules systems view contains definition for stored procedures, triggers, functions and views. Prior to SQL Server 2005 the sys.syscomments table was used to obtain object definition source code.

```
USE AdventureWorks2012;
SELECT object_id, LEFT(definition,64) AS DefinitionPrefix
FROM sys.SQL_Modules ORDER BY object_id;
GO  -- (52 row(s) affected) - Partial results.
```

object_id	DefinitionPrefix
7671075	CREATE VIEW [Sales].[vStoreWithContacts] AS SELECT s.[
23671132	CREATE VIEW [Sales].[vStoreWithAddresses] AS SELECT s.

Forcing Users out of a Database

This method is used as "last resort" by DBA-s when all users must be exiting a database.

```
Use master;
Declare @dbname sysname = 'AdventureWorks2012',  @spid int;
Select @spid = min(spid) from master.dbo.sysprocesses where dbid = db_id(@dbname)
While @spid Is Not Null  Begin   Execute ('Kill ' + @spid);
    Select @spid = min(spid) from master.dbo.sysprocesses
    where dbid = db_id(@dbname) and spid > @spid;  End
Exec  sp_who;
```

CHAPTER 8: Advanced Database Architecture

Retrieving the Full Definition of a Stored Procedure

```
SELECT          schema_name(schema_id)              AS SchemaName,
                object_Name(m.object_ID)            AS ObjectName,
                definition                          AS ObjectDefinition
FROM   sys.SQL_Modules m
  INNER JOIN sys.objects o      ON m.object_id=o.object_id
WHERE  object_Name(m.object_ID) = 'uspGetBillOfMaterials'
GO
```

```
SchemaName          ObjectName              ObjectDefinition
dbo             uspGetBillOfMaterials       CREATE PROCEDURE [dbo].[uspGetBillOfMaterials]
  @StartProductID [int],
  @CheckDate [datetime]
AS
BEGIN
  SET NOCOUNT ON;

  -- Use recursive query to generate a multi-level Bill of Material (i.e. all level 1
  -- components of a level 0 assembly, all level 2 components of a level 1 assembly)
  -- The CheckDate eliminates any components that are no longer used in the product on this date.
  WITH [BOM_cte]([ProductAssemblyID], [ComponentID], [ComponentDesc], [PerAssemblyQty], [StandardCost], [ListPrice],
[BOMLevel], [RecursionLevel]) -- CTE name and columns
    AS (
      SELECT b.[ProductAssemblyID], b.[ComponentID], p.[Name], b.[PerAssemblyQty], p.[StandardCost], p.[ListPrice], b.[BOMLevel],
0 -- Get the initial list of components for the bike assembly
      FROM [Production].[BillOfMaterials] b
        INNER JOIN [Production].[Product] p
        ON b.[ComponentID] = p.[ProductID]
      WHERE b.[ProductAssemblyID] = @StartProductID
        AND @CheckDate >= b.[StartDate]
        AND @CheckDate <= ISNULL(b.[EndDate], @CheckDate)
      UNION ALL
      SELECT b.[ProductAssemblyID], b.[ComponentID], p.[Name], b.[PerAssemblyQty], p.[StandardCost], p.[ListPrice], b.[BOMLevel],
[RecursionLevel] + 1 -- Join recursive member to anchor
      FROM [BOM_cte] cte
        INNER JOIN [Production].[BillOfMaterials] b
        ON b.[ProductAssemblyID] = cte.[ComponentID]
        INNER JOIN [Production].[Product] p
        ON b.[ComponentID] = p.[ProductID]
      WHERE @CheckDate >= b.[StartDate]
        AND @CheckDate <= ISNULL(b.[EndDate], @CheckDate)
      )
  -- Outer select from the CTE
  SELECT b.[ProductAssemblyID], b.[ComponentID], b.[ComponentDesc], SUM(b.[PerAssemblyQty]) AS [TotalQuantity] ,
b.[StandardCost], b.[ListPrice], b.[BOMLevel], b.[RecursionLevel]
  FROM [BOM_cte] b
  GROUP BY b.[ComponentID], b.[ComponentDesc], b.[ProductAssemblyID], b.[BOMLevel], b.[RecursionLevel], b.[StandardCost],
b.[ListPrice]
  ORDER BY b.[BOMLevel], b.[ProductAssemblyID], b.[ComponentID]      OPTION (MAXRECURSION 25)
END;
```

CHAPTER 8: Advanced Database Architecture

Snowflake Schema Data Warehouse Design

If the following DW design were Star Schema, the DimProduct would be a flat dimension including DimProductSubcategory and DimProductCategory. In Snowflake Schema the dimension tables follow 3NF relational design.

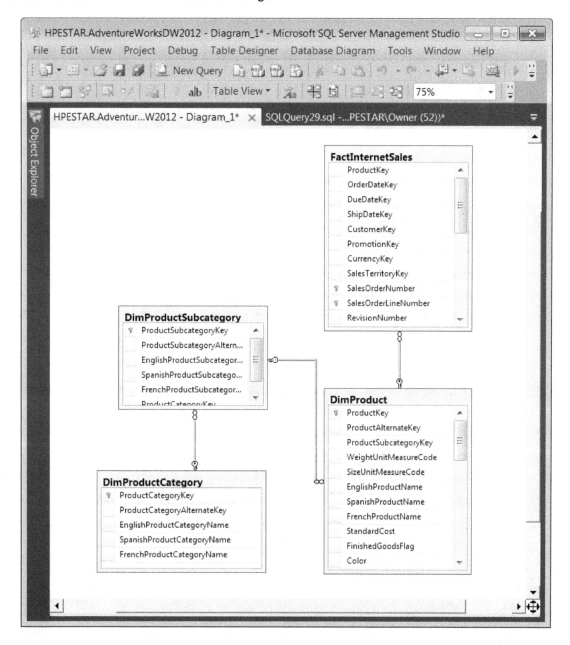

Object Explorer Table Editor

A table editor is available for directly editing data in a table. It is designed for limited use. First we create a test table, Department, then we launch the editor.

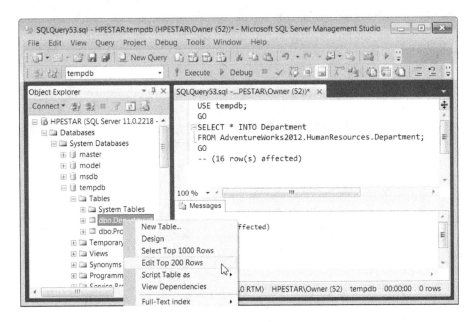

We added row 17 just by typing it in, then investigated the right click drop-down menu.

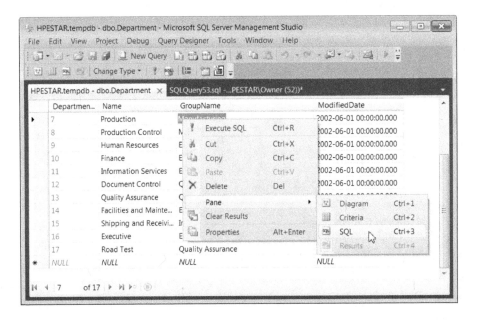

All Tables Row Count without the COUNT() Function

Here is quick way to get a row count, not exact like COUNT(*) but really fast.

```
USE AdventureWorks2012;

SELECT  CONCAT(SCHEMA_NAME(schema_id),'.',o.name )        AS TableName,
        FORMAT(max(i.rows),'###,###,###')                AS Rows
FROM    sys.sysobjects o
    INNER JOIN sys.sysindexes i
      ON o.id = i.id
    INNER JOIN sys.objects oo
      ON o.id = oo.object_id
WHERE   xtype = 'u'
    AND OBJECTPROPERTY(o.id,N'IsUserTable') = 1
GROUP BY schema_id, o.name
ORDER BY max(i.rows) DESC, TableName;
GO
-- (71 row(s) affected)  -- Partial results.
```

TableName	Rows
Sales.SalesOrderDetail	121,317
Production.TransactionHistory	113,443
Production.TransactionHistoryArchive	89,253
Production.WorkOrder	72,591
Production.WorkOrderRouting	67,131
Sales.SalesOrderHeader	31,465
Sales.SalesOrderHeaderSalesReason	27,647
Person.BusinessEntity	20,777
Person.EmailAddress	19,972
Person.Password	19,972
Person.Person	19,972
Person.PersonPhone	19,972
Sales.Customer	19,820
Person.Address	19,614
Person.BusinessEntityAddress	19,614
Sales.CreditCard	19,118
Sales.PersonCreditCard	19,118
Sales.CurrencyRate	13,532
Purchasing.PurchaseOrderDetail	8,845
Purchasing.PurchaseOrderHeader	4,012
Production.BillOfMaterials	2,679
dbo.DatabaseLog	1,597
Production.ProductInventory	1,069
Person.BusinessEntityContact	909
Production.ProductDescription	762

Column Properties Page in Object Explorer

Object Explorer right click on a column launches the column properties page.
Production.Product table ProductNumber column properties. No changes can be performed on
this page. To change the table, we have to launch the table designer.

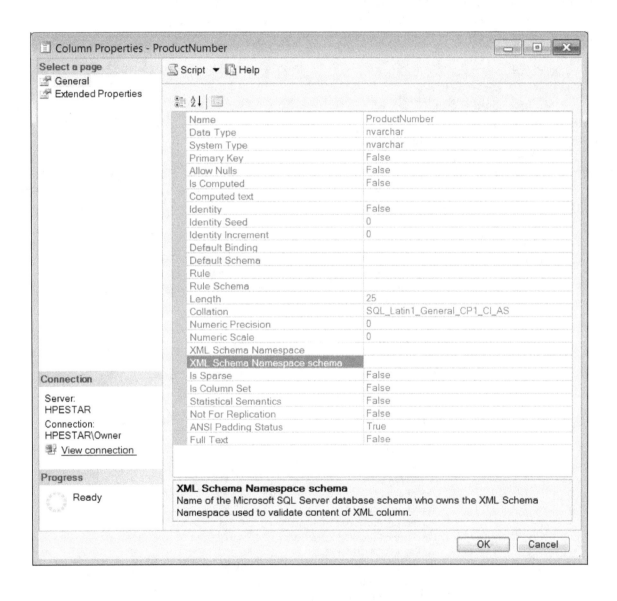

Listing All Columns with PK, FK & IDENTITY Properties

There are various ways for retrieving column properties including the COLUMNPROPERTY() function.

```
USE AdventureWorks2012;

SELECT c.TABLE_CATALOG                                          AS DatabaseName,
    c.TABLE_SCHEMA                                              AS SchemaName,
    c.TABLE_NAME                                                AS TableName,
    c.COLUMN_NAME                                               AS ColumnName,
    Columnproperty(Object_id(CONCAT(c.TABLE_SCHEMA,'.',c.TABLE_NAME)),
                    c.COLUMN_NAME, 'ISIDENTITY')                AS IsIdentity,
    CASE
      WHEN CONSTRAINT_NAME IN (SELECT NAME
                FROM   sys.objects
                WHERE  TYPE = 'PK') THEN 1
      ELSE 0   END                                             AS IsPrimaryKey,
    CASE
      WHEN CONSTRAINT_NAME IN (SELECT NAME
                FROM   sys.objects
                WHERE  TYPE = 'F') THEN 1
      ELSE 0   END                                             AS IsForeignKey
FROM   INFORMATION_SCHEMA.TABLES t
    INNER JOIN INFORMATION_SCHEMA.COLUMNS c
        ON c.TABLE_CATALOG = t.TABLE_CATALOG
            AND c.TABLE_SCHEMA = t.TABLE_SCHEMA
            AND c.TABLE_NAME = t.TABLE_NAME
    LEFT JOIN INFORMATION_SCHEMA.KEY_COLUMN_USAGE u
        ON c.TABLE_CATALOG = u.TABLE_CATALOG
            AND c.TABLE_SCHEMA = u.TABLE_SCHEMA
            AND c.TABLE_NAME = u.TABLE_NAME
            AND c.COLUMN_NAME = u.COLUMN_NAME
WHERE  TABLE_TYPE = 'BASE TABLE'
ORDER  BY SchemaName,   TableName,   c.ORDINAL_POSITION;
GO
-- (534 row(s) affected) - Partial results.
```

DatabaseName	SchemaName	TableName	ColumnName	IsIdentity	IsPrimaryKey	IsForeignKey
AdventureWorks2012	Person	EmailAddress	BusinessEntityID	0	0	1
AdventureWorks2012	Person	EmailAddress	BusinessEntityID	0	1	0
AdventureWorks2012	Person	EmailAddress	EmailAddressID	1	1	0
AdventureWorks2012	Person	EmailAddress	EmailAddress	0	0	0

CHAPTER 8: Advanced Database Architecture

The Collation Column Property & the COLLATE Clause

Each text column requires the collation property. The server & databases also have collation property as defaults only. When the database collation is changed, the actual column collations remain the same. New table columns will inherit the database default collation. New databases inherit the server collation. A column collation can be changed with ALTER TABLE. To change all text collations in a database may prove to be a big task.

```
USE tempdb;

SELECT * INTO Product FROM AdventureWorks2012.Production.Product;
-- (504 row(s) affected)

ALTER TABLE Product ALTER COLUMN Name nvarchar(50)
            COLLATE SQL_Latin1_General_CP1_CS_AS null;
-- Command(s) completed successfully.
```

Text operations with different collations result in error.

```
SELECT COUNT(*) FROM Product p
            INNER JOIN AdventureWorks2012.Production.Product aw12
            ON p.Name = aw12.Name;
GO

/*  Msg 468, Level 16, State 9, Line 3
Cannot resolve the collation conflict between "SQL_Latin1_General_CP1_CI_AS" and
"SQL_Latin1_General_CP1_CS_AS" in the equal to operation.   */
```

We can correct it in the query with the COLLATE clause. We can use a specific collation on one side of the expression, or the easy to remember DATABASE_DEFAULT.

```
SELECT COUNT(*) FROM Product p
            INNER JOIN AdventureWorks2012.Production.Product aw12
            ON p.Name = aw12.Name COLLATE DATABASE_DEFAULT;
-- 504
```

Restoring the original column collation.

```
ALTER TABLE Product alter column ProductName varchar(40)
            COLLATE SQL_Latin1_General_CP1_CI_AS null;
```

Listing All Database & Server Collations

Database collations can be enumerated by a query, while there is special function for server collations. QUOTENAME() function forms proper object names.

```
USE AdventureWorks2012;
GO


SELECT CONCAT(QUOTENAME(s.name), '.', QUOTENAME(t.name),
              '.', QUOTENAME(c.name))                        AS ColumnName,
              c.collation_name                               AS Collation
FROM sys.schemas s
  INNER JOIN sys.tables t
    ON t.schema_id = s.schema_id
  INNER JOIN sys.columns c
    ON c.object_id = t.object_id
WHERE collation_name is not null
ORDER BY ColumnName;
-- (104 row(s) affected) - Partial results.
```

ColumnName	Collation
[HumanResources].[Employee].[NationalIDNumber]	SQL_Latin1_General_CP1_CI_AS
[HumanResources].[Shift].[Name]	SQL_Latin1_General_CP1_CI_AS
[Person].[Address].[AddressLine1]	SQL_Latin1_General_CP1_CI_AS
[Person].[Address].[AddressLine2]	SQL_Latin1_General_CP1_CI_AS

All server collations can be obtained from a table-valued system function.

```
use master;
select  name                                      AS Name,
        COLLATIONPROPERTY(name, 'CodePage')       AS CodePage,
        LEFT(description,80)                       AS Description
from sys.fn_HelpCollations() order by Name;
-- (3885 row(s) affected) - Partial results;
```

Name	CodePage	Description
Modern_Spanish_CS_AS_KS_WS	1252	Modern-Spanish, case-sensitive, accent-sensitive, kanatype-sensitive, width-sens
Modern_Spanish_CS_AS_WS	1252	Modern-Spanish, case-sensitive, accent-sensitive, kanatype-insensitive, width-se
Mohawk_100_BIN	1252	Mohawk-100, binary sort
Mohawk_100_BIN2	1252	Mohawk-100, binary code point comparison sort
Mohawk_100_CI_AI	1252	Mohawk-100, case-insensitive, accent-insensitive, kanatype-insensitive, width-in

CHAPTER 8: Advanced Database Architecture

Designing Table for Multi-Language Support with UNICODE

Let's script the DimProductSubcategory table from AdventureWorks2012 to demonstrate multi-language support. nvarchar data type is for UNICODE data with each character 2 bytes. It has sufficient capacity to hold even Chinese, Japanese and Korean letters among others.

```
CREATE TABLE dbo.DimProductSubcategory(
        ProductSubcategoryKey int IDENTITY(1,1) NOT NULL,
        ProductSubcategoryAlternateKey int NULL,
        EnglishProductSubcategoryName nvarchar(50) NOT NULL,
        SpanishProductSubcategoryName nvarchar(50) NOT NULL,
        FrenchProductSubcategoryName nvarchar(50) NOT NULL,
        ProductCategoryKey int NULL,
        CONSTRAINT PK_DimProductSubcategory_ProductSubcategoryKey
              PRIMARY KEY CLUSTERED (ProductSubcategoryKey ASC),
        CONSTRAINT AK_DimProductSubcategory_ProductSubcategoryAlternateKey
              UNIQUE NONCLUSTERED (ProductSubcategoryAlternateKey ASC ) );
```

Since there are no COLLATE clauses for the English, Spanish & French names, the collation is the database default. The DATABASEPROPERTYEX() function can be used to retrieve it.

```
SELECT DATABASEPROPERTYEX('AdventureWorksDW2012', 'Collation');
-- SQL_Latin1_General_CP1_CI_AS
```

To get a Spanish language sort, we have to add the COLLATE clause to the ORDER BY clause.

```
SELECT * FROM DimProductSubcategory
ORDER BY SpanishProductSubcategoryName COLLATE Modern_Spanish_CI_AS_WS;
-- (37 row(s) affected) - Partial results.
```

ProductSubcateg oryKey	ProductSubcategoryAlte rnateKey	EnglishProductSubcateg oryName	SpanishProductSubcateg oryName	FrenchProductSubcateg oryName	ProductCatego ryKey
4	4	Handlebars	Barra	Barre d'appui	2
2	2	Road Bikes	Bicicleta de carretera	Vélo de route	1
1	1	Mountain Bikes	Bicicleta de montaña	VTT	1
3	3	Touring Bikes	Bicicleta de paseo	Vélo de randonnée	1
8	8	Cranksets	Bielas	Pédalier	2
36	36	Pumps	Bomba	Pompe	4

Find all collations for a culture.

```
SELECT name, description = LEFT(description, 60) FROM   sys.fn_HelpCollations()
WHERE  name LIKE '%german%'  ORDER BY name;  -- (52 row(s) affected)
```

CHAPTER 8: Advanced Database Architecture

CHAPTER 9: Exporting & Importing Data

Saving a T-SQL Script as .sql File

Any T-SQL script can be saved as .sql file. One easy way is saving from Management Studio Query Editor. Here is the script we will save.

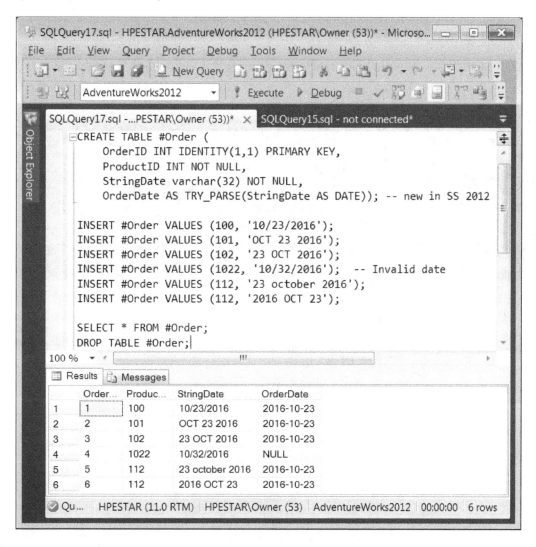

Click on File, click on Save .. As, choose a path and enter the file name for the script.

To load it back: click on File, click on Open File, locate file in Open File dialog pop-up.

Executing a .sql Script File Using SQLCMD

The SQLCMD command line utility can be used to execute a .sql script file typically with the -i (input) and -o (output) options. **Note: with any of the Command Prompt utilities the command line should not be broken with carriage return or line feed (CR/LF), it has to be one long line.**

SQLCMD -S"HPESTAR" -Uyourlogin -Psecret007 -i "f:\data\sql\tryparsedemo.sql" -o"f:\data\result\tryparsedemo.txt"

"HPESTAR" is the name of the SQL Server. With Windows authentication:

SQLCMD -S"HPESTAR" -i "f:\data\sql\tryparsedemo.sql" -o"f:\data\result\tryparsedemo.txt"

```
Command Prompt

Microsoft Windows [Version 6.1.7601]
Copyright (c) 2009 Microsoft Corporation.  All rights reserved.

C:\Users\Owner>SQLCMD -S"HPESTAR"  -i "f:\data\sql\tryparsedemo.sql" -o"f:\data\
result\tryparsedemo.txt"

C:\Users\Owner>_
```

The output file collects warnings, messages, errors and results.

```
tryparsedemo - Notepad
File  Edit  Format  View  Help
(1 rows affected)

(1 rows affected)

(1 rows affected)

(1 rows affected)

(1 rows affected)

(1 rows affected)
OrderID  ProductID  StringDate          OrderDate
-------  ---------  ------------------  ----------------
      1        100  10/23/2016          2016-10-23
      2        101  OCT 23 2016         2016-10-23
      3        102  23 OCT 2016         2016-10-23
      4       1022  10/32/2016          NULL
      5        112  23 october 2016     2016-10-23
      6        112  2016 OCT 23         2016-10-23

(6 rows affected)
```

Making a T-SQL Script Rerunnable

It takes special attention to make a T-SQL script re-executable as many times as desired. A CREATE VIEW script can only be executed once.

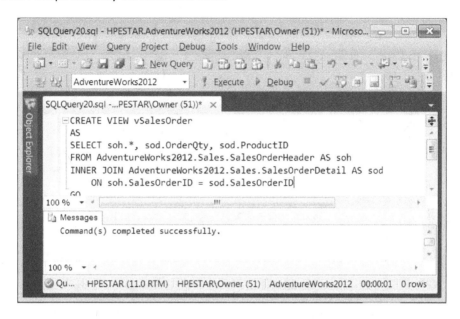

Repeat execution gives an error.

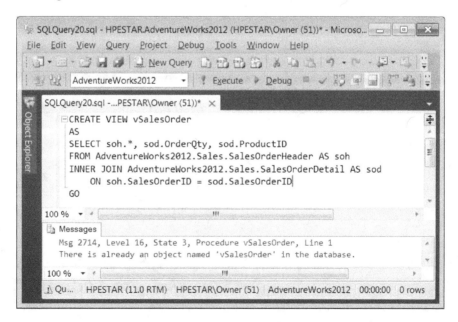

IF...ELSE Conditional Way to Make a Script Rerunnable

IF...ELSE is frequently the solution to prepare a rerunnable script. In this instance, first we check if the view exists. If it doesn't exist, we just go ahead and create it. If indeed it exists, we drop it first, then create it again.

bcp Usage for Exporting & Importing Data

bcp (Bulk Copy Program) is a command line utility for moving data. The Production.Product table is exported to a flat file with bcp using Windows authentication.

For SQL Server authentication, add the "-Uyourlogin -Pyourpasswrd" parameters. **Note: the command must be one long line without breaks.**

```
Command Prompt                                                    _  □  ✕

Microsoft Windows [Version 6.1.7601]
Copyright (c) 2009 Microsoft Corporation.  All rights reserved.

C:\Users\Owner>bcp AdventureWorks2012.Production.Product out F:\data\export\prod
uctz.txt -w -T -S"HPESTAR"

Starting copy...
SQLState = S1000, NativeError = 0
Error = [Microsoft][SQL Server Native Client 11.0]Warning: BCP import with a for
mat file will convert empty strings in delimited columns to NULL.

504 rows copied.
Network packet size (bytes): 4096
Clock Time (ms.) Total     : 125     Average : (4032.00 rows per sec.)

C:\Users\Owner>
```

The **results of a query execution** can be exported with bcp as well using the queryout option. Rule is the same, no carriage return or line feed in the command no matter how long is it. The command can be edited in SSMS Query Editor and pasted into Command Prompt with Right Mouse Click Paste. CTRL-V does not work.

```
Command Prompt                                                    _  □  ✕

C:\Users\Owner>bcp "SELECT × from AdventureWorks2012.HumanResources.Department"
queryout F:\data\export\departmentz.txt -w -T -S"HPESTAR"

Starting copy...

16 rows copied.
Network packet size (bytes): 4096
Clock Time (ms.) Total     : 453     Average : (35.32 rows per sec.)

C:\Users\Owner>
```

CHAPTER 9: Exporting & Importing Data

Importing Data with the bcp Utility

Importing is very similar to exporting. For better control though it is necessary to use a format file. First we create an empty table for the data.

```
use tempdb;
select  TOP 0 * into product1 from AdventureWorks2012.Production.Product;
go
```

We are ready to execute the bcp import command.

Checking the results.

Exporting Data with SQL Server Import and Export Wizard

We will export a view query results to a new Excel worksheet. The SELECT query returns 8,914 rows from the vPersonDemographics view.

Starting the SSIS Import and Export Wizard

We start the SSIS Import/Export Wizard by a Right Click on the database in Object Explorer. It does not matter much if we choose Import Data or Export data since it only presets the destination or source pages respectively.

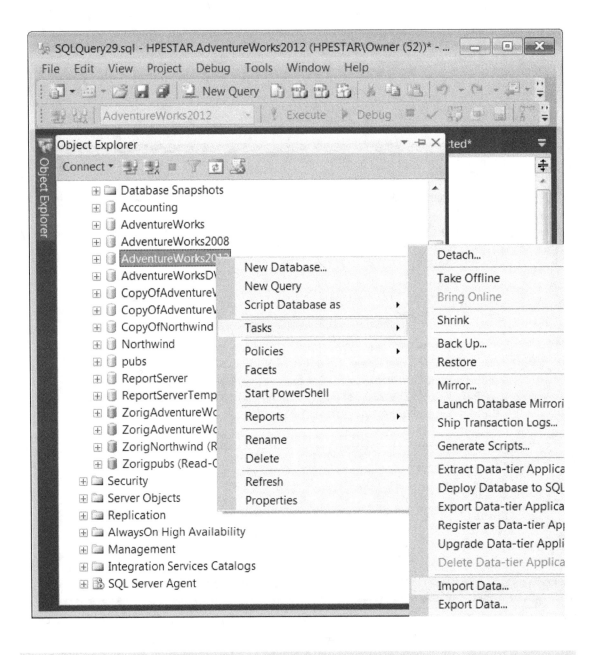

Optional Wizard Starting Welcome Screen

There is a checkmark option on the bottom to turn it off.

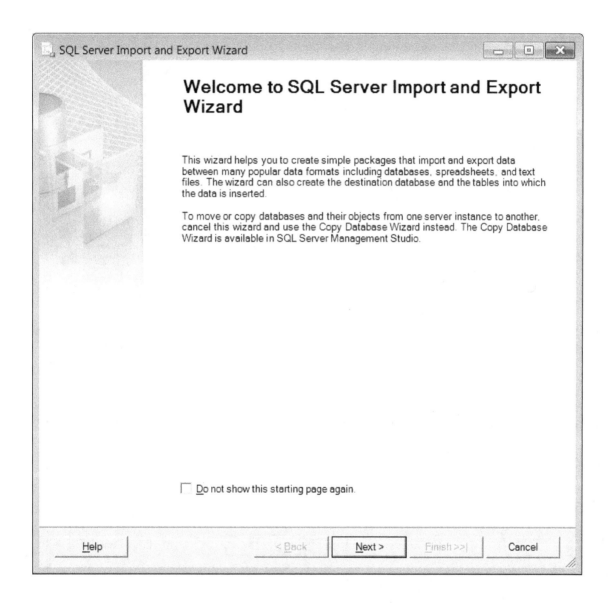

Configuring the Data Source Page

The data source is a database, therefore the server and database must be set up on this page.

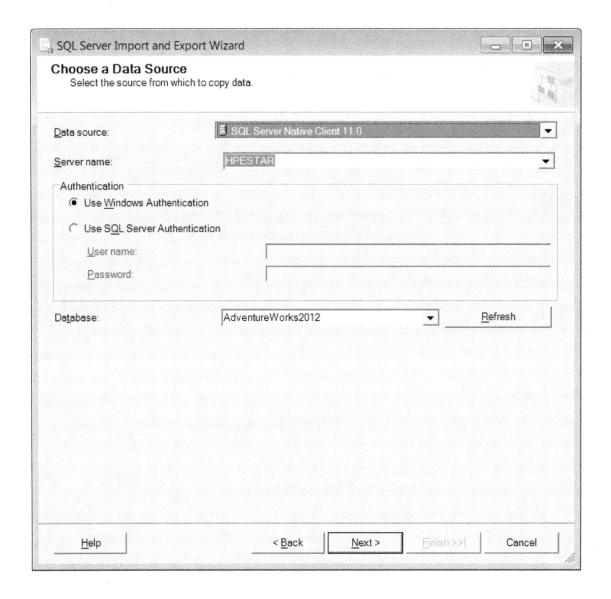

Configuring the Destination Page
The destination is a new Excel worksheet. Path & name must be given.

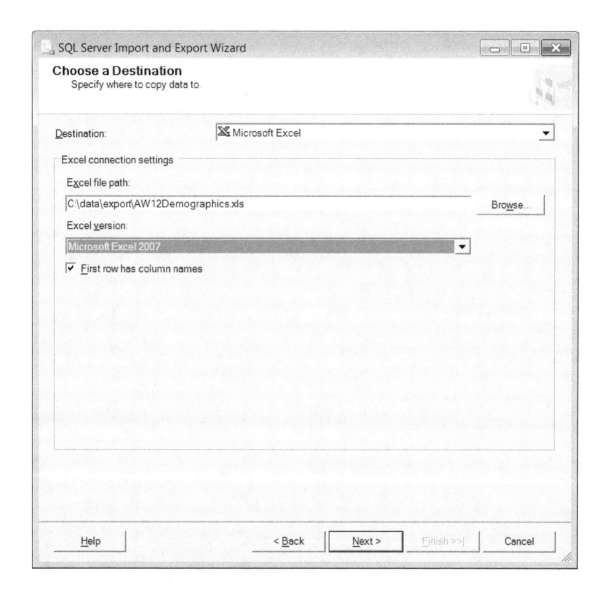

Specifying Table/View or Query Source

The Wizard logic branches based on what radio button we choose. If the choose table/view source, the next dialog box offers the entire list of tables/views in the database for checkmark selection.

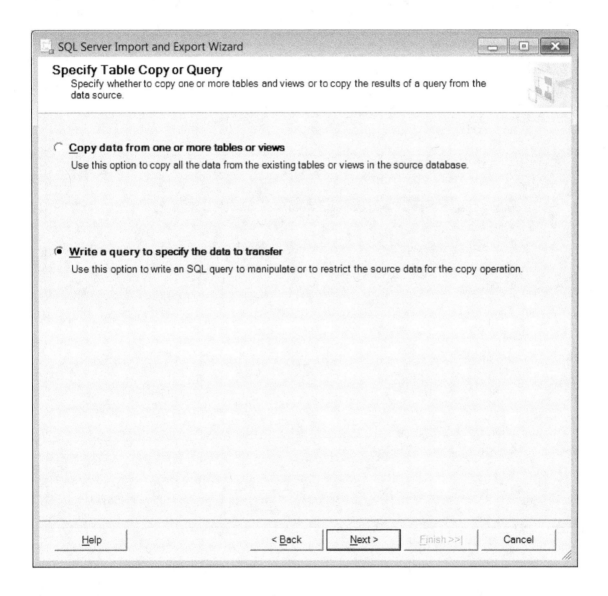

Entering the Query Source

We should use a tested query in order to avoid a failure in the execution of the generated SSIS package. Parse option is available for syntax checking.

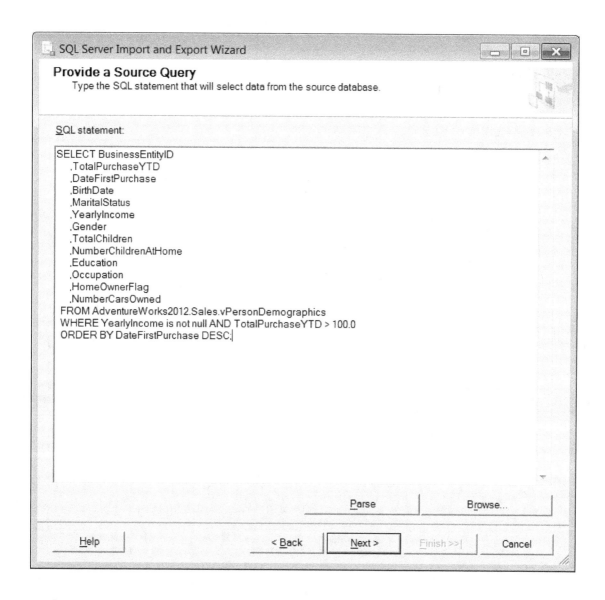

Option to Edit Mappings & Review Data

If you trust the Wizard, you can just click "Next". Otherwise, you can edit column mappings and review the data.

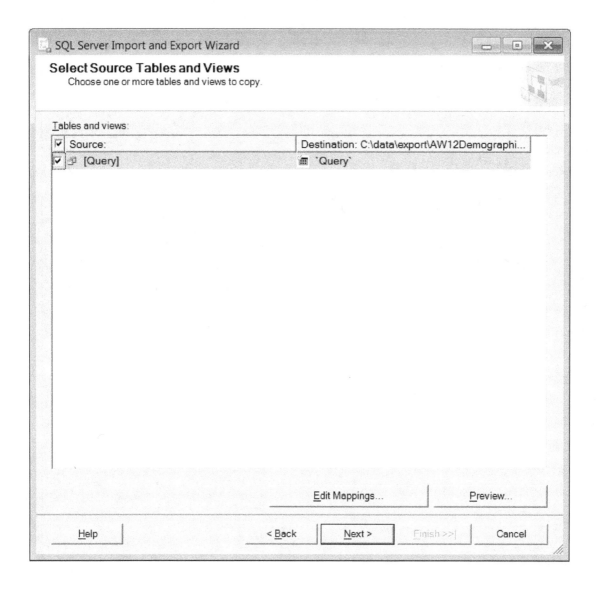

Edit Mappings & Preview

The next Wizard screen offers popup windows for editing the column mappings, changing the CREATE TABLE SQL and preview the data. We don't perform any change.

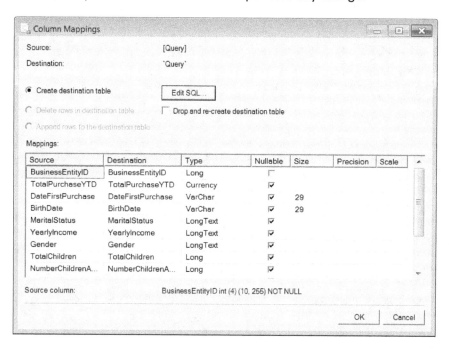

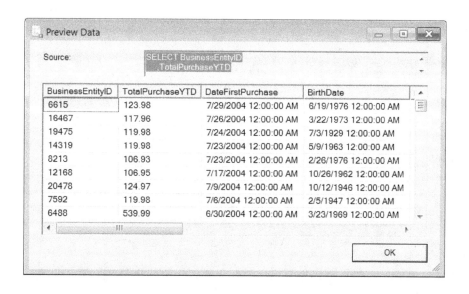

Review Data Type Mappings

Column data mappings can be reviewed in detail on this dialog box.

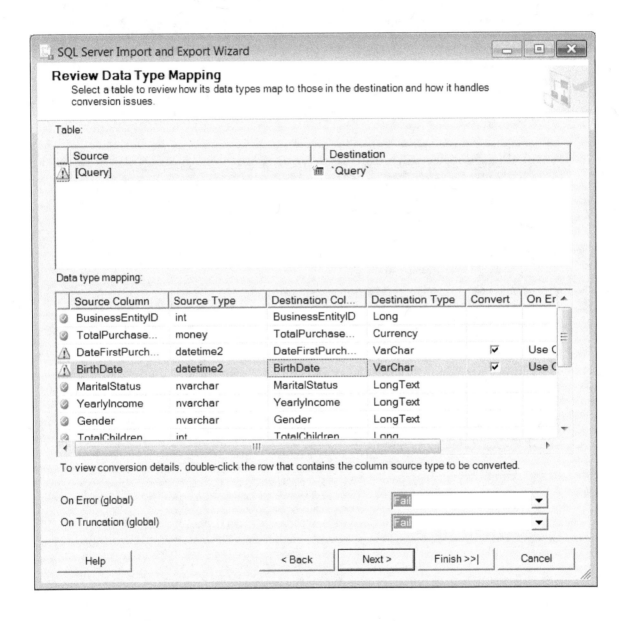

Save and/or Run Package

The Wizard generated SSIS package can be saved for future use or enhancements. If we run it immediately without saving, it will just go away after execution.

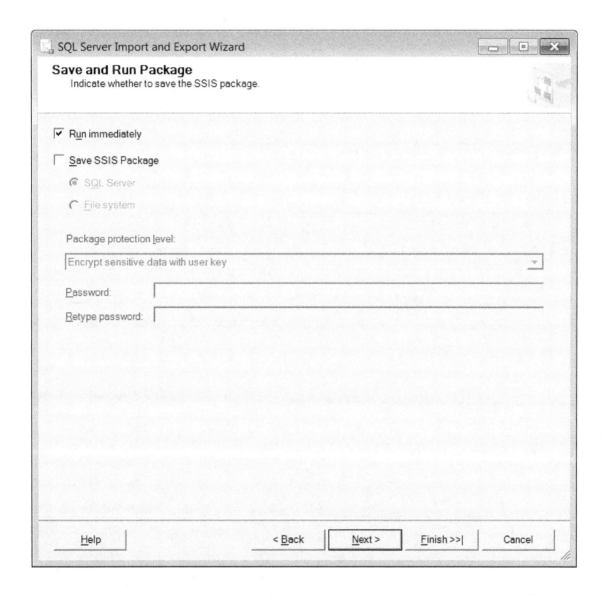

Verification Screen before Execution

At this point we still can go back and make changes should it be necessary. Once we click on Finish and we did not checkmark Save, the package will execute and goes away on success or failure.

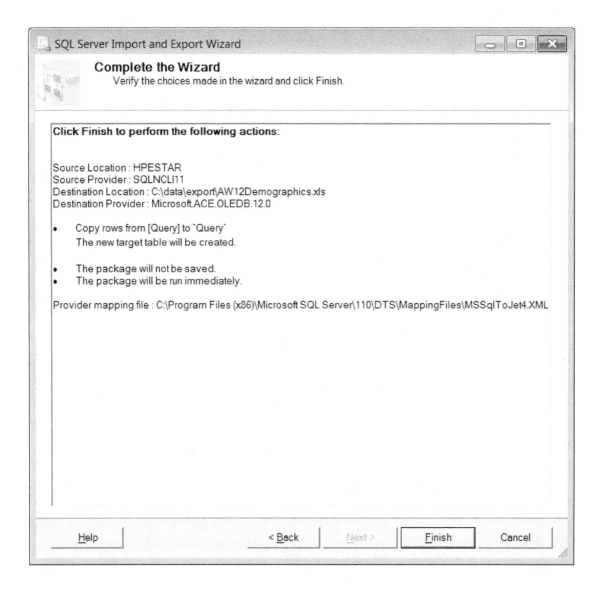

Execution Results Screen

If there are errors in the execution of the package, they will show in this window. The current Wizard generated SSIS package executed successfully.

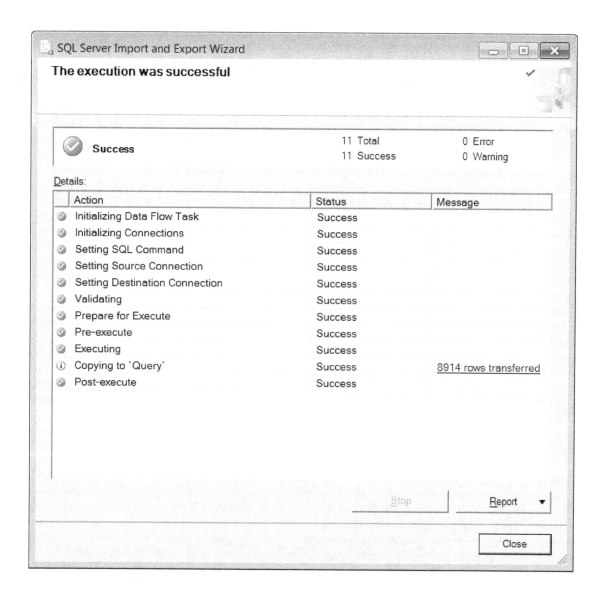

Checking Results in Excel

If the double click on the destination filename, the transferred data is displayed by Excel.

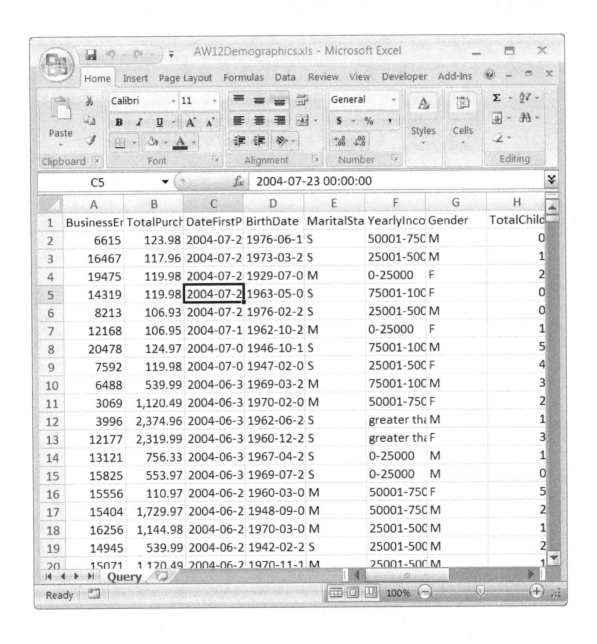

Importing Data with SQL Server Import and Export Wizard

Importing with the Wizard is very similar to the exporting process. We are going to import the just created AW12Demographics.xls Excel worksheet into a new database table. We start the Wizard the same as for export. First we configure the source as Excel worksheet.

Specify Data Source

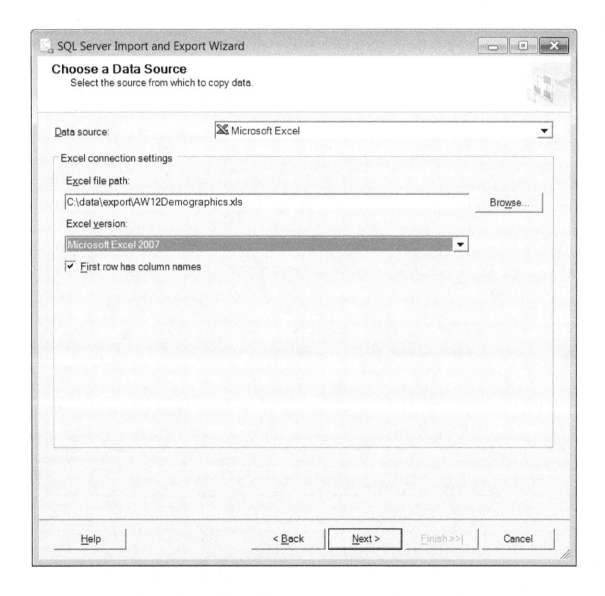

Specify Data Destination as Database

AdventureWorks2012 is the destination for the data movement.

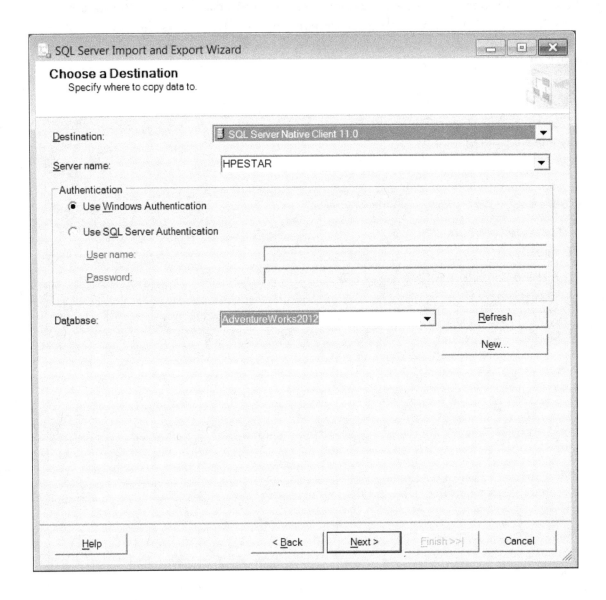

Excel Worksheet Source Is Considered a Table

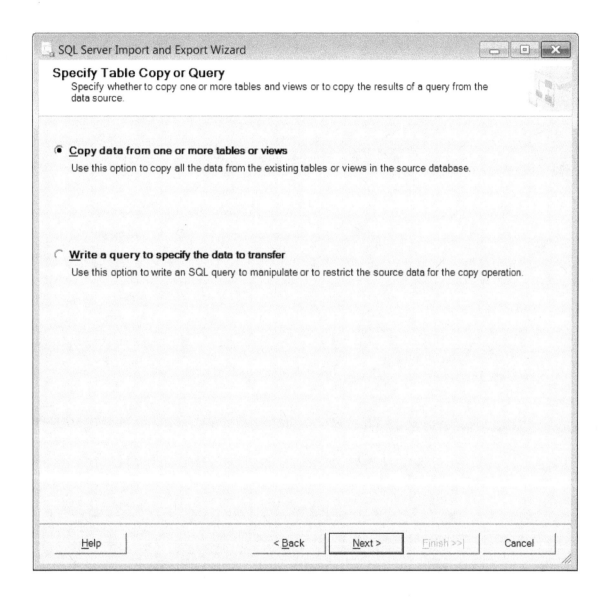

Select Excel Sheet and Assign Database Table Name

All the data is on the 'Query' sheet.

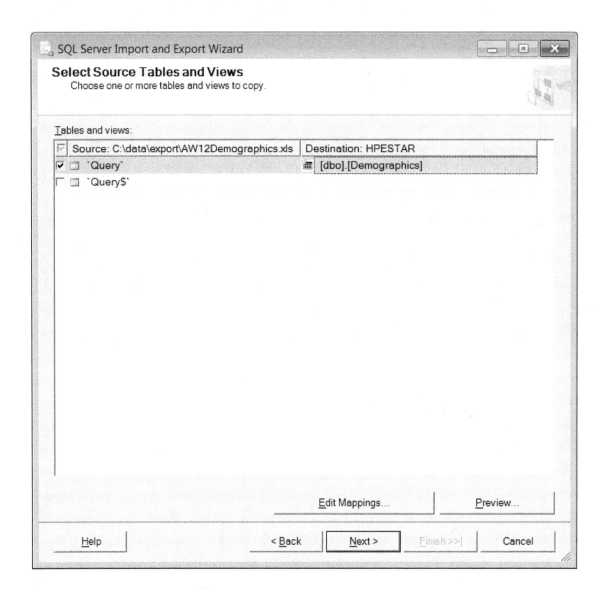

Column Mappings & CREATE TABLE Edit Panels

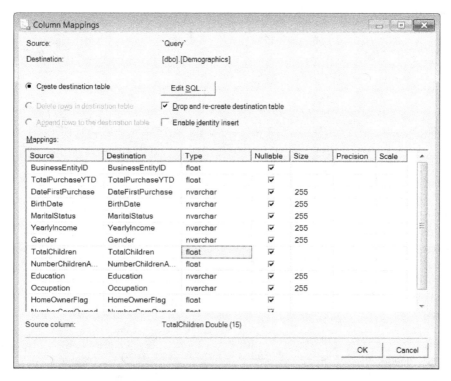

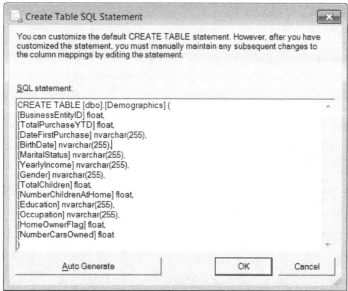

Source Data Inspection with Preview Data

This is a very important step. If the data does not look correct here, it will not be correct in the database table either.

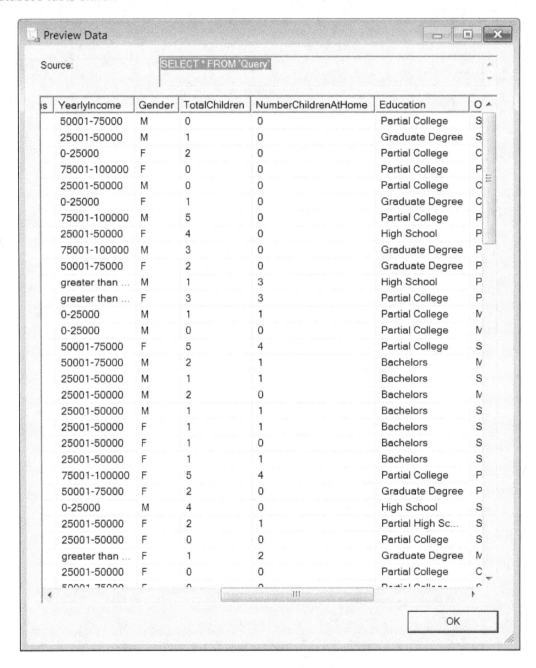

Indicate Saving and/or Run the SSIS Package

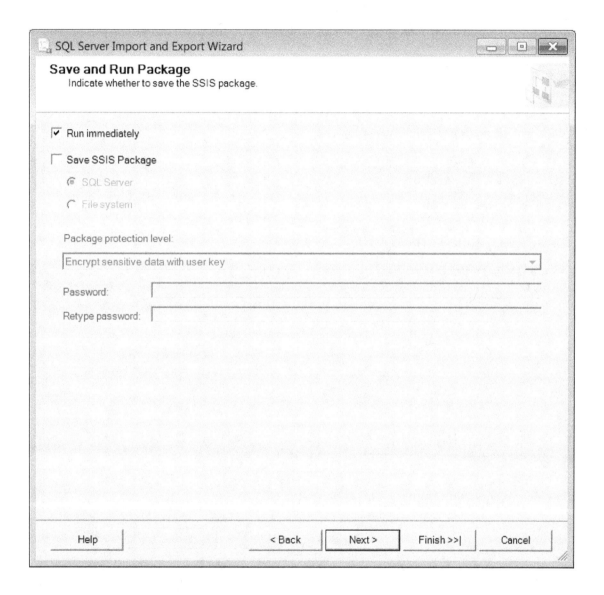

The Final Release Screen for Execution

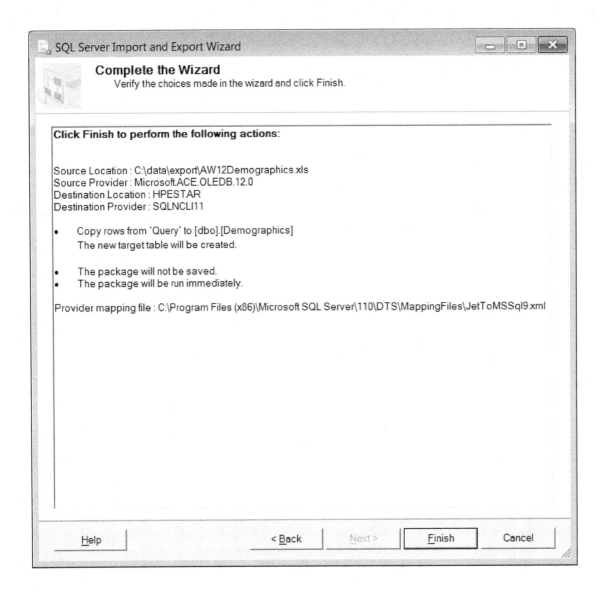

Successful Execution Screen

In case of errors, hyperlink to errors will display.

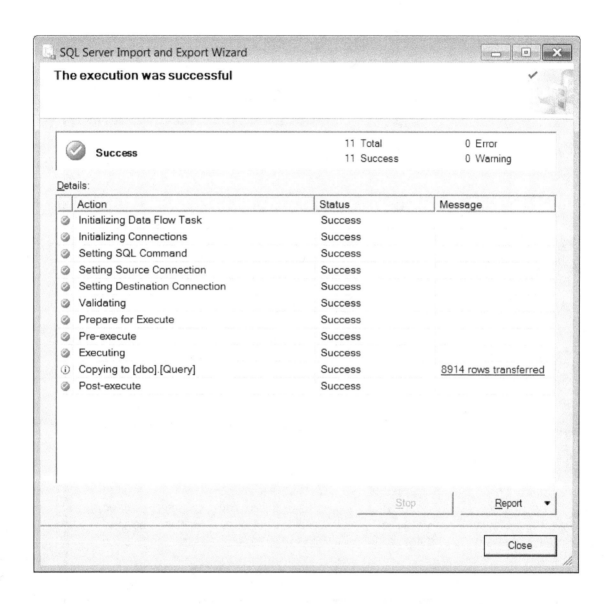

Check New Table in Database

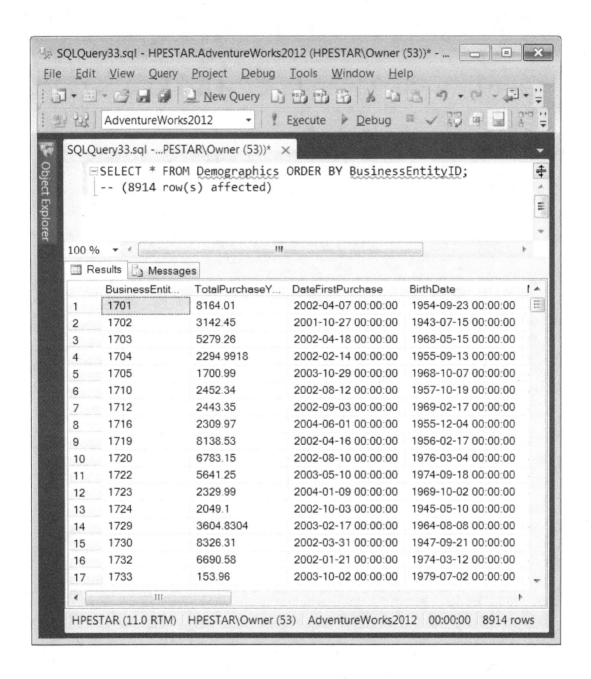

Exporting Database Table to Excel

The Wizard sequence is very similar to exporting query results. We shall export
Sales.SalesOrderHeader table.

Specify Destination

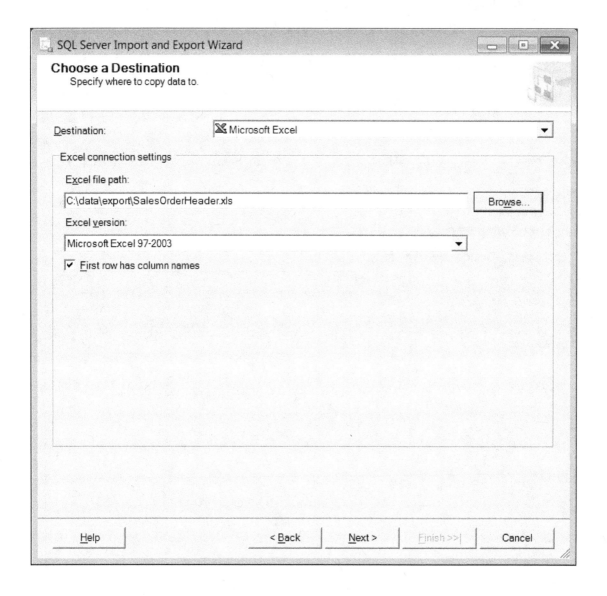

Choose Table Copy or Query

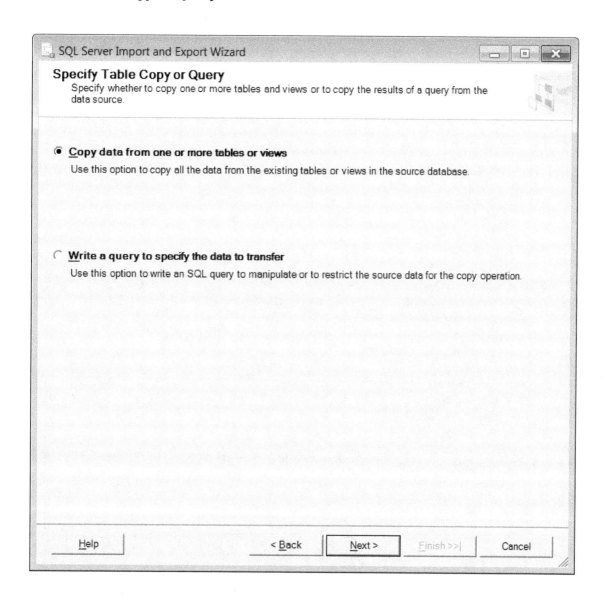

Checkmark Source Table

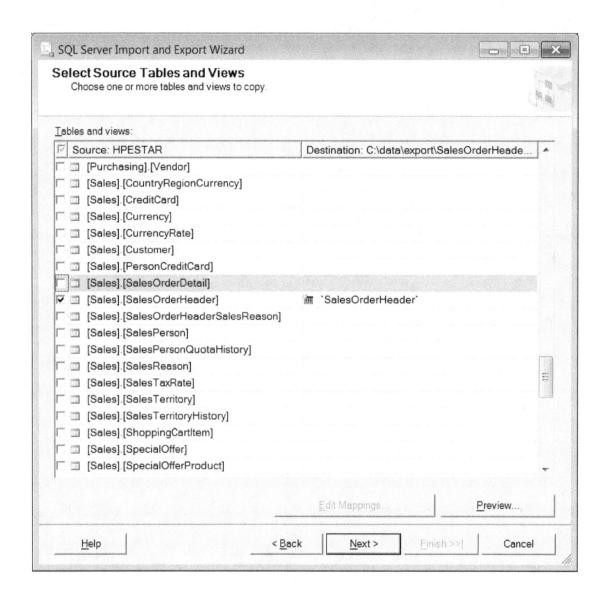

Check Data Type Mapping

Save and/or Run Package

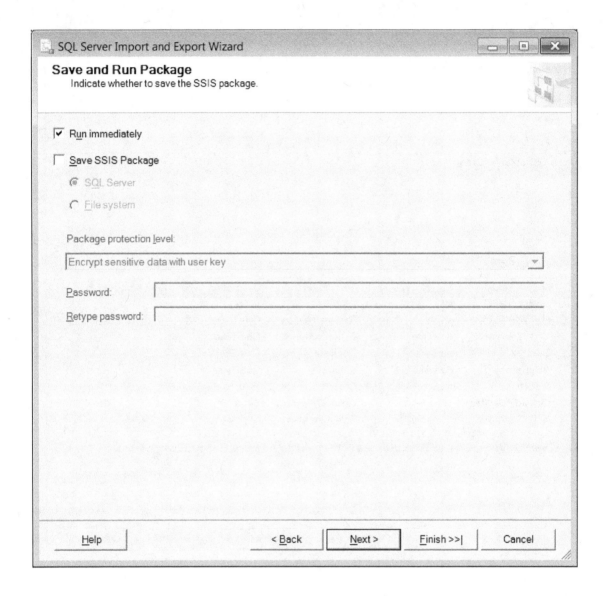

Complete the Wizard

Successful Execution Screen

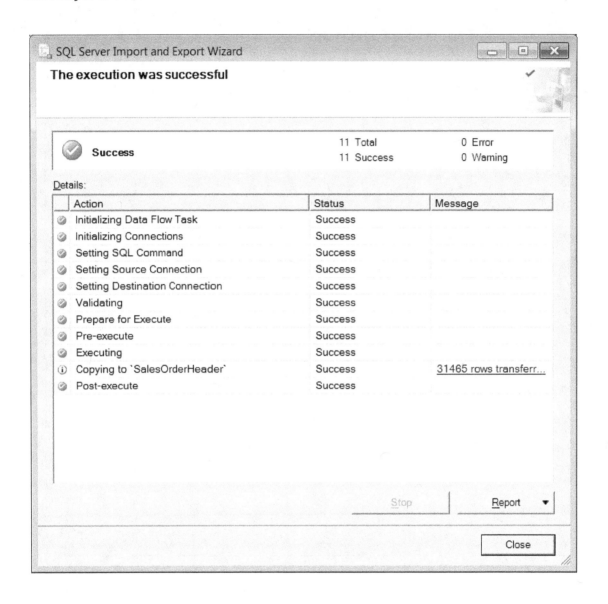

Check File in Folder and Data in Excel

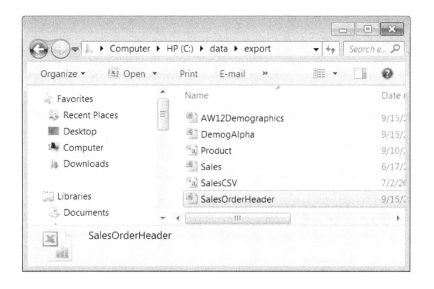

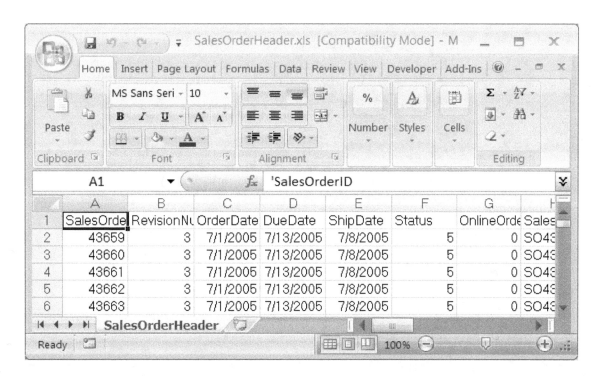

Command Prompt Commands List by HELP

Command Prompt commands can be used for data transport as well including COPY & XCOPY. We can get the entire command list by typing the "HELP" command. It is like a time machine back to the programming style of 1960-s.

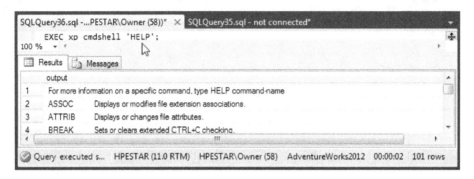

Command List

ASSOC	Displays or modifies file extension associations.
ATTRIB	Displays or changes file attributes.
BREAK	Sets or clears extended CTRL+C checking.
BCDEDIT	Sets properties in boot database to control boot loading.
CACLS	Displays or modifies access control lists (ACLs) of files.
CALL	Calls one batch program from another.
CD	Displays the name of or changes the current directory.
CHCP	Displays or sets the active code page number.
CHDIR	Displays the name of or changes the current directory.
CHKDSK	Checks a disk and displays a status report.
CHKNTFS	Displays or modifies the checking of disk at boot time.
CLS	Clears the screen.
CMD	Starts a new instance of the Windows command interpreter.
COLOR	Sets the default console foreground and background colors.
COMP	Compares the contents of two files or sets of files.
COMPACT	Displays or alters the compression of files on NTFS partitions.
CONVERT	Converts FAT volumes to NTFS. You cannot convert the current drive.
COPY	Copies one or more files to another location.
DATE	Displays or sets the date.
DEL	Deletes one or more files.
DIR	Displays a list of files and subdirectories in a directory.
DISKCOMP	Compares the contents of two floppy disks.
DISKCOPY	Copies the contents of one floppy disk to another.
DISKPART	Displays or configures Disk Partition properties.
DOSKEY	Edits command lines, recalls Windows commands, and creates macros.
DRIVERQUERY	Displays current device driver status and properties.
ECHO	Displays messages, or turns command echoing on or off.
ENDLOCAL	Ends localization of environment changes in a batch file.
ERASE	Deletes one or more files.
EXIT	Quits the CMD.EXE program (command interpreter).
FC	Compares two files or sets of files, and displays the differences between them.
FIND	Searches for a text string in a file or files.

FINDSTR	Searches for strings in files.
FOR	Runs a specified command for each file in a set of files.
FORMAT	Formats a disk for use with Windows.
FSUTIL	Displays or configures the file system properties.
FTYPE	Displays or modifies file types used in file extension associations.
GOTO	Directs the Windows command interpreter to a labeled line in a batch program.
GPRESULT	Displays Group Policy information for machine or user.
GRAFTABL	Enables Windows to display an extended character set in graphics mode.
HELP	Provides Help information for Windows commands.
ICACLS	Display, modify, backup, or restore ACLs for files and directories.
IF	Performs conditional processing in batch programs.
LABEL	Creates, changes, or deletes the volume label of a disk.
MD	Creates a directory.
MKDIR	Creates a directory.
MKLINK	Creates Symbolic Links and Hard Links
MODE	Configures a system device.
MORE	Displays output one screen at a time.
MOVE	Moves one or more files from one directory to another directory.
OPENFILES	Displays files opened by remote users for a file share.
PATH	Displays or sets a search path for executable files.
PAUSE	Suspends processing of a batch file and displays a message.
POPD	Restores the previous value of the current directory saved by PUSHD.
PRINT	Prints a text file.
PROMPT	Changes the Windows command prompt.
PUSHD	Saves the current directory then changes it.
RD	Removes a directory.
RECOVER	Recovers readable information from a bad or defective disk.
REM	Records comments (remarks) in batch files or CONFIG.SYS.
REN	Renames a file or files.
RENAME	Renames a file or files.
REPLACE	Replaces files.
RMDIR	Removes a directory.
ROBOCOPY	Advanced utility to copy files and directory trees
SET	Displays, sets, or removes Windows environment variables.
SETLOCAL	Begins localization of environment changes in a batch file.
SC	Displays or configures services (background processes).
SCHTASKS	Schedules commands and programs to run on a computer.
SHIFT	Shifts the position of replaceable parameters in batch files.
SHUTDOWN	Allows proper local or remote shutdown of machine.
SORT	Sorts input.
START	Starts a separate window to run a specified program or command.
SUBST	Associates a path with a drive letter.
SYSTEMINFO	Displays machine specific properties and configuration.
TASKLIST	Displays all currently running tasks including services.
TASKKILL	Kill or stop a running process or application.
TIME	Displays or sets the system time.
TITLE	Sets the window title for a CMD.EXE session.
TREE	Graphically displays the directory structure of a drive or path.
TYPE	Displays the contents of a text file.
VER	Displays the Windows version.
VERIFY	Tells Windows whether to verify that your files are written correctly to a disk.
VOL	Displays a disk volume label and serial number.
XCOPY	Copies files and directory trees.
WMIC	Displays WMI information inside interactive command shell.

CHAPTER 9: Exporting & Importing Data

BULK INSERT Command

BULK INSERT is a T-SQL command which corresponds to bcp "in" action for uploading a file into a database table. The command includes an optional format file. Generally it is a good idea to use format file with BULK INSERT and bcp for more reliable and successful data transfer.

Format File Generation with bcp

Format file can be created manually by an editor or automatically by bcp. Execute at Command Prompt as one line with no breaks to create a non-XML format file:

```
bcp AdventureWorks2012.HumanResources.Department format nul -T -n -f
f:\data\bcpdemo\hrdept.fmt
```

The generated format file:

```
11.0
4
1    SQLSMALLINT    0    2     ""   1   DepartmentID        ""
2    SQLNCHAR       2    100   ""   2   Name                SQL_Latin1_General_CP1_CI_AS
3    SQLNCHAR       2    100   ""   3   GroupName           SQL_Latin1_General_CP1_CI_AS
4    SQLDATETIME    0    8     ""   4   ModifiedDate        ""
```

11.0 refers to SQL Server 2012 internal version number.

Export Data with bcp Format File Option

We use the format file for exporting the data at Command Prompt.

```
bcp AdventureWorks2012.HumanResources.Department out  f:\data\bcpdemo\hrdept.txt  -f
f:\data\bcpdemo\hrdept.fmt  -T
```

This is how the exported data looks in Notepad:

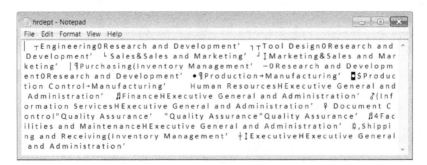

Import Data with BULK INSERT Format File Option

The same format file can be used to import the data into the database with BULK INSERT. First we create an empty table for the data import.

```
USE tempdb;
SELECT TOP(0)
        [DepartmentID] = CONVERT(INT, DepartmentID) --prevent IDENTITY inheritance
        ,[Name]
        ,[GroupName]
        ,[ModifiedDate]
INTO Department
FROM [AdventureWorks2012].[HumanResources].[Department];
GO
-- (0 row(s) affected)
```

```
BULK INSERT Department
        FROM 'f:\data\bcpdemo\hrdept.txt'
        WITH (FORMATFILE = 'f:\data\bcpdemo\hrdept.fmt');
GO
-- (16 row(s) affected)
```

```
SELECT TOP (3) * FROM Department ORDER BY NEWID();
GO
```

DepartmentID	Name	GroupName	ModifiedDate
14	Facilities and Maintenance	Executive General and Administration	2002-06-01 00:00:00.000
15	Shipping and Receiving	Inventory Management	2002-06-01 00:00:00.000
3	Sales	Sales and Marketing	2002-06-01 00:00:00.000

We can use the -n native mode for exporting data and DATAFILETYPE for importing.

```
bcp AdventureWorks2012.HumanResources.Shift out f:\temp\shift.txt -n -T
```

```
CREATE TABLE [Shift](
        [ShiftID] [tinyint]  NOT NULL,
        [Name] [dbo].[Name] NOT NULL,
        [StartTime] [time](7) NOT NULL,
        [EndTime] [time](7) NOT NULL,
        [ModifiedDate] [datetime] NOT NULL,
);
```

```
BULK INSERT Shift    FROM 'f:\temp\shift.txt'    WITH (DATAFILETYPE='native');
```

CHAPTER 9: Exporting & Importing Data

Importing & Exporting Images

Importing & exporting images and other binary large objects (BLOB) requires special techniques. We use OPENROWSET BULK method to import an image.

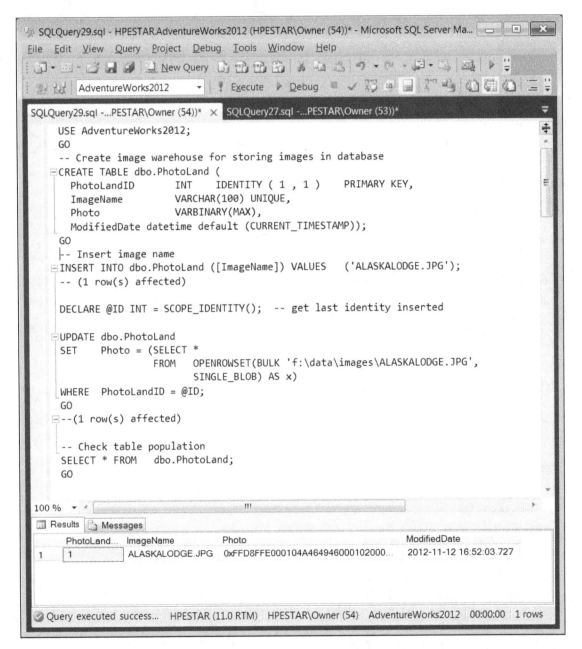

Exporting Image with bcp

The bcp command can be used to export an image. In the following demo, it is executed from xp_cmdshell. **NOTE: on most production servers the xp_cmdshell option is disabled due to security concerns.**

```
DECLARE  @Command NVARCHAR(4000);

-- Keep the command on ONE LINE - here it wraps around
SET @Command = 'bcp "SELECT Photo FROM AdventureWorks2012.dbo.PhotoLand WHERE
PhotoLandID=1"  queryout "F:\temp\ALASKALODGE.jpg" -T -n' ;

PRINT @Command -- debugging

EXEC xp_cmdshell   @Command;
GO
/*NULL
Starting copy...
NULL
1 rows copied.
Network packet size (bytes): 4096
Clock Time (ms.) Total    : 203   Average : (4.93 rows per sec.)
NULL */
```

Building a bcp Format File Interactively for Image Export

Exporting All Images from Table

The content of the previously created bcp format file.

```
11.0
1
1    SQLBINARY    0    0    ""  1    LargePhoto        ""
```

T-SQL script for exporting all images to the file system from Production.ProductPhoto table LargePhoto column.

```
USE AdventureWorks2012;
GO


DECLARE @Command  VARCHAR(4000), @PhotoID  INT,  @ImageFileName VARCHAR(128) ;
DECLARE PHOTOcursor CURSOR  FOR
        SELECT ProductPhotoID,  LargePhotoFileName FROM  Production.ProductPhoto
        WHERE  LargePhotoFileName != 'no_image_available_large.gif';


OPEN PHOTOcursor FETCH NEXT FROM PHOTOcursor INTO @PhotoID,  @ImageFileName;


WHILE (@@FETCH_STATUS = 0) -- Cursor loop
  BEGIN
-- No carriage return or new line in bcp command string!
   SET @Command = CONCAT('bcp "SELECT LargePhoto FROM
AdventureWorks2012.Production.ProductPhoto WHERE ProductPhotoID = ',
   convert(VARCHAR,@PhotoID) + '" queryout "f:\data\images\productphoto\',
   @ImageFileName,'" -T -f "f:\data\images\bcpimage.fmt" ');


   PRINT @Command -- debugging
   EXEC xp_cmdshell @Command, no_output;


   FETCH NEXT FROM PHOTOcursor  INTO @PhotoID,    @ImageFileName;
  END; -- cursor loop


CLOSE PHOTOcursor; DEALLOCATE PHOTOcursor;
GO
```

Product Photo Icons in the ProductPhoto Folder
The folder contains 100 exported product photos. The photos cannot be visualized in SSMS. but in the file system or SSRS reports. The following is a partial list of image icons.

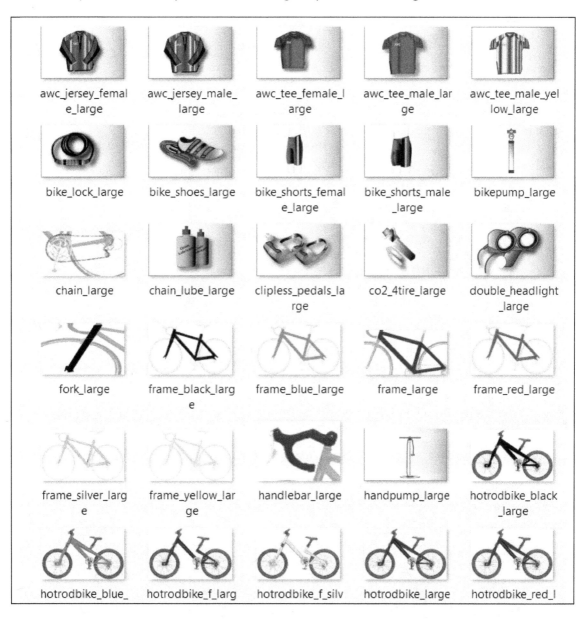

In SSIS the Export Column & Import Column Transformations can be used for exporting and importing a set of images to and from folders.

CHAPTER 9: Exporting & Importing Data

Importing Data into hierarchyid

Data can be imported into a hierarchyid tree table two ways:

- ➢ Using string representation of hierarchyid values instead of hex
- ➢ Using hierarchyid system functions

Both methods of importing data into an orgchart (tree) table demonstrated.

```
CREATE TABLE dbo.Employee
(   ID INT IDENTITY(1,1) PRIMARY KEY,       Position hierarchyid UNIQUE,
    LastName varchar(30) NOT NULL,          FirstName varchar(30) NOT NULL,
    Title varchar(70) NOT NULL,             CreatedDate date default (CURRENT_TIMESTAMP)  );
```

```
-- Applying string representation of hierarchyid
INSERT INTO dbo.Employee(Position, FirstName, LastName, Title)    VALUES
        (hierarchyid::Parse( '/'), 'Charles', 'Lancaster', 'CEO'),
        (hierarchyid::Parse( '/1/'), 'Bill', 'Origo', 'Production Vice President'),
        (hierarchyid::Parse( '/1/1/'), 'Linda', 'Smith', 'Production Manager'),
        (hierarchyid::Parse( '/2/'), 'Michael', 'Ditto','Finance Vice President'),
        (hierarchyid::Parse( '/2/1/'), 'LeBlanc', 'O''Brien', 'Finance Manager'),
        (hierarchyid::Parse( '/2/1/1/'), 'Dan', 'Brutto', 'Finance Assistant'),
        (hierarchyid::Parse( '/1/1/1/'), 'Ronny', 'Dinno', 'Production Clerk');
```

```
-- Altenate way of inserting a node with hierarchyid system functions
DECLARE @boss hierarchyid, @empid hierarchyid, @prevempid hierarchyid;
SELECT @boss = Position FROM Employee WHERE LastName='Smith' AND FirstName='Linda';
SELECT @prevempid = Position FROM Employee WHERE LastName='Dinno' AND
        FirstName='Ronny';
SET @empid = @Boss.GetDescendant(@prevempid, null);
SELECT @boss, @empid;  -- 0x5AC0          0x5ADA
INSERT INTO Employee(Position, LastName, FirstName, Title)
VALUES (@empid, 'Desserone', 'Sue', 'Production Supervisor');
```

```
-- Verify structure
SELECT ID, Position.ToString() AS StringHierarchy, Position,  FirstName, LastName, Title, CreatedDate
FROM dbo.Employee ORDER BY Position;
```

ID	StringHierarchy	Position	FirstName	LastName	Title	CreatedDate
1	/	0x	Charles	Lancaster	CEO	2018-05-07
2	/1/	0x58	Bill	Origo	Production Vice President	2018-05-07
3	/1/1/	0x5AC0	Linda	Smith	Production Manager	2018-05-07
7	/1/1/1/	0x5AD6	Ronny	Dinno	Production Clerk	2018-05-07
8	/1/1/2/	0x5ADA	Sue	Desserone	Production Supervisor	2018-05-07
4	/2/	0x68	Michael	Ditto	Finance Vice President	2018-05-07
5	/2/1/	0x6AC0	LeBlanc	O'Brien	Finance Manager	2018-05-07
6	/2/1/1/	0x6AD6	Dan	Brutto	Finance Assistant	2018-05-07

CHAPTER 10: Enterprise Information Security

Principals, Securables and Permissions

Principals
Principals, individual or collection, can request SQL Server resources.

Windows-level principals
- ➤ Windows domain login
- ➤ Windows local login
- ➤ Windows group (collection)

SQL Server-level principals
- ➤ SQL Server login
- ➤ SQL Server login mapped to a Windows login
- ➤ SQL Server login mapped to a Windows group
- ➤ SQL Server login mapped to a certificate e.g. ##MS_SQLResourceSigningCertificate##
- ➤ SQL Server login mapped to an asymmetric key
- ➤ Server role (collection, not mapped)
- ➤ sa login (not mapped)

Database-level principals
- ➤ Database user   (mapped to SQL login)
- ➤ Database user mapped to a Windows login
- ➤ Database user mapped to a Windows group
- ➤ Database user mapped to a certificate
- ➤ Database user mapped to an asymmetric key
- ➤ Database role (collection, not mapped)
- ➤ Application role (collection, not mapped)
- ➤ Public role (collection, not mapped)
- ➤ guest user (not mapped)
- ➤ INFORMATION_SCHEMA schema entity user (not mapped)
- ➤ sys schema entity user (not mapped)

SQL Server Built-in Permissions Hierarchy

The sys.fn_builtin_permissions system function returns a list of the built-in permissions hierarchy of SQL Server.

SELECT * FROM master.sys.fn_builtin_permissions(default)
ORDER BY class_desc, permission_name;   -- (214 row(s) affected)

class_desc	permission_name	type	covering_permission_name	parent_class_desc	parent_covering_permission_name
APPLICATION ROLE	ALTER	AL	CONTROL	DATABASE	ALTER ANY APPLICATION ROLE
APPLICATION ROLE	CONTROL	CL		DATABASE	CONTROL
APPLICATION ROLE	VIEW DEFINITION	VW	CONTROL	DATABASE	VIEW DEFINITION
ASSEMBLY	ALTER	AL	CONTROL	DATABASE	ALTER ANY ASSEMBLY
ASSEMBLY	CONTROL	CL		DATABASE	CONTROL
ASSEMBLY	REFERENCES	RF	CONTROL	DATABASE	REFERENCES
ASSEMBLY	TAKE OWNERSHIP	TO	CONTROL	DATABASE	CONTROL
ASSEMBLY	VIEW DEFINITION	VW	CONTROL	DATABASE	VIEW DEFINITION
ASYMMETRIC KEY	ALTER	AL	CONTROL	DATABASE	ALTER ANY ASYMMETRIC KEY
ASYMMETRIC KEY	CONTROL	CL		DATABASE	CONTROL
ASYMMETRIC KEY	REFERENCES	RF	CONTROL	DATABASE	REFERENCES
ASYMMETRIC KEY	TAKE OWNERSHIP	TO	CONTROL	DATABASE	CONTROL
ASYMMETRIC KEY	VIEW DEFINITION	VW	CONTROL	DATABASE	VIEW DEFINITION
AVAILABILITY GROUP	ALTER	AL	CONTROL	SERVER	ALTER ANY AVAILABILITY GROUP
AVAILABILITY GROUP	CONTROL	CL		SERVER	CONTROL SERVER
AVAILABILITY GROUP	TAKE OWNERSHIP	TO	CONTROL	SERVER	CONTROL SERVER
AVAILABILITY GROUP	VIEW DEFINITION	VW	CONTROL	SERVER	VIEW ANY DEFINITION
CERTIFICATE	ALTER	AL	CONTROL	DATABASE	ALTER ANY CERTIFICATE
CERTIFICATE	CONTROL	CL		DATABASE	CONTROL
CERTIFICATE	REFERENCES	RF	CONTROL	DATABASE	REFERENCES
CERTIFICATE	TAKE OWNERSHIP	TO	CONTROL	DATABASE	CONTROL
CERTIFICATE	VIEW DEFINITION	VW	CONTROL	DATABASE	VIEW DEFINITION
CONTRACT	ALTER	AL	CONTROL	DATABASE	ALTER ANY CONTRACT
CONTRACT	CONTROL	CL		DATABASE	CONTROL
CONTRACT	REFERENCES	RF	CONTROL	DATABASE	REFERENCES
CONTRACT	TAKE OWNERSHIP	TO	CONTROL	DATABASE	CONTROL
CONTRACT	VIEW DEFINITION	VW	CONTROL	DATABASE	VIEW DEFINITION
DATABASE	ALTER	AL	CONTROL	SERVER	ALTER ANY DATABASE
DATABASE	ALTER ANY APPLICATION ROLE	ALAR	ALTER	SERVER	CONTROL SERVER
DATABASE	ALTER ANY ASSEMBLY	ALAS	ALTER	SERVER	CONTROL SERVER
DATABASE	ALTER ANY ASYMMETRIC KEY	ALAK	ALTER	SERVER	CONTROL SERVER
DATABASE	ALTER ANY CERTIFICATE	ALCF	ALTER	SERVER	CONTROL SERVER
DATABASE	ALTER ANY CONTRACT	ALSC	ALTER	SERVER	CONTROL SERVER
DATABASE	ALTER ANY DATABASE AUDIT	ALDA	ALTER	SERVER	ALTER ANY SERVER AUDIT
DATABASE	ALTER ANY DATABASE DDL TRIGGER	ALTG	ALTER	SERVER	CONTROL SERVER
DATABASE	ALTER ANY DATABASE EVENT NOTIFICATION	ALED	ALTER	SERVER	ALTER ANY EVENT NOTIFICATION
DATABASE	ALTER ANY DATASPACE	ALDS	ALTER	SERVER	CONTROL SERVER
DATABASE	ALTER ANY FULLTEXT CATALOG	ALFT	ALTER	SERVER	CONTROL SERVER
DATABASE	ALTER ANY MESSAGE TYPE	ALMT	ALTER	SERVER	CONTROL SERVER
DATABASE	ALTER ANY REMOTE SERVICE BINDING	ALSB	ALTER	SERVER	CONTROL SERVER
DATABASE	ALTER ANY ROLE	ALRL	ALTER	SERVER	CONTROL SERVER
DATABASE	ALTER ANY ROUTE	ALRT	ALTER	SERVER	CONTROL SERVER
DATABASE	ALTER ANY SCHEMA	ALSM	ALTER	SERVER	CONTROL SERVER

DATABASE	ALTER ANY SERVICE	ALSV	ALTER	SERVER	CONTROL SERVER
DATABASE	ALTER ANY SYMMETRIC KEY	ALSK	ALTER	SERVER	CONTROL SERVER
DATABASE	ALTER ANY USER	ALUS	ALTER	SERVER	CONTROL SERVER
DATABASE	AUTHENTICATE	AUTH	CONTROL	SERVER	AUTHENTICATE SERVER
DATABASE	BACKUP DATABASE	BADB	CONTROL	SERVER	CONTROL SERVER
DATABASE	BACKUP LOG	BALO	CONTROL	SERVER	CONTROL SERVER
DATABASE	CHECKPOINT	CP	CONTROL	SERVER	CONTROL SERVER
DATABASE	CONNECT	CO	CONNECT REPLICATION	SERVER	CONTROL SERVER
DATABASE	CONNECT REPLICATION	CORP	CONTROL	SERVER	CONTROL SERVER
DATABASE	CONTROL	CL		SERVER	CONTROL SERVER
DATABASE	CREATE AGGREGATE	CRAG	ALTER	SERVER	CONTROL SERVER
DATABASE	CREATE ASSEMBLY	CRAS	ALTER ANY ASSEMBLY	SERVER	CONTROL SERVER
DATABASE	CREATE ASYMMETRIC KEY	CRAK	ALTER ANY ASYMMETRIC KEY	SERVER	CONTROL SERVER
DATABASE	CREATE CERTIFICATE	CRCF	ALTER ANY CERTIFICATE	SERVER	CONTROL SERVER
DATABASE	CREATE CONTRACT	CRSC	ALTER ANY CONTRACT	SERVER	CONTROL SERVER
DATABASE	CREATE DATABASE	CRDB		SERVER	CREATE ANY DATABASE
DATABASE	CREATE DATABASE DDL EVENT NOTIFICATION	CRED	ALTER ANY DATABASE EVENT NOTIFICATION	SERVER	CREATE DDL EVENT NOTIFICATION
DATABASE	CREATE DEFAULT	CRDF	ALTER	SERVER	CONTROL SERVER
DATABASE	CREATE FULLTEXT CATALOG	CRFT	ALTER ANY FULLTEXT CATALOG	SERVER	CONTROL SERVER
DATABASE	CREATE FUNCTION	CRFN	ALTER	SERVER	CONTROL SERVER
DATABASE	CREATE MESSAGE TYPE	CRMT	ALTER ANY MESSAGE TYPE	SERVER	CONTROL SERVER
DATABASE	CREATE PROCEDURE	CRPR	ALTER	SERVER	CONTROL SERVER
DATABASE	CREATE QUEUE	CRQU	ALTER	SERVER	CONTROL SERVER
DATABASE	CREATE REMOTE SERVICE BINDING	CRSB	ALTER ANY REMOTE SERVICE BINDING	SERVER	CONTROL SERVER
DATABASE	CREATE ROLE	CRRL	ALTER ANY ROLE	SERVER	CONTROL SERVER
DATABASE	CREATE ROUTE	CRRT	ALTER ANY ROUTE	SERVER	CONTROL SERVER
DATABASE	CREATE RULE	CRRU	ALTER	SERVER	CONTROL SERVER
DATABASE	CREATE SCHEMA	CRSM	ALTER ANY SCHEMA	SERVER	CONTROL SERVER
DATABASE	CREATE SERVICE	CRSV	ALTER ANY SERVICE	SERVER	CONTROL SERVER
DATABASE	CREATE SYMMETRIC KEY	CRSK	ALTER ANY SYMMETRIC KEY	SERVER	CONTROL SERVER
DATABASE	CREATE SYNONYM	CRSN	ALTER	SERVER	CONTROL SERVER
DATABASE	CREATE TABLE	CRTB	ALTER	SERVER	CONTROL SERVER
DATABASE	CREATE TYPE	CRTY	ALTER	SERVER	CONTROL SERVER
DATABASE	CREATE VIEW	CRVW	ALTER	SERVER	CONTROL SERVER
DATABASE	CREATE XML SCHEMA COLLECTION	CRXS	ALTER	SERVER	CONTROL SERVER
DATABASE	DELETE	DL	CONTROL	SERVER	CONTROL SERVER
DATABASE	EXECUTE	EX	CONTROL	SERVER	CONTROL SERVER
DATABASE	INSERT	IN	CONTROL	SERVER	CONTROL SERVER
DATABASE	REFERENCES	RF	CONTROL	SERVER	CONTROL SERVER
DATABASE	SELECT	SL	CONTROL	SERVER	CONTROL SERVER
DATABASE	SHOWPLAN	SPLN	CONTROL	SERVER	ALTER TRACE
DATABASE	SUBSCRIBE QUERY NOTIFICATIONS	SUQN	CONTROL	SERVER	CONTROL SERVER
DATABASE	TAKE OWNERSHIP	TO	CONTROL	SERVER	CONTROL SERVER
DATABASE	UPDATE	UP	CONTROL	SERVER	CONTROL SERVER
DATABASE	VIEW DATABASE STATE	VWDS	CONTROL	SERVER	VIEW SERVER STATE
DATABASE	VIEW DEFINITION	VW	CONTROL	SERVER	VIEW ANY DEFINITION
ENDPOINT	ALTER	AL	CONTROL	SERVER	ALTER ANY ENDPOINT
ENDPOINT	CONNECT	CO	CONTROL	SERVER	CONTROL SERVER
ENDPOINT	CONTROL	CL		SERVER	CONTROL SERVER
ENDPOINT	TAKE OWNERSHIP	TO	CONTROL	SERVER	CONTROL SERVER
ENDPOINT	VIEW DEFINITION	VW	CONTROL	SERVER	VIEW ANY DEFINITION
FULLTEXT CATALOG	ALTER	AL	CONTROL	DATABASE	ALTER ANY FULLTEXT CATALOG
FULLTEXT CATALOG	CONTROL	CL		DATABASE	CONTROL
FULLTEXT CATALOG	REFERENCES	RF	CONTROL	DATABASE	REFERENCES
FULLTEXT CATALOG	TAKE OWNERSHIP	TO	CONTROL	DATABASE	CONTROL
FULLTEXT CATALOG	VIEW DEFINITION	VW	CONTROL	DATABASE	VIEW DEFINITION
FULLTEXT STOPLIST	ALTER	AL	CONTROL	DATABASE	ALTER ANY FULLTEXT CATALOG

CHAPTER 10: Enterprise Information Security

FULLTEXT STOPLIST	CONTROL	CL		DATABASE	CONTROL
FULLTEXT STOPLIST	REFERENCES	RF	CONTROL	DATABASE	REFERENCES
FULLTEXT STOPLIST	TAKE OWNERSHIP	TO	CONTROL	DATABASE	CONTROL
FULLTEXT STOPLIST	VIEW DEFINITION	VW	CONTROL	DATABASE	VIEW DEFINITION
LOGIN	ALTER	AL	CONTROL	SERVER	ALTER ANY LOGIN
LOGIN	CONTROL	CL		SERVER	CONTROL SERVER
LOGIN	IMPERSONATE	IM	CONTROL	SERVER	CONTROL SERVER
LOGIN	VIEW DEFINITION	VW	CONTROL	SERVER	VIEW ANY DEFINITION
MESSAGE TYPE	ALTER	AL	CONTROL	DATABASE	ALTER ANY MESSAGE TYPE
MESSAGE TYPE	CONTROL	CL		DATABASE	CONTROL
MESSAGE TYPE	REFERENCES	RF	CONTROL	DATABASE	REFERENCES
MESSAGE TYPE	TAKE OWNERSHIP	TO	CONTROL	DATABASE	CONTROL
MESSAGE TYPE	VIEW DEFINITION	VW	CONTROL	DATABASE	VIEW DEFINITION
OBJECT	ALTER	AL	CONTROL	SCHEMA	ALTER
OBJECT	CONTROL	CL		SCHEMA	CONTROL
OBJECT	DELETE	DL	CONTROL	SCHEMA	DELETE
OBJECT	EXECUTE	EX	CONTROL	SCHEMA	EXECUTE
OBJECT	INSERT	IN	CONTROL	SCHEMA	INSERT
OBJECT	RECEIVE	RC	CONTROL	SCHEMA	CONTROL
OBJECT	REFERENCES	RF	CONTROL	SCHEMA	REFERENCES
OBJECT	SELECT	SL	RECEIVE	SCHEMA	SELECT
OBJECT	TAKE OWNERSHIP	TO	CONTROL	SCHEMA	CONTROL
OBJECT	UPDATE	UP	CONTROL	SCHEMA	UPDATE
OBJECT	VIEW CHANGE TRACKING	VWCT	CONTROL	SCHEMA	VIEW CHANGE TRACKING
OBJECT	VIEW DEFINITION	VW	CONTROL	SCHEMA	VIEW DEFINITION
REMOTE SERVICE BINDING	ALTER	AL	CONTROL	DATABASE	ALTER ANY REMOTE SERVICE BINDING
REMOTE SERVICE BINDING	CONTROL	CL		DATABASE	CONTROL
REMOTE SERVICE BINDING	TAKE OWNERSHIP	TO	CONTROL	DATABASE	CONTROL
REMOTE SERVICE BINDING	VIEW DEFINITION	VW	CONTROL	DATABASE	VIEW DEFINITION
ROLE	ALTER	AL	CONTROL	DATABASE	ALTER ANY ROLE
ROLE	CONTROL	CL		DATABASE	CONTROL
ROLE	TAKE OWNERSHIP	TO	CONTROL	DATABASE	CONTROL
ROLE	VIEW DEFINITION	VW	CONTROL	DATABASE	VIEW DEFINITION
ROUTE	ALTER	AL	CONTROL	DATABASE	ALTER ANY ROUTE
ROUTE	CONTROL	CL		DATABASE	CONTROL
ROUTE	TAKE OWNERSHIP	TO	CONTROL	DATABASE	CONTROL
ROUTE	VIEW DEFINITION	VW	CONTROL	DATABASE	VIEW DEFINITION
SCHEMA	ALTER	AL	CONTROL	DATABASE	ALTER ANY SCHEMA
SCHEMA	CONTROL	CL		DATABASE	CONTROL
SCHEMA	CREATE SEQUENCE	CRSO	ALTER	DATABASE	CONTROL
SCHEMA	DELETE	DL	CONTROL	DATABASE	DELETE
SCHEMA	EXECUTE	EX	CONTROL	DATABASE	EXECUTE
SCHEMA	INSERT	IN	CONTROL	DATABASE	INSERT
SCHEMA	REFERENCES	RF	CONTROL	DATABASE	REFERENCES
SCHEMA	SELECT	SL	CONTROL	DATABASE	SELECT
SCHEMA	TAKE OWNERSHIP	TO	CONTROL	DATABASE	CONTROL
SCHEMA	UPDATE	UP	CONTROL	DATABASE	UPDATE
SCHEMA	VIEW CHANGE TRACKING	VWCT	CONTROL	DATABASE	CONTROL
SCHEMA	VIEW DEFINITION	VW	CONTROL	DATABASE	VIEW DEFINITION
SEARCH PROPERTY LIST	ALTER	AL	CONTROL	DATABASE	ALTER ANY FULLTEXT CATALOG
SEARCH PROPERTY LIST	CONTROL	CL		DATABASE	CONTROL
SEARCH PROPERTY LIST	REFERENCES	RF	CONTROL	DATABASE	REFERENCES
SEARCH PROPERTY LIST	TAKE OWNERSHIP	TO	CONTROL	DATABASE	CONTROL
SEARCH PROPERTY LIST	VIEW DEFINITION	VW	CONTROL	DATABASE	VIEW DEFINITION
SERVER	ADMINISTER BULK OPERATIONS	ADBO	CONTROL SERVER		
SERVER	ALTER ANY AVAILABILITY GROUP	ALAG	CONTROL SERVER		
SERVER	ALTER ANY CONNECTION	ALCO	CONTROL SERVER		
SERVER	ALTER ANY CREDENTIAL	ALCD	CONTROL SERVER		
SERVER	ALTER ANY DATABASE	ALDB	CONTROL SERVER		
SERVER	ALTER ANY ENDPOINT	ALHE	CONTROL SERVER		
SERVER	ALTER ANY EVENT	ALES	CONTROL SERVER		

	NOTIFICATION				
SERVER	ALTER ANY EVENT SESSION	AAES	CONTROL SERVER		
SERVER	ALTER ANY LINKED SERVER	ALLS	CONTROL SERVER		
SERVER	ALTER ANY LOGIN	ALLG	CONTROL SERVER		
SERVER	ALTER ANY SERVER AUDIT	ALAA	CONTROL SERVER		
SERVER	ALTER ANY SERVER ROLE	ALSR	CONTROL SERVER		
SERVER	ALTER RESOURCES	ALRS	CONTROL SERVER		
SERVER	ALTER SERVER STATE	ALSS	CONTROL SERVER		
SERVER	ALTER SETTINGS	ALST	CONTROL SERVER		
SERVER	ALTER TRACE	ALTR	CONTROL SERVER		
SERVER	AUTHENTICATE SERVER	AUTH	CONTROL SERVER		
SERVER	CONNECT SQL	COSQ	CONTROL SERVER		
SERVER	CONTROL SERVER	CL			
SERVER	CREATE ANY DATABASE	CRDB	ALTER ANY DATABASE		
SERVER	CREATE AVAILABILITY GROUP	CRAC	ALTER ANY AVAILABILITY GROUP		
SERVER	CREATE DDL EVENT NOTIFICATION	CRDE	ALTER ANY EVENT NOTIFICATION		
SERVER	CREATE ENDPOINT	CRHE	ALTER ANY ENDPOINT		
SERVER	CREATE SERVER ROLE	CRSR	ALTER ANY SERVER ROLE		
SERVER	CREATE TRACE EVENT NOTIFICATION	CRTE	ALTER ANY EVENT NOTIFICATION		
SERVER	EXTERNAL ACCESS ASSEMBLY	XA	UNSAFE ASSEMBLY		
SERVER	SHUTDOWN	SHDN	CONTROL SERVER		
SERVER	UNSAFE ASSEMBLY	XU	CONTROL SERVER		
SERVER	VIEW ANY DATABASE	VWDB	VIEW ANY DEFINITION		
SERVER	VIEW ANY DEFINITION	VWAD	CONTROL SERVER		
SERVER	VIEW SERVER STATE	VWSS	ALTER SERVER STATE		
SERVER ROLE	ALTER	AL	CONTROL	SERVER	ALTER ANY SERVER ROLE
SERVER ROLE	CONTROL	CL		SERVER	CONTROL SERVER
SERVER ROLE	TAKE OWNERSHIP	TO	CONTROL	SERVER	CONTROL SERVER
SERVER ROLE	VIEW DEFINITION	VW	CONTROL	SERVER	VIEW ANY DEFINITION
SERVICE	ALTER	AL	CONTROL	DATABASE	ALTER ANY SERVICE
SERVICE	CONTROL	CL		DATABASE	CONTROL
SERVICE	SEND	SN	CONTROL	DATABASE	CONTROL
SERVICE	TAKE OWNERSHIP	TO	CONTROL	DATABASE	CONTROL
SERVICE	VIEW DEFINITION	VW	CONTROL	DATABASE	VIEW DEFINITION
SYMMETRIC KEY	ALTER	AL	CONTROL	DATABASE	ALTER ANY SYMMETRIC KEY
SYMMETRIC KEY	CONTROL	CL		DATABASE	CONTROL
SYMMETRIC KEY	REFERENCES	RF	CONTROL	DATABASE	REFERENCES
SYMMETRIC KEY	TAKE OWNERSHIP	TO	CONTROL	DATABASE	CONTROL
SYMMETRIC KEY	VIEW DEFINITION	VW	CONTROL	DATABASE	VIEW DEFINITION
TYPE	CONTROL	CL		SCHEMA	CONTROL
TYPE	EXECUTE	EX	CONTROL	SCHEMA	EXECUTE
TYPE	REFERENCES	RF	CONTROL	SCHEMA	REFERENCES
TYPE	TAKE OWNERSHIP	TO	CONTROL	SCHEMA	CONTROL
TYPE	VIEW DEFINITION	VW	CONTROL	SCHEMA	VIEW DEFINITION
USER	ALTER	AL	CONTROL	DATABASE	ALTER ANY USER
USER	CONTROL	CL		DATABASE	CONTROL
USER	IMPERSONATE	IM	CONTROL	DATABASE	CONTROL
USER	VIEW DEFINITION	VW	CONTROL	DATABASE	VIEW DEFINITION
XML SCHEMA COLLECTION	ALTER	AL	CONTROL	SCHEMA	ALTER
XML SCHEMA COLLECTION	CONTROL	CL		SCHEMA	CONTROL
XML SCHEMA COLLECTION	EXECUTE	EX	CONTROL	SCHEMA	EXECUTE
XML SCHEMA COLLECTION	REFERENCES	RF	CONTROL	SCHEMA	REFERENCES
XML SCHEMA COLLECTION	TAKE OWNERSHIP	TO	CONTROL	SCHEMA	CONTROL
XML SCHEMA COLLECTION	VIEW DEFINITION	VW	CONTROL	SCHEMA	VIEW DEFINITION

USER & CURRENT USER Functions

"WHO AM I" login/user information can be obtained via USER system functions. Here is the list of available functions for that purpose.

Command	Output
SELECT USER;	dbo
SELECT CURRENT_USER;	dbo
SELECT USER_NAME();	dbo
SELECT USER_ID();	1
SELECT DATABASE_PRINCIPAL_ID();	1
SELECT SYSTEM_USER;	HPESTAR\Owner
SELECT SUSER_NAME();	HPESTAR\Owner
SELECT SUSER_SNAME();	HPESTAR\Owner
SELECT ORIGINAL_LOGIN();	HPESTAR\Owner
SELECT SUSER_ID();	259
SELECT USER_SID();	0x0105000000000000051500000083A66141640B5ED2C6FD4509E9030000
SELECT SUSER_SID();	0x0105000000000000051500000083A66141640B5ED2C6FD4509E9030000

If the right click and choose Properties Window in Query Editor, we get connection information.

Database Schemas

Schemas are containters of database objects.

CREATE Script of Sales Schema

USE [AdventureWorks2012]

/****** Object: Schema [Sales]   Script Date: 6/27/2016 3:22:12 PM ******/
CREATE SCHEMA [Sales]

CHAPTER 10: Enterprise Information Security

Object Explorer Schema Properties

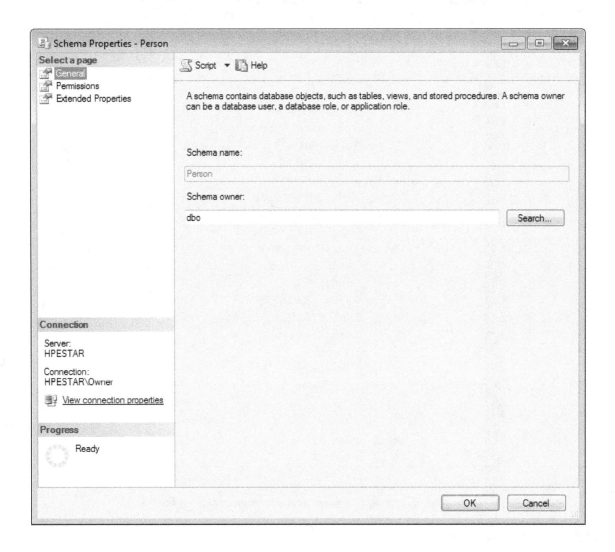

Schema Properties Permissions Page

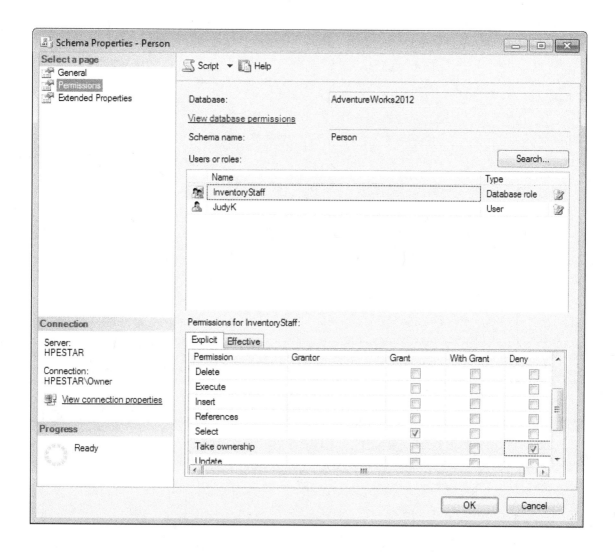

View Database Permissions Page

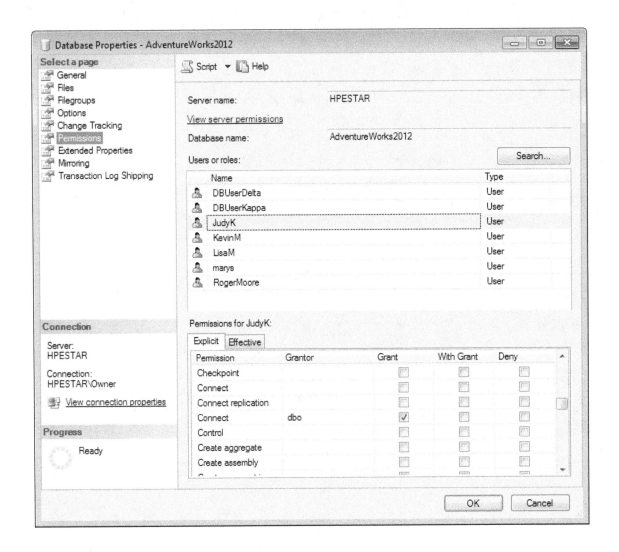

View Server Permissions Page

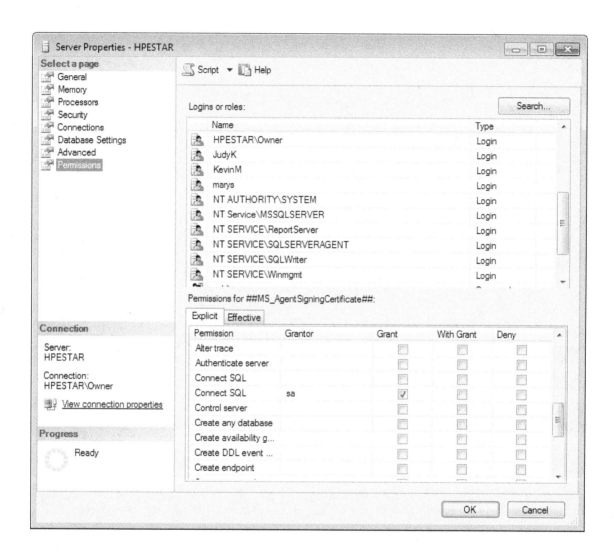

Extended Properties (Data Dictionary) Page

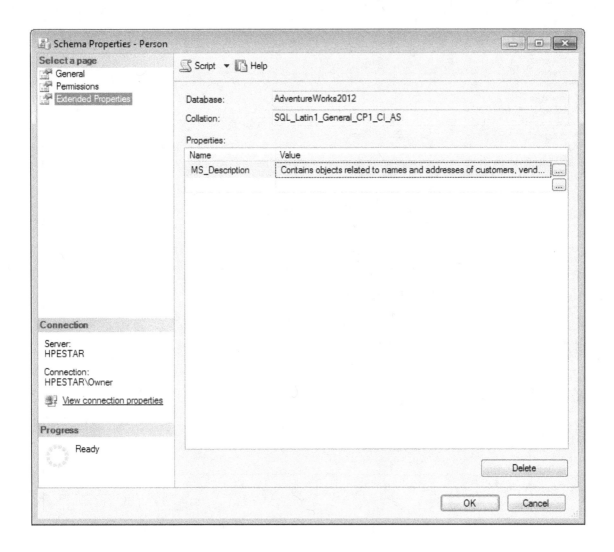

CREATE LOGIN & CREATE USER Statements

Login is a server-level security object. User is a database-level security object.

USE master;

CREATE LOGIN UserKappa WITH password = '007Password';

You can use one or multiple databases of your choice to make the server login a database user.

USE AdventureWorks2012;
CREATE USER DBUserKappa FOR LOGIN UserKappa;
GO

Find out WHO AM I as a login and a user?

SELECT SYSTEM_USER;   -- HPESTAR\Owner

SELECT CURRENT_USER;   -- dbo

I logged into SSMS as HPESTAR\Owner which is dbo (database owner) in AdventureWorks2012.

We can switch login context with the EXECUTE AS command.

EXECUTE AS LOGIN = 'UserKappa';   -- Command(s) completed successfully.

SELECT SYSTEM_USER;   -- UserKappa

SELECT CURRENT_USER;   -- DBUserKappa

Because the user has no permissions in the db, no rows are returned.

SELECT * FROM sys.objects;   -- (0 row(s) affected)

Return to original login context with the REVERT command.

REVERT;

SELECT SYSTEM_USER;   -- HPESTAR\Owner
SELECT CURRENT_USER;   -- dbo

SELECT * FROM sys.objects;   -- (622 row(s) affected)

CHAPTER 10: Enterprise Information Security

Create User from a Certificate

User can be created mapped to a certificate instead of a server login. CREATE MASTER KEY only once for the database

```
/*
CREATE MASTER KEY ENCRYPTION BY PASSWORD = '007EnglishSpy';
-- Command(s) completed successfully.
*/
```

```
CREATE CERTIFICATE InventoryLondon001
   WITH SUBJECT = 'London Warehouse Managers',
   EXPIRY_DATE = '03/31/2016';
GO -- Command(s) completed successfully.
```

```
CREATE USER LisaM FOR CERTIFICATE InventoryLondon001;
-- Command(s) completed successfully.
```

```
EXEC sp_helpuser LisaM;
```

UserName	RoleName	LoginName	DefDBName	DefSchemaName	UserID	SID
LisaM	public	NULL	NULL	NULL	13	0x0106000000000000901000000D30F312388D5BD7F8C1FC76CA88B143F592A85B5

MSDN Article: **Securing SQL Server**   http://bit.ly/16yIiWp
http://msdn.microsoft.com/en-us/library/bb283235(v=sql.105).aspx

Security tab in Object Explorer.

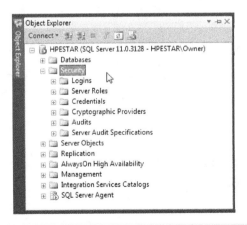

Login Properties in Object Explorer

Login Properties General Screen

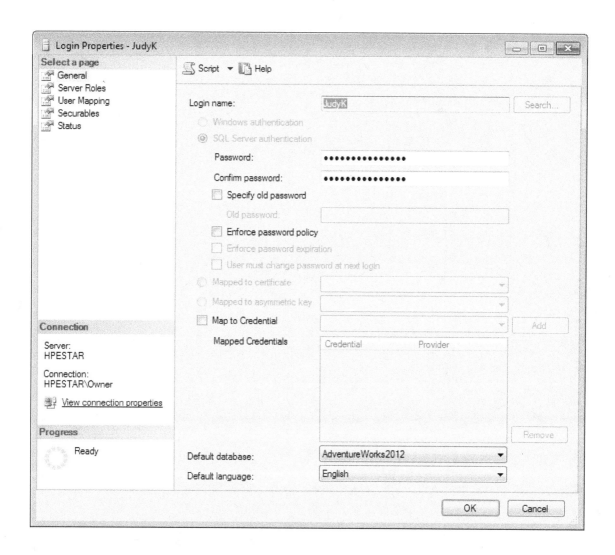

Login Properties Server Roles Page

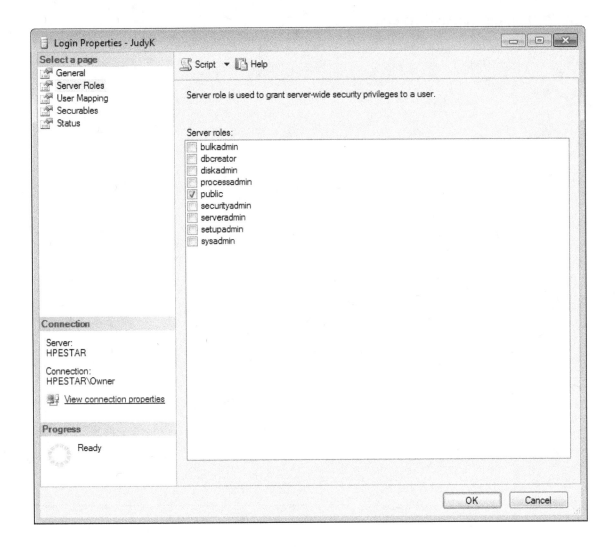

Login Properties Users Mapping Dialog Box

Login mapped as database user.

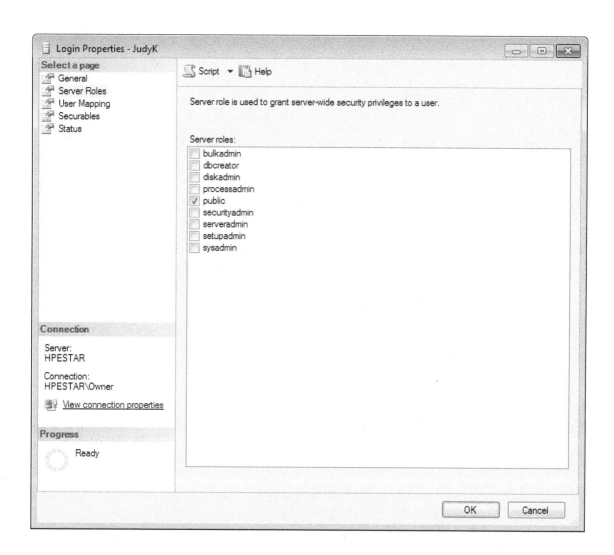

Login Properties Securables Page

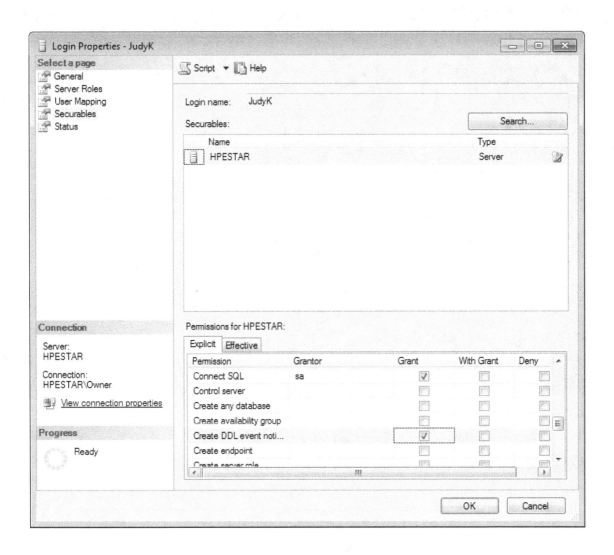

Login Properties Status Page

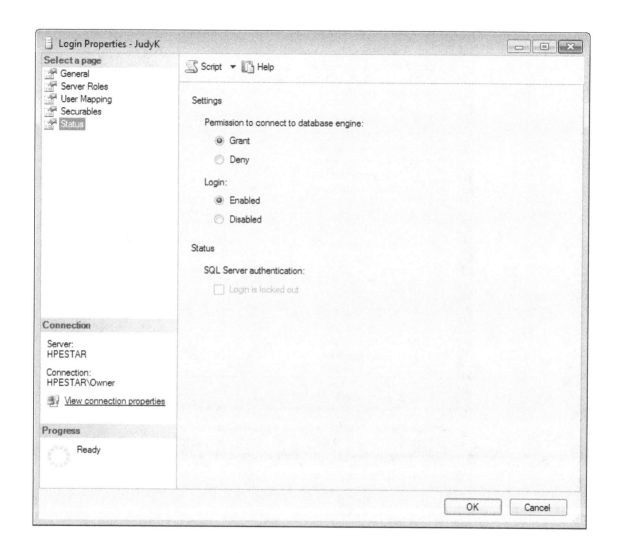

The Database Security & Users Tab

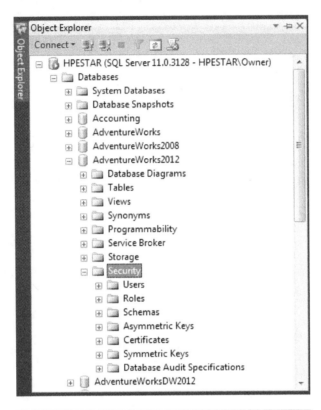

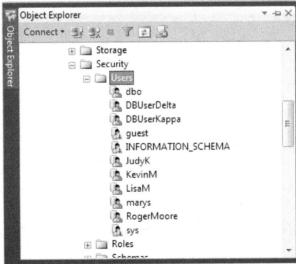

Server Roles & Database Roles

Instead of permissioning server logins and database users, we permission server roles and database roles. Server logins can belong to multiple server roles and database users can belong to multiple database roles.

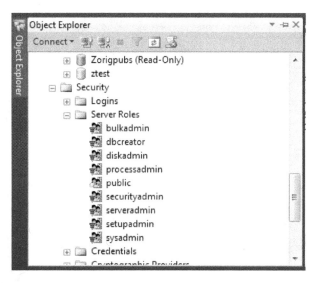

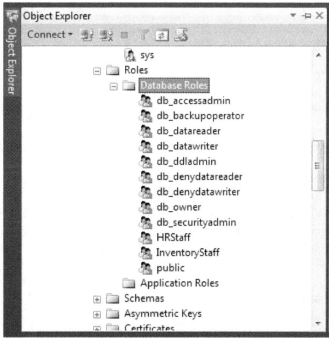

Scripting Server Login from Object Explorer

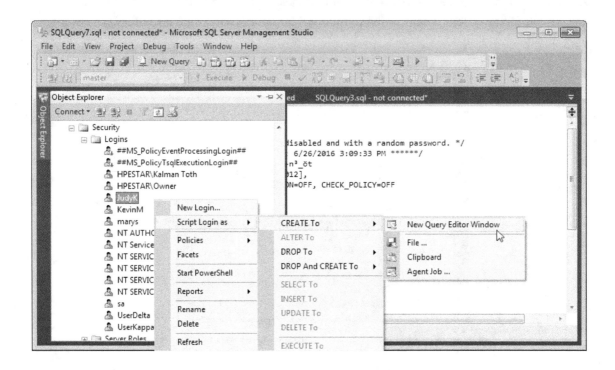

Generated T-SQL Scipt

```
USE [master]
GO


/* For security reasons the login is created disabled and with a random password. */
/****** Object:  Login [JudyK]    Script Date: 6/26/2016 3:09:33 PM ******/
CREATE LOGIN [JudyK] WITH PASSWORD=N'ÓÅ¡Ç-ø+Ç-n³_†öt È‰êFÁõOŠíø5',
DEFAULT_DATABASE=[AdventureWorks2012],
DEFAULT_LANGUAGE=[us_english], CHECK_EXPIRATION=OFF, CHECK_POLICY=OFF
GO


ALTER LOGIN [JudyK] DISABLE
GO
```

Scripting Database User

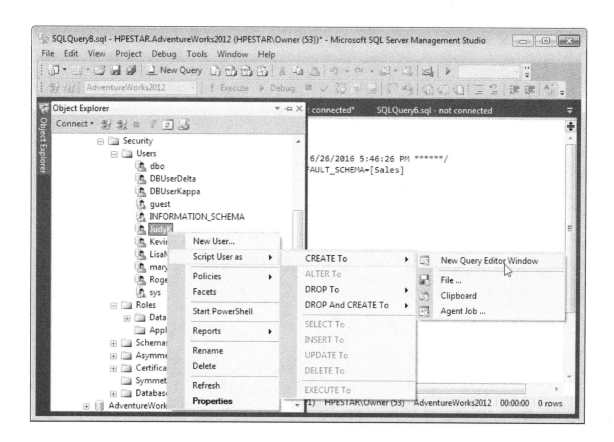

Generated T-SQL Script

USE [AdventureWorks2012]
GO

/****** Object: User [JudyK]   Script Date: 6/26/2016 5:46:26 PM ******/

CREATE USER [JudyK] FOR LOGIN [JudyK] WITH DEFAULT_SCHEMA=[Sales]
GO

CHAPTER 10: Enterprise Information Security

SECURABLES

Securables are resources to which the authorization system regulates access.

Securable scope: Server

Endpoint
Login
Database

Securable scope: Database

User
Role
Application role
Assembly
Message Type
Route
Service
Remote Service Binding
Fulltext Catalog
Certificate
Asymmetric Key
Symmetric Key
Contract
Schema

Securable scope: Schema

Type
XML Schema Collection
Object

Objects Class

Aggregate
Constraint
Function
Procedure
Queue
Statistic
Synonym
Table
View

Database User Properties in Object Explorer

Database User Properties Screen

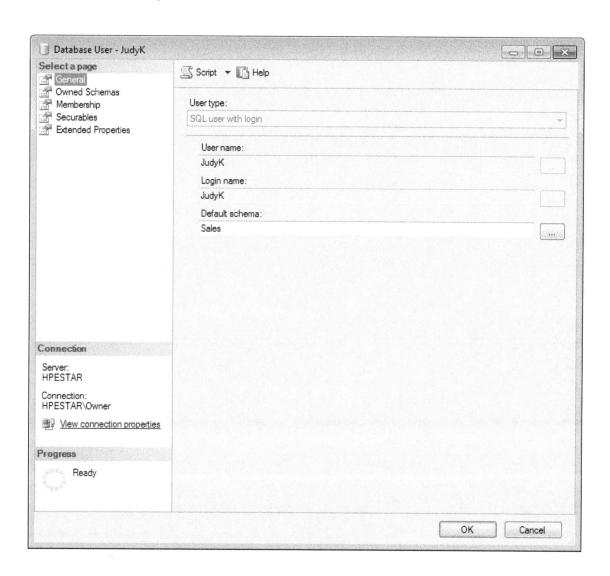

Database User Owned Schemas Page

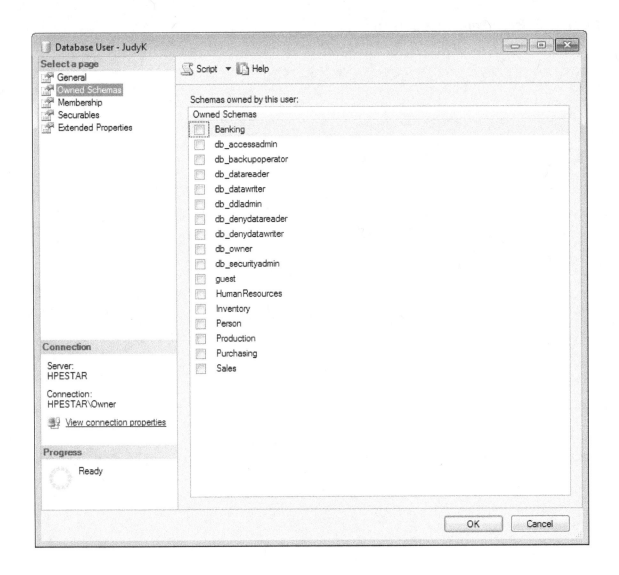

Database User Role Membership Page

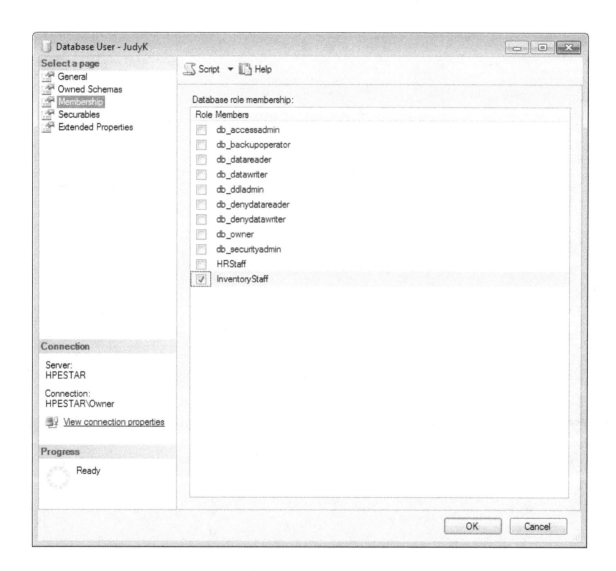

Database User Securables Screen

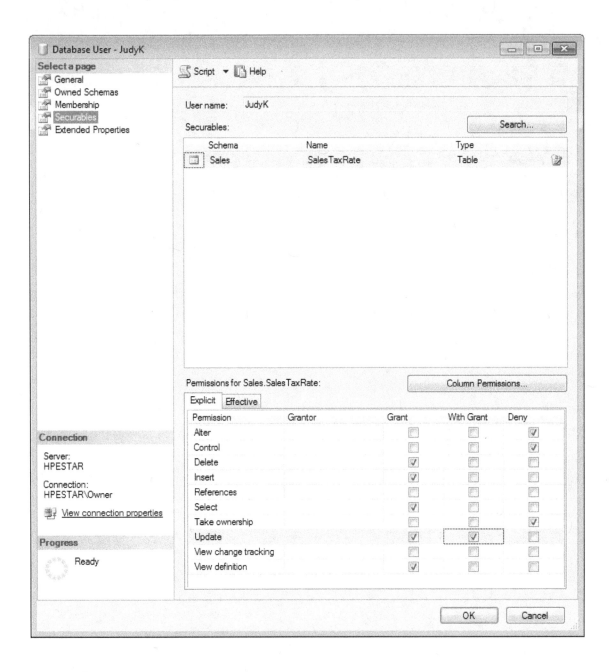

Database User Extended Properties (Data Dictionary) Page

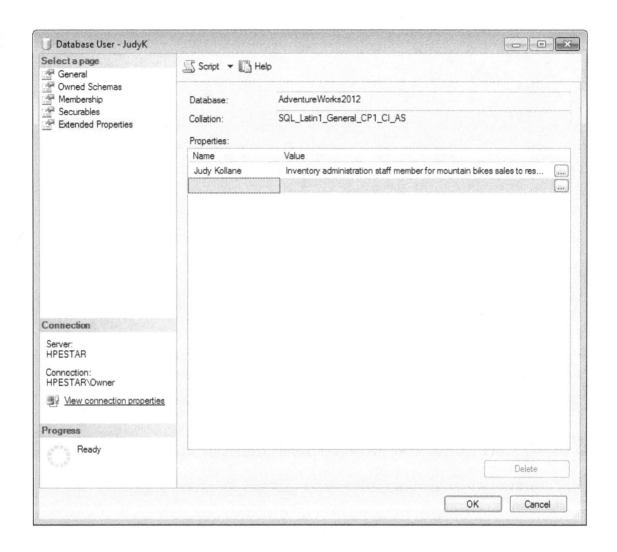

SELECT Permission Can Be Refined to Column Permissions

Granting Permissions

GRANT statement sets permissioning of database objects (securables) to users/roles.

Because the user has no permissions for the Product table SELECT denied error is returned.

```
EXECUTE AS LOGIN = 'UserOmega'
SELECT * FROM Production.Product;
/*
Msg 229, Level 14, State 5, Line 2
The SELECT permission was denied on the object 'Product', database 'AdventureWorks2012',
schema 'Production'.
*/
```

```
REVERT
```

Who am I? I am the "dbo" (db_owner - database owner), so I have the authority to grant
permissions. On the server level I am sysadmin, so I can do anything without any restriction.

```
SELECT SUSER_NAME(), USER_NAME();
-- HPESTAR\Owner       dbo
```

```
GRANT SELECT ON Production.Product TO UserOmega
GO
```

```
EXECUTE AS LOGIN = 'UserOmega'
SELECT * FROM Production.Product;
GO
-- (504 row(s) affected)
```

```
REVERT
```

MSDN Article: **Permissions Hierarchy (Database Engine)**   http://bit.ly/150mXFY
http://msdn.microsoft.com/en-us/library/ms191465(v=sql.105).aspx

Listing Permissions in the Database

```
USE AdventureWorks2012;

SELECT        dp.NAME              AS PrincipalName,
              dp.type_desc         AS PrincipalTypeDesc,
              s.NAME               AS SchemaName,
              o.NAME               AS ObjectName,
              o.TYPE_DESC          AS TypeDesc,
              p.permission_name    AS PermissionName,
              p.state_desc         AS PermissionStateDesc
FROM   sys.database_permissions p
   LEFT OUTER JOIN sys.all_objects o
       ON p.major_id = o.OBJECT_ID
   INNER JOIN sys.database_principals dp
       ON p.grantee_principal_id = dp.principal_id
   INNER JOIN sys.schemas s
       ON s.schema_id = o.schema_id
ORDER  BY        PrincipalName,
                 SchemaName,
                 ObjectName;
```

Principal Name	PrincipalTypeDesc	Schema Name	ObjectName	TypeDesc	Permission Name	PermissionStateDesc
guest	SQL_USER	dbo	fn_diagramobjects	SQL_SCALAR_FUNCTION	EXECUTE	DENY
guest	SQL_USER	dbo	sp_alterdiagram	SQL_STORED_PROCEDURE	EXECUTE	DENY
guest	SQL_USER	dbo	sp_creatediagram	SQL_STORED_PROCEDURE	EXECUTE	DENY
guest	SQL_USER	dbo	sp_dropdiagram	SQL_STORED_PROCEDURE	EXECUTE	DENY
guest	SQL_USER	dbo	sp_helpdiagramdefinition	SQL_STORED_PROCEDURE	EXECUTE	DENY
guest	SQL_USER	dbo	sp_helpdiagrams	SQL_STORED_PROCEDURE	EXECUTE	DENY
guest	SQL_USER	dbo	sp_renamediagram	SQL_STORED_PROCEDURE	EXECUTE	DENY
Inventory Staff	DATABASE_ROLE	dbo	uspProductInventoryLocation	SQL_STORED_PROCEDURE	CONTROL	DENY
Inventory Staff	DATABASE_ROLE	dbo	vInventory	VIEW	INSERT	GRANT
Inventory Staff	DATABASE_ROLE	dbo	vInventory	VIEW	SELECT	GRANT
Inventory Staff	DATABASE_ROLE	dbo	vInventory	VIEW	UPDATE	GRANT
JudyK	SQL_USER	Sales	SalesTaxRate	USER_TABLE	ALTER	DENY
JudyK	SQL_USER	Sales	SalesTaxRate	USER_TABLE	CONTROL	DENY

JudyK	SQL_USER	Sales	SalesTaxRate	USER_TABLE	DELETE	GRANT
JudyK	SQL_USER	Sales	SalesTaxRate	USER_TABLE	INSERT	GRANT
JudyK	SQL_USER	Sales	SalesTaxRate	USER_TABLE	SELECT	GRANT
JudyK	SQL_USER	Sales	SalesTaxRate	USER_TABLE	TAKE OWNERSHIP	DENY
JudyK	SQL_USER	Sales	SalesTaxRate	USER_TABLE	UPDATE	GRANT_WITH_GRANT_OPTION
JudyK	SQL_USER	Sales	SalesTaxRate	USER_TABLE	VIEW DEFINITION	GRANT
public	DATABASE_ROLE	dbo	fn_diagramobjects	SQL_SCALAR_FUNCTION	EXECUTE	GRANT
public	DATABASE_ROLE	dbo	sp_alterdiagram	SQL_STORED_PROCEDURE	EXECUTE	GRANT
public	DATABASE_ROLE	dbo	sp_creatediagram	SQL_STORED_PROCEDURE	EXECUTE	GRANT
public	DATABASE_ROLE	dbo	sp_dropdiagram	SQL_STORED_PROCEDURE	EXECUTE	GRANT
public	DATABASE_ROLE	dbo	sp_helpdiagramdefinition	SQL_STORED_PROCEDURE	EXECUTE	GRANT
public	DATABASE_ROLE	dbo	sp_helpdiagrams	SQL_STORED_PROCEDURE	EXECUTE	GRANT
public	DATABASE_ROLE	dbo	sp_renamediagram	SQL_STORED_PROCEDURE	EXECUTE	GRANT
public	DATABASE_ROLE	sys	all_columns	VIEW	SELECT	GRANT
public	DATABASE_ROLE	sys	all_objects	VIEW	SELECT	GRANT
public	DATABASE_ROLE	sys	all_parameters	VIEW	SELECT	GRANT
public	DATABASE_ROLE	sys	all_sql_modules	VIEW	SELECT	GRANT
public	DATABASE_ROLE	sys	all_views	VIEW	SELECT	GRANT
public	DATABASE_ROLE	sys	allocation_units	VIEW	SELECT	GRANT
public	DATABASE_ROLE	sys	assemblies	VIEW	SELECT	GRANT
public	DATABASE_ROLE	sys	assembly_files	VIEW	SELECT	GRANT
public	DATABASE_ROLE	sys	assembly_modules	VIEW	SELECT	GRANT
public	DATABASE_ROLE	sys	assembly_references	VIEW	SELECT	GRANT
public	DATABASE_ROLE	sys	assembly_types	VIEW	SELECT	GRANT
public	DATABASE_ROLE	sys	asymmetric_keys	VIEW	SELECT	GRANT
public	DATABASE_ROLE	sys	certificates	VIEW	SELECT	GRANT
public	DATABASE_ROLE	sys	change_tracking_tables	VIEW	SELECT	GRANT
public	DATABASE_ROLE	sys	check_constraints	VIEW	SELECT	GRANT
public	DATABASE_ROLE	sys	column_store_dictionaries	VIEW	SELECT	GRANT

CHAPTER 10: Enterprise Information Security

public	DATABASE_ROLE	sys	column_store_segments	VIEW	SELECT	GRANT
public	DATABASE_ROLE	sys	column_type_usages	VIEW	SELECT	GRANT
public	DATABASE_ROLE	sys	column_xml_schema_collection_usages	VIEW	SELECT	GRANT
public	DATABASE_ROLE	sys	columns	VIEW	SELECT	GRANT
public	DATABASE_ROLE	sys	computed_columns	VIEW	SELECT	GRANT
public	DATABASE_ROLE	sys	conversation_endpoints	VIEW	SELECT	GRANT
public	DATABASE_ROLE	sys	conversation_groups	VIEW	SELECT	GRANT
public	DATABASE_ROLE	sys	conversation_priorities	VIEW	SELECT	GRANT
public	DATABASE_ROLE	sys	crypt_properties	VIEW	SELECT	GRANT
public	DATABASE_ROLE	sys	data_spaces	VIEW	SELECT	GRANT
public	DATABASE_ROLE	sys	database_audit_specification_details	VIEW	SELECT	GRANT
public	DATABASE_ROLE	sys	database_audit_specifications	VIEW	SELECT	GRANT
public	DATABASE_ROLE	sys	database_files	VIEW	SELECT	GRANT
public	DATABASE_ROLE	sys	database_permissions	VIEW	SELECT	GRANT
public	DATABASE_ROLE	sys	database_principals	VIEW	SELECT	GRANT
public	DATABASE_ROLE	sys	database_role_members	VIEW	SELECT	GRANT
public	DATABASE_ROLE	sys	default_constraints	VIEW	SELECT	GRANT
public	DATABASE_ROLE	sys	destination_data_spaces	VIEW	SELECT	GRANT
public	DATABASE_ROLE	sys	event_notifications	VIEW	SELECT	GRANT
public	DATABASE_ROLE	sys	events	VIEW	SELECT	GRANT
public	DATABASE_ROLE	sys	extended_procedures	VIEW	SELECT	GRANT
public	DATABASE_ROLE	sys	extended_properties	VIEW	SELECT	GRANT
public	DATABASE_ROLE	sys	filegroups	VIEW	SELECT	GRANT
public	DATABASE_ROLE	sys	filetable_system_defined_objects	VIEW	SELECT	GRANT
public	DATABASE_ROLE	sys	filetables	VIEW	SELECT	GRANT
public	DATABASE_ROLE	sys	foreign_key_columns	VIEW	SELECT	GRANT
public	DATABASE_ROLE	sys	foreign_keys	VIEW	SELECT	GRANT
public	DATABASE_ROLE	sys	fulltext_catalogs	VIEW	SELECT	GRANT
public	DATABASE_	sys	fulltext_index_catalog_usages	VIEW	SELECT	GRANT

			ROLE			
public	DATABASE_ROLE	sys	fulltext_index_columns	VIEW	SELECT	GRANT
public	DATABASE_ROLE	sys	fulltext_index_fragments	VIEW	SELECT	GRANT
public	DATABASE_ROLE	sys	fulltext_indexes	VIEW	SELECT	GRANT
public	DATABASE_ROLE	sys	fulltext_stoplists	VIEW	SELECT	GRANT
public	DATABASE_ROLE	sys	fulltext_stopwords	VIEW	SELECT	GRANT
public	DATABASE_ROLE	sys	function_order_columns	VIEW	SELECT	GRANT
public	DATABASE_ROLE	sys	identity_columns	VIEW	SELECT	GRANT
public	DATABASE_ROLE	sys	index_columns	VIEW	SELECT	GRANT
public	DATABASE_ROLE	sys	indexes	VIEW	SELECT	GRANT
public	DATABASE_ROLE	sys	internal_tables	VIEW	SELECT	GRANT
public	DATABASE_ROLE	sys	key_constraints	VIEW	SELECT	GRANT
public	DATABASE_ROLE	sys	key_encryptions	VIEW	SELECT	GRANT
public	DATABASE_ROLE	sys	message_type_xml_schema_collection_usages	VIEW	SELECT	GRANT
public	DATABASE_ROLE	sys	module_assembly_usages	VIEW	SELECT	GRANT
public	DATABASE_ROLE	sys	numbered_procedure_parameters	VIEW	SELECT	GRANT
public	DATABASE_ROLE	sys	numbered_procedures	VIEW	SELECT	GRANT
public	DATABASE_ROLE	sys	objects	VIEW	SELECT	GRANT
public	DATABASE_ROLE	sys	parameter_type_usages	VIEW	SELECT	GRANT
public	DATABASE_ROLE	sys	parameter_xml_schema_collection_usages	VIEW	SELECT	GRANT
public	DATABASE_ROLE	sys	parameters	VIEW	SELECT	GRANT
public	DATABASE_ROLE	sys	partition_functions	VIEW	SELECT	GRANT
public	DATABASE_ROLE	sys	partition_parameters	VIEW	SELECT	GRANT
public	DATABASE_ROLE	sys	partition_range_values	VIEW	SELECT	GRANT
public	DATABASE_ROLE	sys	partition_schemes	VIEW	SELECT	GRANT
public	DATABASE_ROLE	sys	partitions	VIEW	SELECT	GRANT
public	DATABASE_ROLE	sys	plan_guides	VIEW	SELECT	GRANT
public	DATABASE_ROLE	sys	procedures	VIEW	SELECT	GRANT
public	DATABASE_ROLE	sys	registered_search_properties	VIEW	SELECT	GRANT

CHAPTER 10: Enterprise Information Security

public	DATABASE_ROLE	sys	registered_search_property_lists	VIEW	SELECT	GRANT
public	DATABASE_ROLE	sys	remote_service_bindings	VIEW	SELECT	GRANT
public	DATABASE_ROLE	sys	routes	VIEW	SELECT	GRANT
public	DATABASE_ROLE	sys	schemas	VIEW	SELECT	GRANT
public	DATABASE_ROLE	sys	selective_xml_index_namespaces	VIEW	SELECT	GRANT
public	DATABASE_ROLE	sys	selective_xml_index_paths	VIEW	SELECT	GRANT
public	DATABASE_ROLE	sys	sequences	VIEW	SELECT	GRANT
public	DATABASE_ROLE	sys	service_contract_message_usages	VIEW	SELECT	GRANT
public	DATABASE_ROLE	sys	service_contract_usages	VIEW	SELECT	GRANT
public	DATABASE_ROLE	sys	service_contracts	VIEW	SELECT	GRANT
public	DATABASE_ROLE	sys	service_message_types	VIEW	SELECT	GRANT
public	DATABASE_ROLE	sys	service_queue_usages	VIEW	SELECT	GRANT
public	DATABASE_ROLE	sys	service_queues	VIEW	SELECT	GRANT
public	DATABASE_ROLE	sys	services	VIEW	SELECT	GRANT
public	DATABASE_ROLE	sys	spatial_index_tessellations	VIEW	SELECT	GRANT
public	DATABASE_ROLE	sys	spatial_indexes	VIEW	SELECT	GRANT
public	DATABASE_ROLE	sys	sql_dependencies	VIEW	SELECT	GRANT
public	DATABASE_ROLE	sys	sql_modules	VIEW	SELECT	GRANT
public	DATABASE_ROLE	sys	stats	VIEW	SELECT	GRANT
public	DATABASE_ROLE	sys	stats_columns	VIEW	SELECT	GRANT
public	DATABASE_ROLE	sys	symmetric_keys	VIEW	SELECT	GRANT
public	DATABASE_ROLE	sys	synonyms	VIEW	SELECT	GRANT
public	DATABASE_ROLE	sys	syscolumns	VIEW	SELECT	GRANT
public	DATABASE_ROLE	sys	syscomments	VIEW	SELECT	GRANT
public	DATABASE_ROLE	sys	sysconstraints	VIEW	SELECT	GRANT
public	DATABASE_ROLE	sys	sysdepends	VIEW	SELECT	GRANT
public	DATABASE_ROLE	sys	sysfilegroups	VIEW	SELECT	GRANT
public	DATABASE_ROLE	sys	sysfiles	VIEW	SELECT	GRANT
public	DATABASE_	sys	sysforeignkeys	VIEW	SELECT	GRANT

	ROLE					
public	DATABASE_ROLE	sys	sysfulltextcatalogs	VIEW	SELECT	GRANT
public	DATABASE_ROLE	sys	sysindexes	VIEW	SELECT	GRANT
public	DATABASE_ROLE	sys	sysindexkeys	VIEW	SELECT	GRANT
public	DATABASE_ROLE	sys	sysmembers	VIEW	SELECT	GRANT
public	DATABASE_ROLE	sys	sysobjects	VIEW	SELECT	GRANT
public	DATABASE_ROLE	sys	syspermissions	VIEW	SELECT	GRANT
public	DATABASE_ROLE	sys	sysprotects	VIEW	SELECT	GRANT
public	DATABASE_ROLE	sys	sysreferences	VIEW	SELECT	GRANT
public	DATABASE_ROLE	sys	system_columns	VIEW	SELECT	GRANT
public	DATABASE_ROLE	sys	system_objects	VIEW	SELECT	GRANT
public	DATABASE_ROLE	sys	system_parameters	VIEW	SELECT	GRANT
public	DATABASE_ROLE	sys	system_sql_modules	VIEW	SELECT	GRANT
public	DATABASE_ROLE	sys	system_views	VIEW	SELECT	GRANT
public	DATABASE_ROLE	sys	systypes	VIEW	SELECT	GRANT
public	DATABASE_ROLE	sys	sysusers	VIEW	SELECT	GRANT
public	DATABASE_ROLE	sys	table_types	VIEW	SELECT	GRANT
public	DATABASE_ROLE	sys	tables	VIEW	SELECT	GRANT
public	DATABASE_ROLE	sys	transmission_queue	VIEW	SELECT	GRANT
public	DATABASE_ROLE	sys	trigger_events	VIEW	SELECT	GRANT
public	DATABASE_ROLE	sys	triggers	VIEW	SELECT	GRANT
public	DATABASE_ROLE	sys	type_assembly_usages	VIEW	SELECT	GRANT
public	DATABASE_ROLE	sys	types	VIEW	SELECT	GRANT
public	DATABASE_ROLE	sys	views	VIEW	SELECT	GRANT
public	DATABASE_ROLE	sys	xml_indexes	VIEW	SELECT	GRANT
public	DATABASE_ROLE	sys	xml_schema_attributes	VIEW	SELECT	GRANT
public	DATABASE_ROLE	sys	xml_schema_collections	VIEW	SELECT	GRANT
public	DATABASE_ROLE	sys	xml_schema_component_placements	VIEW	SELECT	GRANT
public	DATABASE_ROLE	sys	xml_schema_components	VIEW	SELECT	GRANT

public	DATABASE_ ROLE	sys	xml_schema_elements	VIEW	SELECT	GRANT
public	DATABASE_ ROLE	sys	xml_schema_facets	VIEW	SELECT	GRANT
public	DATABASE_ ROLE	sys	xml_schema_model_groups	VIEW	SELECT	GRANT
public	DATABASE_ ROLE	sys	xml_schema_namespaces	VIEW	SELECT	GRANT
public	DATABASE_ ROLE	sys	xml_schema_types	VIEW	SELECT	GRANT
public	DATABASE_ ROLE	sys	xml_schema_wildcard_namesp aces	VIEW	SELECT	GRANT
public	DATABASE_ ROLE	sys	xml_schema_wildcards	VIEW	SELECT	GRANT

Listing Permissions for a Principal

Principals are entities (logins, users, roles) that can request SQL Server resources.

```
USE AdventureWorks2012;
```

```
SELECT          dp.NAME              AS PrincipalName,
                dp.type_desc         AS PrincipalTypeDesc,
                s.NAME               AS SchemaName,
                o.NAME               AS ObjectName,
                o.TYPE_DESC          AS TypeDesc,
                p.permission_name    AS PermissionName,
                p.state_desc         AS PermissionStateDesc
FROM   sys.database_permissions p
   LEFT OUTER JOIN sys.all_objects o          ON p.major_id = o.OBJECT_ID
   INNER JOIN sys.database_principals dp       ON p.grantee_principal_id = dp.principal_id
   INNER JOIN sys.schemas s                    ON s.schema_id = o.schema_id
WHERE dp.NAME = 'JudyK'
ORDER  BY       PrincipalName,       SchemaName,       ObjectName;
```

PrincipalName	PrincipalTypeDesc	SchemaName	ObjectName	TypeDesc	PermissionName	PermissionStateDesc
JudyK	SQL_USER	Sales	SalesTaxRate	USER_TABLE	VIEW DEFINITION	GRANT
JudyK	SQL_USER	Sales	SalesTaxRate	USER_TABLE	UPDATE	GRANT_WITH_GRANT_OPTION
JudyK	SQL_USER	Sales	SalesTaxRate	USER_TABLE	TAKE OWNERSHIP	DENY
JudyK	SQL_USER	Sales	SalesTaxRate	USER_TABLE	SELECT	GRANT
JudyK	SQL_USER	Sales	SalesTaxRate	USER_TABLE	INSERT	GRANT
JudyK	SQL_USER	Sales	SalesTaxRate	USER_TABLE	DELETE	GRANT
JudyK	SQL_USER	Sales	SalesTaxRate	USER_TABLE	CONTROL	DENY
JudyK	SQL_USER	Sales	SalesTaxRate	USER_TABLE	ALTER	DENY

CHAPTER 11: Managing Users Permissions

Built-in and Implied permissions

The following permissions can be granted.

```
USE master;
go
```

```
SELECT *
FROM    sys.fn_builtin_permissions(DEFAULT)
ORDER  BY class_desc, permission_name;
go
```

class_desc	permission_name	type	covering_permission_name	parent_class_desc	parent_covering_permission_name
APPLICATION ROLE	ALTER	AL	CONTROL	DATABASE	ALTER ANY APPLICATION ROLE
APPLICATION ROLE	CONTROL	CL		DATABASE	CONTROL
APPLICATION ROLE	VIEW DEFINITION	VW	CONTROL	DATABASE	VIEW DEFINITION
ASSEMBLY	ALTER	AL	CONTROL	DATABASE	ALTER ANY ASSEMBLY
ASSEMBLY	CONTROL	CL		DATABASE	CONTROL
ASSEMBLY	REFERENCES	RF	CONTROL	DATABASE	REFERENCES
ASSEMBLY	TAKE OWNERSHIP	TO	CONTROL	DATABASE	CONTROL
ASSEMBLY	VIEW DEFINITION	VW	CONTROL	DATABASE	VIEW DEFINITION
ASYMMETRIC KEY	ALTER	AL	CONTROL	DATABASE	ALTER ANY ASYMMETRIC KEY
ASYMMETRIC KEY	CONTROL	CL		DATABASE	CONTROL
ASYMMETRIC KEY	REFERENCES	RF	CONTROL	DATABASE	REFERENCES
ASYMMETRIC KEY	TAKE OWNERSHIP	TO	CONTROL	DATABASE	CONTROL
ASYMMETRIC KEY	VIEW DEFINITION	VW	CONTROL	DATABASE	VIEW DEFINITION
AVAILABILITY GROUP	ALTER	AL	CONTROL	SERVER	ALTER ANY AVAILABILITY GROUP
AVAILABILITY GROUP	CONTROL	CL		SERVER	CONTROL SERVER
AVAILABILITY GROUP	TAKE OWNERSHIP	TO	CONTROL	SERVER	CONTROL SERVER
AVAILABILITY GROUP	VIEW DEFINITION	VW	CONTROL	SERVER	VIEW ANY DEFINITION
CERTIFICATE	ALTER	AL	CONTROL	DATABASE	ALTER ANY CERTIFICATE

CERTIFICATE	CONTROL	CL		DATABASE	CONTROL
CERTIFICATE	REFERENCES	RF	CONTROL	DATABASE	REFERENCES
CERTIFICATE	TAKE OWNERSHIP	TO	CONTROL	DATABASE	CONTROL
CERTIFICATE	VIEW DEFINITION	VW	CONTROL	DATABASE	VIEW DEFINITION
CONTRACT	ALTER	AL	CONTROL	DATABASE	ALTER ANY CONTRACT
CONTRACT	CONTROL	CL		DATABASE	CONTROL
CONTRACT	REFERENCES	RF	CONTROL	DATABASE	REFERENCES
CONTRACT	TAKE OWNERSHIP	TO	CONTROL	DATABASE	CONTROL
CONTRACT	VIEW DEFINITION	VW	CONTROL	DATABASE	VIEW DEFINITION
DATABASE	ALTER	AL	CONTROL	SERVER	ALTER ANY DATABASE
DATABASE	ALTER ANY APPLICATION ROLE	ALAR	ALTER	SERVER	CONTROL SERVER
DATABASE	ALTER ANY ASSEMBLY	ALAS	ALTER	SERVER	CONTROL SERVER
DATABASE	ALTER ANY ASYMMETRIC KEY	ALAK	ALTER	SERVER	CONTROL SERVER
DATABASE	ALTER ANY CERTIFICATE	ALCF	ALTER	SERVER	CONTROL SERVER
DATABASE	ALTER ANY CONTRACT	ALSC	ALTER	SERVER	CONTROL SERVER
DATABASE	ALTER ANY DATABASE AUDIT	ALDA	ALTER	SERVER	ALTER ANY SERVER AUDIT
DATABASE	ALTER ANY DATABASE DDL TRIGGER	ALTG	ALTER	SERVER	CONTROL SERVER
DATABASE	ALTER ANY DATABASE EVENT NOTIFICATION	ALED	ALTER	SERVER	ALTER ANY EVENT NOTIFICATION
DATABASE	ALTER ANY DATASPACE	ALDS	ALTER	SERVER	CONTROL SERVER
DATABASE	ALTER ANY FULLTEXT CATALOG	ALFT	ALTER	SERVER	CONTROL SERVER
DATABASE	ALTER ANY MESSAGE TYPE	ALMT	ALTER	SERVER	CONTROL SERVER
DATABASE	ALTER ANY REMOTE SERVICE BINDING	ALSB	ALTER	SERVER	CONTROL SERVER
DATABASE	ALTER ANY ROLE	ALRL	ALTER	SERVER	CONTROL SERVER

DATABASE	ALTER ANY ROUTE	ALRT	ALTER	SERVER	CONTROL SERVER
DATABASE	ALTER ANY SCHEMA	ALSM	ALTER	SERVER	CONTROL SERVER
DATABASE	ALTER ANY SERVICE	ALSV	ALTER	SERVER	CONTROL SERVER
DATABASE	ALTER ANY SYMMETRIC KEY	ALSK	ALTER	SERVER	CONTROL SERVER
DATABASE	ALTER ANY USER	ALUS	ALTER	SERVER	CONTROL SERVER
DATABASE	AUTHENTICATE	AUTH	CONTROL	SERVER	AUTHENTICATE SERVER
DATABASE	BACKUP DATABASE	BADB	CONTROL	SERVER	CONTROL SERVER
DATABASE	BACKUP LOG	BALO	CONTROL	SERVER	CONTROL SERVER
DATABASE	CHECKPOINT	CP	CONTROL	SERVER	CONTROL SERVER
DATABASE	CONNECT	CO	CONNECT REPLICATION	SERVER	CONTROL SERVER
DATABASE	CONNECT REPLICATION	CORP	CONTROL	SERVER	CONTROL SERVER
DATABASE	CONTROL	CL		SERVER	CONTROL SERVER
DATABASE	CREATE AGGREGATE	CRAG	ALTER	SERVER	CONTROL SERVER
DATABASE	CREATE ASSEMBLY	CRAS	ALTER ANY ASSEMBLY	SERVER	CONTROL SERVER
DATABASE	CREATE ASYMMETRIC KEY	CRAK	ALTER ANY ASYMMETRIC KEY	SERVER	CONTROL SERVER
DATABASE	CREATE CERTIFICATE	CRCF	ALTER ANY CERTIFICATE	SERVER	CONTROL SERVER
DATABASE	CREATE CONTRACT	CRSC	ALTER ANY CONTRACT	SERVER	CONTROL SERVER
DATABASE	CREATE DATABASE	CRDB		SERVER	CREATE ANY DATABASE
DATABASE	CREATE DATABASE DDL EVENT NOTIFICATION	CRED	ALTER ANY DATABASE EVENT NOTIFICATION	SERVER	CREATE DDL EVENT NOTIFICATION
DATABASE	CREATE DEFAULT	CRDF	ALTER	SERVER	CONTROL SERVER
DATABASE	CREATE FULLTEXT CATALOG	CRFT	ALTER ANY FULLTEXT CATALOG	SERVER	CONTROL SERVER
DATABASE	CREATE FUNCTION	CRFN	ALTER	SERVER	CONTROL SERVER
DATABASE	CREATE MESSAGE TYPE	CRMT	ALTER ANY MESSAGE TYPE	SERVER	CONTROL SERVER
DATABASE	CREATE	CRPR	ALTER	SERVER	CONTROL SERVER

CHAPTER 11: Managing Users Permissions

	PROCEDURE				
DATABASE	CREATE QUEUE	CRQU	ALTER	SERVER	CONTROL SERVER
DATABASE	CREATE REMOTE SERVICE BINDING	CRSB	ALTER ANY REMOTE SERVICE BINDING	SERVER	CONTROL SERVER
DATABASE	CREATE ROLE	CRRL	ALTER ANY ROLE	SERVER	CONTROL SERVER
DATABASE	CREATE ROUTE	CRRT	ALTER ANY ROUTE	SERVER	CONTROL SERVER
DATABASE	CREATE RULE	CRRU	ALTER	SERVER	CONTROL SERVER
DATABASE	CREATE SCHEMA	CRSM	ALTER ANY SCHEMA	SERVER	CONTROL SERVER
DATABASE	CREATE SERVICE	CRSV	ALTER ANY SERVICE	SERVER	CONTROL SERVER
DATABASE	CREATE SYMMETRIC KEY	CRSK	ALTER ANY SYMMETRIC KEY	SERVER	CONTROL SERVER
DATABASE	CREATE SYNONYM	CRSN	ALTER	SERVER	CONTROL SERVER
DATABASE	CREATE TABLE	CRTB	ALTER	SERVER	CONTROL SERVER
DATABASE	CREATE TYPE	CRTY	ALTER	SERVER	CONTROL SERVER
DATABASE	CREATE VIEW	CRVW	ALTER	SERVER	CONTROL SERVER
DATABASE	CREATE XML SCHEMA COLLECTION	CRXS	ALTER	SERVER	CONTROL SERVER
DATABASE	DELETE	DL	CONTROL	SERVER	CONTROL SERVER
DATABASE	EXECUTE	EX	CONTROL	SERVER	CONTROL SERVER
DATABASE	INSERT	IN	CONTROL	SERVER	CONTROL SERVER
DATABASE	REFERENCES	RF	CONTROL	SERVER	CONTROL SERVER
DATABASE	SELECT	SL	CONTROL	SERVER	CONTROL SERVER
DATABASE	SHOWPLAN	SPLN	CONTROL	SERVER	ALTER TRACE
DATABASE	SUBSCRIBE QUERY NOTIFICATIONS	SUQN	CONTROL	SERVER	CONTROL SERVER
DATABASE	TAKE OWNERSHIP	TO	CONTROL	SERVER	CONTROL SERVER
DATABASE	UPDATE	UP	CONTROL	SERVER	CONTROL SERVER
DATABASE	VIEW DATABASE STATE	VWDS	CONTROL	SERVER	VIEW SERVER STATE
DATABASE	VIEW DEFINITION	VW	CONTROL	SERVER	VIEW ANY DEFINITION
ENDPOINT	ALTER	AL	CONTROL	SERVER	ALTER ANY ENDPOINT
ENDPOINT	CONNECT	CO	CONTROL	SERVER	CONTROL SERVER
ENDPOINT	CONTROL	CL		SERVER	CONTROL SERVER

CHAPTER 11: Managing Users Permissions

ENDPOINT	TAKE OWNERSHIP	TO	CONTROL	SERVER	CONTROL SERVER
ENDPOINT	VIEW DEFINITION	VW	CONTROL	SERVER	VIEW ANY DEFINITION
FULLTEXT CATALOG	ALTER	AL	CONTROL	DATABASE	ALTER ANY FULLTEXT CATALOG
FULLTEXT CATALOG	CONTROL	CL		DATABASE	CONTROL
FULLTEXT CATALOG	REFERENCES	RF	CONTROL	DATABASE	REFERENCES
FULLTEXT CATALOG	TAKE OWNERSHIP	TO	CONTROL	DATABASE	CONTROL
FULLTEXT CATALOG	VIEW DEFINITION	VW	CONTROL	DATABASE	VIEW DEFINITION
FULLTEXT STOPLIST	ALTER	AL	CONTROL	DATABASE	ALTER ANY FULLTEXT CATALOG
FULLTEXT STOPLIST	CONTROL	CL		DATABASE	CONTROL
FULLTEXT STOPLIST	REFERENCES	RF	CONTROL	DATABASE	REFERENCES
FULLTEXT STOPLIST	TAKE OWNERSHIP	TO	CONTROL	DATABASE	CONTROL
FULLTEXT STOPLIST	VIEW DEFINITION	VW	CONTROL	DATABASE	VIEW DEFINITION
LOGIN	ALTER	AL	CONTROL	SERVER	ALTER ANY LOGIN
LOGIN	CONTROL	CL		SERVER	CONTROL SERVER
LOGIN	IMPERSONATE	IM	CONTROL	SERVER	CONTROL SERVER
LOGIN	VIEW DEFINITION	VW	CONTROL	SERVER	VIEW ANY DEFINITION
MESSAGE TYPE	ALTER	AL	CONTROL	DATABASE	ALTER ANY MESSAGE TYPE
MESSAGE TYPE	CONTROL	CL		DATABASE	CONTROL
MESSAGE TYPE	REFERENCES	RF	CONTROL	DATABASE	REFERENCES
MESSAGE TYPE	TAKE OWNERSHIP	TO	CONTROL	DATABASE	CONTROL
MESSAGE TYPE	VIEW DEFINITION	VW	CONTROL	DATABASE	VIEW DEFINITION
OBJECT	ALTER	AL	CONTROL	SCHEMA	ALTER
OBJECT	CONTROL	CL		SCHEMA	CONTROL
OBJECT	DELETE	DL	CONTROL	SCHEMA	DELETE
OBJECT	EXECUTE	EX	CONTROL	SCHEMA	EXECUTE
OBJECT	INSERT	IN	CONTROL	SCHEMA	INSERT
OBJECT	RECEIVE	RC	CONTROL	SCHEMA	CONTROL
OBJECT	REFERENCES	RF	CONTROL	SCHEMA	REFERENCES
OBJECT	SELECT	SL	RECEIVE	SCHEMA	SELECT
OBJECT	TAKE OWNERSHIP	TO	CONTROL	SCHEMA	CONTROL
OBJECT	UPDATE	UP	CONTROL	SCHEMA	UPDATE
OBJECT	VIEW CHANGE TRACKING	VWCT	CONTROL	SCHEMA	VIEW CHANGE TRACKING
OBJECT	VIEW DEFINITION	VW	CONTROL	SCHEMA	VIEW DEFINITION
REMOTE SERVICE BINDING	ALTER	AL	CONTROL	DATABASE	ALTER ANY REMOTE SERVICE BINDING

CHAPTER 11: Managing Users Permissions

REMOTE SERVICE BINDING	CONTROL	CL		DATABASE	CONTROL
REMOTE SERVICE BINDING	TAKE OWNERSHIP	TO	CONTROL	DATABASE	CONTROL
REMOTE SERVICE BINDING	VIEW DEFINITION	VW	CONTROL	DATABASE	VIEW DEFINITION
ROLE	ALTER	AL	CONTROL	DATABASE	ALTER ANY ROLE
ROLE	CONTROL	CL		DATABASE	CONTROL
ROLE	TAKE OWNERSHIP	TO	CONTROL	DATABASE	CONTROL
ROLE	VIEW DEFINITION	VW	CONTROL	DATABASE	VIEW DEFINITION
ROUTE	ALTER	AL	CONTROL	DATABASE	ALTER ANY ROUTE
ROUTE	CONTROL	CL		DATABASE	CONTROL
ROUTE	TAKE OWNERSHIP	TO	CONTROL	DATABASE	CONTROL
ROUTE	VIEW DEFINITION	VW	CONTROL	DATABASE	VIEW DEFINITION
SCHEMA	ALTER	AL	CONTROL	DATABASE	ALTER ANY SCHEMA
SCHEMA	CONTROL	CL		DATABASE	CONTROL
SCHEMA	CREATE SEQUENCE	CRSO	ALTER	DATABASE	CONTROL
SCHEMA	DELETE	DL	CONTROL	DATABASE	DELETE
SCHEMA	EXECUTE	EX	CONTROL	DATABASE	EXECUTE
SCHEMA	INSERT	IN	CONTROL	DATABASE	INSERT
SCHEMA	REFERENCES	RF	CONTROL	DATABASE	REFERENCES
SCHEMA	SELECT	SL	CONTROL	DATABASE	SELECT
SCHEMA	TAKE OWNERSHIP	TO	CONTROL	DATABASE	CONTROL
SCHEMA	UPDATE	UP	CONTROL	DATABASE	UPDATE
SCHEMA	VIEW CHANGE TRACKING	VWCT	CONTROL	DATABASE	CONTROL
SCHEMA	VIEW DEFINITION	VW	CONTROL	DATABASE	VIEW DEFINITION
SEARCH PROPERTY LIST	ALTER	AL	CONTROL	DATABASE	ALTER ANY FULLTEXT CATALOG
SEARCH PROPERTY LIST	CONTROL	CL		DATABASE	CONTROL
SEARCH PROPERTY LIST	REFERENCES	RF	CONTROL	DATABASE	REFERENCES
SEARCH PROPERTY LIST	TAKE OWNERSHIP	TO	CONTROL	DATABASE	CONTROL
SEARCH PROPERTY LIST	VIEW DEFINITION	VW	CONTROL	DATABASE	VIEW DEFINITION
SERVER	ADMINISTER BULK OPERATIONS	ADBO	CONTROL SERVER		
SERVER	ALTER ANY AVAILABILITY GROUP	ALAG	CONTROL SERVER		

CHAPTER 11: Managing Users Permissions

SERVER	ALTER ANY CONNECTION	ALCO	CONTROL SERVER		
SERVER	ALTER ANY CREDENTIAL	ALCD	CONTROL SERVER		
SERVER	ALTER ANY DATABASE	ALDB	CONTROL SERVER		
SERVER	ALTER ANY ENDPOINT	ALHE	CONTROL SERVER		
SERVER	ALTER ANY EVENT NOTIFICATION	ALES	CONTROL SERVER		
SERVER	ALTER ANY EVENT SESSION	AAES	CONTROL SERVER		
SERVER	ALTER ANY LINKED SERVER	ALLS	CONTROL SERVER		
SERVER	ALTER ANY LOGIN	ALLG	CONTROL SERVER		
SERVER	ALTER ANY SERVER AUDIT	ALAA	CONTROL SERVER		
SERVER	ALTER ANY SERVER ROLE	ALSR	CONTROL SERVER		
SERVER	ALTER RESOURCES	ALRS	CONTROL SERVER		
SERVER	ALTER SERVER STATE	ALSS	CONTROL SERVER		
SERVER	ALTER SETTINGS	ALST	CONTROL SERVER		
SERVER	ALTER TRACE	ALTR	CONTROL SERVER		
SERVER	AUTHENTICATE SERVER	AUTH	CONTROL SERVER		
SERVER	CONNECT SQL	COSQ	CONTROL SERVER		
SERVER	CONTROL SERVER	CL			
SERVER	CREATE ANY DATABASE	CRDB	ALTER ANY DATABASE		
SERVER	CREATE AVAILABILITY GROUP	CRAC	ALTER ANY AVAILABILITY GROUP		
SERVER	CREATE DDL EVENT NOTIFICATION	CRDE	ALTER ANY EVENT NOTIFICATION		
SERVER	CREATE ENDPOINT	CRHE	ALTER ANY ENDPOINT		
SERVER	CREATE SERVER ROLE	CRSR	ALTER ANY SERVER ROLE		
SERVER	CREATE TRACE EVENT	CRTE	ALTER ANY EVENT		

CHAPTER 11: Managing Users Permissions

	NOTIFICATION		NOTIFICATION		
SERVER	EXTERNAL ACCESS ASSEMBLY	XA	UNSAFE ASSEMBLY		
SERVER	SHUTDOWN	SHDN	CONTROL SERVER		
SERVER	UNSAFE ASSEMBLY	XU	CONTROL SERVER		
SERVER	VIEW ANY DATABASE	VWDB	VIEW ANY DEFINITION		
SERVER	VIEW ANY DEFINITION	VWAD	CONTROL SERVER		
SERVER	VIEW SERVER STATE	VWSS	ALTER SERVER STATE		
SERVER ROLE	ALTER	AL	CONTROL	SERVER	ALTER ANY SERVER ROLE
SERVER ROLE	CONTROL	CL		SERVER	CONTROL SERVER
SERVER ROLE	TAKE OWNERSHIP	TO	CONTROL	SERVER	CONTROL SERVER
SERVER ROLE	VIEW DEFINITION	VW	CONTROL	SERVER	VIEW ANY DEFINITION
SERVICE	ALTER	AL	CONTROL	DATABASE	ALTER ANY SERVICE
SERVICE	CONTROL	CL		DATABASE	CONTROL
SERVICE	SEND	SN	CONTROL	DATABASE	CONTROL
SERVICE	TAKE OWNERSHIP	TO	CONTROL	DATABASE	CONTROL
SERVICE	VIEW DEFINITION	VW	CONTROL	DATABASE	VIEW DEFINITION
SYMMETRIC KEY	ALTER	AL	CONTROL	DATABASE	ALTER ANY SYMMETRIC KEY
SYMMETRIC KEY	CONTROL	CL		DATABASE	CONTROL
SYMMETRIC KEY	REFERENCES	RF	CONTROL	DATABASE	REFERENCES
SYMMETRIC KEY	TAKE OWNERSHIP	TO	CONTROL	DATABASE	CONTROL
SYMMETRIC KEY	VIEW DEFINITION	VW	CONTROL	DATABASE	VIEW DEFINITION
TYPE	CONTROL	CL		SCHEMA	CONTROL
TYPE	EXECUTE	EX	CONTROL	SCHEMA	EXECUTE
TYPE	REFERENCES	RF	CONTROL	SCHEMA	REFERENCES
TYPE	TAKE OWNERSHIP	TO	CONTROL	SCHEMA	CONTROL
TYPE	VIEW DEFINITION	VW	CONTROL	SCHEMA	VIEW DEFINITION
USER	ALTER	AL	CONTROL	DATABASE	ALTER ANY USER
USER	CONTROL	CL		DATABASE	CONTROL
USER	IMPERSONATE	IM	CONTROL	DATABASE	CONTROL
USER	VIEW DEFINITION	VW	CONTROL	DATABASE	VIEW DEFINITION

CHAPTER 11: Managing Users Permissions

XML SCHEMA COLLECTION	ALTER	AL	CONTROL	SCHEMA	ALTER
XML SCHEMA COLLECTION	CONTROL	CL		SCHEMA	CONTROL
XML SCHEMA COLLECTION	EXECUTE	EX	CONTROL	SCHEMA	EXECUTE
XML SCHEMA COLLECTION	REFERENCES	RF	CONTROL	SCHEMA	REFERENCES
XML SCHEMA COLLECTION	TAKE OWNERSHIP	TO	CONTROL	SCHEMA	CONTROL
XML SCHEMA COLLECTION	VIEW DEFINITION	VW	CONTROL	SCHEMA	VIEW DEFINITION

We can query a particular class the following manner.

```
SELECT *
FROM   sys.fn_builtin_permissions(N'SCHEMA');
-- (12 row(s) affected)
```

> MSDN Article: **Covering/Implied Permissions (Database Engine)** http://bit.ly/11LWdIJ
> http://msdn.microsoft.com/en-us/library/ms177450(v=sql.105).aspx

Public database role permissions

```
SELECT  a.class_desc,
        a.permission_name,
        a.state_desc,
        b.name AS 'Role'
FROM   sys.server_permissions a
    INNER JOIN sys.server_principals b      ON a.grantee_principal_id = b.principal_id
WHERE  b.name = 'public';
```

class_desc	permission_name	state_desc	Role
SERVER	VIEW ANY DATABASE	GRANT	public
ENDPOINT	CONNECT	GRANT	public
ENDPOINT	CONNECT	GRANT	public
ENDPOINT	CONNECT	GRANT	public
ENDPOINT	CONNECT	GRANT	public

Securables Hierarchy

The securable scopes (nested hierarchies) are server, database, and schema.

Server				
	Endpoint			
	Login			
	Database			
		User		
		Role		
		Application role		
		Assembly		
		Message Type		
		Route		
		Service		
		Remote Service Binding		
		Fulltext Catalog		
		Certificate		
		Asymmetric Key		
		Symmetric Key		
		Contract		
		Schema		
			Type	
			XML Schema Collection	
			Object	
				Aggregate
				Constraint
				Function
				Procedure
				Queue
				Statistic
				Synonym
				Table
				View

Security Related Command Scripting

Here are the main security related system views with sample content listings.

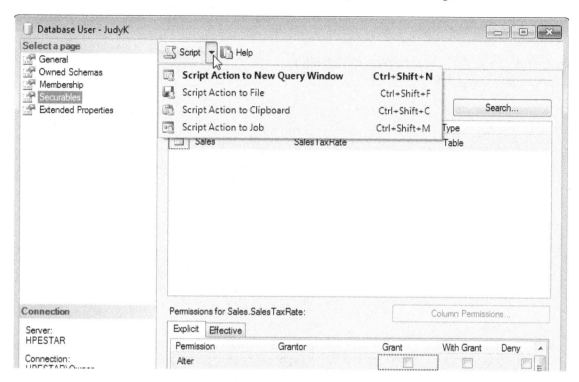

Scripting GRANT, REVOKE & DENY Commands

```
use [AdventureWorks2012]
GO
GRANT VIEW DEFINITION ON [Sales].[SalesTaxRate] TO [JudyK]
```

```
use [AdventureWorks2012]
GO
REVOKE VIEW DEFINITION ON [Sales].[SalesTaxRate] TO [JudyK]
```

```
use [AdventureWorks2012]
GO
DENY VIEW DEFINITION ON [Sales].[SalesTaxRate] TO [JudyK]
```

Password Change for a login by sysadmin

```
ALTER LOGIN KevinW WITH PASSWORD = 'Super&Secret2';
```

CHAPTER 11: Managing Users Permissions

System Administrator (sa -sysadmin) Permissions

I am logged in as a member of the sysadmin fixed server role. Here are my server permissions.

use AdventureWorks2012;

select * from fn_my_permissions(NULL, 'SERVER')
order by permission_name;

entity_name	subentity_name	permission_name
server		ADMINISTER BULK OPERATIONS
server		ALTER ANY AVAILABILITY GROUP
server		ALTER ANY CONNECTION
server		ALTER ANY CREDENTIAL
server		ALTER ANY DATABASE
server		ALTER ANY ENDPOINT
server		ALTER ANY EVENT NOTIFICATION
server		ALTER ANY EVENT SESSION
server		ALTER ANY LINKED SERVER
server		ALTER ANY LOGIN
server		ALTER ANY SERVER AUDIT
server		ALTER ANY SERVER ROLE
server		ALTER RESOURCES
server		ALTER SERVER STATE
server		ALTER SETTINGS
server		ALTER TRACE
server		AUTHENTICATE SERVER
server		CONNECT SQL
server		CONTROL SERVER
server		CREATE ANY DATABASE
server		CREATE AVAILABILITY GROUP
server		CREATE DDL EVENT NOTIFICATION
server		CREATE ENDPOINT
server		CREATE SERVER ROLE
server		CREATE TRACE EVENT NOTIFICATION
server		EXTERNAL ACCESS ASSEMBLY
server		SHUTDOWN
server		UNSAFE ASSEMBLY
server		VIEW ANY DATABASE
server		VIEW ANY DEFINITION

fn_my_permissions Lists Database Permissions

I am logged in as a member of db_owner (dbo) fixed database role.

select * from fn_my_permissions(NULL, 'DATABASE')
order by permission_name;

entity_name	subentity_name	permission_name
database		ALTER
database		ALTER ANY APPLICATION ROLE
database		ALTER ANY ASSEMBLY
database		ALTER ANY ASYMMETRIC KEY
database		ALTER ANY CERTIFICATE
database		ALTER ANY CONTRACT
database		ALTER ANY DATABASE AUDIT
database		ALTER ANY DATABASE DDL TRIGGER
database		ALTER ANY DATABASE EVENT NOTIFICATION
database		ALTER ANY DATASPACE
database		ALTER ANY FULLTEXT CATALOG
database		ALTER ANY MESSAGE TYPE
database		ALTER ANY REMOTE SERVICE BINDING
database		ALTER ANY ROLE
database		ALTER ANY ROUTE
database		ALTER ANY SCHEMA
database		ALTER ANY SERVICE
database		ALTER ANY SYMMETRIC KEY
database		ALTER ANY USER
database		AUTHENTICATE
database		BACKUP DATABASE
database		BACKUP LOG
database		CHECKPOINT
database		CONNECT
database		CONNECT REPLICATION
database		CONTROL
database		CREATE AGGREGATE
database		CREATE ASSEMBLY
database		CREATE ASYMMETRIC KEY
database		CREATE CERTIFICATE
database		CREATE CONTRACT
database		CREATE DATABASE
database		CREATE DATABASE DDL EVENT NOTIFICATION
database		CREATE DEFAULT

database		CREATE FULLTEXT CATALOG
database		CREATE FUNCTION
database		CREATE MESSAGE TYPE
database		CREATE PROCEDURE
database		CREATE QUEUE
database		CREATE REMOTE SERVICE BINDING
database		CREATE ROLE
database		CREATE ROUTE
database		CREATE RULE
database		CREATE SCHEMA
database		CREATE SERVICE
database		CREATE SYMMETRIC KEY
database		CREATE SYNONYM
database		CREATE TABLE
database		CREATE TYPE
database		CREATE VIEW
database		CREATE XML SCHEMA COLLECTION
database		DELETE
database		EXECUTE
database		INSERT
database		REFERENCES
database		SELECT
database		SHOWPLAN
database		SUBSCRIBE QUERY NOTIFICATIONS
database		TAKE OWNERSHIP
database		UPDATE
database		VIEW DATABASE STATE
database		VIEW DEFINITION

Example for what I can do as member of the sysadmin (sa) role

```
CREATE EVENT NOTIFICATION NotifyDDLDBA
ON DATABASE
FOR ALTER_TABLE
TO SERVICE 'DBAsupport',
  'ECFED6C2-59FF-49B5-B06C-7D8AC834DB8B';
```

CHAPTER 11: Managing Users Permissions

Server Role Permissions

We can get a list of server roles by executing a system procedure.

EXEC sp_helpsrvrole;
go

ServerRole	Description
sysadmin	System Administrators
securityadmin	Security Administrators
serveradmin	Server Administrators
setupadmin	Setup Administrators
processadmin	Process Administrators
diskadmin	Disk Administrators
dbcreator	Database Creators
bulkadmin	Bulk Insert Administrators

Another system procedure lists the permissions for each role.

EXEC sp_srvrolepermission sysadmin;

ServerRole	Permission
sysadmin	Add extended procedures
sysadmin	Add member to bulkadmin
sysadmin	Add member to dbcreator
sysadmin	Add member to diskadmin
sysadmin	Add member to processadmin
sysadmin	Add member to securityadmin
sysadmin	Add member to serveradmin
sysadmin	Add member to setupadmin
sysadmin	Add member to sysadmin
sysadmin	Add/drop to/from db_accessadmin
sysadmin	Add/drop to/from db_backupoperator
sysadmin	Add/drop to/from db_datareader
sysadmin	Add/drop to/from db_datawriter
sysadmin	Add/drop to/from db_ddladmin
sysadmin	Add/drop to/from db_denydatareader
sysadmin	Add/drop to/from db_denydatawriter
sysadmin	Add/drop to/from db_owner
sysadmin	Add/drop to/from db_securityadmin
sysadmin	Add/drop/configure linked servers

CHAPTER 11: Managing Users Permissions

sysadmin	All DDL but GRANT, REVOKE, DENY
sysadmin	ALTER DATABASE
sysadmin	BACKUP DATABASE
sysadmin	BACKUP LOG
sysadmin	BULK INSERT
sysadmin	CHECKPOINT
sysadmin	Complete SETUSER SQL user
sysadmin	Constraints on System tables
sysadmin	CREATE DATABASE
sysadmin	Create indices on system tables
sysadmin	Create/delete/modify system tables
sysadmin	dbcc change 'on' rules
sysadmin	dbcc checkalloc
sysadmin	dbcc checkdb
sysadmin	dbcc checkfilegroup
sysadmin	dbcc checkident
sysadmin	dbcc checktable
sysadmin	dbcc cleantable
sysadmin	dbcc dbreindex
sysadmin	dbcc dropcleanbuffers
sysadmin	dbcc freeproccache
sysadmin	dbcc inputbuffer
sysadmin	dbcc outputbuffer
sysadmin	dbcc pintable
sysadmin	dbcc proccache
sysadmin	dbcc setcpuweight
sysadmin	dbcc setioweight
sysadmin	dbcc show_statistics
sysadmin	dbcc showcontig
sysadmin	dbcc showoptweights
sysadmin	DBCC ShrinkDatabase
sysadmin	dbcc shrinkfile
sysadmin	dbcc traceon/off
sysadmin	dbcc updateusage
sysadmin	DELETE permission on any object
sysadmin	DENY
sysadmin	DISK INIT
sysadmin	DROP DATABASE
sysadmin	EXECUTE any procedure
sysadmin	Extend database
sysadmin	GRANT

sysadmin	Grant/deny/revoke CREATE DATABASE
sysadmin	INSERT permission on any object
sysadmin	KILL
sysadmin	Mark a stored procedure as startup
sysadmin	Raiserror With Log
sysadmin	Read the error log
sysadmin	RECONFIGURE
sysadmin	REFERENCES permission on any table
sysadmin	RESTORE DATABASE
sysadmin	RESTORE LOG
sysadmin	REVOKE
sysadmin	SELECT permission on any object
sysadmin	SHUTDOWN
sysadmin	sp_addapprole
sysadmin	sp_addlinkedsrvlogin
sysadmin	sp_addlogin
sysadmin	sp_addrole
sysadmin	sp_addrolemember
sysadmin	sp_addumpdevice
sysadmin	sp_adduser
sysadmin	sp_altermessage
sysadmin	sp_approlepassword
sysadmin	sp_change_users_login
sysadmin	sp_changedbowner
sysadmin	sp_changeobjectowner
sysadmin	sp_configure
sysadmin	sp_dbcmptlevel
sysadmin	sp_defaultdb
sysadmin	sp_defaultlanguage
sysadmin	sp_denylogin
sysadmin	sp_diskdefault
sysadmin	sp_dropapprole
sysadmin	sp_dropdevice
sysadmin	sp_droplinkedsrvlogin
sysadmin	sp_droplogin
sysadmin	sp_dropremotelogin
sysadmin	sp_droprole
sysadmin	sp_droprolemember
sysadmin	sp_dropuser
sysadmin	sp_fulltext_catalog
sysadmin	sp_fulltext_column

sysadmin	sp_fulltext_database
sysadmin	sp_fulltext_service
sysadmin	sp_fulltext_table
sysadmin	sp_grantdbaccess
sysadmin	sp_grantlogin
sysadmin	sp_helplogins
sysadmin	sp_password
sysadmin	sp_recompile
sysadmin	sp_refreshview
sysadmin	sp_remoteoption
sysadmin	sp_remoteoption (update)
sysadmin	sp_rename
sysadmin	sp_renamedb
sysadmin	sp_revokedbaccess
sysadmin	sp_revokelogin
sysadmin	sp_tableoption
sysadmin	sp_updatestats
sysadmin	TRUNCATE TABLE
sysadmin	UPDATE permission on any object
sysadmin	USE to a suspect database

EXEC sp_srvrolepermission securityadmin;

ServerRole	Permission
securityadmin	Add member to securityadmin
securityadmin	Grant/deny/revoke CREATE DATABASE
securityadmin	Read the error log
securityadmin	sp_addlinkedsrvlogin
securityadmin	sp_addlogin
securityadmin	sp_defaultdb
securityadmin	sp_defaultlanguage
securityadmin	sp_denylogin
securityadmin	sp_droplinkedsrvlogin
securityadmin	sp_droplogin
securityadmin	sp_dropremotelogin
securityadmin	sp_grantlogin
securityadmin	sp_helplogins
securityadmin	sp_password
securityadmin	sp_remoteoption (update)
securityadmin	sp_revokelogin

EXEC sp_srvrolepermission serveradmin;

ServerRole	Permission
serveradmin	Add member to serveradmin
serveradmin	dbcc freeproccache
serveradmin	RECONFIGURE
serveradmin	SHUTDOWN
serveradmin	sp_configure
serveradmin	sp_fulltext_service
serveradmin	sp_tableoption

EXEC sp_srvrolepermission setupadmin;

ServerRole	Permission
setupadmin	Add member to setupadmin
setupadmin	Add/drop/configure linked servers
setupadmin	Mark a stored procedure as startup

EXEC sp_srvrolepermission processadmin;

ServerRole	Permission
processadmin	Add member to processadmin
processadmin	KILL

EXEC sp_srvrolepermission diskadmin;

ServerRole	Permission
diskadmin	Add member to diskadmin
diskadmin	DISK INIT
diskadmin	sp_addumpdevice
diskadmin	sp_diskdefault
diskadmin	sp_dropdevice

EXEC sp_srvrolepermission dbcreator;

ServerRole	Permission
dbcreator	Add member to dbcreator
dbcreator	ALTER DATABASE
dbcreator	CREATE DATABASE
dbcreator	DROP DATABASE
dbcreator	Extend database
dbcreator	RESTORE DATABASE
dbcreator	RESTORE LOG
dbcreator	sp_renamedb

EXEC sp_srvrolepermission bulkadmin;

ServerRole	Permission
bulkadmin	Add member to bulkadmin
bulkadmin	BULK INSERT

Database Role Permissions

The sp_helprole and sp_helprolemember system procedures can be used to investigate database security metadata. The db_... roles are called fixed database roles.

use AdventureWorks2012;

exec sp_helprole;
go

RoleName	RoleId	IsAppRole
public	0	0
InventoryStaff	7	0
HRStaff	8	0
db_owner	16384	0
db_accessadmin	16385	0
db_securityadmin	16386	0
db_ddladmin	16387	0
db_backupoperator	16389	0
db_datareader	16390	0
db_datawriter	16391	0
db_denydatareader	16392	0
db_denydatawriter	16393	0

exec sp_helprolemember db_owner;

DbRole	MemberName	MemberSID
db_owner	dbo	0x01

Role permissions can be checked by sp_dbfixedrolepermission system procedure.

exec sp_dbfixedrolepermission db_owner;

DbFixedRole	Permission
db_owner	Add/drop to/from db_accessadmin
db_owner	Add/drop to/from db_backupoperator
db_owner	Add/drop to/from db_datareader
db_owner	Add/drop to/from db_datawriter
db_owner	Add/drop to/from db_ddladmin
db_owner	Add/drop to/from db_denydatareader
db_owner	Add/drop to/from db_denydatawriter

db_owner	Add/drop to/from db_owner
db_owner	Add/drop to/from db_securityadmin
db_owner	All DDL but GRANT, REVOKE, DENY
db_owner	BACKUP DATABASE
db_owner	BACKUP LOG
db_owner	CHECKPOINT
db_owner	dbcc checkalloc
db_owner	dbcc checkdb
db_owner	dbcc checkfilegroup
db_owner	dbcc checkident
db_owner	dbcc checktable
db_owner	dbcc cleantable
db_owner	dbcc dbreindex
db_owner	dbcc proccache
db_owner	dbcc show_statistics
db_owner	dbcc showcontig
db_owner	dbcc shrinkdatabase
db_owner	dbcc shrinkfile
db_owner	dbcc updateusage
db_owner	DELETE permission on any object
db_owner	DENY
db_owner	EXECUTE any procedure
db_owner	GRANT
db_owner	INSERT permission on any object
db_owner	REFERENCES permission on any table
db_owner	REVOKE
db_owner	SELECT permission on any object
db_owner	sp_addapprole
db_owner	sp_addrole
db_owner	sp_addrolemember
db_owner	sp_approlepassword
db_owner	sp_change_users_login
db_owner	sp_changeobjectowner
db_owner	sp_dbcmptlevel
db_owner	sp_dropapprole
db_owner	sp_droprole
db_owner	sp_droprolemember
db_owner	sp_dropuser
db_owner	sp_fulltext_catalog
db_owner	sp_fulltext_column
db_owner	sp_fulltext_database

db_owner	sp_fulltext_table
db_owner	sp_grantdbaccess
db_owner	sp_recompile
db_owner	sp_refreshview
db_owner	sp_rename
db_owner	sp_revokedbaccess
db_owner	sp_tableoption
db_owner	TRUNCATE TABLE
db_owner	UPDATE permission on any object

exec sp_dbfixedrolepermission db_accessadmin;

DbFixedRole	Permission
db_accessadmin	sp_dropuser
db_accessadmin	sp_grantdbaccess
db_accessadmin	sp_revokedbaccess

exec sp_dbfixedrolepermission db_securityadmin;

DbFixedRole	Permission
db_securityadmin	DENY
db_securityadmin	GRANT
db_securityadmin	REVOKE
db_securityadmin	sp_addapprole
db_securityadmin	sp_addrole
db_securityadmin	sp_addrolemember
db_securityadmin	sp_approlepassword
db_securityadmin	sp_changeobjectowner
db_securityadmin	sp_dropapprole
db_securityadmin	sp_droprole
db_securityadmin	sp_droprolemember

exec sp_dbfixedrolepermission db_ddladmin;

DbFixedRole	Permission
db_ddladmin	All DDL but GRANT, REVOKE, DENY
db_ddladmin	dbcc cleantable
db_ddladmin	dbcc show_statistics
db_ddladmin	dbcc showcontig
db_ddladmin	REFERENCES permission on any table
db_ddladmin	sp_changeobjectowner

CHAPTER 11: Managing Users Permissions

db_ddladmin	sp_fulltext_column
db_ddladmin	sp_fulltext_table
db_ddladmin	sp_recompile
db_ddladmin	sp_rename
db_ddladmin	sp_tableoption
db_ddladmin	TRUNCATE TABLE

exec sp_dbfixedrolepermission db_backupoperator;

DbFixedRole	Permission
db_backupoperator	BACKUP DATABASE
db_backupoperator	BACKUP LOG
db_backupoperator	CHECKPOINT

exec sp_dbfixedrolepermission db_datareader;

DbFixedRole	Permission
db_datareader	SELECT permission on any object

exec sp_dbfixedrolepermission db_datawriter;

DbFixedRole	Permission
db_datawriter	DELETE permission on any object
db_datawriter	INSERT permission on any object
db_datawriter	UPDATE permission on any object

exec sp_dbfixedrolepermission db_denydatareader;

DbFixedRole	Permission
db_denydatareader	No SELECT permission on any object

exec sp_dbfixedrolepermission db_denydatawriter;

DbFixedRole	Permission
db_denydatawriter	No DELETE permission on any object
db_denydatawriter	No INSERT permission on any object
db_denydatawriter	No UPDATE permission on any object

List All Roles for a User

All users are in the public role by default.

```
DECLARE @UserName sysname;
SET @UserName= 'JudyK';
WITH cteRoles (role_principal_id)
   AS (SELECT role_principal_id
      FROM   sys.database_role_members
      WHERE  member_principal_id = USER_ID(@UserName)
      UNION ALL
      SELECT dbrm.role_principal_id
      FROM   sys.database_role_members dbrm
         INNER JOIN cteRoles cte
            ON dbrm.member_principal_id = cte.role_principal_id)
SELECT DISTINCT USER_NAME(role_principal_id) AS RoleName
FROM   cteRoles
UNION ALL
SELECT 'public'
ORDER  BY RoleName;
```

RoleName
InventoryStaff
public

Object Ownership Within the Database

Each object must have an owner. The default owner is the dbo. Query to find the owner.

```
USE AdventureWorks2012;
```

```
SELECT * FROM   sys.database_principals
WHERE  principal_id IN (SELECT OBJECTPROPERTY(
            OBJECT_ID(N'HumanResources.vEmployee'),  'ownerid'));
```

name	principal_id	type	type_desc	default_schema_name	create_date
	modify_date	owning_principal_id	sid	is_fixed_role	authentication_type
	authentication_type_desc		default_language_name		default_language_lcid
RogerMoore	10	C	CERTIFICATE_MAPPED_USER	NULL	2013-05-14
09:32:59.217	2013-05-14 09:32:59.217		NULL		
	0x0106000000000000901000000A63C316F57F204F50AA6006971891342A5B59A89				
	0	0	NONE	NULL	NULL

```
SELECT * FROM  sys.database_principals  WHERE  principal_id
IN (SELECT OBJECTPROPERTY(OBJECT_ID(N'Production.Product' ),  'ownerid'));
```

```
name    principal_id  type    type_desc      default_schema_name  create_date
        modify_date    owning_principal_id  sid     is_fixed_role authentication_type
        authentication_type_desc    default_language_name
        default_language_lcid
dbo     1       U       WINDOWS_USER  dbo      2003-04-08 09:10:42.287     2012-03-14
13:14:18.683    NULL    0x01050000000000000515000000A065CF7E784B9B5FE77C877005E28000
        0       3       WINDOWS         NULL    NULL
```

Statement Permissions

Activities involved in creating a database or an item in a database
require a different group of permissions called statement permissions. Examples
for statements requiring statement permission.

> BACKUP DATABASE

> BACKUP LOG

> CREATE DATABASE

> CREATE DEFAULT

> CREATE FUNCTION

> CREATE PROCEDURE

> CREATE LOGIN

> CREATE TABLE

> CREATE VIEW

Implied Permissions

Implied permissions manage those activities that can be performed only by members of
predefined system roles or owners of database objects. As an example, a member of the
sysadmin fixed server role, like sa, inherits automatically full permission to do anything in a SQL
Server instance. Database object owners also have implied permissions that allow them to
perform all activities with the objects they own.

Object Ownership Chains

If a user owns the source object along with the underlying (target) objects it depends on, then the ownership chain is unbroken. If any of the underlying objects is owned by someone else, then the ownership chain is broken.

Articles: **Using Ownership Chains**   http://bit.ly/129t46S
http://msdn.microsoft.com/en-us/library/aa905173(v=sql.80).aspx

Understanding Cross Database Ownership Chaining in SQL Server   http://bit.ly/XhgocL
http://www.mssqltips.com/sqlservertip/1782/understanding-cross-database-ownership-chaining-in-sql-server/

Views As Security Mechanisms

Instead of permissioning tables we can create views and grant access to the views only not the underlying table(s). This methods adds lots of flexibility to permissioning.

MSDN Article: **Using Views as Security Mechanisms**   http://bit.ly/13cOczl
http://msdn.microsoft.com/en-us/library/aa905180(v=sql.80).aspx

Stored Procedures as Security Mechanisms

Stored procedures, similarly to views, can be permissioned for execution instead of providing access to the underlying objects.

MSDN Article: **Using Stored Procedures as Security Mechanisms** http://bit.ly/19E5tUm
http://msdn.microsoft.com/en-us/library/aa905166(v=sql.80).aspx

Ownership Display in Object Explorer Details

Warning: Regular Object Explorer does not display ownership.

CHAPTER 11: Managing Users Permissions

Object Dependencies

A database object, such as a stored procedure, may depend on other objects for example tables. Also the other way around: some other objects may be dependent on this object. Dependency display in Object Explorer is launched by right click on object.

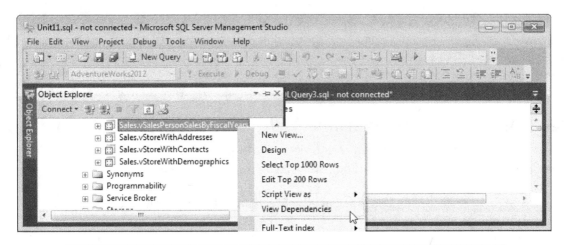

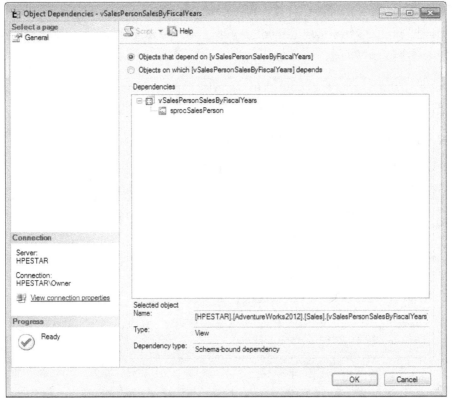

Objects on Which This View Object Depends

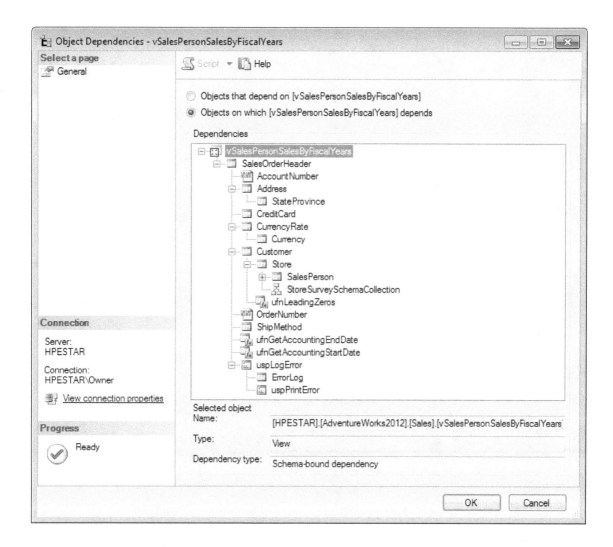

MSDN Article: **Object Dependencies (General Page)** http://bit.ly/19Hypei
http://msdn.microsoft.com/en-us/library/ms188972(v=sql.105).aspx

Objects That Depend On Production.Product Table

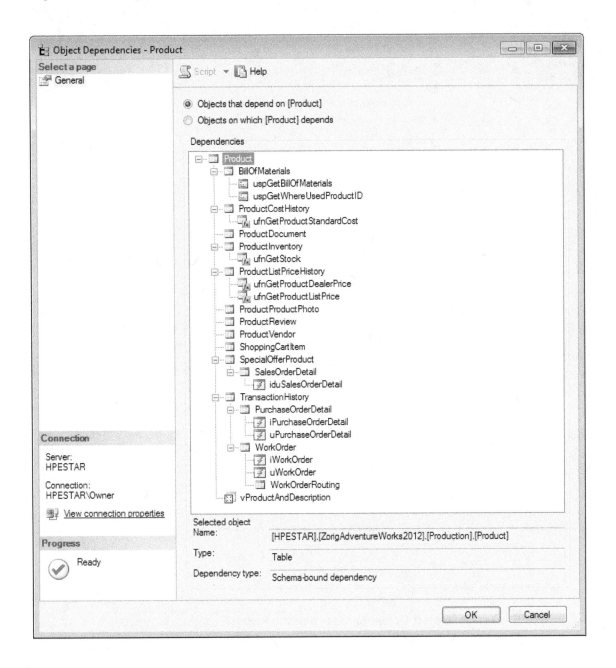

Objects on Which Production.Product Table Depends

Notice the tables hierarchy: Product --> ProductSubcategory --> ProductCategory.

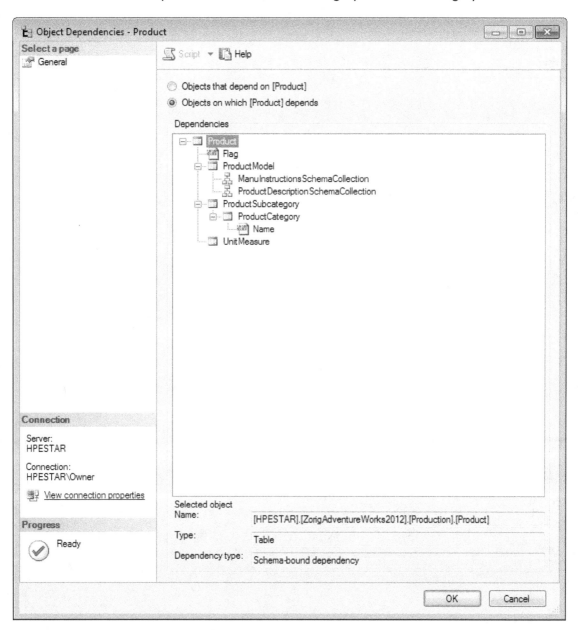

Objects That Depend on uSalesOrdersHeader Trigger

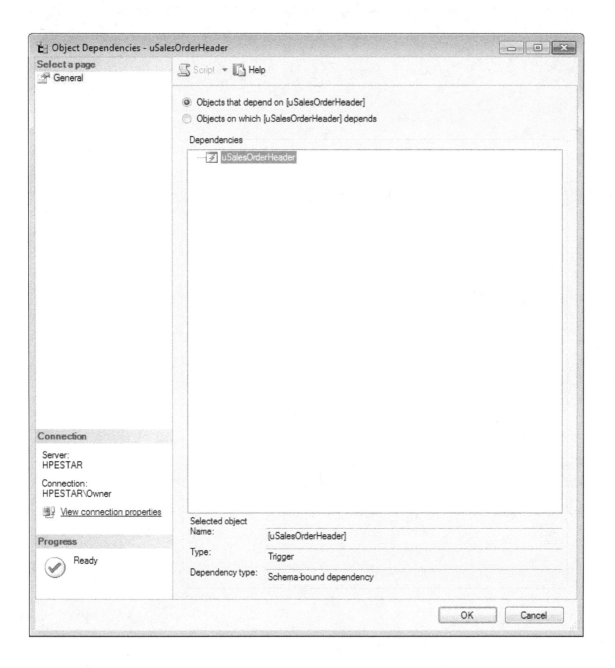

Objects on Which uSalesOrderHeader Trigger Depends

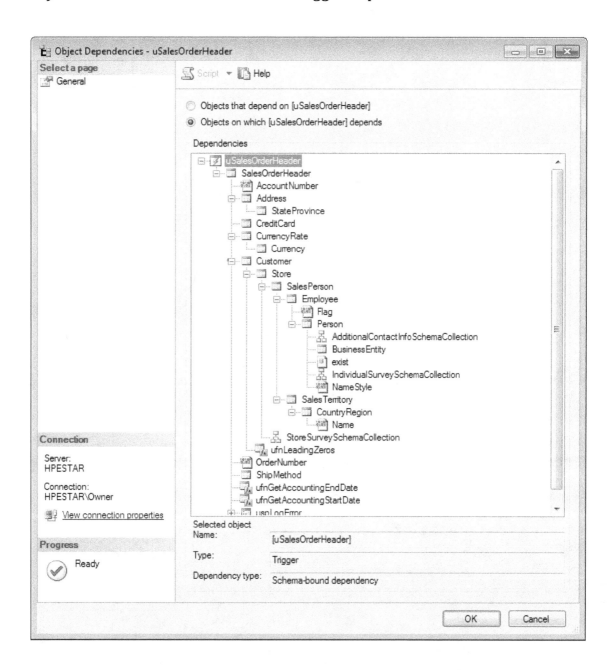

Objects Dependent on ufnGetContactInformation UDF

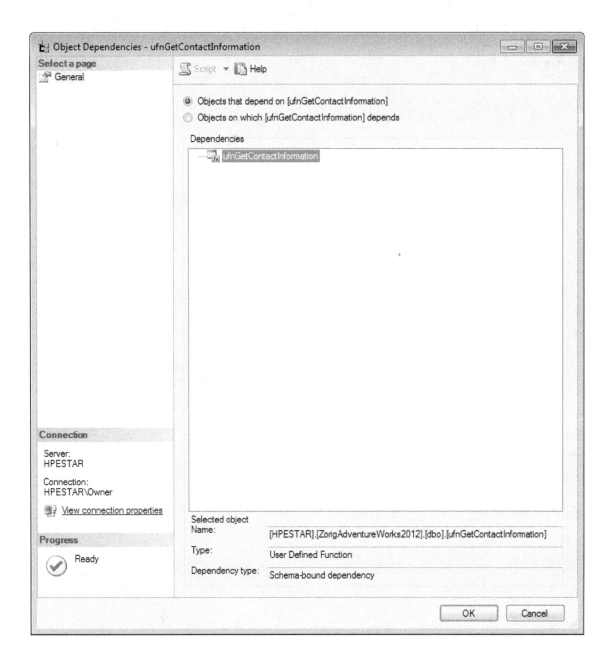

Objects on Which ufnGetContactInformation Function (UDF) Depends

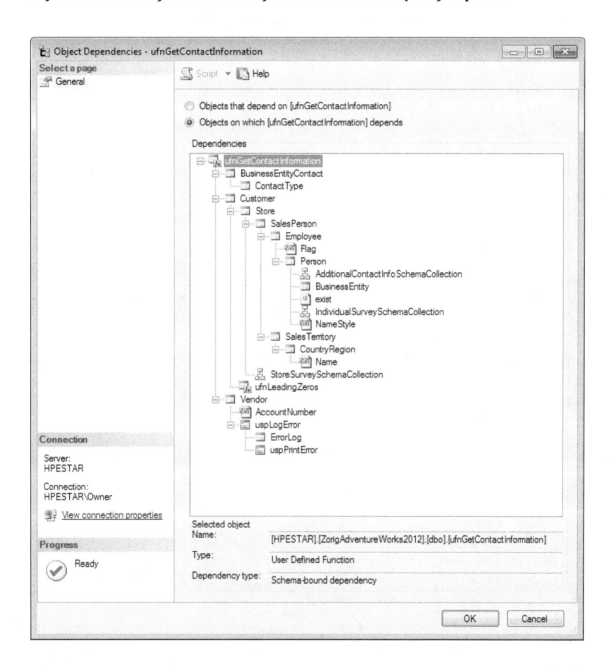

Programmatic Object Dependency Check

System views are available to extract dependency data programmatically. Dependency information is very important in development, production debugging and changes to a production database system.

```
SELECT  ReferencingObject = CONCAT(SCHEMA_NAME(o1.schema_id), '.',o1.name),
        ReferencedObject = CONCAT(SCHEMA_NAME(o2.schema_id),'.',
                                            ed.referenced_entity_name),

        ColumnName = c.name,
        ReferencedObjectType = o2.type_desc,
        ReferencingObjecType = o1.type_desc
FROM   AdventureWorks2012.sys.sql_expression_dependencies ed
    INNER JOIN AdventureWorks2012.sys.objects o1
        ON ed.referencing_id = o1.object_id
    INNER JOIN AdventureWorks2012.sys.objects o2
        ON ed.referenced_id = o2.object_id
    INNER JOIN AdventureWorks2012.sys.sql_dependencies d
        ON ed.referencing_id = d.object_id
          AND d.referenced_major_id = ed.referenced_id
    INNER JOIN sys.columns c
        ON c.object_id = ed.referenced_id
          AND d.referenced_minor_id = c.column_id
WHERE  CONCAT(SCHEMA_NAME(o1.schema_id), '.' ,  o1.name) = 'Sales.vSalesPerson'
ORDER  BY ReferencedObject,
    c.column_id;
```

ReferencingObject	ReferencedObject	ColumnName	ReferencedObjectType	ReferencingObjecType
Sales.vSalesPerson	HumanResources.Employee	BusinessEntityID	USER_TABLE	VIEW
Sales.vSalesPerson	HumanResources.Employee	JobTitle	USER_TABLE	VIEW
Sales.vSalesPerson	Person.Address	AddressID	USER_TABLE	VIEW
Sales.vSalesPerson	Person.Address	AddressLine1	USER_TABLE	VIEW
Sales.vSalesPerson	Person.Address	AddressLine2	USER_TABLE	VIEW
Sales.vSalesPerson	Person.Address	City	USER_TABLE	VIEW
Sales.vSalesPerson	Person.Address	StateProvinceID	USER_TABLE	VIEW
Sales.vSalesPerson	Person.Address	PostalCode	USER_TABLE	VIEW
Sales.vSalesPerson	Person.BusinessEntityAddress	BusinessEntityID	USER_TABLE	VIEW
Sales.vSalesPerson	Person.BusinessEntityAddress	AddressID	USER_TABLE	VIEW
Sales.vSalesPerson	Person.CountryRegion	CountryRegionCode	USER_TABLE	VIEW
Sales.vSalesPerson	Person.CountryRegion	Name	USER_TABLE	VIEW
Sales.vSalesPerson	Person.EmailAddress	BusinessEntityID	USER_TABLE	VIEW
Sales.vSalesPerson	Person.EmailAddress	EmailAddress	USER_TABLE	VIEW
Sales.vSalesPerson	Person.Person	BusinessEntityID	USER_TABLE	VIEW
Sales.vSalesPerson	Person.Person	Title	USER_TABLE	VIEW
Sales.vSalesPerson	Person.Person	FirstName	USER_TABLE	VIEW
Sales.vSalesPerson	Person.Person	MiddleName	USER_TABLE	VIEW

Sales.vSalesPerson	Person.Person	LastName	USER_TABLE	VIEW
Sales.vSalesPerson	Person.Person	Suffix	USER_TABLE	VIEW
Sales.vSalesPerson	Person.Person	EmailPromotion	USER_TABLE	VIEW
Sales.vSalesPerson	Person.PersonPhone	BusinessEntityID	USER_TABLE	VIEW
Sales.vSalesPerson	Person.PersonPhone	PhoneNumber	USER_TABLE	VIEW
Sales.vSalesPerson	Person.PersonPhone	PhoneNumberTypeID	USER_TABLE	VIEW
Sales.vSalesPerson	Person.PhoneNumberType	PhoneNumberTypeID	USER_TABLE	VIEW
Sales.vSalesPerson	Person.PhoneNumberType	Name	USER_TABLE	VIEW
Sales.vSalesPerson	Person.StateProvince	StateProvinceID	USER_TABLE	VIEW
Sales.vSalesPerson	Person.StateProvince	CountryRegionCode	USER_TABLE	VIEW
Sales.vSalesPerson	Person.StateProvince	Name	USER_TABLE	VIEW
Sales.vSalesPerson	Sales.SalesPerson	BusinessEntityID	USER_TABLE	VIEW
Sales.vSalesPerson	Sales.SalesPerson	TerritoryID	USER_TABLE	VIEW
Sales.vSalesPerson	Sales.SalesPerson	SalesQuota	USER_TABLE	VIEW
Sales.vSalesPerson	Sales.SalesPerson	SalesYTD	USER_TABLE	VIEW
Sales.vSalesPerson	Sales.SalesPerson	SalesLastYear	USER_TABLE	VIEW
Sales.vSalesPerson	Sales.SalesTerritory	TerritoryID	USER_TABLE	VIEW
Sales.vSalesPerson	Sales.SalesTerritory	Name	USER_TABLE	VIEW
Sales.vSalesPerson	Sales.SalesTerritory	Group	USER_TABLE	VIEW

Same query executed for dbo.uspGetBillOfMaterials stored procedure.

ReferencingObject	ReferencedObject	ColumnName	ReferencedObjectType	ReferencingObjecType
dbo.uspGetBillOfMaterials	Production.BillOfMaterials	ProductAssemblyID	USER_TABLE	SQL_STORED_PROCEDURE
dbo.uspGetBillOfMaterials	Production.BillOfMaterials	ComponentID	USER_TABLE	SQL_STORED_PROCEDURE
dbo.uspGetBillOfMaterials	Production.BillOfMaterials	StartDate	USER_TABLE	SQL_STORED_PROCEDURE
dbo.uspGetBillOfMaterials	Production.BillOfMaterials	EndDate	USER_TABLE	SQL_STORED_PROCEDURE
dbo.uspGetBillOfMaterials	Production.BillOfMaterials	BOMLevel	USER_TABLE	SQL_STORED_PROCEDURE
dbo.uspGetBillOfMaterials	Production.BillOfMaterials	PerAssemblyQty	USER_TABLE	SQL_STORED_PROCEDURE
dbo.uspGetBillOfMaterials	Production.Product	ProductID	USER_TABLE	SQL_STORED_PROCEDURE
dbo.uspGetBillOfMaterials	Production.Product	Name	USER_TABLE	SQL_STORED_PROCEDURE
dbo.uspGetBillOfMaterials	Production.Product	StandardCost	USER_TABLE	SQL_STORED_PROCEDURE
dbo.uspGetBillOfMaterials	Production.Product	ListPrice	USER_TABLE	SQL_STORED_PROCEDURE

CHAPTER 11: Managing Users Permissions

Enumerating Dependencies by Object Type

The following query lists dependencies in AdventureWorks2012 database for stored procedures, views, triggers and table-valued functons.

```
SELECT
        ReferencingObjectType = o1.type,
        ReferencingObject =
                CONCAT(SCHEMA_NAME(o1.schema_id), '.', o1.name),
        ReferencedObject =
                CONCAT(SCHEMA_NAME(o2.schema_id), '.', ed.referenced_entity_name),
        ReferencedObjectType = o2.type
FROM
                sys.sql_expression_dependencies ed
    INNER JOIN sys.objects o1
        ON ed.referencing_id = o1.object_id
    INNER JOIN sys.objects o2
        ON ed.referenced_id = o2.object_id
WHERE  o1.type IN ( 'P', 'TR', 'V', 'TF' )
ORDER  BY       ReferencingObjectType,
                ReferencingObject,
                ReferencedObject;
GO
```

ReferencingObject Type	ReferencingObject	ReferencedObject	ReferencedObject Type
P	dbo.uspGetBillOfMaterials	Production.BillOfMaterials	U
P	dbo.uspGetBillOfMaterials	Production.Product	U
P	dbo.uspGetEmployeeManagers	HumanResources.Employee	U
P	dbo.uspGetEmployeeManagers	Person.Person	U
P	dbo.uspGetManagerEmployees	HumanResources.Employee	U
P	dbo.uspGetManagerEmployees	Person.Person	U
P	dbo.uspGetWhereUsedProductID	Production.BillOfMaterials	U
P	dbo.uspGetWhereUsedProductID	Production.Product	U
P	dbo.uspLogError	dbo.ErrorLog	U
P	dbo.uspLogError	dbo.uspPrintError	P
P	dbo.uspSearchCandidateResumes	HumanResources.JobCandidate	U
P	HumanResources.uspUpdateEmployeeHireInfo	dbo.uspLogError	P
P	HumanResources.uspUpdateEmployeeHireInfo	HumanResources.Employee	U
P	HumanResources.uspUpdateEmployeeHireInfo	HumanResources.EmployeePayHistory	U
P	HumanResources.uspUpdateEmployeeLogin	dbo.uspLogError	P
P	HumanResources.uspUpdateEmployeeLogin	HumanResources.Employee	U
P	HumanResources.uspUpdateEmployeePe	dbo.uspLogError	P

	rsonalInfo		
P	HumanResources.uspUpdateEmployeePersonalInfo	HumanResources.Employee	U
TF	dbo.ufnGetContactInformation	HumanResources.Employee	U
TF	dbo.ufnGetContactInformation	Person.BusinessEntityContact	U
TF	dbo.ufnGetContactInformation	Person.ContactType	U
TF	dbo.ufnGetContactInformation	Person.Person	U
TF	dbo.ufnGetContactInformation	Purchasing.Vendor	U
TF	dbo.ufnGetContactInformation	Sales.Customer	U
TF	dbo.ufnGetContactInformation	Sales.Store	U
TR	Person.iuPerson	Person.Person	U
TR	Production.iWorkOrder	dbo.uspLogError	P
TR	Production.iWorkOrder	dbo.uspPrintError	P
TR	Production.iWorkOrder	Production.TransactionHistory	U
TR	Production.uWorkOrder	dbo.uspLogError	P
TR	Production.uWorkOrder	dbo.uspPrintError	P
TR	Production.uWorkOrder	Production.TransactionHistory	U
TR	Purchasing.dVendor	dbo.uspLogError	P
TR	Purchasing.dVendor	dbo.uspPrintError	P
TR	Purchasing.iPurchaseOrderDetail	dbo.uspLogError	P
TR	Purchasing.iPurchaseOrderDetail	dbo.uspPrintError	P
TR	Purchasing.iPurchaseOrderDetail	Production.TransactionHistory	U
TR	Purchasing.iPurchaseOrderDetail	Purchasing.PurchaseOrderDetail	U
TR	Purchasing.iPurchaseOrderDetail	Purchasing.PurchaseOrderHeader	U
TR	Purchasing.uPurchaseOrderDetail	dbo.uspLogError	P
TR	Purchasing.uPurchaseOrderDetail	dbo.uspPrintError	P
TR	Purchasing.uPurchaseOrderDetail	Production.TransactionHistory	U
TR	Purchasing.uPurchaseOrderDetail	Purchasing.PurchaseOrderDetail	U
TR	Purchasing.uPurchaseOrderDetail	Purchasing.PurchaseOrderHeader	U
TR	Purchasing.uPurchaseOrderHeader	dbo.uspLogError	P
TR	Purchasing.uPurchaseOrderHeader	dbo.uspPrintError	P
TR	Purchasing.uPurchaseOrderHeader	Purchasing.PurchaseOrderHeader	U
TR	Sales.iduSalesOrderDetail	dbo.uspLogError	P
TR	Sales.iduSalesOrderDetail	dbo.uspPrintError	P
TR	Sales.iduSalesOrderDetail	Person.Person	U
TR	Sales.iduSalesOrderDetail	Production.TransactionHistory	U
TR	Sales.iduSalesOrderDetail	Sales.Customer	U
TR	Sales.iduSalesOrderDetail	Sales.SalesOrderDetail	U
TR	Sales.iduSalesOrderDetail	Sales.SalesOrderHeader	U
TR	Sales.uSalesOrderHeader	dbo.ufnGetAccountingEndDate	FN
TR	Sales.uSalesOrderHeader	dbo.ufnGetAccountingStartDate	FN
TR	Sales.uSalesOrderHeader	dbo.uspLogError	P
TR	Sales.uSalesOrderHeader	dbo.uspPrintError	P
TR	Sales.uSalesOrderHeader	Sales.SalesOrderHeader	U
TR	Sales.uSalesOrderHeader	Sales.SalesPerson	U
TR	Sales.uSalesOrderHeader	Sales.SalesTerritory	U
V	HumanResources.vEmployee	HumanResources.Employee	U
V	HumanResources.vEmployee	Person.Address	U
V	HumanResources.vEmployee	Person.BusinessEntityAddress	U
V	HumanResources.vEmployee	Person.CountryRegion	U
V	HumanResources.vEmployee	Person.EmailAddress	U
V	HumanResources.vEmployee	Person.Person	U
V	HumanResources.vEmployee	Person.PersonPhone	U
V	HumanResources.vEmployee	Person.PhoneNumberType	U
V	HumanResources.vEmployee	Person.StateProvince	U

CHAPTER 11: Managing Users Permissions

V	HumanResources.vEmployeeDepartment	HumanResources.Department	U
V	HumanResources.vEmployeeDepartment	HumanResources.Employee	U
V	HumanResources.vEmployeeDepartment	HumanResources.EmployeeDepartmentHistory	U
V	HumanResources.vEmployeeDepartment	Person.Person	U
V	HumanResources.vEmployeeDepartment History	HumanResources.Department	U
V	HumanResources.vEmployeeDepartment History	HumanResources.Employee	U
V	HumanResources.vEmployeeDepartment History	HumanResources.EmployeeDepartmentHistory	U
V	HumanResources.vEmployeeDepartment History	HumanResources.Shift	U
V	HumanResources.vEmployeeDepartment History	Person.Person	U
V	HumanResources.vJobCandidate	HumanResources.JobCandidate	U
V	HumanResources.vJobCandidateEducation	HumanResources.JobCandidate	U
V	HumanResources.vJobCandidateEmployment	HumanResources.JobCandidate	U
V	Person.vAdditionalContactInfo	Person.Person	U
V	Person.vStateProvinceCountryRegion	Person.CountryRegion	U
V	Person.vStateProvinceCountryRegion	Person.CountryRegion	U
V	Person.vStateProvinceCountryRegion	Person.CountryRegion	U
V	Person.vStateProvinceCountryRegion	Person.StateProvince	U
V	Person.vStateProvinceCountryRegion	Person.StateProvince	U
V	Person.vStateProvinceCountryRegion	Person.StateProvince	U
V	Person.vStateProvinceCountryRegion	Person.StateProvince	U
V	Person.vStateProvinceCountryRegion	Person.StateProvince	U
V	Person.vStateProvinceCountryRegion	Person.StateProvince	U
V	Person.vStateProvinceCountryRegion	Person.StateProvince	U
V	Production.vProductAndDescription	Production.Product	U
V	Production.vProductAndDescription	Production.Product	U
V	Production.vProductAndDescription	Production.Product	U
V	Production.vProductAndDescription	Production.Product	U
V	Production.vProductAndDescription	Production.ProductDescription	U
V	Production.vProductAndDescription	Production.ProductDescription	U
V	Production.vProductAndDescription	Production.ProductDescription	U
V	Production.vProductAndDescription	Production.ProductModel	U
V	Production.vProductAndDescription	Production.ProductModel	U
V	Production.vProductAndDescription	Production.ProductModel	U
V	Production.vProductAndDescription	Production.ProductModelProductDescriptionCulture	U
V	Production.vProductAndDescription	Production.ProductModelProductDescriptionCulture	U
V	Production.vProductAndDescription	Production.ProductModelProductDescriptionCulture	U
V	Production.vProductAndDescription	Production.ProductModelProductDescriptionCulture	U
V	Production.vProductModelCatalogDescription	Production.ProductModel	U
V	Production.vProductModelInstructions	Production.ProductModel	U
V	Purchasing.vVendorWithAddresses	Person.Address	U
V	Purchasing.vVendorWithAddresses	Person.AddressType	U
V	Purchasing.vVendorWithAddresses	Person.BusinessEntityAddress	U
V	Purchasing.vVendorWithAddresses	Person.CountryRegion	U

CHAPTER 11: Managing Users Permissions

V	Purchasing.vVendorWithAddresses	Person.StateProvince	U
V	Purchasing.vVendorWithAddresses	Purchasing.Vendor	U
V	Purchasing.vVendorWithContacts	Person.BusinessEntityContact	U
V	Purchasing.vVendorWithContacts	Person.ContactType	U
V	Purchasing.vVendorWithContacts	Person.EmailAddress	U
V	Purchasing.vVendorWithContacts	Person.Person	U
V	Purchasing.vVendorWithContacts	Person.PersonPhone	U
V	Purchasing.vVendorWithContacts	Person.PhoneNumberType	U
V	Purchasing.vVendorWithContacts	Purchasing.Vendor	U
V	Sales.vIndividualCustomer	Person.Address	U
V	Sales.vIndividualCustomer	Person.AddressType	U
V	Sales.vIndividualCustomer	Person.BusinessEntityAddress	U
V	Sales.vIndividualCustomer	Person.CountryRegion	U
V	Sales.vIndividualCustomer	Person.EmailAddress	U
V	Sales.vIndividualCustomer	Person.Person	U
V	Sales.vIndividualCustomer	Person.PersonPhone	U
V	Sales.vIndividualCustomer	Person.PhoneNumberType	U
V	Sales.vIndividualCustomer	Person.StateProvince	U
V	Sales.vIndividualCustomer	Sales.Customer	U
V	Sales.vPersonDemographics	Person.Person	U
V	Sales.vSalesPerson	HumanResources.Employee	U
V	Sales.vSalesPerson	Person.Address	U
V	Sales.vSalesPerson	Person.BusinessEntityAddress	U
V	Sales.vSalesPerson	Person.CountryRegion	U
V	Sales.vSalesPerson	Person.EmailAddress	U
V	Sales.vSalesPerson	Person.Person	U
V	Sales.vSalesPerson	Person.PersonPhone	U
V	Sales.vSalesPerson	Person.PhoneNumberType	U
V	Sales.vSalesPerson	Person.StateProvince	U
V	Sales.vSalesPerson	Sales.SalesPerson	U
V	Sales.vSalesPerson	Sales.SalesTerritory	U
V	Sales.vSalesPersonSalesByFiscalYears	HumanResources.Employee	U
V	Sales.vSalesPersonSalesByFiscalYears	Person.Person	U
V	Sales.vSalesPersonSalesByFiscalYears	Sales.SalesOrderHeader	U
V	Sales.vSalesPersonSalesByFiscalYears	Sales.SalesPerson	U
V	Sales.vSalesPersonSalesByFiscalYears	Sales.SalesTerritory	U
V	Sales.vStoreWithAddresses	Person.Address	U
V	Sales.vStoreWithAddresses	Person.AddressType	U
V	Sales.vStoreWithAddresses	Person.BusinessEntityAddress	U
V	Sales.vStoreWithAddresses	Person.CountryRegion	U
V	Sales.vStoreWithAddresses	Person.StateProvince	U
V	Sales.vStoreWithAddresses	Sales.Store	U
V	Sales.vStoreWithContacts	Person.BusinessEntityContact	U
V	Sales.vStoreWithContacts	Person.ContactType	U
V	Sales.vStoreWithContacts	Person.EmailAddress	U
V	Sales.vStoreWithContacts	Person.Person	U
V	Sales.vStoreWithContacts	Person.PersonPhone	U
V	Sales.vStoreWithContacts	Person.PhoneNumberType	U
V	Sales.vStoreWithContacts	Sales.Store	U
V	Sales.vStoreWithDemographics	Sales.Store	U

CHAPTER 11: Managing Users Permissions

Find All sp-s Where Column Used

When we have to change a column, then first we have to do a research where is it used. The T-SQL scripts finds all stored procedures where Production.Product table ProductID column is used.

```sql
USE AdventureWorks2012;

DECLARE @SchemaName sysname = N'Production';
DECLARE @TableName sysname = N'Product';
DECLARE @ColumnName sysname = N'ProductID';

SELECT CONCAT(QUOTENAME(refing.referencing_schema_name), N'.',
        QUOTENAME(refing.referencing_entity_name)) AS SprocName
FROM   sys.dm_sql_referencing_entities(CONCAT(QUOTENAME(
                        ISNULL(@SchemaName, N'dbo')),
                        N'.', QUOTENAME(@TableName)),   'object' ) refing
    CROSS APPLY sys.dm_sql_referenced_entities(CONCAT(
            QUOTENAME(refing.referencing_schema_name),      N'.',
            QUOTENAME(refing.referencing_entity_name)), 'object') refed
WHERE  EXISTS(SELECT *
        FROM   sys.objects
        WHERE  refing.referencing_id = object_id   AND type = 'P')
    AND refed.referenced_schema_name = @SchemaName
    AND refed.referenced_entity_name = @TableName
    AND refed.referenced_minor_name = @ColumnName
ORDER  BY SprocName;
GO
```

SprocName
[dbo].[rptSalesByQuarter]
[dbo].[sprocGetProductList]
[dbo].[sprocProduct]
[dbo].[sprocProductDatetimestamp]
[dbo].[sprocProductLineAnalysis]
[dbo].[sprocProductList]
[dbo].[uspGetBillOfMaterials]
[dbo].[uspGetWhereUsedProductID]
[dbo].[uspProductByColor]
[dbo].[uspProductInventoryLocation]
[dbo].[uspProductsBySubcat]

Transferring a Table from a Schema to Another

Tables can be transferred from one schema to another schema.

```
USE CopyOfAdventureWorks2012;
GO
```

We can check Schema Ownership with a query.

```
SELECT s.name AS SchemaName,
    u.name AS Owner
FROM   sys.schemas s
    JOIN sys.database_principals u
    ON s.principal_id = u.principal_id
WHERE  s.schema_id < 16384
ORDER  BY SchemaName;
GO
```

SchemaName	Owner
Banking	dbo
dbo	dbo
guest	guest
HumanResources	dbo
INFORMATION_SCHEMA	INFORMATION_SCHEMA
Person	dbo
Production	dbo
Purchasing	dbo
Sales	dbo
sys	sys

Objects in schema can be queried as well.

```
SELECT ObjectName=o.name,
    SchemaName=s.name,
    ObjectType=o.type_desc
FROM   sys.objects o
    JOIN sys.schemas s
    ON o.schema_id = s.schema_id
      AND s.name = 'Person'
ORDER  BY ObjectName;
GO
-- (70 row(s) affected)
```

CHAPTER 11: Managing Users Permissions

ObjectName	SchemaName	ObjectType
Address	Person	USER_TABLE
AddressType	Person	USER_TABLE
BusinessEntity	Person	USER_TABLE
BusinessEntityAddress	Person	USER_TABLE
BusinessEntityContact	Person	USER_TABLE
CK_Person_EmailPromotion	Person	CHECK_CONSTRAINT
CK_Person_PersonType	Person	CHECK_CONSTRAINT
ContactType	Person	USER_TABLE
CountryRegion	Person	USER_TABLE
DF_Address_ModifiedDate	Person	DEFAULT_CONSTRAINT
DF_Address_rowguid	Person	DEFAULT_CONSTRAINT
DF_AddressType_ModifiedDate	Person	DEFAULT_CONSTRAINT
DF_AddressType_rowguid	Person	DEFAULT_CONSTRAINT
DF_BusinessEntity_ModifiedDate	Person	DEFAULT_CONSTRAINT
DF_BusinessEntity_rowguid	Person	DEFAULT_CONSTRAINT
DF_BusinessEntityAddress_ModifiedDate	Person	DEFAULT_CONSTRAINT
DF_BusinessEntityAddress_rowguid	Person	DEFAULT_CONSTRAINT
DF_BusinessEntityContact_ModifiedDate	Person	DEFAULT_CONSTRAINT
DF_BusinessEntityContact_rowguid	Person	DEFAULT_CONSTRAINT
DF_ContactType_ModifiedDate	Person	DEFAULT_CONSTRAINT
DF_CountryRegion_ModifiedDate	Person	DEFAULT_CONSTRAINT
DF_EmailAddress_ModifiedDate	Person	DEFAULT_CONSTRAINT
DF_EmailAddress_rowguid	Person	DEFAULT_CONSTRAINT
DF_Password_ModifiedDate	Person	DEFAULT_CONSTRAINT
F_Password_rowguid	Person	DEFAULT_CONSTRAINT
DF_Person_EmailPromotion	Person	DEFAULT_CONSTRAINT
DF_Person_ModifiedDate	Person	DEFAULT_CONSTRAINT
DF_Person_NameStyle	Person	DEFAULT_CONSTRAINT
DF_Person_rowguid	Person	DEFAULT_CONSTRAINT
DF_PersonPhone_ModifiedDate	Person	DEFAULT_CONSTRAINT
DF_PhoneNumberType_ModifiedDate	Person	DEFAULT_CONSTRAINT
DF_StateProvince_IsOnlyStateProvinceFlag	Person	DEFAULT_CONSTRAINT
DF_StateProvince_ModifiedDate	Person	DEFAULT_CONSTRAINT
DF_StateProvince_rowguid	Person	DEFAULT_CONSTRAINT
EmailAddress	Person	USER_TABLE
FK_Address_StateProvince_StateProvinceID	Person	FOREIGN_KEY_CONSTRAINT
FK_BusinessEntityAddress_Address_AddressID	Person	FOREIGN_KEY_CONSTRAINT
FK_BusinessEntityAddress_AddressType_AddressTypeID	Person	FOREIGN_KEY_CONSTRAINT
FK_BusinessEntityAddress_BusinessEntity_BusinessEntityID	Person	FOREIGN_KEY_CONSTRAINT
FK_BusinessEntityContact_BusinessEntity_BusinessEntityID	Person	FOREIGN_KEY_CONSTRAINT
FK_BusinessEntityContact_ContactType_ContactTypeID	Person	FOREIGN_KEY_CONSTRAINT
FK_BusinessEntityContact_Person_PersonID	Person	FOREIGN_KEY_CONSTRAINT
FK_EmailAddress_Person_BusinessEntityID	Person	FOREIGN_KEY_CONSTRAINT
FK_Password_Person_BusinessEntityID	Person	FOREIGN_KEY_CONSTRAINT
FK_Person_BusinessEntity_BusinessEntityID	Person	FOREIGN_KEY_CONSTRAINT
FK_PersonPhone_Person_BusinessEntityID	Person	FOREIGN_KEY_CONSTRAINT
FK_PersonPhone_PhoneNumberType_PhoneNumberTypeID	Person	FOREIGN_KEY_CONSTRAINT
FK_StateProvince_CountryRegion_CountryRegionCode	Person	FOREIGN_KEY_CONSTRAINT
FK_StateProvince_SalesTerritory_TerritoryID	Person	FOREIGN_KEY_CONSTRAINT
iuPerson	Person	SQL_TRIGGER
Password	Person	USER_TABLE
Person	Person	USER_TABLE
PersonPhone	Person	USER_TABLE
PhoneNumberType	Person	USER_TABLE
PK_Address_AddressID	Person	PRIMARY_KEY_CONSTRAINT
PK_AddressType_AddressTypeID	Person	PRIMARY_KEY_CONSTRAINT
PK_BusinessEntity_BusinessEntityID	Person	PRIMARY_KEY_CONSTRAINT
PK_BusinessEntityAddress_BusinessEntityID_AddressID_AddressTypeID	Person	PRIMARY_KEY_CONSTRAINT
PK_BusinessEntityContact_BusinessEntityID_PersonID_ContactTypeID	Person	PRIMARY_KEY_CONSTRAINT
PK_ContactType_ContactTypeID	Person	PRIMARY_KEY_CONSTRAINT
PK_CountryRegion_CountryRegionCode	Person	PRIMARY_KEY_CONSTRAINT
PK_EmailAddress_BusinessEntityID_EmailAddressID	Person	PRIMARY_KEY_CONSTRAINT

CHAPTER 11: Managing Users Permissions

PK_Password_BusinessEntityID	Person	PRIMARY_KEY_CONSTRAINT
PK_Person_BusinessEntityID	Person	PRIMARY_KEY_CONSTRAINT
PK_PersonPhone_BusinessEntityID_PhoneNumber_PhoneNumberTypeID	Person	PRIMARY_KEY_CONSTRAINT
PK_PhoneNumberType_PhoneNumberTypeID	Person	PRIMARY_KEY_CONSTRAINT
PK_StateProvince_StateProvinceID	Person	PRIMARY_KEY_CONSTRAINT
StateProvince	Person	USER_TABLE
vAdditionalContactInfo	Person	VIEW
vStateProvinceCountryRegion	Person	VIEW

Command to transfer the Person.Person table from Person schema to HumanResources schema.

```
ALTER SCHEMA HumanResources TRANSFER Person.Person;
GO
--Command(s) completed successfully.
```

We can verify the transfer.

```
SELECT ObjectName=o.name,
    SchemaName=s.name,
    ObjectType=o.type_desc
FROM   sys.objects o
    JOIN sys.schemas s
     ON o.schema_id = s.schema_id
       AND s.name = 'HumanResources'
ORDER  BY ObjectName;
GO
-- Partial results
```

ObjectName	SchemaName	ObjectType
Person	HumanResources	USER_TABLE

```
exec sp_help 'Person.Person';
go
```

```
/*
Msg 15009, Level 16, State 1, Procedure sp_help, Line 79
The object 'Person.Person' does not exist in database 'CopyOfAdventureWorks2012'
or is invalid for this operation.
*/
```

CHAPTER II: Managing Users Permissions

Investigating the transferred table object in the HumanResources Schema

```
exec sp_help 'HumanResources.Person';
go
```

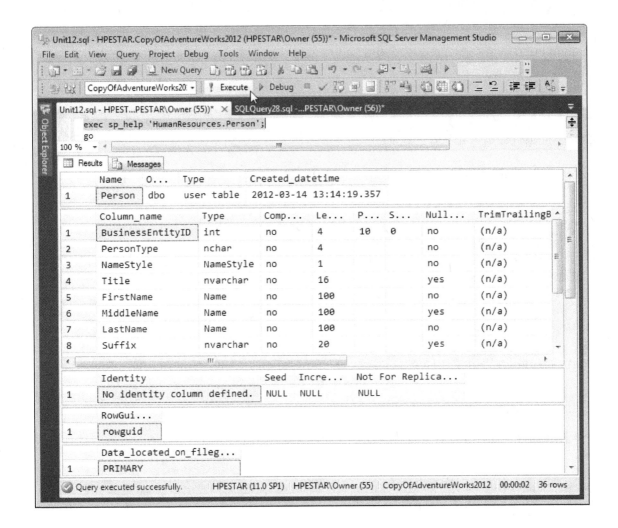

Article: **DBA Best Practices Tips**   http://bit.ly/115raco
http://www.mssqltips.com/sql-server-tip-category/53/dba-best-practices/

Developing Permissions Strategy

Security and permissioning is a complex topic which requires quite an expertise to do it right. Checking my permissions as sysadmin & dbo. I can impersonate a user with "EXECUTE AS" and use the same commands to check permissions of the impersonated user.

```
USE AdventureWorks2012;
SELECT * FROM fn_my_permissions('Sales', 'SCHEMA') ORDER BY permission_name;
```

entity_name	subentity_name	permission_name
Sales		ALTER
Sales		CONTROL
Sales		CREATE SEQUENCE
Sales		DELETE
Sales		EXECUTE
Sales		INSERT
Sales		REFERENCES
Sales		SELECT
Sales		TAKE OWNERSHIP
Sales		UPDATE
Sales		VIEW CHANGE TRACKING
Sales		VIEW DEFINITION

Server level permissions.

```
SELECT * FROM fn_my_permissions(NULL, NULL);    -- (31 row(s) affected)
```

Explicit permissions granted on stored procedures.

```
SELECT SPROC=o.name, UserName=dpr.name
FROM   sys.objects o
    INNER JOIN sys.database_permissions dp
    ON dp.major_id = o.object_id
    INNER JOIN sys.database_principals dpr
    ON dp.grantee_principal_id = dpr.principal_id
WHERE  o.[type] = 'P'   AND dp.permission_name = 'EXECUTE'   AND dp.state IN ('G','W');
```

SPROC	UserName
sp_dropdiagram	public
sp_alterdiagram	public
sp_renamediagram	public
sp_creatediagram	public
sp_helpdiagramdefinition	public
sp_helpdiagrams	public

Small IT Shop Permissions Strategy

There is no professional DBA.

- ➢ Use as few logins as possible.
- ➢ Give db_owner (dbo) rights to logins.

_/_/_/_/_/_/ This is not best practice, simply forced practice. _/_/_/_/_/_/

Medium IT Shop Permissions Strategy

There is a DBA with limited time for security.

- ➢ DBA & lead developers db_owner rights on production.
- ➢ Developers logins on development server with db_owner rights.

Enterprise IT Shop Permissions Strategy

There is dedicated DBA for security.

- ➢ Object and statement level implementation of security
- ➢ on all servers: production, standby, QA, staging/content,
- ➢ development.

- ➢ Only DBAs can make changes in production and QA.

- ➢ The goal when planning the security model in your database
- ➢ servers is to give the least permissions as possible.
- ➢ That way, users can view and/or modify only the data
- ➢ they are in charge of.

- ➢ Address issues with application using the 'sa' login
- ➢ or xp_cmdshell (not good practices).

- ➢ Develop security standards or use 3rd party product.

> Articles: **Database Engine Permission Basics**   http://bit.ly/r6Bt4r
> http://blogs.msdn.com/b/sqlsecurity/archive/2011/08/25/database-engine-permission-basics.aspx
>
> **SQL Server Security Best Practices**   http://bit.ly/dTE0ye
> http://www.greensql.com/content/sql-server-security-best-practices

CHAPTER 12: Database Backup Strategies

CHAPTER 12: Database Backup Strategies

FULL Database Backup

Backup & restore is something a DBA has to know inside-out.

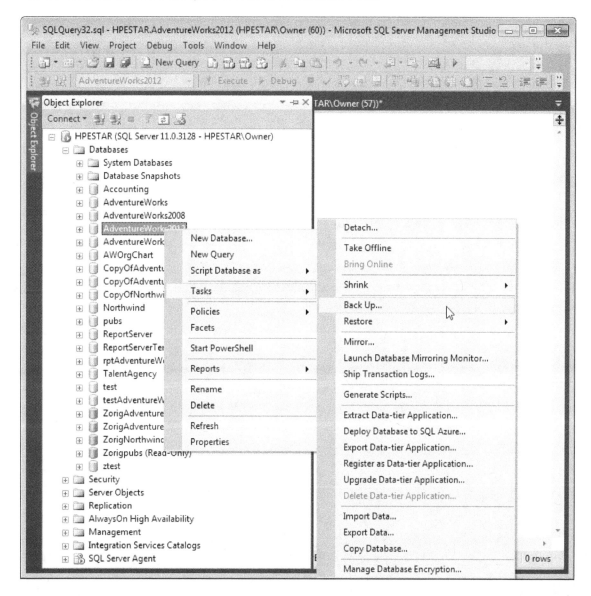

Backup Database General Page

If we intend to backup to a new backup file, the disk file list window must be empty(use Remove), otherwise the backup will split between backup sets (files).

If I don't change anything the new backup file will be appended to AW2012.bak (default behaviour).

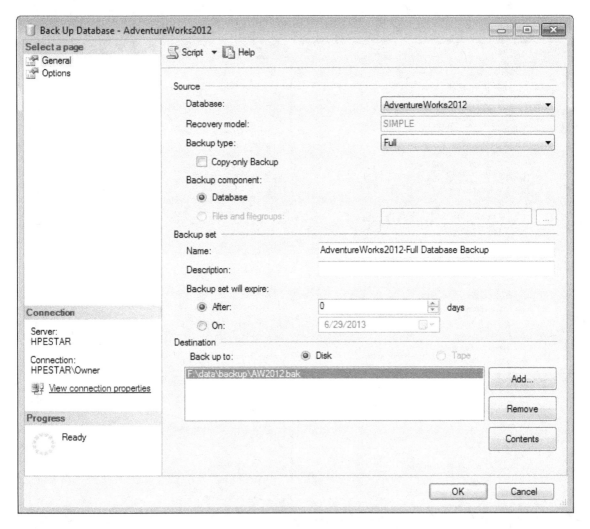

Remove the Default Backup File

A backup file can contain multiple backups of different kind. For example, a mixture of FULL and TRANSACTION backups.

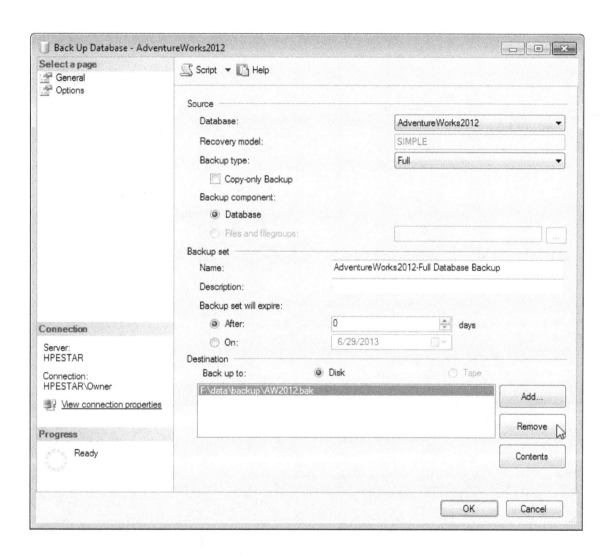

Add a New Backup File

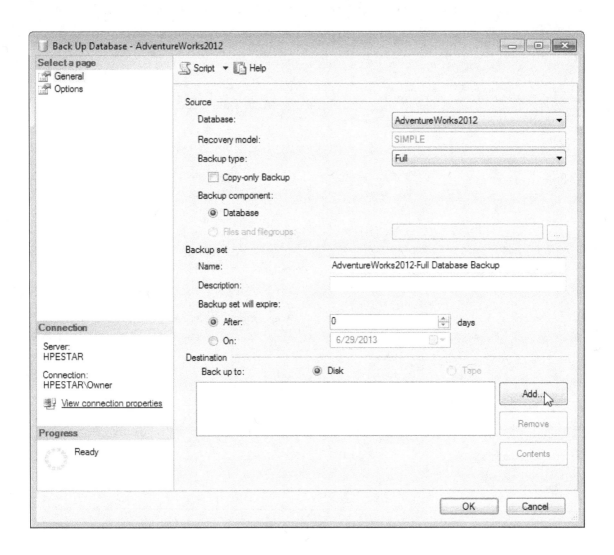

Define a Backup Destination as a New File

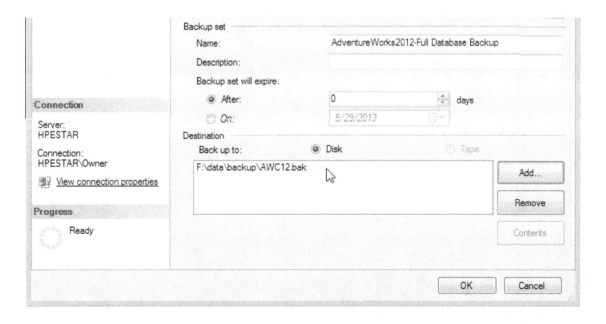

The File(s) window displays the new destination file

Backup Database Options Page

We checkmark the optional Verify backup box.

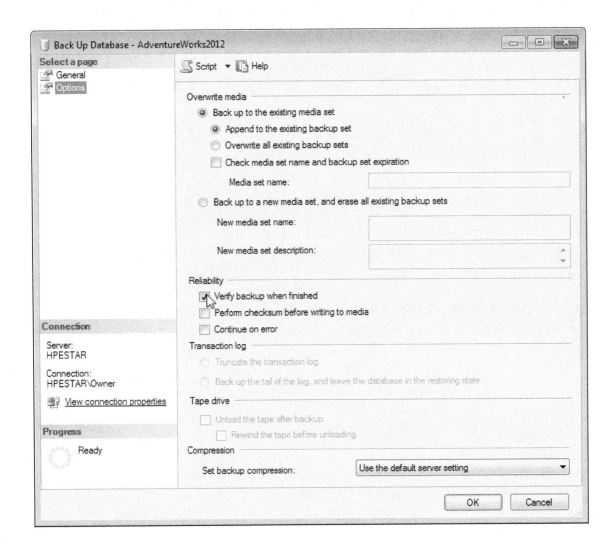

Generating a Backup Database Script

We are ready to start the backup, but first we generate a T-SQL backup script.

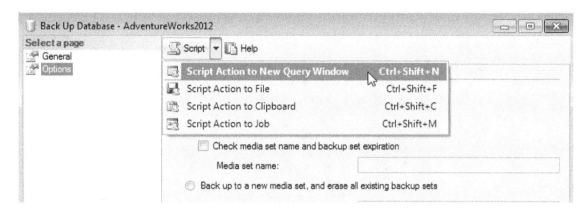

The Generated Script

First part is the backup, second part is the verification.

```
BACKUP DATABASE [AdventureWorks2012] TO  DISK = N'F:\data\backup\AWC12.bak'
WITH NOFORMAT, NOINIT,
NAME = N'AdventureWorks2012-Full Database Backup',
SKIP, NOREWIND, NOUNLOAD,  STATS = 10
GO

declare @backupSetId as int

select @backupSetId = position from msdb..backupset
where database_name=N'AdventureWorks2012'
and backup_set_id=(select max(backup_set_id)
from msdb..backupset where database_name=N'AdventureWorks2012' )
if @backupSetId is null
begin
raiserror(N'Verify failed. Backup information for database ''AdventureWorks2012'' not found.',
16, 1)
 end

RESTORE VERIFYONLY FROM
DISK = N'F:\data\backup\AWC12.bak'
WITH  FILE = @backupSetId,  NOUNLOAD,  NOREWIND
GO
```

CHAPTER 12: Database Backup Strategies

Starting Backup Execution

Clicking on OK start execution, the window changes to greyed out mode. Progress is shown in lower right.

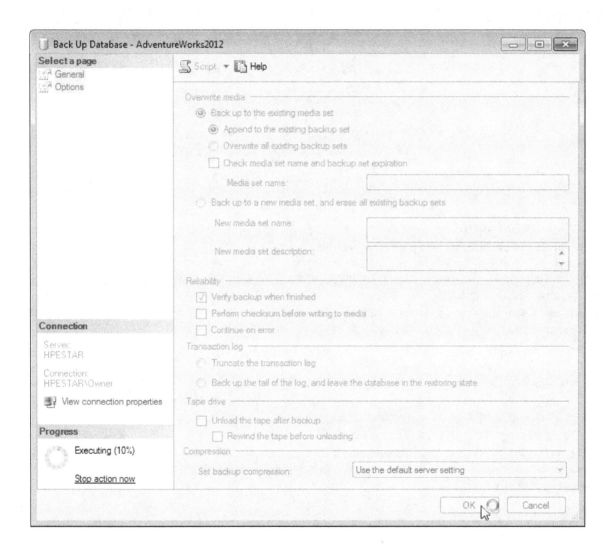

Finish Popup Box

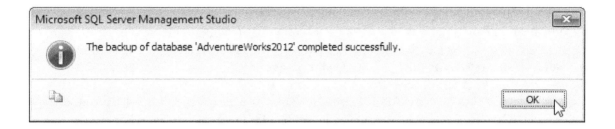

Checking the Content of a Backup File

We have to use the RESTORE command to look inside a database backup file for content information.

RESTORE HEADERONLY FROM DISK = N'F:\data\backup\AWC12.bak';

Backup type code	Meaning
1	Database
2	Transaction log
4	File
5	Differential database
6	Differential file
7	Partial
8	Differential partial

BackupName   BackupDescription   BackupType   ExpirationDate Compressed
        Position   DeviceType   UserName   ServerName   DatabaseName
        DatabaseVersion   DatabaseCreationDate BackupSize   FirstLSN   LastLSN
        CheckpointLSN DatabaseBackupLSN   BackupStartDate   BackupFinishDate
        SortOrder   CodePage   UnicodeLocaleId   UnicodeComparisonStyle
        CompatibilityLevel   SoftwareVendorId   SoftwareVersionMajor
        SoftwareVersionMinor SoftwareVersionBuild   MachineName Flags   BindingID
        RecoveryForkID Collation   FamilyGUID   HasBulkLoggedData   IsSnapshot
        IsReadOnly   IsSingleUser   HasBackupChecksums IsDamaged   BeginsLogChain
        HasIncompleteMetaData   IsForceOffline IsCopyOnly   FirstRecoveryForkID
        ForkPointLSN   RecoveryModel DifferentialBaseLSN   DifferentialBaseGUID
        BackupTypeDescription BackupSetGUID CompressedBackupSize Containment

```
AdventureWorks2012-Full Database Backup      NULL    1        NULL    0        1        2
        HPESTAR\Owner           HPESTAR          AdventureWorks2012  706      2012-05-19
02:43:09.000    419871744       1663000000306000252 1663000000316300001
        1663000000306000252 1360000003863100274 2013-06-29 18:19:58.000        2013-
06-29 18:20:17.000    52      0       1033    196609 110      4608    11       0        3128
        HPESTAR         512     4EA0C5BD-7035-4F72-BF9C-595DC083159A        05AE789E-
3AD5-46ED-9B30-B1E52C418B00        SQL_Latin1_General_CP1_CI_AS            EB72F9D9-
7BB8-4BA2-A4D3-F697D6D5DD85        0       0       0       0        0        0        0
        0       0       0       05AE789E-3AD5-46ED-9B30-B1E52C418B00        NULL    SIMPLE
        NULL    NULL    Database        6F4182DD-C32C-434C-A896-CF767FC4640E
        419871744       0
```

Adding a second backup to the same file.

```
BACKUP DATABASE [AdventureWorks2012] TO  DISK = N'F:\data\backup\AWC12.bak';
```

```
Processed 50944 pages for database 'AdventureWorks2012', file 'AdventureWorks2012_Data'
on file 2.
Processed 80 pages for database 'AdventureWorks2012', file 'FSAlpha' on file 2.
Processed 5 pages for database 'AdventureWorks2012', file 'AdventureWorks2012_Log' on file
2.
BACKUP DATABASE successfully processed 51029 pages in 19.513 seconds (20.430 MB/sec).
```

Checking the file content again, we can see information on two database full backups.

```
RESTORE HEADERONLY FROM DISK = N'F:\data\backup\AWC12.bak';
```

```
BackupName    BackupDescription       BackupType      ExpirationDate Compressed
        Position        DeviceType      UserName        ServerName      DatabaseName
        DatabaseVersion         DatabaseCreationDate BackupSize       FirstLSN        LastLSN
        CheckpointLSN DatabaseBackupLSN       BackupStartDate         BackupFinishDate
        SortOrder       CodePage        UnicodeLocaleId         UnicodeComparisonStyle
        CompatibilityLevel      SoftwareVendorId        SoftwareVersionMajor
        SoftwareVersionMinor SoftwareVersionBuild    MachineName Flags    BindingID
        RecoveryForkID Collation        FamilyGUID      HasBulkLoggedData       IsSnapshot
        IsReadOnly      IsSingleUser    HasBackupChecksums IsDamaged        BeginsLogChain
        HasIncompleteMetaData   IsForceOffline IsCopyOnly       FirstRecoveryForkID
        ForkPointLSN    RecoveryModel DifferentialBaseLSN       DifferentialBaseGUID
        BackupTypeDescription BackupSetGUID CompressedBackupSize Containment
```

AdventureWorks2012-Full Database Backup   NULL   1   NULL   0   1   2
          HPESTAR\Owner   HPESTAR   AdventureWorks2012   706   2012-05-19
02:43:09.000   419871744   1663000000306000252 1663000000316300001
          1663000000306000252 1360000003863100274 2013-06-29 18:19:58.000   2013-
06-29 18:20:17.000   52   0   1033   196609 110   4608   11   0   3128
          HPESTAR   512   4EA0C5BD-7035-4F72-BF9C-595DC083159A   05AE789E-
3AD5-46ED-9B30-B1E52C418B00   SQL_Latin1_General_CP1_CI_AS   EB72F9D9-
7BB8-4BA2-A4D3-F697D6D5DD85   0   0   0   0   0   0   0
          0   0   0   05AE789E-3AD5-46ED-9B30-B1E52C418B00   NULL   SIMPLE
          NULL   NULL   Database   6F4182DD-C32C-434C-A896-CF767FC4640E
          419871744   0

NULL   NULL   1   NULL   0   2   2   HPESTAR\Owner   HPESTAR
          AdventureWorks2012   706   2012-05-19 02:43:09.000   419870720
          1663000001962100174 1663000001969300001 1663000001962100174
          1663000000306000252 2013-06-30 06:49:10.000   2013-06-30 06:49:30.000
          52   0   1033   196609 110   4608   11   0   3128   HPESTAR
          512   4EA0C5BD-7035-4F72-BF9C-595DC083159A   05AE789E-3AD5-46ED-9B30-
B1E52C418B00 SQL_Latin1_General_CP1_CI_AS   EB72F9D9-7BB8-4BA2-A4D3-
F697D6D5DD850   0   0   0   0   0   0   0   0   0
          05AE789E-3AD5-46ED-9B30-B1E52C418B00   NULL   SIMPLE NULL   NULL
          Database   451A921C-A4CE-4F39-A9D3-9ADE25F49869   419870720   0

Checking Backup File Content in Object Explorer

We can check the file content using Object Explorer GUI interface as well. Similarly we have to use the RESTORE command.

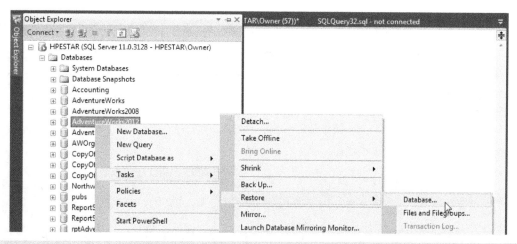

Restore Database General Window

By default the last backup (Position 2) is displayed.

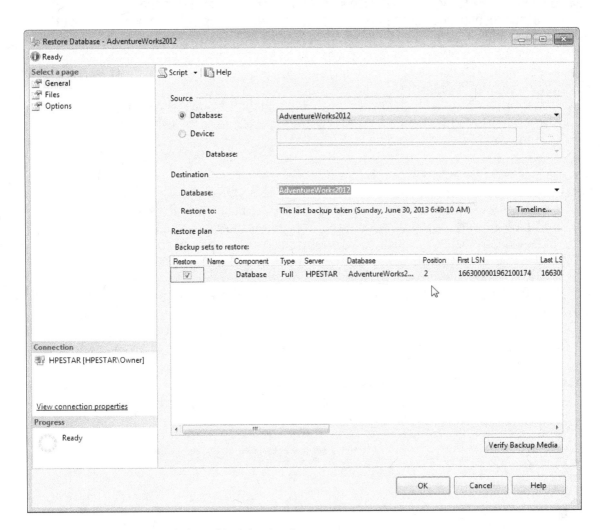

Radio button Device and click on file selection button.

Add the backup file to the backup media window.

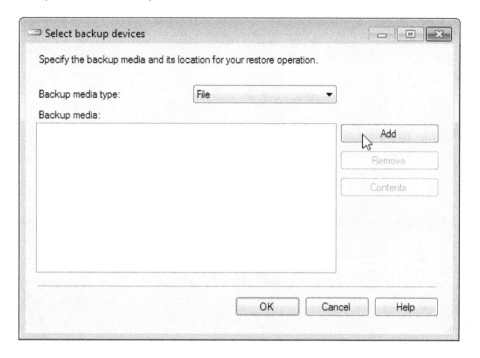

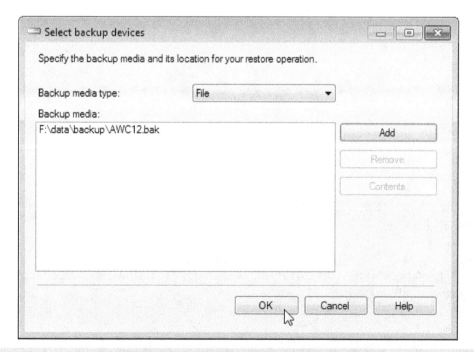

Last backup information of a database backup file

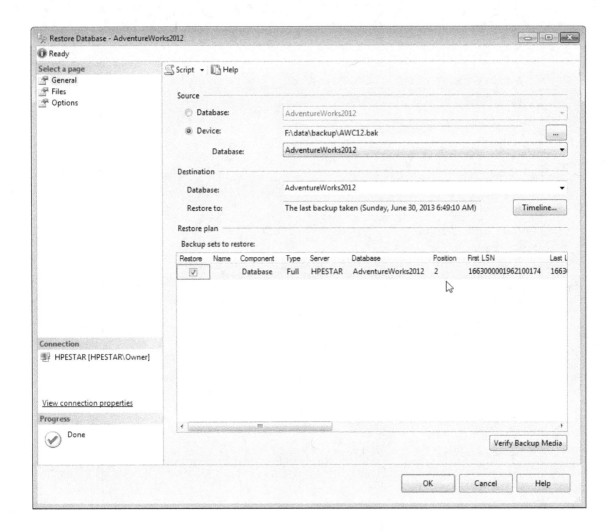

When restoring a database the filenumber (FILE =..) indicates which backup should be used in a file with multiple backups.

```
USE [master]
RESTORE DATABASE [AdventureWorks2012] FROM  DISK = N'F:\data\backup\AWC12.bak'
WITH  FILE = 2,  NOUNLOAD,  STATS = 5
GO
```

CHAPTER 12: Database Backup Strategies

Getting Backup File Timeline Information

Graphical timeline information is available by pressing the Timeline button.

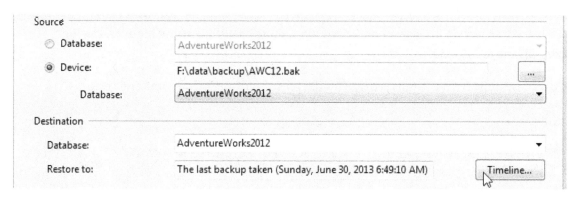

The timeline display shows the two full backups in the backup file.

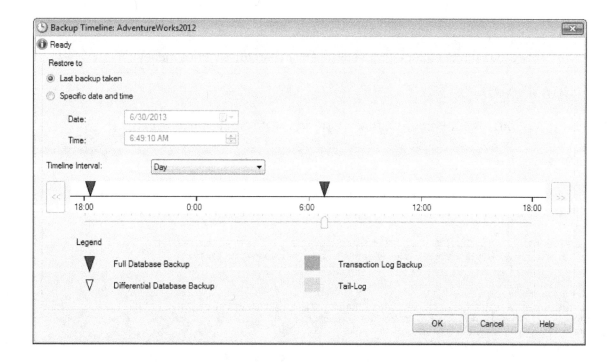

Transaction Log Backup

Transaction log backup captures the transactions list the last full backup or last transaction backup. **Usually** it is significantly **smaller** in size then a full backup and executes faster. **However, if transaction intensive operations were done like REBUILDing indexes, the log backup file maybe sizable**.

The database must be in the full recovery model for transaction log backups and restores.

```
USE [master]
GO
ALTER DATABASE [AdventureWorks2012] SET RECOVERY FULL WITH NO_WAIT
GO
```

A third full backup created into the same backup file because full - log backups must be completly synchronized.

```
BACKUP DATABASE [AdventureWorks2012] TO  DISK = N'F:\data\backup\AWC12.bak';
```

We create transactions for the log file by creating a table and populating it.

```
USE AdventureWorks2012;
CREATE TABLE Prod1 (ProductID int, ProductName nvarchar(70), ListPrice money);
GO
--(1 row(s) affected)
```

```
INSERT INTO Prod1 SELECT ProductID, Name, ListPrice FROM Production.Product;
GO
-- (504 row(s) affected)
```

Prior to pressing OK on the following Options page script can be generated. Second part is the verification.

```
BACKUP LOG [AdventureWorks2012] TO  DISK = N'F:\data\backup\AWC12.bak' WITH NOFORMAT, NOINIT,
NAME = N'AdventureWorks2012-Transaction Log  Backup', SKIP, NOREWIND, NOUNLOAD,  STATS = 10
GO
```

```
declare @backupSetId as int
select @backupSetId = position from msdb..backupset where database_name=N'AdventureWorks2012'
and backup_set_id=(select max(backup_set_id) from msdb..backupset
where database_name=N'AdventureWorks2012' )
if @backupSetId is null begin raiserror(N'Verify failed. Backup information for database ''AdventureWorks2012'' not found.', 16, 1)
end
RESTORE VERIFYONLY FROM  DISK = N'F:\data\backup\AWC12.bak'
WITH  FILE = @backupSetId, NOUNLOAD, NOREWIND
GO
```

CHAPTER 12: Database Backup Strategies

Transaction Log Backup General Page

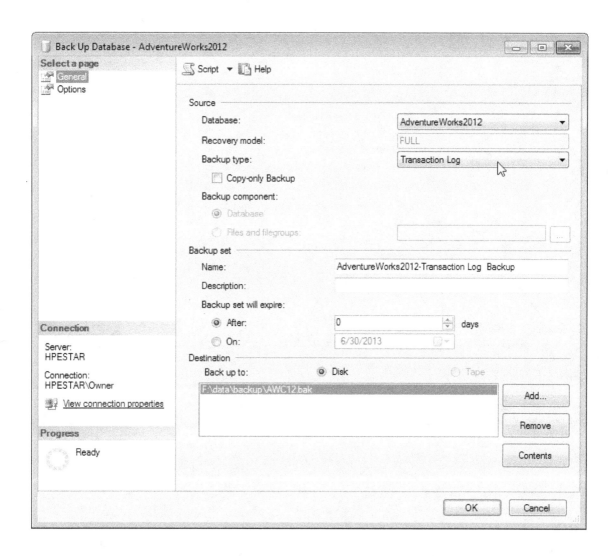

Transaction Log Backup Options Page

Verify backup is checkmarked.

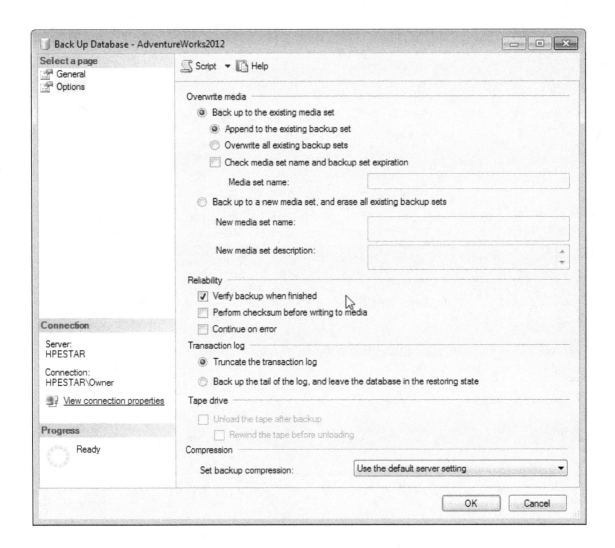

Checking Server Log for Backup Information

Since database backup is a significant event, it is logged in SQL Server log.

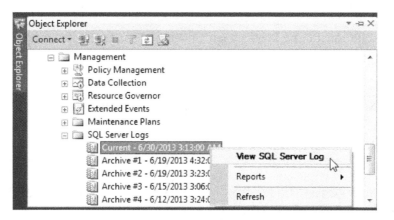

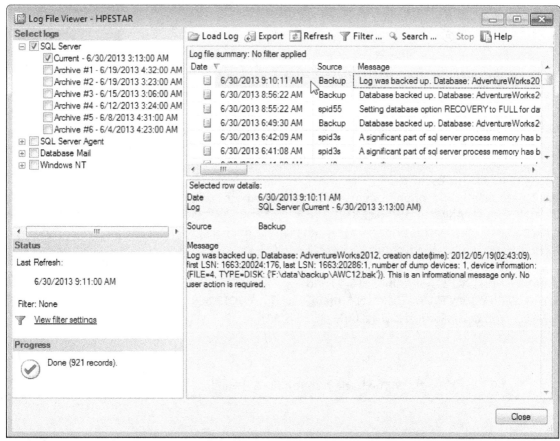

Transaction Log Backup Using Script

A second table is added and populated prior to the transaction log backup.

```
USE AdventureWorks2012;
CREATE TABLE Prod2 (ProductID int, ProductName nvarchar(70), ListPrice money);
GO
--(1 row(s) affected)
```

```
INSERT INTO Prod2 SELECT ProductID, Name, ListPrice FROM Production.Product;
GO
-- (504 row(s) affected)
```

```
USE master;
BACKUP LOG [AdventureWorks2012] TO  DISK = N'F:\data\backup\AWC12.bak' WITH
NOFORMAT, NOINIT,
NAME = N'AdventureWorks2012-Transaction Log  Backup', SKIP, NOREWIND, NOUNLOAD,
STATS = 10
GO
```

```
100 percent processed.
Processed 12 pages for database 'AdventureWorks2012', file 'AdventureWorks2012_Log' on file
5.
BACKUP LOG successfully processed 12 pages in 0.097 seconds (0.890 MB/sec).
```

```
declare @backupSetId as int
select @backupSetId = position from msdb..backupset where
database_name=N'AdventureWorks2012'
and backup_set_id=(select max(backup_set_id) from msdb..backupset
where database_name=N'AdventureWorks2012' )
if @backupSetId is null begin raiserror(N'Verify failed. Backup information for database
''AdventureWorks2012'' not found.', 16, 1) end
RESTORE VERIFYONLY FROM  DISK = N'F:\data\backup\AWC12.bak'
WITH  FILE = @backupSetId,  NOUNLOAD,  NOREWIND
GO
```

```
The backup set on file 5 is valid.
```

Checking Timeline for Full & Log Backup Sequence

The current sequence should be 3 full backups and 2 transaction log backups. The last (3rd) full backup and the 2 transaction log backups form a complete synchronized backup sequence which can be used for database restore (restore full, restore log1, restore log2).

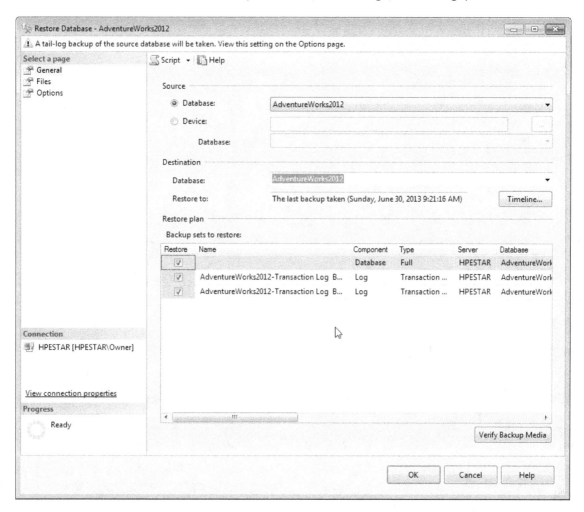

Backup File Timeline Display

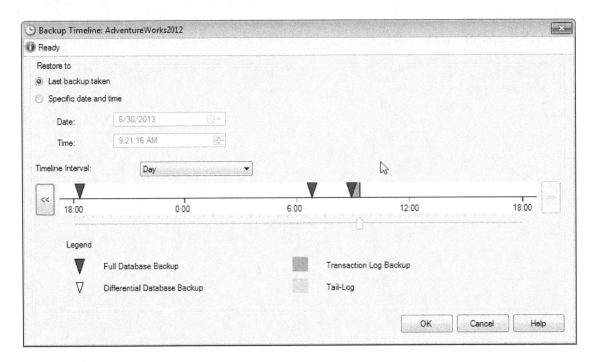

Checking backup file content with T-SQL command.

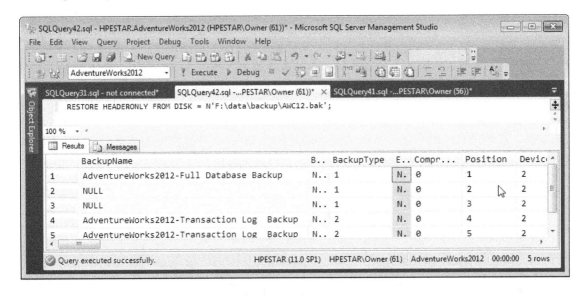

Backup File Contents Display via Contents Button

The Contents button is accessible from Backup Database general page.

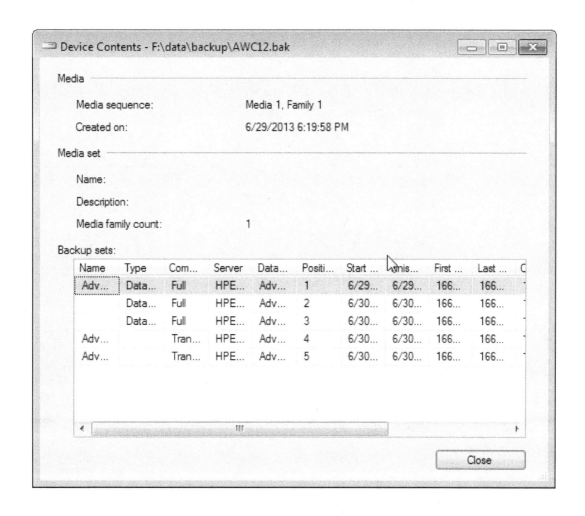

Differential Database Backup

Differential database backup creates a backup set since the last full backup. A new backup file is designated in the first step. Typically .bak, .trn & .diff file extensions are used, but that is only by convention, not a requirement.

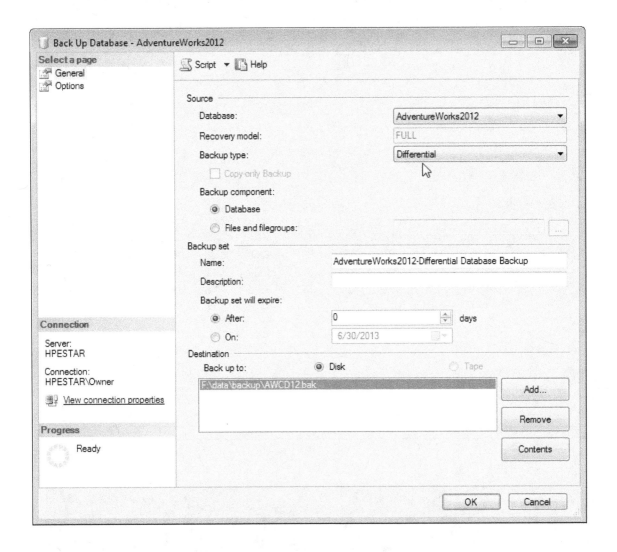

Differential Backup Option Page

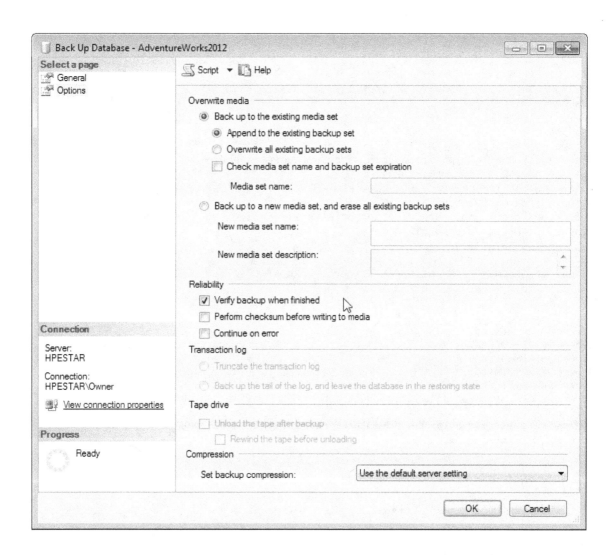

Generated T-SQL Script

First batch is the backup, second batch is the verification step.

> A DBA should always save T-SQL scripts of GUI actions.

```
BACKUP DATABASE [AdventureWorks2012] TO  DISK = N'F:\data\backup\AWCD12.bak'
WITH  DIFFERENTIAL , NOFORMAT, NOINIT,
NAME = N'AdventureWorks2012-Differential Database Backup', SKIP, NOREWIND,
NOUNLOAD,  STATS = 10
GO
```

```
declare @backupSetId as int
select @backupSetId = position from msdb..backupset where
database_name=N'AdventureWorks2012'
and backup_set_id=(select max(backup_set_id) from msdb..backupset where
database_name=N'AdventureWorks2012' )
if @backupSetId is null begin raiserror(N'Verify failed. Backup information for
database ''AdventureWorks2012''
not found.', 16, 1) end

RESTORE VERIFYONLY FROM  DISK = N'F:\data\backup\AWCD12.bak' WITH  FILE =
@backupSetId,  NOUNLOAD,  NOREWIND
GO
```

```
10 percent processed.
20 percent processed.
30 percent processed.
41 percent processed.
51 percent processed.
Processed 296 pages for database 'AdventureWorks2012', file 'AdventureWorks2012_Data'
on file 1.
Processed 0 pages for database 'AdventureWorks2012', file 'FSAlpha' on file 1.
Processed 1 pages for database 'AdventureWorks2012', file 'AdventureWorks2012_Log' on
file 1.
100 percent processed.
BACKUP DATABASE WITH DIFFERENTIAL successfully processed 297 pages in 0.333 seconds
(6.948 MB/sec).
The backup set on file 1 is valid.
```

Check the content of the database backup file.

```
RESTORE HEADERONLY FROM DISK = N'F:\data\backup\AWCD12.bak';
```

	BackupName	B.	BackupType	E...	C...	Position	DeviceType	UserName
1	AdventureWorks2012-Differential Database Backup	N	5	N...	0	1	2	HPESTAR\C

Configuring A Backup Device

Backup device is a symbolic setup for a physical backup device. Configuration is launched from Server Objects --> Backup Devices in Object Explorer.

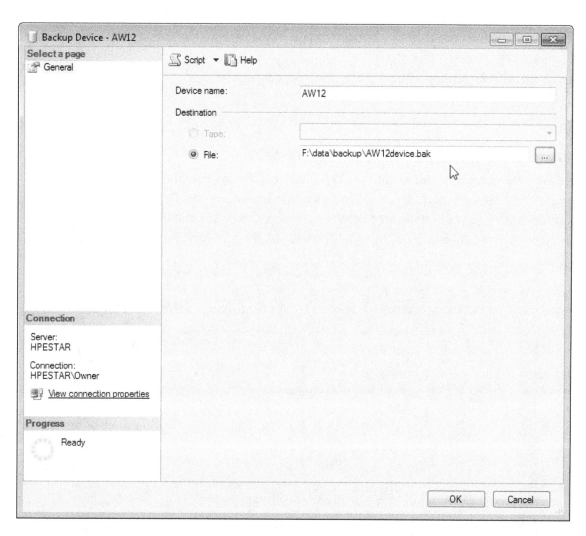

Generated script.

```
USE [master]
GO
EXEC master.dbo.sp_addumpdevice  @devtype = N'disk', @logicalname = N'AW12',
@physicalname = N'F:\data\backup\AW12device.bak'
```

CHAPTER 12: Database Backup Strategies

BACKUP DATABASE with Datestamp

The backup filename can be changed at will to reflect the backup date.

```
BACKUP DATABASE [AdventureWorks2012] TO  DISK = N'F:\data\backup\AW20161023.bak';
```

```
-- Dynamic backup filename with datestamp
DECLARE @Filename nvarchar(64) = CONCAT(N'F:\data\backup\AW', CONVERT(varchar,
CONVERT(DATE, getdate())),'.bak');
BACKUP DATABASE [AdventureWorks2012] TO  DISK = @Filename;
-- AW2018-08-23.bak
```

Export Data-tier Application - Azure SQL

The export file (.bacpac) includes both the definitions of the objects in the database and all of the data in the tables. Export launching sequence. Windows Azure SQL Database Import / Export operations can copy databases between Windows Azure SQL Database servers, or can migrate databases between the SQL Server Database Engine and Windows Azure SQL Database.

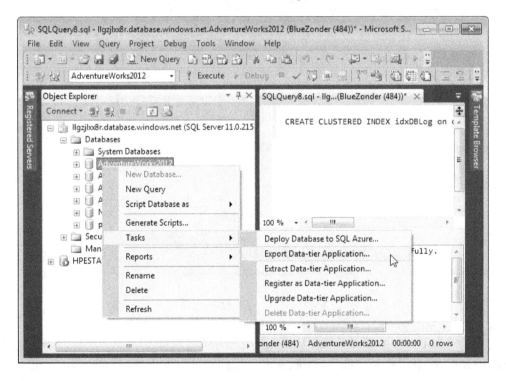

Introduction Page

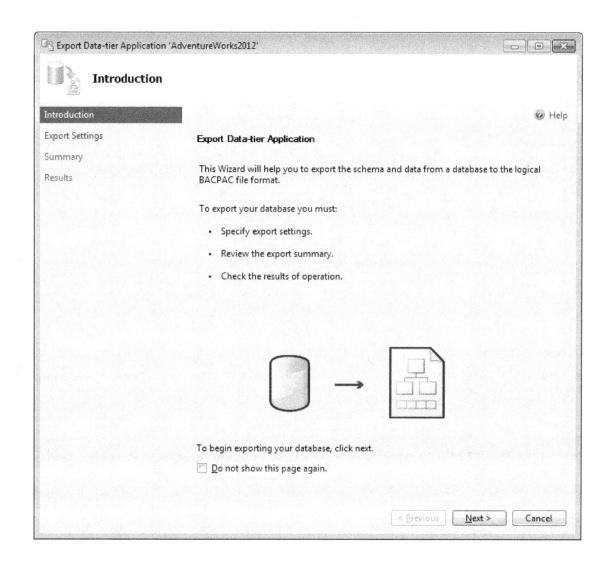

Export Settings

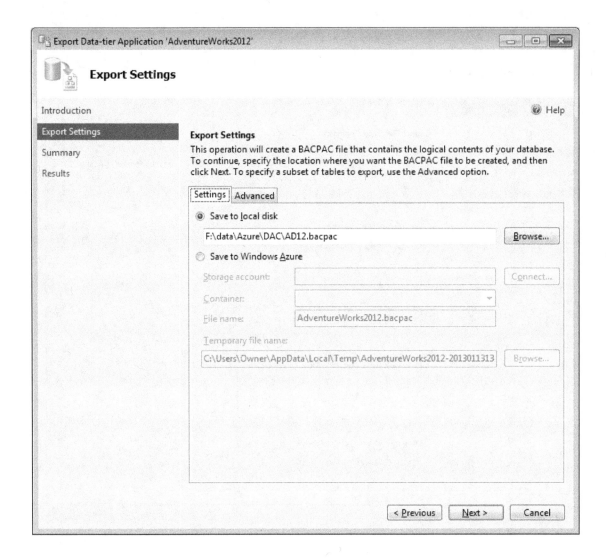

Advanced Export Settings

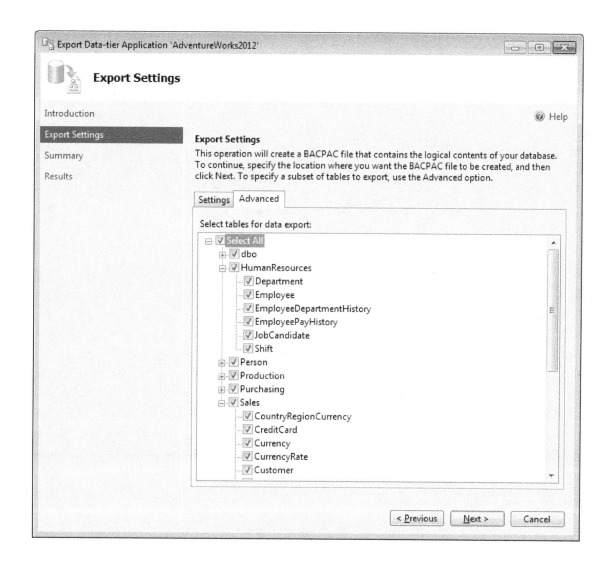

Summary

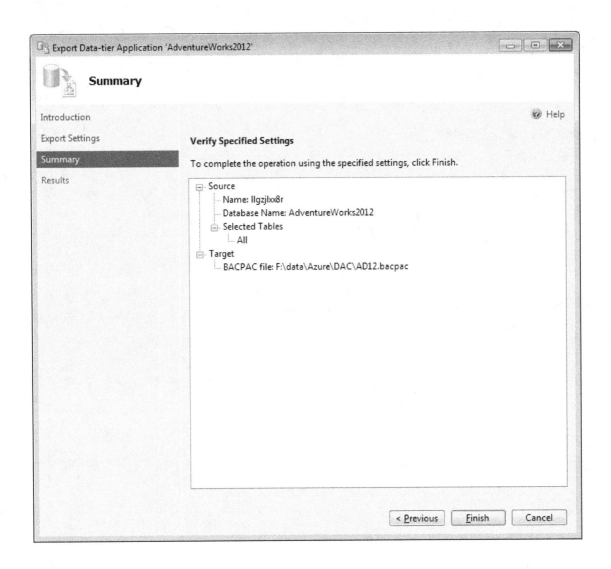

Progress

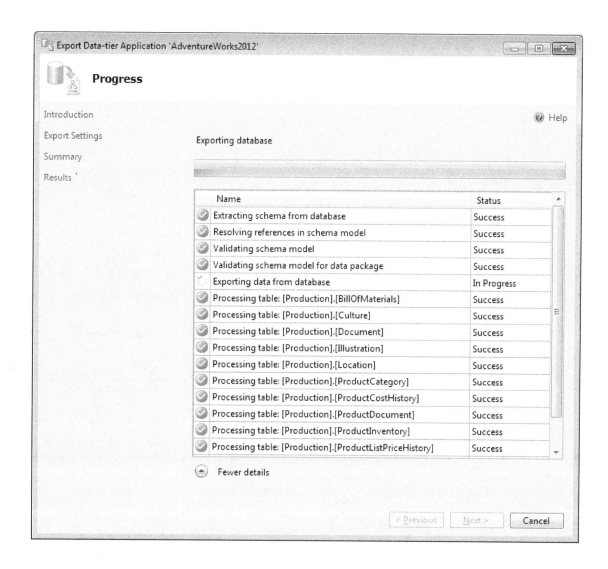

Operation Complete - Elapsed Time 2 Minutes

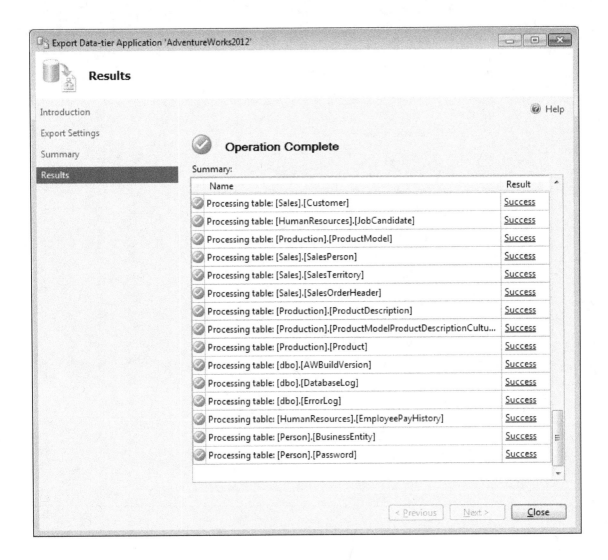

Import Data-tier Application

Import recreates the database from the .bacpac file.

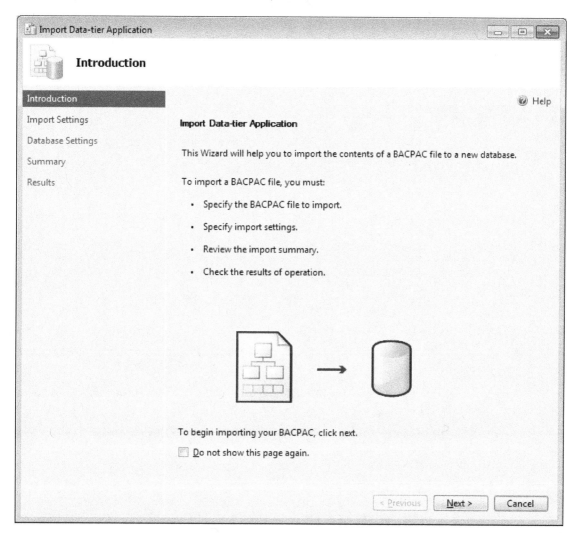

Import Settings

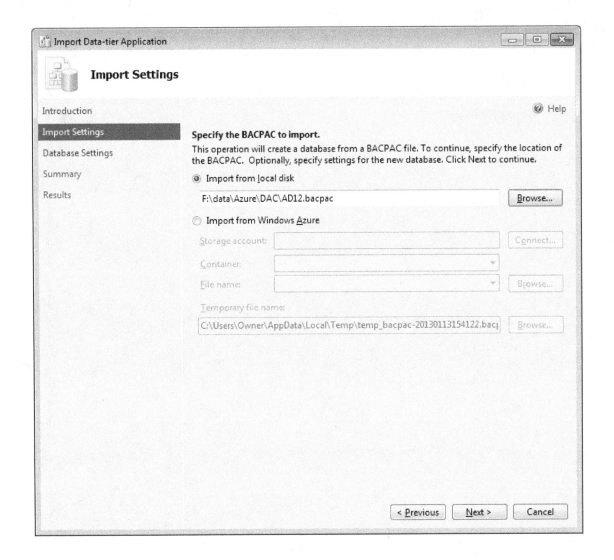

Database Settings

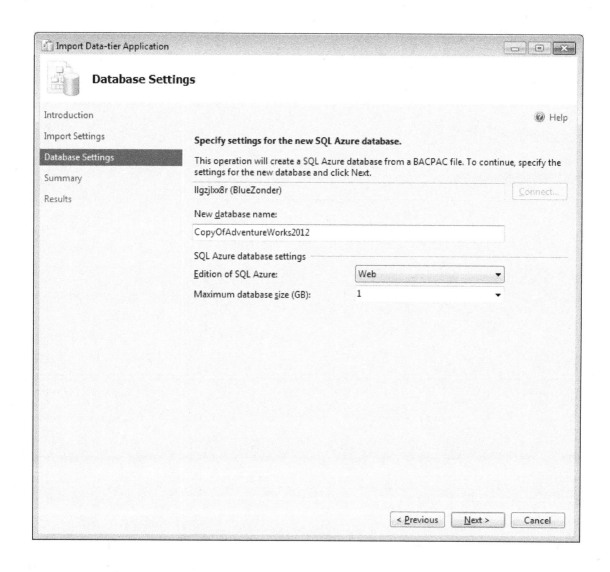

Summary

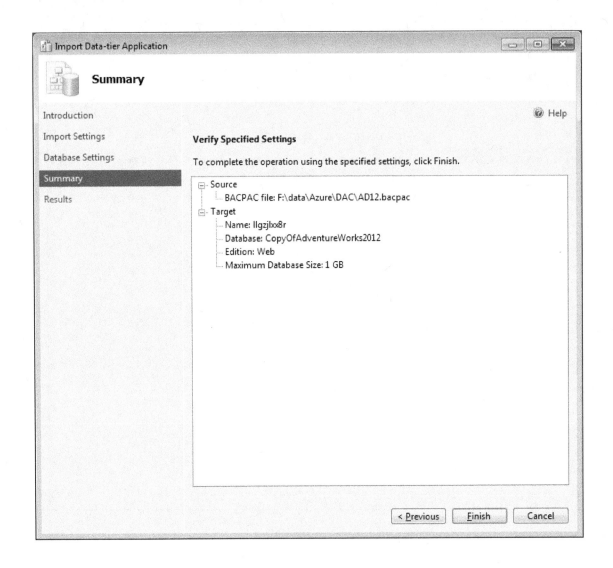

Importing Progress

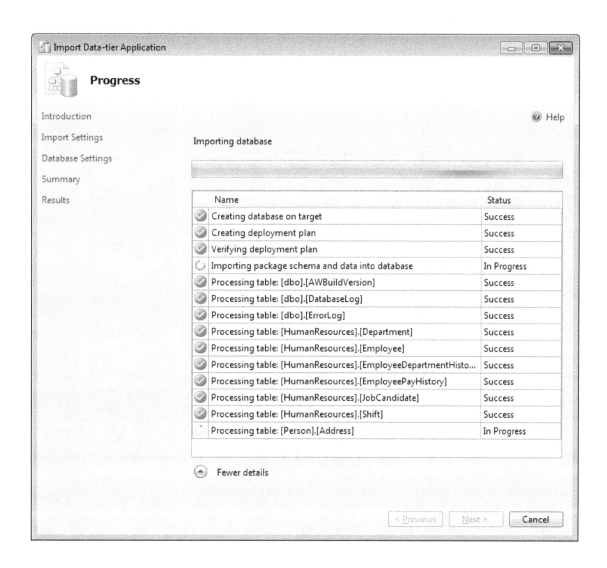

Operation Complete - Elapsed Time 20 Minutes

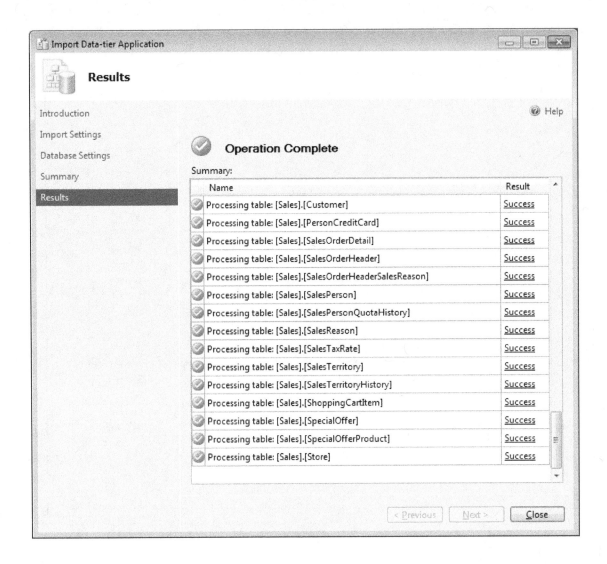

Deploy Data-tier Application

A data-tier application (DAC) is an entity that contains all of the database & SQL Server instance objects used by an application. The DAC package file can be generated by Visual Studio, SSMS Extract Data-tier Application or some utilities.

> MSDN Articles
> **Understanding Data-tier Applications**
> http://msdn.microsoft.com/en-us/library/ee240739(v=sql.105).aspx
>
> **Deploying Data-tier Applications**
> http://msdn.microsoft.com/en-us/library/ee210580(v=sql.105).aspx

The deployment file type is .dacpac.

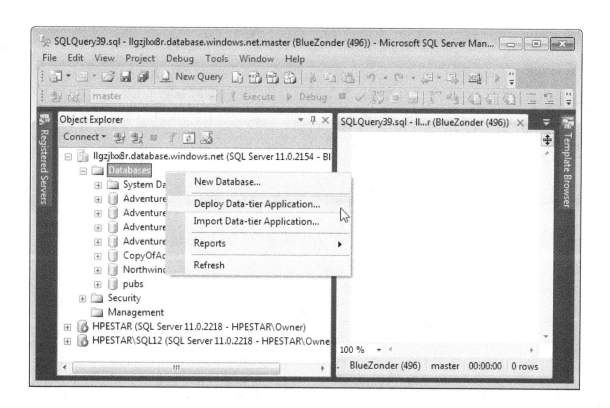

The Introduction Page Explains the Process

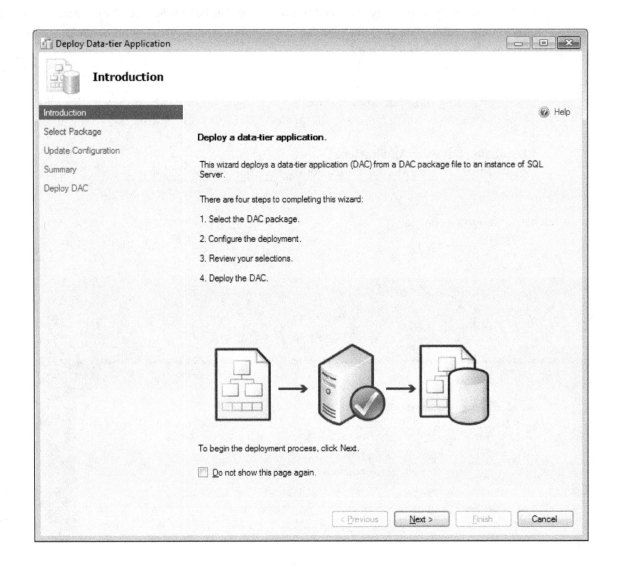

Select the DAC Package to Deploy

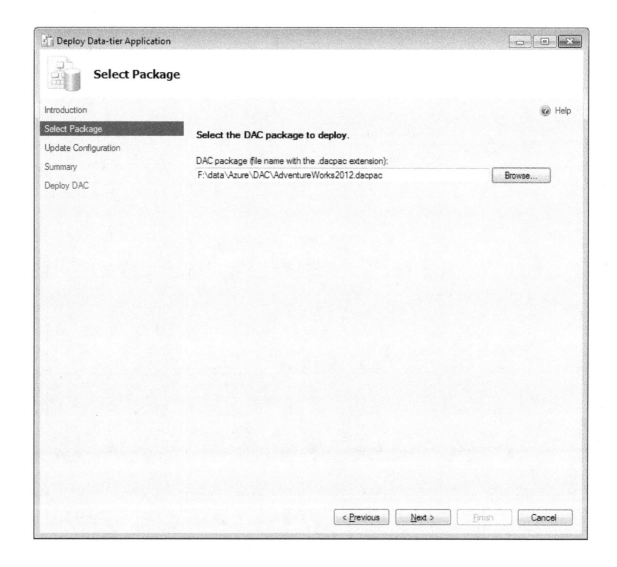

Configure the Database Deployment Properties

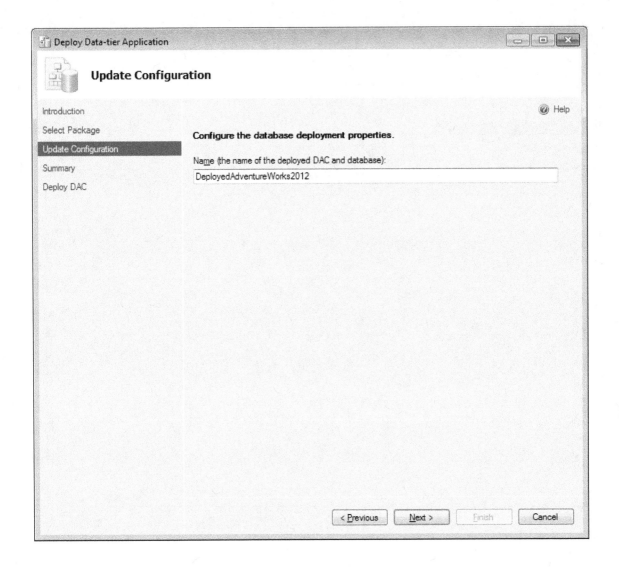

Summary screen follows. Click Finish to start processing.

Object Explorer View After Deployment - Runtime around 1 minute
All tables are empty in deployed database. All objects are defined.

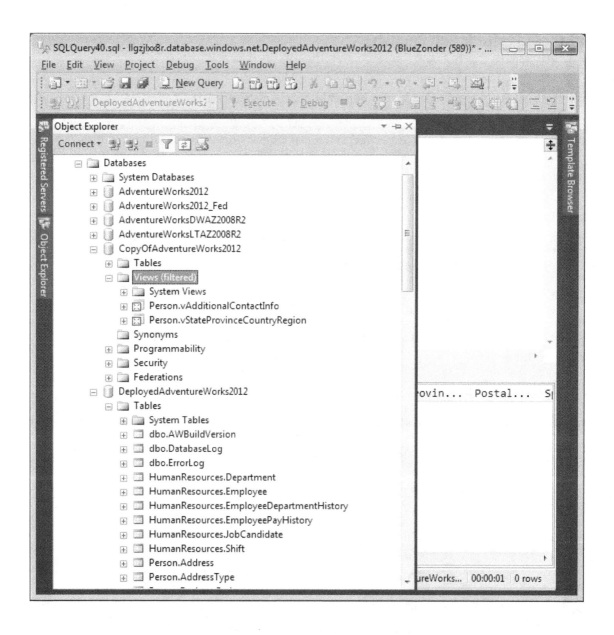

Popular Backup Plans

Backup is the most important task for a Database Administrator. It is necessary to do a test restore periodically in order to validate the backups.

Nightly or Periodic Full Backup

Database can be recovered to the time of the last backup.

Nightly Full Backup & Daytime Transaction Log Backup

Typically log backup is scheduled every 15 minutes between 8am and 6pm. Database can be recovered to a point-in-time up to the time of the last log backup

Weekend Full, Nightly Differential and Daytime Log Backup

Point-in-time recovery is supported. Assumption is that the differential backup is faster than the full backup.

> For log recovery, each transaction log file must be restored in order. For differential recovery, only the last differential file has to be restored.

Example: To recover to Thursday 11:40 am: restore weekend full backup, WED differential backup, THU transaction log backups in order till 11:00 am. All restores are with norecovery except the last one.

The database restore page sequences automatically the backups for a most recent restore.

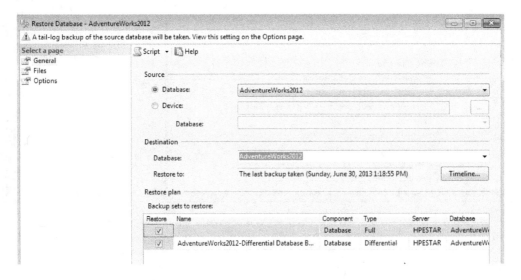

Copy-Only Database Backup

Copy-only backup does not interrupt the point-in-time recovery sequence backups. Assume log-shipping is setup. Doing a regular log backup to file abc.trn would break log-shipping. Log-shipping uses the point-in-time recovery principle with predefined times like 15 minutes log backups.

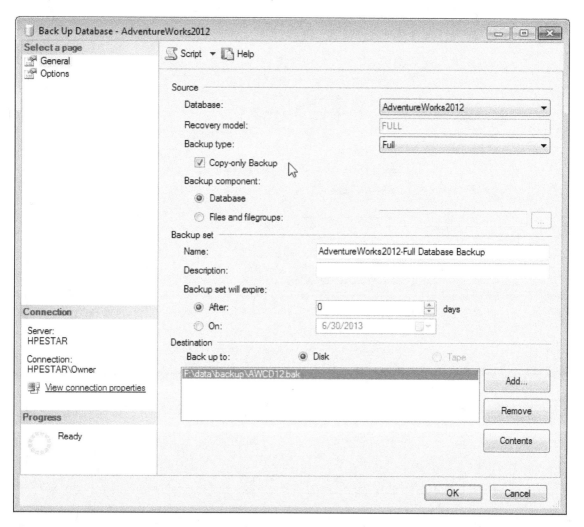

Generated Script

```
BACKUP DATABASE [AdventureWorks2012] TO  DISK = N'F:\data\backup\AWCD12.bak' WITH  COPY_ONLY,
NOFORMAT, NOINIT,  NAME = N'AdventureWorks2012-Full Database Backup', SKIP, NOREWIND, NOUNLOAD,  STATS
= 10
GO
```

CHAPTER 12: Database Backup Strategies

Tail of the Log Backup

Tail of the log backup performs a log backup and puts the database into the recovery mode **preventing further transactions**. This method is used when a database has to be copied over to another server usually at geographical distance in a consistent manner.

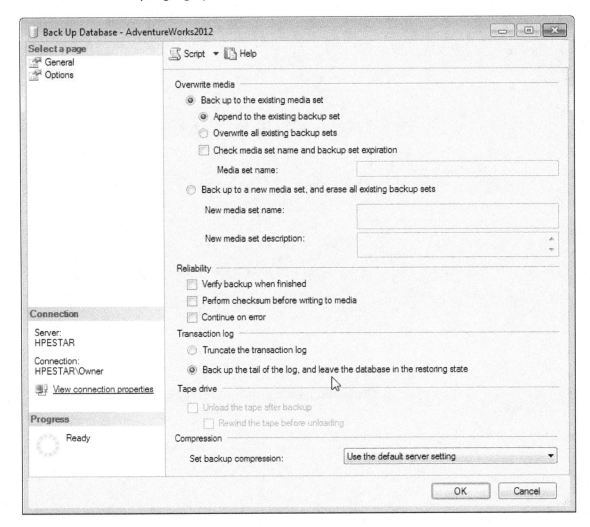

Generated Script

```
BACKUP LOG [AdventureWorks2012] TO  DISK = N'F:\data\backup\AWCD12.bak' WITH
NO_TRUNCATE , NOFORMAT, NOINIT,  NAME = N'AdventureWorks2012-Transaction Log  Backup',
SKIP, NOREWIND, NOUNLOAD, NORECOVERY , STATS = 10
GO
```

CHAPTER 12: Database Backup Strategies

CHAPTER 13: Database Restore Scenarios

A MUST Know-How for a DBA

A DBA may not know all administration tasks, nonetheless, BACKUP & RESTORE are absolute must. Practice, practice, practice.

Restore Database from Full Backup with Overwrite

First a full backup created.

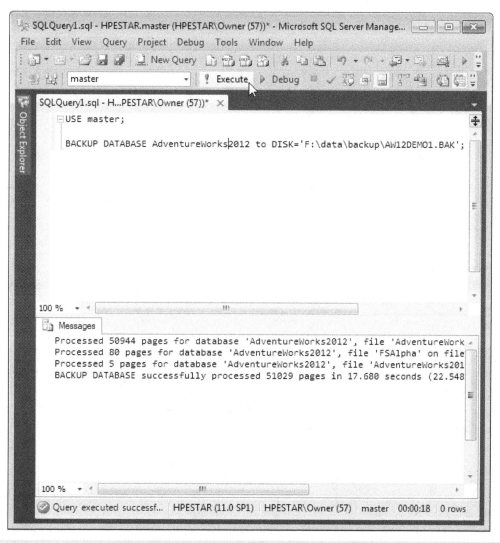

Launching RESTORE DATABASE in Object Explorer

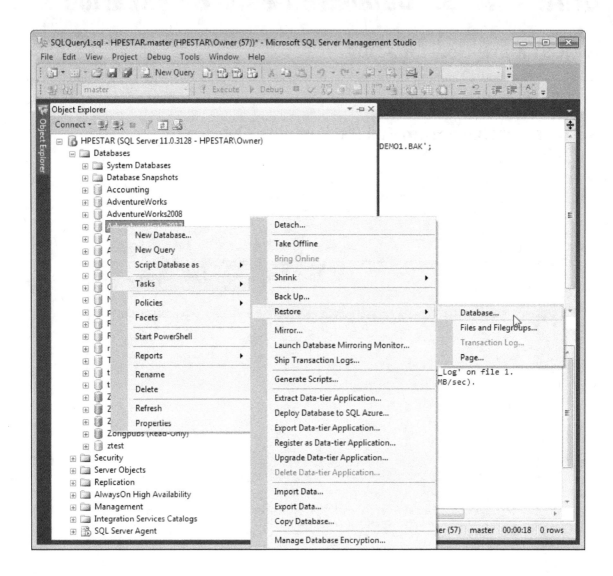

Restore Database General Page
Verification can be performed prior to restore.

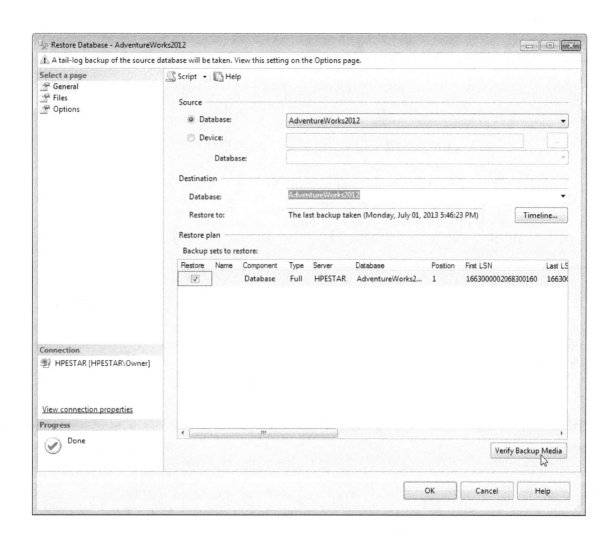

Restore Database Files Page

Optionally the database files can be relocated and renamed (not done here).

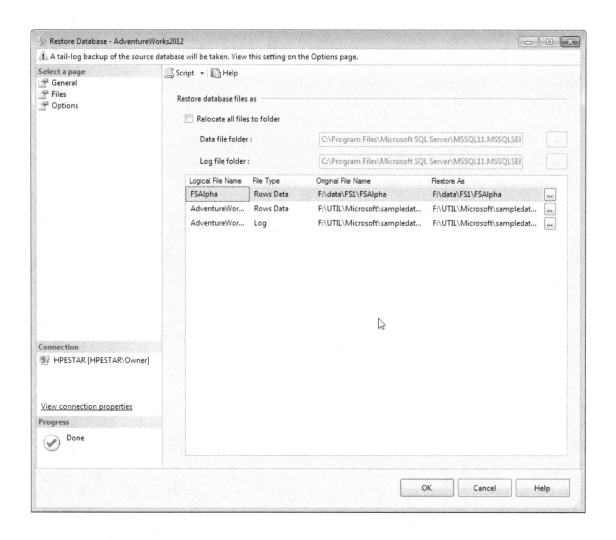

Restore Database Options Page

Checkmark the Overwrite box. Restore with RECOVERY means the database will be accessible after restore. NORECOVERY is the opposite option.

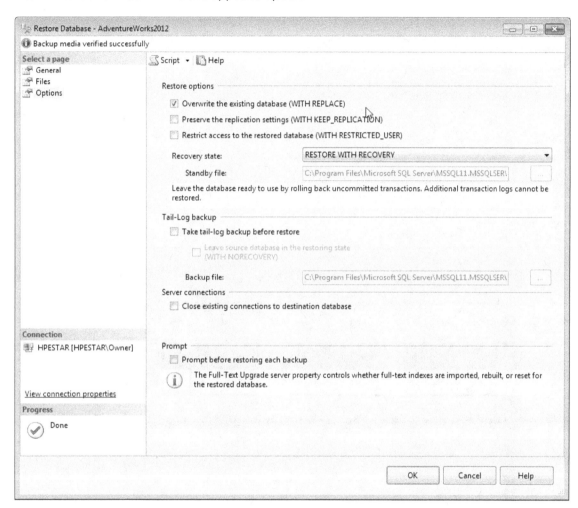

Generated T-SQL Script

```
USE [master]
RESTORE DATABASE [AdventureWorks2012] FROM  DISK =
N'F:\data\backup\AW12DEMO1.BAK'
WITH  FILE = 1,  NOUNLOAD,  REPLACE,  STATS = 5
```

CHAPTER 13: Database Restore Scenarios

Restore Failure Due to Users in the Database

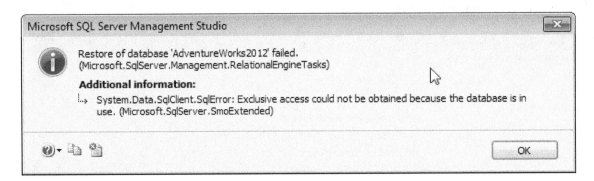

Checking Database Use with Activity Monitor

We can see one user (actually myself) for AdventureWorks2012. We can also check with sp_who or sp_who2.

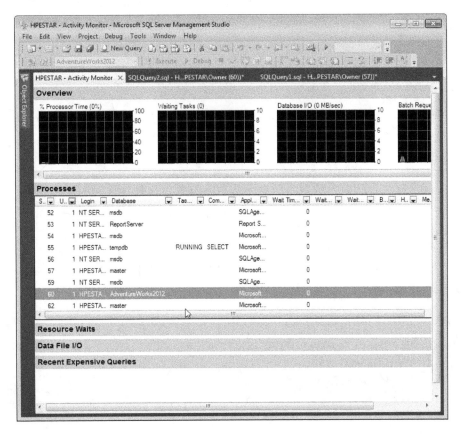

The Generated Script Window is the User

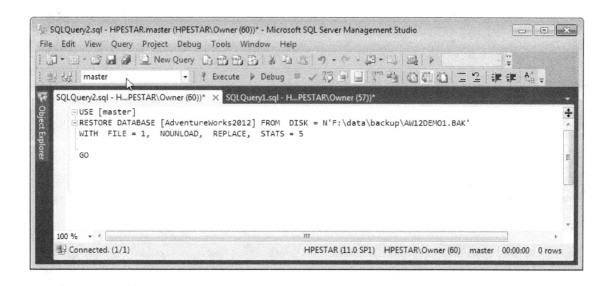

Repositioning to the master database

Executing the RESTORE DATABASE and the Action is Successful

The GUI restore database offers only the cancel option after the error. Lucky that the script was generated.

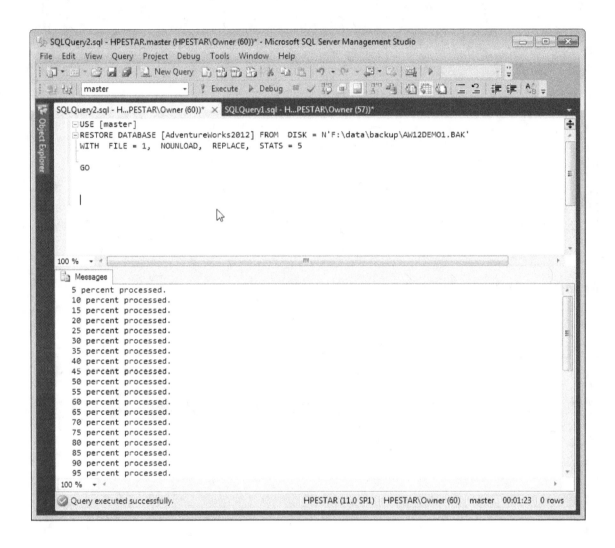

Restore into New Database

We can create a copy of a database by restoring it under a new name or on a different server. Tail-log backup would pick up the transactions between the full backup was taken and now.

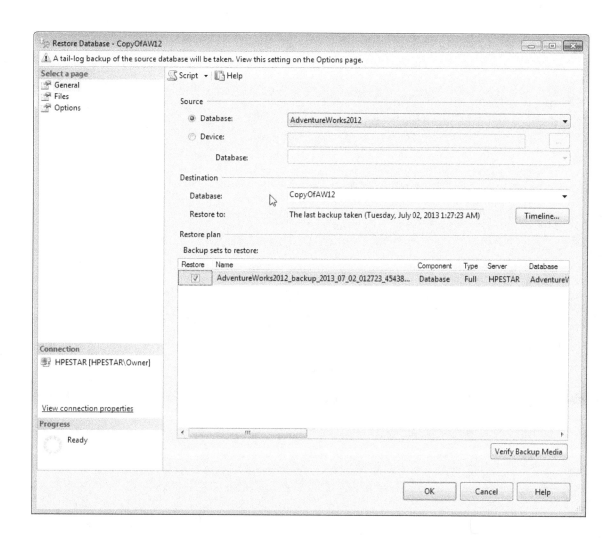

Restore Database Files Page

Folders are setup for the new database files. File names are unchanged.

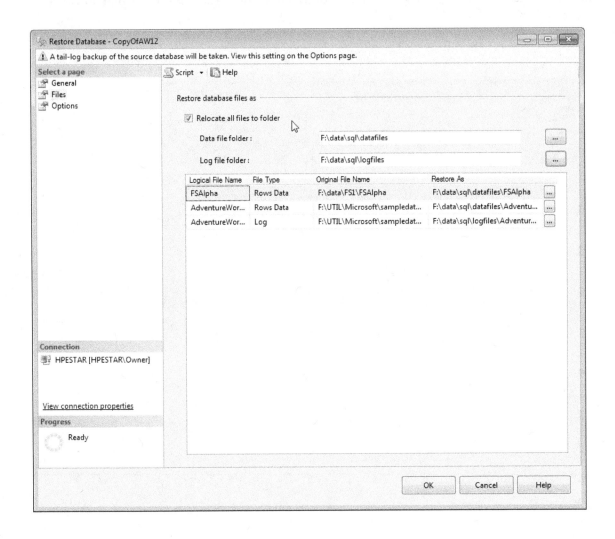

Restore Database Options Page
Tail-log backup option uncheckmarked.

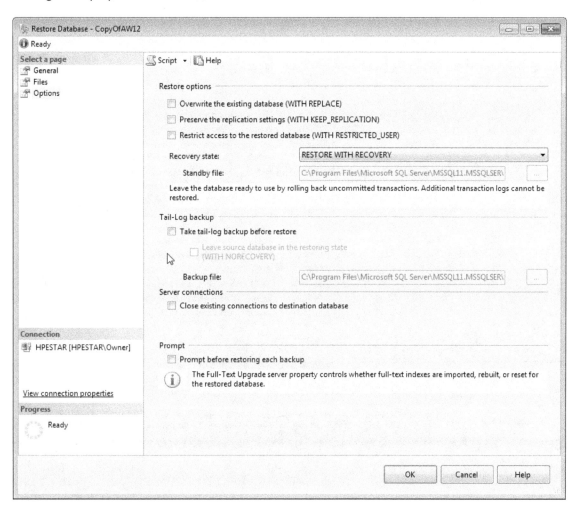

Generated Script

```
USE [master]
RESTORE DATABASE [CopyOfAW12] FROM
DISK = N'F:\data\backup\AdventureWorks2012\AdventureWorks2012_backup_2013_07_02_012723_4543858.bak'
WITH  FILE = 1,
MOVE N'FSAlpha' TO N'F:\data\sql\datafiles\FSAlpha',
MOVE N'AdventureWorks2012_Data' TO N'F:\data\sql\datafiles\AdventureWorks2012_Data.mdf',
MOVE N'AdventureWorks2012_Log' TO N'F:\data\sql\logfiles\AdventureWorks2012_log.ldf',
NOUNLOAD,  STATS = 5
```

CHAPTER 13: Database Restore Scenarios

Confirming Restore in SQL Server Log

Since RESTORE DATABASE is a major event, there is a SQL Server log entry about it.

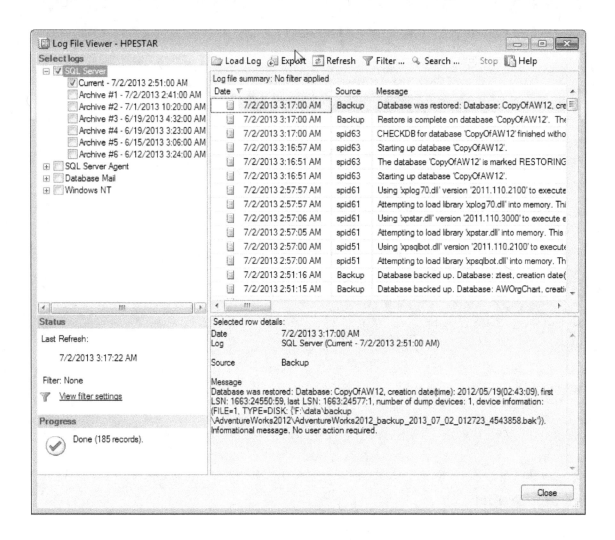

Restore Full Backup & All Log Backups

Assume a hardware disaster happened in the middle of the day at 1:50PM. The database must be restored on the same physical server (after repair) or a different server up to the last transaction log backup. All the transaction logs must be restored in order: 8:00, 8:15, 8:30, 8:45 and so on. A full backup and a number of transaction log backups were stored into backup device AW12 (similarly it can be done with a backup file).

NOTE: If backups are stored in different files, it requires manual effort to organize them into a valid restore chain.

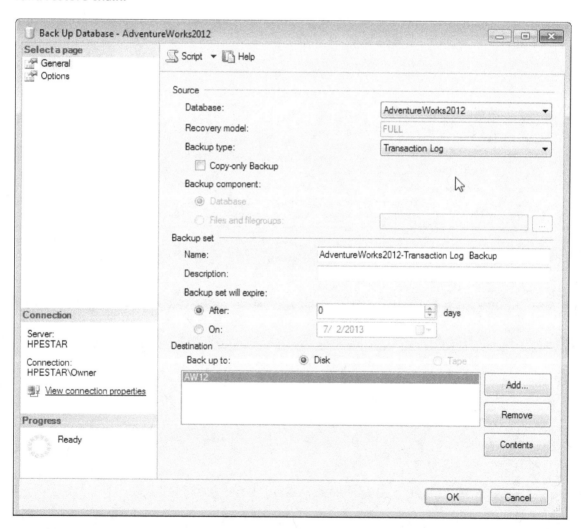

Contents of the Backup Device
One full backup and 5 transaction log backups.

The following query was executed between transaction log backups (SOD1 - SOD5):

`SELECT * INTO SOD5 FROM Sales.SalesOrderHeader;`

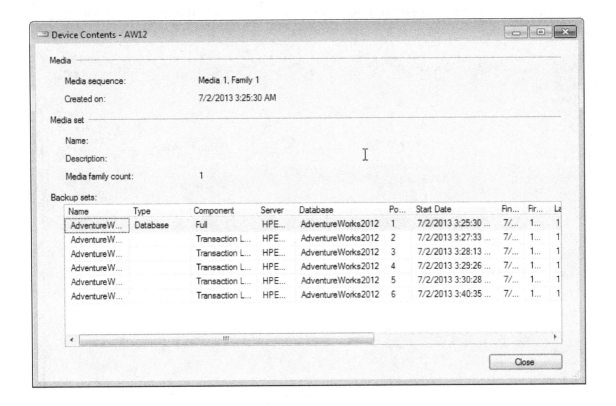

Backup Timeline Display

The timeline display shows that around 3:25 AM a full backup was taken and the last transaction log backup around 3:40 AM. It does not show how many log backups were taken. Since we did not choose Specific date and time (restore to a point-in-time), it will restore to the last transaction log backup taken as shown by the slider.

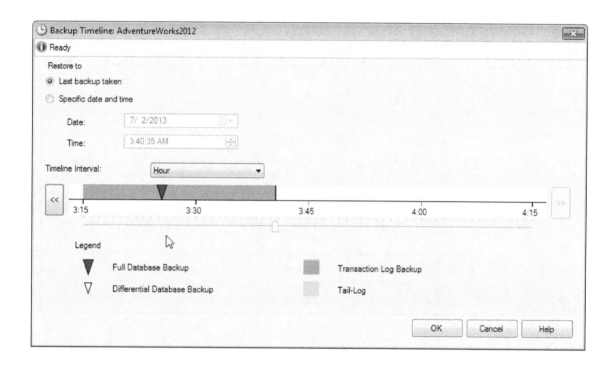

Restore Database General Page

All users should exit from this database. As a DBA you could send an email notification. The KILL command can be used to force out lingering processes.

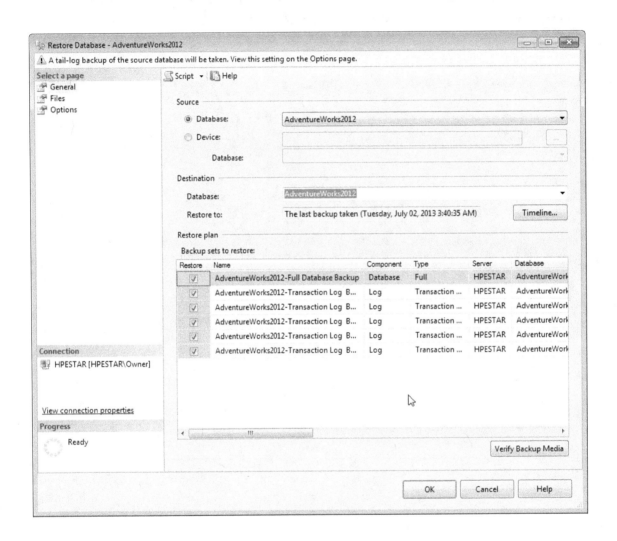

Restore Database Files Page

No changes on this pages.

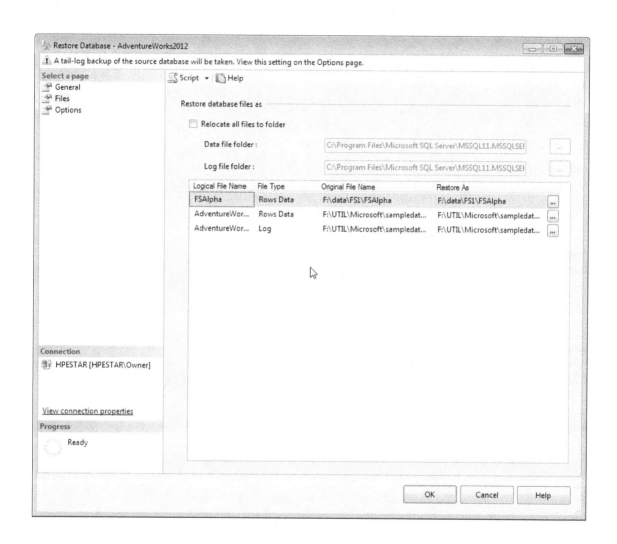

Restore Database Options Page

Tail-log backup uncheckmarked. Overwrite is checkmarked. Script is generated and the GUI restore is cancelled. Instead the restore script will be executed in a query editor window.

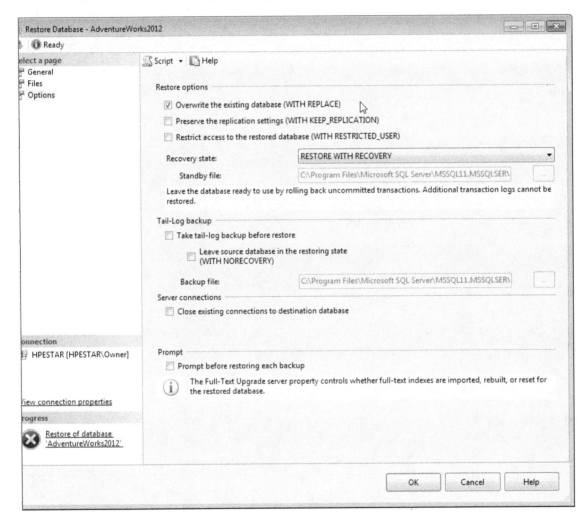

Generated Script

```
USE [master]
RESTORE DATABASE [AdventureWorks2012] FROM [AW12] WITH FILE = 1, NORECOVERY, NOUNLOAD, REPLACE, STATS = 5
RESTORE LOG [AdventureWorks2012] FROM [AW12] WITH FILE = 2, NORECOVERY, NOUNLOAD, STATS = 5
RESTORE LOG [AdventureWorks2012] FROM [AW12] WITH FILE = 3, NORECOVERY, NOUNLOAD, STATS = 5
RESTORE LOG [AdventureWorks2012] FROM [AW12] WITH FILE = 4, NORECOVERY, NOUNLOAD, STATS = 5
RESTORE LOG [AdventureWorks2012] FROM [AW12] WITH FILE = 5, NORECOVERY, NOUNLOAD, STATS = 5
RESTORE LOG [AdventureWorks2012] FROM [AW12] WITH FILE = 6, NOUNLOAD, STATS = 5
```

Execution of the Combination Restore Chain

Only the last restore is done with RECOVERY(default). NORECOVERY leaves the database unusable for users until the completion of restore script. If the backup files are out of order or a transaction log backup file is broken, the restore will fail. Everything went OK this time.

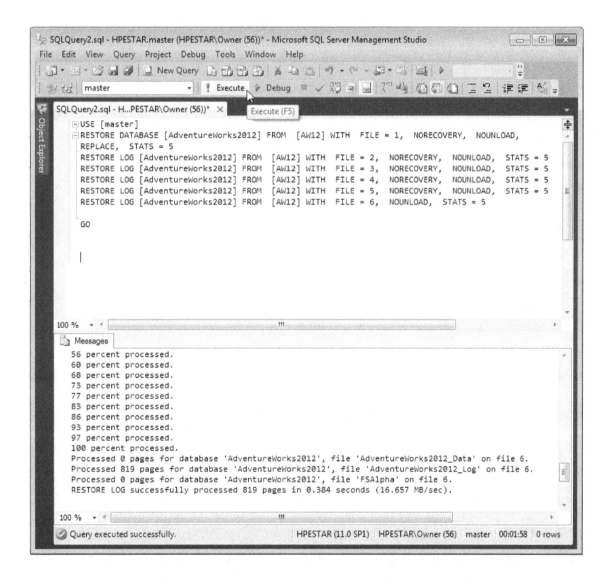

Point-in-Time Database Restore

Another (not a hardware) disaster scenario: a user updated 1 million records my mistake around 2pm. DBA gets request to restore database as of 1pm prior to the erroneous updates. The full and transactin log backups are used again but the restore stops at the requested time.

Same setup as in the previous restore database scenario except that we select point-in-time in the timeline dialog window.

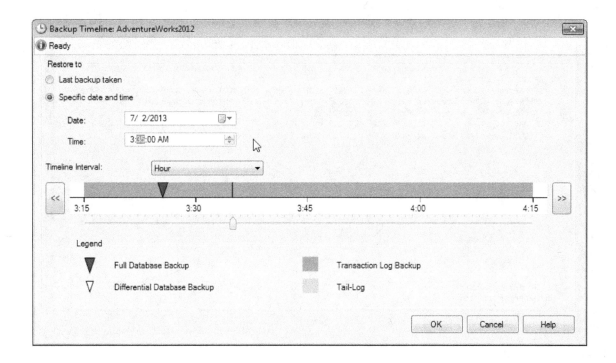

Generated Script

```
USE [master]
RESTORE DATABASE [AdventureWorks2012] FROM [AW12] WITH FILE = 1, NORECOVERY, NOUNLOAD,
REPLACE, STATS = 5
RESTORE LOG [AdventureWorks2012] FROM [AW12] WITH FILE = 2, NORECOVERY, NOUNLOAD, STATS = 5
RESTORE LOG [AdventureWorks2012] FROM [AW12] WITH FILE = 3, NORECOVERY, NOUNLOAD, STATS = 5
RESTORE LOG [AdventureWorks2012] FROM [AW12] WITH FILE = 4, NORECOVERY, NOUNLOAD, STATS = 5
RESTORE LOG [AdventureWorks2012] FROM [AW12] WITH FILE = 5, NORECOVERY, NOUNLOAD, STATS = 5
RESTORE LOG [AdventureWorks2012] FROM [AW12] WITH FILE = 6, NOUNLOAD, STATS = 5,
STOPAT = N'2013-07-02T03:35:00'
```

Point-in-Time Restore Execution

SOD5 is not in table list due to the early termination of restore.

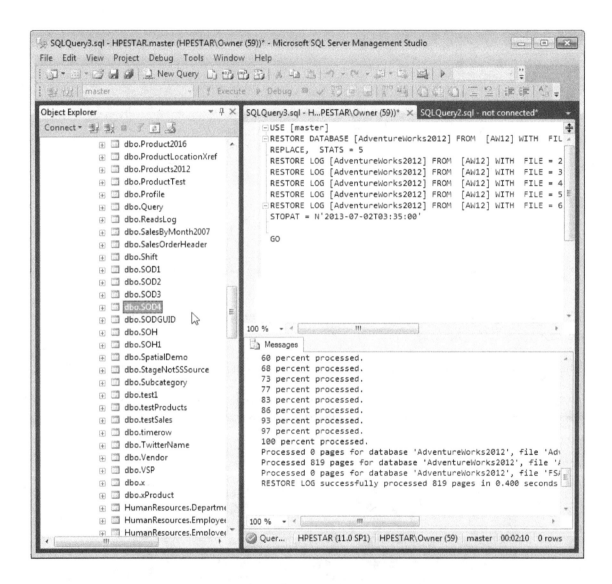

Full, Differential & Transaction Log Restore Scenario

The concept is that full backup takes long, for example, 5 hours (only weekend maintenance window is sufficient for it), differential backup 20 minutes and transaction log backup 1 minute.

Backups taken:

➢ SUN 2AM   FULL

➢ TUE - FRI 2AM DIFFERENTIAL

➢ MON-FRI 8AM - 6PM TRANSACTION LOG IN 15 MIN INTERVALS

Restore sequence to THU 1:55PM:

➢ FULL RESTORE

➢ THU DIFFERENTIAL RESTORE

➢ THU TRANSACTION LOGs RESTORE FROM 8AM to 1:45PM IN ORDER

NOTE: DIFFERENTIAL backup requires only the last one to be restored unlike transaction log backups.

All backups must be valid, otherwise the restore can only be performed to the last good backup.

MSDN Article: **Back Up and Restore of SQL Server Databases**　　http://bit.ly/91yCVx http://msdn.microsoft.com/en-us/library/ms187048.aspx

CHAPTER 13: Database Restore Scenarios

CHAPTER 14: Data Integrity & Change Management

Why is Data Integrity Paramount

A business or organization can only operate efficiently with good quality data. Computers were the real engine of economic progress since the 1950-s. Without computers, we would pretty much be at post Second World War level. Computers work with data and produce data. As the saying goes: garbage in, garbage out. Therefore it is our job as database designers, database developers and database administrators to ensure the data integrity in a database. What are the sources of the bad data? They can be data feeds received from various sources,   data entry by people, and bugs in database or application programming. The best way to minimize bugs is putting each piece of new software through rigorous quality assurance (QA) process. To prevent bad data getting into the database there are a number of possibilities: table design, constraints, stored procedures, triggers and application software.

At the lowest level, constraints make up the guarding force over data integrity. The default constraint is different from the rest: it provides predefined default value if no value is provided for a cell (a column in a row), it does not give an error message.

```
USE AdventureWorks2012;
SELECT          ConstraintType = type_desc,  [Count] = COUNT(*)
FROM sys.objects
WHERE type_desc in        (
                          'CHECK_CONSTRAINT',
                          'DEFAULT_CONSTRAINT',
                          'FOREIGN_KEY_CONSTRAINT',
                          'PRIMARY_KEY_CONSTRAINT',
                          'UNIQUE_CONSTRAINT'
                          )
GROUP BY type_desc  ORDER BY type_desc;
```

ConstraintType	Count
CHECK_CONSTRAINT	89
DEFAULT_CONSTRAINT	152
FOREIGN_KEY_CONSTRAINT	90
PRIMARY_KEY_CONSTRAINT	71
UNIQUE_CONSTRAINT	1

Entity Integrity

Entity Integrity defines a row as a unique entity for a particular table. The main enforcing mechanisms are: NOT NULL constraint and unique index. PRIMARY KEY implies not null, and unique index automatically created. In the Production.Product table ProductID is the INT IDENTITY PRIMARY KEY, Name & ProductNumber are NATURAL KEYs and rowguid is a system generated unique key. All four keys are not null and all have unique index defined. The implication is that we can use any of 4 columns for row identification. However, ProductID INT (4 bytes) column is the most efficient row (record) identifier.

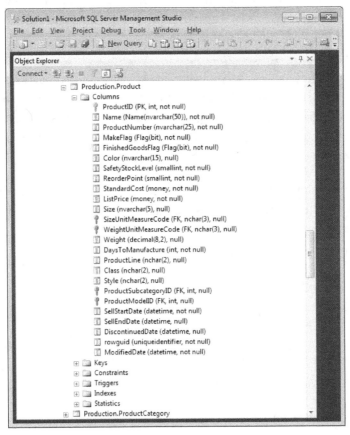

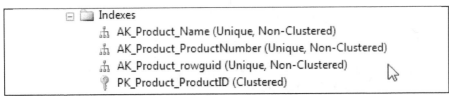

How to Remove Duplicates in a Table

The best way to prevent duplicates is by placing a UNIQUE KEY or unique index on the unique column(s). PRIMARY KEY & UNIQUE KEY constraints automatically create a unique index on the key column(s). If the entire row is a duplicate, removal is real simple with the DISTINCT clause.

```
SELECT DISTINCT * INTO T2 FROM T1;
GO
```

If duplicates are only in one or more columns, then duplicates removal is fairly easy with the ROW_NUMBER method, it is more involved with the GROUP BY method (prior to SQL Server 2005).

```
-- Create test table
USE tempdb;
SELECT          ProductID=CONVERT(int, ProductID),
                ProductName = Name,  ProductNumber,
                ListPrice = ListPrice + 1.00
INTO Product
FROM AdventureWorks2012.Production.Product   WHERE ListPrice > 0.0;
GO  -- (304 row(s) affected)
```

```
-- Unique index prevents duplicates
CREATE UNIQUE INDEX idxProd ON Product(ProductName, ProductNumber);
GO
```

```
 -- Try to insert  duplicates on ProductName & ProductNumber
INSERT INTO Product
SELECT          TOP (100) ProductID=CONVERT(int, ProductID) + 1000,
                ProductName = Name, ProductNumber,
                ListPrice = ListPrice + 2.00
FROM AdventureWorks2008.Production.Product
WHERE ListPrice > 0.0 ORDER BY NEWID();
GO
/* Msg 2601, Level 14, State 1, Line 2
Cannot insert duplicate key row in object 'dbo.Product' with unique index 'idxProd'.
The duplicate key value is (Fender Set - Mountain, FE-6654).
The statement has been terminated.  */
```

```
DROP INDEX Product.idxProd;
GO
```

CHAPTER 14: Data Integrity & Change Management

Rows with Duplicates Can Be Numbered in Ordered or Random Manner

```
-- Insert  100 duplicates on ProductName & ProductNumber
INSERT INTO Product
SELECT          TOP (100) ProductID=CONVERT(int, ProductID) + 1000,
                ProductName = Name, ProductNumber,   ListPrice = ListPrice + 2.00
FROM AdventureWorks2008.Production.Product
WHERE ListPrice > 0.0
ORDER BY NEWID();
GO
```

```
-- Quantify duplicates with GROUP BY query
SELECT ProductName, ProductNumber, [Count] = count(*)
FROM Product
GROUP BY ProductName, ProductNumber
        HAVING count(*) > 1
ORDER BY ProductName, ProductNumber;
GO -- (100 row(s) affected) - Partial results.
```

ProductName	ProductNumber	Count
Bike Wash - Dissolver	CL-9009	2
Classic Vest, L	VE-C304-L	2
Classic Vest, S	VE-C304-S	2
Front Brakes	FB-9873	2
Full-Finger Gloves, M	GL-F110-M	2

```
-- Quantify duplicates with ROW_NUMBER OVER - we don't care about duplicates ordering
;WITH CTE AS (
   SELECT RN=ROW_NUMBER() OVER (PARTITION BY ProductName, ProductNumber
   ORDER BY NEWID() ),  ProductName, ProductNumber
   FROM Product)
SELECT * FROM CTE WHERE RN > 1
ORDER BY ProductName, ProductNumber;
GO -- (100 row(s) affected) - Partial results.
```

RN	ProductName	ProductNumber
2	Bike Wash - Dissolver	CL-9009
2	Classic Vest, L	VE-C304-L
2	Classic Vest, S	VE-C304-S
2	Front Brakes	FB-9873
2	Full-Finger Gloves, M	GL-F110-M

CHAPTER 14: Data Integrity & Change Management

Remove Duplicates with CTE & ROW_NUMBER OVER PARTITION BY

```
-- To removal of duplicates is real easy with CTE & ROW_NUMBER
;WITH CTE AS (
    SELECT RN=ROW_NUMBER() OVER (PARTITION BY ProductName, ProductNumber
    ORDER BY NEWID()),  ProductName, ProductNumber    FROM Product)
DELETE CTE  WHERE RN > 1;
GO -- (100 row(s) affected)


-- Test for duplicates again
SELECT ProductName, ProductNumber, [Count] = count(*)
FROM Product  GROUP BY ProductName, ProductNumber  HAVING count(*) > 1
ORDER BY ProductName, ProductNumber;
GO -- (0 row(s) affected)


SELECT COUNT(*) FROM Product;  -- 304
GO
```

Remove Duplicates with GROUP BY

```
-- Insert  duplicates on ProductName & ProductNumber
INSERT INTO Product    SELECT    TOP (100) ProductID=CONVERT(int, ProductID) + 1000,
                 ProductName = Name, ProductNumber,    ListPrice = ListPrice + 2.00
FROM AdventureWorks2008.Production.Product  WHERE ListPrice > 0.0  ORDER BY NEWID();
GO


-- Sample of conflicting data - It is a business decision what to keep
SELECT TOP (4) * FROM Product WHERE ProductNumber IN
   ( SELECT ProductNumber FROM Product   GROUP BY ProductNumber HAVING count(*) > 1   )
ORDER BY ProductNumber;
```

ProductID	ProductName	ProductNumber	ListPrice
992	Mountain-500 Black, 48	BK-M18B-48	540.9900
1992	Mountain-500 Black, 48	BK-M18B-48	541.9900
993	Mountain-500 Black, 52	BK-M18B-52	540.9900
1993	Mountain-500 Black, 52	BK-M18B-52	541.9900

```
-- Assume it does not matter which duplicate to keep: any ProductID and any ListPrice OK
SELECT ProductID=MIN(ProductID), ProductName, ProductNumber, ListPrice=MIN(ListPrice)
INTO Product1 FROM Product GROUP BY ProductName, ProductNumber ORDER BY ProductID;
GO  -- (304 row(s) affected)
```

CHAPTER 14: Data Integrity & Change Management

Domain Integrity

A domain defines the possible values for a column. Domain Integrity rules enforce the validity data in a column:

Data type	table design
Data length	table design
Nullability	table design
Collation	table design
Allowable values	check constraints - table design
Default value	default constraints - table design

CHECK constraint is used for simple rules such as OrderQty > 0. UDF CHECK constraints can be used for complex rules. In addition, at the development phase, triggers, stored procedures and client-side application software can be developed to enforce Domain Integrity.

Server-side CHECK constraints are the most desirable. Client-side Domain Integrity enforcement is the least desirable. However, it may happen that there is no database expert on the project and developers feel more confident programming data validity rules in the application software. Ultimately what counts is valid data in the database. Usually big-budget projects can do everything the right way due to the availability of expert-level resources in all areas of the software development project. Basic table definition data from INFORMATION_SCHEMA views.

```
SELECT          COLUMN_NAME, ORDINAL_POSITION, DATA_TYPE, IS_NULLABLE,
                CHARACTER_MAXIMUM_LENGTH, COLLATION_NAME, COLUMN_DEFAULT
FROM INFORMATION_SCHEMA.COLUMNS WHERE TABLE_NAME = 'SalesOrderHeader';
```

COLUMN_NAME	ORDINAL_POSITION	DATA_TYPE	IS_NULLABLE	CHARACTER_MAXIMUM_LENGTH	COLLATION_NAME	COLUMN_DEFAULT
SalesOrderID	1	int	NO	NULL	NULL	NULL
RevisionNumber	2	tinyint	NO	NULL	NULL	((0))
OrderDate	3	datetime	NO	NULL	NULL	(getdate())
DueDate	4	datetime	NO	NULL	NULL	NULL
ShipDate	5	datetime	YES	NULL	NULL	NULL
tatus	6	tinyint	NO	NULL	NULL	((1))
OnlineOrderFlag	7	bit	NO	NULL	NULL	((1))
SalesOrderNumber	8	nvarchar	NO	25	SQL_Latin1_General_CP1_CI_AS	NULL
PurchaseOrderNumber	9	nvarchar	YES	25	SQL_Latin1_General_CP1_CI_AS	NULL
AccountNumber	10	nvarchar	YES	15	SQL_Latin1_General_CP1_CI_AS	NULL
CustomerID	11	int	NO	NULL	NULL	NULL
SalesPersonID	12	int	YES	NULL	NULL	NULL
TerritoryID	13	int	YES	NULL	NULL	NULL
BillToAddressID	14	int	NO	NULL	NULL	NULL
ShipToAddressID	15	int	NO	NULL	NULL	NULL
ShipMethodID	16	int	NO	NULL	NULL	NULL
CreditCardID	17	int	YES	NULL	NULL	NULL
CreditCardApprovalCode	18	varchar	YES	15	SQL_Latin1_General_CP1_CI_AS	NULL
CurrencyRateID	19	int	YES	NULL	NULL	NULL
SubTotal	20	money	NO	NULL	NULL	((0.00))
TaxAmt	21	money	NO	NULL	NULL	((0.00))
Freight	22	money	NO	NULL	NULL	((0.00))
TotalDue	23	money	NO	NULL	NULL	NULL
Comment	24	nvarchar	YES	128	SQL_Latin1_General_CP1_CI_AS	NULL
rowguid	25	uniqueidentifier	NO	NULL	NULL	(newid())
ModifiedDate	26	datetime	NO	NULL	NULL	(getdate())

Domain Integrity Summary Display with sp_help

The sp_help system procedure provides a convenient way to display a summary of Domain Integrity definitions for a table.

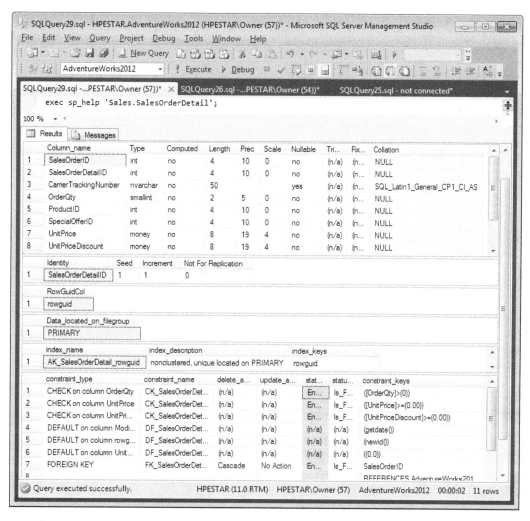

We can query "sys" system views metadata for column definition as well.

```
SELECT * FROM sys.columns
WHERE object_name(object_id) = 'PurchaseOrderHeader'  ORDER BY column_id;
-- (13 row(s) affected) - Partial results.
```

object_id	name	column_id	system_type_id	user_type_id	max_length	precision	scale	collation_name
946102411	PurchaseOrderID	1	56	56	4	10	0	NULL

CHAPTER 14: Data Integrity & Change Management

THE COLUMNPROPERTY() Function

The COLUMNPROPERTY() function can be used for programmatic discovery of column properties. Script to generate SELECT queries for all properties.

```
USE AdventureWorks2012;
GO
```

```
DECLARE @Parms TABLE (Property varchar(32))
INSERT  @Parms VALUES
('AllowsNull'), ('ColumnId'),
('FullTextTypeColumn'), ('IsComputed'),
('IsCursorType'), ('IsDeterministic'),
('IsFulltextIndexed'), ('IsIdentity'),
('IsIdNotForRepl'), ('IsIndexable'),
('IsOutParam'), ('IsPrecise'),
('IsRowGuidCol'), ('IsSystemVerified'),
('IsXmlIndexable'), ('Precision'),
('Scale'), ('StatisticalSemantics'),
('SystemDataAccess'), ('UserDataAccess'),
('UsesAnsiTrim'), ('IsSparse'),
('IsColumnSet')
SELECT CONCAT('SELECT COLUMNPROPERTY( OBJECT_ID(''Person.Person''), ''LastName'', ''',
                Property, ''') AS [', Property, '];')
FROM @Parms
GO  -- Partial results.
```

```
SELECT COLUMNPROPERTY( OBJECT_ID('Person.Person'), 'LastName', 'AllowsNull') AS [AllowsNull];
SELECT COLUMNPROPERTY( OBJECT_ID('Person.Person'), 'LastName', 'ColumnId') AS [ColumnId];
SELECT COLUMNPROPERTY( OBJECT_ID('Person.Person'), 'LastName', 'FullTextTypeColumn') AS [FullTextTypeColumn];
SELECT COLUMNPROPERTY( OBJECT_ID('Person.Person'), 'LastName', 'IsComputed') AS [IsComputed];
SELECT COLUMNPROPERTY( OBJECT_ID('Person.Person'), 'LastName', 'IsCursorType') AS [IsCursorType];
```

Executing the queries, the column properties are returned one by one.

Column List Using System Views & Data Dictionary

We can combine sys. system views with data dictionary description to get a valuable list when working with domain integrity.

```
USE AdventureWorks2012;
SELECT SCHEMA_NAME(T.schema_id)   AS SchemaName,
    T.name                        AS TableName,
    C.name                        AS ColumnName,
    TP.name                       AS ColumnType,
    C.max_length                  AS ColumnLength,
    COALESCE(EP.value, Space(1))  AS ColumnDesc
FROM   sys.tables AS T
    INNER JOIN sys.columns AS C
        ON T.object_id = C.object_id
    INNER JOIN sys.types AS TP
        ON  C.system_type_id = TP.user_type_id
    LEFT JOIN sys.extended_properties AS EP
        ON EP.major_id = T.object_id
            AND EP.minor_id = C.column_id
ORDER  BY SchemaName,  TableName, ColumnName;
GO  -- (643 row(s) affected) - Partial Results.
```

Purchasing	PurchaseOrderHeader	EmployeeID	int	4	Employee who created the purchase order. Foreign key to Employee.BusinessEntityID.
Purchasing	PurchaseOrderHeader	Freight	money	8	Shipping cost.
Purchasing	PurchaseOrderHeader	ModifiedDate	datetime	8	Date and time the record was last updated.
Purchasing	PurchaseOrderHeader	OrderDate	datetime	8	Purchase order creation date.
Purchasing	PurchaseOrderHeader	PurchaseOrderID	int	4	Primary key.
Purchasing	PurchaseOrderHeader	PurchaseOrderID	int	4	Clustered index created by a primary key constraint.
Purchasing	PurchaseOrderHeader	RevisionNumber	tinyint	1	Incremental number to track changes to the purchase order over time.
Purchasing	PurchaseOrderHeader	RevisionNumber	tinyint	1	Nonclustered index.
Purchasing	PurchaseOrderHeader	ShipDate	datetime	8	Estimated shipment date from the vendor.
Purchasing	PurchaseOrderHeader	ShipMethodID	int	4	Shipping method. Foreign key to ShipMethod.ShipMethodID.
Purchasing	PurchaseOrderHeader	Status	tinyint	1	Order current status. 1 = Pending; 2 = Approved; 3 = Rejected; 4 = Complete
Purchasing	PurchaseOrderHeader	Status	tinyint	1	Nonclustered index.
Purchasing	PurchaseOrderHeader	SubTotal	money	8	Purchase order subtotal. Computed as SUM(PurchaseOrderDetail.LineTotal)for the appropriate PurchaseOrderID.
Purchasing	PurchaseOrderHeader	TaxAmt	money	8	Tax amount.
Purchasing	PurchaseOrderHeader	TotalDue	money	8	Total due to vendor. Computed as Subtotal + TaxAmt + Freight.
Purchasing	PurchaseOrderHeader	VendorID	int	4	Vendor with whom the purchase order is placed. Foreign key to Vendor.BusinessEntityID.

Declarative Referential Integrity

Referential Integrity refers to ensuring that relationships between tables remain consistent. Declarative means it is part of table setup, not in programming objects like stored procedure. When one table attempts to create a FOREIGN KEY to another (PK) table, Referential Integrity requires that the primary key value exists in the referenced (PK) table. The optional cascading update & cascading delete ensure that changes made to the primary table are reflected in the linked referencing (FK) table. For example, if a row is deleted in the primary table, then all referencing rows are automatically deleted in the linked (FK) table when ON DELETE CASCADE is set. All three Referential Integrity constraint actions are demonstrated by the following script.

```
USE tempdb;

-- Create 2 test tables with PK-FK relationship
CREATE TABLE Product (
        ProductID INT PRIMARY KEY,
        ProductName varchar(50) UNIQUE,
        ProductNumber varchar(20) UNIQUE,
        ListPrice MONEY);
GO
```

```
-- First we test without the DELETE CASCADE action
CREATE TABLE OrderDetail (
        SalesOrderID INT,
        SalesOrderDetailID INT,
        PRIMARY KEY (SalesOrderID, SalesOrderDetailID),
        OrderQty INT ,
        ProductID INT REFERENCES Product(ProductID)  -- ON DELETE CASCADE  );
GO
```

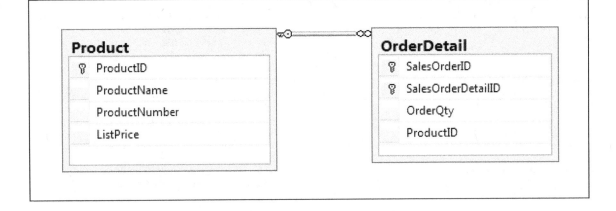

FOREIGN KEY Constraint Protects Two Ways

```
-- Populate test tables
INSERT Product
SELECT ProductID, Name, ProductNumber, ListPrice
FROM AdventureWorks2012.Production.Product
ORDER BY ProductID;
GO
--(504 row(s) affected)
```

```
INSERT OrderDetail
SELECT          SalesOrderID,
                SalesOrderDetailID,
                OrderQty,
                ProductID
FROM AdventureWorks2012.Sales.SalesOrderDetail
ORDER BY SalesOrderID, SalesOrderDetailID;
GO
-- (121317 row(s) affected)
```

-- Attempting to insert into FK table a reference to a non-existing (PK) ProductID
```
INSERT OrderDetail
SELECT          SalesOrderID = 100000,
                SalesOrderDetailID = 1000000,
                OrderQty = 5,
                ProductID = 2000
GO
/* Msg 547, Level 16, State 0, Line 1
The INSERT statement conflicted with the FOREIGN KEY constraint
"FK__OrderDeta__Produ__59FA5E80". The conflict occurred in database "tempdb", table
"dbo.Product", column 'ProductID'.
The statement has been terminated.   */
```

-- Attempting to delete from PK table a ProductID which is referenced from the FK table
```
DELETE Product WHERE ProductID = 800;
GO
/* Msg 547, Level 16, State 0, Line 1
The DELETE statement conflicted with the REFERENCE constraint
"FK__OrderDeta__Produ__59FA5E80". The conflict occurred in database "tempdb", table
"dbo.OrderDetail", column 'ProductID'.
The statement has been terminated.  */
```

ON DELETE CASCADE Action Causes DELETE Chain Reaction

-- Change FOREIGN KEY: specify ON DELETE CASCADE option
-- Lookup FK constraints name
SELECT * FROM INFORMATION_SCHEMA.REFERENTIAL_CONSTRAINTS;

CONSTRAINT_ CATALOG	CONSTRAINT _SCHEMA	CONSTRAINT_NAME	UNIQUE_CONSTRAI NT_CATALOG	UNIQUE_CONSTRAI NT_SCHEMA	UNIQUE_CONSTRAIN T_NAME	MATCH_ OPTION	UPDATE _RULE	DELETE _RULE
tempdb	dbo	FK__OrderDeta__Prod u__0A9D95DB	tempdb	dbo	PK__Product__B40CC 6ED66641298	SIMPLE	NO ACTION	NO ACTION

BEGIN TRANSACTION
GO
ALTER TABLE dbo.OrderDetail DROP CONSTRAINT FK__OrderDeta__Produ__0A9D95DB;
GO
ALTER TABLE dbo.Product SET (LOCK_ESCALATION = TABLE)
GO
COMMIT TRANSACTION -- Command(s) completed successfully.

BEGIN TRANSACTION;
GO
ALTER TABLE dbo.OrderDetail ADD CONSTRAINT FK__OrderDeta__Produ__0A9D95DB
FOREIGN KEY (ProductID) REFERENCES dbo.Product (ProductID) ON DELETE CASCADE;
GO
ALTER TABLE dbo.OrderDetail SET (LOCK_ESCALATION = TABLE);
GO
COMMIT TRANSACTION; -- Command(s) completed successfully.

SELECT * FROM INFORMATION_SCHEMA.REFERENTIAL_CONSTRAINTS;

CONSTRAINT_ CATALOG	CONSTRAINT _SCHEMA	CONSTRAINT_NAME	UNIQUE_CONSTRAI NT_CATALOG	UNIQUE_CONSTRAI NT_SCHEMA	UNIQUE_CONSTRAIN T_NAME	MATCH_ OPTION	UPDATE _RULE	DELETE _RULE
tempdb	dbo	FK__OrderDeta__Prod u__0A9D95DB	tempdb	dbo	PK__Product__B40CC 6ED66641298	SIMPLE	NO ACTION	CASCAD E

SELECT COUNT(*) FROM OrderDetail;
GO -- 121317

-- Cascading DELETE: first DELETE all referencing FK records, then DELETE PK record
DELETE Product WHERE ProductID = 800;
GO
-- (1 row(s) affected)

SELECT COUNT(*) FROM OrderDetail;
GO -- 120822

CHAPTER 14: Data Integrity & Change Management

FOREIGN KEY Constraints Represent the Only Connections Among Tables

While we talk about linked tables in functional terms such as master/header-detail, parent-child, dimension-fact, junction, etc., **there is only a single way to connect tables: FOREIGN KEY references PRIMARY KEY in another table**. We are going to demonstrate it in a grand manner: we will create 290 tables with the names of all the employees of AdventureWorks Cycles (fictional) company in a new test database. We shall connect all of them with FOREIGN KEY constraints: employee (FK table) references manager (PK table).

```
USE master;
GO
CREATE DATABASE AWOrgChart;
GO
USE AWOrgChart;
GO


DECLARE @SQL NVARCHAR(max) = '';

WITH CTE (ID, Emp, Mgr, MgrNode)  -- CTE with column names
    AS
(    SELECT E.BusinessEntityID,
        Emp=CONCAT(P.FirstName, SPACE(1), P.LastName),
        NULL,
        NULL
    FROM   AdventureWorks2012.HumanResources.Employee E
        INNER JOIN AdventureWorks2012.Person.Person P
            ON E.BusinessEntityID = P.BusinessEntityID
    WHERE  E.OrganizationNode = 0x                          -- Root node
    UNION
    SELECT E.BusinessEntityID,
        CONCAT(P.FirstName, SPACE(1), P.LastName)           AS Emp,
        CONCAT(PP.FirstName, SPACE(1), PP.LastName)         AS Mgr,
        E.OrganizationNode.GetAncestor(1)                   AS SuperNode
    FROM   AdventureWorks2012.HumanResources.Employee E
        INNER JOIN AdventureWorks2012.Person.Person P
            ON E.BusinessEntityID = P.BusinessEntityID
        INNER JOIN AdventureWorks2012.HumanResources.Employee EE
            ON ( EE.OrganizationNode = E.OrganizationNode.GetAncestor(1) )
        INNER JOIN AdventureWorks2012.Person.Person PP
            ON EE.BusinessEntityID = PP.BusinessEntityID)
```

```
SELECT @SQL = CONCAT(@SQL, CONCAT('CREATE TABLE ', QUOTENAME(Emp),
                '( ID INT PRIMARY KEY ,',
                  ' MgrID INT ',
                        CASE
                WHEN Mgr IS NOT NULL THEN CONCAT(' REFERENCES ',
                          QUOTENAME(Mgr),   '(ID)')
                ELSE ''   END, '); '))
FROM   CTE;

PRINT @SQL;  -- Partial text.
```

CREATE TABLE [Ken Sánchez](ID INT PRIMARY KEY , MgrID INT);
CREATE TABLE [Terri Duffy](ID INT PRIMARY KEY , MgrID INT REFERENCES [Ken Sánchez](ID));
CREATE TABLE [Roberto Tamburello](ID INT PRIMARY KEY ,   MgrID INT REFERENCES [Terri Duffy](ID));
CREATE TABLE [Rob Walters](ID INT PRIMARY KEY ,   MgrID INT REFERENCES [Roberto Tamburello](ID));
CREATE TABLE [Gail Erickson](ID INT PRIMARY KEY ,   MgrID INT REFERENCES [Roberto Tamburello](ID));
CREATE TABLE [Jossef Goldberg](ID INT PRIMARY KEY ,   MgrID INT REFERENCES [Roberto Tamburello](ID));
CREATE TABLE [Dylan Miller](ID INT PRIMARY KEY ,   MgrID INT REFERENCES [Roberto Tamburello](ID));
CREATE TABLE [Diane Margheim](ID INT PRIMARY KEY ,   MgrID INT REFERENCES [Dylan Miller](ID));
CREATE TABLE [Gigi Matthew](ID INT PRIMARY KEY , MgrID INT REFERENCES [Dylan Miller](ID));
CREATE TABLE [Michael Raheem](ID INT PRIMARY KEY ,   MgrID INT REFERENCES [Dylan Miller](ID));
CREATE TABLE [Ovidiu Cracium](ID INT PRIMARY KEY ,   MgrID INT REFERENCES [Roberto Tamburello](ID));
CREATE TABLE [Thierry D'Hers](ID INT PRIMARY KEY ,   MgrID INT REFERENCES [Ovidiu Cracium](ID));

The functional meaning of Terry Duffy "references" Ken Sanchez: Duffy reports to Sanchez.

```
EXEC sp_executeSQL @SQL;  -- Dynamic SQL execution: create 290 linked tables
GO
```

```
-- USE master;
DROP DATABASE AWOrgChart;
```

CHAPTER 14: Data Integrity & Change Management

Diagram Tool Can Be Used for Organizational Charts

We can use the diagram tool in the AWOrgChart database as an orgchart tool. We add a chosen table to the diagram, for example, [Ken Sanchez]. With the right click menu, we add related tables, set view to table name only & arrange selection. The result is orgchart with the CEO and executive managers.

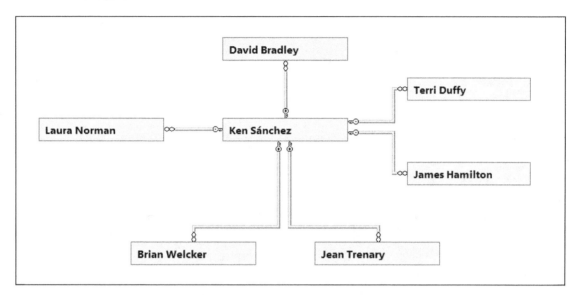

Orgchart starting with [David Hamilton]. Hamilton reports to Krebs (Gold Key).

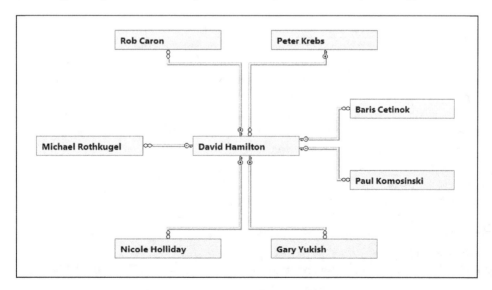

Enterprise-Level Business Rules Enforcement

Enterprise-Level Business Rules can be enforced by stored procedures & triggers on the server-side and application programs on the client-side. While stored procedures & application programs can be used to implement a complex set of business rules, they can only effect the current application. Stored procedure or application cannot catch an UPDATE transaction, for example, coming from a legacy application nobody dares to touch at the IT department. In a way stored procedure can be configured to perform after-the-fact near-real-time updates for recently posted data: configure the stored procedure as SQL Server Agent job and schedule it to run each minute.

Special Role of Triggers

Triggers, on the other hand, can catch, for example, an INSERT to the ProductPrice table, wherever it is coming from; current in-house application software, old in-house application, another profit-center of the enterprise application or 3rd party software package. An example for an enterprise business rule: convert foreign currency pricing to USD in the INSERT record to ProductPrice using the latest conversion rates from the ForeignExchange table. A constraint cannot be used to implement such a rule, a trigger can. Trigger code almost as flexible as stored procedure code. Triggers can also be used for cross-database referential integrity enforcement. While triggers are compiled into one database, they can access tables in another database. Because of their omnipotent nature, triggers are frequently misapplied as fix-it-all tools.

WARNING
Triggers are high maintenance database objects. Triggers are not for junior staff. Dropped/disabled triggers do not "COMPLAIN": stealth behavior.

Triggers are just like silent workhorses. They can be forgotten after months of operation since they don't have to be called explicitly from the client-side application programs, they are event launched on the server-side. DDL trigger can be applied to guard DML triggers, but then someone or something has to guard the DDL trigger as well. On the other hand, a dropped stored procedure causes user error ("complains"). Dropped trigger can cause user error also, but the error cannot easily be traced back the trigger.

The following update trigger will prevent last name update from new software, old software, other department's software or even 3rd party software package.

```
CREATE TRIGGER trgEmployee  ON Employee FOR UPDATE AS
   IF (UPDATE(LastName))                BEGIN
      RAISERROR ('Last name cannot be changed', 16, 1);  ROLLBACK TRAN;  RETURN;    END
GO
```

Product Reorder Trigger

The UPDATE trigger is attached to the Products table. It fires whenever there is an UPDATE for the table, no matter what kind of software application from what part of the world executed the UPDATE statement. **A trigger should never return a result set**. However, there is no error if we try to return a result set with a SELECT statement just like in a stored procedure. For testing & debugging purposes we can return results.

```
USE Northwind
GO


-- Logging table for product reorder notices
CREATE TABLE Reorder (
        ID INT IDENTITY(1,1) PRIMARY KEY,
        Message varchar(256),
        CreateDate datetime default (CURRENT_TIMESTAMP));
GO

IF EXISTS (select * from sys.objects where type='TR' and name = 'trgProductReorder')
        DROP TRIGGER trgProductReorder
GO


CREATE TRIGGER trgProductReorder
ON Products FOR UPDATE
AS
 BEGIN
   SET NOCOUNT ON;
   DECLARE @MsgText    varchar(128),   @QtyOnHand   int,  @ReorderLevel int;
   SELECT @MsgText = CONCAT('Please place a reorder  for ',  Rtrim(ProductName))
   FROM   inserted;

   SELECT @QtyOnHand = UnitsInStock,   @ReorderLevel = ReorderLevel  FROM   inserted;


   IF @QtyOnHand < @ReorderLevel
       INSERT Reorder  (Message)        SELECT @MsgText;

 --select * from deleted -- for testing &debugging only
 --select * from inserted
 --select @MsgText
 END
GO
```

A Trigger Should Never Return A Result Set Like A Stored Procedure

Check Data Manipulation Language (DML) trigger existence with sp_helptrigger system procedure.

```
EXEC sp_helptrigger Products ;
GO
```

trigger_name	trigger_owner	isupdate	isdelete	isinsert	isafter	isinsteadof	trigger_schema
trgProductReorder	dbo	1	0	0	1	0	dbo

```
-- Test trigger
/* For demonstration purposes, the debugging statements in trigger were uncommented */
UPDATE Products
        SET   UnitsInStock = 10
        WHERE  ProductID = 77;
GO
```

SQL Server UPDATE is implemented as complete deleted (old) and inserted (new) rows. Even if 1 byte updated, a complete row deleted and complete row inserted generated for logging.

deleted table row:

Product ID	ProductNa me	Supplier ID	Category ID	QuantityPer Unit	UnitPri ce	**UnitsInSt ock**	UnitsOnOr der	ReorderLe vel	Discontinu ed
77	Original Frankfurter grüne Soße	12	2	12 boxes	13.00	**50**	0	15	0

inserted table row:

Product ID	ProductNa me	Supplier ID	Category ID	QuantityPer Unit	UnitPri ce	**UnitsInSt ock**	UnitsOnOr der	ReorderLe vel	Discontinu ed
77	Original Frankfurter grüne Soße	12	2	12 boxes	13.00	**10**	0	15	0

```
SELECT * FROM   Reorder;
GO
```

ID	Message	CreateDate
1	Please place a reorder for Original Frankfurter grüne Soße	2016-11-25 06:06:45.043

```
DROP TRIGGER trgProductReorder;
DROP TABLE Reorder;
```

CHAPTER 14: Data Integrity & Change Management

Trigger Examples In AdventureWorks2012

List of triggers in the sample database. parent_object_id is the object_id of the trigger parent table. SELF-JOIN is required to get the parent information.

```
USE AdventureWorks2012;
SELECT
    o.name                                              AS TriggerName,
    SCHEMA_NAME(po.schema_id)                           AS TableSchema,
    OBJECT_NAME(o.parent_object_id)                     AS TableName,
    OBJECTPROPERTY( o.object_id, 'ExecIsUpdateTrigger') AS [isupdate],
    OBJECTPROPERTY( o.object_id, 'ExecIsDeleteTrigger') AS [isdelete],
    OBJECTPROPERTY( o.object_id, 'ExecIsInsertTrigger') AS [isinsert],
    OBJECTPROPERTY( o.object_id, 'ExecIsAfterTrigger')  AS [isafter],
    OBJECTPROPERTY( o.object_id, 'ExecIsInsteadOfTrigger') AS [isinsteadof],
    OBJECTPROPERTY( o.object_id, 'ExecIsTriggerDisabled') AS [disabled]
FROM sys.objects AS o
        INNER JOIN sys.objects AS po    ON o.parent_object_id = po.object_id
WHERE o.[type] = 'TR'  ORDER BY TableSchema, TableName, TriggerName;
```

TriggerName	TableSchema	TableName	isupdate	isdelete	isinsert	isafter	isinsteadof	disabled
dEmployee	HumanResources	Employee	0	1	0	0	1	0
iuPerson	Person	Person	1	0	1	1	0	0
iWorkOrder	Production	WorkOrder	0	0	1	1	0	0
uWorkOrder	Production	WorkOrder	1	0	0	1	0	0
iPurchaseOrderDetail	Purchasing	PurchaseOrderDetail	0	0	1	1	0	0
uPurchaseOrderDetail	Purchasing	PurchaseOrderDetail	1	0	0	1	0	0
uPurchaseOrderHeader	Purchasing	PurchaseOrderHeader	1	0	0	1	0	0
dVendor	Purchasing	Vendor	0	1	0	0	1	0
iduSalesOrderDetail	Sales	SalesOrderDetail	1	1	1	1	0	0
uSalesOrderHeader	Sales	SalesOrderHeader	1	0	0	1	0	0

Alternate method of obtaining all triggers information.

```
SELECT * FROM sys.triggers ORDER BY name; -- Partial results.
```

name	object_id	parent_class	parent_class_desc	parent_id	type	type_desc
ddlDatabaseTriggerLog	261575970	0	DATABASE	0	TR	SQL_TRIGGER
dEmployee	1739153241	1	OBJECT_OR_COLUMN	1237579447	TR	SQL_TRIGGER
dVendor	1851153640	1	OBJECT_OR_COLUMN	766625774	TR	SQL_TRIGGER
iduSalesOrderDetail	1819153526	1	OBJECT_OR_COLUMN	1154103152	TR	SQL_TRIGGER
iPurchaseOrderDetail	1771153355	1	OBJECT_OR_COLUMN	850102069	TR	SQL_TRIGGER
iuPerson	1755153298	1	OBJECT_OR_COLUMN	1765581328	TR	SQL_TRIGGER
iWorkOrder	1867153697	1	OBJECT_OR_COLUMN	846626059	TR	SQL_TRIGGER
uPurchaseOrderDetail	1787153412	1	OBJECT_OR_COLUMN	850102069	TR	SQL_TRIGGER
uPurchaseOrderHeader	1803153469	1	OBJECT_OR_COLUMN	946102411	TR	SQL_TRIGGER
uSalesOrderHeader	1835153583	1	OBJECT_OR_COLUMN	1266103551	TR	SQL_TRIGGER
uWorkOrder	1883153754	1	OBJECT_OR_COLUMN	846626059	TR	SQL_TRIGGER

Trigger Can Be Modified in Object Explorer

When the Modify Trigger option is picked, Object Explorer loads it as ALTER TRIGGER script.

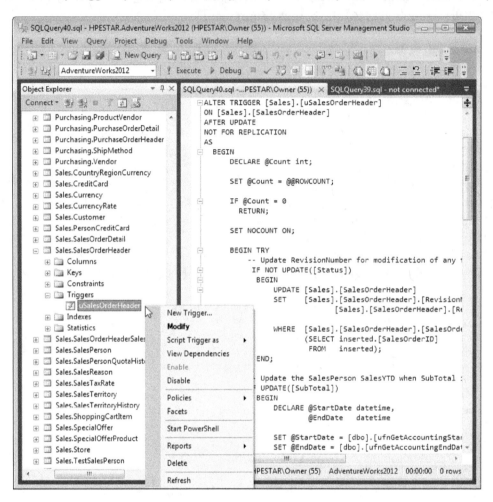

Programmatic way to get trigger definition.

SELECT OBJECT_DEFINITION(object_id('Person.iuPerson'));

| CREATE TRIGGER [Person].[iuPerson] ON [Person].[Person] |
| AFTER INSERT, UPDATE NOT FOR REPLICATION AS |
| BEGIN |
| DECLARE @Count int; |
| SET @Count = @@ROWCOUNT; |
| IF @Count = 0   RETURN; |
| SET NOCOUNT ON; |
| IF UPDATE([BusinessEntityID]) OR UPDATE([Demographics]) |

CHAPTER 14: Data Integrity & Change Management

Change Management

Keeping track of changes is a real challenge in an RDBMS system since the tracking data may become larger than the data being tracked. The simplest change management method: each table should have two table maintenance columns: ModifiedByDate and ModifiedByUser.

Change Auditing with OUTPUT Clause

The OUTPUT clause is excellent for auditing as long as it is programmed when the software is developed. Applying it to existing software requires substantial resources.

```
USE AdventureWorks2012;
GO
-- Create audit table - mmsql create table
CREATE TABLE Production.ProductAudit (
    AuditDate datetime,
    ProductID int,
    ChangedColumn sysname,
    OldPrice money,
    NewPrice money  );
```

```
-- T-SQL update with output clause - insert change info into audit table
UPDATE Production.Product
SET   ListPrice = ListPrice * 1.1
    OUTPUT getdate(), convert(VARCHAR,DELETED.ProductID),
        'ListPrice', convert(VARCHAR,DELETED.ListPrice),
        convert(VARCHAR,INSERTED.ListPrice)
    INTO Production.ProductAudit
WHERE  ListPrice > 0.0 and ListPrice < 100.0;
-- (94 row(s) affected)
```

```
SELECT * FROM Production.ProductAudit;
GO   -- Partial results
```

AuditDate	ProductID	ChangedColumn	OldPrice	NewPrice
2016-07-10 10:01:29.090	707	ListPrice	34.99	38.49
2016-07-10 10:01:29.090	708	ListPrice	34.99	38.49
2016-07-10 10:01:29.090	709	ListPrice	9.50	10.45
2016-07-10 10:01:29.090	710	ListPrice	9.50	10.45
2016-07-10 10:01:29.090	711	ListPrice	34.99	38.49
2016-07-10 10:01:29.090	712	ListPrice	8.99	9.89

Change Management By Built-in Methods

Data in the database can be tracked by two methods: Change Data Capture (asynchronous) and Change Tracking (synchronous).

> MSDN Article: **Track Data Changes (SQL Server)** http://bit.ly/yA4x8q
> http://msdn.microsoft.com/en-us/library/bb933994.aspx

Change Data Capture

Quote: "**Change data capture** records insert, update, and delete activity that is applied to a SQL Server table. This makes the details of the changes available in an easily consumed relational format. Column information and the metadata that is required to apply the changes to a target environment is captured for the modified rows and stored in change tables that mirror the column structure of the tracked source tables. Table-valued functions are provided to allow systematic access to the change data by consumers. A good example of a data consumer that is targeted by this technology is an extraction, transformation, and loading (ETL) application. An ETL application incrementally loads change data from SQL Server source tables to a data warehouse or data mart. Although the representation of the source tables within the data warehouse must reflect changes in the source tables, an end-to-end technology that refreshes a replica of the source is not appropriate. Instead, you need a reliable stream of change data that is structured so that consumers can apply it to dissimilar target representations of the data. SQL Server change data capture provides this technology."

> MSDN Article: **About Change Data Capture (SQL Server)** http://bit.ly/5s17UI
> http://msdn.microsoft.com/en-us/library/cc645937.aspx

Change Tracking

Quote: "Change tracking is a lightweight solution that provides an efficient change tracking mechanism for applications. Typically, to enable applications to query for changes to data in a database and access information that is related to the changes, application developers had to implement custom change tracking mechanisms. Creating these mechanisms usually involved a lot of work and frequently involved using a combination of triggers, timestamp columns, new tables to store tracking information, and custom cleanup processes."

> MSDN Article: **About Change Tracking (SQL Server)** http://bit.ly/3eVOq
> http://msdn.microsoft.com/en-us/library/bb933875.aspx

CHAPTER 15: Getting Started with SSIS

SSIS stands for SQL Server Integration Services.

Quote: "Access And Integrate With Any Heterogeneous Data Source

Access data from any heterogeneous data source whether Microsoft or non-Microsoft sources or whether structured, application, cloud or real-time data.

Access data from any third party source including SQL Server, Oracle, Teradata, DB2, ODBC, OLE DB, text files, and the Microsoft Entity Framework.

Integrate data from business workflows in Microsoft BizTalk Server for SAP, ERP, CRM, Web Service, and mainframe applications.

Bring data from the cloud with Data Sync, ADO.NET connectivity to SQL Azure, and data from the Azure Marketplace data market.

Capture real-time data from sensors and other complex event streams by using Microsoft SQL Server StreamInsight technologies. "

Article: **Integration Services**	http://bit.ly/10p4MEI
http://www.microsoft.com/en-us/sqlserver/solutions-technologies/enterprise-information-management/integration-services.aspx	

Single SSIS Service for All SS Instances

A single SSIS service is shared by all the instances of SQL Server (default MSSQLSERVER and named SQL12).

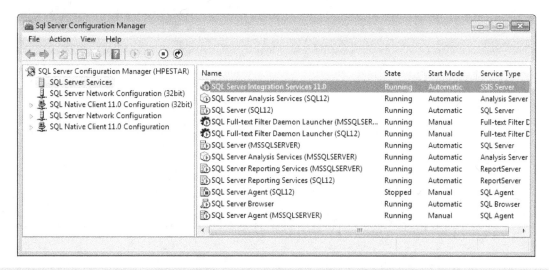

Starting a New SSIS Project in SSDT 2012

SQL Server Data TOOLS (SSDT) is the design/maintain environment for SSIS packages not Management Studio.

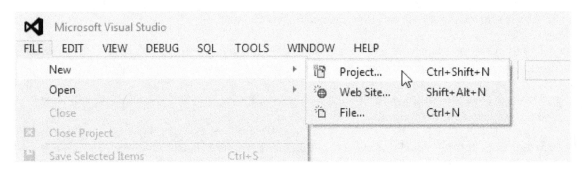

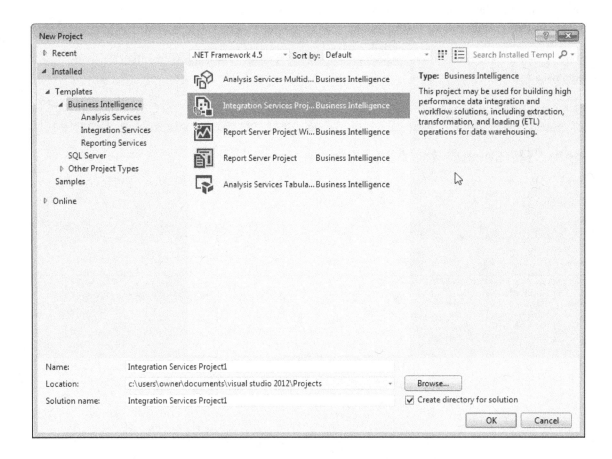

Studio Environment for Design

Reviewing a Working SSIS Package

This demo SSIS package routs input rows into normal and expensive products using the Conditional Split transformation. Data flow has transformations, control flow has tasks.

Data Flow for the Package

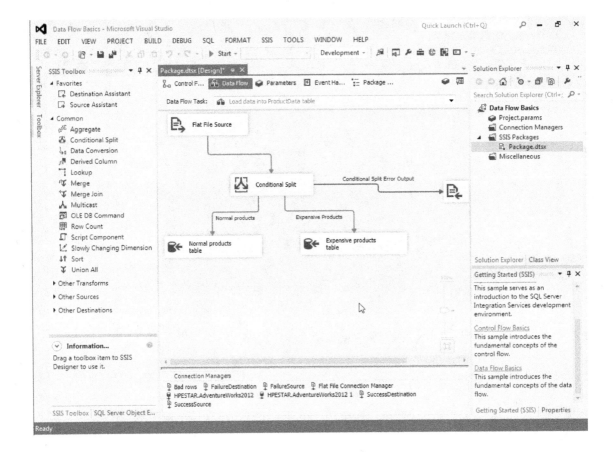

Control Flow for the Package

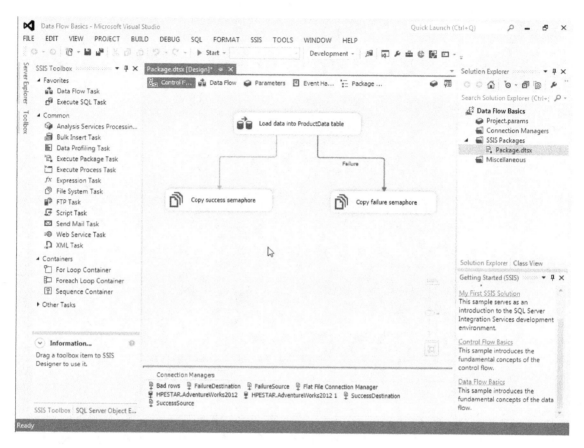

Success Semaphore Folder

Similar folder for Failure Semaphore.

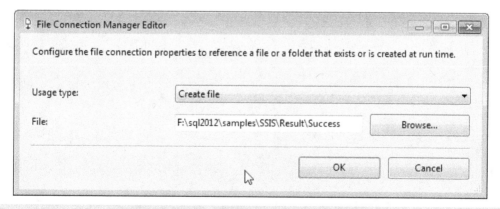

Flat File Connection Manager

This is the data source.

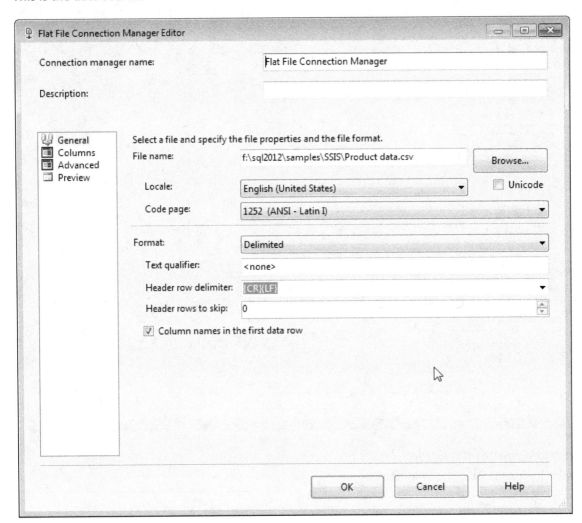

Preview of the Data in the Source File

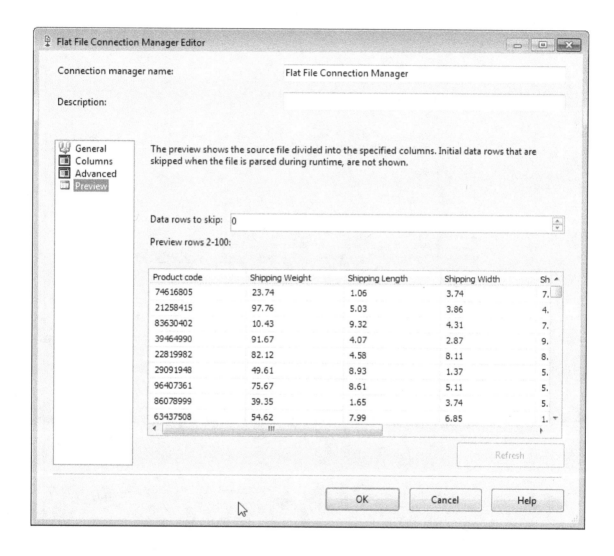

Columns Page

Row and column delimiter can be configured.

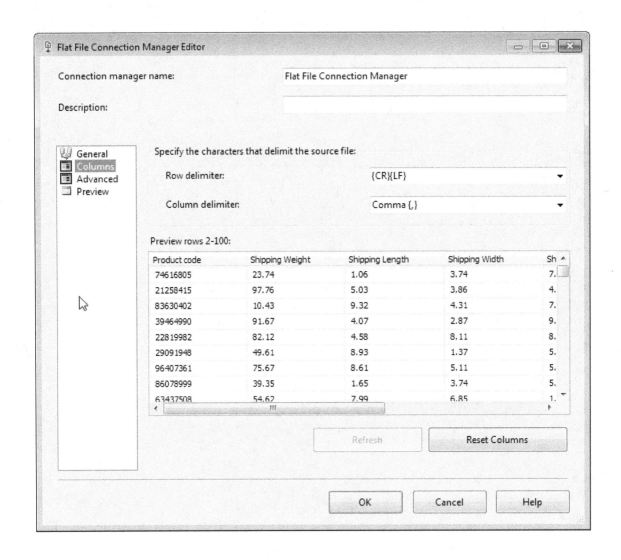

Advanced Page

Each column properties can be configured. DT_I4 corresponds to INT in T-SQL.

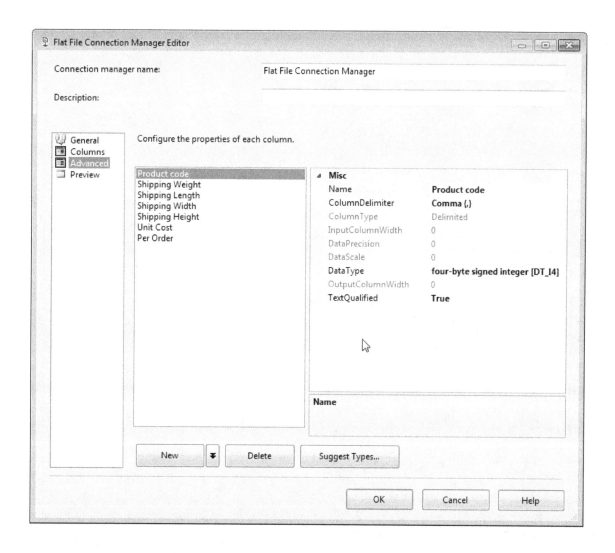

Output Destination

AdventureWorks2012 database is the target.

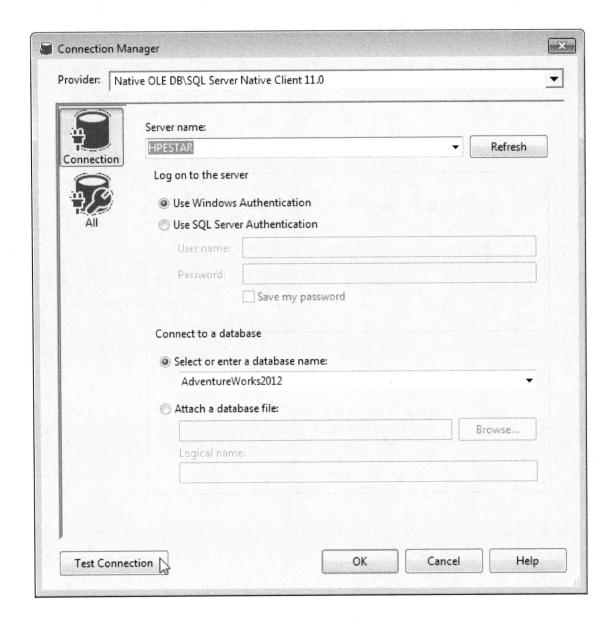

Success Source

The file from Success Source will be copied over with text added to Success Semaphore upon successful completion.

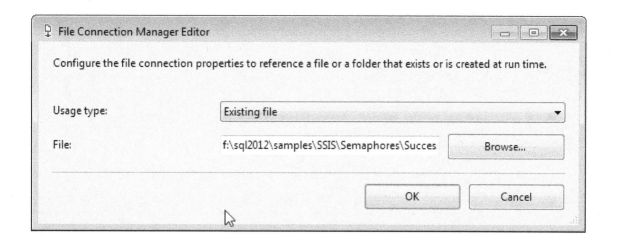

Currently the semaphores are empty flat files.

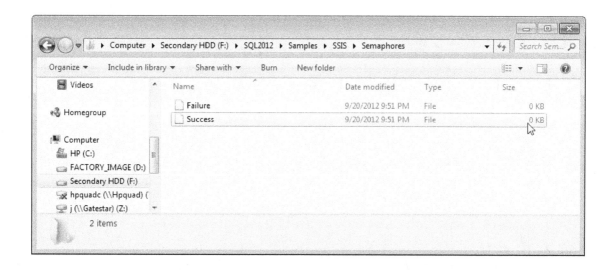

Flat File for Bad Rows

Rejects from the input stream output into this file.

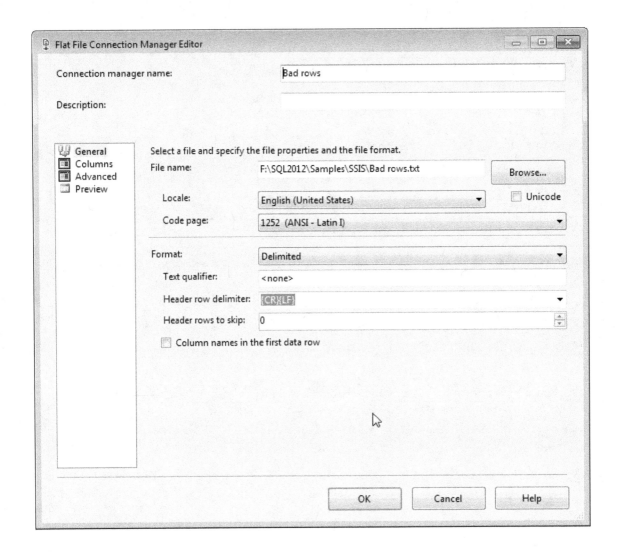

Tasks in the Control Flow

There are 3 tasks: a data flow task and 2 file system tasks.

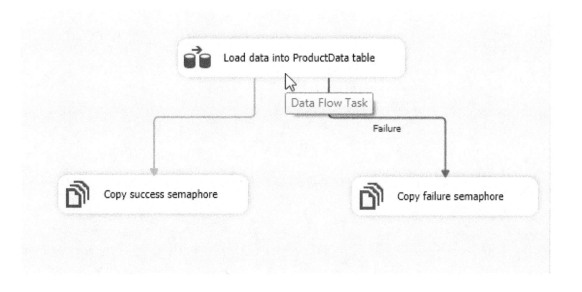

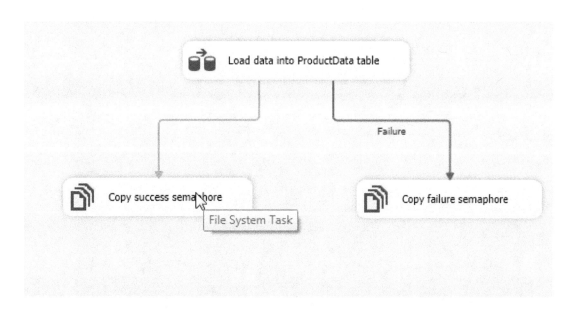

Success and Failure Precedence Constraints

These are the lines connecting the the Control Flow tasks.

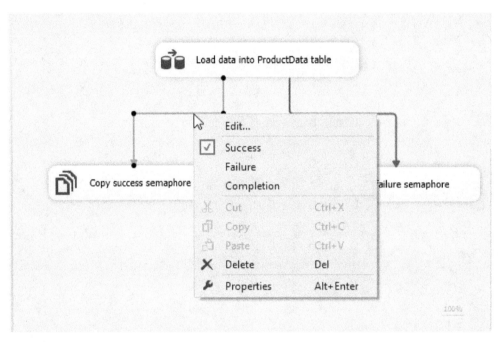

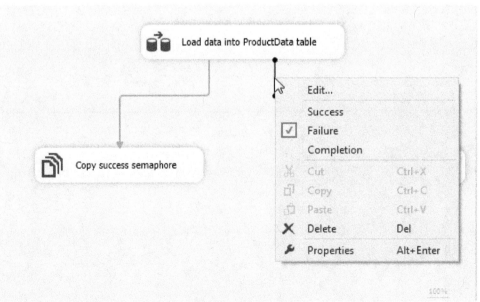

Data Flow Elements

There is a single source file.

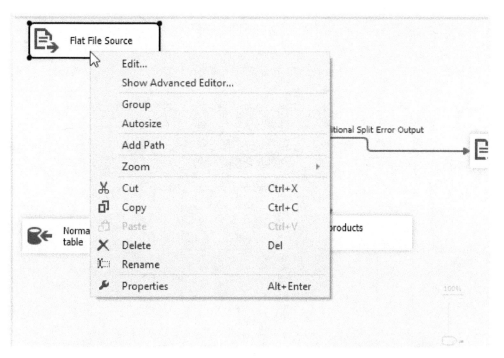

Data Flow Path

Data flow path shows how the data flows from source to destination.

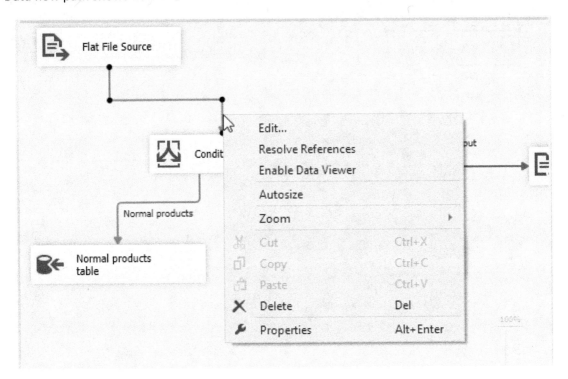

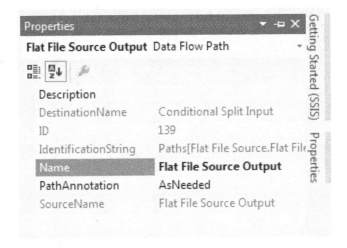

Conditional Split Setup

If UnitCost / Qty > 5 then it is considered expensive product.

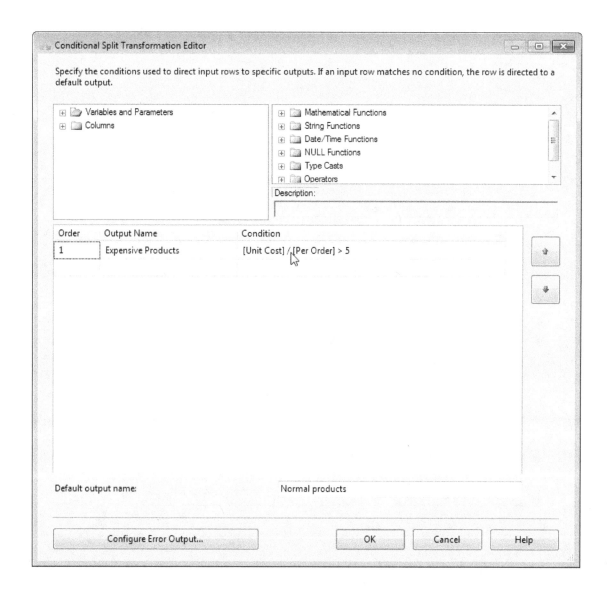

Expensive Products Output Table Destination

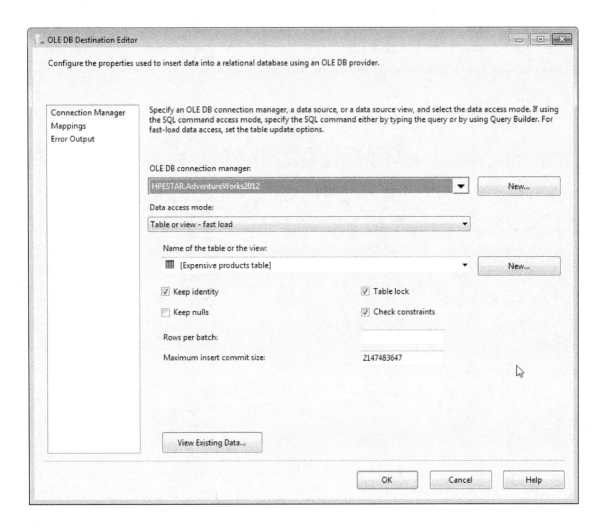

SSIS Package Execution in Debug Mode

Data source split to 81 expensive products and 18 normal products. No error output.

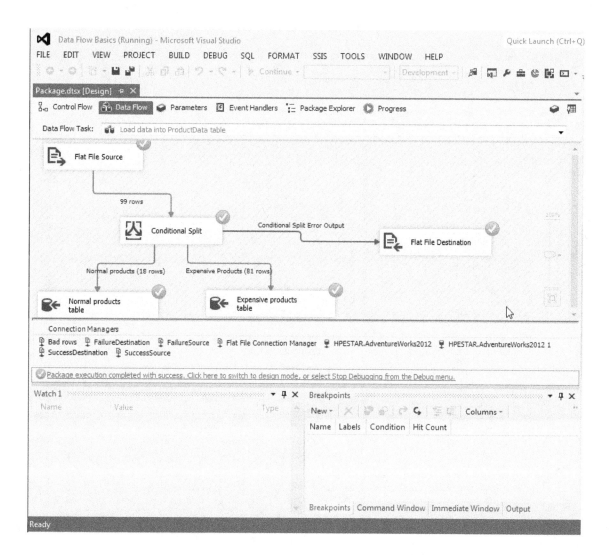

Expensive Products Table Output

The reason for the 648 lines: the SSIS package has been executed multiple times (8) appending 81 rows to the table each time.

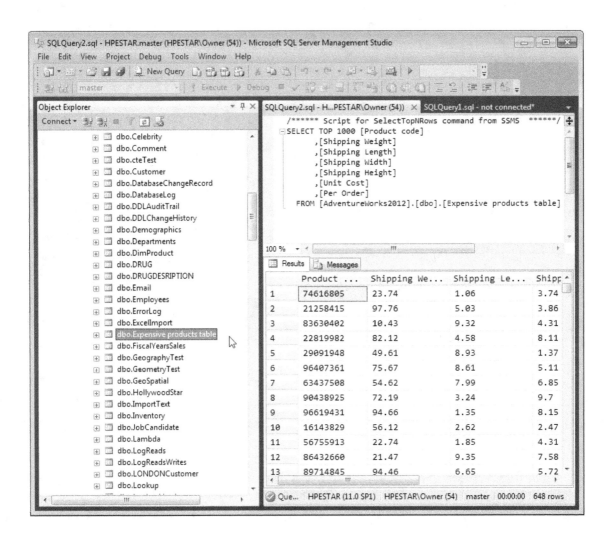

CHAPTER 16: Automation with SQL Server Agent

SQL Server Agent

SQL Server Agent is a job scheduler and execution facility which works in conjunction with SQL Server. A job can consists of one or more job steps, administrative tasks such as database backup, execution of a program or REBUILDing indexes. If database mail is configured, SQL Server Agent jobs can be configured for email messaging.

> MSDN Article: **SQL Server Agent**   http://bit.ly/r9twX
> http://msdn.microsoft.com/en-us/library/ms189237.aspx

Configuring Database Mail

Using database mail warnings, error messages and reports can be emailed. Right click on Management --> Database Mail to launch the Wizard.

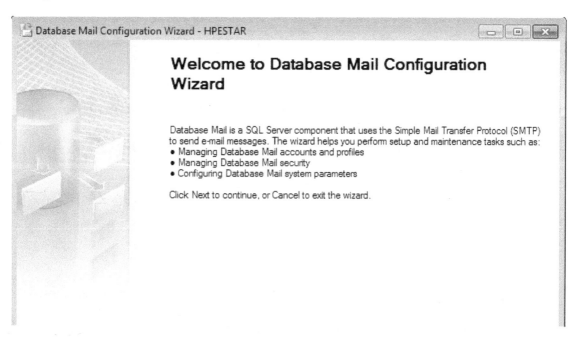

Set Configuration Task Selection

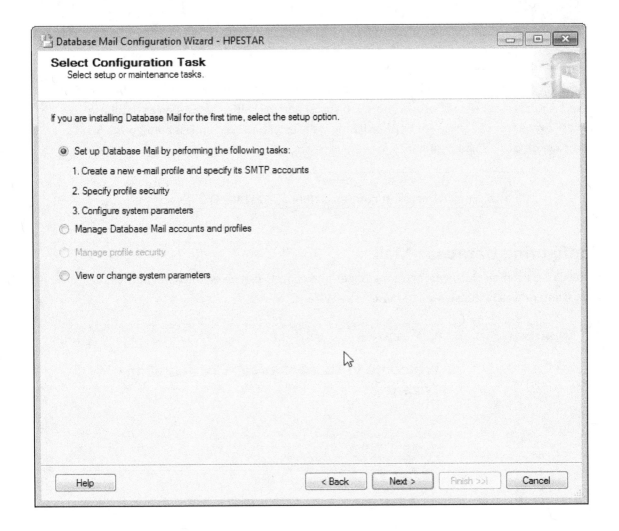

New Profile Page

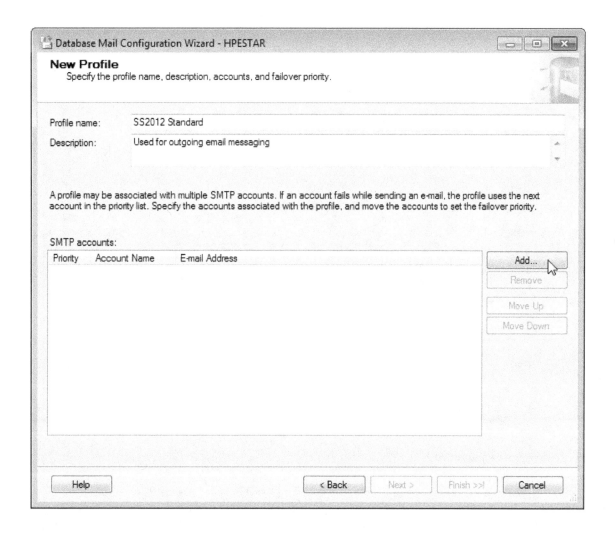

New Database Mail Account Page
**NOTE: mail.optonline.net is a live SMTP account on this server. It should be replaced with
your SMTP live account.**

Profile Security Page

Note: SS2012 Standard & SQL2012 Standard are configured similarly.

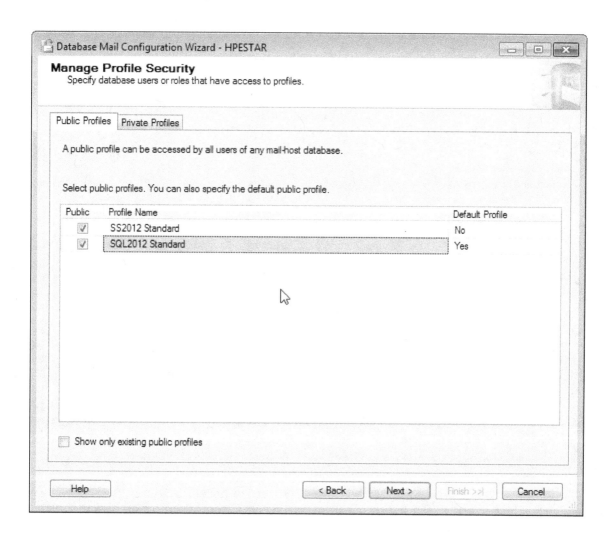

System Paramaters Page

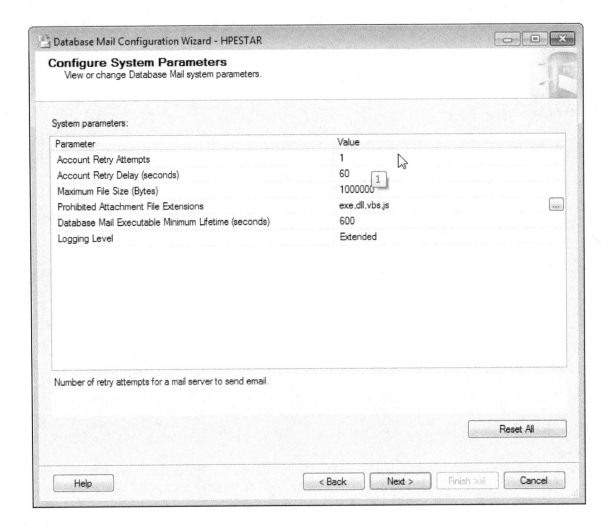

Complete the Wizard Page

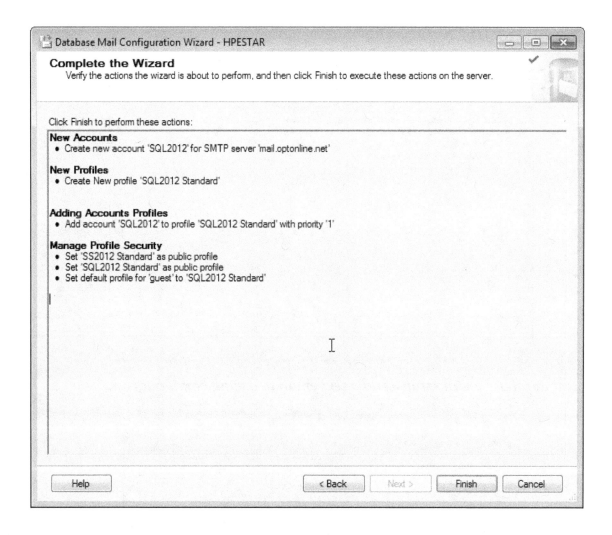

Creation Page

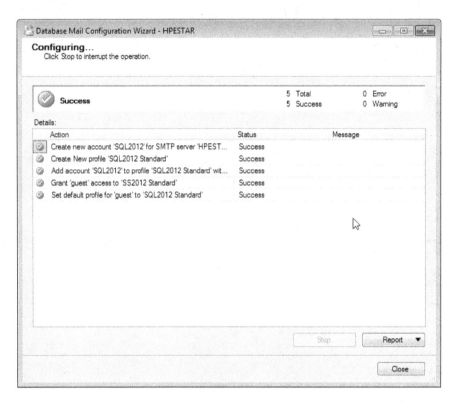

To test database email setup, send a test email to a valid email address.

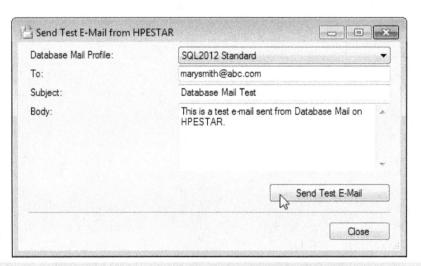

SQL Server Agent Configuration

The various components of SQL Server Agent require configuration settings.

Enable Mail Profile for SQL Server Agent Use

Sql Server Agent should be restarted after this step.

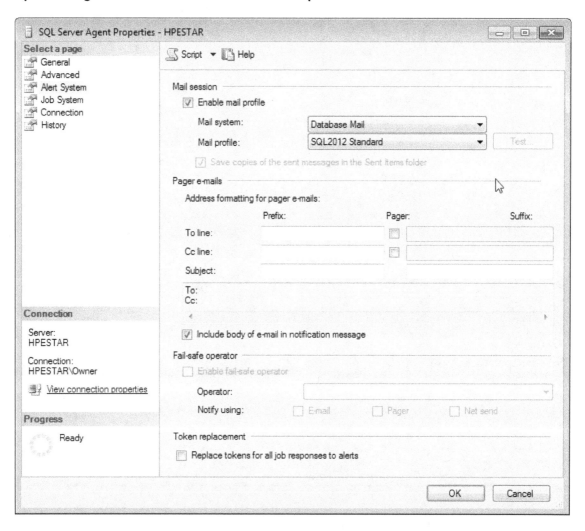

Setting up a New Operator

Operators are IT staff members operating SQL Server and the network.

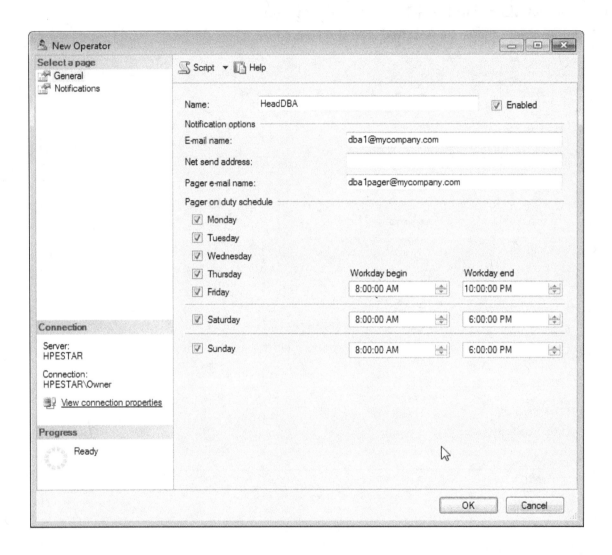

Alert Configuration

Alerts can be setup for different warning and error events.

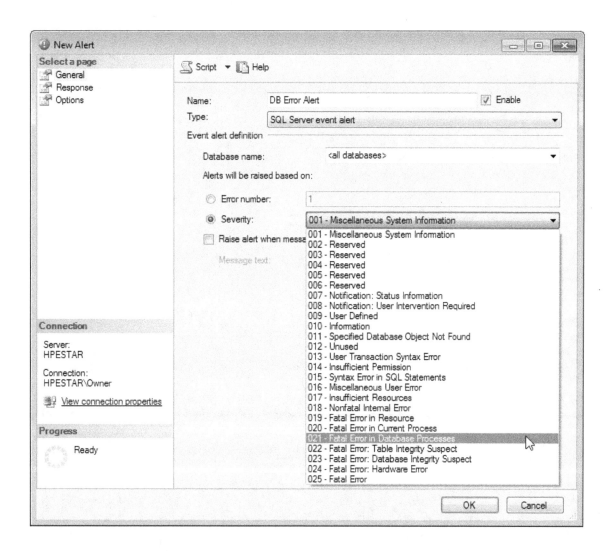

Alert Response Page

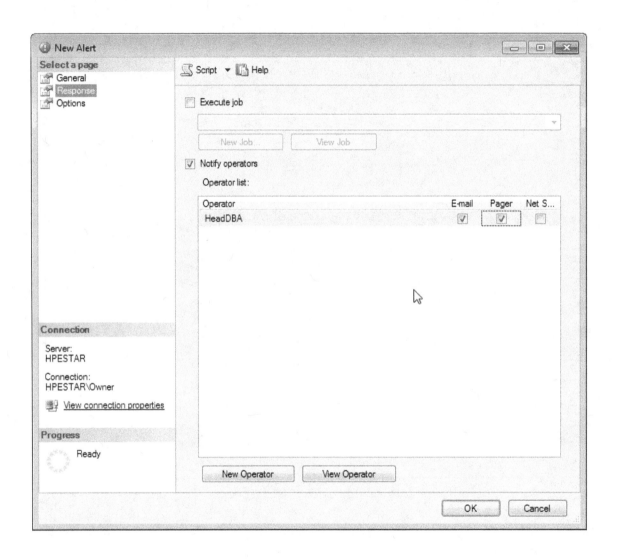

Alert Options Page

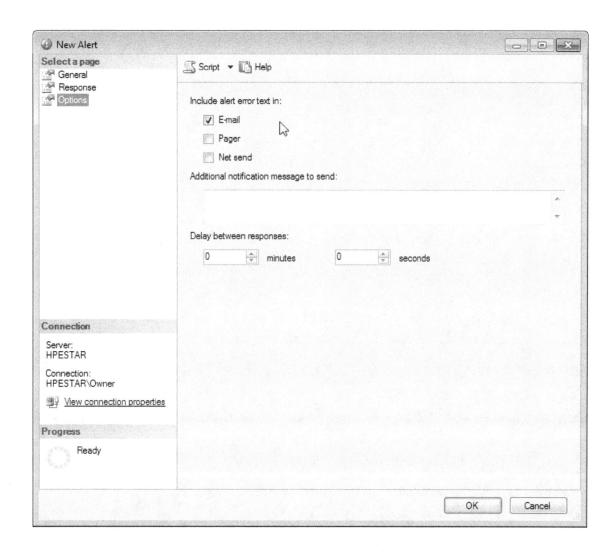

Reviewing the Properties of a Job

The AW12 MaintenancePlan.Subplan_1 job was setup by the Dabase Maintenance Plan Wizard.

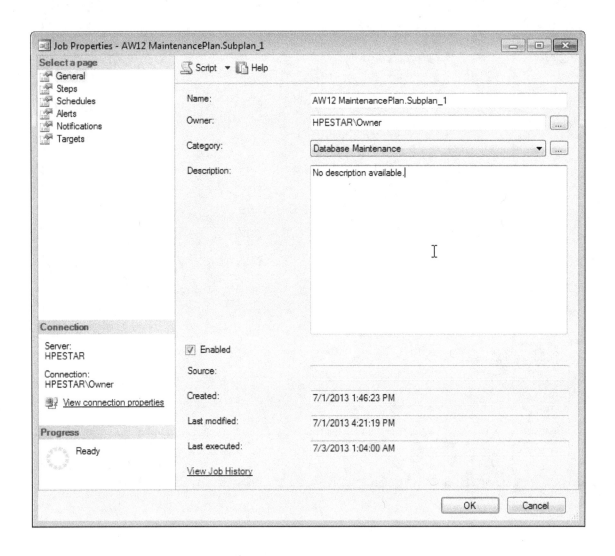

Job Steps Page

This job has only 1 step. A large job may have 20 steps.

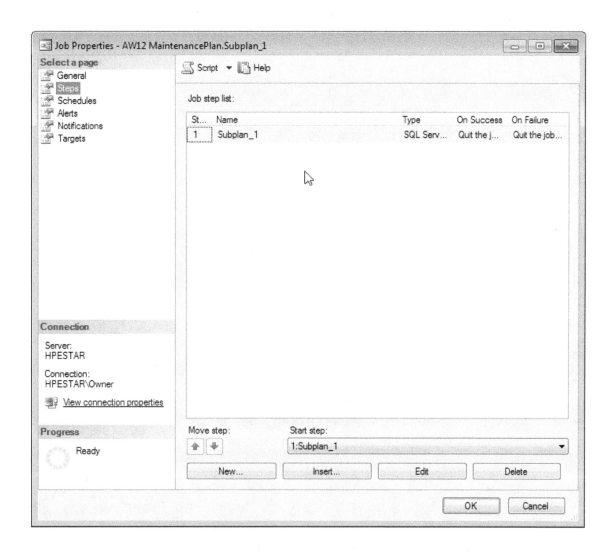

Job Step Page

The job step is to execute an SSIS package created by the Maintenance Wizard.

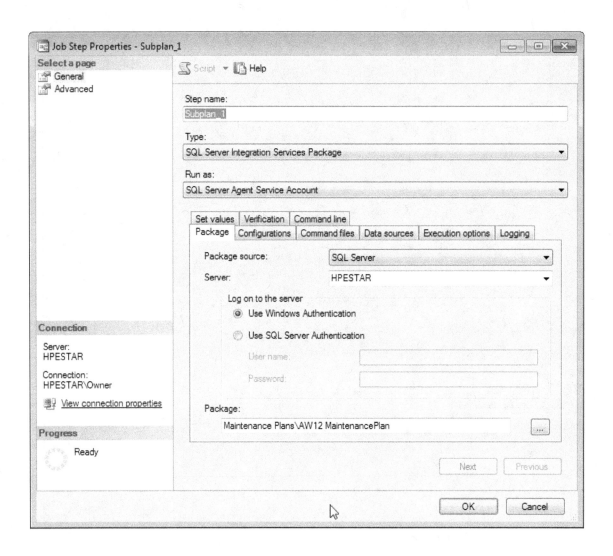

Job Step Advanced Page

For a multi-step job the On success action and On failure action defines the work flow branching logic.

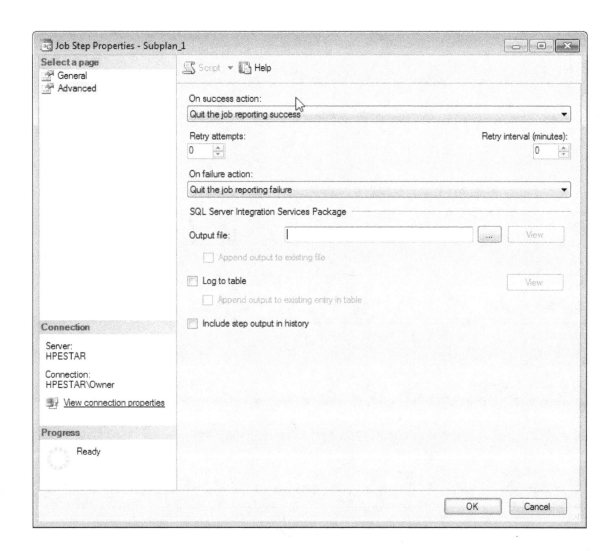

Schedules Page

There is one schedule for this job. Multiple schedules are supported providing flexibility.

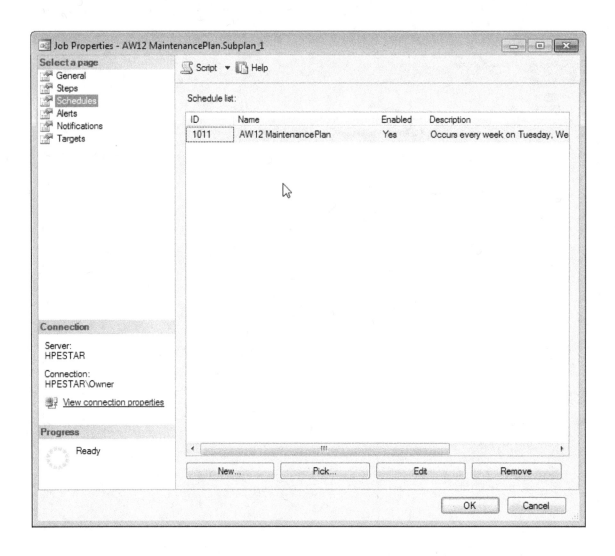

Schedule Setup

A bit confusing: basically daily schedule but Occurs: positioned at Weekly.

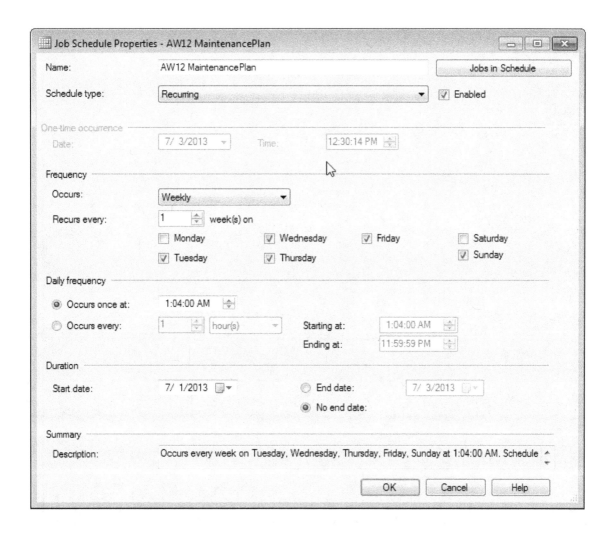

Alert Page

There is no alert setup for this job.

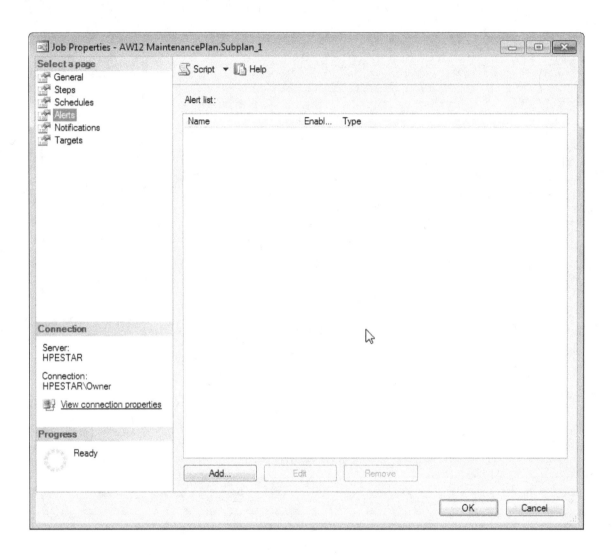

Notifications Page

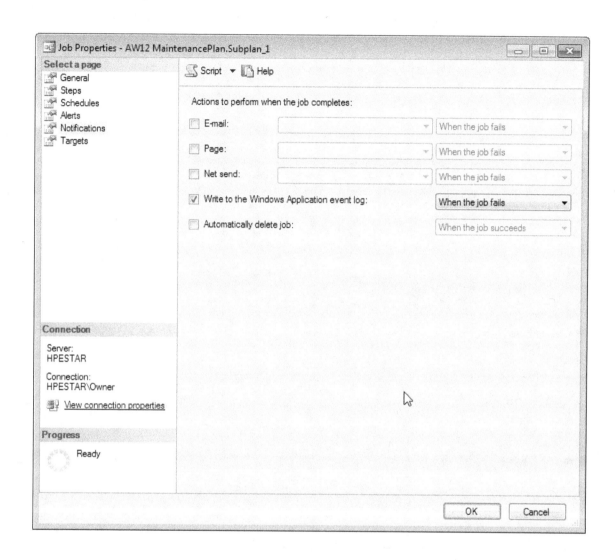

Job Activity Monitor

Job Activity Monitor lists latest job execution histories and provides job management, such as start/stop, functions.

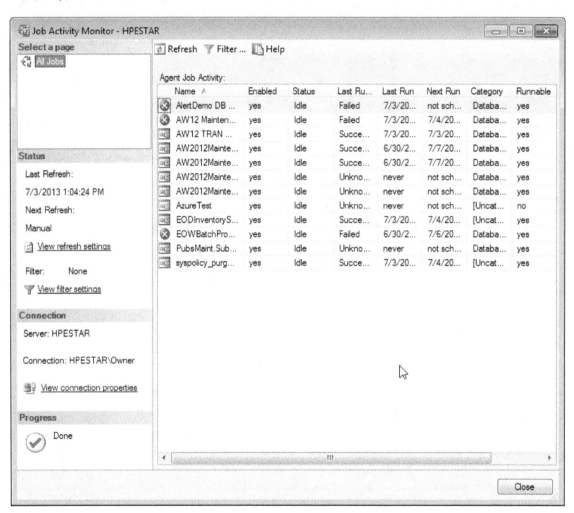

T-SQL script for job activity

```
USE msdb ;
GO
EXEC dbo.sp_help_jobactivity ;
GO
```

Email Send from a Job

We can even send the result set of a query.

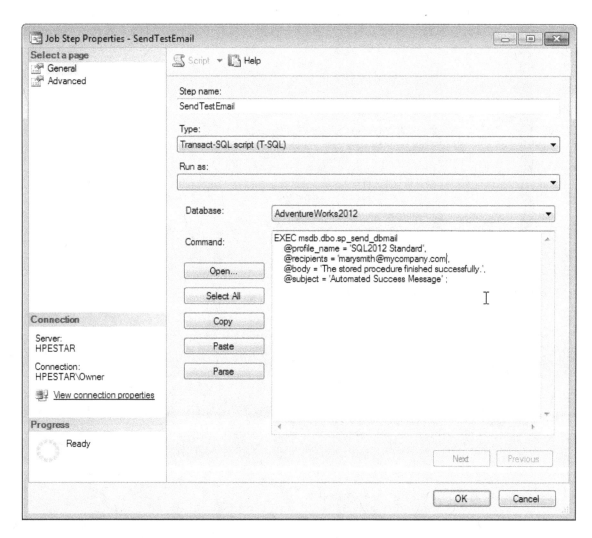

Programmatic Job Execution

Jobs can be executed programmatically. Program flow will not wait for job to finish.

```
EXEC msdb.dbo.sp_start_job N'SendTestEmail';
GO
-- Job 'SendTestEmail' started successfully.
```

CHAPTER 16: Automation with SQL Server Agent

Execute Job Manually

This job has no schedule. It can be executed manually.

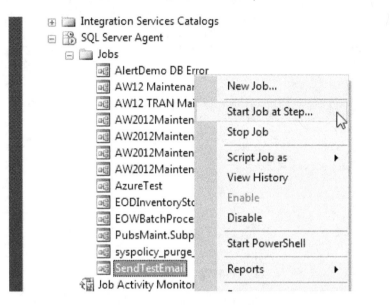

Received email message in Outlook

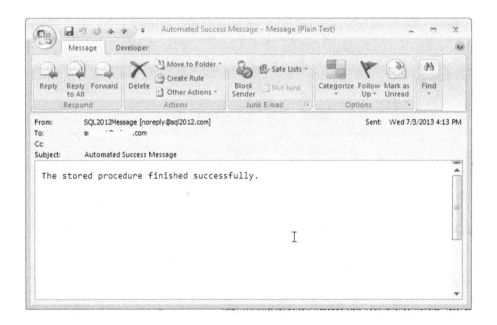

Setting Job Error Notification

Job step has an error (no such table) on purpose.

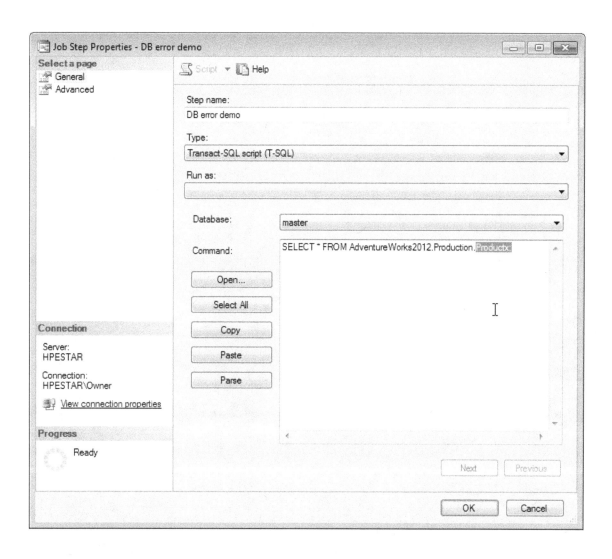

Job Notifications Page

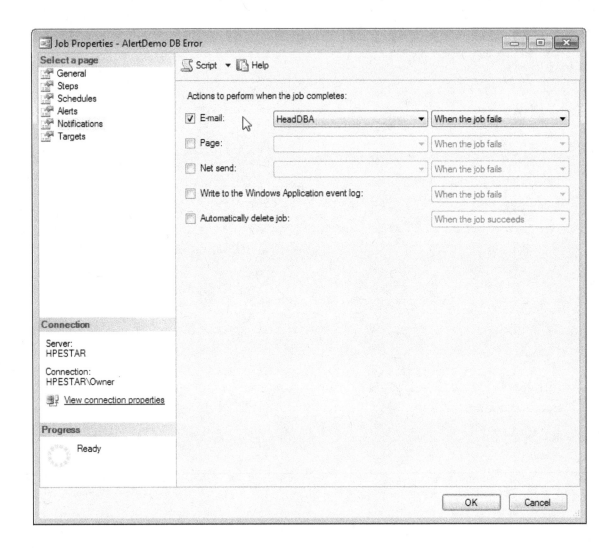

Job with Email Alert Execution

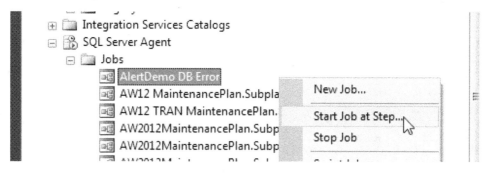

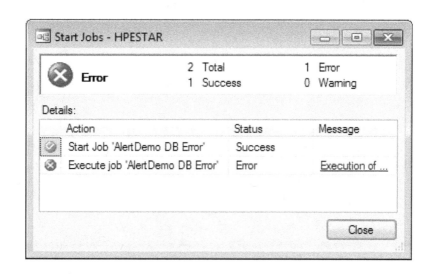

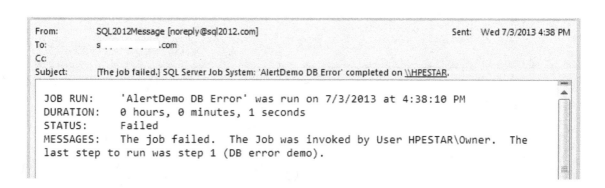

Create Job

Job creation is fairly simple and effective with the GUI tool in Object Explorer

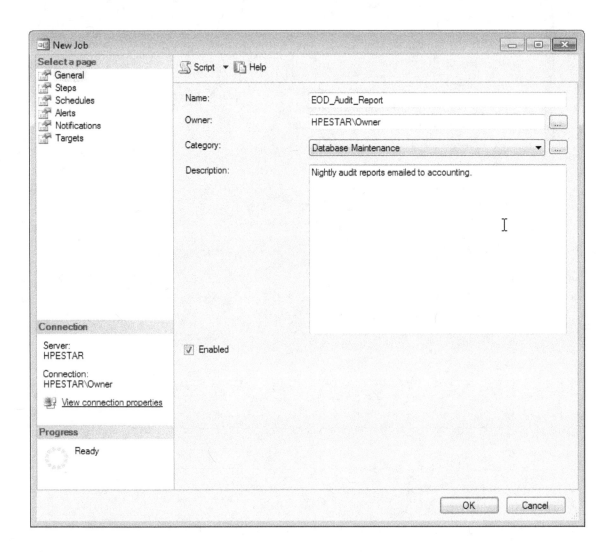

Define a New Job Step

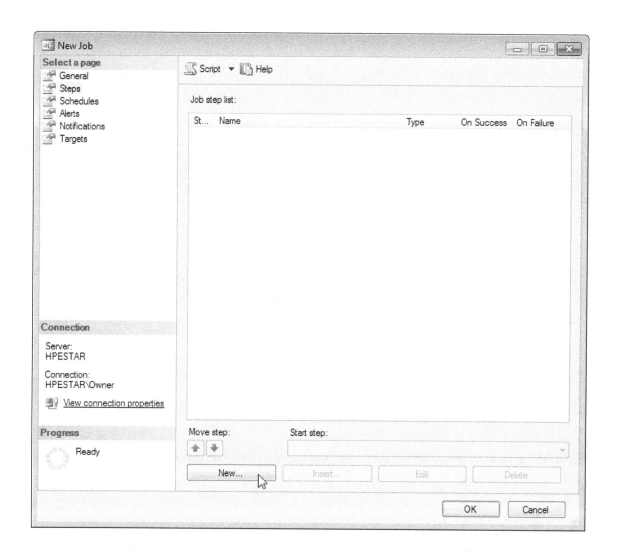

SalesSummary Job Step

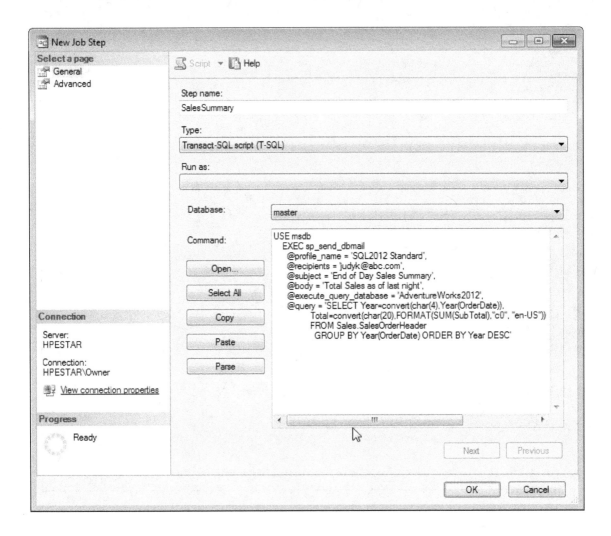

New Job Step Advanced Page

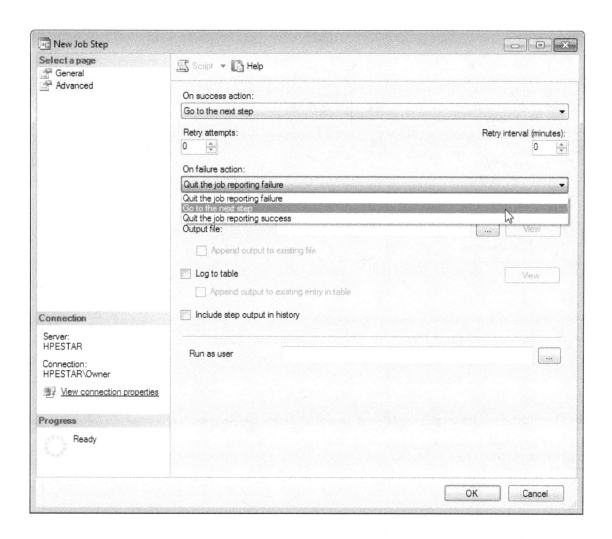

Designing a Product Summary Query

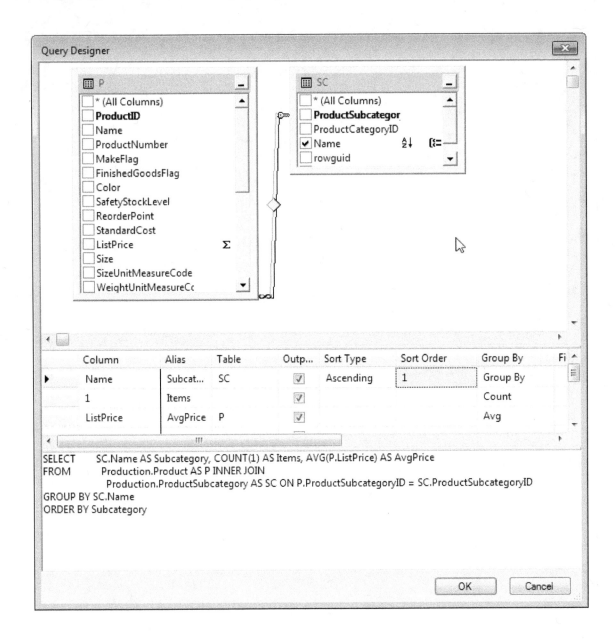

Second Job Step

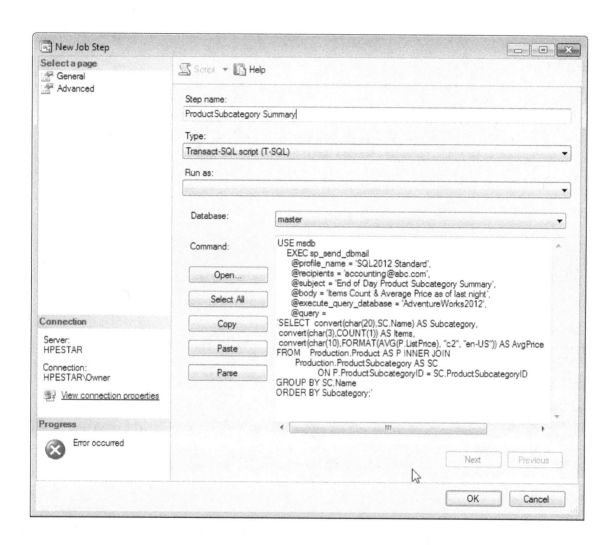

Defined Job Steps

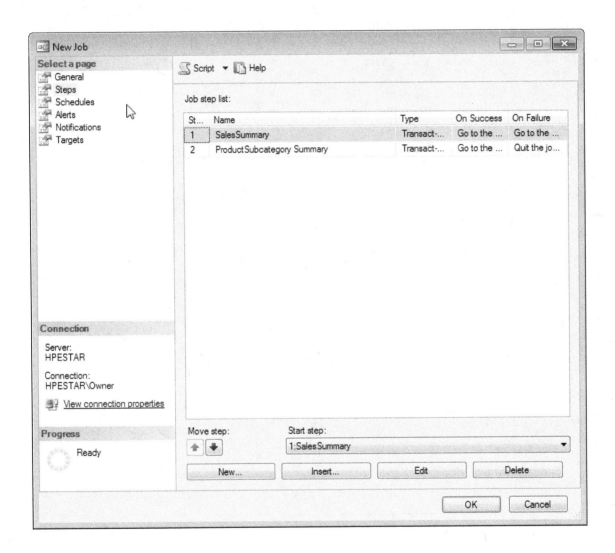

Schedule Configuration

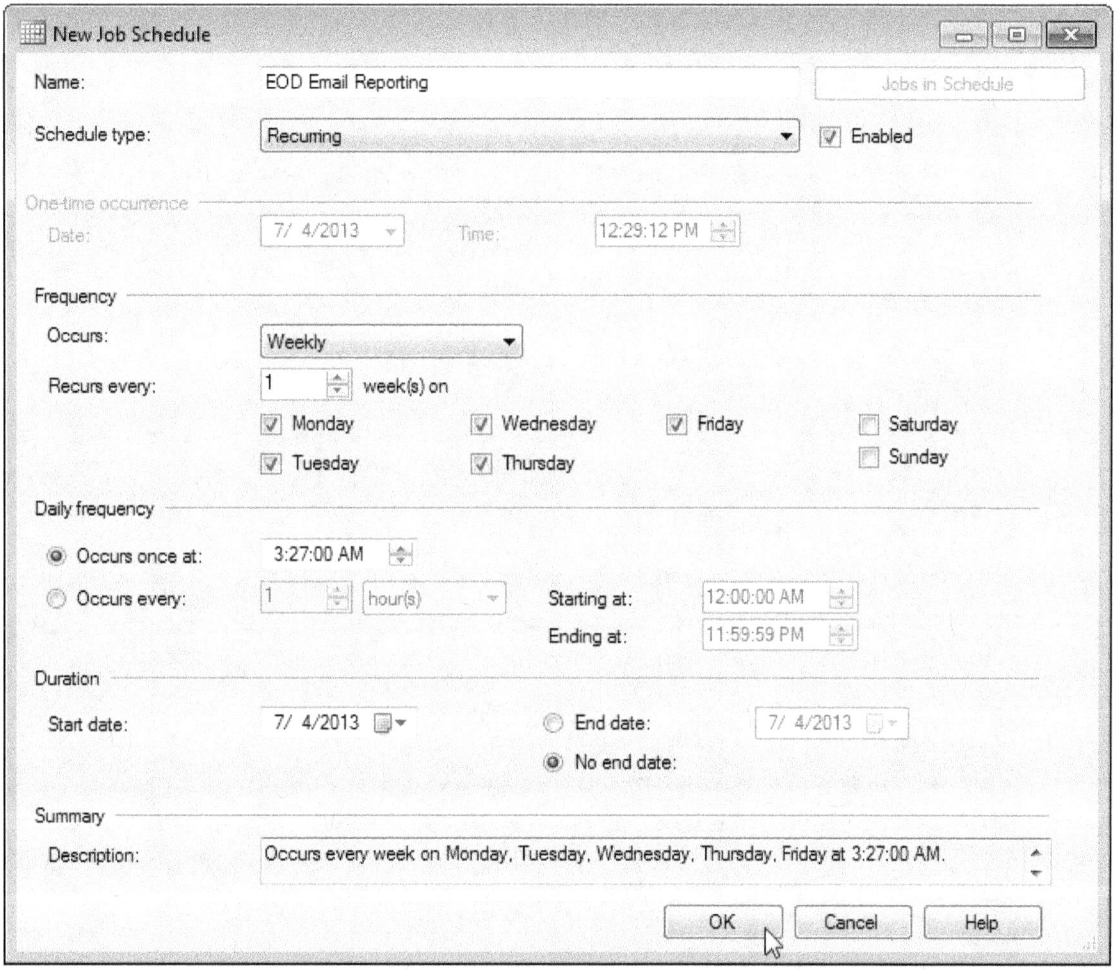

Email Reports after Job Execution

Here is one of emailed reports after manual execution of the job. A job can be executed manually, programmatically and by schedule.

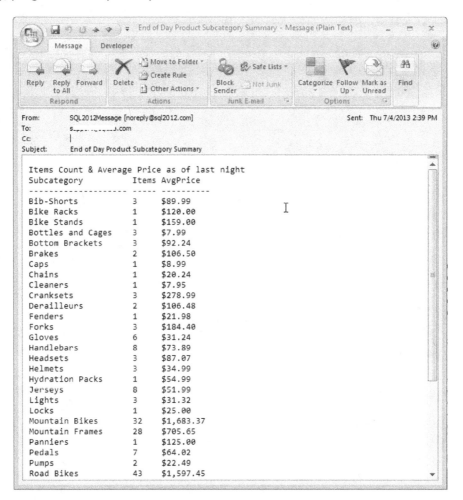

Automating Report Distribution

Instead of 100 users going online during the day and running the same report again and again, automatic delivery can be configured via a SQL Server Agent job. The job runs the report only once during the night and emails it to the distribution list which can be an email group also. At the same time performance of the RDBMS system improves since the report query is executed only once during the night instead of 100 times during the busy hours.

Job Creation via T-SQL Script

Jobs can be created by T-SQL programming as well. Here is the complete script of the EOD job.

```
USE [msdb]
GO
/****** Object:  Job [EOD_Audit_Report]    Script Date: 7/5/2016 10:20:27 AM ******/
BEGIN TRANSACTION
DECLARE @ReturnCode INT
SELECT @ReturnCode = 0
/****** Object:  JobCategory [Database Maintenance]    Script Date: 7/5/2016 10:20:27 AM ******/
IF NOT EXISTS (SELECT name FROM msdb.dbo.syscategories WHERE name=N'Database Maintenance' AND
category_class=1)
BEGIN
EXEC @ReturnCode = msdb.dbo.sp_add_category @class=N'JOB', @type=N'LOCAL', @name=N'Database
Maintenance'
IF (@@ERROR <> 0 OR @ReturnCode <> 0) GOTO QuitWithRollback
END
DECLARE @jobId BINARY(16)
EXEC @ReturnCode =  msdb.dbo.sp_add_job @job_name=N'EOD_Audit_Report',
                @enabled=1,
                @notify_level_eventlog=0,
                @notify_level_email=0,
                @notify_level_netsend=0,
                @notify_level_page=0,
                @delete_level=0,
                @description=N'Nightly audit reports emailed to accounting.',
                @category_name=N'Database Maintenance',
                @owner_login_name=N'HPESTAR\Owner', @job_id = @jobId OUTPUT
IF (@@ERROR <> 0 OR @ReturnCode <> 0) GOTO QuitWithRollback
/****** Object:  Step [SalesSummary]    Script Date: 7/5/2016 10:20:27 AM ******/
EXEC @ReturnCode = msdb.dbo.sp_add_jobstep @job_id=@jobId, @step_name=N'SalesSummary',
                @step_id=1,
                @cmdexec_success_code=0,
                @on_success_action=3,
                @on_success_step_id=0,
                @on_fail_action=3,
                @on_fail_step_id=0,
                @retry_attempts=0,
                @retry_interval=0,
                @os_run_priority=0, @subsystem=N'TSQL',
                @command=N'USE msdb
  EXEC sp_send_dbmail
    @profile_name = "SQL2012 Standard",
    @recipients = "accounting@abc.com",
    @subject = "End of Day Sales Summary",
    @body = "Total Sales as of last night",
    @execute_query_database = "AdventureWorks2012",
    @query = "SELECT Year=convert(char(4),Year(OrderDate)),
        Total=convert(char(20),FORMAT(SUM(SubTotal),""c0"", ""en-US""))
        FROM Sales.SalesOrderHeader
```

```
                GROUP BY Year(OrderDate) ORDER BY Year DESC''',
                    @database_name=N'master',
                    @flags=0
IF (@@ERROR <> 0 OR @ReturnCode <> 0) GOTO QuitWithRollback
/****** Object:  Step [ProductSubcategory Summary]    Script Date: 7/5/2016 10:20:27 AM ******/
EXEC @ReturnCode = msdb.dbo.sp_add_jobstep @job_id=@jobId, @step_name=N'ProductSubcategory Summary',
                    @step_id=2,
                    @cmdexec_success_code=0,
                    @on_success_action=1,
                    @on_success_step_id=0,
                    @on_fail_action=2,
                    @on_fail_step_id=0,
                    @retry_attempts=0,
                    @retry_interval=0,
                    @os_run_priority=0, @subsystem=N'TSQL',
                    @command=N'USE msdb
  EXEC sp_send_dbmail
    @profile_name = ''SQL2012 Standard'',
    @recipients = ''accounting@abc.com'',
    @subject = ''End of Day Product Subcategory Summary'',
    @body = ''Items Count & Average Price as of last night'',
    @execute_query_database = ''AdventureWorks2012'',
    @query =
''SELECT  convert(char(20),SC.Name) AS Subcategory,
 convert(char(3),COUNT(1)) AS Items,
 convert(char(10),FORMAT(AVG(P.ListPrice), ''''c2'''', ''''en-US'''')) AS AvgPrice
FROM    Production.Product AS P INNER JOIN
     Production.ProductSubcategory AS SC
           ON P.ProductSubcategoryID = SC.ProductSubcategoryID
GROUP BY SC.Name  ORDER BY Subcategory;''',
                    @database_name=N'master',
                    @flags=0
IF (@@ERROR <> 0 OR @ReturnCode <> 0) GOTO QuitWithRollback
EXEC @ReturnCode = msdb.dbo.sp_update_job @job_id = @jobId, @start_step_id = 1
IF (@@ERROR <> 0 OR @ReturnCode <> 0) GOTO QuitWithRollback
EXEC @ReturnCode = msdb.dbo.sp_add_jobschedule @job_id=@jobId, @name=N'EOD Email Reporting',
                    @enabled=1, @freq_type=8, @freq_interval=62, @freq_subday_type=1,
                    @freq_subday_interval=0, @freq_relative_interval=0,      @freq_recurrence_factor=1,
                    @active_start_date=20130704, @active_end_date=99991231,
                    @active_start_time=32700,
                    @active_end_time=235959,
                    @schedule_uid=N'aca338d8-7f7e-4eec-961b-fca1304b9085'
IF (@@ERROR <> 0 OR @ReturnCode <> 0) GOTO QuitWithRollback
EXEC @ReturnCode = msdb.dbo.sp_add_jobserver @job_id = @jobId, @server_name = N'(local)'
IF (@@ERROR <> 0 OR @ReturnCode <> 0) GOTO QuitWithRollback
COMMIT TRANSACTION
GOTO EndSave
QuitWithRollback:
  IF (@@TRANCOUNT > 0) ROLLBACK TRANSACTION
EndSave:
GO
```

CHAPTER 17: Replication for Data Distribution

Overview

Quote: "Replication is a set of technologies for copying and distributing data and database objects from one database to another and then synchronizing between databases to maintain consistency. Using replication, you can distribute data to different locations and to remote or mobile users over local and wide area networks, dial-up connections, wireless connections, and the Internet.

Transactional replication is typically used in server-to-server scenarios that require high throughput, including: improving scalability and availability; data warehousing and reporting; integrating data from multiple sites; integrating heterogeneous data; and offloading batch processing. Merge replication is primarily designed for mobile applications or distributed server applications that have possible data conflicts. Common scenarios include: exchanging data with mobile users; consumer point of sale (POS) applications; and integration of data from multiple sites. Snapshot replication is used to provide the initial data set for transactional and merge replication; it can also be used when complete refreshes of data are appropriate. With these three types of replication, SQL Server provides a powerful and flexible system for synchronizing data across your enterprise."

> MSDN Article: **SQL Server Replication**   http://bit.ly/dc8nfw
> http://msdn.microsoft.com/en-us/library/ms151198.aspx

Quote: "SQL Replication can solve many problems in running database-driven applications. The publication/subscriber model isn't completely easy to understand, the complexities of scripting and monitoring replication systems takes some thought. Here, at last, is a series of articles that takes care to produce a jargon-free approach to SQL Server Replication of all types."

> Article: **Stairway to SQL Server Replication**   http://bit.ly/zOl5eR
> http://www.sqlservercentral.com/stairway/72401/

Replicate the titles Table of pubs from the Default Instance to a Named Instance

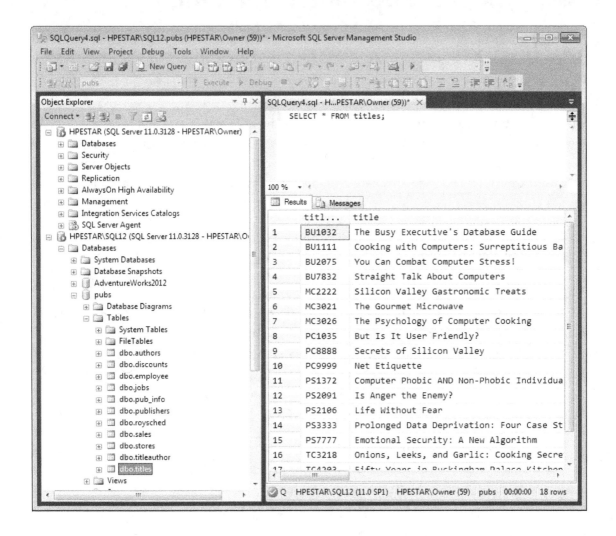

Replication Configuration

Object Explorer has excellent GUI tools to configure replication. Launch configuration from the right click drop-down menu.

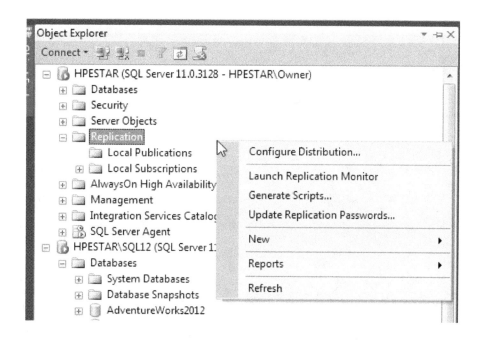

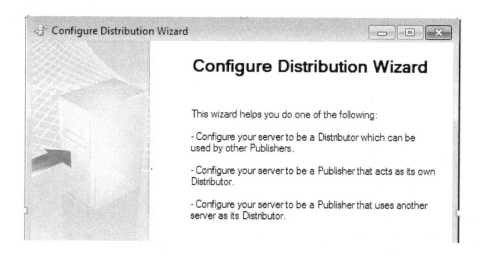

Source Server Will Be Its Own Distributor

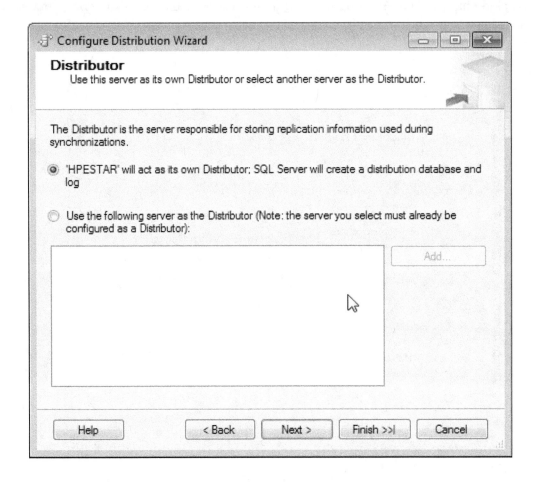

SQL Server Agent Page

SQL Server Agent has a pivotal role in executing replication processes.

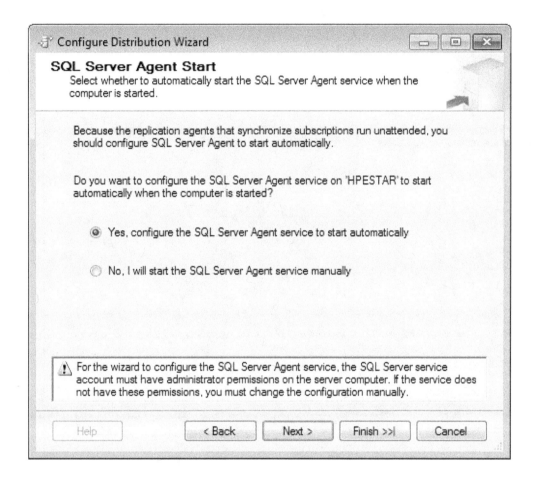

Snapshot Folder Configuration Page

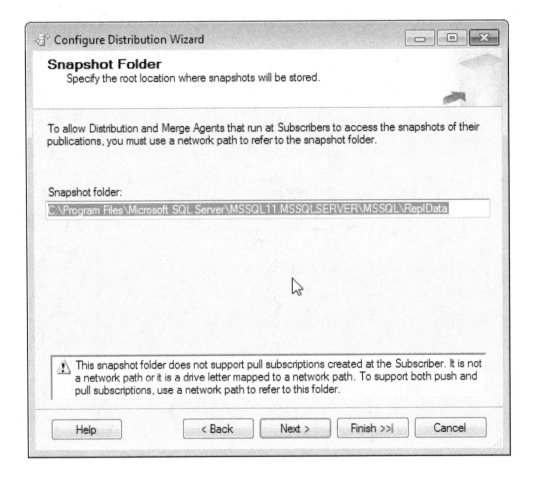

Distribution Database Setup

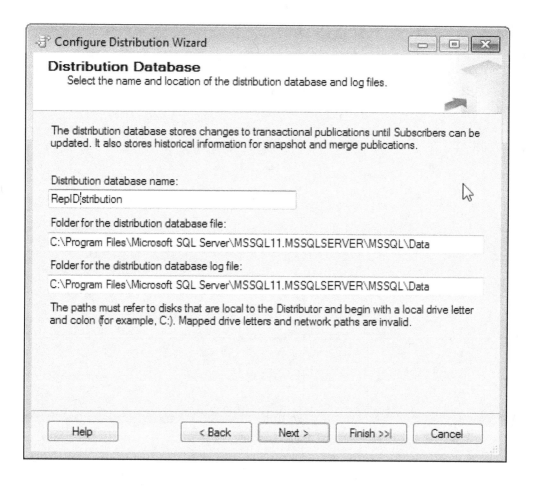

Currently One Publisher Uses the Distributor

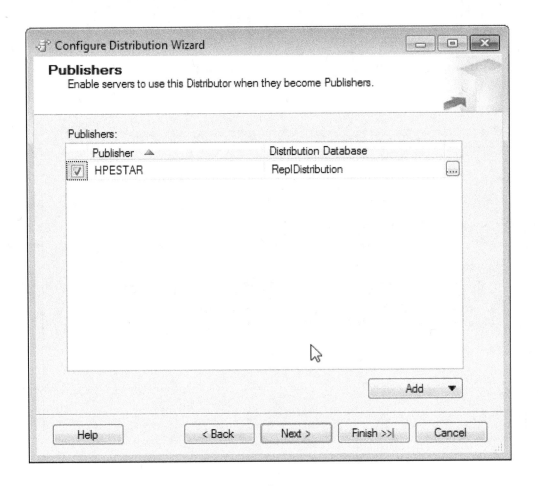

Wizard Actions Screen

It is generally a good idea to save script when using GUI configuration.

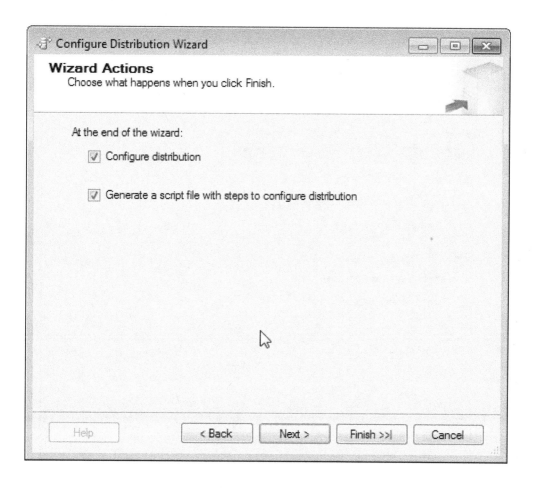

Script File Properties Page

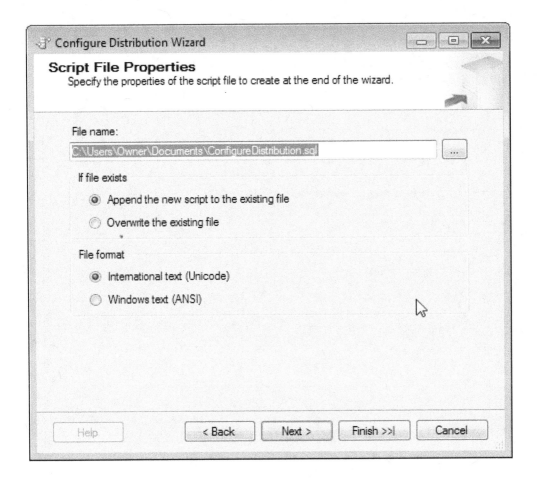

Complete the Wizard Page

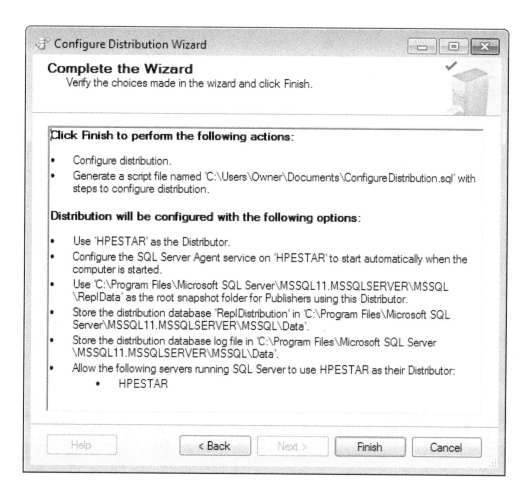

Distributor Properties Page

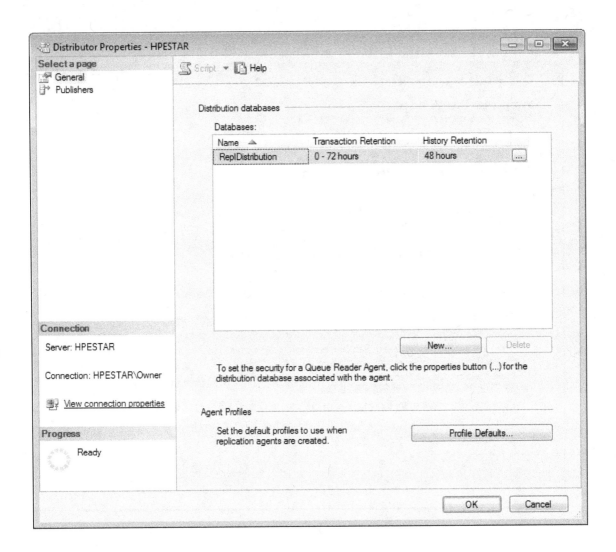

Configuring a New Publication

Publication Database Selection

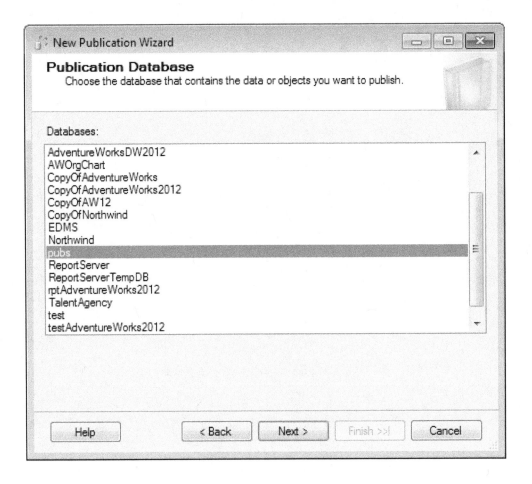

Publication Type Page

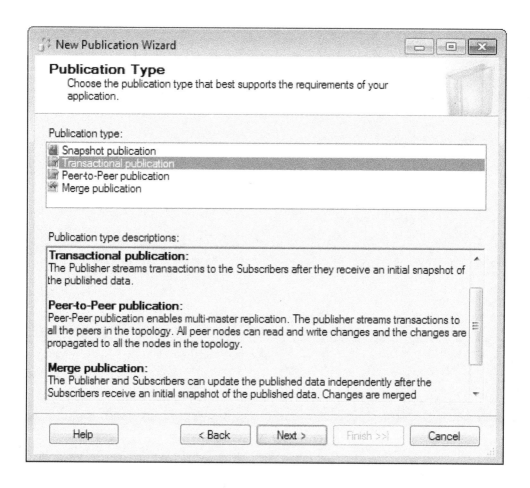

Articles to Publish Page

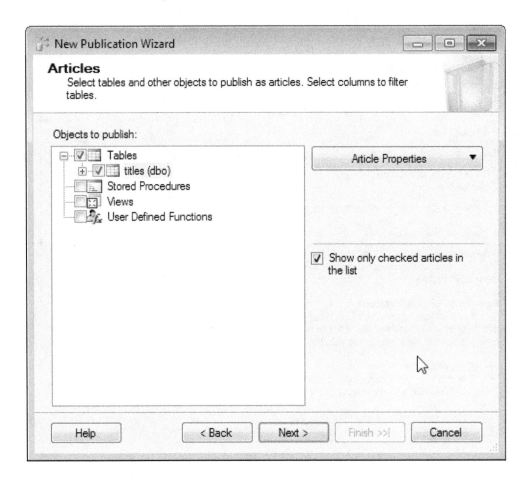

Filter Table Rows Page

Snapshot Options Page

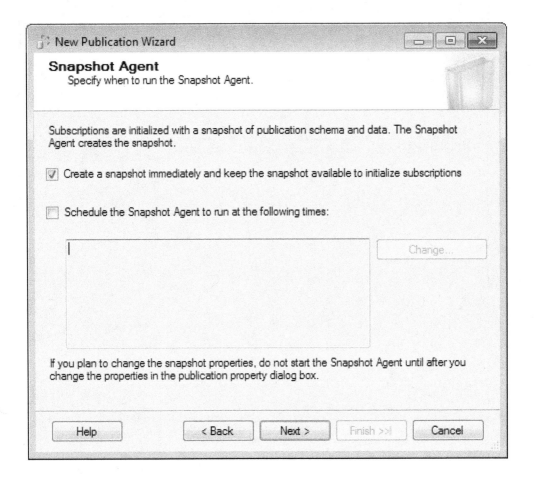

Security Account Settings

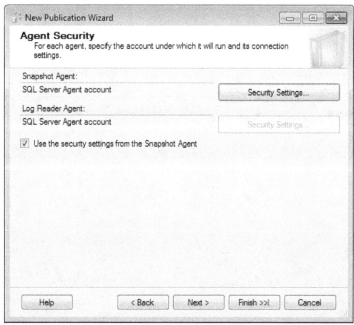

Wizard Actions Page

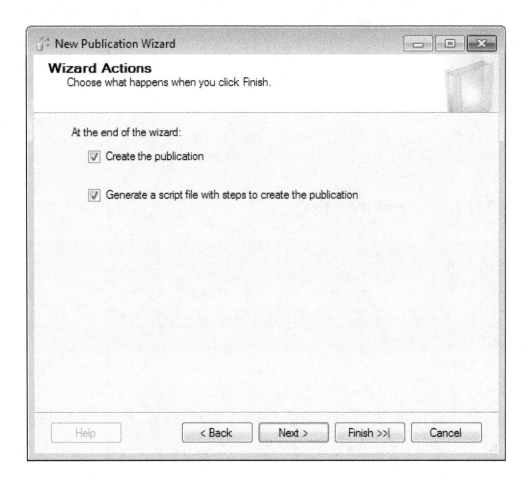

Script Files Properties Page

It is very important to save the script. It can be used for recovery or programmatic way of setting up replication on another computer.

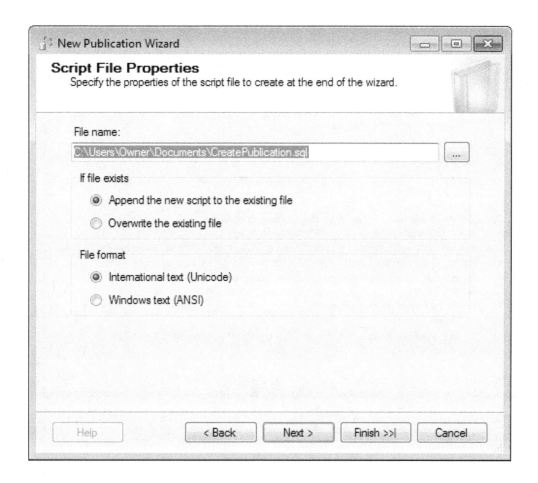

Complete the Wizard Page

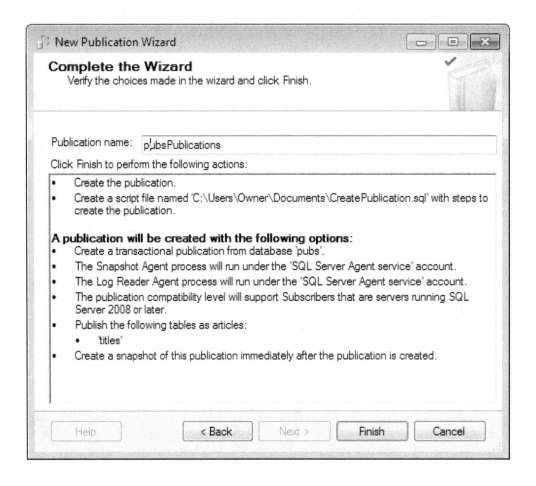

Publication Properties General Page

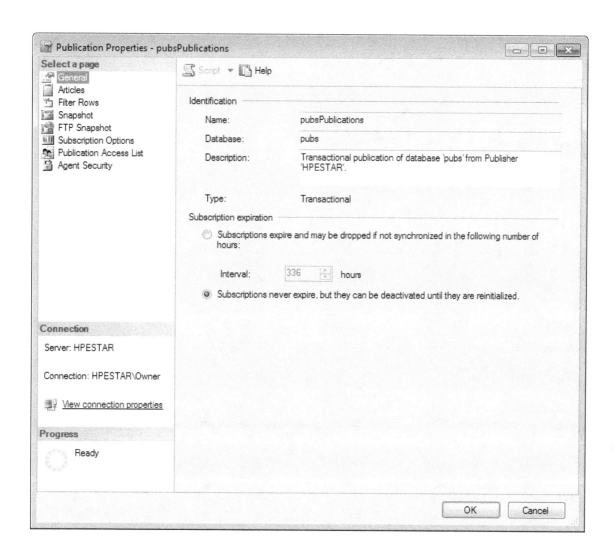

Publication Properties Articles Page

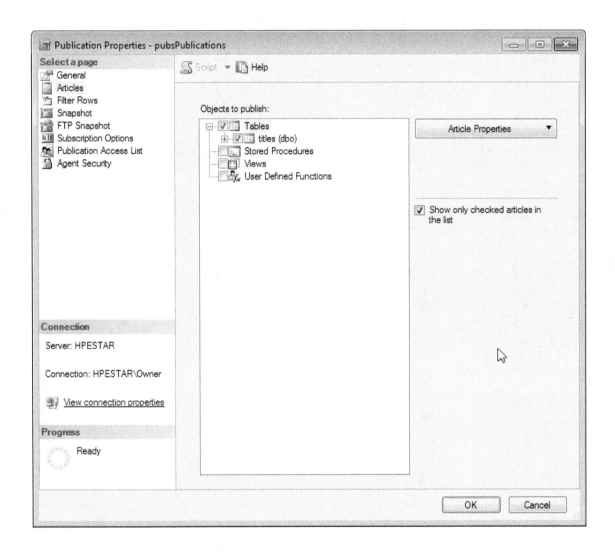

Configuring a Subscriber

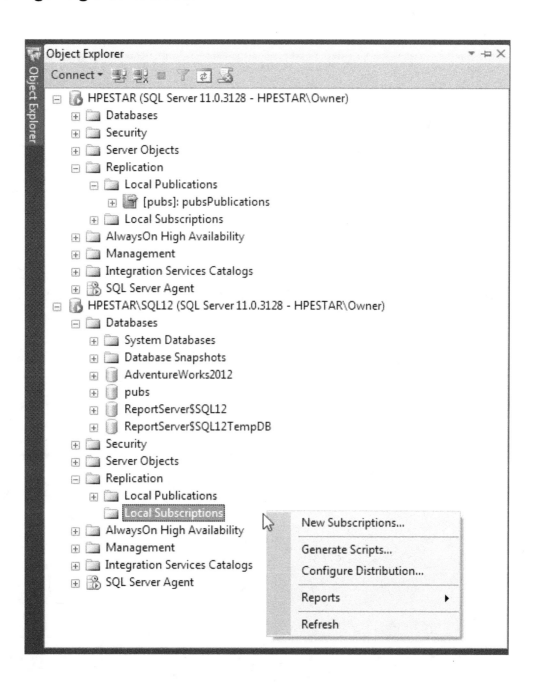

New Subscription Wizard

Identify Publisher Page

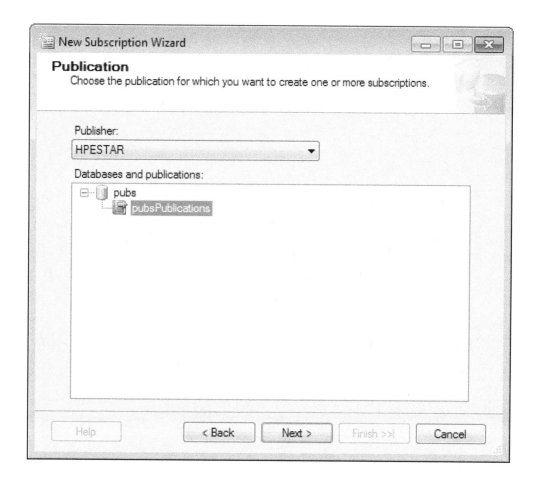

Distribution Agent Location Page

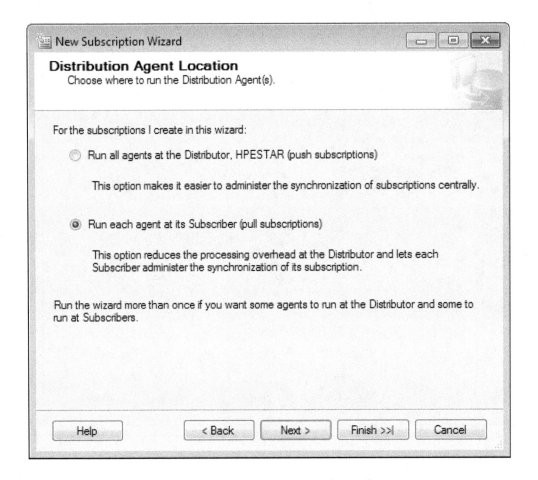

Subscribers Page

Distribution Agent Security Page

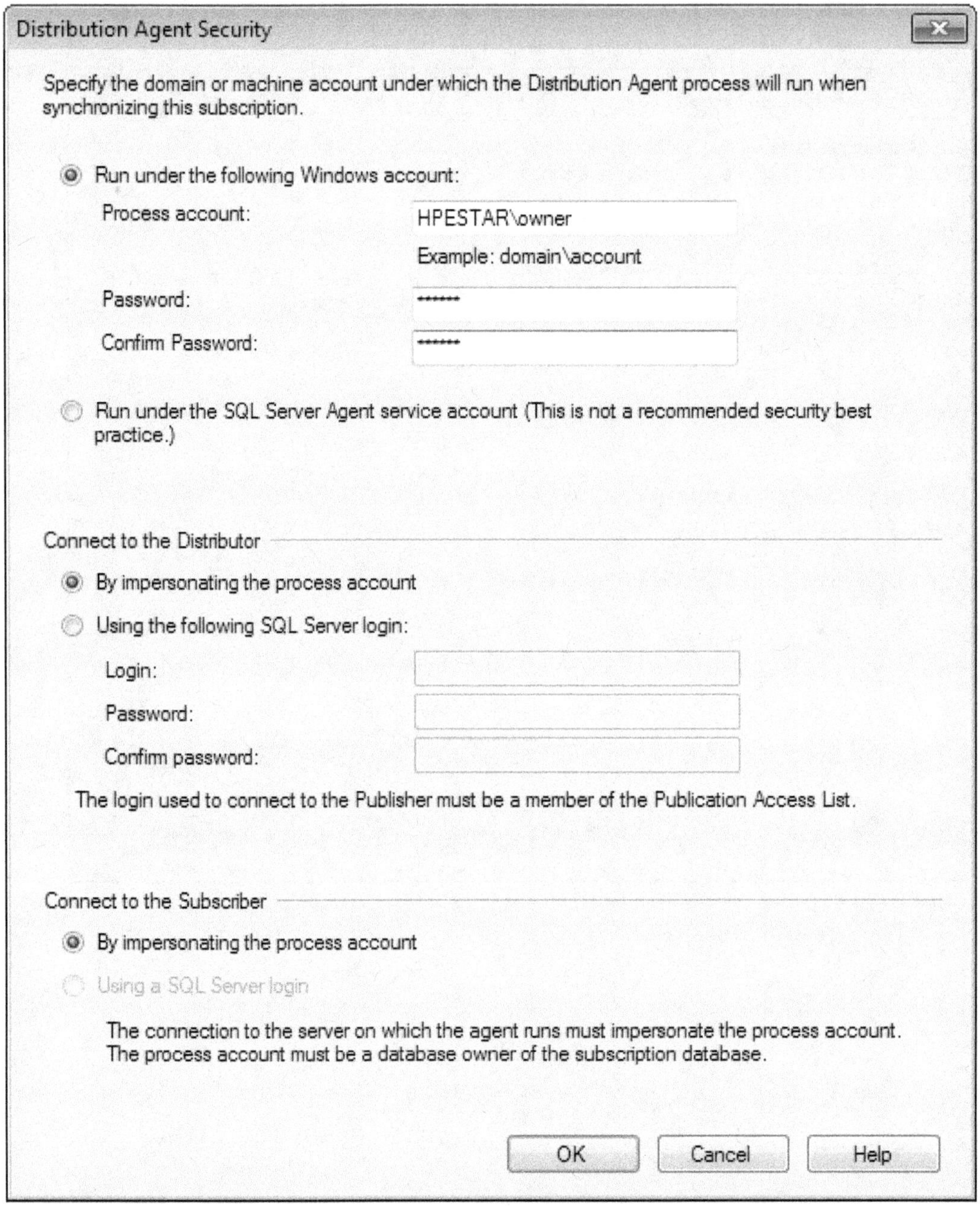

Distribution Agent Security Page

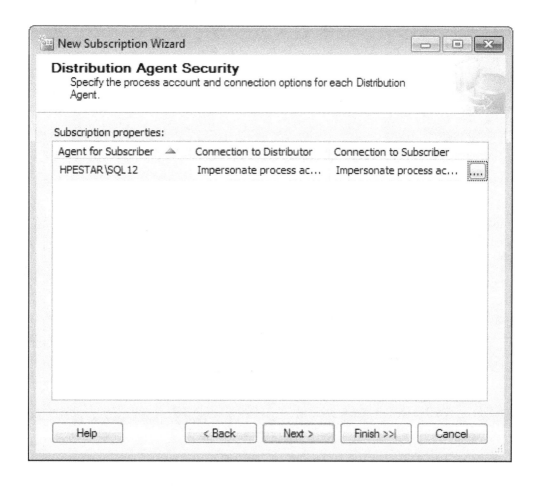

Synchronization Schedule Page

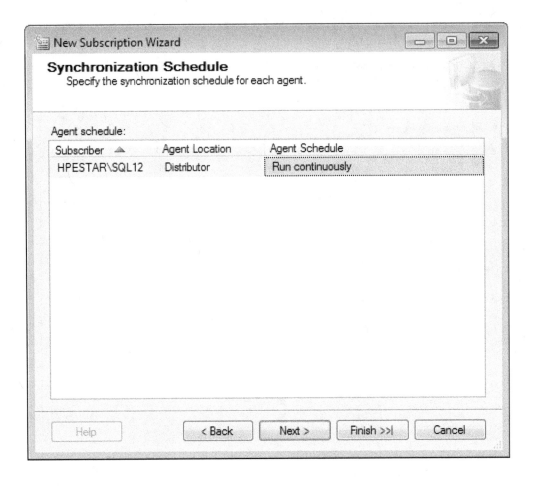

Initialize Subscriptions Page

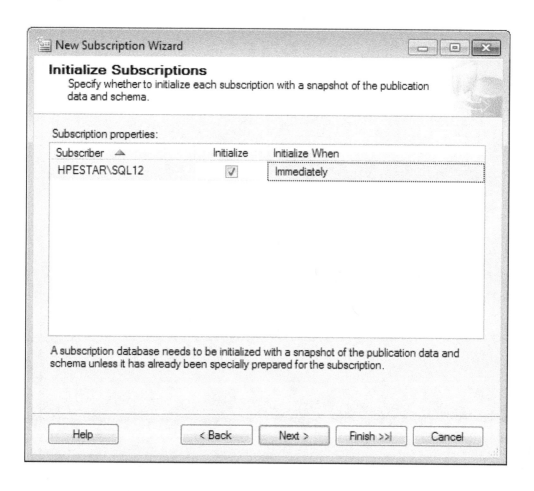

Wizard Actions Page

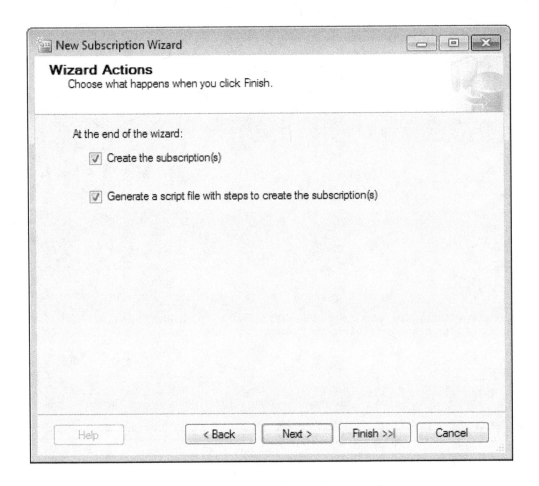

Script File Properties Page

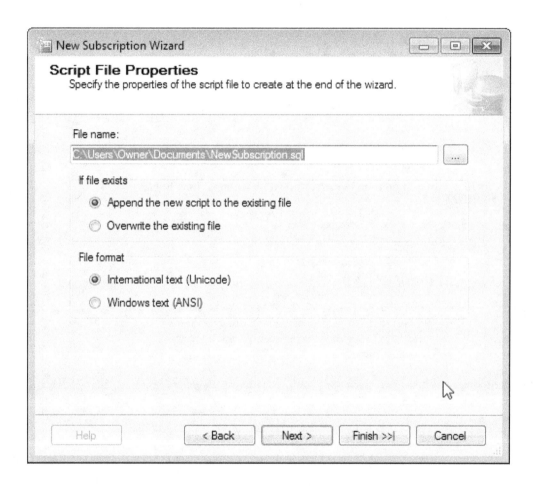

Complete the Wizard Page

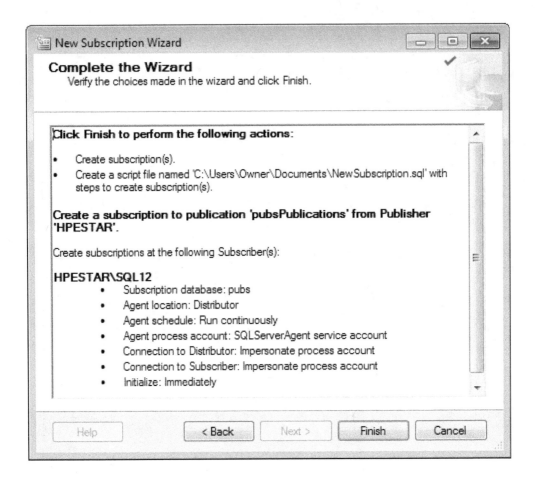

Creating Subscriptions Page

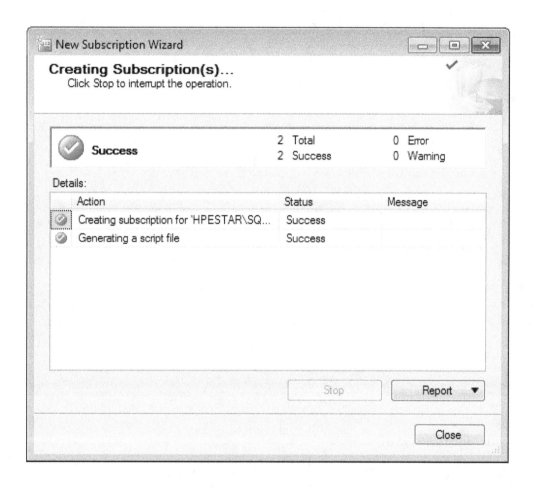

Verifying Transactional Replication

At the publisher pubs database we insert a record into the titles table.

```
INSERT INTO [dbo].[titles]
    VALUES
        ( 'MK3030', 'Columbus & Queen Isabella',
          'fiction', 1389, 19.95, 5000.0, 10, 0.0,
          'A new look at the complex relationship between a man and a woman who changed world history',
          '2016-06-02');
```

Testing at subscriber a second later.

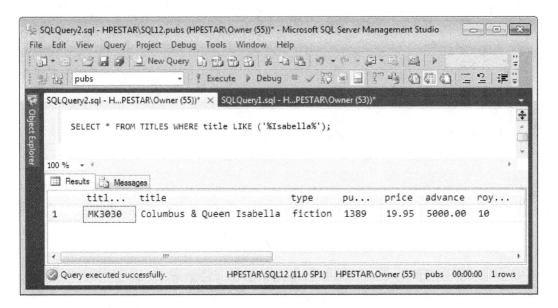

Replication Monitor at Subscriber

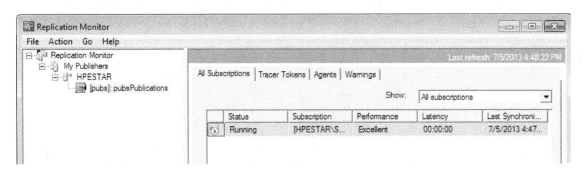

Replication Monitor at Publisher

Launching from right click drop-down menu.

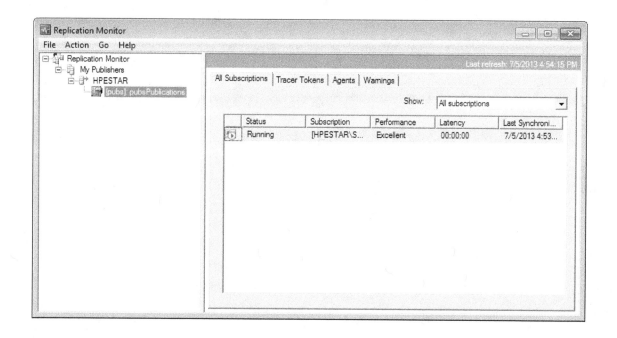

CHAPTER 17: Replication for Data Distribution

Reviewing Subscriber Job History

Green arrow indicates everything is OK.

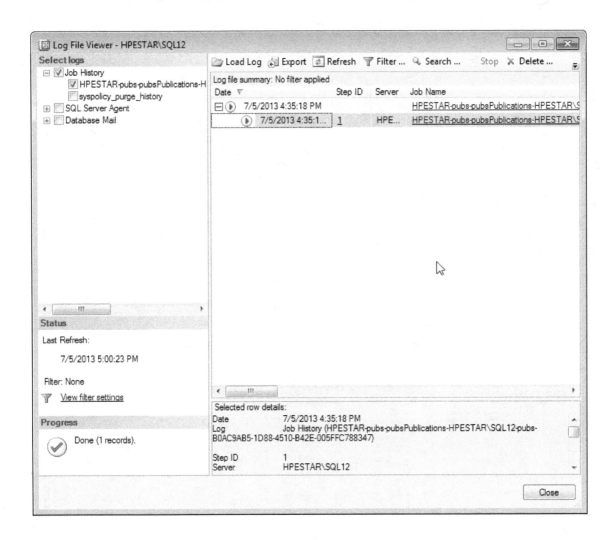

CHAPTER 18: Log-Shipping & Database Mirroring for Standby

Log Shipping

Log shipping involves sending the database transaction log from the production server to the standby server in every 15 minutes or so and restoring the log on the standby server. Naturally, the databases must be synchronized to start the log-shipping process. In case of disaster with the production server database, the standby takes over with some data loss. The standby computer can be in the same computer room as the production server, same building, same city, same state or thousands miles away.

Transaction Log Shipping Page of Database Properties

MSDN Articles: **About Log Shipping (SQL Server)**   http://bit.ly/daWQXB
http://msdn.microsoft.com/en-us/library/ms187103.aspx
Configure Log Shipping (SQL Server)   http://bit.ly/P9gt0P
http://msdn.microsoft.com/en-us/library/ms190640.aspx

Database Mirroring

Database mirroring is similar technology to log-shipping, it is more automated and failover can happen with a few seconds blackout period as opposed to over half an hour (typical) with log-shipping.

Database Properties Mirroring Page

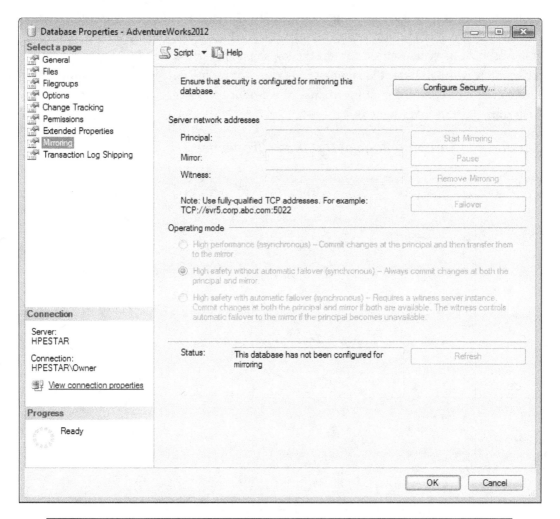

MSDN Articles: **Database Mirroring (SQL Server)**   http://bit.ly/i2i2OE
http://msdn.microsoft.com/en-us/library/ms189852.aspx
Setting Up Database Mirroring (SQL Server)   http://bit.ly/10C9Swm
http://msdn.microsoft.com/en-us/library/ms190941.aspx

CHAPTER 19: AlwaysOn & Clustering for High Availability

SQL Server Clustering

Quote: "**SQL Server Clustering technology**
SQL Server clustering is a high-availability technology that helps companies meet their availability and uptime goals. This technology ensures that mission-critical services, applications, and data will be constantly available in case of any kind of failure or disaster. Being an automatic technology, it allows one physical server to take control over tasks and responsibilities of another one that failed. SQL Server cluster shares tasks and services between cluster nodes, each of which can contain one or more shared disks grouped into logical units called resource groups.

Basics of Clustering
Every virtual server is shown on a network as a system. If a virtual server contains SQL Server resources, clients connected to it may access resources on its current host node. If the current host fails, the resource group will be transferred to another node within the cluster. It is critical to set failover order for each instance in clusters having more than two nodes or instances.

 The aim of clustering is to provide availability to clients by supplying a system with an automatic failover mechanism. During the failure there will be a short database server interruption on all clusters. Clustering is a part of a big strategy to help reduce application downtime."

Article: **SQL Server Clustering technology**	http://bit.ly/16nRriC
http://sql.starwindsoftware.com/sql-server-clustering-technology	

Quote: "**Key Concept:** A Windows Failover Cluster uses shared storage– typically, this shared storage is on a SAN. When a SQL Server instance is installed on the cluster, system and user databases are required to be on the shared storage. That allows the cluster to move the SQL instance to any server (or "node") in the cluster whenever you request, or if one of the nodes is having a problem. There is only one copy of the data, but the network name and SQL Server service for the instance can be made active from any cluster node.

Translation: A failover cluster basically gives you the ability to have all the data for a SQL Server instance installed in something like a share that can be accessed from different servers. It will always have the same instance name, SQL Agent jobs, Linked Servers and Logins wherever you bring it up. You can even make it always use the same IPAddress and port– so no users of the SQL Server have to know where it is at any given time."

Article: An Introduction to SQL Server Clusters http://bit.ly/zWGgTP http://www.brentozar.com/archive/2012/02/introduction-sql-server-clusters/	

Quote: "**Active Nodes Versus Passive Nodes**
A Windows Failover Cluster can support up to sixteen nodes; however, most clustering deployment is only two nodes. A single SQL Server 2012 instance can run on only a single node at a time; and should a failover occur, the failed instance can failover to another node. Clusters of three or more physical nodes should be considered when you need to cluster many SQL Server instances.

In a two-node Windows Failover Cluster with SQL Server, one of the physical nodes is considered the active node, and the second one is the passive node for that single SQL Server instance. It doesn't matter which of the physical servers in the cluster is designated as active or passive, but you should specifically assign one node as the active and the other as the passive. This way, there is no confusion about which physical server is performing which role at the current time.

When referring to an active node, this particular node is currently running a SQL Server instance accessing that instance's databases, which are located on a shared disk array. When referring to a passive node, this particular node is not currently running the SQL Server. When a node is passive, it is not running the production databases, but it is in a state of readiness"

Article: How SQL Server Clustering Works, Part 1 http://bit.ly/1a90l7A http://www.confio.com/logicalread/how-sql-server-clustering-works-part-1-w02/#.UdxY4BDD9xA	

MSDN Articles: **SQL Server Failover Cluster Installation** http://bit.ly/13JzOh4 http://msdn.microsoft.com/en-us/library/hh231721.aspx	
Create a New SQL Server Failover Cluster (Setup) http://bit.ly/aWQMTp http://msdn.microsoft.com/en-us/library/ms179530.aspx	

Alwayson Availability Groups

Quote: "**Understanding The AlwaysOn Feature**
AlwaysOn is a new High Availability (HA) and Disaster Recovery (DR) solution in SQL Server 2012 which improves high availability and protects data of your mission critical applications. AlwaysOn lets you utilize your current hardware and provides a flexible and simplified configuration, deployment and management experience. AlwaysOn is common name for two high availability and disaster recovery solutions:

AlwaysOn Failover Cluster Instance (FCI)
 This is an enhancement to the existing SQL Server failover clustering (which is based on Windows Server Failover Cluster (WSFC)) which provides higher availability of SQL Server instance after failover. Some of the enhancements in AlwaysOn Failover Cluster Instance over the existing SQL Server failover clustering are:

- o   For improved site protection you can now set up multisite failover clustering
- o   You can now define flexible failover policy to better control instance failover
- o   You now have better and improved diagnostics capabilities out of the box

AlwaysOn Availability Group (AG)
This is a completely new HA/DR feature and combines best of failover clustering and database mirroring. It allows you to create a group of databases which failover together as a unit from one replica/instance of SQL Server to another replica/instance of SQL Server in the same availability group. Each availability group that we create, allows you to create one (and only) availability group listener which is nothing but a Virtual Network Name (VNN) to be used by clients to connect to the availability group."

> Article: **Using The AlwaysOn Feature of SQL Server 2012**   http://bit.ly/172lO0d
> http://www.sql-server-performance.com/2013/alwayson-clustering-failover/

Quote: "**Why HA SQL is Important**

Highly available (HA) SQL Server services are the cornerstone of many enterprise database applications. Few enterprise solutions today are deployed on non-HA SQL. Without an HA mechanism for database services, enterprise applications and e-commerce websites cannot offer maximum available uptime. Even perfectly managed servers require periodic restarts for updates and maintenance; and you always need to be prepared for equipment failure such as extended outages of particular servers or disk drives.

The traditional way to offer HA SQL is by creating a SQL Server failover cluster based on shared storage. That is, a storage area network (SAN) presents shelves of disk drives to two or more servers at the same time ("shared storage"). The SAN and shared storage is often the most expensive component in the datacenter. Public cloud solutions abstract you from the storage, and usually don't offer the kind of infrastructure you would need to run a conventional HA SQL failover cluster with shared storage in the cloud.

HA SQL for the public cloud

A drag on projects looking for ways to move workloads to the public cloud is the lack of HA SQL support on infrastructure-class SQL services. In the Microsoft public cloud, Windows Azure, you can rent a slice of SQL Azure, which is highly available; however, many commercial applications won't install correctly against a SQL Azure backend. Applications running with a SQL Azure backend are generally conceived as Azure applications and written to support SQL Azure specifically. There is a demand to run HA SQL as infrastructure in public and hybrid cloud solutions.

To achieve infrastructure-class SQL services, you can install SQL Server inside a Windows Azure Infrastructure-as-a-Service (IaaS) class virtual machine (VM), and this works as expected. Your SQL server will be subject to the SLA of a single Azure IaaS VM instance. Windows Azure VMs by default have their virtual hard drives (VHDs) geo-replicated to a second Azure datacenter, providing a degree of protection against failure of some Azure hardware. Take note, Windows Azure geo-replicated VHD storage is not an HA solution."

> Article:
> **SQL Server 2012 AlwaysOn: High Availability database for cloud data centers**
> http://tek.io/UlKuuh
> http://www.techrepublic.com/blog/datacenter/sql-server-2012-alwayson-high-availability-database-for-cloud-data-centers/5885

> MSDN Articles: **SQL AlwaysOn Team Blog**   http://bit.ly/fwqzat
> http://blogs.msdn.com/b/sqlalwayson/
>
> **Overview of AlwaysOn Availability Groups (SQL Server)**   http://bit.ly/LjMzEb
> http://msdn.microsoft.com/en-us/library/ff877884.aspx

CHAPTER 20: Preparation for Disaster & Recovery

Maintenance Plan Wizard

The Wizard is the DBA's best friend! It automatically prepares a complex maintenance plan for one or more databases. The Wizard can be launched from the Management tab in Object Explorer. The objective is a maintenance plan for AdventureWorks2012 sample database.

Nightly Full Backup Plan

The purpose is recovery to the previous night in case of disaster. Also STATISTICS is updated to support query performance.

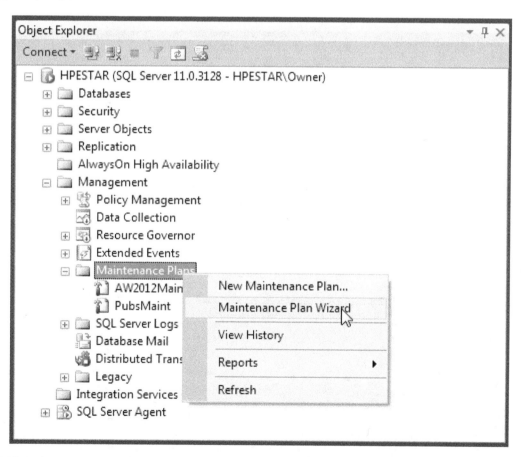

CHAPTER 20: Preparation for Disaster & Recovery

Maintenace Plan Wizard Welcome Page

Assign a Name to the New Plan & Setup Schedule

Setup a Nightly Job Execution Schedule

This is the scheduler for SQL Server Agent.

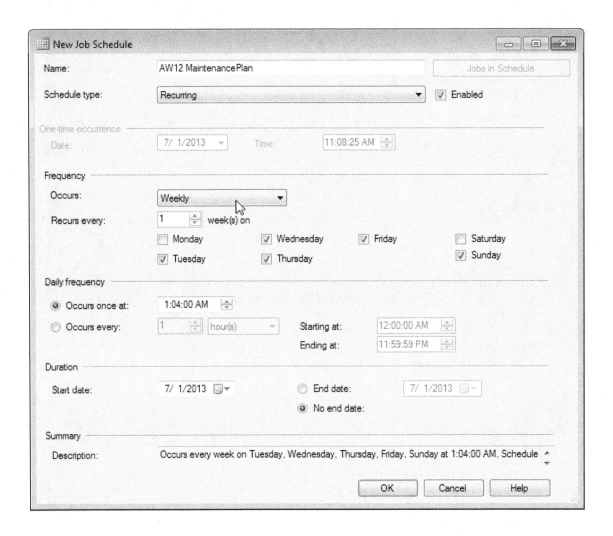

Scheduling Page After Job Schedule Setup

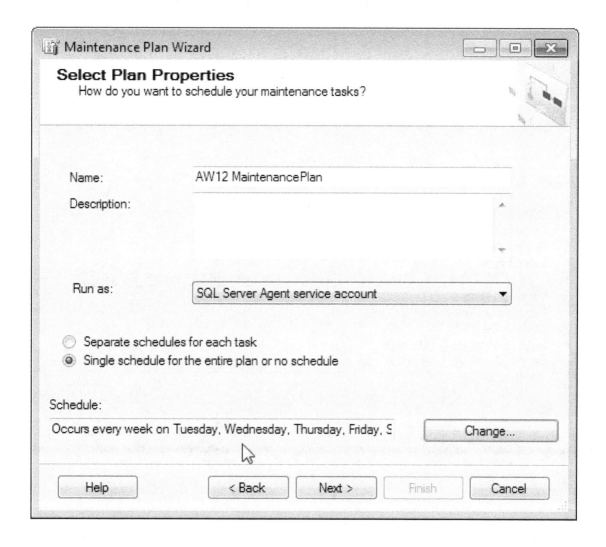

Define Database Maintenance Tasks

A new maintance plan will be defined to REBUILD indexes every weekend.

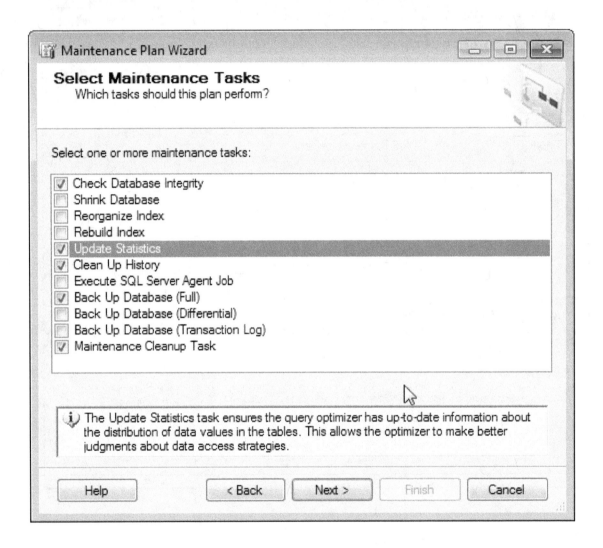

Define Task Order

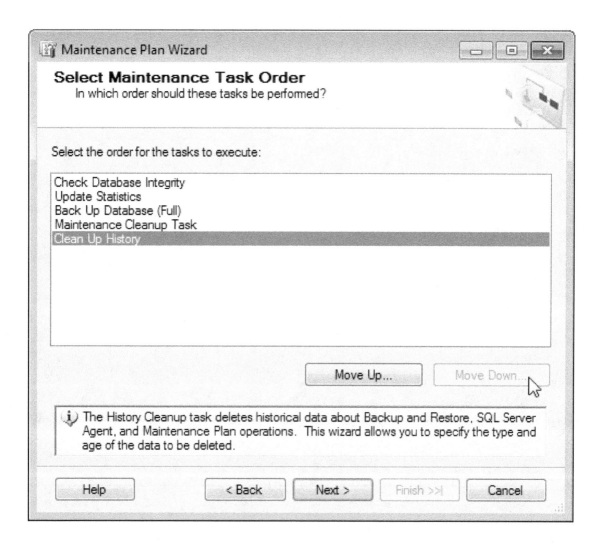

Database Integrity Check Setup

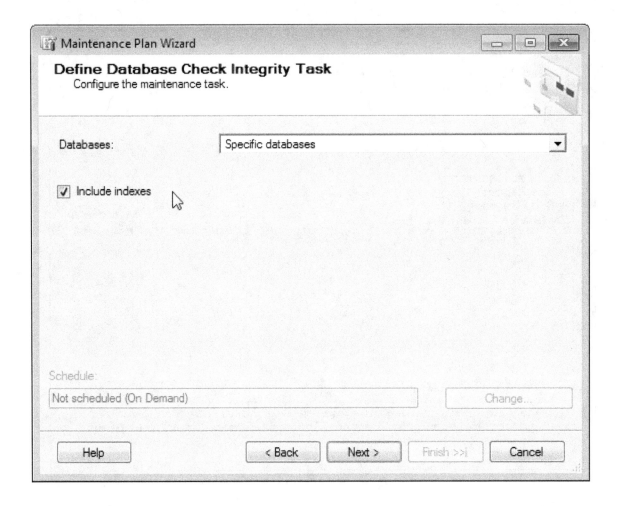

Statistictics Update Definition Page

While the All existing statistics and Full scan are desirable options, there may not be sufficient time in the nightly maintenance window.

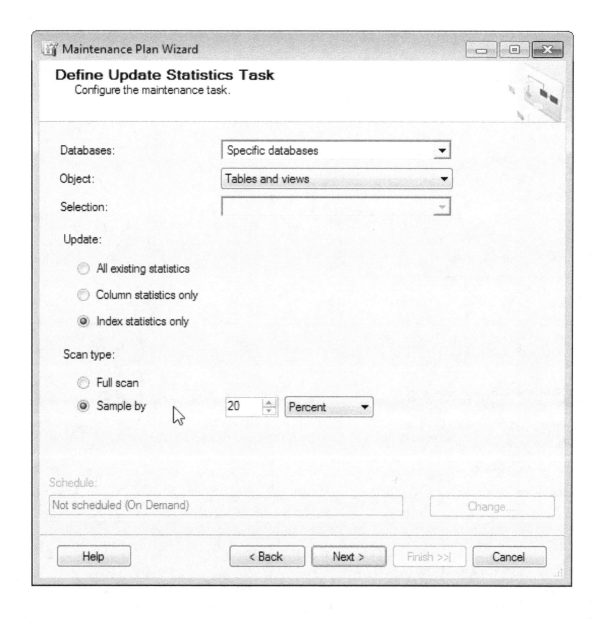

Database Backup Definition

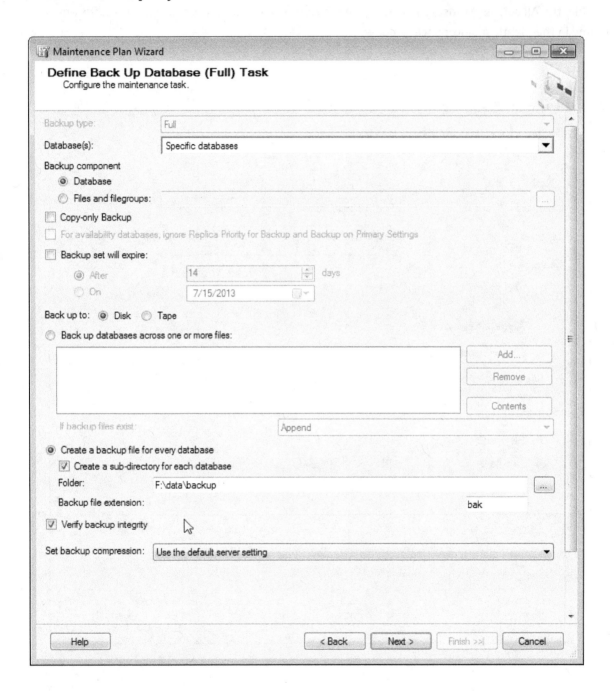

Cleanup Task Definition Page

History Cleanup Task Page

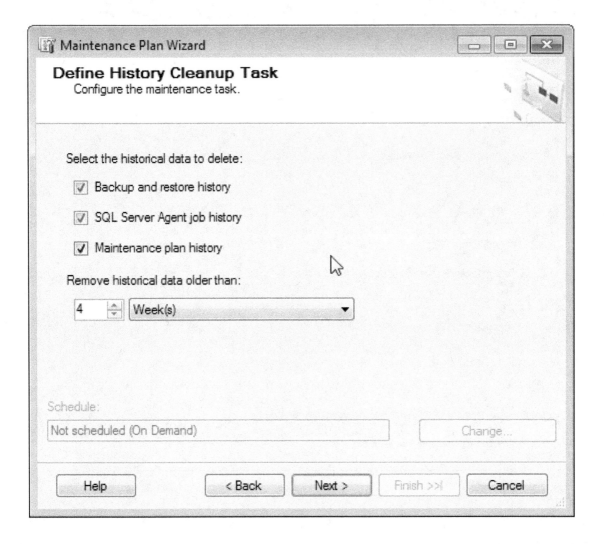

Report Options Page

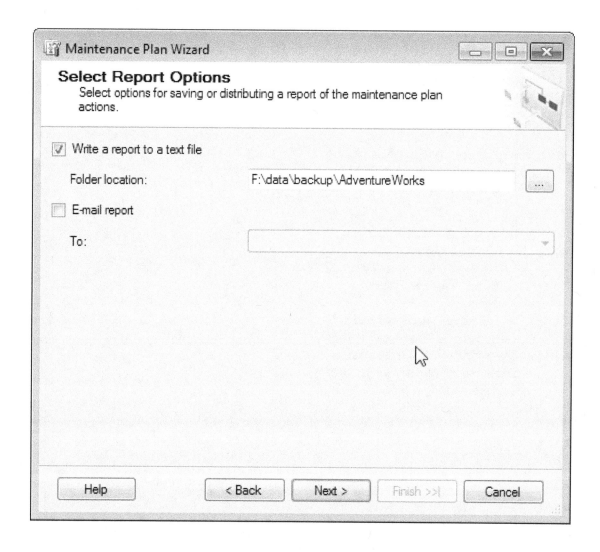

Plan Summary Page

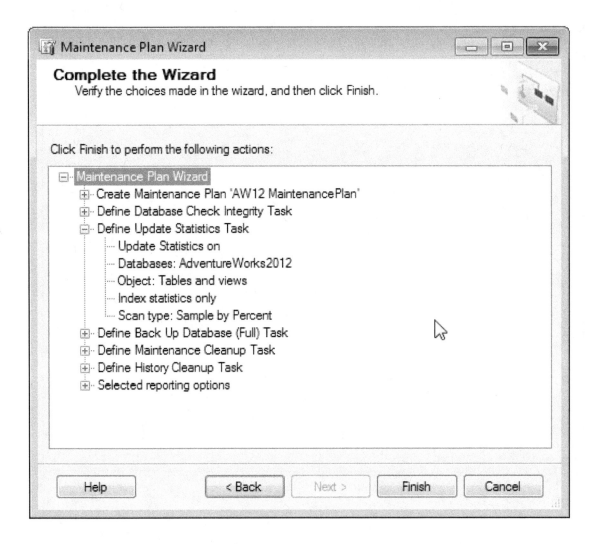

Maintenance Plan Creation Screen

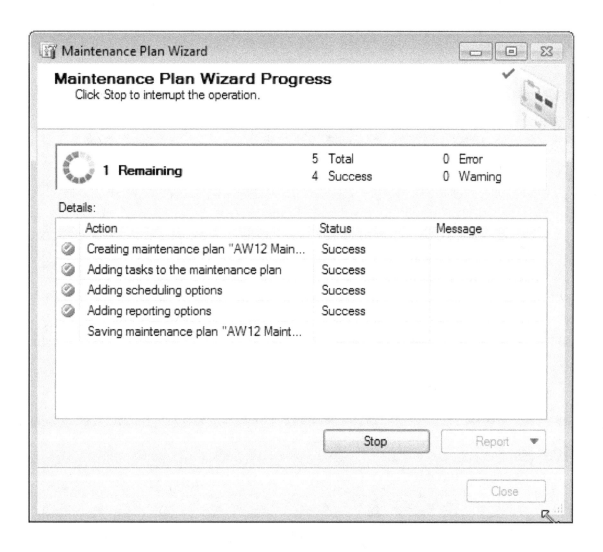

Daytime Transaction Log Backup Plan

To recover to point-in-time (e.g. middle of the day), a periodic transaction log backup plan must be prepared. Typically log backup is fast unless some massive operations, like index REBUILD, taking place. Combination of full & log backup is the basis of log-shipping as well.

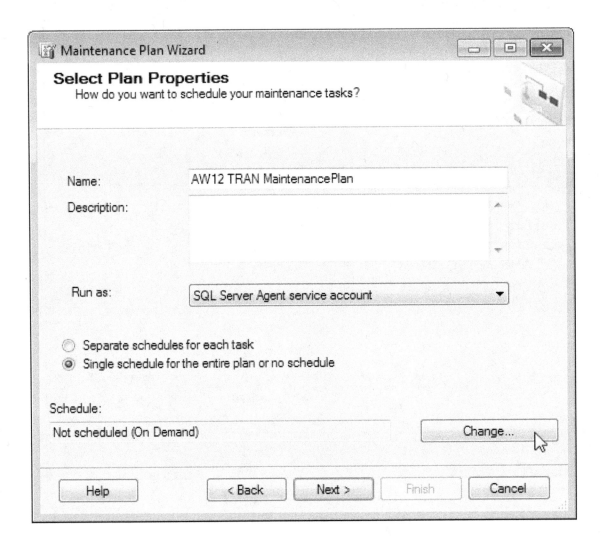

Setting of a Log Backup Schedule

Take a transaction log backup during business hours from 8am to 7pm every 15 minutes. Note: if Saturday & Sunday is to be excluded, then 5 single day only schedules should be setup to cover MON-FRI.

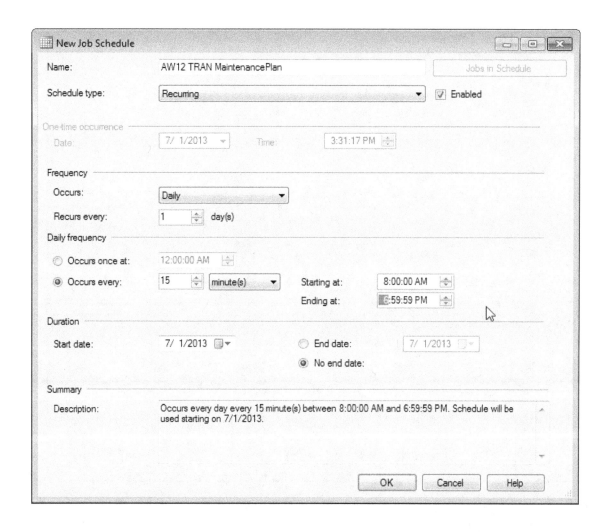

Schedule Information at Bottom

Task Selection Page

Typically Full backup is the slowest and Transaction Log backup is the fastest.

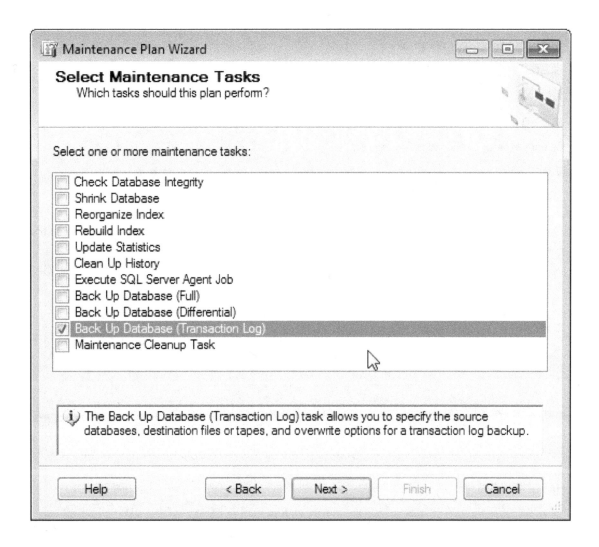

Tasks Reordering Page

Configuring the Log Backup

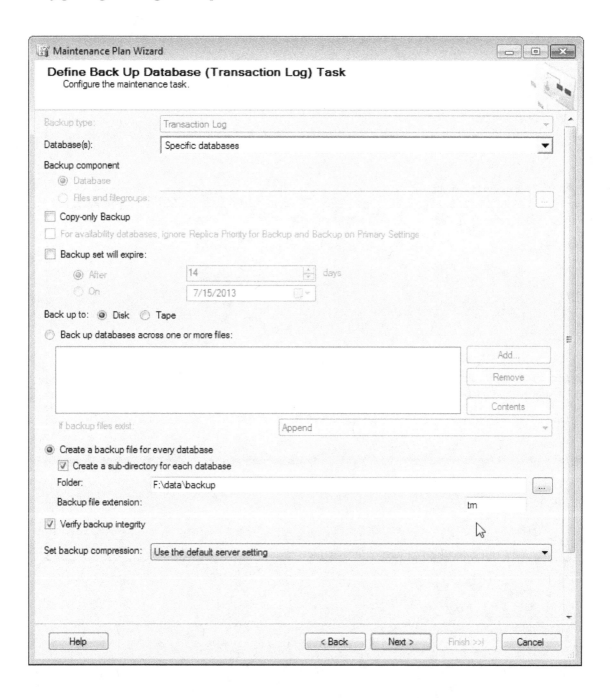

Report Options Setup

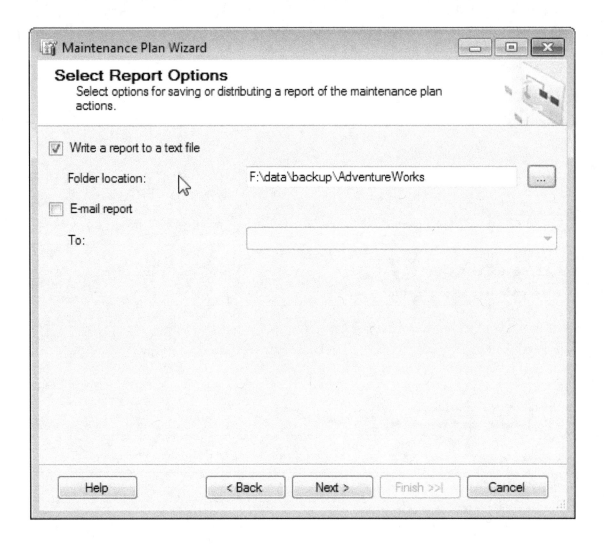

Maintenance Summary

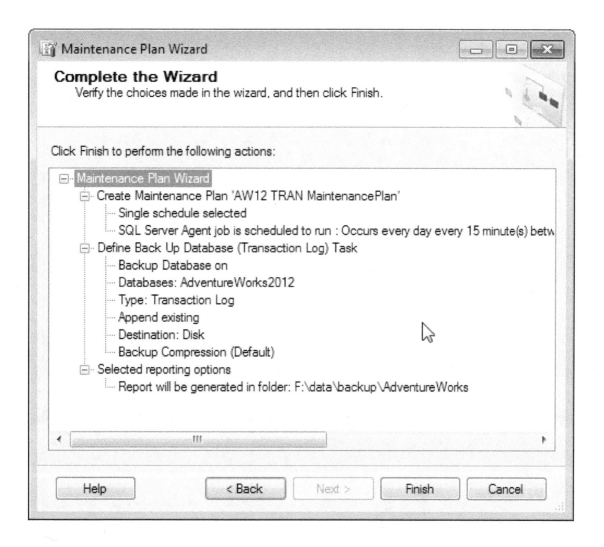

Plan Creation Page

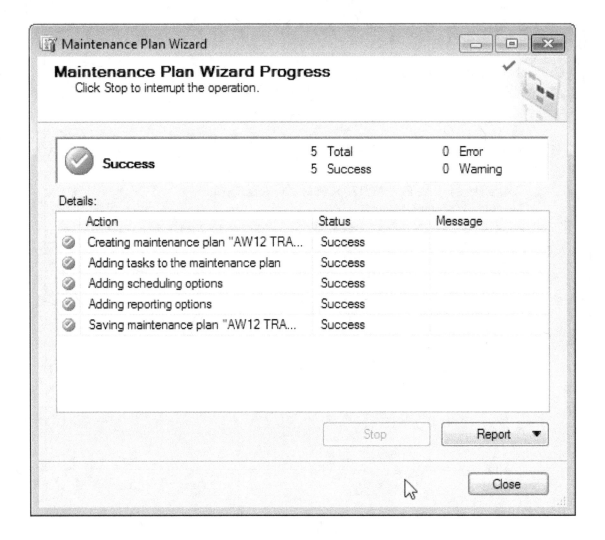

Checking Maintenance Plan Setup

SQL Server Agent Jobs

The Wizard creates one or more SQL Server Agent jobs to carry out the defined maintenance tasks.

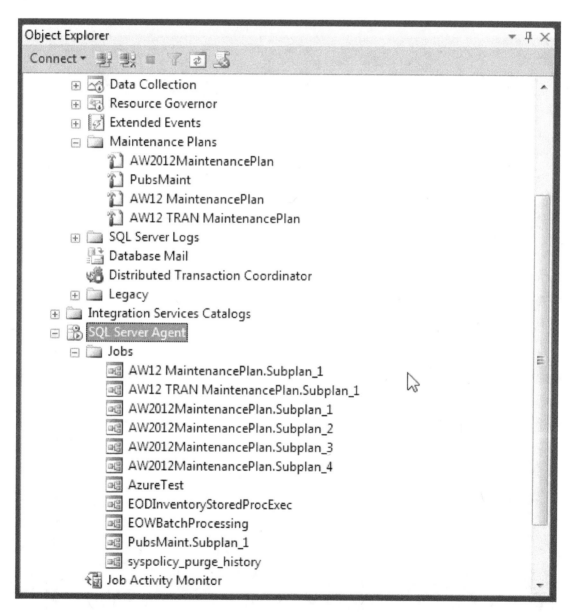

Maintenance Plan Modify Option

Right click drop-down menu on maintenance Plan. Modify can be used to inspect the plan and make changes.

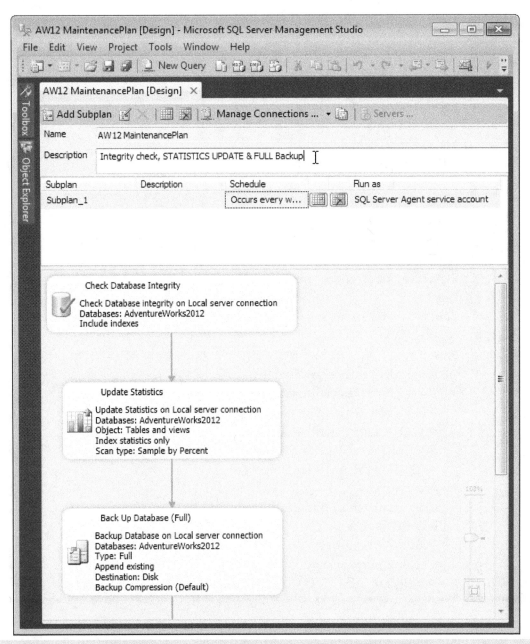

Editing STATISTICS UPDATE

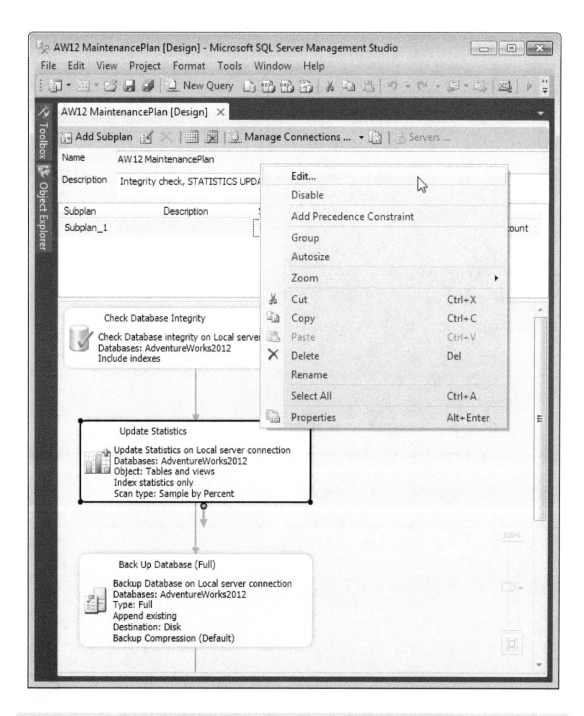

STATISTICS UPDATE Sampling Rate Change

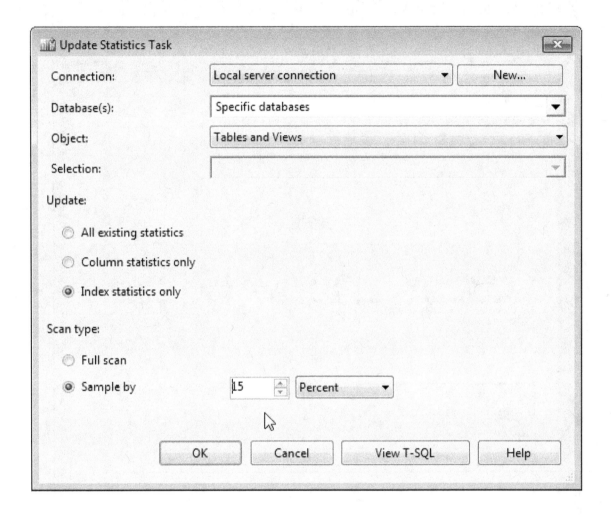

View T-SQL Window

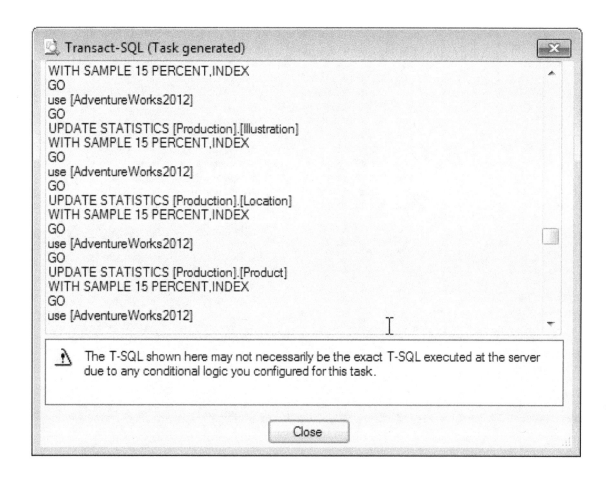

Viewing Maintenance Plan History

Right-click on plan menu has history tab option.

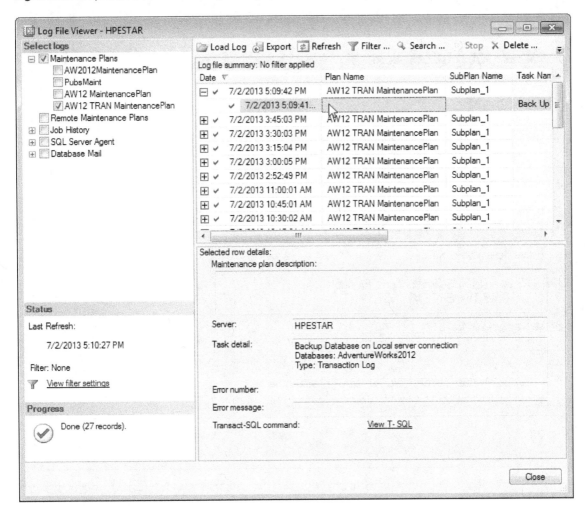

Executed T-SQL

```
EXECUTE master.dbo.xp_create_subdir N''F:\data\backup\AdventureWorks2012''
GO
BACKUP LOG [AdventureWorks2012] TO  DISK =
N''F:\data\backup\AdventureWorks2012\AdventureWorks2012_backup_2013_07_02_170941_8844407.trn'' WITH NOFORMAT, NOINIT,  NAME =
N''AdventureWorks2012_backup_2013_07_02_170941_8844407'', SKIP, REWIND, NOUNLOAD,  STATS = 10
GO
declare @backupSetId as int
select @backupSetId = position from msdb..backupset where database_name=N''AdventureWorks2012'' and backup_set_id=(select
max(backup_set_id) from msdb..backupset where database_name=N''AdventureWorks2012'' )
if @backupSetId is null begin raiserror(N''Verify failed. Backup information for database ''''AdventureWorks2012'''' not found.'', 16, 1) end
RESTORE VERIFYONLY FROM  DISK = N''F:\data\backup\AdventureWorks2012\AdventureWorks2012_backup_2013_07_02_170941_8844407.trn''
WITH FILE = @backupSetId, NOUNLOAD, NOREWIND
```

CHAPTER 20: Preparation for Disaster & Recovery

Disaster Recovery Scenario

Full backup is taken nightly. Transaction log backups during normal working hours every 15 minutes. Disaster strike. Management asks the DBA to restore the database on the same (if fixed) or different server. Restore database screen with automatic sequencing of available database backups. Verify backup media is suggested provided there is time.

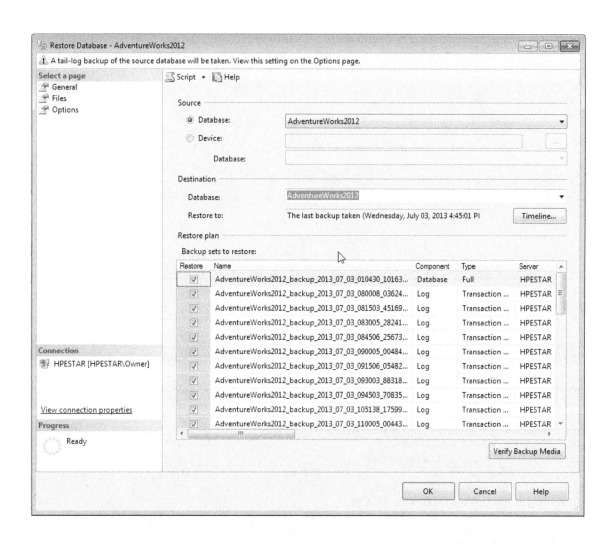

Timeline Display

We can restore to 4:45PM or any point-in-time before that. Management is consulted. The decision is 4:45PM (all transaction logs restored).

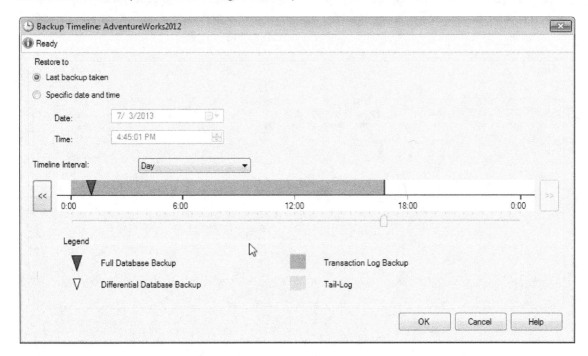

Generated Script

```
USE [master]
RESTORE DATABASE [AdventureWorks2012] FROM  DISK =
N'F:\data\backup\AdventureWorks2012\AdventureWorks2012_backup_2013_07_03_010430_1016340.bak' WITH
FILE = 1,  NORECOVERY,  NOUNLOAD,  REPLACE,  STATS = 5
RESTORE LOG [AdventureWorks2012] FROM  DISK =
N'F:\data\backup\AdventureWorks2012\AdventureWorks2012_backup_2013_07_03_080008_0362434.trn' WITH
FILE = 1,  NORECOVERY,  NOUNLOAD,  STATS = 5
RESTORE LOG [AdventureWorks2012] FROM  DISK =
N'F:\data\backup\AdventureWorks2012\AdventureWorks2012_backup_2013_07_03_081503_4516973.trn' WITH
FILE = 1,  NORECOVERY,  NOUNLOAD,  STATS = 5
RESTORE LOG [AdventureWorks2012] FROM  DISK =
N'F:\data\backup\AdventureWorks2012\AdventureWorks2012_backup_2013_07_03_083005_2824105.trn' WITH
FILE = 1,  NORECOVERY,  NOUNLOAD,  STATS = 5
RESTORE LOG [AdventureWorks2012] FROM  DISK =
N'F:\data\backup\AdventureWorks2012\AdventureWorks2012_backup_2013_07_03_084506_2567387.trn' WITH
FILE = 1,  NORECOVERY,  NOUNLOAD,  STATS = 5
RESTORE LOG [AdventureWorks2012] FROM  DISK =
N'F:\data\backup\AdventureWorks2012\AdventureWorks2012_backup_2013_07_03_090005_0048497.trn' WITH
FILE = 1,  NORECOVERY,  NOUNLOAD,  STATS = 5
```

```
RESTORE LOG [AdventureWorks2012] FROM  DISK =
N'F:\data\backup\AdventureWorks2012\AdventureWorks2012_backup_2013_07_03_091506_0548209.trn' WITH
FILE = 1, NORECOVERY, NOUNLOAD, STATS = 5
RESTORE LOG [AdventureWorks2012] FROM  DISK =
N'F:\data\backup\AdventureWorks2012\AdventureWorks2012_backup_2013_07_03_093003_8831864.trn' WITH
FILE = 1, NORECOVERY, NOUNLOAD, STATS = 5
RESTORE LOG [AdventureWorks2012] FROM  DISK =
N'F:\data\backup\AdventureWorks2012\AdventureWorks2012_backup_2013_07_03_094503_7083553.trn' WITH
FILE = 1, NORECOVERY, NOUNLOAD, STATS = 5
RESTORE LOG [AdventureWorks2012] FROM  DISK =
N'F:\data\backup\AdventureWorks2012\AdventureWorks2012_backup_2013_07_03_105138_1759985.trn' WITH
FILE = 1, NORECOVERY, NOUNLOAD, STATS = 5
RESTORE LOG [AdventureWorks2012] FROM  DISK =
N'F:\data\backup\AdventureWorks2012\AdventureWorks2012_backup_2013_07_03_110005_0044381.trn' WITH
FILE = 1, NORECOVERY, NOUNLOAD, STATS = 5
RESTORE LOG [AdventureWorks2012] FROM  DISK =
N'F:\data\backup\AdventureWorks2012\AdventureWorks2012_backup_2013_07_03_111504_9269151.trn' WITH
FILE = 1, NORECOVERY, NOUNLOAD, STATS = 5
RESTORE LOG [AdventureWorks2012] FROM  DISK =
N'F:\data\backup\AdventureWorks2012\AdventureWorks2012_backup_2013_07_03_113001_0227221.trn' WITH
FILE = 1, NORECOVERY, NOUNLOAD, STATS = 5
RESTORE LOG [AdventureWorks2012] FROM  DISK =
N'F:\data\backup\AdventureWorks2012\AdventureWorks2012_backup_2013_07_03_114501_4261866.trn' WITH
FILE = 1, NORECOVERY, NOUNLOAD, STATS = 5
RESTORE LOG [AdventureWorks2012] FROM  DISK =
N'F:\data\backup\AdventureWorks2012\AdventureWorks2012_backup_2013_07_03_120001_7813566.trn' WITH
FILE = 1, NORECOVERY, NOUNLOAD, STATS = 5
RESTORE LOG [AdventureWorks2012] FROM  DISK =
N'F:\data\backup\AdventureWorks2012\AdventureWorks2012_backup_2013_07_03_121501_3078443.trn' WITH
FILE = 1, NORECOVERY, NOUNLOAD, STATS = 5
RESTORE LOG [AdventureWorks2012] FROM  DISK =
N'F:\data\backup\AdventureWorks2012\AdventureWorks2012_backup_2013_07_03_123001_7570143.trn' WITH
FILE = 1, NORECOVERY, NOUNLOAD, STATS = 5
RESTORE LOG [AdventureWorks2012] FROM  DISK =
N'F:\data\backup\AdventureWorks2012\AdventureWorks2012_backup_2013_07_03_124501_7674855.trn' WITH
FILE = 1, NORECOVERY, NOUNLOAD, STATS = 5
RESTORE LOG [AdventureWorks2012] FROM  DISK =
N'F:\data\backup\AdventureWorks2012\AdventureWorks2012_backup_2013_07_03_130001_5884033.trn' WITH
FILE = 1, NORECOVERY, NOUNLOAD, STATS = 5
RESTORE LOG [AdventureWorks2012] FROM  DISK =
N'F:\data\backup\AdventureWorks2012\AdventureWorks2012_backup_2013_07_03_131501_1663276.trn' WITH
FILE = 1, NORECOVERY, NOUNLOAD, STATS = 5
RESTORE LOG [AdventureWorks2012] FROM  DISK =
N'F:\data\backup\AdventureWorks2012\AdventureWorks2012_backup_2013_07_03_133001_6707181.trn' WITH
FILE = 1, NORECOVERY, NOUNLOAD, STATS = 5
RESTORE LOG [AdventureWorks2012] FROM  DISK =
N'F:\data\backup\AdventureWorks2012\AdventureWorks2012_backup_2013_07_03_134501_2881502.trn' WITH
FILE = 1, NORECOVERY, NOUNLOAD, STATS = 5
RESTORE LOG [AdventureWorks2012] FROM  DISK =
N'F:\data\backup\AdventureWorks2012\AdventureWorks2012_backup_2013_07_03_140002_4273867.trn' WITH
FILE = 1, NORECOVERY, NOUNLOAD, STATS = 5
```

CHAPTER 20: Preparation for Disaster & Recovery

RESTORE LOG [AdventureWorks2012] FROM DISK =
N'F:\data\backup\AdventureWorks2012\AdventureWorks2012_backup_2013_07_03_141501_2762267.trn' WITH
FILE = 1, NORECOVERY, NOUNLOAD, STATS = 5
RESTORE LOG [AdventureWorks2012] FROM DISK =
N'F:\data\backup\AdventureWorks2012\AdventureWorks2012_backup_2013_07_03_143001_4646465.trn' WITH
FILE = 1, NORECOVERY, NOUNLOAD, STATS = 5
RESTORE LOG [AdventureWorks2012] FROM DISK =
N'F:\data\backup\AdventureWorks2012\AdventureWorks2012_backup_2013_07_03_144501_5692649.trn' WITH
FILE = 1, NORECOVERY, NOUNLOAD, STATS = 5
RESTORE LOG [AdventureWorks2012] FROM DISK =
N'F:\data\backup\AdventureWorks2012\AdventureWorks2012_backup_2013_07_03_150001_9046819.trn' WITH
FILE = 1, NORECOVERY, NOUNLOAD, STATS = 5
RESTORE LOG [AdventureWorks2012] FROM DISK =
N'F:\data\backup\AdventureWorks2012\AdventureWorks2012_backup_2013_07_03_151501_7106769.trn' WITH
FILE = 1, NORECOVERY, NOUNLOAD, STATS = 5
RESTORE LOG [AdventureWorks2012] FROM DISK =
N'F:\data\backup\AdventureWorks2012\AdventureWorks2012_backup_2013_07_03_153001_9379526.trn' WITH
FILE = 1, NORECOVERY, NOUNLOAD, STATS = 5
RESTORE LOG [AdventureWorks2012] FROM DISK =
N'F:\data\backup\AdventureWorks2012\AdventureWorks2012_backup_2013_07_03_154501_2810547.trn' WITH
FILE = 1, NORECOVERY, NOUNLOAD, STATS = 5
RESTORE LOG [AdventureWorks2012] FROM DISK =
N'F:\data\backup\AdventureWorks2012\AdventureWorks2012_backup_2013_07_03_160001_1641873.trn' WITH
FILE = 1, NORECOVERY, NOUNLOAD, STATS = 5
RESTORE LOG [AdventureWorks2012] FROM DISK =
N'F:\data\backup\AdventureWorks2012\AdventureWorks2012_backup_2013_07_03_161501_0215463.trn' WITH
FILE = 1, NORECOVERY, NOUNLOAD, STATS = 5
RESTORE LOG [AdventureWorks2012] FROM DISK =
N'F:\data\backup\AdventureWorks2012\AdventureWorks2012_backup_2013_07_03_163000_9831157.trn' WITH
FILE = 1, NORECOVERY, NOUNLOAD, STATS = 5
RESTORE LOG [AdventureWorks2012] FROM DISK =
N'F:\data\backup\AdventureWorks2012\AdventureWorks2012_backup_2013_07_03_164501_5903090.trn' WITH
FILE = 1, NOUNLOAD, STATS = 5

Restore database took 4 minutes

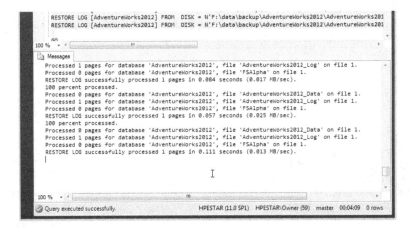

Scripting Data from Database for Safe-keeping

Not only objects but also table contents can be scripted provided the table is modest size. Launch the Script Wizard and choose the Production .Product table. Related 3rd party tools: **redgates SQL Compare & SQL Data Compare**.

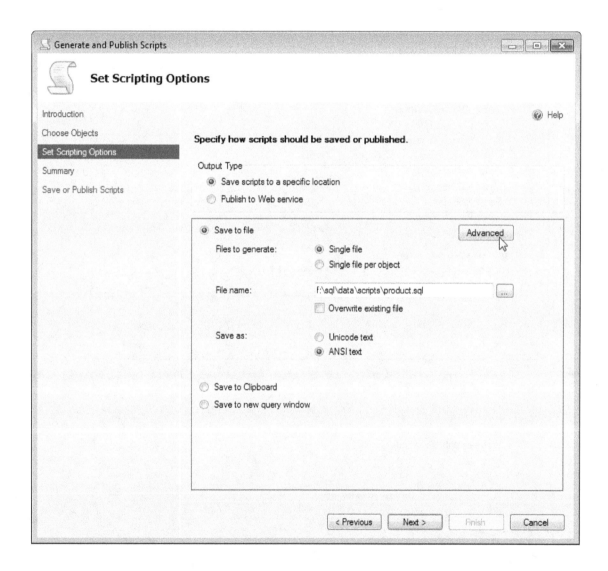

Choose Data Only on the Advanced Screen

Generated INSERT Script

Partial results.

```
USE [AdventureWorks2012]
GO
SET IDENTITY_INSERT [Production].[Product] ON

INSERT [Production].[Product] ([ProductID], [Name], [ProductNumber], [MakeFlag],
[FinishedGoodsFlag], [Color], [SafetyStockLevel], [ReorderPoint], [StandardCost], [ListPrice],
[Size], [SizeUnitMeasureCode], [WeightUnitMeasureCode], [Weight], [DaysToManufacture],
[ProductLine], [Class], [Style], [ProductSubcategoryID], [ProductModelID], [SellStartDate],
[SellEndDate], [DiscontinuedDate], [rowguid], [ModifiedDate]) VALUES (1, N'Adjustable Race',
N'AR-5381', 0, 0, NULL, 1000, 750, 0.0000, 0.0000, NULL, NULL, NULL, NULL, 0, NULL, NULL,
NULL, NULL, NULL, CAST(0x0000921E00000000 AS DateTime), NULL, NULL, N'694215b7-08f7-
4c0d-acb1-d734ba44c0c8', CAST(0x00009A5C00A53CF8 AS DateTime))
INSERT [Production].[Product] ([ProductID], [Name], [ProductNumber], [MakeFlag],
[FinishedGoodsFlag], [Color], [SafetyStockLevel], [ReorderPoint], [StandardCost], [ListPrice],
[Size], [SizeUnitMeasureCode], [WeightUnitMeasureCode], [Weight], [DaysToManufacture],
[ProductLine], [Class], [Style], [ProductSubcategoryID], [ProductModelID], [SellStartDate],
[SellEndDate], [DiscontinuedDate], [rowguid], [ModifiedDate]) VALUES (2, N'Bearing Ball', N'BA-
8327', 0, 0, NULL, 1000, 750, 0.0000, 0.0000, NULL, NULL, NULL, NULL, 0, NULL, NULL, NULL,
NULL, NULL, CAST(0x0000921E00000000 AS DateTime), NULL, NULL, N'58ae3c20-4f3a-4749-
a7d4-d568806cc537', CAST(0x00009A5C00A53CF8 AS DateTime))
INSERT [Production].[Product] ([ProductID], [Name], [ProductNumber], [MakeFlag],
[FinishedGoodsFlag], [Color], [SafetyStockLevel], [ReorderPoint], [StandardCost], [ListPrice],
[Size], [SizeUnitMeasureCode], [WeightUnitMeasureCode], [Weight], [DaysToManufacture],
[ProductLine], [Class], [Style], [ProductSubcategoryID], [ProductModelID], [SellStartDate],
[SellEndDate], [DiscontinuedDate], [rowguid], [ModifiedDate]) VALUES (3, N'BB Ball Bearing',
N'BE-2349', 1, 0, NULL, 800, 600, 0.0000, 0.0000, NULL, NULL, NULL, NULL, 1, NULL, NULL, NULL,
NULL, NULL, CAST(0x0000921E00000000 AS DateTime), NULL, NULL, N'9c21aed2-5bfa-4f18-
bcb8-f11638dc2e4e', CAST(0x00009A5C00A53CF8 AS DateTime))
INSERT [Production].[Product] ([ProductID], [Name], [ProductNumber], [MakeFlag],
[FinishedGoodsFlag], [Color], [SafetyStockLevel], [ReorderPoint], [StandardCost], [ListPrice],
[Size], [SizeUnitMeasureCode], [WeightUnitMeasureCode], [Weight], [DaysToManufacture],
[ProductLine], [Class], [Style], [ProductSubcategoryID], [ProductModelID], [SellStartDate],
[SellEndDate], [DiscontinuedDate], [rowguid], [ModifiedDate]) VALUES (4, N'Headset Ball
Bearings', N'BE-2908', 0, 0, NULL, 800, 600, 0.0000, 0.0000, NULL, NULL, NULL, NULL, 0, NULL,
NULL, NULL, NULL, NULL, CAST(0x0000921E00000000 AS DateTime), NULL, NULL, N'ecfed6cb-
51ff-49b5-b06c-7d8ac834db8b', CAST(0x00009A5C00A53CF8 AS DateTime))
INSERT [Production].[Product] ([ProductID], [Name], [ProductNumber], [MakeFlag],
[FinishedGoodsFlag], [Color], [SafetyStockLevel], [ReorderPoint], [StandardCost], [ListPrice],
[Size], [SizeUnitMeasureCode], [WeightUnitMeasureCode], [Weight], [DaysToManufacture],
```

Populating Table from Data Script

First a table has to be created.

```
SELECT TOP (0) * INTO CopyOfProduct FROM Production.Product;
```

Second step is replace all table name to CopyOfProduct. Third, execute the script.

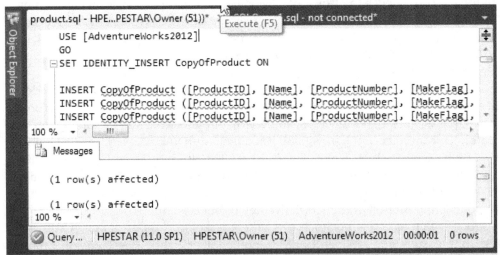

CHAPTER 21: Monitoring, Troubleshooting & Maintenance

Monitoring Tools

There are a number of ways to monitor the functioning and performance of SQL Server and the databases:

- ➢ Activity Monitor
- ➢ Server Standard Reports
- ➢ Database Standard Reports
- ➢ Peformance DMV/DMF Queries
- ➢ SQL Server Profiler
- ➢ Server-side Tracing
- ➢ Perfmon Counters

MSDN Article: **Monitoring SQL Server Performance** http://bit.ly/12k4MGl
http://msdn.microsoft.com/en-us/library/ee377023(v=bts.10).aspx

SQL Server Profiler

Profiler tracing is a GUI fun way of monitoring SQL Server. Nonetheless the "boring" programmatic Server-side Tracing is the more efficient way of tracing.

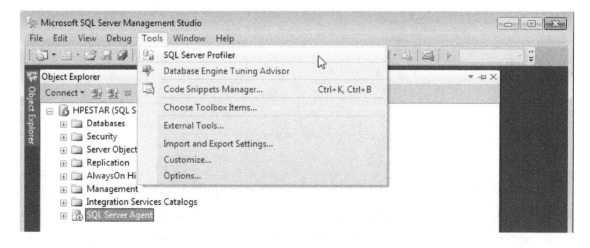

Profiler Connection to the Database Engine

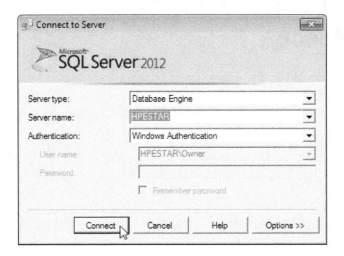

Template Selection

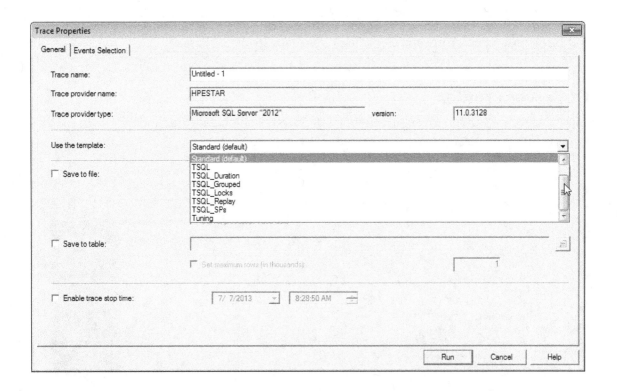

Trace Events Selection

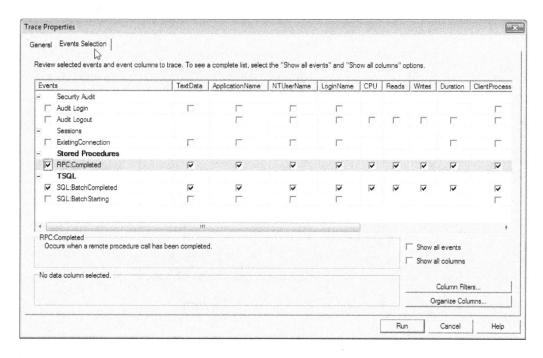

Defining Column Filter to Parse Text for Search Term

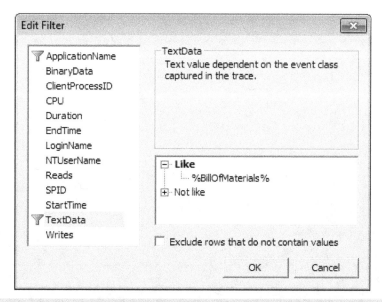

Organize Columns Dialog Box

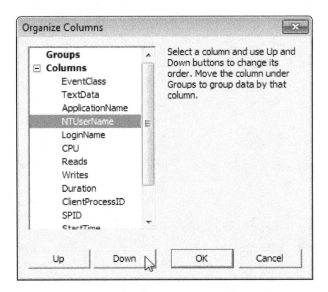

Show All Events Makes All Events Available for Selection

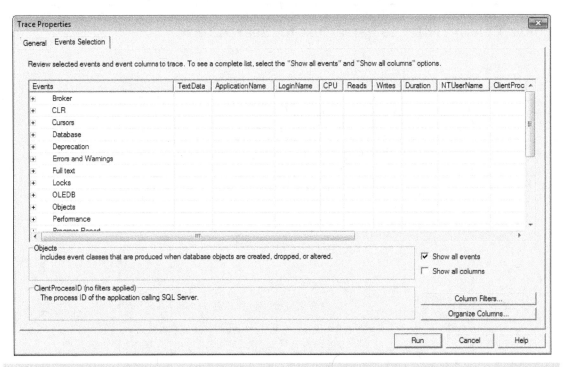

Show All Columns Makes Additional Columns Available for Selection

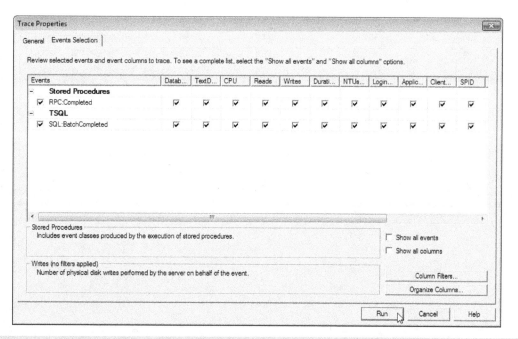

Starting the Trace

Generating Database Activity in Query Editor

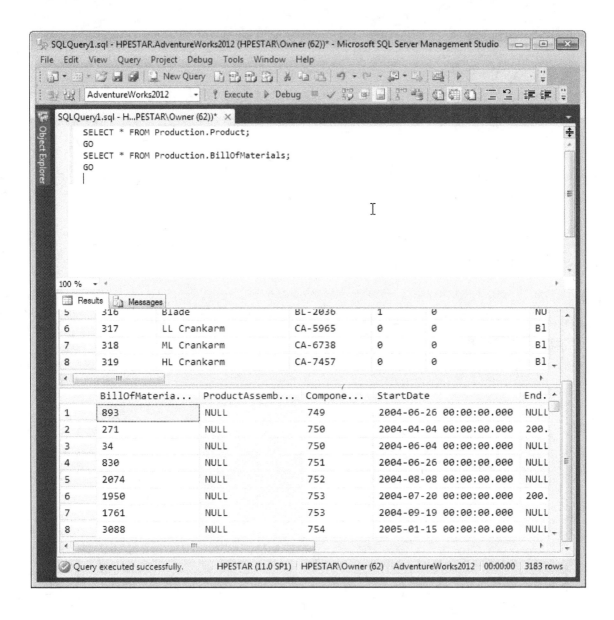

Viewing Profiler Live Trace Display

The Production.Product query is not in the trace due to the column filter. The RPC:Completed trace is system generated, considered "noise" for our purposes.

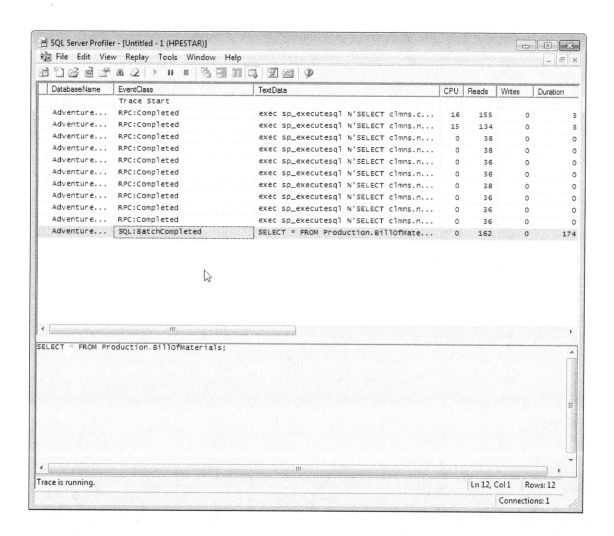

Changing Trace Properties

Trace can also be stopped or paused on the same drop-down menu.

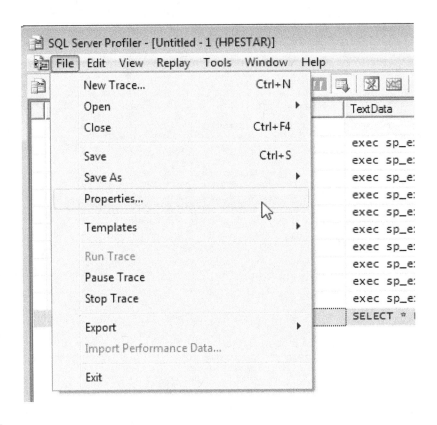

Adding Additional Column Filter

We need to filter out IntelliSense generated traffic.

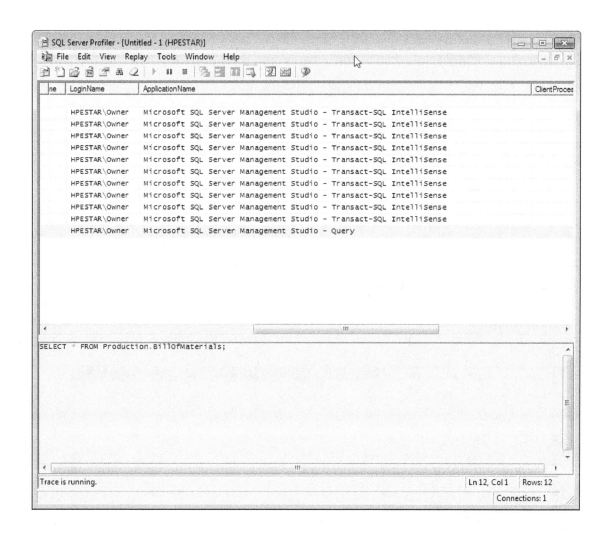

Trace Should Be Stopped Prior to Changing Properties

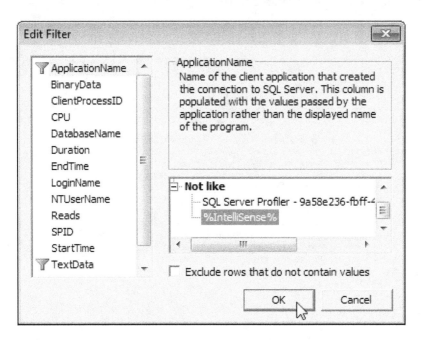

Retesting Scripts

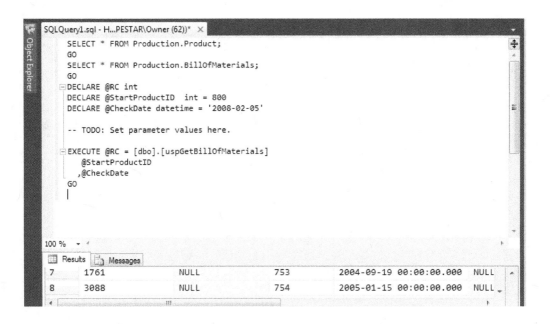

Viewing the Updated Profiler Trace Live

Saving Trace as Template

For future reuse we can save the trace as a template.

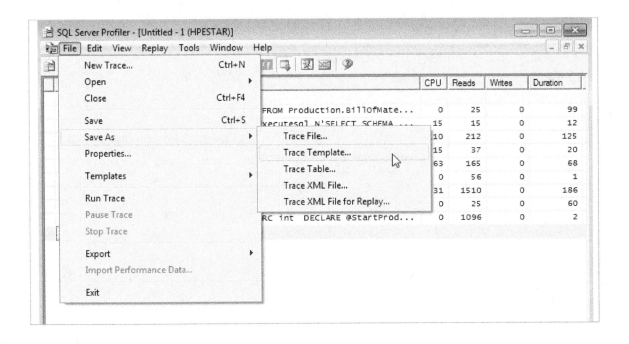

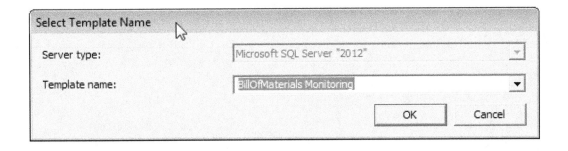

Generating Trace Script

For programmatic control and safe-keeping, GUI setup trace can be scripted.

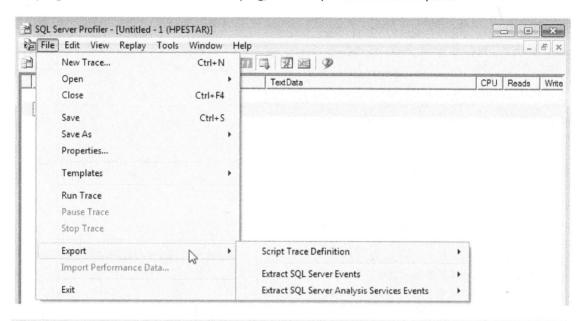

```
/****************************************************/
/* Created by: SQL Server 2012  Profiler      *//* Date: 07/07/2018 01:05:15 PM      */
/****************************************************/
-- Create a Queue
declare @rc int
declare @TraceID int
declare @maxfilesize bigint
set @maxfilesize = 5
-- Please replace the text InsertFileNameHere, with an appropriate
-- filename prefixed by a path, e.g., c:\MyFolder\MyTrace. The .trc extension
-- will be appended to the filename automatically. If you are writing from
-- remote server to local drive, please use UNC path and make sure server has
-- write access to your network share
exec @rc = sp_trace_create @TraceID output, 0, N'InsertFileNameHere', @maxfilesize, NULL
if (@rc != 0) goto error
-- Client side File and Table cannot be scripted   -   Set the events
declare @on bit
set @on = 1
exec sp_trace_setevent @TraceID, 10, 1, @on
exec sp_trace_setevent @TraceID, 10, 9, @on
exec sp_trace_setevent @TraceID, 10, 2, @on
```

```
exec sp_trace_setevent @TraceID, 10, 10, @on
exec sp_trace_setevent @TraceID, 10, 6, @on
exec sp_trace_setevent @TraceID, 10, 11, @on
exec sp_trace_setevent @TraceID, 10, 12, @on
exec sp_trace_setevent @TraceID, 10, 13, @on
exec sp_trace_setevent @TraceID, 10, 14, @on
exec sp_trace_setevent @TraceID, 10, 15, @on
exec sp_trace_setevent @TraceID, 10, 16, @on
exec sp_trace_setevent @TraceID, 10, 17, @on
exec sp_trace_setevent @TraceID, 10, 18, @on
exec sp_trace_setevent @TraceID, 10, 35, @on
exec sp_trace_setevent @TraceID, 12, 1, @on
exec sp_trace_setevent @TraceID, 12, 9, @on
exec sp_trace_setevent @TraceID, 12, 11, @on
exec sp_trace_setevent @TraceID, 12, 6, @on
exec sp_trace_setevent @TraceID, 12, 10, @on
exec sp_trace_setevent @TraceID, 12, 12, @on
exec sp_trace_setevent @TraceID, 12, 13, @on
exec sp_trace_setevent @TraceID, 12, 14, @on
exec sp_trace_setevent @TraceID, 12, 15, @on
exec sp_trace_setevent @TraceID, 12, 16, @on
exec sp_trace_setevent @TraceID, 12, 17, @on
exec sp_trace_setevent @TraceID, 12, 18, @on
exec sp_trace_setevent @TraceID, 12, 35, @on
-- Set the Filters
declare @intfilter int
declare @bigintfilter bigint
exec sp_trace_setfilter @TraceID, 1, 0, 6, N'%BillOfMaterials%'
exec sp_trace_setfilter @TraceID, 10, 0, 7, N'SQL Server Profiler - 9a58e236-fbff-43f5-908b-
af90cbbcf128'
exec sp_trace_setfilter @TraceID, 10, 0, 7, N'%IntelliSense%'
exec sp_trace_setfilter @TraceID, 10, 0, 7, N'SQL Server Profiler - cbb24c4e-dde4-4058-a5be-
e904aa5d1b61'
-- Set the trace status to start
exec sp_trace_setstatus @TraceID, 1
-- display trace id for future references
select TraceID=@TraceID
goto finish
error:
select ErrorCode=@rc
finish:
go
```

Saving Profiler Trace to Table or File

Trace can be saved to a table or a file. For high-volume db tracing, file is recommended.

System Generated Trace Without Filters

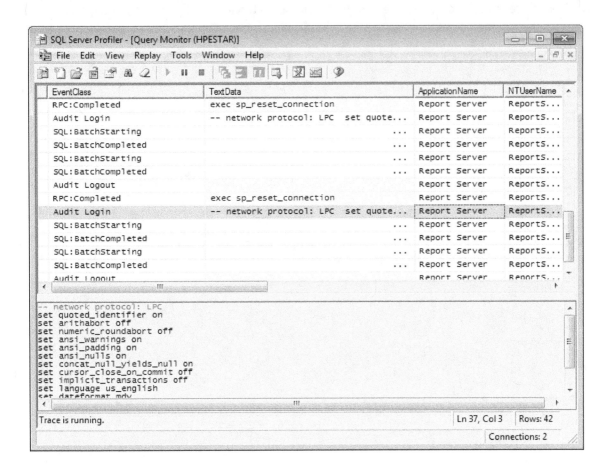

Analyzing Saved Trace

Trace can be analyzed just like data in other table. If the trace is a file, the fn_trace_gettable system function returns it as a virtual table.

> MSDN Article: **View and Analyze Traces with SQL Server Profiler**   http://bit.ly/eIavq
> http://msdn.microsoft.com/en-us/library/ms175848.aspx

The Reads column is very important since "reads" reduction is the typical goal of query optimization.   Duration is shown in milliseconds or microseconds based on options setting. Duration includes blocking as well hence it can be a misleading performance metrics.

Analyzing Trace Table Data in Query Editor

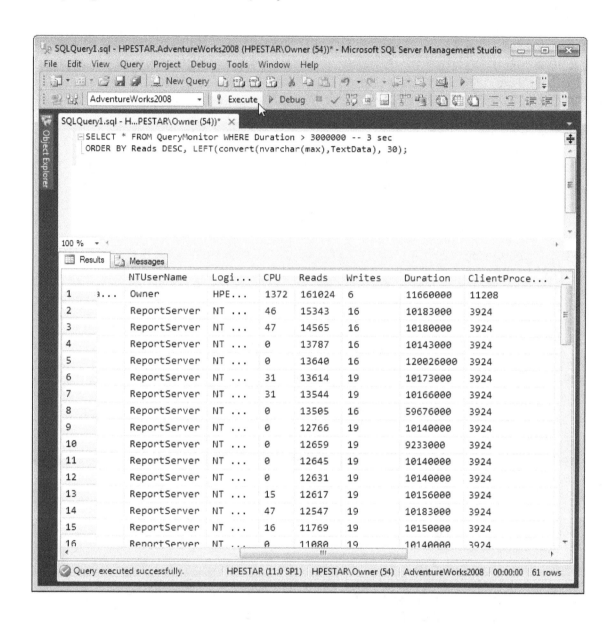

SQL Server Default Trace

The default trace keeps track of significant meta data events such CREATE TABLE.

```
EXEC sp_configure 'default trace enabled'                    -- run value 1:   default trace enabled
/* Enable default trace script
EXEC sp_configure 'default trace enabled', 1
RECONFIGURE
GO   */
-- Trace file information
SELECT * FROM  sys.traces
GO
-- C:\Program Files\Microsoft SQL Server\MSSQL11.MSSQLSERVER\MSSQL\Log\log_109.trc
 -- Current default trace rollover file
DECLARE @Path varchar(256) = (SELECT CONVERT(varchar(256), VALUE)
  FROM  ::fn_trace_getinfo(0)
  WHERE  property = 2);
SELECT @Path
-- C:\Program Files\Microsoft SQL Server\MSSQL11.MSSQLSERVER\MSSQL\Log\log_109.trc
-- Query the default trace rollover file for altered objects
SELECT loginname   AS LoginName,
    loginsid,
    spid,
    hostname    AS HostName,
    applicationname,
    servername   AS ServerName,
    databasename AS DatabaseName,
    objectName,
    e.category_id,
    cat.name    AS CategoryName,
    textdata,
    starttime,
    e.name     AS EventName
FROM  ::fn_trace_gettable(@Path, 0)
    INNER JOIN sys.trace_events e
        ON eventclass = trace_event_id
    INNER JOIN sys.trace_categories AS cat
        ON e.category_id = cat.category_id
WHERE  databasename = 'AdventureWorks2012'
    AND objectname IS NULL
    -- AND e.name = 'Object:Altered'
```

For additional analysis the virtual table can be saved with SELECT....INTO as a permanent table.

CHAPTER 21: Monitoring, Troubleshooting & Maintenance

Reviewing & Replaying Saved Traces

Saved traces (table or file) can be loaded into Profiler and reviewed. Replay trace is also possible but certain rules must be followed.

> MSDN Article: **Replay a Trace File (SQL Server Profiler)** http://bit.ly/1aZiUy1
> http://msdn.microsoft.com/en-us/library/ms189604.aspx

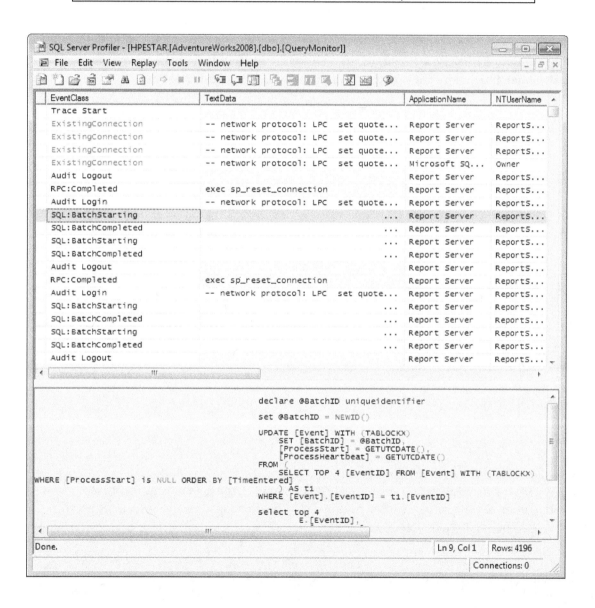

Server-Side Tracing

Server-side tracing (programmatic) saving to the server disk is suggested for production databases. The following is true for server-side tracing as well. A server-side trace can be designed in Profiler and scripted upon completion.

Quote: "Use SQL Server Profiler to monitor only the events in which you are interested. If traces are becoming too large, you can filter them based on the information you want, so that only a subset of the event data is collected. **Monitoring too many events adds overhead to the server and the monitoring process, and can cause the trace file or trace table to grow very large, especially when the monitoring process takes place over a long period of time.**"

> MSDN Article: **SQL Server Profiler Templates and Permissions**   http://bit.ly/9A6JZ
> http://msdn.microsoft.com/en-us/library/ms187929.aspx

Read a trace file with SELECT. Use SELECT... INTO to make it into a table.

```
SELECT *
FROM fn_trace_gettable('D:\data\tracelog\YourTraceFile.trc', default)
```

> MSDN Article: **Server-Side Tracing and Collection**   http://bit.ly/ibh6QA
> http://technet.microsoft.com/en-us/library/cc293613.aspx

```
/* Start of the batch */

declare @ReturnCode int
declare @TraceID int
declare @maxfilesize bigint
set @maxfilesize = 5

/* Replace the text InsertFileNameHere, with an appropriate  filename prefixed by a path, e.g.,
c:\MyFolder\MyTrace. The .trc extension will be appended to the filename automatically. If you
are writing from  remote server to local drive,  use UNC path and make sure server has  write
access to your network share.  */


exec @ReturnCode = sp_trace_create @TraceID output, 0, N'InsertFileNameHere',
@maxfilesize, NULL
if (@ReturnCode != 0) goto error
```

CHAPTER 21: Monitoring, Troubleshooting & Maintenance

/* Set the trace events. */

```
declare @on bit
set @on = 1
exec sp_trace_setevent @TraceID, 10, 15, @on
exec sp_trace_setevent @TraceID, 10, 16, @on
exec sp_trace_setevent @TraceID, 10, 1, @on
exec sp_trace_setevent @TraceID, 10, 9, @on
exec sp_trace_setevent @TraceID, 10, 17, @on
exec sp_trace_setevent @TraceID, 10, 2, @on
exec sp_trace_setevent @TraceID, 10, 10, @on
exec sp_trace_setevent @TraceID, 10, 18, @on
exec sp_trace_setevent @TraceID, 10, 11, @on
exec sp_trace_setevent @TraceID, 10, 12, @on
exec sp_trace_setevent @TraceID, 10, 13, @on

exec sp_trace_setevent @TraceID, 10, 6, @on
exec sp_trace_setevent @TraceID, 10, 14, @on
exec sp_trace_setevent @TraceID, 12, 15, @on
exec sp_trace_setevent @TraceID, 12, 16, @on
exec sp_trace_setevent @TraceID, 12, 1, @on
exec sp_trace_setevent @TraceID, 12, 9, @on
exec sp_trace_setevent @TraceID, 12, 17, @on
exec sp_trace_setevent @TraceID, 12, 6, @on
exec sp_trace_setevent @TraceID, 12, 10, @on
exec sp_trace_setevent @TraceID, 12, 14, @on
exec sp_trace_setevent @TraceID, 12, 18, @on
exec sp_trace_setevent @TraceID, 12, 11, @on
exec sp_trace_setevent @TraceID, 12, 12, @on
exec sp_trace_setevent @TraceID, 12, 13, @on
```

/* Set the column filters for the trace. */

```
declare @intfilter int
declare @bigintfilter bigint
exec sp_trace_setfilter @TraceID, 10, 0, 7, N'SQL Server Profiler - c7150cea-7535-41df-a3ba-
e5c12616a80f'
set @bigintfilter = 3000000
exec sp_trace_setfilter @TraceID, 13, 0, 4, @bigintfilter
```

CHAPTER 21: Monitoring, Troubleshooting & Maintenance

```
/* Set the trace status to start.  */
exec sp_trace_setstatus @TraceID, 1
goto finish
error:
select ErrorCode=@ReturnCode
finish:
go
```

Test if Profiler Trace is Running

A DMV query can be applied.

SELECT * FROM sys.dm_exec_sessions WHERE program_name LIKE 'SQL Server Profiler%' ;

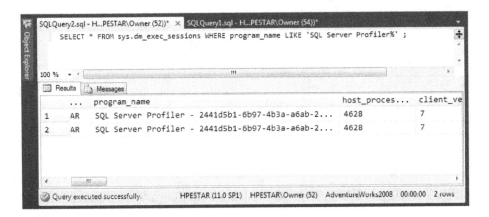

Test if Server-Side Trace is Running

An fn_trace_getinfo system function query can be used. If property 5 is 1 then running.

SELECT * from ::fn_trace_getinfo(default);

CHAPTER 21: Monitoring, Troubleshooting & Maintenance

Windows Performance Monitor

Perfmon can be launched from the Tools menu of SQL Server Profiler.

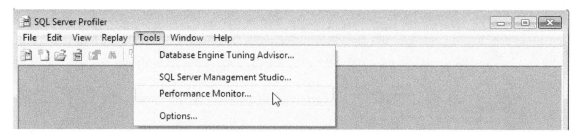

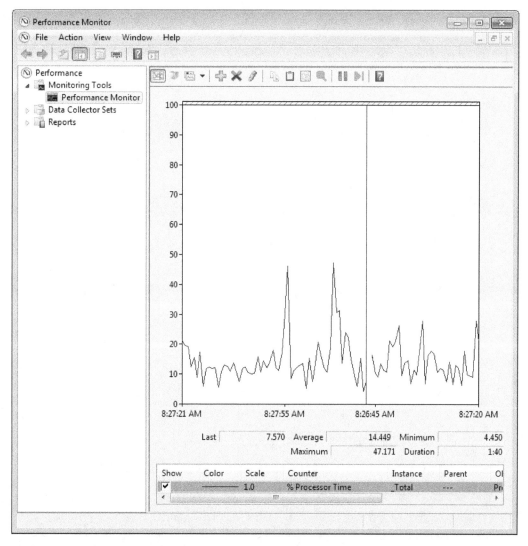

Adding a New Counter for Tracing

In addition to Windows performance counters, Perfmon has specific SQL Server related counters.

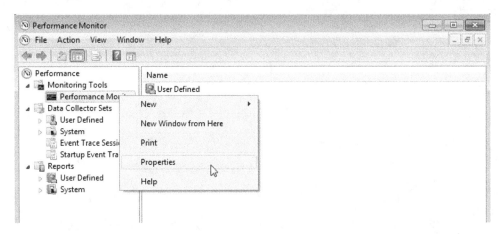

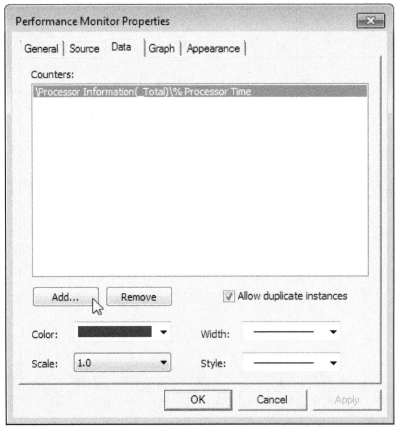

Add Physical Disk Counters

Typically each group has a number of counters. Remove ones which of no interest.

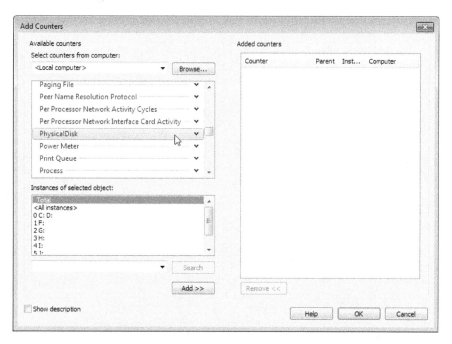

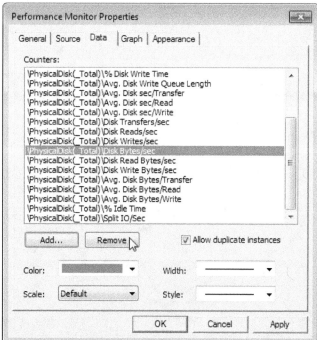

Four Additional Counters Added for Monitoring

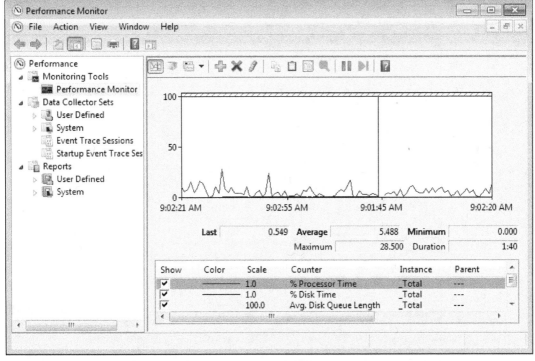

Generating Test Load with a WHILE Loop

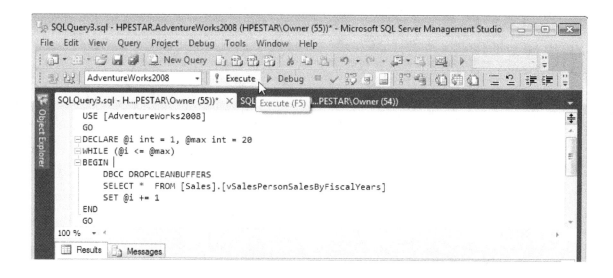

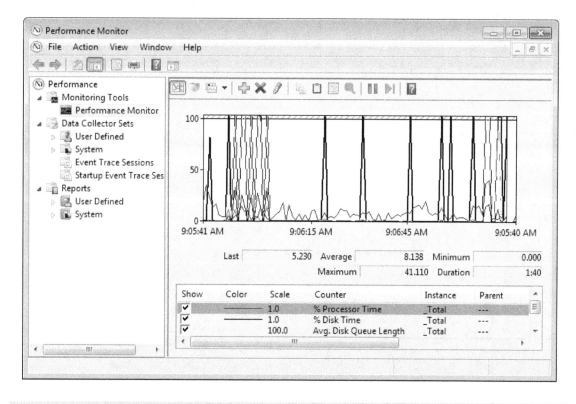

Performance Monitor is Feature Rich

Counters can be saved for future analysis. Profiler and Perfmon tracings can be combined to relate query executions to Perfmon charts.

Articles: **Integrating Profiler and PerfMon Log Files**   http://bit.ly/bffyox
http://www.sqlteam.com/article/integrating-profiler-and-perfmon-log-files

Combining Profiler and Perfmon Data   http://bit.ly/jb8f77
http://www.sanssql.com/2010/10/combining-profiler-and-perfmon-data.html

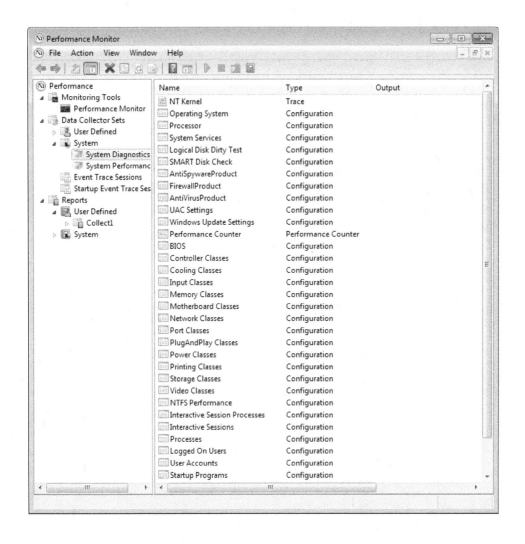

CHAPTER 22: Indexing, Query Optimization & Performance Tuning

Optimization Basics

Optimization revolves around techniques for the reduction of the resource requirements to carry out an operation such as a SELECT query. There are two ways to do optimization:

> ➢ Engineering the query / script the optimal way
> ➢ Creating indexes on the tables

In both instances the usual objective is "reads" (logical 8K page reads) reduction. While the final objective is the "duration" reduction, that measure involves blocking as well so it is not as reliable as the "reads" measure. Using the first software engineering technique, we aim to eliminate unneeded operations or find a replacement which is less resource intensive. The second indexing technique is purely "reads" reduction in focus, we are not changing the query or the script. T-SQL has 2 statistics commands for taking basic performance measures. For even tests, we don't want to use cache memory (fast), but only disk (slow). A "cold" execute of a query may take 8 seconds, while the next (using cache) 1 second only.

```
USE AdventureWorks2012;
DBCC DROPCLEANBUFFERS;  -- Forces reload of data pages (forces disk io) in cache buffer memory
SET STATISTICS IO ON; SET STATISTICS TIME ON;
        EXEC uspGetBillOfMaterials 801, '2008-01-05';
SET STATISTICS TIME OFF; SET STATISTICS IO OFF;  -- Messages
```

DBCC execution completed. If DBCC printed error messages, contact your system administrator.
SQL Server parse and compile time:
  CPU time = 0 ms, elapsed time = 0 ms.

 SQL Server Execution Times:
  CPU time = 0 ms, elapsed time = 0 ms.
Table 'Product'. Scan count 0, logical reads 178, physical reads 3, read-ahead reads 0, lob logical reads 0, lob physical reads 0, lob read-ahead reads 0.
Table 'BillOfMaterials'. Scan count 90, logical reads 181, physical reads 4, read-ahead reads 0, lob logical reads 0, lob physical reads 0, lob read-ahead reads 0.
Table 'Worktable'. Scan count 2, logical reads 510, physical reads 0, read-ahead reads 0, lob logical reads 0, lob physical reads 0, lob read-ahead reads 0.

 SQL Server Execution Times:
  CPU time = 16 ms, elapsed time = 6 ms.

 SQL Server Execution Times:
  CPU time = 16 ms, elapsed time = 6 ms.

No Disk IO Needed When All Pages for a Query Are in Buffer Cache

When we execute a query shortly after the previous execution, most pages may still be on cache memory, thus reduction in the need for (slow) disk io.

```
USE AdventureWorks2012;
SET STATISTICS IO ON;
SET STATISTICS TIME ON;
        EXEC uspGetBillOfMaterials 801, '2008-01-05';
SET STATISTICS TIME OFF;  SET STATISTICS IO OFF;
GO -- Messages
```

SQL Server parse and compile time:
   CPU time = 0 ms, elapsed time = 0 ms.

SQL Server Execution Times:
   CPU time = 0 ms, elapsed time = 0 ms.
Table 'Product'. Scan count 0, logical reads 178, **physical reads 0**, read-ahead reads 0, lob logical reads 0, lob physical reads 0, lob read-ahead reads 0.
Table 'BillOfMaterials'. Scan count 90, logical reads 181, **physical reads 0,** read-ahead reads 0, lob logical reads 0, lob physical reads 0, lob read-ahead reads 0.
Table 'Worktable'. Scan count 2, logical reads 510, physical reads 0, read-ahead reads 0, lob logical reads 0, lob physical reads 0, lob read-ahead reads 0.

SQL Server Execution Times:
   CPU time = 0 ms, elapsed time = 2 ms.

SQL Server Execution Times:
   CPU time = 0 ms, elapsed time = 2 ms.

We can see that physical reads have been eliminated, hence the faster execution. Note, however, timing will vary due to server activities. Therefore, to obtain good measurements we should average over multiple executions, for example 3, 11 or 31. When we monitor a similar execution sequence in SQL Server Profiler, we can see that the logical reads (Reads) were the same but the execution was faster (2 milliseconds) the second time due to the lack of disk io (physical reads). Note: STATISTICS IO and Profiler are 2 different piece of software, hence the difference in figures.

CPU	Reads	Writes	Duration
0	1096	0	7
0	1096	0	2

Optimizing a Query by Reengineering

Less fancy way of saying is rewriting the query. Consider an INNER JOIN query with a view which may look simple until we look at the view underlying code. The database engine has to expand the view definition "on the fly" and develop a plan for the more complex query.

```
USE [AdventureWorks2012]
GO
DBCC DROPCLEANBUFFERS;
SET STATISTICS IO ON;
SET STATISTICS TIME ON;
SELECT  LTRIM(CONCAT(ISNULL(Title,''),SPACE(1), FullName))          AS SalesPerson,
        JobTitle, SalesTerritory, FORMAT([2008],'c0','en-US')       AS [2008]
FROM [Sales].[vSalesPersonSalesByFiscalYears] VSP
  INNER JOIN Person.Person P
   ON CONCAT(FirstName, ' ', MiddleName, ' ', LastName) = VSP.FullName
ORDER BY [2008] DESC;
SET STATISTICS TIME OFF;  SET STATISTICS IO OFF;
```

SalesPerson	JobTitle	SalesTerritory	2008
Linda C Mitchell	Sales Representative	Southwest	$4,251,369
Jae B Pak	Sales Representative	United Kingdom	$4,116,871
Michael G Blythe	Sales Representative	Northeast	$3,763,178
Jillian Carson	Sales Representative	Central	$3,189,418
Ranjit R Varkey Chudukatil	Sales Representative	France	$3,121,616
José Edvaldo Saraiva	Sales Representative	Canada	$2,604,541
Shu K Ito	Sales Representative	Southwest	$2,458,536
Tsvi Michael Reiter	Sales Representative	Southeast	$2,315,186
Rachel B Valdez	Sales Representative	Germany	$1,827,067
Mr. Tete A Mensa-Annan	Sales Representative	Northwest	$1,576,562
David R Campbell	Sales Representative	Northwest	$1,573,013
Garrett R Vargas	Sales Representative	Canada	$1,453,719
Lynn N Tsoflias	Sales Representative	Australia	$1,421,811
Pamela O Ansman-Wolfe	Sales Representative	Northwest	$1,352,577

DBCC execution completed. If DBCC printed error messages, contact your system administrator.

(14 row(s) affected)

Table 'Worktable'. Scan count 0, logical reads 0, physical reads 0, read-ahead reads 0, lob logical reads 0, lob physical reads 0, lob read-ahead reads 0.

Table 'SalesOrderHeader'. Scan count 5, logical reads 865, physical reads 2, read-ahead reads 784, lob logical reads 0, lob physical reads 0, lob read-ahead reads 0.

Table 'Employee'. Scan count 0, logical reads 28, physical reads 1, read-ahead reads 0, lob logical reads 0, lob physical reads 0, lob read-ahead reads 0.

Table 'Person'. Scan count 5, logical reads 4240, physical reads 2, read-ahead reads 3817, lob logical reads 0, lob physical reads 0, lob read-ahead reads 0.

Table 'SalesTerritory'. Scan count 0, logical reads 28, physical reads 1, read-ahead reads 0, lob logical reads 0, lob physical reads 0, lob read-ahead reads 0.

Table 'SalesPerson'. Scan count 0, logical reads 34, physical reads 1, read-ahead reads 0, lob logical reads 0, lob physical reads 0, lob read-ahead reads 0.

Table 'Worktable'. Scan count 0, logical reads 0, physical reads 0, read-ahead reads 0, lob logical reads 0, lob physical reads 0, lob read-ahead reads 0.

SQL Server Execution Times:
  CPU time = 172 ms, elapsed time = 1162 ms.

JOIN on INT Columns Faster Than on nvarchar Strings

Our suspicion is that JOINing on nvarchar fields may be improved if we replace it with JOIN on INT columns (4 bytes). Actually, we are in luck, it is just an easy rewrite of the query.

```
USE [AdventureWorks2012]
GO
DBCC DROPCLEANBUFFERS;
SET STATISTICS IO ON;
SET STATISTICS TIME ON;
SELECT  LTRIM(CONCAT(ISNULL(Title,''),SPACE(1), FullName))          AS SalesPerson,
        JobTitle, SalesTerritory, FORMAT([2008],'c0','en-US')       AS [2008]
FROM [Sales].[vSalesPersonSalesByFiscalYears] VSP
  INNER JOIN Person.Person P
    ON P.BusinessEntityID = VSP.SalesPersonID  ORDER BY [2008] DESC;
SET STATISTICS TIME OFF;  SET STATISTICS IO OFF;
GO
```

```
DBCC execution completed. If DBCC printed error messages, contact your system administrator.

(14 row(s) affected)
Table 'Person'. Scan count 0, logical reads 90, physical reads 2, read-ahead reads 0, lob logical reads 0, lob physical reads 0, lob read-ahead reads 0.
Table 'SalesOrderHeader'. Scan count 14, logical reads 12333, physical reads 9, read-ahead reads 352, lob logical reads 0, lob physical reads 0, lob read-ahead reads 0.
Table 'Employee'. Scan count 0, logical reads 28, physical reads 2, read-ahead reads 0, lob logical reads 0, lob physical reads 0, lob read-ahead reads 0.
Table 'SalesTerritory'. Scan count 0, logical reads 28, physical reads 1, read-ahead reads 0, lob logical reads 0, lob physical reads 0, lob read-ahead reads 0.
Table 'SalesPerson'. Scan count 1, logical reads 2, physical reads 1, read-ahead reads 0, lob logical reads 0, lob physical reads 0, lob read-ahead reads 0.

SQL Server Execution Times:
  CPU time = 16 ms,  elapsed time = 68 ms.
```

When we compare the statistics we observe the elimination of 2 worktables and we reduced the "reads" on the Person table by the more efficient JOIN. The low CPU in the Profiler comparison screenshot indicative of the simpler JOIN. Even though the total "reads" are higher, the indexed INT JOIN proves to be quite advantageous over varchar JOIN as reflected in the lower CPU figure.

CPU	Reads	Writes	Duration
0	0	0	0
236	5314	0	1144
0	0	0	0
78	14194	0	302

Examining the Actual Execution Plan

There are two execution plan which can be turned by clicking on the corresponding icons: estimated and actual. The execution plan can be helpful with missing indexes and improvement considerations. Understanding a complex execution plan requires extensive studying and experience.

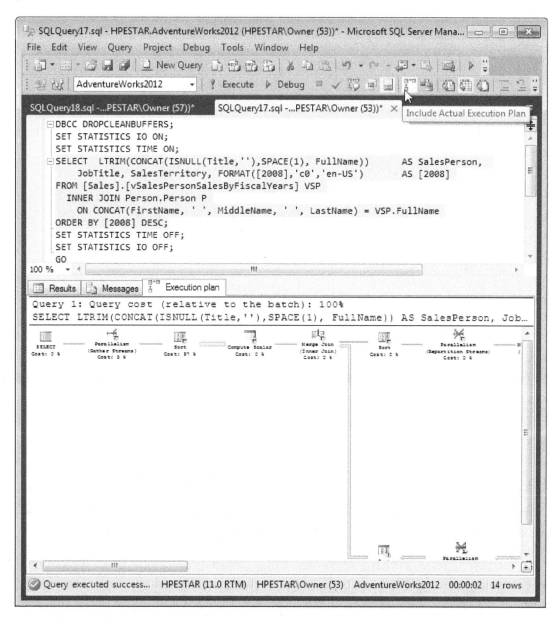

Comparing Execution Plan Cost Summary Pop-ups

When hovering with the mouse over the SELECT on the left side of the execution plan, a cost summary panel pops up.

SELECT		SELECT	
Cached plan size	120 KB	Cached plan size	96 KB
Degree of Parallelism	4	Degree of Parallelism	1
Estimated Operator Cost	0 (0%)	Estimated Operator Cost	0 (0%)
Memory Grant	1018816	Estimated Subtree Cost	1.60204
Estimated Subtree Cost	15132.9	Memory Grant	7352
Estimated Number of Rows	2608890	Estimated Number of Rows	1306.27

Statement

```
SELECT LTRIM(CONCAT(ISNULL
(Title,''),SPACE(1), FullName)) AS
SalesPerson,
JobTitle, SalesTerritory, FORMAT
([2008],'c0','en-US') AS [2008]
FROM [Sales].
[vSalesPersonSalesByFiscalYears] VSP
   INNER JOIN Person.Person P
   ON CONCAT(FirstName, ' ',
MiddleName, ' ', LastName) =
VSP.FullName
ORDER BY [2008] DESC;
```

Statement

```
SELECT LTRIM(CONCAT(ISNULL
(Title,''),SPACE(1), FullName)) AS
SalesPerson,
JobTitle, SalesTerritory, FORMAT
([2008],'c0','en-US') AS [2008]
FROM [Sales].
[vSalesPersonSalesByFiscalYears] VSP
   INNER JOIN Person.Person P
   ON P.BusinessEntityID =
VSP.SalesPersonID
ORDER BY [2008] DESC;
```

Side by side comparison of the cost panels shows dramatic differences. Cost of 15,132 versus 1.6 are simply shocking. The example powerfully illustrates the challenges in query optimization whereby relatively simple rewrite may result in huge performance improvement. We cannot say much about the optimization state of a query just by looking at cost. Only when we compare it to a different version of the query we can say if worsened, improved or much improved. We can also notice the huge difference in rows: 2.6 million vs. 1,300. Memory requirement for the nvarchar JOIN is over a million grants, while only 7 thousands for the INT JOIN.

Poorly written query not only slow in execution but very resource intensive as well, therefore it slows down other queries executing simultaneously. Hence the need to optimize queries especially frequently executed ones.

An extreme bad query can bring down the mightiest server to its "knees". We can see why just by looking at this very simple example with bad and good INNER JOINs.

Optimizing with Multi Statements Query Using Temporary Tables

Assume that the fast INT JOIN is not available. Another technique: instead of a single statement query multi statements since we have more control over the execution plan. In the current example we are forcing the optimizer to evaluate the view query first and store the results into a temporary table. Note: messages shows the long (real) name of #VSP temporary table, personalized to this connection.

```
DBCC DROPCLEANBUFFERS;
SET STATISTICS IO ON;
SET STATISTICS TIME ON;
SELECT * INTO #VSP FROM [Sales].[vSalesPersonSalesByFiscalYears];


SELECT  LTRIM(CONCAT(ISNULL(Title,''),SPACE(1), FullName))          AS SalesPerson,
        JobTitle, SalesTerritory, FORMAT([2008],'c0','en-US')       AS [2008]
FROM #VSP
 INNER JOIN Person.Person P
  ON CONCAT(FirstName, ' ', MiddleName, ' ', LastName) = #VSP.FullName
ORDER BY [2008] DESC;
SET STATISTICS TIME OFF;
SET STATISTICS IO OFF;
GO
DROP TABLE #VSP
```

Messages

```
DBCC execution completed. If DBCC printed error messages, contact your system administrator.
Table 'SalesOrderHeader'. Scan count 14, logical reads 12452, physical reads 9, read-ahead reads 352, lob logical reads 0, lob physical reads 0, lob read-ahead reads 0.
Table 'Person'. Scan count 0, logical reads 42, physical reads 2, read-ahead reads 0, lob logical reads 0, lob physical reads 0, lob read-ahead reads 0.
Table 'Employee'. Scan count 0, logical reads 28, physical reads 2, read-ahead reads 0, lob logical reads 0, lob physical reads 0, lob read-ahead reads 0.
Table 'SalesTerritory'. Scan count 0, logical reads 28, physical reads 1, read-ahead reads 0, lob logical reads 0, lob physical reads 0, lob read-ahead reads 0.
Table 'SalesPerson'. Scan count 1, logical reads 2, physical reads 1, read-ahead reads 0, lob logical reads 0, lob physical reads 0, lob read-ahead reads 0.

(14 row(s) affected)

(1 row(s) affected)

 SQL Server Execution Times:
   CPU time = 94 ms,  elapsed time = 362 ms.
 SQL Server parse and compile time:
   CPU time = 0 ms, elapsed time = 70 ms.
 SQL Server parse and compile time:
   CPU time = 0 ms, elapsed time = 236 ms.

(14 row(s) affected)
Table 'Person'. Scan count 1, logical reads 3826, physical reads 0, read-ahead reads 3817, lob logical reads 0, lob physical reads 0, lob read-ahead reads 0.
Table 'Worktable'. Scan count 1, logical reads 42166, physical reads 0, read-ahead reads 0, lob logical reads 0, lob physical reads 0, lob read-ahead reads 0.
Table '#VSP_____000000000074'. Scan count
1, logical reads 1, physical reads 0, read-ahead reads 0, lob logical reads 0, lob physical reads 0, lob read-ahead reads 0.

(1 row(s) affected)

 SQL Server Execution Times:
   CPU time = 266 ms,  elapsed time = 832 ms.
```

Obstacle: Worktable 42K "reads" Cannot Be Decreased

This course of action is not as good as the JOIN on the INT (integer) keys. Yet the combination of costs came down to 6, a reasonable figure relatively speaking. The Estimated Number of Rows are "reasonable" as well, just like the Memory Grants.

CPU	Reads	Writes	Duration
125	15849	3	1155
203	42536	123	356

SELECT INTO		SELECT	
Cached plan size	120 KB	Cached plan size	32 KB
Degree of Parallelism	1	Degree of Parallelism	1
Estimated Operator Cost	0 (0%)	Estimated Operator Cost	0 (0%)
Estimated Subtree Cost	1.6378	Memory Grant	1024
Estimated Number of Rows	1306.27	Estimated Subtree Cost	4.18429
		Estimated Number of Rows	19972

Statement (SELECT INTO)
```
SELECT * INTO #VSP FROM [Sales].
[vSalesPersonSalesByFiscalYears];
```

Statement (SELECT)
```
SELECT LTRIM(CONCAT(ISNULL
(Title,''),SPACE(1), FullName)) AS
SalesPerson,
JobTitle, SalesTerritory, FORMAT
([2008],'c0','en-US') AS [2008]
FROM #VSP
  INNER JOIN Person.Person P
    ON #VSP.FullName = CONCAT
(FirstName, ' ', MiddleName, ' ',
LastName)
ORDER BY [2008] DESC;
```

The 42K "reads" is huge, in this case on an internal work table which is outside our direct control, however, indirectly we may be able to influence it. The common goal of optimization is "reads" reduction usually with indexing if the query is engineered correctly. With indexing we may be able to bring down the reads to 500 or even 50.

Optimizing with Covering Index

We can achieve miracles in query optimization with indexing but at a cost: index represents an overhead since it slows down some operations such as INSERT or DELETE and it has to be maintained. First we add a computed column to the Person.Person table, them create a "covering" index on it which includes the Title used in the SELECT clause. Note: computed column and covering index are "luxury" items which are used to support **business critical queries** only. In a covering index all columns are present in the index for the query as keys or included column. **Note: there is no "free lunch" with indexing only tradeoff**. Covering index tends to be wide and may slow down other than the target queries.

```
ALTER TABLE Person.Person ADD FullName
        AS CONCAT(FirstName, ' ', MiddleName, ' ', LastName)          PERSISTED;
GO
--Command(s) completed successfully.
```

```
CREATE INDEX idxFullName
              on Person.Person(FullName) INCLUDE (Title);
GO
-- Command(s) completed successfully.
```

```
-- DROP INDEX Person.Person.idxFullName;
```

The new query using the new column in the INNER JOIN:

```
SELECT  LTRIM(CONCAT(ISNULL(Title,''),SPACE(1), #VSP.FullName))     AS SalesPerson,
        JobTitle, SalesTerritory, FORMAT([2008],'c0','en-US')       AS [2008]
FROM #VSP
 INNER JOIN Person.Person P
  ON P.FullName = #VSP.FullName
```

The result is simply amazing: the 42K "reads" on the work table is gone. The 123 "writes" are gone as well. Duration is not a stable measure because it includes blocking as well. If there is no blocking duration is proportionally higher with higher CPU, Reads & Writes.

CPU	Reads	Writes	Duration
140	15802	1	551
16	81	0	117

Optimizing with Indexing

The general rule is that all JOIN keys and WHERE condition columns should be indexed. Since PRIMARY KEY is automatically indexed, the rule means that all FOREIGN KEYS should be indexed since that is not automatic.

```
USE tempdb;
SELECT [SalesOrderID]
    ,CONVERT(INT,[SalesOrderDetailID]) AS [SalesOrderDetailID] -- inhibit identity inheritence
    ,[CarrierTrackingNumber], [OrderQty], [ProductID], [SpecialOfferID] ,[UnitPrice]
    ,[UnitPriceDiscount],[LineTotal],[rowguid],[ModifiedDate]
INTO SOD FROM [AdventureWorks2012].[Sales].[SalesOrderDetail];
GO -- (121317 row(s) affected)
INSERT SOD SELECT * FROM SOD;   -- increase size of table by duplicating itself
GO 5    /* Beginning execution loop  (121317 row(s) affected) (242634 row(s) affected)
(485268 row(s) affected)  (970536 row(s) affected)
(1941072 row(s) affected)  Batch execution completed 5 times. */
SELECT FORMAT(COUNT(*), '###,###,###') FROM SOD; -- 3,882,144
SELECT * INTO Product FROM AdventureWorks2012.Production.Product;
```

The Larger the Table the More Benefits of Indexing

```
DBCC DROPCLEANBUFFERS;  SET STATISTICS IO ON; SET STATISTICS TIME ON;
        SELECT * FROM SOD INNER JOIN Product P
              ON SOD.ProductID = P.ProductID     WHERE P.ProductID = 800;
SET STATISTICS TIME OFF;   SET STATISTICS IO OFF;
```

```
DBCC execution completed. If DBCC printed error messages, contact your system administrator.
(15840 row(s) affected)
Table 'SOD'. Scan count 5, logical reads 54796, physical reads 0, read-ahead reads 1719, lob logical reads 0, lob physical reads 0, lob
read-ahead reads 0.
Table 'Product'. Scan count 1, logical reads 14, physical reads 0, read-ahead reads 0, lob logical reads 0, lob physical reads 0, lob
read-ahead reads 0.
Table 'Worktable'. Scan count 0, logical reads 0, physical reads 0, read-ahead reads 0, lob logical reads 0, lob physical reads 0, lob
read-ahead reads 0.
SQL Server Execution Times:
  CPU time = 483 ms,  elapsed time = 845 ms.
```

MSDN Article: **Clustered and Nonclustered Indexes Described**
http://msdn.microsoft.com/en-us/library/ms190457.aspx

Create Unique Nonclustered & Clustered Indexes

```
CREATE CLUSTERED INDEX idxPrd ON SOD(ProductID);
CREATE UNIQUE INDEX idxPrd ON Product(ProductID);
GO


DBCC DROPCLEANBUFFERS; SET STATISTICS IO ON; SET STATISTICS TIME ON;
        SELECT * FROM SOD INNER JOIN Product P
                ON SOD.ProductID = P.ProductID     WHERE P.ProductID = 800;
SET STATISTICS TIME OFF;  SET STATISTICS IO OFF;
GO
```

DBCC execution completed. If DBCC printed error messages, contact your system administrator.
SQL Server parse and compile time:
CPU time = 0 ms, elapsed time = 2 ms.
(15840 row(s) affected)
Table 'SOD'. Scan count 1, logical reads 210, physical reads 0, read-ahead reads 206, lob logical reads 0, lob physical reads 0, lob read-ahead reads 0.
Table 'Product'. Scan count 0, logical reads 3, physical reads 0, read-ahead reads 0, lob logical reads 0, lob physical reads 0, lob read-ahead reads 0.
(1 row(s) affected)
SQL Server Execution Times:
CPU time = 47 ms, elapsed time = 517 ms.

Check Data & Indexes Fragmentation on a Table

The sys.dm_db_index_physical_stats Dynamic Management Function (DMF) can be used to obtain index fragmentation information(Ye Olde Way: DBCC SHOWCONTIG). The clustered index line represents the data fragmentation. 20% fragmentation is considered low, 80% considered high.

```
SELECT object_NAME(object_id) AS TableName, i ndex_id,
        index_type_desc, FORMAT(avg_fragmentation_in_percent, 'p0') AS PcntFrag
        FROM sys.dm_db_index_physical_stats(DB_ID(N'AdventureWorks2012'),
            OBJECT_ID(N'AdventureWorks2012.Sales.SalesOrderDetail'), NULL, NULL , 'LIMITED');
```

TableName	index_id	index_type_desc	PcntFrag
SalesOrderDetail	1	CLUSTERED INDEX	21 %
SalesOrderDetail	2	NONCLUSTERED INDEX	0 %
SalesOrderDetail	3	NONCLUSTERED INDEX	11 %
SalesOrderDetail	10	NONCLUSTERED INDEX	0 %
SalesOrderDetail	13	NONCLUSTERED INDEX	90 %

> MSDN Article: **Reorganize and Rebuild Indexes**
> http://msdn.microsoft.com/en-us/library/ms189858.aspx

CHAPTER 22: Indexing, Query Optimization & Performance Tuning

Clustered Index for Business Critical Query Support

Clustered index is another "luxury" item in optimization since there can only be one on a table and 0 to many nonclustered indexes. In this example nonclustered index does some improvement, but not significant. Cleanup commands for the indexing example script.

-- DROP INDEX SOD.idxPrd; DROP INDEX Product.idxPrd;
DROP TABLE SOD; DROP TABLE Product;

SQL Profiler statistics on the sequence of batches we sent to the server from SSMS Query Editor.

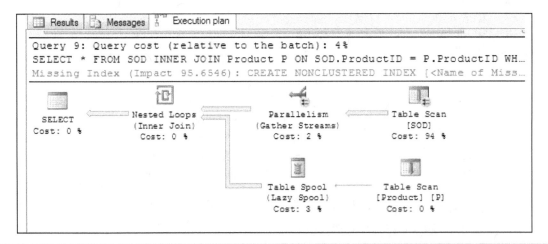

TextData	CPU	Reads	Writes	Duration	SPID	EventClass
USE tempdb;	0	0	0	0	53	SQL:BatchCompleted
SELECT [SalesOrderID] ,CONVE...	218	3327	672	782	53	SQL:BatchCompleted
INSERT SOD SELECT * FROM SOD; -...	796	496577	2968	832	53	SQL:BatchCompleted
INSERT SOD SELECT * FROM SOD; -...	1685	1026720	3103	1700	53	SQL:BatchCompleted
INSERT SOD SELECT * FROM SOD; -...	3354	2086787	6433	3505	53	SQL:BatchCompleted
INSERT SOD SELECT * FROM SOD; -...	6645	4207017	12832	6709	53	SQL:BatchCompleted
INSERT SOD SELECT * FROM SOD; -...	13229	8447507	25504	13339	53	SQL:BatchCompleted
/* Beginning execution loop (121...	719	55189	9	249	53	SQL:BatchCompleted
DBCC DROPCLEANBUFFERS; SET STATI...	732	57035	1	1182	53	SQL:BatchCompleted
CREATE CLUSTERED INDEX idxPrd ON ...	15398	133236	51211	13607	53	SQL:BatchCompleted
DBCC DROPCLEANBUFFERS; SET STATI...	109	225	0	497	53	SQL:BatchCompleted
-- DROP INDEX SOD.idxPrd -- DROP...	16	480	0	147	53	SQL:BatchCompleted

We can see the reads of 57,035 decreased to 225 after creating the indexes. Not only we speeded up this query but other queries as well by decreasing the load on the server. The execution plan displays **table scan** prior to index creation.

Query 9: Query cost (relative to the batch): 4%
SELECT * FROM SOD INNER JOIN Product P ON SOD.ProductID = P.ProductID WH...
Missing Index (Impact 95.6546): CREATE NONCLUSTERED INDEX [<Name of Miss...

SELECT
Cost: 0 %

Nested Loops
(Inner Join)
Cost: 0 %

Parallelism
(Gather Streams)
Cost: 2 %

Table Scan
[SOD]
Cost: 94 %

Table Spool
(Lazy Spool)
Cost: 3 %

Table Scan
[Product] [P]
Cost: 0 %

CHAPTER 22: Indexing, Query Optimization & Performance Tuning

Execution Plan after Index Creation & Cost Comparison

The execution plan shows clustered index seek instead of table scan after index creation. Generally our aim with indexing is to replace table scan or index scan with index seek.

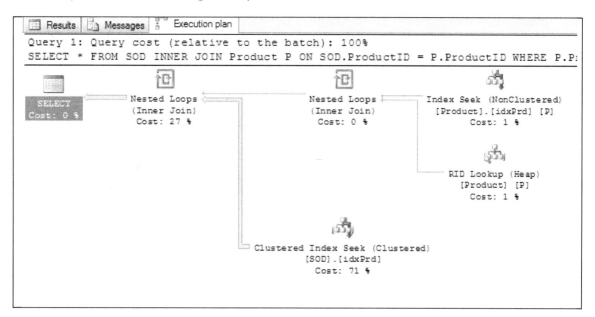

Cost comparison before and after index create reflects a very significant improvement in cost, roughly 200 fold.

SELECT		SELECT	
Cached plan size	56 KB	Cached plan size	56 KB
Degree of Parallelism	4	Degree of Parallelism	1
Estimated Operator Cost	0 (0%)	Estimated Operator Cost	0 (0%)
Estimated Subtree Cost	45.4362	Estimated Subtree Cost	0.247049
Memory Grant	72	Estimated Number of Rows	15840
Estimated Number of Rows	15513.1		

Statement

SELECT * FROM SOD INNER JOIN
Product P
    ON SOD.ProductID = P.ProductID
  WHERE P.ProductID = 800;

Statement

SELECT * FROM SOD INNER JOIN Product
P
    ON SOD.ProductID = P.ProductID
  WHERE P.ProductID = 800;

Non-SARGable Predicates Force Index Scan

The term SARGable stands for Search ARGument ABLE. It means the WHERE clause OR join ON clause predicate written such a way that the database engine can use the index on the column. Basically means if we form an expression with the indexed column, index scan will be performed instead of index seek, in other words, index will not be used to speed up the query. The (SOD.ProductID +1 - 1) expression in the ON clause causes clustered index scan. The relative query costs are 1% (SARGable) and 99% (non-SARGable) in the batch of 2 queries.

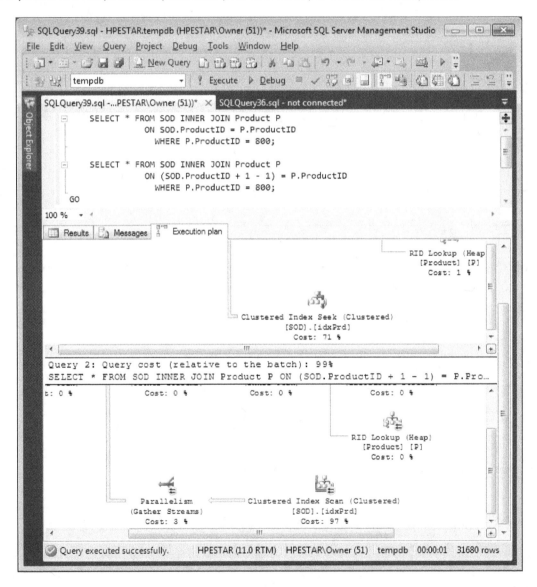

SARGable Predicate Construction

It is a challenge to remember all the time to make the predicate SARGable. Frequently, so much easier to make it non-SARGable.

YEAR(OrderDate) = 2016 AND MONTH(OrderDate) = 10   -- non-SARGable

OrderDate >= '2016-10-01' AND OrderDate < DATEADD(MM,1, '2016-10-01') -- SARGable

The payoff can be great as shown by the previous SARGable & non-SARGable examples, duration in msec.

CPU	Reads	Writes	Duration
125	223	0	668
1527	51451	0	11497

Clustered Index Seek (Clustered)		**Clustered Index Scan (Clustered)**	
Scanning a particular range of rows from a clustered index.		Scanning a clustered index, entirely or only a range.	
Physical Operation	Clustered Index Seek	**Physical Operation**	Clustered Index Scan
Logical Operation	Clustered Index Seek	**Logical Operation**	Clustered Index Scan
Actual Execution Mode	Row	**Actual Execution Mode**	Row
Estimated Execution Mode	Row	**Estimated Execution Mode**	Row
Storage	RowStore	**Actual Number of Rows**	15840
Actual Number of Rows	15840	**Actual Number of Batches**	0
Actual Number of Batches	0	**Estimated I/O Cost**	37.8224
Estimated Operator Cost	0.174279 (71%)	**Estimated Operator Cost**	39.9576 (97%)
Estimated I/O Cost	0.156698	**Estimated CPU Cost**	2.13526
Estimated CPU Cost	0.017581	**Estimated Subtree Cost**	39.9576
Estimated Subtree Cost	0.174279	**Number of Executions**	4
Number of Executions	1	**Estimated Number of Executions**	1
Estimated Number of Executions	1	**Estimated Number of Rows**	15840
Estimated Number of Rows	15840	**Estimated Row Size**	112 B
Estimated Row Size	112 B	**Actual Rebinds**	0
Actual Rebinds	0	**Actual Rewinds**	0
Actual Rewinds	0	**Ordered**	False
Ordered	True	**Node ID**	58
Node ID	54		

Object
[tempdb].[dbo].[SOD].[idxPrd]
Output List
[tempdb].[dbo].[SOD].SalesOrderID, [tempdb].[dbo].
[SOD].SalesOrderDetailID, [tempdb].[dbo].
[SOD].CarrierTrackingNumber, [tempdb].[dbo].
[SOD].OrderQty, [tempdb].[dbo].[SOD].ProductID, [tempdb].
[dbo].[SOD].SpecialOfferID, [tempdb].[dbo].[SOD].UnitPrice,
[tempdb].[dbo].[SOD].UnitPriceDiscount, [tempdb].[dbo].
[SOD].LineTotal, [tempdb].[dbo].[SOD].rowguid, [tempdb].
[dbo].[SOD].ModifiedDate
Seek Predicates
Seek Keys[1]: Prefix: [tempdb].[dbo].[SOD].ProductID =
Scalar Operator((800))

Predicate
([tempdb].[dbo].[SOD].[ProductID]+(1)-(1))=(800)
Object
[tempdb].[dbo].[SOD].[idxPrd]
Output List
[tempdb].[dbo].[SOD].SalesOrderID, [tempdb].[dbo].
[SOD].SalesOrderDetailID, [tempdb].[dbo].
[SOD].CarrierTrackingNumber, [tempdb].[dbo].
[SOD].OrderQty, [tempdb].[dbo].[SOD].ProductID, [tempdb].
[dbo].[SOD].SpecialOfferID, [tempdb].[dbo].[SOD].UnitPrice,
[tempdb].[dbo].[SOD].UnitPriceDiscount, [tempdb].[dbo].
[SOD].LineTotal, [tempdb].[dbo].[SOD].rowguid, [tempdb].
[dbo].[SOD].ModifiedDate

Stored Procedure Parameter Sniffing & Prevention

When SQL Server database engine compiles a stored procedure, it may use the actual parameters supplied to prepare an execution plan. If the parameters are atypical, the plan may be slow for typical parameters. For consistent stored procedure performance parameter sniffing should be eliminated. A telltale sign of parameter sniffing when suddenly a stored procedure executes in 2 minutes, as an example, instead of the usual 10 seconds. *This is different when the first (cold from disk) execution of a stored procedure is much longer than the second & on (warm since pages in buffer memory) execution.* Parameter sniffing may show up also as 5 minutes execution in one environment (like application) and 2 seconds in another (like SSMS).

```
Technet Article
Batch Compilation, Recompilation, and Plan Caching Issues in SQL Server 2005
http://technet.microsoft.com/en-us/library/cc966425.aspx
```

First prevention method: remap parameters to local variables and use those only.

```
USE AdventureWorks2012;
GO
CREATE PROCEDURE uspProductByColor @pcolor varchar(20)   AS BEGIN
        DECLARE @color varchar(20) = @pcolor;            -- remapping
        SET NOCOUNT ON;
        SELECT * FROM Production.Product WHERE Color = @color  ORDER BY name;    END
```

```
EXEC uspProductByColor 'Red';  -- 38 rows returned
```

Second prevention method: RECOMPILE stored procedure at each execution (for large procedure compilation time may be significant).

```
CREATE PROCEDURE uspProductByColor @pcolor varchar(20)
WITH RECOMPILE AS BEGIN  SET NOCOUNT ON;
  SELECT * FROM Production.Product WHERE Color = @pcolor     ORDER BY name;    END
```

Optimizing with MERGE

Single statement MERGE can perform better than multi statements INSERT/UPDATE/DELETE.

```
Technet Article:  Optimizing MERGE Statement Performance
http://technet.microsoft.com/en-us/library/cc879317(v=sql.105).aspx
```

CHAPTER 22: Indexing, Query Optimization & Performance Tuning

Stress Testing a View with Include Client Statistics Feature

Client Statistics feature can be turned by icon or right click drop-down menu option. It calculates averages for up to 10 trials. DBCC DROPCLEANBUFFERS equalizes the tests by purging thecached data pages from buffer memory. Note: server load will influence timings. Query drop-down has option to Reset Client Statistics.

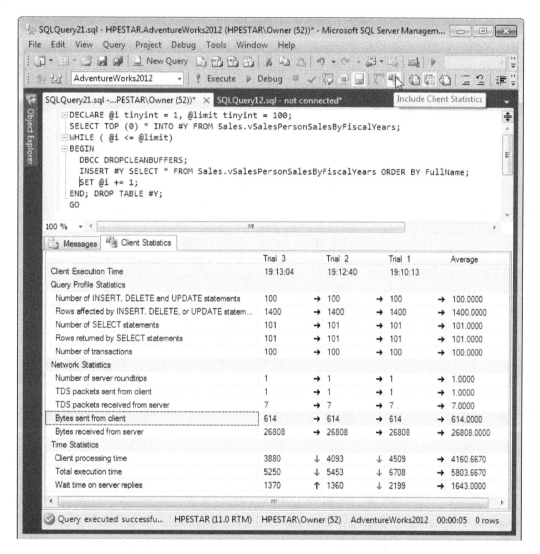

Maximum Capacity Specifications for SQL Server
http://msdn.microsoft.com/en-us/library/ms143432.aspx

CHAPTER 22: Indexing, Query Optimization & Performance Tuning

10 Point Optimization Guide

Performance tuning and optimization are a huge topic. We only touch the tip of the iceberg. Nonetheless, the important elements of optimization can be summarized quite easily. It starts with prioritizing what is business critical, what is not. If 500 users are unhappy with a stored procedure, that is business critical. If one user is unhappy with a slow report, that is not business critical, unless that user is the CEO.

1. REBUILD indexes every weekend. Use FILLFACTOR for dynamic tables with lots of INSERTs. FILLFACTOR 70 means 70% data and 30% empty space. Free database maintenance scripts at http://ola.hallengren.com/ - SQL Server Backup, Integrity Check, and Index and Statistics Maintenance.

2. UPDATE STATISTICS every night. The database engine query optimizer uses the statistics to prepare efficient execution plans.

3. Eliminate missing indexes. All FOREIGN KEY & WHERE condition columns should be considered for indexing.

4. Optimize all business critical queries. WHERE & ON clause predicates should be SARGable.

5. Examine execution plan for business critical queries to make sure they are efficient.

6. Optimize all business critical stored procedures. In a sproc all queries should be optimized and looping should be kept at an absolute minimum. Non-scalable cursors should be avoided.

7. Server memory max should be set in server properties. That is quite a challenge with 32-bit OS. For 64 bit OS with 65GB of memory, max memory should be set to 55GB, as a general guideline, to leave enough room for SS and other program operations.

8. Disk configuration should be optimized. Article: http://technet.microsoft.com/en-us/library/cc966412.aspx .

9. Operational solutions for performance problems which cannot be readily resolved due to lack of resources. For example, external feed arrives 11AM every day and promptly uploaded in 1/2 hour thus slowing down the system and annoying users. Instead schedule uploading with SQL Server Agent to low use time like 11pm.

10. Database design should be efficient. Narrow and fixed row size tables are the best performant. Note: frequently database design is frozen, "as is" , for budget reasons or a 3rd party package. Even in a such a case, index & statistics maintenance can improve performance.

CHAPTER 22: Indexing, Query Optimization & Performance Tuning

Object Explorer GUI REBUILD Indexes

The indexes can be rebuilt in SSMS Object Explorer using Graphical User Interface. REBUILD indexes updates statistics as well. T-SQL command syntax example:

ALTER INDEX ALL ON [Sales].[SalesOrderDetail] REBUILD WITH (FILLFACTOR = 90);

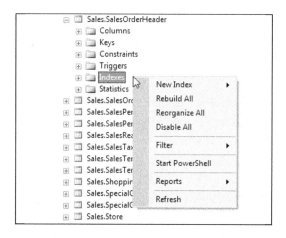

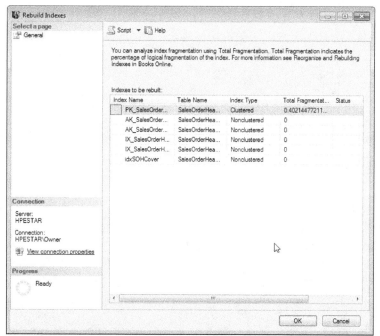

Optimization Guide MSDN Article: **Improving SQL Server Performance**
http://msdn.microsoft.com/en-us/library/ff647793.aspx

CHAPTER 22: Indexing, Query Optimization & Performance Tuning

UPDATE STATISTICS on All Tables Stored Procedure

The UPDATE STATISTICS on all tables stored procedure has one parameter: the sample percent for scanning. Lower the number, faster the update. WITH FULLSCAN option does 100% sampling, it may be slow for large tables. Create & execute stored procedure script.

```
CREATE PROCEDURE sprocUpdateAllStats (@Sample int)  AS
BEGIN
DECLARE @SQL AS NVARCHAR(1024), @Table sysname, @Schema sysname;
DECLARE curAllTables CURSOR FOR
        SELECT TABLE_SCHEMA, TABLE_NAME  FROM INFORMATION_SCHEMA.TABLES
        WHERE TABLE_TYPE='BASE TABLE'  ORDER BY TABLE_SCHEMA, TABLE_NAME;
OPEN curAllTables;  FETCH NEXT FROM curAllTables  INTO @Schema, @Table;
 WHILE (@@FETCH_STATUS = 0)  BEGIN
  SET @SQL =   CONCAT('UPDATE STATISTICS ',
               QUOTENAME( @Schema),'.', QUOTENAME( @Table),
               ' WITH SAMPLE ', CONVERT(char(3), @sample), ' PERCENT;');
--             ' WITH FULLSCAN; ');
  PRINT @SQL;      -- UPDATE STATISTICS [Sales].[Store] WITH SAMPLE 10 PERCENT;
  EXEC sp_executesql @SQL;
  FETCH NEXT FROM curAllTables          INTO @Schema, @Table;
END -- while
CLOSE curAllTables;  DEALLOCATE curAllTables;
END
GO
```

```
EXEC sprocUpdateAllStats 10;
```

Check update status of STATISTICS for a table. SELECT from DMV CROSS APPLY with DMF.

```
SELECT name, last_updated, rows, rows_sampled   FROM sys.stats AS ST        -- DMV
CROSS APPLY sys.dm_db_stats_properties(ST.object_id, ST.stats_id) AS SP      -- DMF
WHERE ST.object_id = object_id('Sales.SalesOrderHeader') ORDER BY name;
-- (28 row(s) affected) - Partial results.
```

name	last_updated	rows	rows_sampled
IX_SalesOrderHeader_CustomerID	2018-05-05 04:38:14.5300000	31468	31468
IX_SalesOrderHeader_SalesPersonID	2018-05-05 04:38:14.5630000	31468	31468
PK_SalesOrderHeader_SalesOrderID	2018-05-05 04:38:14.7330000	31468	31468

Blocking of a Query by Another Query

SQL Server applies locks at the row, page and table level in order to maintain data integrity. If another query tries to operate on the locked part, it may get blocked. It is easy to see how blocking can degrade the performance of the server. We can simulate blocking. In connection 1 we execute and leave open a transaction. In connection 2 we execute a query which intends to operate on the locked table. The result is blocking of connection 2 query by connection 1 query.

```
-- Connection 1
BEGIN TRAN;
UPDATE HumanResources.Shift SET ModifiedDate = convert(datetime, ModifiedDate);
-- ROLLBACK TRAN;
```

```
-- Connection 2
BEGIN TRAN;
UPDATE HumanResources.Shift SET ModifiedDate = convert(datetime, ModifiedDate);
COMMIT TRAN;
```

Checking blocking by **sp_who** system procedure (exec sp_who in a 3rd connection) and **Activity Monitor** (right click on server menu). The Activity Monitor chart even shows the Head Blocker which is very helpful to trace the source of a blocking chain. A quick resolution is killing the head blocker (kill 55). Long term fix is making the blocking query efficient.

	spid	ecid	status	loginame	hostname	blk	dbname	cmd
36	52	0	runnable	HPES...	HPEST...	0	master	SELECT
37	53	0	sleeping	NT SE...	HPEST...	0	ReportServer	AWAITING COMMAND
38	54	0	sleeping	HPES...	HPEST...	0	master	AWAITING COMMAND
39	55	0	sleeping	HPES...	HPEST...	0	AdventureWorks2012	AWAITING COMMAND
40	56	0	sleeping	NT SE...	HPEST...	0	ReportServer	AWAITING COMMAND
41	57	0	suspended	HPES...	HPEST...	55	AdventureWorks2012	UPDATE

S...	U...	Login	Dat...	Tas...	Com...	Appl...	Wait Tim...	Wait...	Wait...	Blocked By	Head Blocker	Me...
51	1	HPESTA...	master			Microsoft...	0					
52	1	HPESTA...	master			Microsoft...	0					
53	1	NT SER...	ReportS...			Report S...	0					
54	1	HPESTA...	master	RUNNING	SELECT	Microsoft...	0					
55	1	HPESTA...	Adventur...			Microsoft...	0				1	
56	1	NT SER...	ReportS...			Report S...	0					
57	1	HPESTA...	Adventur...	SUSPEN...	UPDATE	Microsoft...	172568	LCK_M_U	keylock ...	55		

CHAPTER 22: Indexing, Query Optimization & Performance Tuning

Activity Monitor

The Activity Monitor provides real time operational information in list and graphical chart formats based on operational DMV-s.

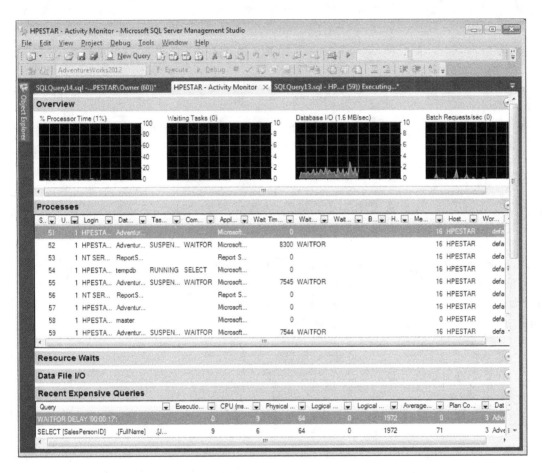

Operational Solutions for Performance Problems

Frequently real fix cannot be carried out quickly or at all for a performance issue due to software complexities and limited expert-level resources. In such a case we have to think about implementing operational solutions:

> Users complain about slow online reports. Setup reports as night jobs with automatic email distribution.

> Reports slow OLTP activities. Restore last night DB backup under new name as reporting DB. Usually, only a small fraction of reports need to be real-time.

Server & Database Standard Reports

The Server Standard Reports can be accessed via the right click on server drop-down menu in SSMS Object Explorer (top left). The Database Standard Reports can be accessed via the right click on database drop down menu (top right). The reports are based on Dynamic Management Views (DMV-s). They represent operational data since the last restart of the server. At the bottom, partial display of the Index Usage Statistics report.

Server Dashboard	Disk Usage
Configuration Changes History	Disk Usage by Top Tables
Schema Changes History	Disk Usage by Table
Scheduler Health	Disk Usage by Partition
Memory Consumption	Backup and Restore Events
Activity - All Blocking Transactions	All Transactions
Activity - All Cursors	All Blocking Transactions
Activity - Top Cursors	Top Transactions by Age
Activity - All Sessions	Top Transactions by Blocked Transactions Count
Activity - Top Sessions	Top Transactions by Locks Count
Activity - Dormant Sessions	Resource Locking Statistics by Objects
Activity - Top Connections	Object Execution Statistics
Top Transactions by Age	Database Consistency History
Top Transactions by Blocked Transactions Count	Index Usage Statistics
Top Transactions by Locks Count	Index Physical Statistics
Performance - Batch Execution Statistics	Schema Changes History
Performance - Object Execution Statistics	User Statistics
Performance - Top Queries by Average CPU Time	
Performance - Top Queries by Average IO	
Performance - Top Queries by Total CPU Time	
Performance - Top Queries by Total IO	
Service Broker Statistics	
Transaction Log Shipping Status	

HumanResources.Employee

Index Name	Index Type	# User Seeks	# User Scans	# User Updates
PK_Employee_BusinessEntityID	CLUSTERED	697	0	0

HumanResources.Shift

Index Name	Index Type	# User Seeks	# User Scans	# User Updates
PK_Shift_ShiftID	CLUSTERED	0	5	5

Person.Person

CHAPTER 22: Indexing, Query Optimization & Performance Tuning

Server Dashboard

The Server Dashboard contains important high-level information about the server.

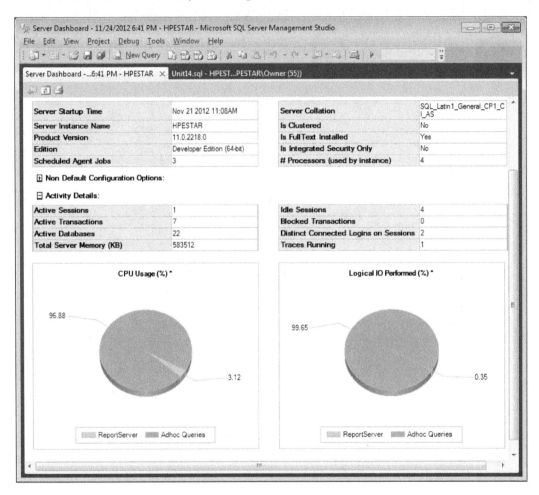

Segment from Performance - Top Queries by Total CPU Time report.

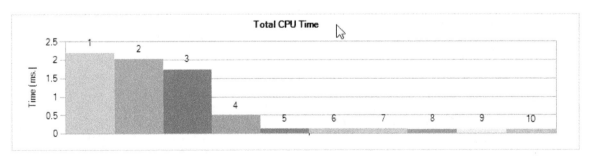

CHAPTER 22: Indexing, Query Optimization & Performance Tuning

Batching Large INSERT, UPDATE & DELETE

Batch processing jobs best executed at low use time like night or weekend. Frequently, however, we may not have a choice, we have to run them during transactional activities. We can minimize conflict by breaking down a large job to small batches and providing 1 second or so wait time for other queries to execute. During that 1 second hundreds of short transactions may execute. DELETE from large tables may prove to be very slow due to restructuring of the index pages.

```
USE tempdb;
SELECT  ProductID=CONVERT(int, ProductID), ProductName=Name,
        ProductNumber, ListPrice, Color, Size
INTO Product FROM AdventureWorks2008.Production.Product;
```

```
INSERT Product SELECT * FROM Product;  -- Double table rows at each execution
GO 16
/* .....   (16515072 row(s) affected)
Batch execution completed 16 times.   */
SELECT FORMAT(COUNT(*),'###,###,###') FROM Product;   -- 33,030,144
GO
CREATE CLUSTERED INDEX idxProductID
                on Product(ProductID);
GO -- 12 minutes 44 seconds
```

```
DECLARE @BatchSize int = 10000;
WHILE (@@ROWCOUNT > 0)   BEGIN     WAITFOR DELAY '00:00:01';
        DELETE TOP (@BatchSize) FROM Product    WHERE ProductNumber = 'CA-5965';
END
GO   -- 3 minutes 8 seconds
/*(10000 row(s) affected)
(10000 row(s) affected)
(10000 row(s) affected)
(10000 row(s) affected)
(10000 row(s) affected)
(10000 row(s) affected)
(5536 row(s) affected)
(0 row(s) affected)*/
```

```
SELECT FORMAT(COUNT(*),'###,###,###') FROM Product;   -- 32,964,608  -- 5 seconds
GO
DROP TABLE tempdb.dbo.Product;
```

CHAPTER 22: Indexing, Query Optimization & Performance Tuning

Database Engine Tuning Advisor

The Database Engine Tuning Advisor (DETA or DTA) provides indexing & statistics recommendations based on the supplied workload. A single query can be analyzed as well, right click Query drop-down menu.

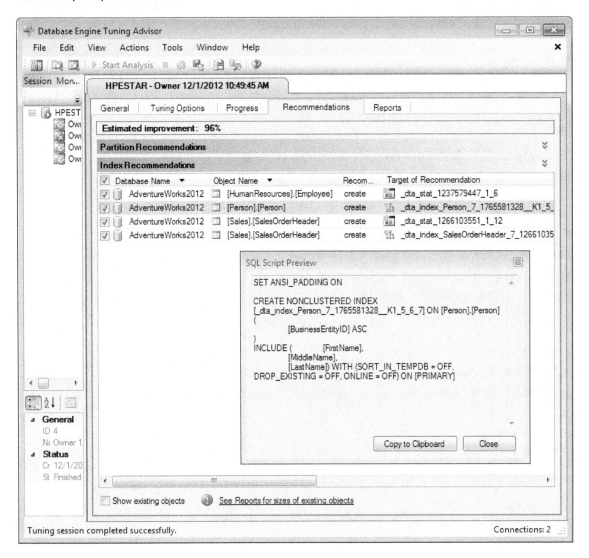

DBCC HELP Command

With the DBCC HELP command you can get syntax assistance with any of the DBCC commands.

DBCC HELP (checkdb);

CHAPTER 22: Indexing, Query Optimization & Performance Tuning

CHAPTER 23: Installing Azure SQL & Sample Cloud DBs

SQL Azure - Enterprise in the Clouds

Microsoft Windows Azure account is available at:

> **Windows Azure** portal
> http://www.windowsazure.com/en-us/
> Your **Windows Azure SQL Database** management portal
> https://yourazuresqlserver.database.windows.net

At the time of writing this book, there is a 90-day free trial package available which includes an SQL database. Credit card is required for an Azure account. One form of verification: a code is sent to your mobile phone.

Creating Database Using the Azure Portal

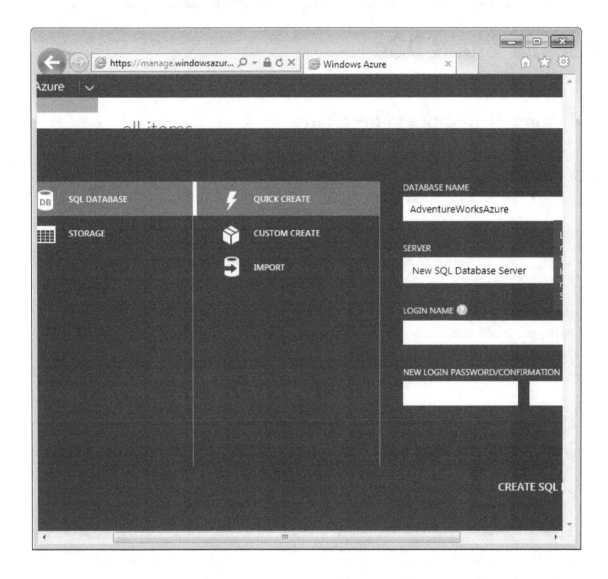

Database can also be created from a Command Prompt utility, SQLCMD, an application program and SQL Server Management Studio. Connection to Windows Azure SQL Database server required and permission to create a database.

Getting Started with Azure SQL Database

Basic configuration has to be done online such as setting Azure SQL server login & password, and setting up firewall rules so you can use Management Studio and other client software from your computer. The configuration processes are automated to a large degree and user-friendly. The best part: once you are finished with configuration, you can continue with the "friendly skies" from the friendly Management Studio environment.

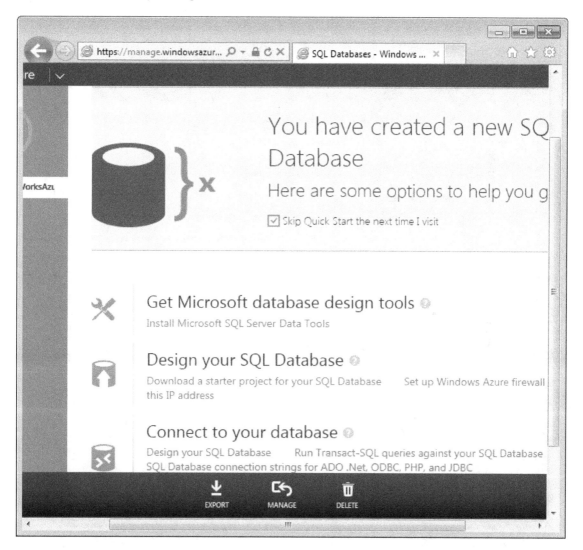

Connecting Azure SQL Server from 2012 Management Studio

You can connect to the Azure SQL Server after setting up a firewall rule for your computer IP using the regular dialog box with SQL Server authentication. The server name is: yourazureserver.database.windows.net. The login & password is what you configured on Azure. Some server & login information has been blanked out on the following screenshot. The Azure T-SQL is different from SQL Server 2012 T-SQL

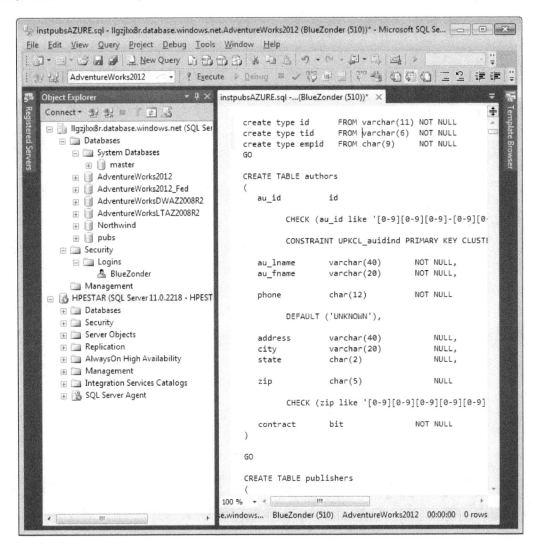

We can get SQL Azure version information by a SELECT:

```
select @@version  -- Microsoft SQL Azure (RTM) - 11.0.2065.0 Aug 29 2012 18:41:07
```

Installing AdventureWorks2012 for Azure SQL

There is a special download site for SQL Azure AdventureWorks sample databases

> Download site: **Adventure Works for Azure SQL Database**
> http://msftdbprodsamples.codeplex.com/releases/view/37304

Download 2 files:

- ➢ AdventureWorks2012ForWindowsAzureSQLDatabase
- ➢ AdventureWorks2008R2AZ.zip

> Download site: **.NET Framework 4 or higher**
> http://msdn.microsoft.com/en-us/vstudio/aa4961

Unzip the zipped files into a directory. In the same directory using Command Prompt run the following command in AdventureWorks directory:

```
CreateAdventureWorksForSQLAzure.cmd yourserverid.database.windows.net
yourserverlogin yourpassword
```

This is going to upload the sample AdventureWorks2012 database into the Azure server using bcp. It takes a few minutes, maybe even an hour if the internet connection is slow. A few tables were created on Azure SQL database but did not populate. The reason of population failure for the Sales.Customer table: it has a computed column AccountNumber.

[AccountNumber] AS (isnull('AW'+[dbo].[ufnLeadingZeros]([CustomerID]),'')),

We shall use SQL Server (SSIS) Import/Export Wizard to transfer the data from SQL Server 2012 AdventureWorks2012 database. Similar upload process for AdventureWorks2012_Fed:

```
CreateAdventureWorksForSQLAzure_Fed yourserverid.database.windows.net
yourserverlogin yourpassword
```

Commands to upload AdventureWorksDWAZ2008R2 database in DW folder & AdventureWorksLTAZ2008R2 database in LT folder.

buildawdwaz.cmd tcp:YOURAZURESERVER.database.windows.net YOURLOGIN YOURPASSWORD

buildawltaz.cmd tcp:YOURAZURESERVER.database.windows.net YOURLOGIN YOURPASSWORD

Checking AdventureWorks2012 Tables Population

We can use database metadata, cursor WHILE loop and dynamic SQL to get the row count for each table.

```sql
DECLARE @SchemaName SYSNAME, @TableName SYSNAME, @TableType varchar(12);
DECLARE @SQL NVARCHAR(MAX);

CREATE TABLE #Population
(      TableName   VARCHAR(256),
       TableType   varchar(12),
       [Population] INT  );

DECLARE curTablesAndViews CURSOR FAST_FORWARD FOR
       SELECT TABLE_SCHEMA, TABLE_NAME, TABLE_TYPE
       FROM  INFORMATION_SCHEMA.TABLES  WHERE  TABLE_TYPE = 'BASE TABLE';

OPEN curTablesAndViews;

FETCH NEXT FROM curTablesAndViews INTO @SchemaName, @TableName, @TableType;

WHILE ( @@FETCH_STATUS = 0 )  BEGIN
   SELECT @SQL = CONCAT('INSERT #Population SELECT ''',
          @SchemaName, '.', @TableName, ''',''',
          @TableType, ''', COUNT(*) as Population ',
          'FROM [', @SchemaName, '].[', @TableName, ']');

   PRINT @SQL -- debugging
   EXEC SP_EXECUTESQL      @SQL;

   FETCH NEXT FROM curTablesAndViews INTO @SchemaName, @TableName, @TableType;
END

CLOSE curTablesAndViews;
DEALLOCATE curTablesAndViews;

-- Return the list of rows counts
SELECT * FROM  #Population  ORDER  BY [Population] DESC;
GO

DROP TABLE #Population;
```

Azure SQL AdventureWorks2012 Tables Population after Upload
Note: Sales.Customer table was populated by SS Import/Export Wizard execution.

TableName	TableType	Population
Sales.SalesOrderDetail	BASE TABLE	121317
Production.TransactionHistory	BASE TABLE	113443
Production.TransactionHistoryArchive	BASE TABLE	89253
Production.WorkOrderRouting	BASE TABLE	67131
Sales.SalesOrderHeader	BASE TABLE	31465
Person.BusinessEntity	BASE TABLE	20777
Person.Password	BASE TABLE	19972
Person.PersonPhone	BASE TABLE	19972
Person.Person	BASE TABLE	19972
Person.EmailAddress	BASE TABLE	19972
Sales.Customer	BASE TABLE	19820
Person.Address	BASE TABLE	19614
Person.BusinessEntityAddress	BASE TABLE	19614
Sales.PersonCreditCard	BASE TABLE	19118
Sales.CreditCard	BASE TABLE	19118
Sales.CurrencyRate	BASE TABLE	13532
Purchasing.PurchaseOrderDetail	BASE TABLE	8845
Purchasing.PurchaseOrderHeader	BASE TABLE	4012
Production.BillOfMaterials	BASE TABLE	2679
Production.ProductInventory	BASE TABLE	1069
Person.BusinessEntityContact	BASE TABLE	909
Production.ProductDescription	BASE TABLE	762
Production.ProductModelProductDescriptionCulture	BASE TABLE	762
Sales.Store	BASE TABLE	701
Sales.SpecialOfferProduct	BASE TABLE	538
Production.Product	BASE TABLE	504
Production.ProductProductPhoto	BASE TABLE	504
Purchasing.ProductVendor	BASE TABLE	460
Production.ProductListPriceHistory	BASE TABLE	395
Production.ProductCostHistory	BASE TABLE	395
HumanResources.EmployeePayHistory	BASE TABLE	316
HumanResources.EmployeeDepartmentHistory	BASE TABLE	296
HumanResources.Employee	BASE TABLE	290
Person.CountryRegion	BASE TABLE	238
Person.StateProvince	BASE TABLE	181
Sales.SalesPersonQuotaHistory	BASE TABLE	163
Production.ProductModel	BASE TABLE	128

Sales.CountryRegionCurrency	BASE TABLE	109
Sales.Currency	BASE TABLE	105
Purchasing.Vendor	BASE TABLE	104
Production.ProductPhoto	BASE TABLE	101
Production.UnitMeasure	BASE TABLE	38
Production.ProductSubcategory	BASE TABLE	37
Production.ProductDocument	BASE TABLE	32
Sales.SalesTaxRate	BASE TABLE	29
Person.ContactType	BASE TABLE	20
Sales.SalesTerritoryHistory	BASE TABLE	17
Sales.SalesPerson	BASE TABLE	17
HumanResources.Department	BASE TABLE	16
Sales.SpecialOffer	BASE TABLE	16
Production.ScrapReason	BASE TABLE	16
Production.Location	BASE TABLE	14
Production.Document	BASE TABLE	13
HumanResources.JobCandidate	BASE TABLE	13
Sales.SalesTerritory	BASE TABLE	10
Sales.SalesReason	BASE TABLE	10
Production.Culture	BASE TABLE	8
Production.Illustration	BASE TABLE	5
Purchasing.ShipMethod	BASE TABLE	5
Production.ProductCategory	BASE TABLE	4
Production.ProductReview	BASE TABLE	4
Person.PhoneNumberType	BASE TABLE	3
Sales.ShoppingCartItem	BASE TABLE	3
HumanResources.Shift	BASE TABLE	3
dbo.AWBuildVersion	BASE TABLE	1
dbo.DatabaseLog	BASE TABLE	0
dbo.ErrorLog	BASE TABLE	0
Sales.SalesOrderHeaderSalesReason	BASE TABLE	0
Person.AddressType	BASE TABLE	0
Production.ProductModelIllustration	BASE TABLE	0
Production.WorkOrder	BASE TABLE	0

We shall populate the last 4 tables with SS Import/Export Wizard from SS 2012 (Earth-based) AdventureWorks2012 database. Full-text index is not supported, therefore a stored procedure using full-text search must be dropped:

DROP PROCEDURE [dbo].[uspSearchCandidateResumes]

CHAPTER 23: Installing Azure SQL & Sample Cloud DBs

Command Prompt Window with Upload Command

```
Command Prompt                                                    _ □ ✕
F:\UTIL\Microsoft\Azure>cd sampledb

F:\UTIL\Microsoft\Azure\sampledb>dir
 Volume in drive F is Secondary HDD
 Volume Serial Number is 96F5-D46B

 Directory of F:\UTIL\Microsoft\Azure\sampledb

01/06/2013  03:27 PM    <DIR>          .
01/06/2013  03:27 PM    <DIR>          ..
01/06/2013  03:27 PM    <DIR>          AdventureWorks
01/06/2013  03:27 PM    <DIR>          AdventureWorks2008R2AZ
01/05/2013  03:17 AM        11,069,693 AdventureWorks2008R2AZ.zip
01/05/2013  03:16 AM        21,383,740 AdventureWorks2012ForSQLAzure.zip
01/06/2013  03:27 PM    <DIR>          AdventureWorks_Federated
01/06/2013  03:27 PM    <DIR>          Data
02/02/2012  02:06 PM             7,168 ExecuteSQL.exe
02/14/2012  10:13 AM            34,644 ReadMe.htm
               4 File(s)     32,495,245 bytes
               6 Dir(s)  1,582,238,818,304 bytes free

F:\UTIL\Microsoft\Azure\sampledb>cd adventureworks

F:\UTIL\Microsoft\Azure\sampledb\AdventureWorks>CreateAdventureWorksForSQLAzure.
cmd yourserverid.database.windows.net yourserverlogin yourpassword
```

Upload in Progress

Note: the error messages are due to the repeat execution of the upload utility.

```
Command Prompt - CreateAdventureWorksForSQLAzure.cmd llgzjlx8r.database.windows.net Blue...   _ □ ✕
1000 rows sent to SQL Server. Total sent: 7000
1000 rows sent to SQL Server. Total sent: 8000
1000 rows sent to SQL Server. Total sent: 9000
1000 rows sent to SQL Server. Total sent: 10000
1000 rows sent to SQL Server. Total sent: 11000
1000 rows sent to SQL Server. Total sent: 12000
1000 rows sent to SQL Server. Total sent: 13000
1000 rows sent to SQL Server. Total sent: 14000
1000 rows sent to SQL Server. Total sent: 15000
1000 rows sent to SQL Server. Total sent: 16000
1000 rows sent to SQL Server. Total sent: 17000
1000 rows sent to SQL Server. Total sent: 18000
1000 rows sent to SQL Server. Total sent: 19000
1000 rows sent to SQL Server. Total sent: 20000
SQLState = 23000, NativeError = 2627
Error = [Microsoft][SQL Server Native Client 11.0][SQL Server]Violation of PRIMA
RY KEY constraint 'PK_BusinessEntity_BusinessEntityID'. Cannot insert duplicate
key in object 'Person.BusinessEntity'. The duplicate key value is (1).
SQLState = 01000, NativeError = 3621
Warning = [Microsoft][SQL Server Native Client 11.0][SQL Server]The statement ha
s been terminated.

BCP copy in failed
Populating Person.ContactType
```

SS Import/Export Wizard for Migrating Data to Azure SQL

We will populate empty Azure tables from SS tables. SSMS Object Explorer view of the cloud and Earth (on-premises) servers.

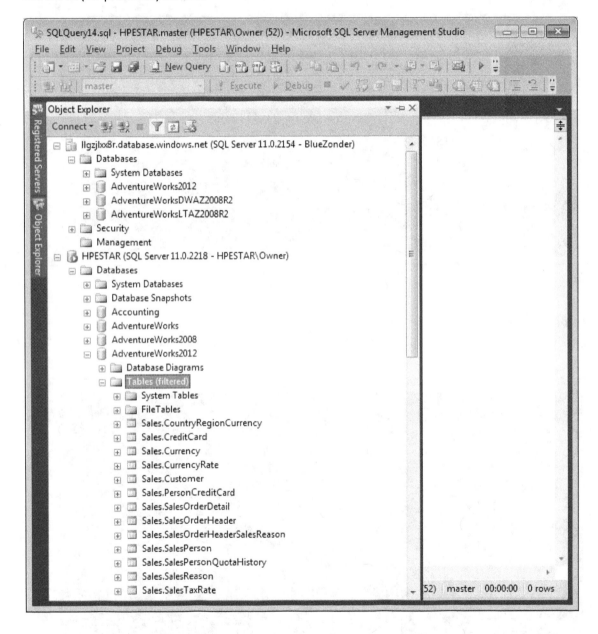

Launching the SS Import/Export Wizard

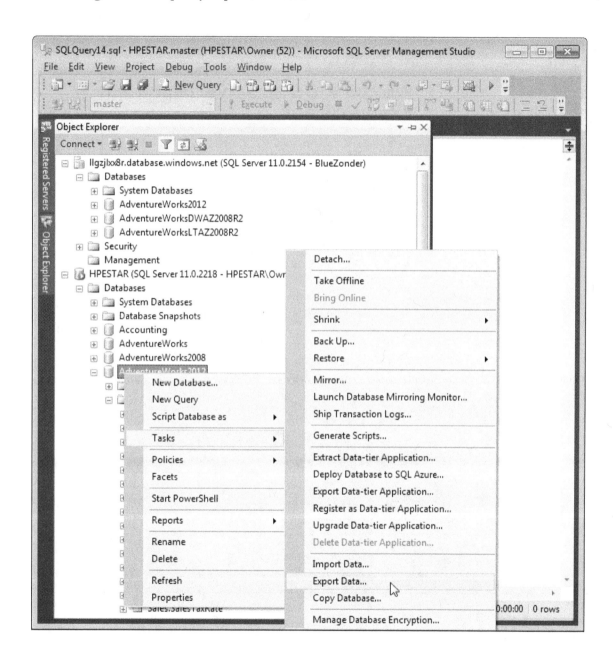

SQL Server Import/Export Wizard Welcome Page

Data Source Page with Automatic Fillin Values

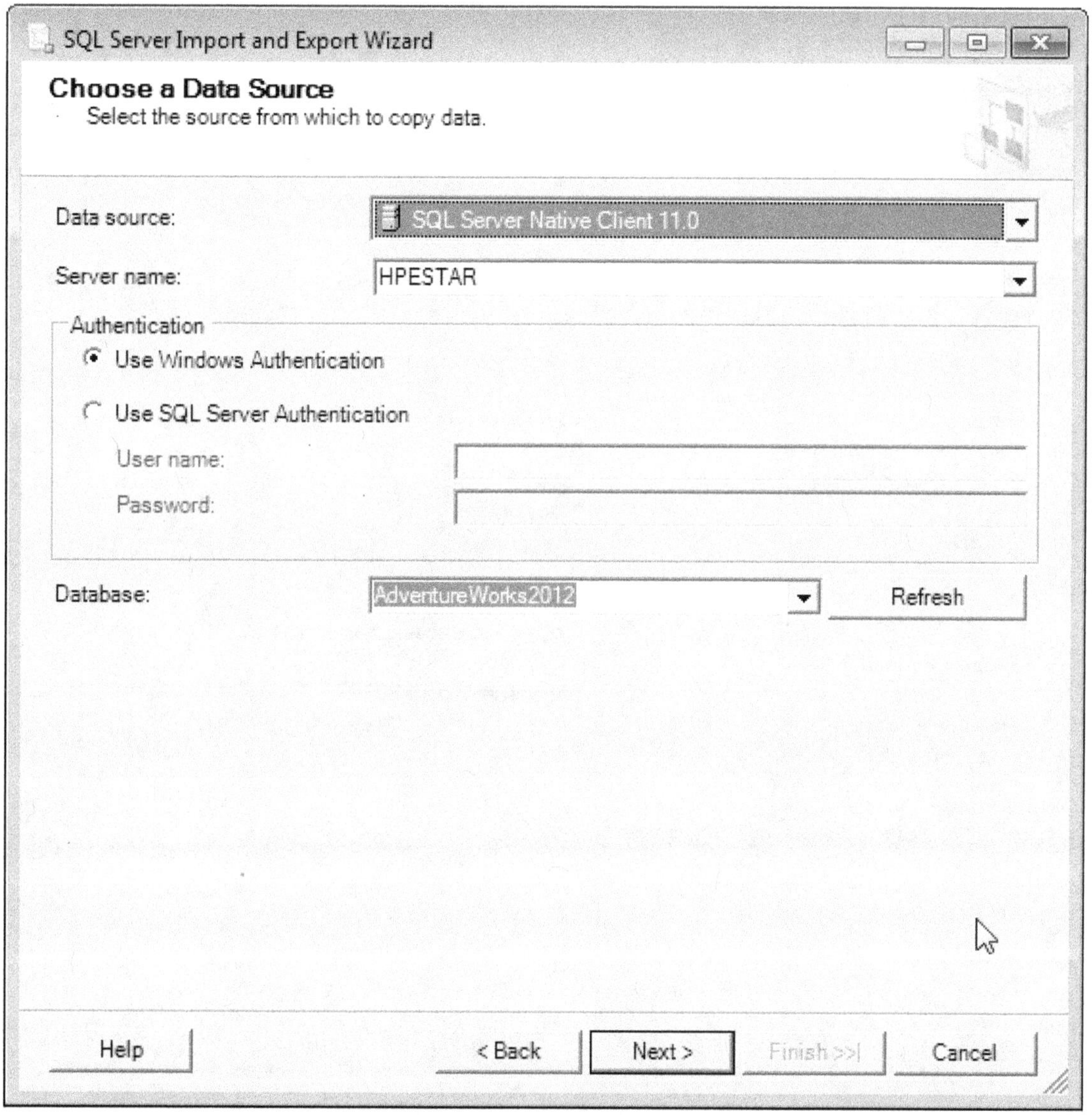

Destination Page - Azure SQL Database

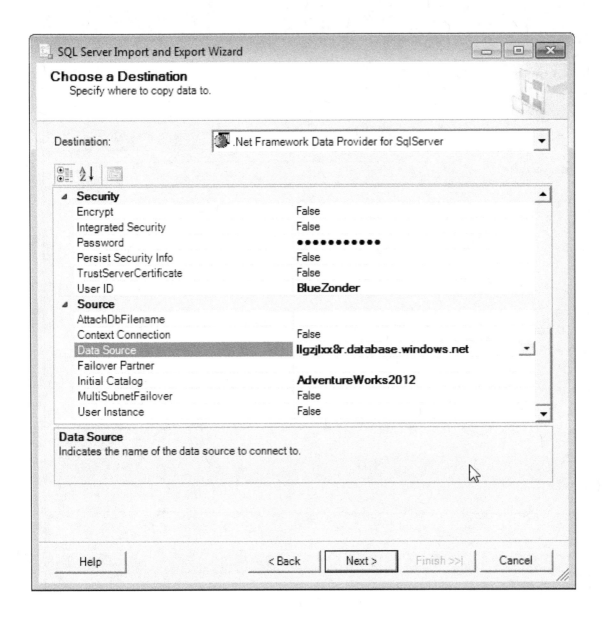

Choose Table Copy or Query Results Copy

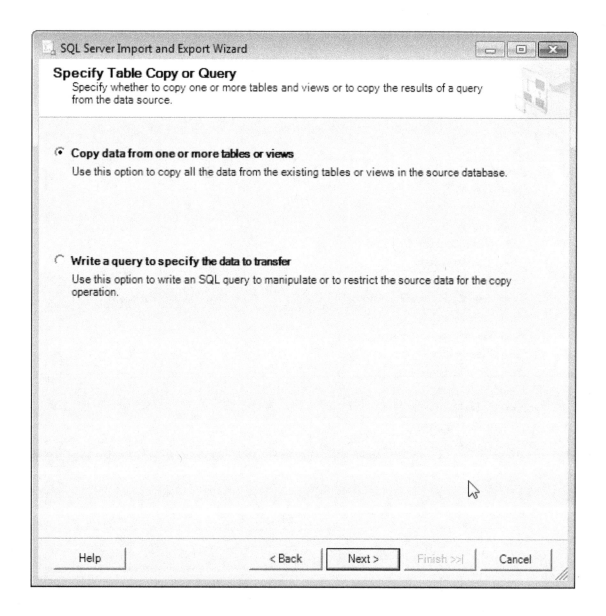

Choose Table to Copy

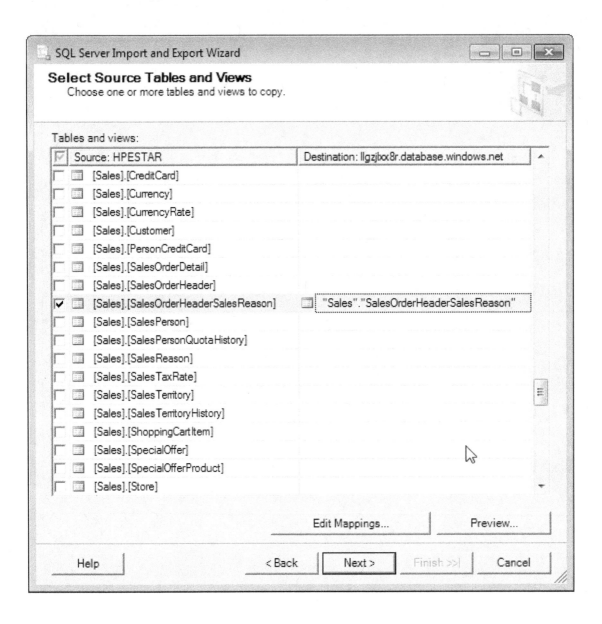

Column Mapping & Preview Data Pages - No Change

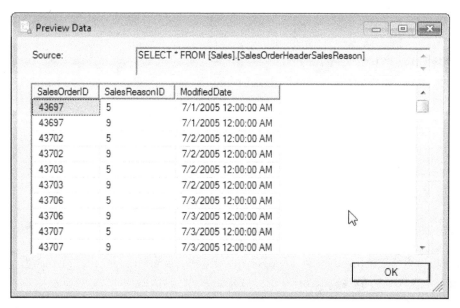

A Computed Column Must Be Mapped with IGNORE

The following page is nor related to the current table transfer, it is just an explanation using the Production.Workorder table tranfer process.

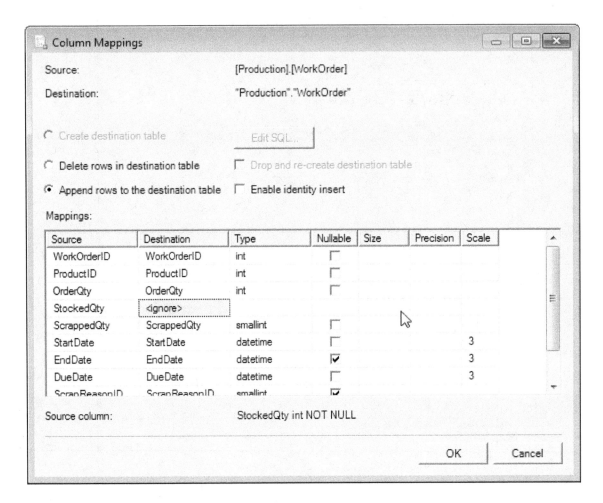

Creating Clustered Index

Create clustered index by script:

```
CREATE CLUSTERED INDEX idxDBLog on databaselog(PostTime, DatabaseUser, Event);
```

A table can only have 1 clustered index and 0 to many nonclustered indexes. Clustered index is a requirement in SQL Azure, exception temporary tables.

CHAPTER 23: Installing Azure SQL & Sample Cloud DBs

Save & Run Options Page

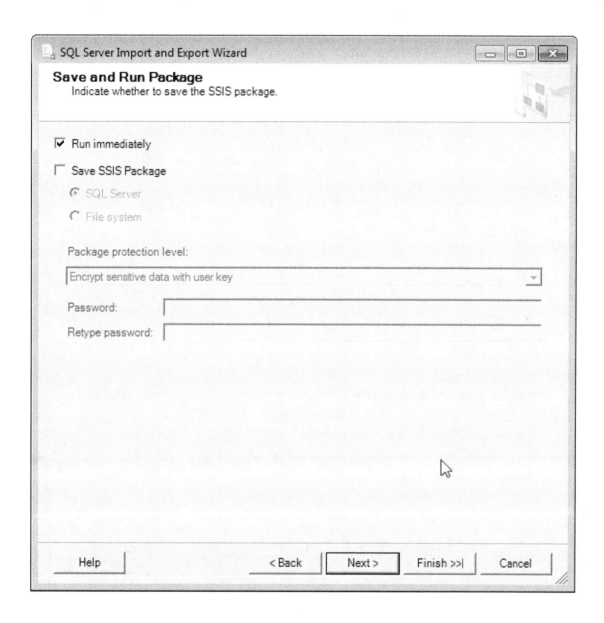

Finish & Execution Page

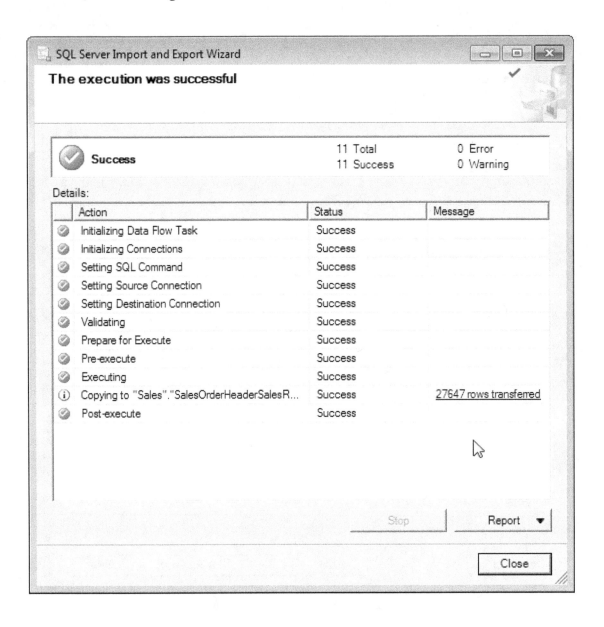

AdventureWorks2012 Final Tables Population

Most of the tables were populated by the upload utility, the rest by SQL Server Import and Export Wizard.

TableName	TableType	Population
Sales.SalesOrderDetail	BASE TABLE	121317
Production.TransactionHistory	BASE TABLE	113443
Production.TransactionHistoryArchive	BASE TABLE	89253
Production.WorkOrder	BASE TABLE	72591
Production.WorkOrderRouting	BASE TABLE	67131
Sales.SalesOrderHeader	BASE TABLE	31465
Sales.SalesOrderHeaderSalesReason	BASE TABLE	27647
Person.BusinessEntity	BASE TABLE	20777
Person.Password	BASE TABLE	19972
Person.Person	BASE TABLE	19972
Person.PersonPhone	BASE TABLE	19972
Person.EmailAddress	BASE TABLE	19972
Sales.Customer	BASE TABLE	19820
Person.Address	BASE TABLE	19614
Person.BusinessEntityAddress	BASE TABLE	19614
Sales.PersonCreditCard	BASE TABLE	19118
Sales.CreditCard	BASE TABLE	19118
Sales.CurrencyRate	BASE TABLE	13532
Purchasing.PurchaseOrderDetail	BASE TABLE	8845
Purchasing.PurchaseOrderHeader	BASE TABLE	4012
Production.BillOfMaterials	BASE TABLE	2679
Production.ProductInventory	BASE TABLE	1069
Person.BusinessEntityContact	BASE TABLE	909
Production.ProductDescription	BASE TABLE	762
Production.ProductModelProductDescriptionCulture	BASE TABLE	762
Sales.Store	BASE TABLE	701
Sales.SpecialOfferProduct	BASE TABLE	538
Production.Product	BASE TABLE	504
Production.ProductProductPhoto	BASE TABLE	504
Purchasing.ProductVendor	BASE TABLE	460
Production.ProductListPriceHistory	BASE TABLE	395
Production.ProductCostHistory	BASE TABLE	395
HumanResources.EmployeePayHistory	BASE TABLE	316
HumanResources.EmployeeDepartmentHistory	BASE TABLE	296
HumanResources.Employee	BASE TABLE	290

Person.CountryRegion	BASE TABLE	238
Person.StateProvince	BASE TABLE	181
Sales.SalesPersonQuotaHistory	BASE TABLE	163
Production.ProductModel	BASE TABLE	128
Sales.CountryRegionCurrency	BASE TABLE	109
Sales.Currency	BASE TABLE	105
Purchasing.Vendor	BASE TABLE	104
Production.ProductPhoto	BASE TABLE	101
Production.UnitMeasure	BASE TABLE	38
Production.ProductSubcategory	BASE TABLE	37
Production.ProductDocument	BASE TABLE	32
Sales.SalesTaxRate	BASE TABLE	29
Person.ContactType	BASE TABLE	20
Sales.SalesPerson	BASE TABLE	17
Sales.SalesTerritoryHistory	BASE TABLE	17
HumanResources.Department	BASE TABLE	16
Sales.SpecialOffer	BASE TABLE	16
Production.ScrapReason	BASE TABLE	16
Production.Location	BASE TABLE	14
Production.Document	BASE TABLE	13
HumanResources.JobCandidate	BASE TABLE	13
Sales.SalesTerritory	BASE TABLE	10
Sales.SalesReason	BASE TABLE	10
Production.Culture	BASE TABLE	8
Production.ProductModelIllustration	BASE TABLE	7
Person.AddressType	BASE TABLE	6
Production.Illustration	BASE TABLE	5
Purchasing.ShipMethod	BASE TABLE	5
Production.ProductCategory	BASE TABLE	4
Production.ProductReview	BASE TABLE	4
Person.PhoneNumberType	BASE TABLE	3
Sales.ShoppingCartItem	BASE TABLE	3
HumanResources.Shift	BASE TABLE	3
dbo.AWBuildVersion	BASE TABLE	1
dbo.DatabaseLog	BASE TABLE	0
dbo.ErrorLog	BASE TABLE	0

AdventureWorksDWAZ2008R2 Tables Population

The upload utility worked without error.

TableName	TableType	Population
dbo.FactInternetSalesReason	BASE TABLE	63877
dbo.FactResellerSales	BASE TABLE	60253
dbo.FactInternetSales	BASE TABLE	59800
dbo.FactFinance	BASE TABLE	39019
dbo.DimCustomer	BASE TABLE	18301
dbo.FactAdditionalInternationalProductDescription	BASE TABLE	15018
dbo.FactCurrencyRate	BASE TABLE	14123
dbo.FactSurveyResponse	BASE TABLE	2700
dbo.ProspectiveBuyer	BASE TABLE	2039
dbo.DimDate	BASE TABLE	1177
dbo.DimReseller	BASE TABLE	695
dbo.DimGeography	BASE TABLE	649
dbo.DimProduct	BASE TABLE	600
dbo.DimEmployee	BASE TABLE	294
dbo.FactSalesQuota	BASE TABLE	162
dbo.FactCallCenter	BASE TABLE	119
dbo.DimCurrency	BASE TABLE	104
dbo.DimAccount	BASE TABLE	99
dbo.DimProductSubcategory	BASE TABLE	37
dbo.DimPromotion	BASE TABLE	16
dbo.DimOrganization	BASE TABLE	14
dbo.DimSalesTerritory	BASE TABLE	11
dbo.DimSalesReason	BASE TABLE	10
dbo.DimDepartmentGroup	BASE TABLE	7
dbo.DimProductCategory	BASE TABLE	4
dbo.DimScenario	BASE TABLE	3
dbo.AdventureWorksDWBuildVersion	BASE TABLE	1
dbo.DatabaseLog	BASE TABLE	0

AdventureWorksLTAZ2008R2 Tables Population

The upload did not have any error.

TableName	TableType	Population
SalesLT.Customer	BASE TABLE	839
SalesLT.ProductDescription	BASE TABLE	755
SalesLT.ProductModelProductDescription	BASE TABLE	755
SalesLT.SalesOrderDetail	BASE TABLE	537
SalesLT.Address	BASE TABLE	446
SalesLT.CustomerAddress	BASE TABLE	413
SalesLT.Product	BASE TABLE	293
SalesLT.ProductModel	BASE TABLE	127
SalesLT.ProductCategory	BASE TABLE	41
SalesLT.SalesOrderHeader	BASE TABLE	32
dbo.BuildVersion	BASE TABLE	1
dbo.ErrorLog	BASE TABLE	0

Migrate pubs & Northwind to Azure SQL Server

First download the sample databases.

> Download Center: **Northwind and pubs Sample Databases for SQL Server 2000**
> http://www.microsoft.com/en-us/download/details.aspx?id=23654

Paste instpubs.sql script into a Query Editor window. It requires manual fixes to make it work. For example, adding PRIMARY KEY with clustered index to some tables prior to population or sp_addtype had to be replaced with CREATE TYPE.

pubs tables population

TableName	TableType	Population
dbo.roysched	BASE TABLE	86
dbo.employee	BASE TABLE	43
dbo.jobs	BASE TABLE	28
dbo.titleauthor	BASE TABLE	25
dbo.authors	BASE TABLE	23
dbo.sales	BASE TABLE	21
dbo.titles	BASE TABLE	18
dbo.pub_info	BASE TABLE	8
dbo.publishers	BASE TABLE	8
dbo.stores	BASE TABLE	6
dbo.discounts	BASE TABLE	3

Installing instnwnd.sql Script

Similarly converting the script, the biggest change was adding PRIMARY KEY with clustered index to some (secondary) tables.

Northwind tables population

TableName	TableType	Population
dbo.Order Details	BASE TABLE	2155
dbo.Orders	BASE TABLE	830
dbo.Customers	BASE TABLE	91
dbo.Products	BASE TABLE	77
dbo.Territories	BASE TABLE	53
dbo.EmployeeTerritories	BASE TABLE	49
dbo.Suppliers	BASE TABLE	29
dbo.Employees	BASE TABLE	9
dbo.Categories	BASE TABLE	8
dbo.Region	BASE TABLE	4
dbo.Shippers	BASE TABLE	3
dbo.CustomerCustomerDemo	BASE TABLE	0
dbo.CustomerDemographics	BASE TABLE	0

CHAPTER 23: Installing Azure SQL & Sample Cloud DBs

Discovering the New SQL Azure Instance

We can start probing the new SQL Server instance in Query Editor & Object Explorer.

```
SELECT @@VERSION;
-- Microsoft SQL Azure (RTM) - 11.0.2154.0 ....
```

```
SELECT @@SERVERNAME;
-- llgzjlxx8r
```

```
-- SS Version, Level (service pack), Edition
SELECT    CONCAT ('Microsoft SQL Azure ',convert(varchar, SERVERPROPERTY('ProductVersion') ), ' -- ',
          convert(varchar, SERVERPROPERTY('ProductLevel') ), ' -- ',convert(varchar, SERVERPROPERTY('Edition') ));
-- Microsoft SQL Azure 11.0.2295.0 -- RTM -- SQL Azure
```

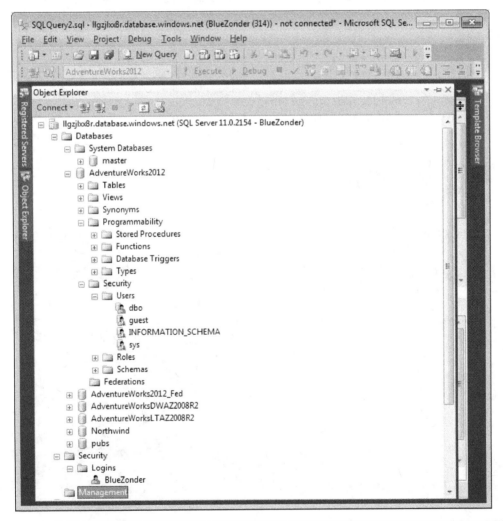

Connecting to 2 SQL Server Instances Simultaneously

SSMS Object Explorer support multiple SS instances connections. Warning: **Production, QA and Development SS instances may look similar, an opportunity to get confused and carry out actions on the wrong server**. Best prevention: **take regular database backups and connect only to one SQL Server instance at one time**.

The first connection is the SQL Azure instance, the second is the SQL Server default instance.

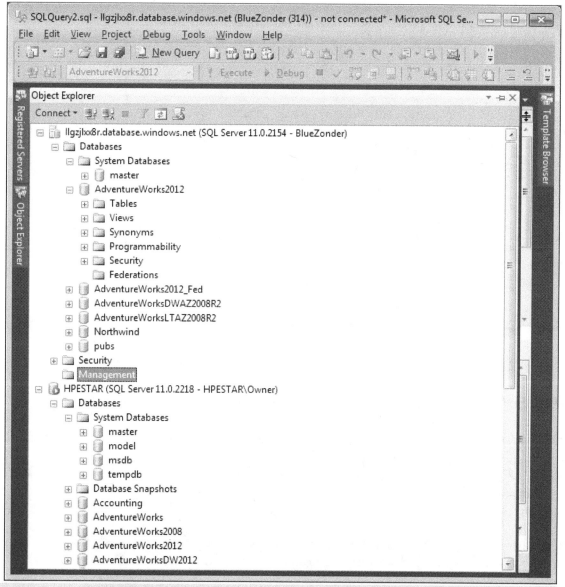

CHAPTER 23: Installing Azure SQL & Sample Cloud DBs

Linked Server to Windows Azure SQL Database

Windows Azure SQL Database server can be configured as linked server from a on-premises SQL Server 2012 (not supported the reverse way). First we have to setup a system DSN.

1. Control Panel, System & Security, Administrative Tools, Data Sources(ODBC), System DSN

2. Add SQL Server Native Client 11.0, "AzureDSN", yourserver. database.windows.net,1433

3. SQL Server authentication: yourazuresqllogin, yourazuresqlpassword

4. Enter default database AdventureWorks2012, Test connection & click "OK"

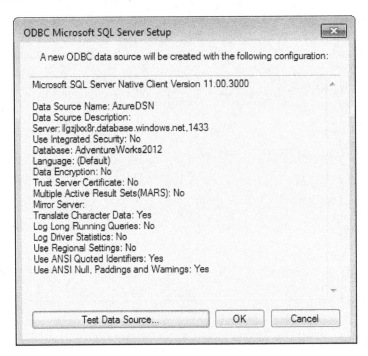

T-SQL Script for Linked Server Setup in On-Premises SQL Serv er

```
USE master;              -- Linked server to Windows Azure SQL Database
EXEC master.dbo.sp_addlinkedserver @server = N'ALPHA_AZURE',
@srvproduct=N'Microsoft OLE DB Provider for ODBC Driver',
@provider=N'MSDASQL', @datasrc='AzureDSN', @location='localhost',
@catalog='AdventureWorks2012';
```

```
EXEC master.dbo.sp_addlinkedsrvlogin @rmtsrvname=N'ALPHA_AZURE', @useself=N'False',
@locallogin=NULL, @rmtuser='yourazuresqllogin', @rmtpassword='yourazuresqlpassword';
```

Querying Azure SQL Database via Linked Server

The queries are executed on-premises SQL Server. The data is from Azure SQL Database.

> Blog: **Linked Server and Distributed Queries against Windows Azure SQL Database**
> http://blogs.msdn.com/b/windowsazure/archive/2012/09/19/announcing-updates-to-windows-azure-sql-database.aspx

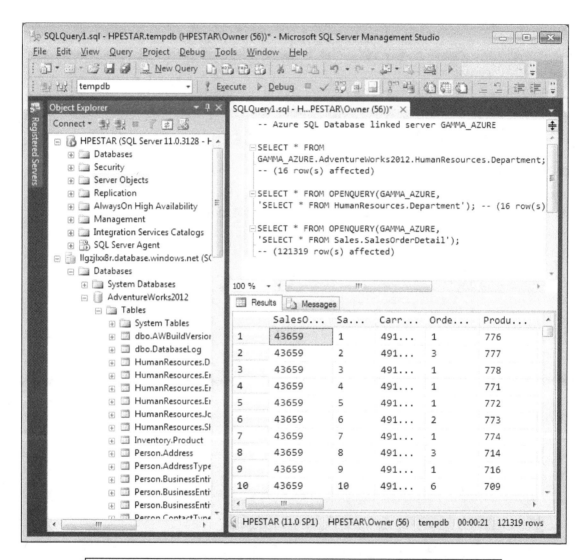

> Note: At the time of book writing some table queries returned errors.
> Example: HumanResources. Shift table with time(7) data type.

SQL Server 2012 BACKUP DATABASE Command

SQL Server 2012 database backup command; the backup filename can be changed at will to reflect the backup date.

```
BACKUP DATABASE [AdventureWorks2012] TO  DISK = N'F:\data\backup\AW20161023.bak';
```

```
-- Dynamic backup filename with datestamp
DECLARE @Filename nvarchar(64) = CONCAT(N'F:\data\backup\AW', CONVERT(varchar,
CONVERT(DATE, getdate())),'.bak');
BACKUP DATABASE [AdventureWorks2012] TO  DISK = @Filename;
-- AW2018-08-23.bak
```

Export Data-tier Application - Azure SQL

The export file (.bacpac) includes both the definitions of the objects in the database and all of the data in the tables. Export launching sequence. Windows Azure SQL Database Import / Export operations can copy databases between Windows Azure SQL Database servers, or can migrate databases between the SQL Server Database Engine and Windows Azure SQL Database.

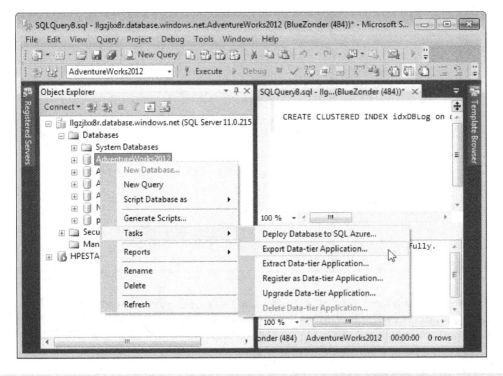

CHAPTER 23: Installing Azure SQL & Sample Cloud DBs

Introduction Page

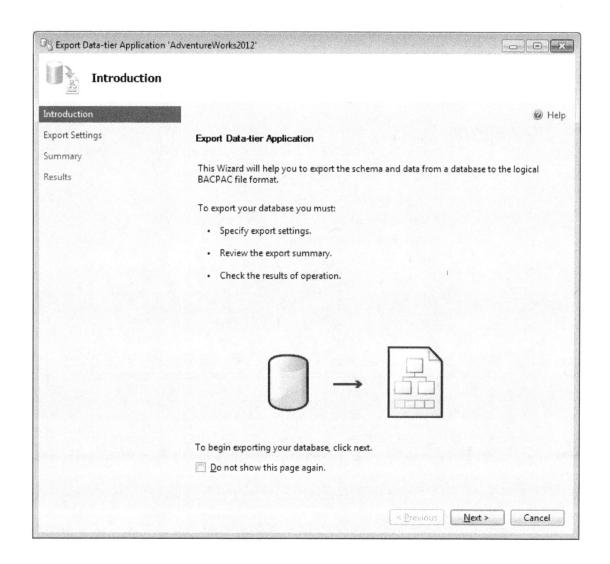

Export Settings

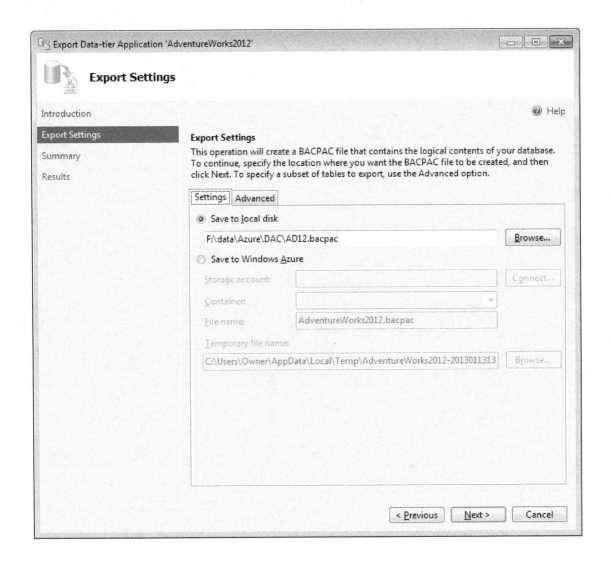

Advanced Export Settings

Summary

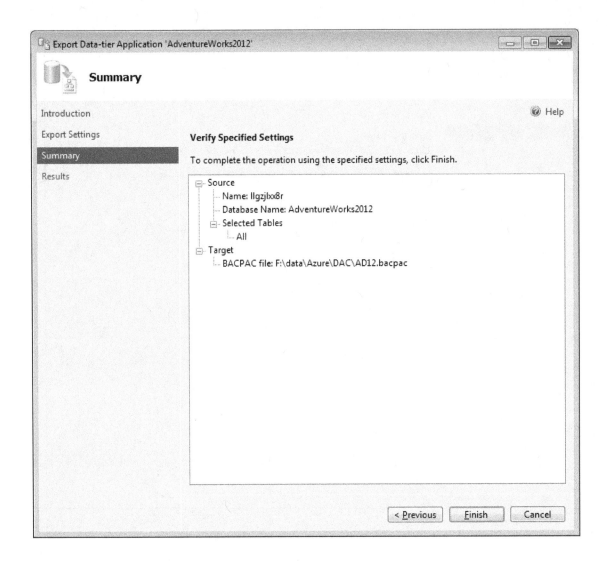

Progress

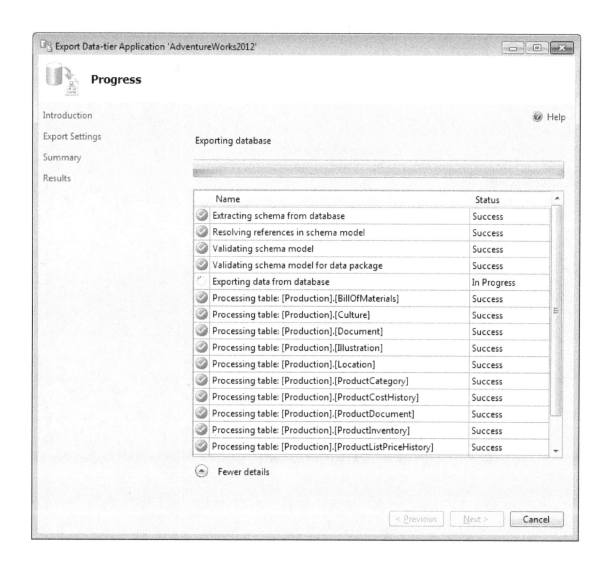

Operation Complete - Elapsed Time 2 Minutes

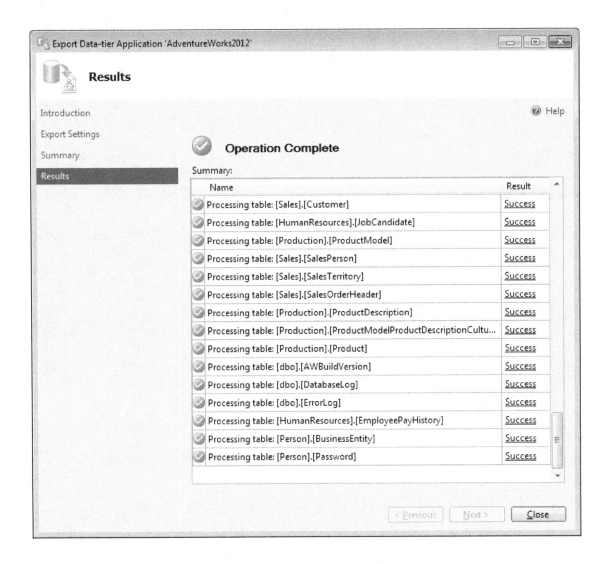

Import Data-tier Application

Import recreates the database from the .bacpac file.

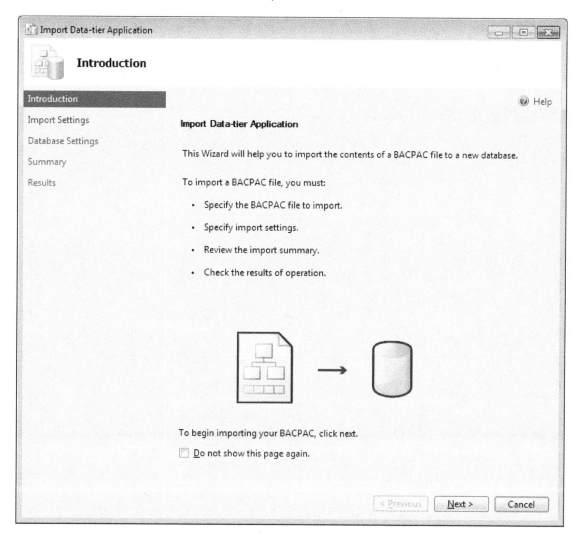

Import Settings

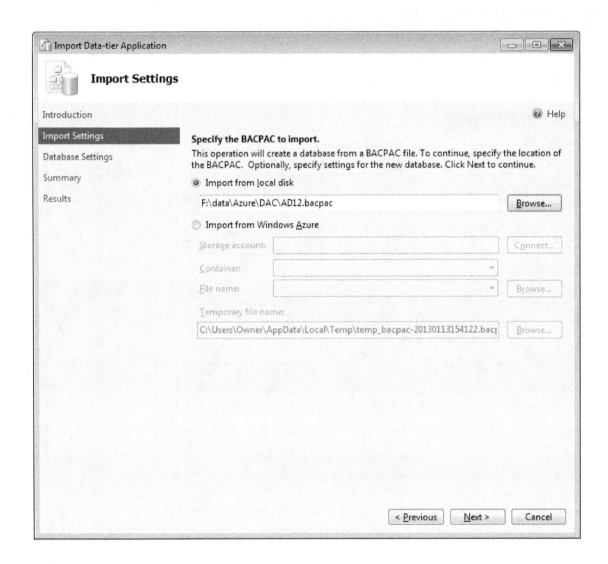

Database Settings

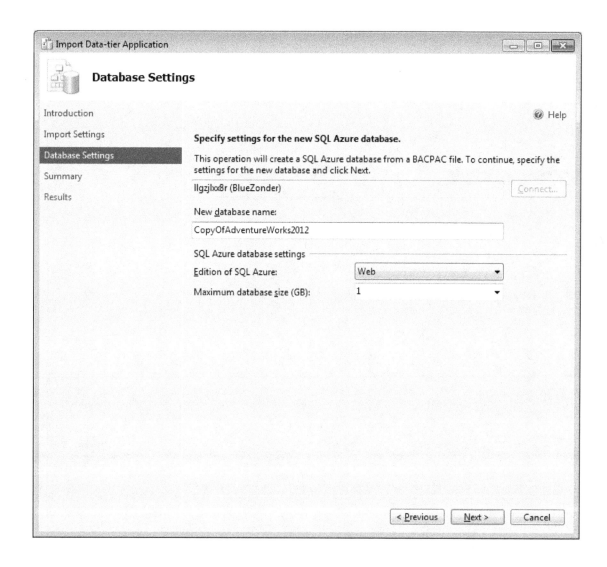

Summary

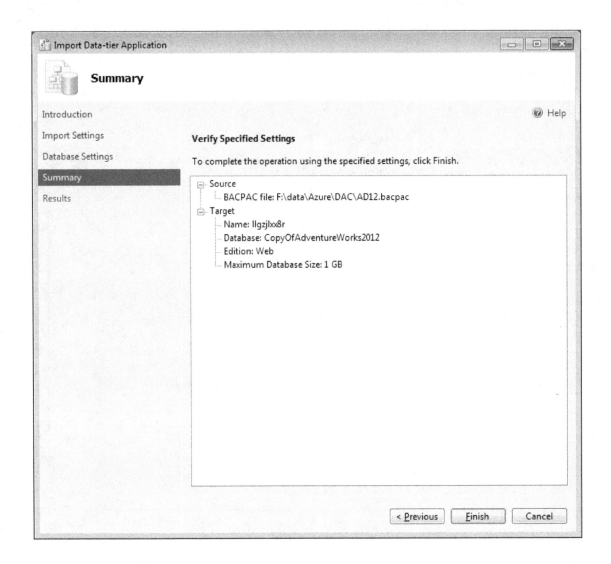

Importing Progress

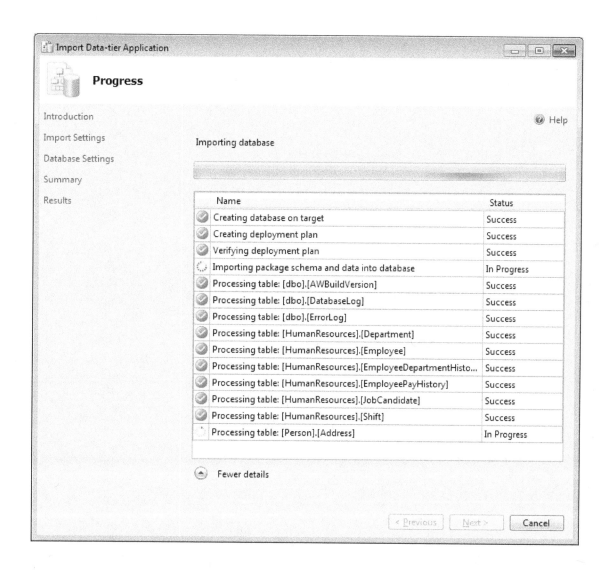

Operation Complete - Elapsed Time 20 Minutes

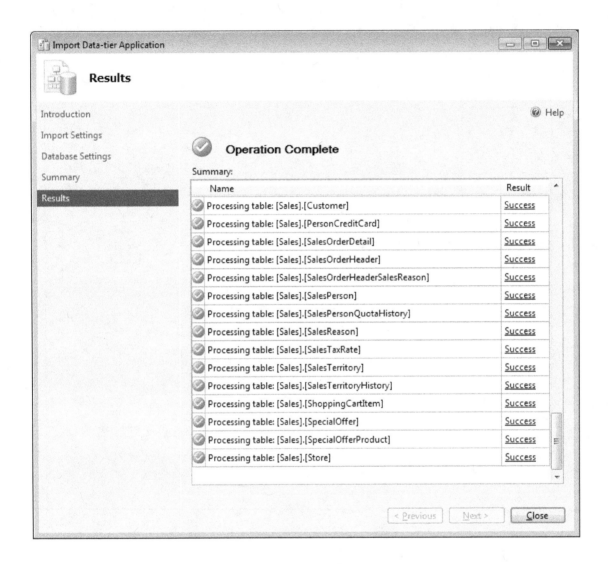

Deploy Data-tier Application

A data-tier application (DAC) is an entity that contains all of the database & SQL Server instance objects used by an application. The DAC package file can be generated by Visual Studio, SSMS Extract Data-tier Application or some utilities.

```
                          MSDN Articles
  Understanding Data-tier Applications
  http://msdn.microsoft.com/en-us/library/ee240739(v=sql.105).aspx

  Deploying Data-tier Applications
  http://msdn.microsoft.com/en-us/library/ee210580(v=sql.105).aspx
```

The deployment file type is .dacpac.

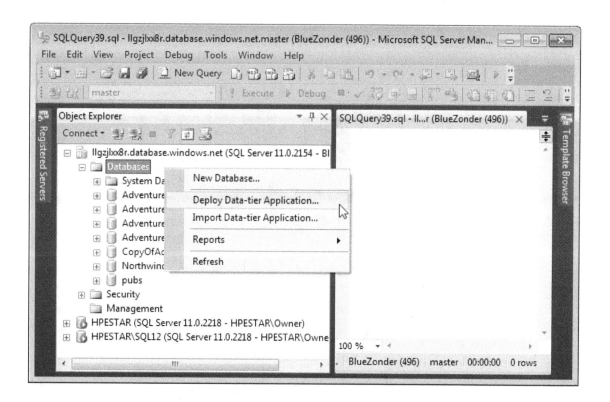

The Introduction Page Explains the Process

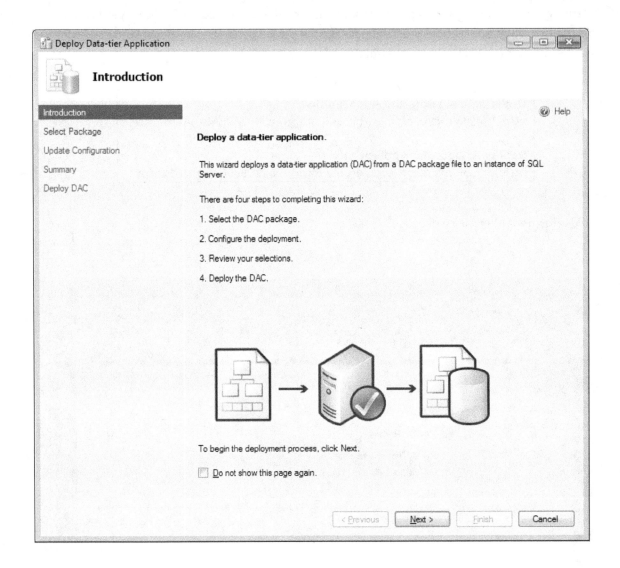

Select the DAC Package to Deploy

Configure the Database Deployment Properties

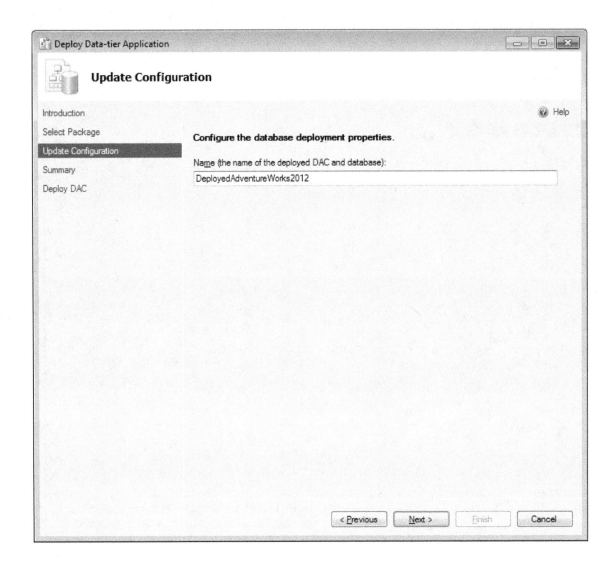

Summary screen follows. Click Finish to start processing.

Object Explorer View After Deployment - Runtime around 1 minute
All tables are empty in deployed database. All objects are defined.

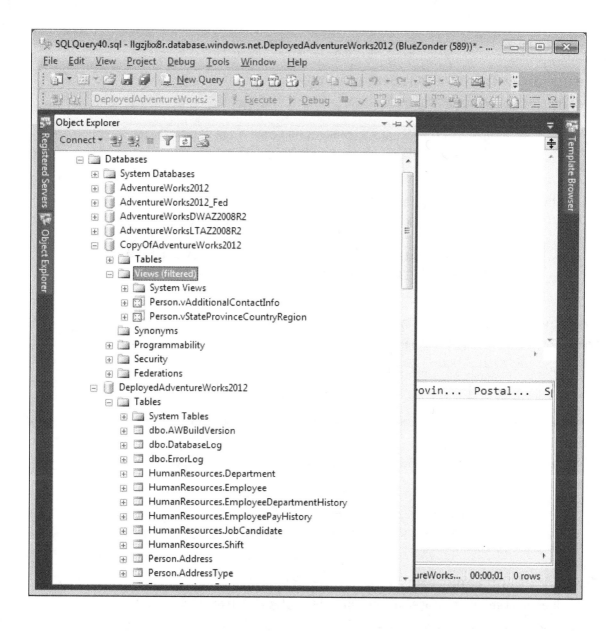

SQL Azure Books Online - BOL

Books Online is available on the web.

> **Windows Azure SQL Database**
> http://msdn.microsoft.com/en-us/library/windowsazure/ee336279.aspx

Unsupported Transact-SQL Statements

A very important section of BOL on unsupported T-SQL statements.

> **Unsupported Transact-SQL Statements (Windows Azure SQL Database)**
> http://msdn.microsoft.com/en-us/library/windowsazure/ee336253.aspx

Partially Supported Transact-SQL Statements

Another very important section of BOL on partially supported T-SQL statements.

> **Partially Supported Transact-SQL Statements (Windows Azure SQL Database)**
> http://msdn.microsoft.com/en-us/library/windowsazure/ee336267.aspx

Windows Azure Platform Management Portal

Windows Azure web management portal.

> Windows Azure Platform Management Portal
> http://msdn.microsoft.com/en-us/library/windowsazure/gg467325.aspx

Administration

Managing Azure SQL server & databases on management portal, migration and trouble-shooting.

> **Administration (Windows Azure SQL Database)**
> http://msdn.microsoft.com/en-us/library/windowsazure/ff394116.aspx

Guidelines and Limitations

Guidelines and Limitations page has very important information about SQL Azure.

> Guidelines and Limitations (Windows Azure SQL Database)
> http://msdn.microsoft.com/en-us/library/windowsazure/ff394102.aspx

Installing SQL Server 2012 AdventureWorks2012

AdventureWorks2012 and other related databases can be installed from the following webpage:
http://msftdbprodsamples.codeplex.com/releases/view/55330

Community Projects & Samples from the Start Menu will bring up the following site:
http://sqlserversamples.codeplex.com/

Installing SQL Server 2012 Northwind & pubs Databases

Northwind and pubs Sample Databases for SQL Server 2000
http://www.microsoft.com/en-us/download/details.aspx?displaylang=en&id=23654

CHAPTER 23: Installing Azure SQL & Sample Cloud DBs

SQL Database Migration Wizard

Download site information.

> **SQL Database Migration Wizard** v3.9.10 & v4.0.13
> http://sqlazuremw.codeplex.com/

Start the **SQLAzureMW** application in the download folder.

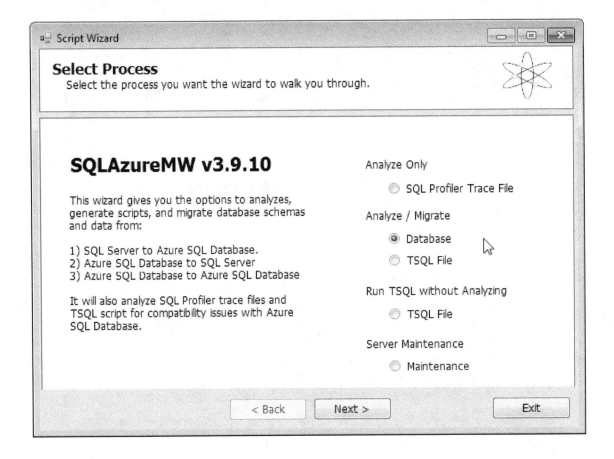

Connecting to Source Server & Database

Connect to Source (on-premises) Server using dialog pop-up and specify database (AdventureWorks).

Select source objects

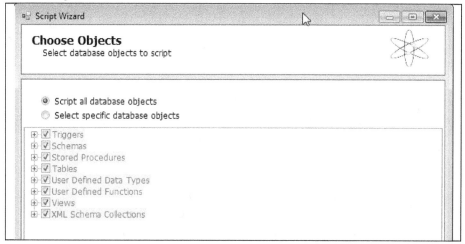

Scripting Summary

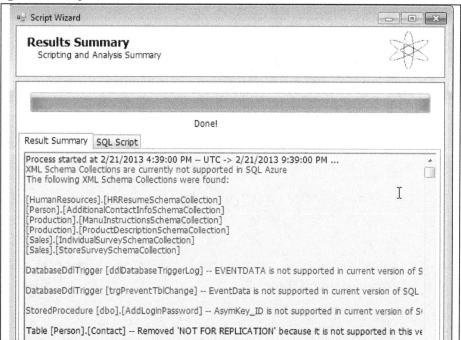

Connecting to Azure SQL Server and Starting the Upload

Connect to target Windows Azure SQL Database server. Usual dialog pop-up for server connection. Choose CREATE DATABASE at next window. New database name is AdventureWorks. Processing the scripts - uploading db objects and content.

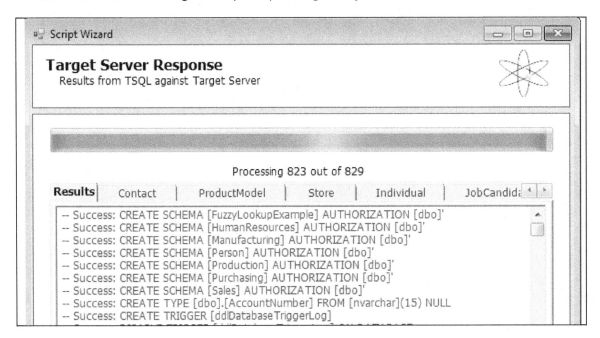

One of the bcp upload command log entries.

```
2/21/2016 4:55:14 PM
 --> Uploading data to PurchaseOrderHeader
 --> BCP Command: bcp.exe "AdventureWorks.Purchasing.PurchaseOrderHeader" in
"c:\SQLAzureMW\BCPData\Purchasing.PurchaseOrderHeader.dat" -E -w -b 10000 -a 16384 -q -S
llgzjlxx8r.database.windows.net -U "BlueZonder@llgzjlxx8r" -P "yyyyyyyyyyy"
*************************
2/21/2016 4:55:55 PM --> Copied 4000 of 4000 (100%)
Clock Time (ms.) Total    : 1498   Average : (2670.23 rows per sec.)
```

There were a few bcp upload errors. They need to be corrected inidividually either by using SQL Server Import/Export Wizard or other ETL tools.

.

Azure SQL Database Differences & Solutions

Some System Views Don't Execute in master DB

Some of the system views give error in master db while work OK in application db. Currently, there is no way of telling which works which not.

```
-- In master db
SELECT * FROM sys.dm_exec_query_stats;
/*  Msg 297, Level 16, State 1, Line 1
The user does not have permission to perform this action.  */
```

```
-- In AdventureWorks2012
SELECT * FROM sys.dm_exec_query_stats;
-- (7 row(s) affected)
```

Solution for USE dbname

USE dbname works only for the current database in the current connection. For a different database, a new connection must be opened. Current database is AdventureWorks2012, open a new connection for Northwind.

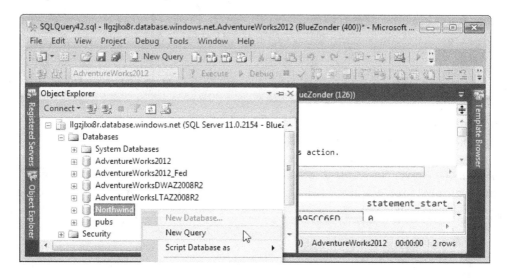

Solution for SELECT INTO

CREATE TABLE first, then INSERT SELECT. Alternative, use the SS Import/Export Wizard.

CHAPTER 23: Installing Azure SQL & Sample Cloud DBs

Solution for 3-part Naming - Cross Database Access

Use the SS Import/Export Wizard or similar data transfer tool.

Solution for Database BACKUP & RESTORE

If the database is not use, Export/Import Data-tier Application is similar to SQL Server 2012 BACKUP & RESTORE commands. However, if the database is in use, Export/Import will not handle transactional consistency.

> MSDN Blog: **Data backup strategies for Windows and SQL Azure**
> http://blogs.msdn.com/b/davidmcg/archive/2011/09/29/data-backup-strategies-for-windows-and-sql-azure.aspx

Solution for Changing Database in SSMS Query Editor

When connection is established to the master database, the drop-down window can be used to change database. It cannot be used for another change, a new connection must be open.

Solution for SQL Server Agent

SQL Server Agent is not supported in Azure SQL. There is no msdb system database.

> Blogs: **I Miss You SQL Server Agent: Part 1**
> http://blogs.msdn.com/b/sqlazure/archive/2010/07/30/10044271.aspx
>
> **I Miss You SQL Server Agent: Part 2**
> http://blogs.msdn.com/b/sqlazure/archive/2010/08/02/10045012.aspx
>
> **Linked Servers to SQL Azure**
> http://blogs.msdn.com/b/sqlcat/archive/2011/03/08/linked-servers-to-sql-azure.aspx
>
> **Build your own SQL Server Agent for Windows Azure SQL Database with the Scheduler**
> http://fabriccontroller.net/blog/posts/build-your-own-sql-server-agent-for-windows-azure-sql-database-with-the-scheduler/

SQL Data Synch - Cloud Replication

SQL Data Synch synchronizes selected data through a Windows Azure SQL Database instance. SQL Data Sync supports synchronizations within or across Windows Azure data centers. SQL Data Sync also supports hybrid configurations of Windows Azure SQL Database instances and Enterprise(on-premises) SQL Server databases. SQL Data Synch is in a way similar to SQL Server Replication in functionality, however, it is technologically different since it is based on

Articles: **SQL Data Sync**
http://msdn.microsoft.com/en-us/library/hh456371.aspx

SQL Data Sync Overview
http://social.technet.microsoft.com/wiki/contents/articles/1821.sql-data-sync-overview.aspx

SSMS: A transport-level error has occurred

The entire error message:

Msg 10053, Level 20, State 0, Line 0

A transport-level error has occurred when sending the request to the server. (provider: TCP Provider, error: 0 - An established connection was aborted by the software in your host machine.)

This is the message when in an SSMS timed-out connection query or script execution attempted. SSMS is trying to reestablish the connection in the background which may take seconds. Execution then should succeed when the execute icon is clicked.

Account & Billing Information

Two system views provide detail usage data for billing: sys.database_usage & sys.bandwidth_usage.

BOL: **Accounts and Billing in Windows Azure SQL Database**
http://msdn.microsoft.com/en-us/library/windowsazure/ee621788.aspx

Azure SQL Database Management Portal

The management portal can be accessed using a special URL:

https://yourservername.database.windows.net

Login and password required, database name is optional.

Query Editing & Running

A simplified version of SSMS Query Editor on-line.

```
SELECT P.Name AS ProductName, L.Name AS Location,
        SUM(PI.Quantity) AS QtyOnHand
FROM Production.Product AS P
    INNER JOIN Production.ProductInventory AS PI ON P.ProductID = PI.ProductID
    INNER JOIN Production.Location AS L ON PI.LocationID = L.LocationID
GROUP BY P.Name, L.Name ORDER BY ProductName, Location ;|
```

Messages   ▼
            Results

1   1069 Row(s)

ProductName	Location	QtyOnHand
Adjustable Race	Miscellaneous Storage	324
Adjustable Race	Subassembly	353
▶ Adjustable Race	Tool Crib	408
All-Purpose Bike Stand	Finished Goods Storage	144

Management icons:

- ➤ "Open" loads a query file from local disk.
- ➤ "Save as" saves query into a folder.
- ➤ "Actual Plan" displays actual execution plan as graphical chart.
- ➤ "Estimated Plan" displays estimated execution plan.

Administration Tools

Summary information is displayed and new database can be created.

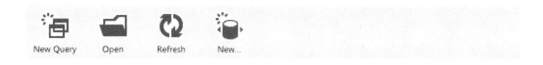

Database Properties

Date Created	1/6/2013 9:37:01 PM
Collation	SQL_Latin1_General_CP1_CI_AS
Read Only	False
Active Users	1
Active Connections	13
Maximum Size	1.00 GB
Space Used	123.36 MB
Free	87%

The **Query Performance** page displays performance related information and statistics on executed queries.

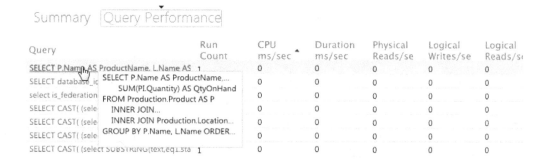

Design Tools

Design tools allow editing/creating/dropping of tables, views and stored procedures.
Dependency information can also be displayed in graphical format.

Tables   Views   Stored Procedures

Search by table name

Schema Name ▲	Table Name ▲	Table Size	Row Count		
Sales	CurrencyRate	1.15 MB	13532	⊘ Edit	(⦂) Dependencies
Sales	Customer	2.18 MB	19820		
Sales	PersonCreditCard	480.00 KB	19118		
Sales	SalesOrderDetail	15.30 MB	121319		
Sales	SalesOrderHeader	7.91 MB	31466	⊘ Edit	(⦂) Dependencies

Dependency subgraph for Sales.SalesOrderHeader table.

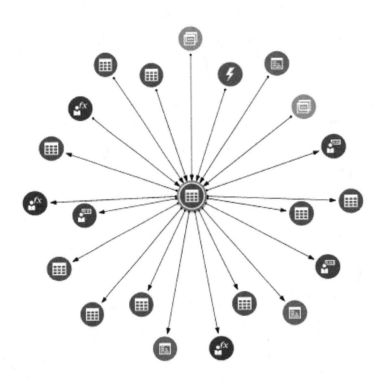

This page is intentionally left blank.

This page is intentionally left blank.

APPENDIX A: Job Interview Questions

Selected Database Design Questions

D1. What is your approach to database design?

D2. Some of our legacy databases are far from 3NF. Can you work in such an environment?

D3. Can UNIQUE KEY be used instead of PRIMARY KEY?

D4. Can a FOREIGN KEY be NULL?

D5. Can a PRIMARY KEY be NULL?

D6. Can a PRIMARY KEY be based on non-clustered unique index?

D7. Do you implement OrderQty > 0 condition as a CHECK constraint or in the application software?

D8. What is a heap?

D9. Can a table have 2 IDENTITY columns, 2 FOREIGN KEYs, 2 PRIMARY KEYs and 2 clustered indexes?

D10. Should each table have a NATURAL KEY or is INT IDENTITY PK sufficient?

D11. How can you prevent entry of "U.S", "USA", etc. instead of "United States" into Country column?

D12. How would you implement ManagerID in an Employee table with EmployeeID as PRIMARY KEY?

D13. How would you implement the relationship between OrderMaster and OrderDetail tables?

D14. Product table has the Color column. Would you create a Color table & change column to ColorID FK?

D15. Can you insert directly into an IDENTITY column?

D16. Which one is better? Composite PRIMARY KEY on NATURAL KEY, or INT IDENTITY PRIMARY KEY & UNIQUE KEY on NATURAL KEY?

D17. What is the lifetime of a regular table created in tempdb?

D18. How many different ways can you connect tables in a database?

D19. How would you connect the Vehicle and Owner tables?

D20. Can you have the same table names in different schemas?

Selected Database Programming Questions

P1. Write a query to list all departments with employee count based on the Department column of Employee table.

P2. Same as above but the Employee table has the DepartmentID column.

P3. Write an INSERT statement for a new "Social Technology" department with GroupName "Sales & Marketing".

P4. Same query es in P2, but the new department should be included even though no employees yet.

P5. Write a query to generate 1000 sequential numbers without a table.

P6. Write a query with SARGable predicate to list all orders from OrderMaster received on 2016-10-23. OrderDate is datetime.

P7. Write a query to add a header record DEPARTMENTNAME to the departments listing from the Department table. If there are 20 departments, the result set should have 21 records.

P8. Make the previous query a derived table in an outer SELECT * query

P9. Write an ORDER BY clause for the previous query with CASE expression to sort DEPARTMENTNAME as first record and alphabetically descending from there on.

P10. Same as above with the IIF conditional.

P11. The table-valued dbo.ufnSplitCSV splits a comma delimited string (input parameter). The Product table has some ProductName-s with comma(s). Write a CROSS APPLY query to return ProductName-s with comma and each split string value from the UDF as separate line. ProductName should repeat for each split part.

ProductName	SplitPart
Full-Finger Gloves, L	Full-Finger Gloves
Full-Finger Gloves, L	L

P12. You need the inserted lines count 10 lines down following the INSERT statement. What should be the statement immediately following the INSERT statement?

P13. What is the result of the second query? What is it called?

SELECT COUNT_BIG(*) FROM Sales.SalesOrderDetail;   -- 121317

SELECT COUNT_BIG(*) FROM Sales.SalesOrderDetail x, Sales.SalesOrderDetail y;

P14. Declare & Assign the string variable @Text varchar(32) the literal '2016/10/23 10:20:12' without the "/" and ":".

P15. You want to add a parameter to a frequently used view. What is the workaround?

P16. When converting up to 40 characters string, can you use varchar instead of varchar(40)?

P17. Can you roll back IDENTITY seeds and table variables with ROLLBACK TRANSACTION?

P18. How do you decide where to place the clustered index?

P19. What is the simplest solution for the collation error: "Cannot resolve collation conflict..."?

P20. Which system table can be used for integer sequence up to 2^12 values?

Selected Database Administration Questions

A1. What was the largest database you administered?
A2. What 3rd party tool did you use for db object and db data compare?
A3. What is the simplest database backup command?
A4. Can a script be created from Object Explorer GUI database restore?
A5. Tape backup is slow. What are the options?
A6. How can you automate database maintenance?
A7. Which is better choice performance wise: 10 SS instance with 1 db each or 1 instance with 10 db-s?
A8. Which is better choice operations wise: 1 huge db or 25 small db-s?
A9. You become in charge of a slow performing database. What 3 things you have to do first?
A10. Should you give minimal or maximal rights to users?
A11. What 2 database objects can be used as security mechanisms?
A12. A stored procedure has to be executed every night except Saturday and Sunday. What can you do?
A13. Flat file has to be uploaded into the database. Which is the best tool: bcp, BULK INSERT or Import/Export Wizard?
A14. What is the best tool to copy a table do a different database?
A15. A manager ask you to manually update 1 million rows due to mistake. What is the first step?
A16. Can transaction log backup peformed in the SIMPLE recovery mode?
A17. Development lead asks you to push 20 updated stored procedures to production. What is the first step?
A18. A developer wants to have xp_cmdshell rights to delete transient files on the production server instead of emailing and burdening you. What is your response?
A19. You have to monitor usage of a stored procedure for a week. What is the right tool?
A20. Why shouldn't the company switch to the free mysql?

This page is intentionally left blank.

This page is intentionally left blank.

This page is intentionally left blank.

APPENDIX B: Job Interview Answers

Selected Database Design Answers

D1. I prefer 3NF design due to high database developer productivity and low maintenance cost.

D2. I did have such projects in the past. I can handle them. Hopefully, introduce some improvements.

D3. Partially yes since UNIQUE KEYs can be FK referenced, fully no. Every table should a PRIMARY KEY.

D4. Yes.

D5. No.

D6. Yes. The default is clustered unique index. Only unique index is required.

D7. CHECK constraint. A server-side object solution is more reliable than code in application software.

D8. A table without clustered index. Database engine generally works better if a table has clustered index.

D9. No, yes, no, no.

D10. A table should be designed with NATURAL KEY(s). INT IDENTITY PK is not a replacement for NK.

D11. Lookup table with UDF CHECK Constraint. UDF checks the Lookup table for valid entries.

D12. ManagerID as a FOREIGN KEY referencing the PRIMARY KEY of the same table; self-referencing.

D13. OrderID PRIMARY KEY of OrderMaster. OrderID & LineItemID composition PK of OrderDetail. OrderID of OrderDetail FK to OrderID of OderMaster.

D14. Yes. It makes sense for color to be in its own table.

D15. No. Only if you SET IDENTITY_INSERT tablename ON.

D16. Meaningless INT IDENTITY PRIMARY KEY with UNIQUE KEY ON NATURAL KEY is better.

D17. Until SQL Server restarted. tempdb starts empty as copy of model database.

D18. There is only one way: FOREIGN KEY constraint.

D19. With the OwnerVehicleXref junction table reflecting many-to-many relationship.

D20. Yes. A table is identified by SchemaName.TableName . dbo is the default schema.

Selected Database Programming Answers

P1. SELECT Department, Employees=COUNT(*) FROM Employee
   GROUP BY Department ORDER BY Department;

P2. SELECT d.Department, Employees = COUNT(EmployeeID) FROM Employee e
   INNER JOIN Department d ON e.DepartmentID = d.DepartmentID
   GROUP BY d.Department ORDER BY Department;

P3. INSERT Department (Name, GroupName) VALUES ('Social Technology', 'Sales & Marketing');

P4. SELECT d.Department, Employees = COUNT(EmployeeID) FROM Employee e
   RIGHT JOIN Department d ON e.DepartmentID = d.DepartmentID
   GROUP BY d.Department ORDER BY Department;

P5. ;WITH Seq AS (SELECT SeqNo = 1 UNION ALL SELECT SeqNo+1 FROM Seq WHERE SeqNo < 100)
   SELECT * FROM Seq;

P6. SELECT * FROM OrderMaster WHERE OrderDate >='20161023'
   AND OrderDate < DATEADD(DD,1,'20161023');

P7. SELECT AllDepartments = 'DEPARTMENTNAME' UNION SELECT Department FROM Department;

P8. SELECT * FROM (SELECT AllDepartments = 'DEPARTMENTNAME' UNION SELECT Name
   FROM HumanResources.Department) x

P9. ORDER BY CASE WHEN AllDepartments = 'DEPARTMENTNAME' THEN 1 ELSE 2 END,
   AllDepartments DESC;

P10. ORDER BY IIF(AllDepartments = 'DEPARTMENTNAME', 1 , 2), AllDepartments DESC;

P11. SELECT ProductName, S.SplitPart FROM Product P CROSS APPLY dbo.ufnSplitCSV (Name) S
   WHERE ProductName like '%,%';

P12. DECLARE @InsertedCount INT = @@ROWCOUNT;

P13. 121317*121317; Cartesian product.

P14. DECLARE @Text varchar(32) =
   REPLACE(REPLACE ('2016/10/23 10:20:12', '/', SPACE(0)), ':', SPACE(0));

P15. Table-valued INLINE user-defined function.

P16. varchar(40). It is a good idea to specify the length always. The default is 30.

P17. No. ROLLBACK has no effect on IDENTITY seeds or table variables. If an INSERT advanced the
IDENTITY seed by 5 during the rollbacked transaction, it will stay that way after the ROLLBACK. It means a
gap in the IDENTITY sequence.

P18. Business critical queries are the determining factor in placing the clustered index. Clustered index
speeds up range queries.

P19. Place "COLLATE DATABASE_DEFAULT" on the right side of the expression.

P20. spt_values table.
SELECT N = number FROM master.dbo.spt_values WHERE type='P' ORDER BY N;

Selected Database Administration Answers

A1. It was only 50GB but it had many internet users so it was a challenge performance wise.

A2. Redgates SQL Compare and SQL Data Compare.

A3. BACKUP DATABASE AdventureWorks2012 TO DISK = 'F:\SQLBackup\AdventureWorks2012.bak';

A4. Yes. The GUI can be cancelled after generation, the script can be saved, executed as is or modified.

A5. Add tapedrives for parallel backup or if the database is small backup to disk first & copy to tape.

A6. Build a maintenance plan using SSMS Object Explorer Maintenance Plan Wizard.

A7. Single SQL Server instance with multiple databases is the better choice.

A8. Single huge db is easier to manage and administer.

A9. Schedule weekend index REBUILD, nightly STATISTICS UPDATE & find missing indexes.

A10. Users should get minimal access rights, just sufficient to perform their jobs.

A11. Views and stored procedures.

A12. Setup the stored procedure as a job with SQL Server Agent and create a schedule.

A13. Import/Export Wizard.

A14. Import/Export Wizard.

A15. Backup the database.

A16. No. Point-in-time recovery requires the FULL recovery mode.

A17. Script the current stored procedures in production and save the source code.

A18. No xp_cmdshell rights to developers. Just burden me. That is why I am being paid.

A19. Server-side tracing.

A20. SS 2012 offers higher capacity, more features & better performance. SS Express is free.

This page is intentionally left blank.

INDEX of SQL Server 2012 Administration

Index of the Most Important Topics

This page is intentionally left blank.

www.ingramcontent.com/pod-product-compliance
Lightning Source LLC
LaVergne TN
LVHW062257060326
832902LV00013B/1931

* 9 7 8 1 4 9 0 9 6 6 9 9 1 *